Praise for *Fifty Years of the Shadow Open Market Committee*

"As the world faces extraordinary sources of volatility, the Hoover Institution's Fifty Years of the Shadow Open Market Committee offers essential ideas for a strong and steady monetary policy. Foremost experts from around the world provide deep insights into the evolution of policy, present challenges, and practical next steps."

—**Lawrence Goodman**, president,
Center for Financial Stability

"For fifty years, the SOMC has held monetary policymakers to account. This retrospective by distinguished economists from around the world sheds light on policy successes and failures. Above all, it demonstrates that, contrary to recent conventional wisdom, money cannot be ignored in understanding inflation."

—**Mervyn King**, governor of the Bank of England,
2003–2013

"For decades, the Shadow Open Market Committee has provided an essential counterpoint to Fed policy decisions and its thinking about the macroeconomy. In the 1970s, the SOMC built the case for using monetary aggregates to control inflation and for the absence of a long-run Phillips curve trade-off. By the mid 2000s, there was substantial convergence in views, with former and future SOMC members playing a role in the Federal Open Market Committee. During the Global Financial Crisis and its aftermath, however, these individuals posted warnings about the Fed's credit market interventions; the weakened boundaries between monetary and fiscal policy; and the reduced reliance on forward-looking actions to control inflation. In the years ahead, the SOMC's guidance will be crucial for the Fed's evolution as it reconsiders its monetary and credit policy framework amid public debate about its role and independence."

—**Robert G. King**, professor of economics at Boston University

"The SOMC has provided an indispensable, alternative appraisal of Federal Reserve monetary policymaking and its effects on the macroeconomy since its inception in 1973. This Hoover Institution volume, in the same spirit, is an invaluable assessment of both the Federal Reserve's—and the SOMC's—hits and misses over the past fifty years."

—**Kevin L. Kliesen**, business economist and research officer,
Federal Reserve Bank of St. Louis

FIFTY YEARS of the SHADOW OPEN MARKET COMMITTEE

The Hoover Institution gratefully acknowledges the following individuals and foundations for their significant support of the ECONOMIC POLICY WORKING GROUP *and this publication:*

Lynde and Harry Bradley Foundation

John A. Gunn and Cynthia Fry Gunn

FIFTY YEARS of the SHADOW OPEN MARKET COMMITTEE

A Retrospective on Its Role in Monetary Policy

EDITED BY Michael D. Bordo, Jeffrey M. Lacker, Mickey D. Levy, and John B. Taylor

CONTRIBUTING AUTHORS

Michael D. Bordo	Robert L. Hetzel	Athanasios Orphanides
Michael J. Boskin	Thomas Hoenig	Charles I. Plosser
James B. Bullard	Peter N. Ireland	Condoleezza Rice
Charles W. Calomiris	Otmar Issing	Georg Rich
John H. Cochrane	Robert G. King	Amit Seru
Steven J. Davis	Donald Kohn	Christina Parajon Skinner
Darrell Duffie	Jeffrey M. Lacker	George S. Tavlas
Roger W. Ferguson Jr.	Andrew T. Levin	John B. Taylor
Esther L. George	Mickey D. Levy	Christopher J. Waller
Charles Goodhart	Deborah Lucas	Kevin Warsh
Robert Heller	Loretta J. Mester	Axel A. Weber
Gregory D. Hess	Bill Nelson	David C. Wheelock

HOOVER INSTITUTION PRESS

STANFORD UNIVERSITY | STANFORD, CALIFORNIA

With its eminent scholars and world-renowned library and archives, the Hoover
Institution seeks to improve the human condition by advancing ideas that
promote economic opportunity and prosperity while securing and safeguarding
peace for America and all mankind. The views expressed in its publications are
entirely those of the authors and do not necessarily reflect the views of the staff,
officers, or Board of Overseers of the Hoover Institution.

hoover.org

Hoover Institution Press Publication No. 741

Hoover Institution at Leland Stanford Junior University, Stanford,
California 94305-6003

First printing 2025

30 29 28 27 26 25   7 6 5 4 3 2 1

Manufactured in the United States of America
Printed on acid-free, archival-quality paper

Cataloging-in-Publication Data is available from the Library of Congress.
ISBN 978-0-8179-2674-8 (cloth)
ISBN 978-0-8179-2676-2 (epub)
ISBN 978-0-8179-2678-6 (PDF)

Contents

Monetarism in Europe and the United Kingdom

The Search for a Nominal Anchor

Keynote Speech: Thoughts on the Economy and Policy Rules at the Federal Open Market Committee

The Fed's Evolving Mandate

The Conduct of Monetary Policy

      Policy Implementation Framework Matters   313
      Bill Nelson

16.   Rate Corridors Depend on Dealer Balance Sheet Capacity   331
      Darrell Duffie

      General Discussion   339
      *Harald Uhlig, Robert G. King, Jeffrey M. Lacker, John H.
      Cochrane, Loretta J. Mester, Darrell Duffie, and Bill Nelson*

Monetary-Fiscal Issues

      Introduction   344
      Michael J. Boskin

17.   Monetary-Fiscal Interactions   347
      John H. Cochrane

18.   Crumbling Boundaries and the Risks to Central Bank
      Independence   367
      Charles I. Plosser

19.   When Are Central Bank Policy Actions Fiscal? Definitions,
      Examples, and a Call for Transparency   379
      Deborah Lucas

      General Discussion   387
      *Michael J. Boskin, Matthew Klein, David Beckworth, Jack
      Krupansky, David Zervos, John H. Cochrane, and Deborah Lucas*

Federal Reserve Credit Policy

      Introduction   394
      Thomas Hoenig

20.   Federal Reserve Credit Policy and the Shadow Open Market
      Committee   395
      Jeffrey M. Lacker

      Discussant Remarks   483
      Amit Seru

      Discussant Remarks   489
      Charles W. Calomiris

Influences of the SOMC and Others Outside the Fed

Preface

Michael D. Bordo, Jeffrey M. Lacker, Mickey D. Levy, and John B. Taylor

On October 13–14, 2024, the Shadow Open Market Committee (SOMC) celebrated its fiftieth anniversary with a conference sponsored by the Hoover Institution at Stanford University. Participants at the conference included current and some past SOMC members, a number of current and former Federal Reserve members, and many Hoover Institution fellows and other monetary policy scholars. The papers presented and panel discussions at the conference considered the Committee's contributions to the conduct of monetary and economic policies over the past half century and the evolution of important topics facing current policymakers. The focus of the conference, in keeping with the original SOMC, was sound policies that would support sustained healthy economic performance.

The Shadow Open Market Committee was established in 1973 by Karl Brunner of the University of Rochester, Allan Meltzer of Carnegie Mellon University, and Anna Schwartz of the National Bureau of Economic Research (and Milton Friedman's coauthor for *A Monetary History of the United States, 1867–1960*). The Committee promoted the idea that the high inflation of the period was a monetary phenomenon and not caused by an eclectic array of factors, which, at the time, was the consensus view. The SOMC successfully promoted the importance of money in the inflationary process and its minority vision eventually won the debate, influencing Paul Volcker in the Fed's successful disinflationary monetary policy.

In the half century since the tumultuous 1970s, monetary policy issues have evolved, and the SOMC has continued to conduct research and provide policy advice on central bank policymaking. The range of the SOMC's expertise has broadened as the Fed and global central banks have expanded their roles and the scope of monetary policy. Many current SOMC members are in academics; three are former Fed members; and several others are former high-level Fed staffers.

The conference proceedings reflect the half-century evolution of the critical issues facing central bank policies, with an eye toward current issues and how to improve the conduct of monetary policy. The current environment sets the stage for the importance of the Fed's getting things right. The 2020s bout of inflation dispelled the notion that the inflation of the 1970s was history that would not be repeated. Although inflation has receded toward the Fed's 2% target, the dramatic rise in the general price level, and the Fed's recent missteps, affect current economic behavior and resonate with the public.

The Fed's understatement of the unprecedented surge in money supply that the earlier SOMC had warned about, and its reliance on discretion rather than rules like the Taylor rule—both of which have been a focus of current SOMC research—provided the perfect backdrop for discussing the history of the SOMC and the evolution of monetary policy.

The papers and discussions at the conference highlighted the benefits of rules-based monetary policy, along with the important role of a nominal anchor. The international influences of monetarism and the SOMC in Europe and the United Kingdom were described by leading central bankers of Europe and the United Kingdom. The Fed's evolving interpretation of its dual mandate and how it implemented policy to achieve its objective was considered. The importance of transparency and the Fed's credibility received close attention.

The evolution of the Fed's operating procedures from free reserves to the corridor and floor systems and how short-term funding markets have been affected was also discussed. The history of the Fed's involvement in providing credit was reviewed. Consistent with the SOMC's long-standing support of responsible fiscal policy, a panel considered fiscal issues and the interaction between monetary and fiscal policies. Widespread concerns about persistent budget deficits and rising debt were considered from different angles. A concluding panel of former Fed members discussed how the SOMC and other outsiders influenced the Fed's conduct of monetary policy.

At the conclusion of the conference, it was widely agreed that over the years the SOMC had provided valuable research and recommendations on the Fed's monetary policy, and enthusiastic participants wholeheartedly encouraged the Committee to continue its constructive critiques of central bank policies in the pursuit of improving economic and financial performance.

Introduction to Conference and Keynote Speech

Michael Bordo, a member of the Shadow Open Market Committee, provided introductory remarks that described the origins of the SOMC and introduced keynote speaker John Taylor of the Hoover Institution. Bordo noted that many of the stances of the SOMC were closely aligned with the beliefs and research of the scholars at the Hoover Institution and of John Taylor in particular—sound money, an emphasis on rules-based policies, and heightened transparency. He noted that beyond Taylor's major contributions to the economic profession and the understanding of the Fed's monetary policy, he has been a long-standing friend of the SOMC and was the driving force that made this conference a reality.

Taylor's speech focused on the benefits of systematic rules-based guidelines, and how adhering to the Taylor rule would have avoided major policy mistakes. He used charts to show that while the Fed's interest-rate policies frequently followed policies that were consistent with Taylor rule estimates of the federal funds rate, there were several distinct periods of wide deviations, particularly the 1970s, the early 2000s, and the 2020s. The deviations in the 1970s and 2020s led to bouts of inflation, while the early 2000s led to costly financial stresses.

Taylor encouraged the Federal Reserve to use the Taylor rule as a guideline in its conduct of monetary policy rather than rely on discretion and judgment. He also described how global central banks often sent monetary policies off course by deviating from rules-based policy prescriptions. Taylor focused particularly on the experiences of Latin American nations that had suffered from costly bouts of inflation. He encouraged cooperation of international monetary policies by global central banks.

Several of the questions from the dinner audience focused on the international aspects of recent monetary policy and inflation. Taylor described that while each nation and central bank faced different circumstances, a 2% inflation target would be a useful starting point, and emphasized that the objective of stable low inflation would be a valuable benchmark for Latin American nations.

Opening Remarks

The Hoover Institution's director and former secretary of state Condoleezza Rice opened the conference, setting the international stage for the conduct of US monetary policy. She warned that the international architecture that had been presumed to be characterized by cooperation was threatened by "populism, nativism, isolationism, and protectionism." She described the early efforts to fully integrate China into the international economy as an experiment. But the realities of China maintaining its principles as a state-owned and Marxist economy while it has grown into a global economic powerhouse has conflicted with and threatened the international economic order.

Rice described Russia's invasion of Ukraine as "another sad experiment" that further isolates Russia. "While it differs from China's integration experiment, Russia's long-term isolation still bodes poorly for the health of the international system."

Rice then described some important economic issues that US politicians have tended to sidestep. The benefits of free trade have been replaced by sanctions, on-shoring, friend-shoring, and pulling back from the international economic order. Politicians have also sidestepped addressing persistent deficits and the government's mounting borrowing. In these uncharted waters, Rice emphasized the importance of "the steady hand of the Federal Reserve and our monetary policy."

History of the Shadow Open Market Committee and Its Influences

In the first session, Michael Bordo and Mickey Levy, two members of the Shadow Open Market Committee, presented a lengthy paper, "The Fifty-Year History of the Shadow Open Market Committee and the Evolution of Monetary Policy," and two discussants, George Tavlas of the National Bank of Greece and David Wheelock of the Federal Reserve Bank of St. Louis, provided formal comments.

Bordo and Levy described the origins of the SOMC and how the Committee was built on the monetarist school led by Milton Friedman. The high inflation and disarray of economic and monetary policy during the 1970s provided a perfect time for establishing the SOMC. They described how the SOMC's straightforward monetarist prescriptions drew significant attention to money in the policy debate and likely influenced the Paul Volcker–led Fed's successful disinflationary monetary policy in the late 1970s.

They then assessed the evolution of the policy research and recommendations of the SOMC and the theoretical foundations and implementation of monetary policy since the 1970s. Bordo and Levy described how the SOMC continued to make monetary policy recommendations in the 1980s and 1990s based on monetary base growth, and this lost relevance. But during this period, its research and policy recommendations that emphasized the importance of rules-based policies, advocacy of an official low inflation target, and the importance of credibility and transparency, were on the mark.

Bordo and Levy described how the modern SOMC addresses a wide array of monetary and financial regulatory issues. It continues to argue for rules-based policies and recommends that the Fed pursue a narrower scope of policies, including staying clear of credit provision, and focus on policies that are within its ability to achieve.

In their comments, George Tavlas and David Wheelock added critically important interpretations of the 1970s and the early years of the SOMC, and the benefits of monetarism. Tavlas focused on the inflation bouts of the 1970s and the 2020s. He highlighted the important theoretical contributions of Friedman, noting that Friedman advocated targeting M2 while the SOMC favored the monetary base. Tavlas described how Fed chair Arthur Burns was politically motivated and incorrect on important technical details, and concluded: "During the 1970s, Friedman and the SOMC got it right." With the volatility of money demand in the 1990s, targeting money growth lost its allure, and in the early 1990s, Tavlas concluded, "The mantle of policy rules had passed from Milton Friedman to John Taylor."

Wheelock emphasized the important role the Federal Reserve Bank of St. Louis played in the prominence of monetarism in the monetary policy debate and the SOMC's history. He highlighted the key role Bill Poole played as president of the St. Louis Fed in advocating monetarism and the importance of rules and, more recently, that of James Bullard, also president of the Federal Reserve Bank of St. Louis, who promoted a systematic approach to the conduct of monetary policy, including a modified Taylor rule.

In the Q&A discussion that followed, several conference participants added historical insights. Jerry Jordan, former SOMC member and former president of the Federal Reserve Bank of Cleveland, emphasized that President Ronald Reagan provided invaluable support for Volcker and the Fed's successful disinflation even though its short-run costs were recession with high unemployment. Several remarked that the SOMC's continued worries in the 1980s about a rebound in inflation were not alarmist but rather were consistent with the high inflation expectations of professional forecasters.

Monetarism in Europe and the United Kingdom

The next session addressed influences of the SOMC and monetarism in Europe and the United Kingdom, featuring leading central bankers Georg Rich, former director of the Swiss National Bank (SNB); Axel Weber, former president of the Deutsche Bundesbank; Otmar Issing, former chief economist of the Bundesbank and the European Central Bank (ECB); and Charles Goodhart, former chief economist of the Bank of England. Each provided remarks on their experiences that emphasized the important role of money in the conduct of monetary policy and some of the critical dilemmas they faced and the strategic decisions they made. The panel was moderated by Charles Plosser, former president of the Federal Reserve Bank of Philadelphia. Plosser noted that the distinguished global central bankers were very influential in the development of central banking.

Georg Rich noted the influence of Karl Brunner on the Swiss National Bank, which, after the Swiss franc was floated in 1971, targeted money growth. Rich noted the success of this policy: "Tight control of money allowed the SNB to reduce inflation to low levels." He described in detail that the SNB switched to multiyear money targets in the 1980s and in 1999 abandoned money targeting in favor of three-year inflation targeting while keeping a close eye on money trends.

Otmar Issing described how the Bundesbank introduced its money-supply target in 1974 and modified it in a way described as "pragmatic monetarism," in which money supply was not targeted but played a prominent role. When he became a member of the Executive Board of the ECB, he introduced the "two-pillar strategy" in which monetary policy is guided by monetary and economic analysis. He concluded that "whatever one may call 'monetarism' today, one cannot simply ignore the importance of the development of the money supply for inflation."

Charles Goodhart noted that while supply shocks of both the 1970s and 2020s generated global inflation, the differences in inflation between the US, UK, and Germany were "closely matched by the differences in money supply." Goodhart found that while the SOMC received little media coverage outside the US, he explained how Karl Brunner had been closely followed and his advice was sought out by Margaret Thatcher and the Bank of England.

Axel Weber described how he and Issing had instituted the ECB Watchers Conference as "an open platform for dialogue," but the debates have evolved and become much more one-sided, a place where criticism is discouraged. He stated that the central banks' adoption of average inflation targeting has been "an inadequately designed monetary policy framework." One result is that "although inflation rates are back around 2%, the loss of purchasing power remains substantially due to these cumulative price increases."

The lively discussion covered both history and the current situation. In response to Michael Bordo's question about the influence of the concept of "stability culture," Issing emphasized that Germany's pursuit of price stability was a direct function of its historic, hugely disruptive inflationary mistakes in the 1920s and 1940s, but the fears of inflation and instability were not uniform across Europe. Matthew Klein asked about Switzerland's experience in the 2020s, and Georg Rich emphasized that the SNB had been the first central bank to tighten policy and that helped keep inflation low. Axel Weber expressed concerns about the lagged impact of higher inflation, noting that wages are now catching up, and said it was too early for central bankers to declare victory. Issing described how labor unions' demands for higher wages were a threat to low inflation. Charles Goodhart noted that high budget deficits also posed an inflation risk.

Search for a Nominal Anchor

In the next session, Kevin Warsh, former member of the Board of Governors of the Federal Reserve System, moderated papers presented by SOMC members Peter Ireland and Greg Hess and monetary policy scholar Robert Hetzel. In his introductory remarks, Warsh identified seeming contradictions in current policymakers and expressed the view that policymakers should go back to the basics, including following the money stock. He noted, "Is it right for a central bank to take credit for a soft landing if it does not take responsibility for the inflation surge that preceded it?" He criticized the Fed's flexible average inflation targeting put in place in August 2020 and highlighted the dramatic expansion of the Fed's balance sheet.

Peter Ireland provided a detailed review of the SOMC's preferred money-based strategy and described the differences between the models advocated by Allan Meltzer and Karl Brunner and those favored by Robert Samuelson and Robert Solow (and others) based on a Phillips curve that posited a trade-off between inflation and the unemployment rate. He described the impact of the advent of the Taylor rule that was based on interest rates and how the SOMC has always preferred a transparent and rules-based approach to monetary policymaking. He discussed the importance of nominal GDP as an anchor in conducting monetary policy and the objective of low inflation. Ireland concluded: "Had policymakers paid more attention to the behavior of the monetary base and the broader monetary aggregates, the return to high inflation in 2021 . . . would likely have been avoided."

Robert Hetzel provided a rigorous assessment of what is required for the Fed to successfully pursue a nominal anchor. He described historical and current external factors such as fiscal policy shocks including deficits and the economy that present challenges to the Fed. He argued that a rules-based monetary policy is required and that the monetary policies that follow the established rules must be transparent and their impacts on the economy and inflation must be predictable. Hetzel's bottom line is that a nominal anchor must be rooted in expectations of price stability along the lines of the Volcker–Greenspan era.

Hess took to heart the importance of the concept of a nominal anchor and traced its historical origins to Robert Barro. For Barro, "the presence of a nominal anchor includes not just an ability to deliver price stability, but also a framework for delivering the price stability goal and routinizing and constraining policy actions to be free from political decision-making and discretion." Hess continued to describe the Fed's interpretation of the nominal anchor as stipulating that "its long run inflation goal will be twinned with a flexible monetary policy strategy that will systematically return inflation . . . to its long run value of 2%." Hess concluded by describing how the Fed deviated from its framework following the COVID-19 pandemic, which contributed to higher inflation.

In response to a question about how the Fed should avoid groupthink, Warsh highlighted the importance of genuine openness to intellectual ideas and the need to be humble. He noted that within the Fed there tends to be pushback on ideas that are inconsistent with the median forecast of the Fed. John Cochrane expressed what he saw as two problems with M2: first, that the Fed does not control M2, and second, that because M2 is exogenous, maybe "the price level controls M2" rather than the other way around. Peter Ireland responded that while the Fed does not directly control M2, we should not be happy with the recent inflation and conduct of monetary policy and instead should be reassessing alternatives that would improve monetary policy and avoid costly mistakes.

Keynote Luncheon Speech

Chris Waller, governor of the Federal Reserve System, provided the keynote luncheon speech. Athanasios Orphanides moderated the speech and took questions from the audience. Waller provided a detailed assessment of current economic and inflation conditions and the Fed's considerations as it deliberated on the conduct of monetary policy. He noted that economic performance had been healthy, with higher growth than the Fed had anticipated. Inflation had declined significantly, and while it was still above the Fed's 2% target, the Fed remained confident that it would recede to its target. Waller then described how the Fed is aware of different rules like the Taylor rule and variations on it that could help the Fed achieve its dual mandate. He concluded that "while rules are valuable in helping analyze policy options, they have limitations," including limitations of the data and risk management issues. Under current circumstances, Waller noted that the Fed had "a considerable extent of policy restrictiveness to remove, and if the economy continues in its current sweet spot, this will happen gradually."

Athanasios Orphanides asked several questions about r^*, the natural rate of interest. Waller said that one of his biggest concerns regarding the outlook for r^* is the sustainability of fiscal policy, since with persistent deficit spending the supply of Treasury securities will start growing faster than demand, pushing up yields. David Zervos suggested that the Fed's balance sheet was not getting sufficient attention. Waller noted that there was no economic theory that determines the optimal size of the balance sheet, and that changes in the balance sheet do have a modest impact on bond yields; he agreed that the Fed's balance sheet requires more attention.

David Beckworth asked about Waller's early prediction that inflation would decline without significant increases in the unemployment rate. Waller noted how his research on the Beveridge curve led him to believe the Fed was at the steep part of the trade-off between job vacancies and job ratio, which proved to be correct. Now his concern is that we are at the flatter portion of the curve, and unemployment is more vulnerable. But he continued to believe there would be an economic soft landing without recession.

The Fed's Evolving Interpretation and Implementation of Its Dual Mandate

This session, which was moderated by Hoover Institution senior fellow Steve Davis, included presentations by three SOMC members: Athanasios Orphanides, Andrew Levin, and James Bullard, who recently joined the SOMC after retiring as president of the Federal Reserve Bank of St. Louis.

Orphanides assessed the history of the Fed's interpretation of its mandate, describing how it was muddled and "has not explicitly recognized price stability as the primary goal of monetary policy." He described how in the 1970s and in the recent past, the Fed placed more emphasis on the elusive goal of maximum employment, and that on both occasions, the Fed's strategy proved insufficiently resilient, and high inflation followed. He concluded: "To improve its policy strategy the Fed ought to revert to earlier interpretations of its mandate that acknowledge the primacy of price stability as a policy guide."

Bullard's paper analyzed the evolution of intellectual thinking in economics and how it influenced the actual conduct of monetary policy. Volcker's successful disinflationary process stemmed in part from innovations in monetarist thinking but also highlighted the critical role policymaker credibility has in achieving desirable outcomes. The successes of the Federal Reserve Bank of St. Louis in conducting innovative research that influenced monetary policy encouraged the Fed's other regional banks. Bullard described how the evolution of the real business cycle model that assumed efficient market allocations of resources subsequently incorporated monetary policy with interest rates as intermediate targets. The New Keynesian models incorporated frictions that required government intervention, including an active role of monetary policy, to achieve desired outcomes.

Bullard concluded with two challenges facing the Fed. First is the introduction of heterogeneities into New Keynesian models that create more need for policymakers to achieve more complex objectives. Second, Japan, with its high government debt-to-GDP ratio but very low inflation and interest rates, poses a perplexing dilemma for monetary policy.

Andy Levin addressed governance issues pertaining to the Fed, arguing that while the Fed's independence is critically important, its conduct of policy would be improved if it had better outside supervision. He explained how the Fed used its own accounting rules rather than generally accepted accounting principles and that it was exempt from the government's General Accounting Office (GAO) audits and review. Levin argued that this had resulted in the Fed's acting in one voice, like a corporate board of directors. He noted that there was insufficient cost-benefit analysis and pointed to the costs to the taxpayers and risks involved. Among other recommendations, Levin said that Congress should have more access to internal Fed information.

In the discussion that followed, Davis weighed in on Bullard's emphasis on the Fed's credibility. He noted that if credibility was so important, why doesn't the Fed and other central banks devote more to understanding and developing a measure of credibility that could be used in real time? There were several comments on Andy Levin's urging for external review of the Fed. John Cochrane stated that while he favored external reviews, he believes the Fed is already a fairly well-run bureaucracy. Andy responded that there was always need for improvement, and referred to the sizable losses the Fed had imposed on taxpayers stemming from its large purchases of long-duration securities when interest rates were artificially low. Bullard said that the Fed was already under examination by outside reviewers, and that the GAO is part of Congress and would not be appropriate as an external reviewer of the Fed, recommending instead the US inspector general's office.

The Conduct of Monetary Policy

In the next session, three noted experts dug into the details of the Fed's operating procedures, and how they had evolved. The panelists were: Loretta Mester, former president of the Federal Reserve Bank of Cleveland; Bill Nelson, chief economist at the Bank Policy Institute; and Darrell Duffie, of Stanford University and the Hoover Institution. The panel was moderated by Robert King of Boston University.

Mester described how the Fed's enlarged balance sheet following the Global (or Great) Financial Crisis (GFC) required it to shift the management of its effective federal funds rate from a scarce-reserves system that relied on a corridor system to an ample-reserves system that used a floor system. She emphasized that while the floor system ensures that the Fed has very good interest-rate control, it is more complex and involves costs, including those generated by the Fed's increased role in the short-term funding market. Despite some of the problems with the current system, Mester concluded, "I think the transition costs of returning to a scarce-reserves system would not be insignificant."

Bill Nelson described how the dramatic increase in the Fed's balance sheet, from 6% of GDP before the GFC to 25%, involved many costs, including the Fed's dominance in the short-term funding market and an associated withering of the interbank lending market. He showed how the current floor system reinforces the Fed's growing balance sheet and had led the Fed to become more complacent about the enlarged size of its balance sheet. Nelson concluded that the Fed should move toward reducing the size of its balance sheet: "While expanding the balance sheet through emergency lending and quantitative easing served a legitimate purpose when the federal funds rate was near zero, there is a building consensus across the major central banks that the costs of a floor system outweigh the benefits."

Darrell Duffie took a more cautious stance and recommended against lowering reserves to the point that banks are forced to deal with less than they feel they need. He described how capital requirements imposed on foreign banks put more pressure on US domestic banks' funding, and spikes in quarter-end repo rates created instability that impacts the implementation of monetary policy.

Duffie emphasized that the biggest problem facing the short-term funding market was the growth of federal government debt that had dramatically increased the ratio of US Treasuries to total primary-dealer assets. He noted that the sheer volumes of daily transactions of the repo market had come to overwhelm the fed funds transactions between banks: "The bond market is getting too big relative to bank balance sheets. And that's not the fault of the Fed, it's the fault of the fiscal authority. It's borrowing so much money that the quantity of bonds that need to get financing in the repo market is growing by leaps and bounds relative to the sizes of the banks that intermediate those markets."

Harald Uhlig initiated the discussion by asking why there is so much focus on the federal funds rate when under the floor system the actual fed funds rate is unimportant. Mester responded by emphasizing that the role the fed funds rate plays as a target is a very important communications tool for the Fed. Duffie reiterated that banks have enormous demands for reserves to meet their liquidity needs for regulatory requirements and payment needs through the course of a business day, and these needs should determine the magnitude of "ample" reserves.

Monetary-Fiscal Issues

Michael Boskin of the Hoover Institution chaired the next session on monetary-fiscal issues, which featured presentations by John Cochrane of the Hoover Institution; Charles Plosser, former president of the Federal Reserve Bank of Philadelphia and SOMC member; Deborah Lucas of MIT and the SOMC; and Patrick Kehoe of Stanford University. Boskin set the backdrop for the session, describing how federal government spending and debt have risen dramatically, primarily due to the rapid growth of outlays on entitlement programs, while funds for defense and national security had been insufficient. He emphasized that while the deeply troubling longer-run projections of soaring government debt are widely understood, neither presidential candidate recommended any programmatic spending cuts that would even slow the rise in the debt.

Kehoe provided a historic assessment of government debt during peacetimes and wars. He described how, historically, the government's finances had improved during peacetime periods, with lower debt-to-GDP ratios, which better prepared it to finance war efforts. Jumps in spending during wars were financed by a combination of higher taxes and borrowing. Kehoe described the clear deviation from this pattern in recent decades of peace with a run-up in government debt, which he viewed as irresponsible because it places the government in a poor position to face the next crisis.

In his presentation, Plosser emphasized the importance of central banks' maintaining their independence, which requires them not to have unrestricted powers and to be accountable. He expressed worries that the boundaries between monetary and fiscal policies have eroded, which poses a risk to central bank independence. He noted that the broadened mandate and scope of the Fed's responsibilities are beyond its capabilities. Plosser described how the Fed's long-standing policy of a "Treasuries only" portfolio ended in 2008 with the Fed's purchases of mortgage-backed securities (MBS), and how paying interest on excess reserves created problems and has adversely affected the monetary transmission channels.

To restore the boundaries between fiscal and monetary policies, Plosser provided the following recommendations: The Fed should return to an all-Treasuries portfolio; it should reduce the size of its balance sheet; and it should reform its emergency lending authorities under section 13(3) so that fiscal policymakers have responsibility for lending decisions.

Lucas's presentation focused on the accounting of the Fed's actions that are fiscal. She began with the premise that a central bank policy action is fiscal if it causes a direct transfer of value to or from the federal government. The Fed's fiscal activities were ramped up during the GFC and in its numerous credit facilities provided in the CARES Act during the COVID pandemic. She described how the accounting of the Fed's remittances to the Treasury, which are measured as reductions in deficit spending, are misleading and dangerous. Her suggestions for improvement include holding the Fed accountable for its fiscal actions; forcing it to adopt an explicit cost-benefit mindset; reducing pressures on the Fed to undertake fiscal actions that the rest of government wants to avoid accountability for; and discouraging efforts by the legislative and executive branches that curtail the Fed's independence.

Cochrane emphasized how the recent bout of inflation was a perfect example of the dominant role of fiscal deficits as the source of inflation and how it supported his fiscal theory of the price level. In response to the Global Financial Crisis in 2008, the government promised fiscal stimulus now and debt repayment later. In contrast, Cochrane viewed the government's surge in deficit spending in response to the 2020–21 pandemic as a true "helicopter drop" in which the government made clear that the rise in debt wouldn't be repaid. The normalization of interest rates raises deficits and poses a serious constraint on monetary policy.

Cochrane noted that the Congressional Budget Office's long-run projections of a rising ratio of debt to GDP are actually optimistic by presuming no disruptions to sustained economic growth and moderate interest rates. He concluded that one solution that would reduce the risks of higher government debt and inflation was stronger real economic growth.

Boskin applauded Lucas's calls for improved transparency and accurate accounting, and Cochrane's mention of the benefits of more economic growth. He noted the dramatic evolution of the budget from primarily government purchases to resources redistribution. He described the history of failures to institute fiscal rules, and underlined Kehoe's suggestion for a capital and operating budget to provide better definition of government spending.

In the subsequent discussion, Matthew Klein wondered why the government's deficit spending in response to the GFC didn't lead to higher inflation, and David Zervos pointed out that Japan's government debt is 250% of GDP, most of which has been monetized by the Bank of Japan, yet Japan's inflation has remained very low. Cochrane noted that Japan has unique characteristics. In the US, the government indicated during the GFC its intention to repay its rising debt, while its deficit spending in response to COVID was primarily distributing checks to people with no thought of repayment.

The Fed in Credit Markets: From "Lender of Last Resort" to "Too Big to Fail" to "Financial Market Savior"

This panel was moderated by Thomas Hoenig, former president of the Federal Reserve Bank of Kansas City. Jeff Lacker, former president of the Federal Reserve Bank of Richmond and SOMC member, presented a lengthy paper on the historical evolution of the theory and practice of Fed lending, and the SOMC's critique of the Fed's lending practices. Lacker noted that when the Fed was established, it viewed lending as the operational mechanism for maintaining monetary stability.

According to Lacker, who took a narrow interpretation of the appropriate role the Fed should play in providing credit and its lender-of-last-resort function, "the scale and scope of the Federal Reserve's credit extension increased dramatically in the 21st century." He continued: "The accumulation of precedents set the stage for the Great Financial Crisis, and recently, the Fed's pandemic credit market interventions." Lacker described the Fed's role in credit markets as an evolution from maintaining monetary stability by acting as a classical lender of last resort when the Fed was founded, to accommodating too-big-to-fail financial institutions as a "Reluctant Samaritan" in the late twentieth century, to broad twenty-first-century financial market crisis interventions in which the Fed has become the "Sell-Side Savior." Lacker emphasized that there was no internal research that provided analytical support or guidance for the Fed's increasing interventionism, and that credit programs were not grounded in economic analysis.

Lacker tracked the evolution of the SOMC's commentary on the Fed's credit lending. Following the GFC, the SOMC worried about the Fed's expanded role in credit and recommended a Treasury-Fed "credit accord" that would establish boundaries for Fed lending.

Discussant Amit Seru of the Stanford Business School agreed with much of Lacker's analysis and argued that the Fed's governance practices and its heavy reliance on discretion rather than principles and rules had undercut its effectiveness and credibility. He pointed to problems posed by the revolving door from employment at the Fed to private-sector jobs. Seru showed empirically that the CAMELS ratings that were widely used by bank supervisors for evaluating commercial bank stability relied heavily on the discretion and subjectivity of the supervisors, rather than numeric rules. He expressed concern about the high leverage at banks.

Seru emphasized that the Fed's assessment of credit and bank supervision needed a commitment toward rules over discretion, consistent and principled decision making, and transparency.

Charles Calomiris praised the valuable historical content and thoroughness of Lacker's paper, but, in contrast to Lacker, took a broader view of the Fed's appropriate role as lender of last resort. In particular, he argued that the Fed's open market operations are not an effective countercyclical tool when systematic losses of bank equity reduce banks' capacity to provide credit. Consistent with this broader interpretation, to fulfill the lender-of-last-resort role, the Fed must include many tools to respond to different shocks to the banking system, including providing credit.

Importantly, Calomiris emphasized that while he takes a broad view of lender of last resort, he completely agrees with Lacker and the SOMC that such lending programs must be provided systematically and transparently, a practice that has not been followed by the Fed.

In response to several questions about the failure of Silicon Valley Bank (SVB), Calomiris emphasized that the SVB problem was one of insolvency, based on its risky portfolio of long-dated bonds and extraordinarily high share of uninsured deposits, rather than a problem of liquidity. Calomiris argued that the Treasury's (FDIC's) bailout of SVB was political, based on the Treasury's perception of the need to provide financial backing to the uninsured depositors, and suggested that there were other ways to resolve the problem.

Panel on Influence of the SOMC and Others Outside the Fed

This very lively concluding panel included four former Fed members: Don Kohn and Roger Ferguson, both of whom served as vice chairs of the Board of Governors of the Fed; Robert Heller, a former governor of the Fed; and Esther George, former president of the Federal Reserve Bank of Kansas City. Deborah Lucas moderated the panel.

All panelists emphasized that the Fed has evolved significantly and become more open to outside influences. Don Kohn said that during the 1970s, while academics often interacted with Fed staffers, Arthur Burns had a very limited tolerance of discussion about monetary policy, and Fed governors and Federal Reserve Bank presidents were discouraged from giving public speeches. He noted that the SOMC's focus on monetary base targets in the 1980s and 1990s would never gain traction, since the Fed was focused on interest rates, and the Fed followed closely the development of interest rate–based rules like the Taylor rule and variations on it. Kohn reflected on history and observed that Volcker and Greenspan achieved desired outcomes of low inflation, but did not follow rules, and emphasized the importance of targeting low inflation.

Ferguson began by stating: "Modern-day central bankers are notoriously proud of their ability to avoid outside influences," but there has been a tremendous evolution toward the Fed's listening to outsiders. He broke the outsiders into three groups: academics, including the SOMC; other central bankers; and financial markets. He focused on the concept of price stability and inflation targeting as two critically important tenets of Fed policy that were heavily influenced by outside thinking. He noted that the institution of inflation targeting by leading global central bankers in the early 1990s had a significant effect on the Fed's thinking and conduct of monetary policy. He described how the Fed's evolution toward transparency, accelerated by Fed chair Ben Bernanke, increased the Fed's interaction with outsiders.

Robert Heller described his early days as an economics professor at UCLA and how he was influenced by Karl Brunner and his then-assistant Jerry Jordan—who would become a leading monetarist and director of research at the Federal Reserve Bank of St. Louis, and later a member of the SOMC and president of the Federal Reserve Bank of Cleveland. Heller noted the importance of the linkages between money and inflation, lamenting that in the modern era the Fed does not pay attention to trends in money. He described how he had become a Fed governor when Volcker was chair. Heller described how Volcker closely controlled the Fed and strongly discouraged other Fed members from public statements. Heller spoke very warmly of his experiences at the Fed and related how his children designed what is now the official flag of the Federal Reserve System.

George used the recent decline of dissents at Federal Open Market Committee (FOMC) meetings as a focal point to discuss how the balance between rigorous discussion about policies and forming a consensus enhances the Fed's credibility. As a Fed member who occasionally dissented, George said there were plenty of disagreements within the FOMC about policy, and she never felt inhibited about expressing her views. But she did emphasize that as an institution, the Fed has a very strong consensus orientation, stating that the Fed's operating model "has evolved toward the need for a strong culture of collaboration and consensus in governance and staffing in their operations."

Much of the follow-up discussion focused on fiscal policy and how it influences monetary policy. Kohn noted that fiscal policies have a significant impact on aggregate demand as well as supply, and the minutes of the FOMC meetings in 2020–21 suggest that there was seemingly little discussion of the unprecedented deficit spending at the Fed. He stated that the Fed "has pulled back too far from commenting on the implications for the macroeconomy of the fiscal policy." Ferguson expressed caution about the Fed and its members making public statements about fiscal policy, but said he was worried that the size of the Fed's balance sheet could lead to misuse. He concluded, "I worry less about fiscal policy per se, and much more about something that might be described as fiscal dominance or the misuse of the Fed's balance sheet for this broader range of tools."

Fed Governor Chris Waller weighed in on the topic from the audience, stating that while he views the persistently high deficits as unsustainable, "I'm not gonna tell Congress how to fix that problem . . . that's what we avoid." Nevertheless, Waller worries that the growing supply of Treasuries will eventually outrun demand and push up interest rates, and the Fed will have to deal with it.

Welcoming Remarks

Condoleezza Rice

The Economic Policy Working Group at the Hoover Institution is a vital forum that allows us to reflect on the great institutions that have spurred tremendous growth and prosperity. This reflection could not come at a more opportune moment. Today, the world faces a number of extraordinary circumstances that challenge the existing international economic architecture. Chief among them is the return of the four horsemen of the apocalypse—populism, nativism, isolationism, and protectionism—which threaten the spirit of international cooperation and free-market exchange.

We have come to take the extraordinary international economy for granted. The world's democracies have steered these institutions and as a result, the international system has been relatively peaceful. Today, the emergence of the China experiment tests our existing institutions. I call it exactly that because it was something of an experiment to try to integrate China fully into the international economy. Under Deng Xiaoping, the country came out of its isolation. But really, it only intended to emerge from its isolation on the economic side while maintaining its principles of a state-owned and Marxist economy at the center. For a while, there was some liberalization and privatization of the Chinese economy. Still, we said of China: It's not possible to have both economic liberalization and political control. And when Xi Jinping came to power in 2013, he decided to take political control.

China's effects on the international economy have been pronounced, both as a manufacturing powerhouse and through investments like the Belt and Road Initiative. When George Shultz and Ronald Reagan started the G7, the seven largest economies in the world were all democracies. That is not the case today, and it is unknown as to how this will play out for the international system. These uncharted waters beg the steady hand of the Federal Reserve and our monetary policy to influence trade competitiveness and counter economic pressures exerted by our autocratic adversaries.

Russia's invasion of Ukraine offers another sad experiment. After Russia's brutal military aggression in 2022, Russia was ripped out of the international economy with the valence of sanctions and restrictions. These measures are unlikely to stop anytime soon, and Russia is a more isolated economy now than it has been since well before Mikhail Gorbachev. We forget that Russia once chose autarky, as they called it, not integration. At no point in its history was more than 1% of the Soviet GDP accounted for by international trade. Russia, however, attempted integration at the nation's inception but is now, thirty years later, sitting on the sidelines of the international economy. While it differs from China's integration experiment, Russia's long-term isolation still bodes poorly for the health of the international system.

As we think about this international economy and the backdrop of this conference, how long has it been since you've heard a politician in the United States say the words "free trade"? It has become for both parties a kind of third rail, replaced instead by discussions of tariffs, by sanctions, by on-shoring, friend-shoring, national shoring, and a pullback from the international economy that was supposed to operate first and foremost on efficiencies.

No politician ever speaks about deficits and what we do about the fact that we continue to borrow money that we do not have. When I was provost of Stanford, I used to say to the departments and the deans, "I'm not the federal government; I can't print money." Well, the federal government, of course, takes that to an extreme, and we see no slowing down there. The economic landscape is extraordinarily more complex and more difficult than fifty years ago when this conference was founded. It is also a landscape that requires a clearer understanding of what it has intended to do and how well it has functioned.

Some work that we have done at the Hoover Institution shows that some 35% of Americans do not trust markets. I am not sure they even know what they mean by markets. I know that many of my students would not be particularly clear on the concept. As such, there is a clear educational imperative for both our policymakers and the next generation. We must renew our commitment to the free-market principles that have anchored our institutions and created a prosperous international economy for so long.

Rules Versus Discretion over the Last Fifty Years

Introduction

Michael D. Bordo

The Shadow Open Market Committee was founded in 1973 by Allan Meltzer of Carnegie Mellon University, Karl Brunner of the University of Rochester, and Anna Schwartz of the NBER [National Bureau of Economic Research] to provide a constructive forum for improving monetary policymaking. They promoted the idea that the high inflation of the time was a monetary phenomenon, and not caused by another eclectic array of factors, which at the time was the consensus view. The SOMC's minority vision eventually won the debate. As monetary policy issues have evolved over the half century, the SOMC and research by its members have continued to influence central bank policymaking in the US and abroad.

The SOMC has always emphasized sound money and the importance of a nominal anchor in the conduct of monetary policy rather than a discretionary approach. The SOMC has highlighted the benefits of a rules-based monetary policy rather than a discretionary approach. The SOMC has highlighted the benefits of heightened central bank transparency. On fiscal policy matters, the SOMC has urged fiscal restraint and the importance of the Fed's steering clear of fiscal policy and its involvement through its balance sheet. These stances align closely with the beliefs and research of Hoover Institution scholars.

The range of the SOMC's expertise has broadened as the Fed and global central banks have expanded their roles. Adding to the SOMC's legacy of monetary policy scholarship, SOMC members include noted experts in banking and bank regulation, financial stability, the Fed's expanded balance sheet, and its role in international finance, monetary history, and governance issues. Historically, several members of the SOMC have joined the Fed, and the current SOMC includes several former Fed members.

The current issues facing monetary policymakers are critically important to healthy economic performance, as were those of the past. The SOMC has played an important role as a watchdog on the Fed's policies in the past and promises to do so in the future.

We thank the Hoover Institution and especially John Taylor and Marie-Christine Slakey for hosting and arranging this special conference to highlight the evolution of monetary policy and the SOMC in the last fifty years, and to address the key issues facing today's policymakers. The conference includes participation by SOMC members, leading scholars of the Hoover Institution, and current and former Fed members and foreign central bankers.

John Taylor's famous rule, which is an essential chapter in every central banker's guidebook, and his pioneering research on monetary policy rules have been at the heart of the SOMC's core beliefs for the past three decades. Now we have the privilege of having John tell us about "Rules Versus Discretion over the Past Fifty Years."

1

Rules Versus Discretion over the Last Fifty Years

John B. Taylor

This event represented an important occasion for colleagues and scholars in macroeconomics to come together. It offered a valuable opportunity to discuss the theme, "Rules Versus Discretion over the Last Fifty Years," marking the fiftieth anniversary of the Shadow Open Market Committee (SOMC), which was established in 1973. The retrospective theme, "A Fifty-Year Retrospective on the Shadow Open Market Committee and Its Role in Monetary Policy," was examined at the David and Joan Traitel Building at Stanford University, made possible by the generous support of David and Joan.

Reflecting on Historical Context

First, it is essential to recognize the key figures who played a role in establishing the SOMC, particularly Allan Meltzer, a long-term colleague. I would also like to acknowledge his wife, Marilyn, who was in attendance. Having grown up in Pittsburgh, I have long admired Carnegie Mellon University. Significant contributions from other original members, such as Karl Brunner and Anna Schwartz, must also be acknowledged. Their intellectual legacies, along with the influence of Milton Friedman—who emphasized monetary aggregates— continue to inform our discussions about monetary policy today.

Understanding Monetary Policy Rules

I would like to highlight the importance of policy rules at the outset. I define a rule like my Taylor 1993 one as an instrument rule whereby the central bank sets its policy interest rate in reaction to its key policy objectives: price stability and stability of the real economy. This is in contrast to the earlier monetary aggregate growth rules of Friedman and Meltzer. It is crucial that we do not overlook these rules, as they can easily be forgotten if we are not careful. If you examine table 1.1, from a paper I recently wrote about the Federal

Table 1.1. Monetary policy rules as reported in the Federal Reserve Report, March 3, 2023

Taylor (1993) rule	$R_t^{T93} = r_t^{LR} + \pi_t + 0.5(\pi_t - \pi^{LR}) + (u_t^{LR} - u_t)$
Balanced-approach rule	$R_t^{BA} = r_t^{LR} + \pi_t + 0.5(\pi_t - \pi^{LR}) + 2(u_t^{LR} - u_t)$
Balanced-approach (shortfalls) rule	$R_t^{BAS} = r_t^{LR} + \pi_t + 0.5(\pi_t - \pi^{LR}) + 2min\{(u_t^{LR} - u_t), 0\}$
Adjusted Taylor (1993) rule	$R_t^{T93adj} = max\{R_t^{T93} - Z_t, ELB\}$
First-difference rule	$R_t^{FD} = R_{t-1} + 0.5(\pi_t - \pi^{LR}) + (u_t^{LR} - u_t) - (u_{t-4}^{LR} - u_{t-4})$

Note: R_t^{T93}, R_t^{BA}, R_t^{BAS}, R_t^{T93adj}, and R_t^{FD} represent the values of the nominal federal funds rate prescribed by the Taylor (1993), balanced-approach, balanced-approach (shortfalls), adjusted Taylor (1993), and first difference rules, respectively. R_{t-1} denotes the midpoint of the target range for the federal funds rate for quarter $t-1$, u_t is the unemployment rate in quarter t, and r_t^{LR} is the level of the neutral real federal funds rate in the longer run that is expected to be consistent with sustaining maximum employment and inflation at the FOMC's 2% longer-run objective, represented by π^{LR}. π_t denotes the realized four-quarter price inflation for quarter t. In addition, u_t^{LR} is the rate of unemployment expected in the longer run. Z_t is the cumulative sum of past deviations of the federal funds rate from the prescriptions of the Taylor (1993) rule when that rule prescribes setting the federal funds rate below an effective lower bound of 12.5 basis points. The Taylor (1993) rule and other policy rules generally respond to the deviation of real output from its full capacity level. In these equations, the output gap has been replaced with the gap between the rate of unemployment in the longer run and its actual level (using a relationship known as Okun's law) to represent the rules in terms of the unemployment rate. The rules are implemented as responding to core PCE (personal consumption expenditures) inflation rather than to headline PCE inflation because current and near-term core inflation rates tend to outperform headline inflation rates as predictors of the medium-term behavior of headline inflation.

Source: Board of Governors (2023).

Reserve and the monetary policy rules reported in the Fed's documentation, you will see how relevant these rules remain, particularly the Taylor rule. The table shows my original (1993) rule and four popular variants that have been developed since.

The Federal Funds Rate over Time

Figure 1.1 shows the evolution of the effective federal funds rate over the past fifty years, illustrating significant swings and the consequences of adhering to—or deviating from—these policy rules. This chart spans the late 1960s through 2024. Notably, the federal funds rate reached nearly 20% during the challenging economic times of the Great Inflation, underscoring the necessity for rigorous corrective policy measures. Since the 1980s, the Federal Reserve's shift toward a more rules-based approach has likely contributed to the overall decrease in rates. Since the beginning of the twenty-first century, as seen in the figure, the Global Financial Crisis of 2007–9 reflected the Fed's keeping interest rates too low for too long, which precipitated a housing

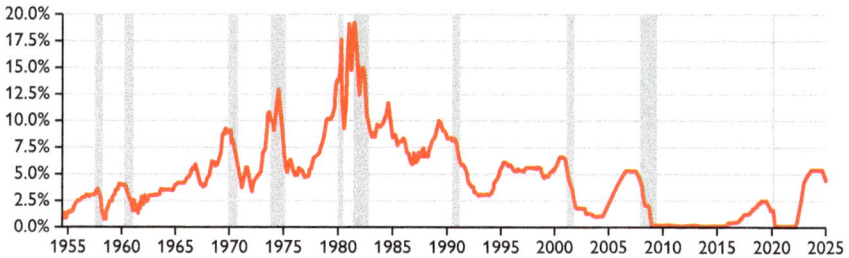

Figure 1.1. The effective federal funds rate.

Source: Board of Governors of the Federal Reserve System via Federal Reserve Bank of St. Louis (FRED).

boom-and-bust. In the subsequent recovery period, the Fed also kept rates too low relative to the rule, as it did during the COVID-19 pandemic. This likely fueled the recent inflationary burst seen at the right of the figure. At present, the goal is to bring interest rates into the ideal range between 2% and 3%.

The Path Forward in Monetary Policy

While historically high rates have posed challenges to the real economy, as recently experienced, our focus today should be on maintaining a target range closer to 2%, possibly 2.5% to 3%. However, achieving this stability continues to be uncertain. It is not solely the Fed's challenge; other countries are also navigating similar situations. Charting the trajectory of the effective funds rate over the past fifty years reveals that we have seen extreme fluctuations in interest rates, and we find ourselves currently in a medium stage, attempting to reduce rates slightly. The success of these efforts remains to be seen.

This, in essence, encapsulates our overarching goal. How can we achieve this? By adhering to a series of established rules as described in table 1.1, one of which—the original Taylor rule—is illustrated in figure 1.2. The Taylor rule is a key framework for monetary policy. It posits that when inflation is at 2% $(p = 2)$ and the GDP gap is zero $(y = 0)$, the interest rate should be set at 4%. This rule has gained significant attention but is part of a broader context that includes similar rules adopted by other central banks, thereby enriching our discussions on contemporary monetary policy.

Below Target: The Consequences of Low Interest Rates

Figure 1.3 allows for a closer analysis of how the federal funds rate has shifted since 2016, noting that decisions made during this period, especially during and after the pandemic, may have inadvertently contributed to rising

$$r = p + 0.5y + 0.5(p - 2) + 2$$

$$r = 1.5p + 0.5y + 1$$

where
  r is the federal funds rate
  p is the inflation rate
  y is the real GDP gap

Figure 1.2. A simple version of the Taylor rule: If inflation is 2% (p = 2) and the GDP gap is 0% (y = 0), then the interest rate r should be 4% (r = 4).

Source: Taylor (1993).

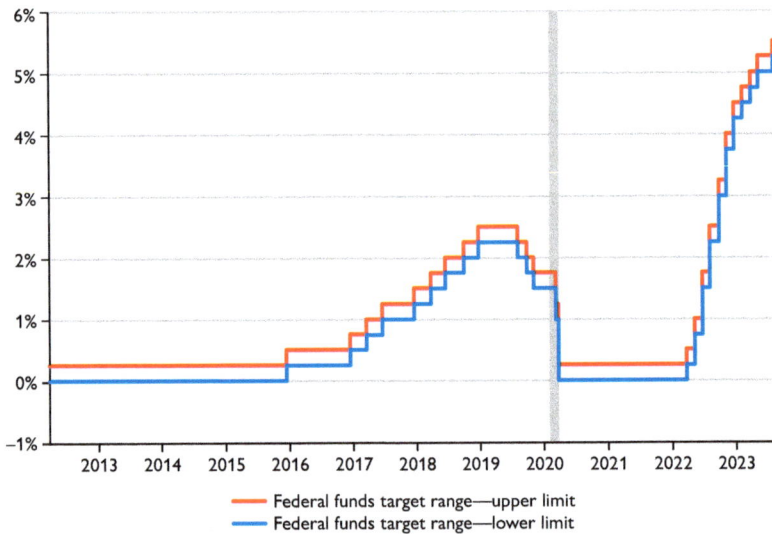

Federal funds target range—upper limit
Federal funds target range—lower limit

Figure 1.3. The Fed held the interest rate lower than the Taylor rule, leading to rising inflation.

Source: Board of Governors of the Federal Reserve System via FRED.

inflation. The signals sent by the Fed regarding interest-rate adjustments have sometimes lacked clarity, resulting in unintended consequences. It is imperative that the Fed aligns its policy rate with established targets to maintain predictability in monetary policy.

The Cost of Low Rates: Historical Context of Inflation

Figure 1.4 provides a historical examination of policy rates, highlighting discrepancies between recommended (based on the Taylor rule) and actual

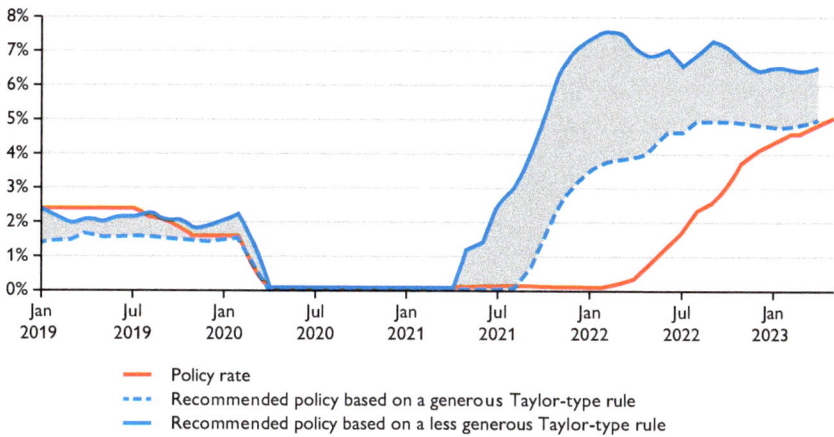

Figure 1.4. This chart, produced by James Bullard, shows that policy was too low, resulting in rising inflation.

Source: James Bullard, Federal Reserve Bank of St. Louis.

rates since January 2019. This underlines the importance of precision in implementing monetary policy. The red line represents the actual policy rate, while the dashed blue line depicts the recommended policy based on a more generous interpretation of the Taylor rule. A less generous interpretation is represented by a less conspicuous straight blue line. The significant gap between these lines reflects the serious consequences of being misaligned with recommended measures.

This illustrates the point I have emphasized in my discussion: One must exercise caution in policy implementation, as deviations can lead to significant risks. While we can debate the specifics, the ideal scenario is to keep rates as close as possible to their target.

Monetary Policy's Global Impact

We must also consider the Fed's role within the global monetary system. Its interactions with other central banks such as the European Central Bank and the People's Bank of China significantly influence domestic policies.

This analysis serves as an illustrative example of the significant deviations observed in the data during specific historical periods. The actual implicit price deflator, presented in figure 1.5, is a reliable measure of the inflation rate. Inflation rates peaked in the 1950s, 1970s, and 1980s before experiencing a substantial decline, except for a recent surge that approached nearly 10%.

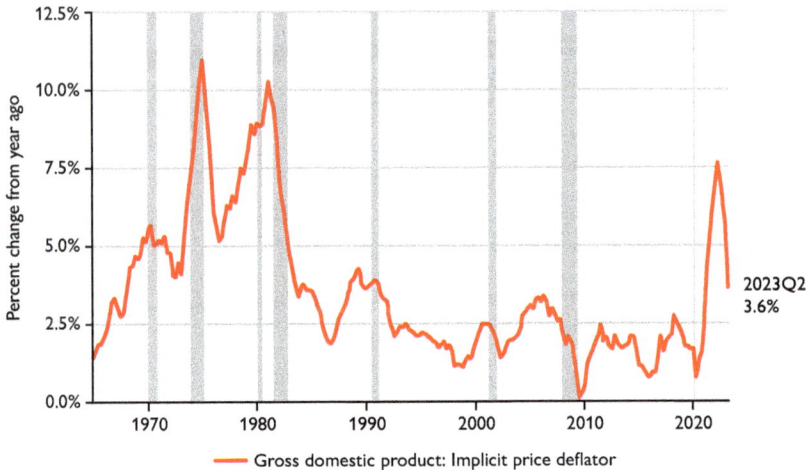

Figure 1.5. The inflation rate rose well above the Fed's target of 4%.

Source: US Bureau of Economic Analysis via FRED.

This domestic price deflator remains a central focus of the Federal Reserve's analysis.

Currently, there is ongoing concern regarding the sustainability of this decline. The Fed has explicitly targeted an inflation rate of 2%, although recent measures indicate levels closer to 2.5% to 3%. It is crucial to avoid inflationary spikes, which deviate from the intended conditions.

Inflation Trends in Latin America and Their Connection to the Fed

Figure 1.6 illustrates inflation rates in Latin America, specifically among Brazil, Chile, Colombia, Mexico, and Peru, collectively referred to as the LA Five (LA5), up to January 2022. These inflation trends closely follow the Fed's actions, indicating that the Fed's influence is not isolated but has ramifications for monetary policies in these countries.

The objective of our reform efforts in the international monetary system should be to foster greater cooperation among all countries—including Russia, China, and Japan—while ensuring alignment where feasible. Pursuing an international framework that incorporates similar rules or strategies to those of the Fed would facilitate enhanced global economic stability.

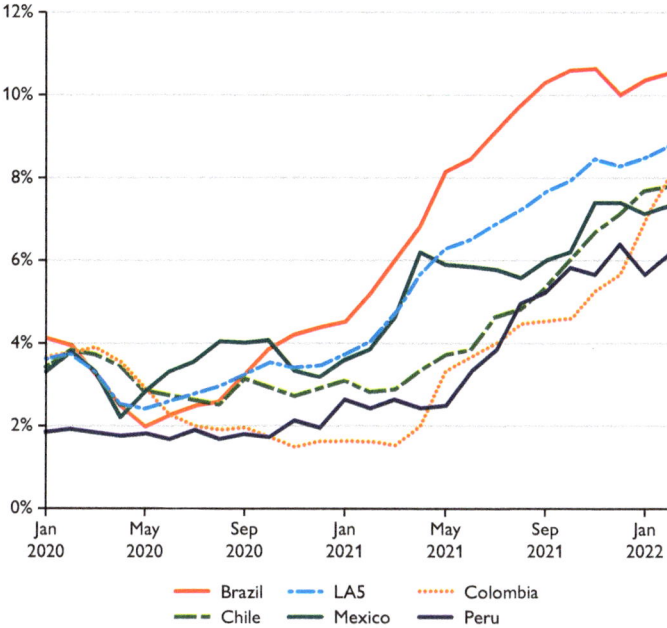

Figure 1.6. Inflation in Latin America from January 2020 to January 2022.
Source: Haver Analytics, national authorities, and IMF staff calculations.

Conclusion

In conclusion, while progress has been made, particularly in the past two to three years, there remains significant work to be done. The ideal scenario envisions a coordinated approach to establish a framework where inflation targets can align internationally, ideally matching the Fed's target of 2%, and contributing to greater global economic stability.

References

Board of Governors (Board of Governors of the Federal Reserve System). 2023. "Monetary Policy Report." Board of Governors of the Federal Reserve System. March 3. https://www.federalreserve.gov/monetarypolicy/files/20230303 _mprfullreport.pdf.

Taylor, John B. 1993. "Discretion versus Policy Rules in Practice." *Carnegie-Rochester Conference Series on Public Policy* 39 (December): 195–214.

MICHAEL D. BORDO: We can take a couple of questions and answers. Questions and then answers. Bill Nelson.

BILL NELSON: Thank you, John. Bill Nelson from the Bank Policy Institute. To prepare for this event, I went back and read some of the original transcripts and research prepared for the very first SOMC meeting.

I was really struck by the disdain that they expressed for caring about interest rates when thinking about monetary policy and the focus that they put on balance sheet items, including money. Of course, your rule is all about interest rates, interest rates that presumably are implemented through fine-tuning operations very much sort of antithetical to some of the things that they held dear.

So I was hoping you could sort of pull those two things together and explain the intellectual connection between your work on rules-based interest-rate policy and the SOMC's original views about what was important and what wasn't important.

JOHN B. TAYLOR: I have been very interested in monetary policy rules all my life, starting before there were interest rate rules, there were just money-growth rules.

My experiences drew me away from money-growth rules but not completely. It is easier to think about what the policy interest rate should be to allow the Fed to reach its main objectives.

Moreover, I think that each country setting its policy rate in the same way would improve global welfare. It might be best if all countries coordinated on say a 2% policy rate.

KEVIN CHEN: Kevin Chen, Horizon Financial. My question is: You mentioned about Japan, right? So Japan has been at a zero interest rate for so long, they tried to increase the rate, it caused such a big turmoil this year. Do you think the Taylor rule should apply to Japan? What's the pros and cons? Let's say if we do increase to 3%, let's say.

TAYLOR: The Bank of Japan talks about the Taylor rule, but that does not mean that they follow it. For many years, their policy rates were well below the Taylor rule, but now they seem to be catching up, which is a good sign. However, the extent of this adjustment remains uncertain, especially considering their significant trading partners, such as China and Russia, which influence their policy decisions. Moreover, I think that the Fed as a global leader in following my rules-based approach would make an important difference and is a key player in this debate.

MICHAEL MORK [PRESIDENT, MORK CAPITAL MANAGEMENT, LLC]: Yes, in 2012 through the pandemic recession, moderate M2 growth produced nominal GDP growth of about 3% a year.

Then the Federal Reserve increased the money supply by 35% and, according to monetarist doctrine a year later, inflation took off. [Jerome] Powell has said that he doesn't pay attention to money anymore. Is this a mistake on Powell's part? And do you think that money was the major cause of the inflation?

TAYLOR: I do not think that rapid money growth was the major cause of the postpandemic inflation, although money growth is a very important component in explaining what happened. Having studied money for most of my life, I recognize its importance, but it is not the sole determinant of economic outcomes. From an international perspective, I think it would be beneficial for countries to align their interest rates more closely with those of the United States, recognizing that specific circumstances may vary. The global solution to keep inflation low is for all countries to coordinate their policy rates at the same level to keep inflation rates in line. So that's my short answer to your very difficult question.

MATTHEW KLEIN [FOUNDER AND PUBLISHER OF THE OVERSHOOT]: Thank you. I'm wondering, particularly in the last chart, there were actually several central banks that raised rates before the Fed, particularly in emerging markets like Brazil and Czechia.

And yet they seem to have had similar, if not worse, inflation outcomes in the United States. I'm just wondering if you could kind of walk through why you think that might have happened. Thank you.

TAYLOR: When different central banks set their policy rates to achieve low inflation, they need to consider their different institutions and market structures in setting wages and prices.

This variability is likely why we observe such diverse economic outcomes across countries. Some nations are faring well, while others are experiencing significant difficulties, highlighting the complexities inherent in formulating effective monetary policy. For instance, many Latin American countries have seen substantial interest-rate hikes alongside rising inflation during this period, and it gives you a sense of what to look for.

BORDO: Thank you.

The Evolution of Monetary Policy

2

The Fifty-Year History of the SOMC and the Evolution of Monetary Policy

Michael D. Bordo and Mickey D. Levy

Introduction and Summary

The Shadow Open Market Committee, a small committee of academic and business economists, was established in the early 1970s by leading monetarist economists Allan Meltzer, Karl Brunner, and Anna Schwartz to promote the argument that inflation was a monetary phenomenon. They emphasized that reducing the rate of growth of the money stock was necessary to lower inflation. This monetarist argument was initiated and championed by Milton Friedman, who had battled since the 1950s with the mainstream Keynesian economists who posited that monetary policy was far less effective than fiscal policy.

The SOMC fashioned itself as an "outside watchdog" of the Federal Reserve's monetary policy setting conducted by its Federal Open Market Committee (FOMC).[1] In the 1970s, it successfully promoted the importance of money and influenced the debate in Congress and at the Fed about how to reduce inflation. Along with other monetarists, the SOMC likely influenced Fed chair Paul Volcker to shift gears in 1979 toward its successful disinflation based on reducing growth of a monetary aggregate—nonborrowed reserves—and allowing short-term interest rates to fluctuate widely.

Over time, two themes have influenced the Fed's monetary policy and the debate about how to conduct it: the evolution of the Fed's interpretation of its dual mandate and the evolution of what "rules" mean in the ongoing debate about the benefits of rules versus discretion. The SOMC's history, which has had distinct phases, reflects these evolving themes.

During the Great Moderation of the 1980s and 1990s, the SOMC continued with its strictly monetarist monetary policy recommendations of targeting money growth without factoring in fluctuations in money demand. It became outdated and fell out of favor as the Fed and the economics profession shifted back toward the targeting of interest rates. The SOMC provided sound advice on other policies. It properly cautioned the Fed against using monetary policy to stabilize the US dollar while advocating flexible exchange rates and free international trade. It promoted sound fiscal policy and argued in favor of rules that would constrain government spending and deficits.

Founding member Allan Meltzer retired from the SOMC in the late 1990s, and SOMC members Charles Plosser and Anna Schwartz became cochairs. Former SOMC members Jerry Jordan and Bill Poole had become influential Fed members, while former Fed member Lee Hoskins joined the SOMC and continued his promotion of price stability, transparency, and accountability.

The SOMC provided wise counsel during the early 2000s, but its following had diminished, and the Fed did not listen to it. Ben McCallum joined the SOMC in 2000 and incorporated the theoretical advances in monetary economics of the 1980s–90s into the Committee's research and underlined its promotion of inflation targeting and rules-based monetary policy. The SOMC's policy statements evolved toward interest rate recommendations while keeping an eye on the monetary aggregates. In 2002, the SOMC argued strenuously that the US would not fall into a Japanese-style deflation as the Fed feared, and urged it to maintain a symmetrical assessment of inflation and raise interest rates. It also warned of the risks to financial stability posed by the housing agencies Fannie Mae and Freddie Mac.

The modern SOMC began to form prior to the Great Financial Crisis (GFC) by attracting new members with strong academic backgrounds and a broad diversity of monetary and financial research interests. New members included Marvin Goodfriend, Michael Bordo, and Charles Calomiris. Subsequently, the SOMC expanded to include Peter Ireland, Athanasios Orphanides, and Plosser (who rejoined after his tenure at the Fed), along with Andrew Levin and Deborah Lucas. The SOMC's newest members are former FOMC members Jeff Lacker and Jim Bullard. The current dominant profile of SOMC members is academic with significant Fed experience.

The SOMC research policy recommendations have evolved and broadened from its strict monetarist foundations, formed by the following core beliefs: sound monetary policy that is guided by systematic rules whose primary objective is stable and low inflation as the best foundation for healthy economic performance; transparency and accountability; and systematic and economically rational approaches to financial regulations.

Looking back on the past half century, the Fed has made three major costly monetary policy errors: the high inflation of the 1970s; its extended low interest rates of the early 2000s, which facilitated the debt-financed housing bubble that evolved into severe financial stresses; and the high inflation of the 2020s. Prior to and during each episode, the SOMC provided warnings and sound policy advice. The SOMC's early warnings about the inflationary impact of unprecedented deficit spending and money growth in 2020–21 were prescient. Unfortunately, the Fed did not heed the SOMC's warnings and recommendations on the last two events.

The SOMC continues to thrive and contribute important research and insights on the Fed's monetary policy, its internal governance, financial regulatory policies, and other economic policies that support sound economic and financial market performance. In an era in which the Fed is most comfortable listening to friendly voices, the SOMC's role as an outside watchdog is critical.

The second section of this paper discusses the origins of the SOMC and the 1970s. The third section covers the SOMC during the Great Moderation of the 1980s–90s. The fourth section describes the SOMC's contributions in the early 2000s. The fifth section discusses the modern-era SOMC and its diverse research and policy recommendation contributions. The sixth section provides concluding remarks. The appendices provide lists of all SOMC members over its history and guest speakers at SOMC meetings and archives of SOMC papers.

The First Phase of the SOMC: Origins and the 1970s

The SOMC was a direct extension of the monetarist campaign in the Keynes-monetarist debate of the 1950s to 1970s. Leading monetarist Milton Friedman (1956) was joined by Homer Jones at the St. Louis Fed, Karl Brunner, Allan Meltzer, and Anna Schwartz, and economists and policymakers in Europe and elsewhere. The monetarist approach to macroeconomics derived from the Chicago tradition going back to the 1920s and before (Tavlas 2023). Its critique of the Keynesian approach, which emphasized the impotence of monetary policy to stabilize aggregate demand and the economy, dominated the macroeconomic and monetary policy debate in the post–World War II era.

Friedman and his principal coauthor Anna Schwartz (and several other prominent coauthors and students) forcefully argued that "money matters," and changes in the quantity of money interacting with a stable money-demand function were the key drivers of nominal income, with its effects first impacting real activity and then the price level (Nelson 2020). This contrasted with the Keynesian view, which emphasized the importance of other sources of aggregate demand, particularly fiscal policies—spending and taxes. A key tenet of Friedman's view was that "inflation is always and everywhere a monetary phenomenon."

In the 1960s, Keynesian and monetarist models and their policy applications developed further and their contrasts were clarified. Keynesian thinking evolved based on the Samuelson and Solow (1960) interpretation of the Phillips curve that provided policymakers a menu of options in the trade-off between inflation and unemployment. Several commonly accepted beliefs were that activist policies could achieve a measurable improvement in outcomes based on the trade-off, and the costs of achieving low inflation were outweighed by the benefits of high employment. Another common belief was that inflation was largely caused by a wide array of nonmonetary factors, especially the monopoly power of strong labor unions and large firms as well as commodity price shocks.

Monetarists Karl Brunner and Allan Meltzer worked tirelessly to promote monetarism. Brunner, who popularized the term "monetarism" in a lecture published in the *Federal Reserve Bank of St. Louis Review* in 1968, and later in 1970 in the *Review of World Economics* (*Weltwirtschaftliches Archiv*; Brunner 1968, 1970), posited six principles of monetarism (also see Laidler 1991).

1. The real economy is essentially stable; relative prices are determined by the operation of free-market forces. This view was in sharp contrast to the dominant Keynesian view in the post–World War II era that the basic instability of the real economy had to be offset by activist fiscal policy.
2. The key sources of shocks to the economy were monetary, induced by central bank errors, in turn based on flawed economic doctrine.
3. Monetary shocks (i.e., changes in the money stock) impacted the real economy in the short run and the price level in the long run. The adjustment mechanism between the short and long runs was determined by the costs of obtaining information.

4. Changes in the money stock largely reflected changes in the monetary base as a consequence of monetary policy actions. The changes in the monetary base interacted with a stable money multiplier, which reflected the portfolio choices of the banking system and the nonbank private sector.
5. The transmission mechanism of monetary policy worked through a portfolio balance mechanism involving changes in the relative prices of financial and nonfinancial assets, which ultimately affected the real price of capital and impacted investment and income.
6. Monetary policy clearly dominated fiscal policy as a tool for economic stabilization.

In Brunner's principles of monetarism, a targeted money-growth rate was the policy rule to be followed and discretionary policies did not play a part.

Brunner and Meltzer prepared a lengthy four-part pamphlet on the conduct of monetary policy for the US House Committee on Banking and Currency. They clearly laid out a monetarist framework for economic policy, discussed past mistakes, and promoted the importance of money (Brunner and Meltzer 1964a, 1964b, 1964c, 1964d; see Bordo 2019). A conference organized by Karl Brunner sponsored by UCLA's Institute for Government and Policy developed and refined many aspects of monetarism (Brunner 1969).

The *Federal Reserve Bank of St. Louis Review* published a debate on the efficacy of monetarist and Keynesian approaches to macroeconomic stability (Andersen 1973; Hetzel 2013). Friedman's (1968) American Economic Association Presidential Address "The Role of Monetary Policy" introduced "unanticipated" versus "anticipated" inflation and argued for the long-run neutrality of money—that the Fed's monetary policy may have a transitory impact on real variables but in the long run only affected inflation. This notion greatly narrowed room for effective countercyclical policies.

Perfect Timing, Right Model

The Great Inflation and the disarray of economic policymaking of the 1970s provided the ideal context for the establishment of the SOMC. Inflation ratcheted up beginning in the mid-1960s, driven by expansive government spending and monetary accommodation through an "even keel" policy when Fed chair William McChesney Martin was pressured by President Lyndon Baines Johnson not to lift rates (Meltzer 2005). Inflation rose from 1.5% in

1965 to 6% in 1969, dipped to 3.5%, and then reaccelerated in 1971. Higher inflationary expectations pushed up bond yields.

Arthur Burns became Fed chair in February 1970. An empirical economist and pioneer with Wesley Clair Mitchell in developing the business cycle tradition of the National Bureau of Economic Research (NBER), Burns believed that inflation was driven by an eclectic array of primarily nonmonetary sources. He did not believe in the effectiveness of monetary policy and favored incomes policies. Burns worked closely with President Richard Nixon to impose wage and price controls in August 1971 and then led the Fed to increase money growth in 1972 to help in Nixon's reelection campaign. In 1973, the resulting acceleration in aggregate demand pushed up inflation despite the difficult-to-administer wage and price controls.

The SOMC held its first meeting in September 1973. It was organized by Meltzer, along with Brunner and Schwartz. The Committee also included business economists who were well connected in financial and media circles and frequently testified before Congress on economic and policy issues. The SOMC's simple monetarist proposal to gradually slow money growth to reduce inflation provided a striking alternative to mainstream economics and the wage and price controls that were a policy failure in every dimension.

Several components contributed to its 1970s success. Its simple money-growth target proposals were easy to understand and could be tracked and monitored. The Committee's communications were well organized, and its policy recommendations attracted attention. Meltzer had obtained ample financing from nonprofit foundations to finance its operations.

The earliest SOMC meetings featured discussions that centered on a policy statement written by Meltzer along with Anna Schwartz, an assessment of current inflation and economic conditions, and written contributions by SOMC members. Papers by SOMC members addressed different aspects of Fed policy and made recommendations on an array of economic, fiscal, and financial issues. An archive of SOMC policy statements and papers by members beginning with the first meeting in September 1973 is at the SOMC website.[2]

Many of the papers set out the basis for targeting money growth and identified past consequences of money-growth deviations. They highlighted the mistakes of discretionary ("fine-tuning") policies and wage and price controls (for example, see Brunner 1974). Jim Meigs (1975) provided analyses that linked money supply to the economy and inflation. Beryl Sprinkel (1975) put forth a proposal for a Federal Reserve annual plan including money-growth targets. Thomas Mayer (1975) argued that the Fed should lobby against pending congressional legislation that would impose credit allocations on commercial banks. Wilson Schmidt (1975) provided an international overview and comments on foreign exchange intervention. Jerry Jordan joined the SOMC in 1976 and provided a series of reports on monetary policy and the economic and inflation outlooks, displaying the growth rates of the monetary base and the broader monetary aggregates (Jordan 1978b). Bob Rasche and James Johannes (1979) provided ongoing analysis of the money multipliers, relating the broad monetary aggregates to the monetary base, and money velocity, relating nominal GDP to money. Erich Heinemann (1977) kept tabs on Federal Reserve policies and current economic conditions. Meltzer (1974) assessed the sources of bank failures and policy remedies. The SOMC policy statements and members' position papers critiqued government fiscal policies, tracking spending, taxes, and deficits, and urged fiscal austerity. Rudy Penner joined the SOMC in 1977 and analyzed fiscal policies (Penner 1977).

These early meetings established the format of the SOMC's semiannual meetings. The SOMC's policy statements and papers by members were presented and debated at Sunday-afternoon meetings attended by a dozen or so nonmember economists. The policy statements (for example, see SOMC 1977) and press releases were reviewed over dinner. At a press conference held on Monday, SOMC members would provide brief comments on their position papers and release the SOMC's policy statement and press release. By Tuesday morning, the SOMC's comments appeared in hundreds of news outlets. Hard copies of the policy statements and SOMC member reports were mailed to a distribution list. This format was followed through the early 2000s.

SOMC Communications

The SOMC's marketing campaign was directed at the media, Congress, and the Fed, and other global central banks. Friendly media, particularly Lindley Clark of *The Wall Street Journal*, promoted the SOMC's ideas. John Berry of *The Washington Post* reported on every SOMC meeting, as did the Associated Press, with its wide correspondent network. Foreign correspondents also covered the SOMC and publicized its ideas and proposals. This helped export the SOMC's platform and proposals to global central banks and policymakers.

Members Allan Meltzer, Jim Meigs, Beryl Sprinkel, and Jerry Jordan highlighted the benefits of the SOMC's money target proposals when they testified before Congress and spoke with the media (Jordan 1978a). Key congressional staff who advocated monetarism, particularly Bob Weintraub of the House Committee on Banking and Currency, incorporated the SOMC ideas and proposals into congressional documents and legislation.

During the decade, there were major theoretical advances in economics, including rational expectations and the Lucas critique that called into question the efficacy of countercyclical policies and fine-tuning, and the trade-off between inflation and unemployment in the Phillips curve (Lucas 1976; Sargent and Wallace 1976). The SOMC's proposals and Committee philosophies were largely consistent with these theoretical advances, although it operated on a less technical level, relying on strict monetarist principles that assumed a simplistic model with stable demand for money. It promoted principles of sound central banking that was based on a simple money-based rule that was transparent and eschewed discretionary fine-tuning. This policy would build credibility. Complementing this money-based rule, the SOMC favored floating exchange rates—and arguing against interventions that attempted to manage currencies—and also advocated free trade and fiscal austerity.

The SOMC's Successful Influences

From its modest but ambitious origins the SOMC garnered much attention for stressing the important role of expansionary money in determining inflation. Basically, the SOMC offered a solution that filled an important gap in the policy space at a time when the persistence of inflation was the biggest economic and social issue. Fed chair Burns was unswayed by the SOMC's monetarist prescriptions and Milton Friedman's ever-expanding presence, and the Fed came under heightened criticism through the decade (Nelson 2025). As inflation ratcheted up, the SOMC's efforts with the media gained significant coverage.

Elsewhere, weekly money-supply data, first initiated by the St. Louis Fed and reported by the Fed, became a key focal point for financial markets and the economic media. Announcements of short-term shifts in the money supply moved financial markets. However misinterpreted, the media and financial coverage brought constant public attention to money. In financial markets struggling with high interest rates and weak stock-market performance, attention was drawn to money, high inflation, and the Fed's ineffectiveness.

The SOMC also made important inroads with Congress. Congressional hearings of the finance and banking committees focused on money growth alongside other important issues. Thanks to well-placed advocates, excerpts of the 1964 Brunner–Meltzer pamphlets on monetarism appeared in select congressional documents. In February 1975, House Concurrent Resolution 124 directed the Fed to "increase the money supply . . . and maintain growth of the money supply commensurate with production, in order to maximize employment and stabilize prices, and require the Federal Reserve to consult with Congress at semiannual hearings before the Committees on Banking concerning its money supply growth targets and other monetary policy actions required in the upcoming six months."[3]

The requirement for the Fed to report to Congress semiannually and to provide money-growth targets was incorporated into the Federal Reserve Reform Act of 1977 and the Full Employment and Balanced Growth Act of 1978, which established the Fed's dual mandate of low inflation and maximum employment. The Fed complied with the congressional resolution and provided money-growth ranges to Congress. However, it did not change its operating procedures to reduce money growth within submitted ranges. In congressional testimony, Burns testified that the dual mandate established by the Humphrey–Hawkins legislation would constrain the independence of the Fed. Following enactment in the late 1970s, the Fed's new dual mandate was not a key focal point for its policy actions—it was overwhelmed by rising inflation, unemployment, and the US dollar crisis—and Burns and his successors G. William Miller and Paul Volcker rarely mentioned it.

Burns and the Fed were an easy target for the SOMC. The wage and price controls he had promoted had been a disaster; inflation rose above 8% even before the first oil shock in October 1973 and surged to 12% when those controls were lifted. The 1973–75 recession was deep and resulted in high unemployment. The stock market was reeling from high inflation and interest rates. Inflation receded to 5% by year-end 1976 and provided a respite, but beginning in 1977, the Fed's ongoing accommodative monetary policy resulted in higher inflation and inflationary expectations.

Monetary policy was in disarray when Burns was replaced by G. William Miller as Fed chair in early 1978. The Fed faced a severe US dollar crisis in 1978 and the second oil shock in 1979. Meltzer blamed the falling US dollar on the Fed's inflationary monetary policies, the disarray of the Carter administration's economic policies, and the deterioration in credibility as the crisis unfolded in the spring of 1978: "The financial markets see that there is no policy. The stock market, the bond market and the foreign exchange market shout their disbelief. . . . They sense that the lack of policy, the drift to controls, and the reliance on stop gaps will continue" (Meltzer 1978). This contrasted sharply with the Carter administration, which blamed the weaker US dollar on higher oil prices.

Inflation was an international phenomenon, and the SOMC made specific recommendations to other central banks to target money growth. However, these recommendations carried little weight, as central bank monetary policies in Austria, Germany, and elsewhere were already dominated by stability cultures that resulted from their historical painful bouts of hyperinflation. In the United Kingdom, a small group of monetarists led by Alan Walters, David Laidler, Michael Parkin, and others urged SOMC-type prescriptions, but their impacts were limited.[4] However, the SOMC's principles may have influenced in subsequent years some small open economies as well as some emerging-market economies to prioritize low inflation and pursue rule-like monetary policy.

SOMC Influences on the Volcker-Led Fed

Paul Volcker, president of the Federal Reserve Bank of New York and FOMC vice chair, was very concerned in the 1970s about the high inflation, a falling US dollar, and the disarray of failing policies, which he worried had resulted in a loss of credibility. As such, he was an inflation hawk and frequently dissented on the FOMC's monetary decisions. While Volcker agreed that in the long run, inflation was a monetary phenomenon and that money growth needed to be slowed, he argued that the volatility of money velocity made money targeting an unreliable policy approach for conducting monetary policy and forecasting near-term inflation and economic activity. However, in public speeches Volcker was relatively sympathetic to the role of money. He made clear that his primary concern was breaking inflationary expectations and regaining credibility (Volcker 1976, 1977).

President Jimmy Carter nominated Volcker to become Fed chair to replace G. William Miller in mid-1979, and in his confirmation hearings, Volcker made clear that the Fed would need to aggressively tighten monetary policy. This differed from the SOMC's prescription of a gradual slowdown in money growth. Brunner (1979), in congressional testimony on the Full Employment Act of 1978, fully recognized the importance of the Fed's reducing inflationary expectations and regaining credibility but argued that the Fed's erratic and unreliable path of monetary policy had created a "murky fog" such that abrupt, aggressive tightening with a sharp slowdown in the monetary base would not be credible and would very likely result in recession. As a result, Brunner favored a gradual approach to lowering inflation.

The broader debate among economists and policymakers centered on the economic costs of reducing inflation. This involved assessments of what it would take to break inflationary expectations and the shape of the short-run Phillips curve. Volcker rejected the gradualist approach as not being up to the task presented by the dire circumstances and believed that aggressive monetary tightening would be required to restore credibility and reduce inflationary expectations.

In October 1979, the Fed dramatically shifted its operating procedures from its long-standing targeting of interest rates to targeting nonborrowed reserves, acknowledging that the new procedure would involve high and volatile short-term interest rates. One interpretation is that this was a major step by the Fed toward acknowledging the importance of controlling money growth as critical to reducing inflation. But it was not the "monetarism" of Friedman, Brunner, and Meltzer that involved targeting the monetary base or a broader monetary aggregate. Rather, the Fed's policy targeted nonborrowed bank reserves, not the monetary base or a broader monetary aggregate, and it did so temporarily to address the emergency situation, not permanently. At the time, Friedman, Brunner, and Meltzer were quite critical of the Volcker strategy (Lindsey et al. 2005; Nelson 2023). It remains uncertain whether Volcker went partway toward controlling money growth on an emergency basis, or whether he was using money targeting as a foil for his aggressive rate increases.

President Carter initially supported Volcker. However, when the Fed raised rates to 17.6% in the spring of 1980, the Carter administration became very concerned about credit markets, believing banks were too lax in supplying credit and consumer demand for credit was too strong. Carter hurriedly announced credit controls to be imposed by the Fed, despite the Fed's objections. This policy backfired and, combined with the soaring interest rates, led to a temporary but severe credit crunch and a very sharp economic recession that lasted only one quarter. In response, the Volcker-led Fed reversed course on interest rates, immediately lowering them to 9%. When the economy quickly rebounded, the Fed raised rates dramatically to 19% by year-end 1980.

President Ronald Reagan supported Paul Volcker's aggressive disinflationary monetary policy, acknowledging it as necessary medicine to reduce inflation, even though it resulted in recession. The Fed began easing interest rates in the summer of 1982 based on evidence that inflation had slowed markedly and banking stresses had mounted. The recession continued until 1982 Q4 and the unemployment rate peaked at 10.8%. While inflation receded, inflationary expectations and bond yields took much longer to recede, frustrating Volcker. In subsequent years, the economy recovered robustly from the back-to-back recessions of 1980–82, the US dollar continued to recover, and financial markets improved. While Volcker's disinflationary policies imposed high short-run costs, the rise in the unemployment rate was less than had been predicted by standard Phillips curve models that had not appropriately incorporated adjustments of inflationary expectations (Hornstein 2008). Meltzer's and Brunner's early criticism of Volcker's aggressive monetary-tightening strategy gradually eased over the 1980s, and they came around to admire Volcker's efforts.

In summary, in the 1970s the SOMC was an important component of a network of monetarist economists that actively advocated for monetary control to reduce inflation. Whether Volcker really believed in the monetarist medicine or used it as a communications camouflage to raise rates dramatically is uncertain. But the SOMC had accomplished most of what it had set out to do and received substantial credit.

Subsequently, Bill Poole, Bob Rasche, and David Wheelock (2013), at an NBER conference, provided a favorable view of the SOMC's monetary policy recommendations. They used simulations of a New Keynesian economic model to show that the gradual stabilization of money growth favored by the SOMC would have outperformed the policies actually implemented by the Fed during the Great Inflation era. Their discussant, Christina Romer (2013), was critical of the SOMC and the Poole-Rasche-Wheelock study. She noted that money velocity was volatile and showed that over the extended period 1973–99, the SOMC's proposed money-growth targets would have resulted in more erratic economic output and would not have been effective in reducing inflation. Her assessment of the SOMC was more charitable in the 1970s but quite critical in the 1980s and 1990s.

The Second Phase of the SOMC's History: The Great Moderation

The dramatic Volcker disinflation ushered in the Great Moderation, the period of the 1980s and 1990s characterized by generally moderate inflation and healthy economic growth. The crisis environment of the high-inflation 1970s dissipated and confidence returned. The focus of monetary and economic policies was to maintain the lower inflation that Volcker had achieved and reverse the damages of the 1970s. Tax cuts and indexing taxes to inflation were the centerpiece of tax reform. The Fed committed policy to low inflation and credibility for low inflation. The Volcker Fed—and more so the Fed under his successor, Alan Greenspan—began to emphasize the importance of preemptive monetary tightening when higher inflation was anticipated. The Fed also began conducting research on the benefits of targeting low inflation.

During the lengthy span of Volcker's (1979–87) and Greenspan's (1987–2006) chairmanships of the Fed, both successfully focused monetary policy on keeping inflation and the unemployment rate moderately low, but neither made the dual mandate the Fed's focal point or referred much to it. Both believed that stable low inflation and inflation expectations were the optimal foundation for achieving sustained healthy growth, and that the Fed's best contribution to achieving this dual mandate was maintaining low inflation. Preemptive tightening was a critical element of their strategy and essential to maintaining credibility. The Fed's aggressive preemptive tightening in 1994 that lowered inflationary expectations and orchestrated an economic soft landing highlighted the Fed's interpretation of how to best achieve its dual mandate during the Great Moderation.

This period was one of transition for the SOMC. Under Meltzer's direction, the SOMC continued its rigid monetarist legacy based on Friedman's notion of a stable money-demand function. After the economy recovered from back-to-back recessions, the SOMC projected that the high inflation of the 1970s would be repeated if the Fed did not slow money growth. The SOMC's short-run forecasts proved incorrect, as inflation remained moderate and inflationary expectations continued to recede (Romer 2013).

As inflation stayed moderate and economic performance remained healthy, the SOMC fell out of favor at the Fed and in the economics community and the media.[5] The SOMC continued to have close followers, and its research on an array of monetary and economic issues provided important insights, but its audience slowly diminished.

Money Demand and Velocity

During the Great Inflation of 1965–82, the velocity of money had fluctuated, reflecting changes in the demand for money that were largely inversely related to inflation and bond yields. Bond yields and money velocity rose markedly during the severe rise in inflation in 1977–80 and then fell sharply during the 1981–82 recession. This defied the monetarists' presumed stability of velocity. In addition, the money multipliers (the broader monetary aggregates divided by the monetary base) also fluctuated. These fluctuations in the monetary transmission channels were reflected in fluctuations of nominal GDP relative to the SOMC's monetary base growth targets. Despite the SOMC's incorrect short-term projections, its 1970s message on the importance of money targeting stood out amid the uncontrolled inflation and the disarray of economic policymaking. However, at the same time, the eclectic array of policies—including wage and price controls, on-and-off increases and reductions in interest rates, WIN buttons, and complaints of price gouging—failed to reduce inflation and interest rates. This made the SOMC's proposal of the slowing of money growth timely and plausible.

In the 1980s, money velocity and the money multipliers continued to fluctuate, reflecting in part financial innovations that had stemmed from the high inflation and interest rates and the binding of financial regulations (like Regulation Q) of the late 1970s. The SOMC's initial response was that the decline in velocity in the early 1980s was a one-time shift rather than the beginning of a structural decline (Meltzer 1983; Johannes and Rasche 1982). It subsequently tracked the changes in velocity and the money multipliers, but the SOMC continued to prescribe targets for monetary base growth (for example, see Rasche 1987). Jordan compared money growth and economic activity to the Fed's semiannual forecasts provided in its Monetary Policy Reports (MPRs) to Congress and cautioned about the importance of considering the lags between money, interest rates, and velocity (for example, Jordan 1985).

The reduced reliability of money-growth targeting as a short-term predictive tool drew criticisms from the Fed, and in late 1982, with inflation receding, it reverted to targeting interest rates. It continued to provide projections of money growth to Congress in its semiannual MPRs, as required by the Full Employment Act of 1978, but referred less and less to money supply. The economics profession had come around to agree with long-run money neutrality—that persistent inflation in the long run is a monetary phenomenon—but the moderation of inflation reinforced challenges to Friedman's notion that inflation is always and everywhere a monetary phenomenon.

The Fed and the media were paying more attention to other factors that affected near-term economic and inflation conditions, including labor markets, global oil prices (which collapsed in 1986), and changes in fiscal policies (including the Deficit Reduction Act of 1984 and the Tax Reform Act of 1986). While the SOMC provided sound advice on many policy issues, such as urging the Fed and other central banks not to manage exchange rates during 1986–88, monetarism lost its allure and the SOMC seemed out of step.

The SOMC overplayed its monetarist hand that had been so influential in the 1970s. It did not modify its model or policy recommendations to incorporate fluctuations in velocity stemming from changes in interest rates and financial innovation and regulation. It overstated the predictive power of short-run fluctuations in money growth. While SOMC members produced important position papers on leading-edge monetary policy topics of inflation targeting and the important role of managing inflationary expectations and credibility, the Committee's message of targeting money growth fell behind theoretical advances and the primary focuses of the Fed.

It is somewhat of a conundrum that the SOMC's monetary policy recommendations continued to rely on a strict monetarist rule of base-money-growth targets. This is particularly apparent since money velocity was clearly exhibiting short-run volatility and Meltzer and Brunner were involved in shepherding some of the important theoretical advances through the journals they edited, the *Journal of Monetary Economics* and the *Journal of Money, Credit and Banking*, and the Carnegie-Rochester Conference on Public Policy. Moreover, Ben McCallum and Marvin Goodfriend, who were close with Meltzer and Brunner and would become SOMC members and heavily influence the Committee, contributed significantly to the advances in macroeconomics and monetary policy thinking during the 1980s and 1990s.[6]

The Fed's thinking on the best way to achieve its dual mandate evolved during the Volcker-Greenspan era, reflecting advances in research on rules. The SOMC emphasized the benefits of rules and the pitfalls of discretionary fine-tuning (Meltzer 1986). A key focus was the effort to develop a monetary policy framework that could systematically achieve a low inflation target while allowing countercyclical responses. In this effort, SOMC members developed different measures of money to facilitate shifts in velocity and financial innovations. Ben McCallum (1988) developed the McCallum rule that was based on the growth of the monetary base adjusted for a four-year moving average of base velocity. Poole (1991) promoted money of zero maturity (MZM) as an alternative money measure.[7] Meltzer and others considered removing foreign currency from money measures (Meltzer 1993). But the Fed clearly favored interest rates as the instrument for conducting monetary policy and remained skeptical about money and the reliability of monetary transmission channels. The economics profession was focusing on interest rates.

Efforts to develop a framework that involved rule-like behavior with a low inflation target that allowed countercyclical policy responses and was based on interest rates were achieved by John Taylor's (1993) innovative Taylor rule. The subsequent Taylor principle that posited that the Fed should respond to rising inflation by increasing interest rates by more than the rise in inflation implied a rise in real rates.

The Taylor rule and Taylor principle quickly gained popularity and traction and proved to be transformative in the monetary policy debate. The Fed became receptive to a guideline that targeted interest rates and allowed for a rational, easy-to-understand approach to countercyclical monetary responses. Fed staff began preparing assessments of the Taylor rule for presentation at every FOMC meeting. Although Greenspan believed strongly in maintaining the Fed's discretion, the Fed publicly discussed its policies in terms of the Taylor rule. This marked a watershed in the evolution of rules in the conduct of monetary policy. From the earlier fixed-price-of-gold rule of the classical gold standard to Friedman's k-percent rule, the Taylor rule provided a systematic way for the Fed to react to deviations of both inflation and output from desired objectives and could be used to achieve the Fed's dual mandate. Of course, it transformed but did not resolve the rules-versus-discretion debate.

The evolving Conduct of Monetary Policy and the SOMC

Beginning in the early 1990s, leading foreign central banks led by New Zealand, Australia, the UK, Sweden, and Canada adopted numeric inflation targets. Central bank inflation targeting became a critical focus of monetary policy and was used strategically for managing inflationary expectations and achieving a low inflation goal (Bernanke et al. 1998). Managing expectations and central bank credibility were infused into macro models and redefined key aspects of the influences of monetary policy.

In the early 1990s, the Fed modified its conduct of monetary policy and communications and became more transparent, although the process proceeded haltingly since Fed chair Greenspan pushed back on full Fed transparency. The SOMC joined many others in emphasizing the benefits of the Fed's establishing an inflation target and becoming more transparent and accountable (Hoskins 1993). Beginning in 1994, the Fed began announcing policy changes at FOMC meetings, a marked shift from its earlier opaque procedure of changing policy through unannounced technical changes conducted by the FOMC's operating desk with private-sector primary dealers in US debt securities. It also introduced announcements at the conclusion of its FOMC meetings of policy "bias," which were intended as forward guidance during the period until the next meeting. These efforts confused rather than clarified.

The SOMC complimented Alan Greenspan for directing the Fed to achieve moderate inflation and its successful preemptive tightening in 1994 but disagreed with his failure to adopt an inflation target that would institutionalize the priority of achieving low inflation, as well as the Fed's lack of transparency. Hoskins (1993) and Goodfriend (2004) characterized Greenspan's practice as "implicit inflation targeting."

The SOMC's Domestic Policy Research and Recommendations in the 1980s and 1990s

The SOMC continued its 1970s practice of closely following fiscal policy. Its concerns about persistent deficits and rising debt led it to propose rules-based fiscal policies that would constrain government spending. Mickey Levy (1985), who replaced Rudy Penner on the SOMC in 1983 when Penner became the director of the Congressional Budget Office, provided detailed reports on the government's fiscal policies and urged the adoption of fiscal guidelines that limited spending and deficits to achieve longer-run responsible budgeting.

In the 1990s, a number of SOMC members contributed papers on fiscal policy with a particular focus on the growing entitlement programs. Levy (1999) emphasized that while the government's cash flow deficit was shrinking, reflecting the post–Cold War reduction in defense spending and the surge in tax revenues generated by the productivity boom and stock market bubble, unfunded liabilities of entitlement programs were raising future debt.

The SOMC did not have a member dedicated to financial regulations and banks, but in 1986, Meltzer helped to set up the Shadow Financial Regulatory Committee (SFRC), which dedicated an entire team of experts to regulatory issues.[8] In response to the collapse in the savings and loan industry, Jordan (1990) and Schwartz (1991) provided recommendations on banking and financial structural reform.

In March 1992, after leaving the SOMC, Jerry Jordan became president of the Federal Reserve Bank of Cleveland, where he continued to promote money rules that would achieve price stability, and pushed back on discretionary fine-tuning policies. Jordan's presence on the Fed was a feather in the cap of the SOMC. He was replaced on the SOMC by Lee Hoskins, former president of the Federal Reserve Bank of Cleveland. Hoskins brought Fed experience and his strong advocacy of rules-based monetary policy and zero inflation to the SOMC. Charles Plosser, who contributed heavily to the development of

the field of real business cycles, also joined the SOMC. Greg Hess, with substantial experience as a Fed researcher, joined the SOMC in 1998.

Evolving toward Interest Rate Recommendations

The SOMC's evolution toward focusing on interest-rate policy recommendations began in the 1990s before Meltzer retired as chair. Throughout
the 1980s and until 1993, the Fed reported on money-growth targets in its
Monetary Policy Reports to Congress and in the chairman's closely followed
Humphrey–Hawkins testimonies. In his testimony to Congress on the Fed's
MPR in July 1993, Greenspan explained that the Fed had officially downgraded money as a policy instrument and indicator of economic activity and
the Fed would focus on interest rates: "At least for the time being . . . M2 has
been downgraded as a reliable indicator of financial conditions in the economy, and no single variable has yet been identified to take its place. . . . One
important guidepost is real interest rates, which have a key bearing on longer-
run spending decisions and inflation prospects. In assessing real rates, the
central issue is their relationship to an equilibrium interest rate, specifically
the real rate level that, if maintained, would keep the economy at its production level overtime" (Greenspan 1993).

Bill Poole (1993) was critical of the Fed's shift to focusing on rates and
downgrading M2 targeting, but while he emphasized the importance of
money, he also acknowledged its weakness and the dilemma that faced the
SOMC. He identified many of the difficulties in targeting real rates but
concluded that if the Fed had been conducting policy by closely adhering
to M2 monetary aggregates, "the outcome may not have been satisfactory."
He emphasized that despite short-term volatility of money demand, the
Fed and other central banks should be aware of the monetary aggregates
and be prepared to respond to sizable deviations of money growth from
the recent experience.

The SOMC continued to recommend money-growth targets through
the 1990s, although it blended in interest rate assessments. In March 1994,
while it urged the Fed to slow money growth, the SOMC Policy Statement
read: "The Federal Reserve continues to suppress the rise in short-term
rates. Last month the Federal Reserve responded belatedly to the recent
increase in the growth of spending with a modest (25 basis point) increase
in short-term interest rates and suggested possible further increases in the
future. This is not enough" (SOMC 1994). In addition, SOMC members
increasingly described policy recommendations in terms of interest rates

in their position papers. In "A Note on Stable Velocity," Meltzer (1998) explained that while the close correlation between monetary base velocity and 10-year Treasury yields persisted in the 1990s, "there is sufficient variability, however, to preclude the use of the relation for forecasting quarterly movements. . . . The same statement is true more generally; no economic relation, or set of relations, permits accurate or reliable quarterly forecasting."

SOMC International Policy Recommendations during the Great Moderation

The SOMC argued strenuously for free trade, cautioned against the Fed's and other central banks' efforts to manage currencies, and was critical of the International Monetary Fund's (IMF) role in international finance. It also dispelled the then-popular notion of the "twin deficits" and the misguided policy recommendations stemming from it. Jan Tumlir (1985), a senior economist at the General Agreement on Tariffs and Trade and an SOMC member during 1980–85, described the economic benefits of free trade and warned about the costs of protectionism. Later, Jagdish Bhagwati (1993), very briefly an SOMC member, analyzed regional free trade agreements and the economic costs of regulations on international trade.

Anna Schwartz (1986) along with Brunner (1987) and Poole (1988) cautioned against central banks' adjusting of monetary policy to manage the US dollar exchange rate and warned about the downside of international policy coordination. Schwartz (1989, 1992) criticized the US's foreign exchange interventions to weaken the US dollar, arguing that unsterilized exchange market intervention was both ineffective and costly, and also analyzed and uncovered the Fed's improper role in warehousing Treasury holdings of foreign exchange (1992). Her findings in an article with Michael Bordo (Bordo and Schwartz 1991) along with research by others likely led to a shift in Fed practices (Bordo et al. 2015).

Schwartz (1995, 1996) was critical of the US's haphazard approach to its Mexican rescue plan in 1994 and questioned whether the US should be providing financial support that would likely perpetuate a continuation of misguided monetary and fiscal policies in Mexico. She questioned the IMF's role and practices as a global lender of last resort without the ability to issue high-powered money (Schwartz 1998). Schwartz also did considerable research with Michael Bordo (1999, 2000) that was highly critical of the IMF's rescues during the Asian crisis of 1997–98 that were viewed as bailouts.

Well-timed Policy Recommendations

The SOMC recommended in September 1993 that the Fed tighten monetary policy to slow growth of money and aggregate demand. The Fed's aggressive monetary tightening beginning in February 1994 successfully reduced inflation and inflationary expectations in a rare mid-cycle economic soft landing. The SOMC applauded the Fed's successful policy.

In 1998 a wave of concerns emerged in financial markets and the media that there would be deflation stemming from a supply glut generated by the productivity boom and from turmoil in Asia. Charles Plosser (1998) pushed back on this assessment in "Exaggerated Risks of Deflation," arguing that persistent inflation was a monetary phenomenon and also stemmed from other sources of excess demand, whereas the higher productivity in select sectors would be associated with a change in relative prices and not deflation. Concerns about inflation would reemerge in the early 2000s.

In 1999, in an environment of strong economic growth, inflation pressures, and a frothy stock market, the SOMC criticized the Fed for delaying tightening monetary policy based on its fears that a liquidity shortage would occur in anticipation of Y2K (that is, the Fed worried that there would be a sharp rise in the demand for currency in anticipation of computer adjustments around the turn of the millennium). The Fed delayed its first interest rate increase until early 2000, and then tightened too much, which led to the mild 2001 recession.

At its September 1998 meeting, the SOMC proudly announced its twenty-fifth anniversary. It reviewed its purpose, identified some of the Fed's policy errors over the quarter century and concluded: "To avoid a return to these mistaken policies, we will continue to urge the Federal Reserve to develop and adopt systematic rules for monetary policy. These rules should aim at a long-term goal of zero inflation. Several other countries have moved decisively in that direction with good results. It is past time for the Federal Reserve to do the same" (SOMC 1998).

Third Phase of the SOMC: The Early 2000s

Allan Meltzer retired from the SOMC in 1999, following a period of productivity-driven economic strength and moderate inflation. Under his leadership, the SOMC's monetarism had made its mark (Meltzer 2000). With inflation low, Meltzer (2005, 2010) turned his attention to writing his monumental three-volume book on the history of the Federal Reserve. A year before, Bill Poole had left the SOMC to become president of the

Federal Reserve Bank of St. Louis, continuing its strong tradition in monetary research. Charles Plosser and Anna Schwartz became cochairs of the SOMC, and the SOMC welcomed two new members, Ben McCallum and Alan Stockman.

These changes in membership initiated several new directions for the SOMC. First, McCallum brought to the SOMC his sizable research contributions to monetary theory and policy, including the development of rational expectations and refinements of the neoclassical model, and rigorous support of policy rules and explicit inflation targeting. This consolidated and reinforced the SOMC's long-standing beliefs and refined the SOMC's perception of the meaning of rules. Alan Stockman added to Anna Schwartz's ongoing rigorous analyses of international trade and addressed issues of corporate governance and tax and fiscal policies.

Second, the SOMC's policy recommendations evolved from money targets to interest rates. While the SOMC continued to keep a close eye on the monetary aggregates, its policy recommendations on interest rates were more closely aligned with the current debate about monetary policy.

Third, the SOMC's research and policy recommendations focused on several critically important issues that heavily influenced the conduct of monetary policy and economic and financial conditions: the Fed's fear of a Japanese-style deflation hitting the US (along with reaching the ZLB, or zero lower bound, on short-term policy rates), and the excessive risks of Fannie Mae and Freddie Mac for overall financial stability. These concerns proved to be prescient.

Consolidating and Expanding the SOMC's Fundamentals

Based on his experiences at the Fed, Lee Hoskins highlighted the failures of discretionary policy and fine-tuning. He argued that the dynamic nature of the economy and constant adjustments of expectations about future policies made it virtually impossible for the Fed to accurately predict economic performance and the impacts of monetary policy (Hoskins 2000). Hoskins (1999) criticized the Fed's new practice of signaling if it had a "bias" in its policy stance following FOMC meetings: "It deflects attention away from more serious and far-reaching changes that would bring real clarity to Fed policymaking such as setting multi-year inflation targets and making predictable responses to deviations from them. The FOMC should build in its hard-earned credibility by improving the predictability of its policy actions rather than attempting to signal its intentions on a selective basis."

McCallum's Focus on Rules and Inflation Targeting

Even though Greenspan pushed back on both a numeric inflation target and full transparency, and coveted the Fed's discretion, the Fed monitored interest rates estimated with the Taylor rule at its FOMC meetings, and Fed members referred to it frequently in speeches. McCallum was a strong advocate of inflation targeting, systematic rules, explicit inflation targeting and transparency. In his first SOMC paper, "The US Deserves a Monetary Standard," McCallum (2000) described the benefits of a low inflation target in an international and historical context. On rules, the SOMC's Policy Statement in November 2002 was clear: "We strongly urge the Fed to adopt more systematic guidelines and explain their decisions in light of the guidelines. The FOMC should be more explicit as to why it believes deviating from the rules is warranted" (SOMC 2002b). The SOMC's reference to rules were no longer to a rigid monetarist rule, rather they represented a systematic and predictable Fed monetary policy reaction function grounded in the dual mandate that would achieve an inflation target.

At the same time, McCallum understood the nuances and misperceptions about monetary policy rules, and was circumspect on the role that rules could play in the conduct of monetary policy. He acknowledged that the Fed and central banks would not be strictly rules-driven, rather that a rule or formula "can systematically and compactly summarize much of the relevant information in a manner that potentially provides a good starting place or 'benchmark' for consideration of policy settings" (McCallum 2002).

In his papers, McCallum analyzed and tracked estimates of the Taylor rule and McCallum rule as a framework for assessing the Fed's monetary policy. The SOMC's policy statements described its recommendations in terms of deviations of actual policies from these rules. These empirical comparisons were updated and posted in semiannual reports of the SOMC proceedings published by the University of Rochester under the direction of Charles Plosser. Beginning in March 2003, they were posted on the SOMC's original (and now defunct) website.[9]

McCallum acknowledged that Greenspan had contributed to the favorable moderate-inflation environment, but he criticized Greenspan for pushing back on explicit inflation targeting (McCallum 2003a). In contrast to Greenspan's "implicit inflation targeting" that did not involve a numeric target and relied on his strong advocacy of policy discretion, McCallum identified as best practice the Bank of England's performance under Governor Mervyn King that relied on inflation targeting that allowed for flexibility to respond to real fluctuations (McCallum 2003b).

International Issues

Alan Stockman (2000, 2004) provided a clear assessment of the factors underlying the rising current account deficit and the US dollar. Anna Schwartz (2000, 2001) remained highly critical of the IMF rescues viewed as bailouts during the Asian crisis of 1997–98 and later (2002) of the Fund's policies in crises in Argentina and Brazil.

Fears of a Japan-Style Deflation and the Fed's Asymmetric Stance

Following the burst of the dot-com bubble and collapse of the stock market, and the mild recession of 2001 and the 9/11 terrorist attacks, inflation fell below 2%. Although the Fed did not have an official inflation target, it became uncomfortable "looking up" at 2% rather than "looking down" at 2%, the condition that had prevailed since the late 1960s. Greenspan (2002) feared deflation, referring to the low-risk, high-cost outcomes of even mild deflation. He overstated Japan's deflation and understated the sizable structural differences between the US and Japanese economies. Fed governor Bernanke (2002) sounded the same alarm about deflation and provided a blueprint of the Fed's ability to ease monetary policy when faced with the ZLB. These concerns led the Fed to adopt an asymmetric interpretation of its dual mandate, tilting its priorities away from low inflation and toward higher inflation, which it argued would be easier and less costly to address. This effective reinterpretation of the Fed's dual mandate would resurface following the Great Financial Crisis.

The SOMC argued strenuously against the Fed's growing concern that the US would fall into a Japan-style deflation (Plosser 2003) and urged it to maintain a symmetrical stance around its low inflation objective (McCallum 2001a). Alan Stockman (2002) emphasized that Japan's deflation was a local issue and the US economy was structurally far different than Japan's. McCallum's (2001b) analysis used the Taylor rule and the McCallum rule to explain that the Bank of Japan (BoJ) had kept monetary policy inadvertently too tight in the 1990s. Faced with the ZLB, he recommended that the BoJ purchase foreign exchange to lower the yen and increase the monetary base.

The Fed brushed aside the SOMC's assessments. The US economy recovered from the mild recession of 2001 and trauma of 9/11, stimulated by monetary ease and fiscal stimulus. At the April SOMC meeting, the SOMC's press release and policy statement urged the Fed to raise rates, stating: "The negative real federal funds rate and excess liquidity are incompatible with stable, low inflation and a sustained healthy economic expansion. . . . As real rates rise with an improving economy, increasing the federal funds rate would not adversely affect the economy" (SOMC 2002a). This proved to be wise advice.

Reflecting its asymmetric assessment of inflation risks, the Fed kept the fed funds rate at 1% through mid-2004, even as the economy reaccelerated and inflation rose above 2%. The negative real rates combined with excessive liquidity and lax risk management by Fannie and Freddie and commercial banks led to a boom in housing activity and prices, excessive debt financing, and a proliferation of financial derivatives based on mortgage-backed securities (MBS) (Taylor 2007).

Fannie and Freddie, Excessive Risk-taking and Fed Policy

Greg Hess (2002), in "Is It Time for Fannie Mae and Freddie Mac to Cut the Cord?" and subsequent articles, emphasized that the mounting resource misallocations and excessive risks that were building through these government-sponsored enterprises (GSEs) could ultimately threaten financial stability, and that these institutions needed to be reformed. Within the Fed, former SOMC member Bill Poole (2001) described the flaws and risks in Fannie and Freddie and was successful in drawing the attention of Fed chair Greenspan and Fed governor Edward M. Gramlich.

The SOMC, along with other concerned parties, continued to express concerns about the excessive risks and leverage of the GSEs and provided pointed recommendations: "Given the interest rate risk exposure on their portfolios, the intermediate legislative solution to avert a potential crisis in the mortgage market is to move the supervision and regulation of these GSE's to the Treasury, to explicitly remove the implicit and explicit benefits that they receive and to significantly raise their capital requirements. Ultimately, however, these institutions should be privatized so that the mortgage market reaps the full rewards of a competitive market environment" (SOMC 2004). Hess (2004) wondered whether a financial crisis could be avoided. Hess (2009) maintained his criticisms of Fannie and Freddie as the GFC unfolded.

The Fed tightened monetary policy between mid-2004 and mid-2006, raising rates from 1% to 5.25%, well above personal consumption expenditures (PCE) inflation, and slowing money growth. The rise in mortgage rates, particularly adjustable-rate mortgages that were the basis for so much housing speculation, generated a reversal in home prices and sales that led to a collapse in the complex derivatives in the MBS market. Certainly, the Fed was not responsible for either the complexities that enveloped the MBS market or supervision of the GSEs, but the combination of low interest rates and forward guidance of very gradual rate increases that kept mortgage rates low fueled the debt-financed-housing boom. Following the Financial Crisis, Bernanke (2010) refuted Taylor's finding that the Fed kept rates too low for too long, arguing that the Fed's extended monetary ease played at most a minor role in contributing to the housing bubble.

In 2006, Plosser left the SOMC to become president of the Federal Reserve Bank of Philadelphia. At the Fed, Plosser was a key architect of the Fed's formal 2012 strategic plan that established an inflation target, and he expressed concerns that the broadened scope of monetary policy and the Fed's expanded balance sheet posed threats to the Fed's independence. Of note, as a pioneer of the real business cycle, Plosser stood out as the only FOMC member to follow and refer to money growth. In 2006, Hoskins retired from the SOMC, and Stockman also retired from the Committee for health reasons. The SOMC took a pause and did not hold meetings during 2007–8 as it regrouped and sought new members.

The Modern Era of the SOMC

The modern SOMC began to jell prior to the Financial Crisis with the addition of three new members: Marvin Goodfriend, Michael Bordo, and Charles Calomiris. Each added academic rigor and a new dimension of expertise to the SOMC. Goodfriend had contributed significantly to the evolution of economic and monetary policy theory (Goodfriend and King 1999) and championed explicit inflation targeting and full transparency to maintain credibility (Goodfriend 2004). These themes tied together the work of McCallum, Hoskins, and Plosser. Bordo was an economic and monetary historian who had worked closely with Anna Schwartz and numerous senior Fed staffers on an array of research projects on the Fed and global central bank policies. He was well-versed in Friedman's economics, the monetarist-Keynesian debate, and the development of the SOMC. Calomiris was a noted expert in banking with a focus on finance and regulation and knowledge of the Fed's historical regulatory policies. While the new members pursued different research agendas, all favored rules-based policies over discretion, inflation targeting, and central bank transparency, and advocated a limited scope of monetary policy; all were anxious to contribute to the SOMC's efforts to advocate sound monetary policy.

Beginning in 2009, the SOMC modified its routine in several ways. First, it invited guest speakers to make presentations at its semiannual meetings. The majority of the guest speakers have been current Fed members, but they have also included fiscal and regulatory policymakers, leading academics, and global central bankers. Appendix II provides a list of guest speakers. The guest speakers were also invited to the SOMC's private premeeting dinners. Their addition to the meetings proved very successful; it enhanced the SOMC's access and communications with the Fed and improved its understanding of the policymaking process. Second, the SOMC's consensus on its core beliefs remained, but based on the diversity of members' research interests, the Committee ceased preparing a policy statement for each meeting. Also, beginning in 2018, the SOMC augmented its semiannual meeting with a third annual meeting sponsored by Chapman University.

The Great Financial Crisis and Its Aftermath
The immediate issue facing the SOMC was the Great Financial Crisis, its shock to financial markets and the economy and the Fed's immediate responses to it. The SOMC had issued warnings of the potential risks of the Fed's low-interest-rate policies of the early 2000s and the excessive leverage and resource misallocations of Fannie and Freddie. The magnitude of the crisis and the scope of the Fed's responses elicited important SOMC policy recommendations.

In response to the unraveling of the MBS market, freezing of financial markets, and sharp economic contraction, the Fed reduced rates to zero and engaged in sizable open market purchases of MBS—i.e., followed a policy of quantitative easing referred to as QE1 (large-scale asset purchases, or LSAPs). Fed chair Bernanke (2008) emphasized that this was credit easing, not quantitative easing, because it involved purchases of MBS and not Treasuries, and pledged that the Fed would unwind these assets on a timely basis in order to avoid inflation. In addition, the Fed's Troubled Asset Relief Program (TARP) infused capital into large systematic important banks and the Fed directly extended over $1 trillion of credit lending—loans to banks and other financial institutions as well as to special-purpose entities to purchase commercial paper and asset-backed securities. In the spring of 2009, the Fed initiated QE2, which involved outright purchases of Treasuries in addition to MBS, while the FDIC extended guarantees on deposits up to $250,000.

Goodfriend's (2009) first SOMC paper, "We Need an 'Accord' for Federal Reserve Credit Policy," was a critically important contribution. It expressed concerns that the Fed's massive extension of credit stepped across the boundary into fiscal policy, since providing credit is an activity that historically had been conducted by the Congress and the president and has direct implications on the government's budget. Moreover, providing credit involves picking winners and losers, which is a political decision and not the province of an independent central bank. He urged the establishment of an agreement analogous to the Treasury-Fed Accord of 1951: "A credit accord should set guidelines for Fed credit policy so that pressure to misuse Fed credit policy for fiscal purposes does not undermine the Fed's independence and impair the central bank's power to stabilize financial markets, inflation, and macroeconomic activity." Goodfriend echoed the concerns expressed by Fed members Charles Plosser (2009) and Jeff Lacker (2009) and urged the Fed to return to a "Treasuries only" balance sheet as soon as reasonably possible. These positions would be repeated in subsequent SOMC papers. Eventually the Fed took policy steps to unwind its direct lending programs, passively reduce its holdings of MBS, and advocate the gradual movement toward an all-Treasuries portfolio.

Bordo (2009) argued that most of the Fed's asset purchases in 2008 had been automatically sterilized, such that they did not increase money growth, suggesting that the Fed had been inadvertently restrictive. Bordo drew analogies to the Great Depression and urged the Fed to ease aggressively to stimulate recovery but then withdraw it soon after the crisis ended, and identify and close insolvent financial institutions.

Calomiris emphasized the need to reform the array of housing subsidies, place limits on the Fed's practice of supporting too-big-to-fail financial institutions, and improve the management of macroprudential risks (Calomiris 2009a). He followed with a position paper on recommendations on minimum bank capital ratio requirements, an issue that was central to the Dodd–Frank Wall Street Reform and Consumer Protection Act of 2010 (Calomiris 2009b).

Goodfriend and McCallum (2009) teamed up in "Exiting Credit Policy to Preserve Sound Monetary Policy" and urged the Fed to exit credit policy as soon as the recovery would allow and to be absolutely transparent in its policies. They addressed a flaw in the newly established floor system of conducting monetary policy in which the effective federal funds rate remained below the floor established by the Fed's designated interest rate on reserves. This resulted from the inability of Fannie Mae and Freddie Mac and the Federal Home Loan Banks to collect interest on reserves left at the Fed, which created a supply-demand disequilibrium in short-term funding markets. To reinforce the interest-rate floor, they recommended that the Fed coordinate with the Treasury and Congress to extend payment of interest on reserves to the

GSEs, despite their status as government enterprises. Goodfriend addressed this issue in detail in subsequent papers.

Bill Poole (2009), who rejoined the SOMC following his 1998–2008 tenure as president of the St. Louis Fed, focused on the unintended consequences of the Fed's too-big-to-fail practices, the failures of bank and federal supervisors and the regulatory agencies, and the problems when capital requirements are too low and not properly structured. He recommended higher capital requirements and credible supervision.

The Fed's QE3 and Expanded Balance Sheet

After the crisis eased, the Fed's focus and concerns evolved toward the slow recovery and lingering weakness in labor markets. The Fed had projected that its zero interest rates and quantitative easing along with fiscal stimulus would generate a strong economic recovery and a rise in inflation. Outside the Fed, based on Milton Friedman's plucking model, Bordo with Joseph Haubrich (2012) had shown that deep recessions accompanied by financial crises should have fast recoveries. That's not what happened. The recovery in aggregate demand was weak, resulting in a slow recovery of the labor-force-participation rate and low inflation.

SOMC members identified several sources of the weak economy. While the Fed's QEs dramatically increased bank reserves and the monetary base, Plosser (2010) and Ireland (2016) argued that the monetary transmission channels had been adversely affected by the Fed's shift to paying interest on excess reserves, the tighter capital requirements it imposed on banks, and more stringent supervision of banks that deterred lending. These factors constrained growth of money and aggregate demand. Levy (2012) attributed the weak recovery to the shock to net wealth associated with the collapse in housing values and the stock market that forced higher saving, resulting in weak consumer spending and a nonacceleration of nominal GDP.

Sluggish economic growth continued in 2012, and the Fed ramped up purchases of Treasuries and MBS through its enhanced quantitative easing program, QE3. The Fed made it clear that with inflation low, the express purpose of QE3 was to increase employment (Bernanke 2012). Thus, rather than unwinding its crisis-management asset purchases, the Fed extended its unconventional monetary policy to pursue its dual mandate. This represented a clear tilt in the Fed's interpretation of its dual mandate and how monetary policy would achieve it.

The SOMC expressed concerns with the expanded scope of the Fed's balance sheet and responsibilities. Goodfriend (2014a, 2014b) addressed the relevance of the Fed's large balance sheet for the conduct of monetary policy and assessed the risks involved in the Fed's practice of effectively borrowing short-duration securities to finance holding longer-term debt securities, including the possible erosion of the Fed's independence. Of note, Goodfriend echoed some of the concerns expressed by Charles Plosser, president of the Federal Reserve Bank of Philadelphia, and Jeff Lacker, president of the Federal Reserve Bank of Richmond.[10]

During the recovery from the GFC, the SOMC was fortunate to attract two new members, Peter Ireland in 2011 and Athanasios Orphanides in 2014. Ireland was a leading expert in monetary policy and the Chicago school of economics who earlier had worked at the Federal Reserve Bank of Richmond with Marvin Goodfriend, Jeff Lacker, and Ben McCallum (a consultant). Orphanides was a former governor of the Central Bank of Cyprus and a member of the Governing Council of the European Central Bank (ECB), and before that a noted senior researcher and senior advisor at the Federal Reserve Board. He had published frequently cited papers (for example, Orphanides 2002) that attributed part of the Fed's policy errors in the Great Inflation to a mismeasured potential output, and had developed the first-difference rule, a variation on the Taylor rule that the Fed closely monitored.

Their contributions quickly made a mark. Ireland (2011) urged the Fed to pursue its low-inflation objective as the best foundation for achieving its dual mandate. He cautioned that too much is asked of the Fed, and the central bank would best achieve its objectives through a commitment to stabilizing nominal variables rather than efforts to fine-tune real variables. Orphanides (2014) first delved into Europe's struggles to emerge from its financial crisis and compared the ECB's monetary policy around the ZLB with the Fed. He then argued that the Fed was too tentative in exiting its zero-interest-rate policy (Orphanides 2015). Many of his subsequent SOMC position papers addressed and tested different aspects of systematic rules for monetary policy.

The SOMC's Core Beliefs

The scope and research interests of the SOMC widened to reflect the expanded scope of the Fed's policies: zero interest rates and an enlarged balance sheet; the sharp decline in oil prices and inflation; the Fed's evolving interpretation of its dual mandate, and new Fed chair Janet Yellen's discretionary prioritization of employment; the Fed's operational conduct of monetary policy; and its role in bank regulation and supervision. The newly enlarged SOMC decided it was an appropriate time to step back and conduct a self-assessment. In 2015, the SOMC held an off-site meeting to discuss the role of the SOMC and what it stood for. The meeting resulted in a statement of the SOMC's Core Beliefs:

- The SOMC takes for granted that US monetary policy will be conducted by the Fed over the foreseeable future.
- It is essential that the central bank be independent from the fiscal authorities and accountable to the legislature. In particular, the central bank should eschew policies that allocate credit.
- Price stability is the best contribution that monetary policy can make to overall macroeconomic performance and for this reason should be the primary objective of the central bank. "Price stability" should be defined to insure that the inflation rate, on average, is not above 2% per year.
- Monetary policy should be conducted in a rule-like manner and be somewhat countercyclical with respect to output and employment, as long as price stability in the long run is not compromised. We expect the central bank to announce the policy rule that it follows so that it can be monitored and held accountable.
- To provide financial stability, the central bank should promote strong capital buffers.
- The SOMC expects the central bank will serve as a lender of last resort. In this role:
  a. The central bank should state its lender of last resort rules clearly in advance;
  b. Such activities should be limited to occasional, temporary well-collateralized lending to solvent, supervised depository institutions at an appropriate interest rate premium; and
  c. More expansive lending should be agreed upon and indemnified in advance by the fiscal authorities.
- The SOMC believes that, by following these basic principles, the Fed would create the monetary and financial framework that best facilitates the efficient functioning of free-market, prosperity-creating, institutions in the US economy.

While the SOMC had evolved and included members with different research interests, its Core Beliefs were strikingly similar to many of the basic tenets of the original SOMC and principles espoused by Karl Brunner close to fifty years earlier in his principles of monetarism.

Following its meeting that reaffirmed its Core Beliefs, the SOMC stepped up its efforts to address a number of broad issues: 1) the Fed's balance sheet, the scope of monetary policy and Fed independence; 2) the evolving interpretation of the Fed's dual mandate; 3) rules versus discretion; 4) the Fed's operational conduct of monetary policy; 4) the SOMC and the COVID-19 pandemic inflation; 5) issues in regulatory policies; and 6) governance of the Federal Reserve.

New SOMC Members

Charles Plosser rejoined the SOMC in 2015 after finishing his 2006–15 tenure as president of the Federal Reserve Bank of Philadelphia. Since the establishment of the SOMC's Core Beliefs, five new members have joined the Committee. Deborah Lucas, a noted scholar in finance, joined in 2017 and added important understanding of cost-benefit analysis of government and Fed credit policies and debt forgiveness. Andrew Levin joined in 2019, bringing decades of experience as a research and policy advisor at the Fed, and an interest in improving the Fed's risk management, governance, and accountability. In 2022, Jeff Lacker joined the SOMC following his presidency of the Federal Reserve Bank of Richmond during 2004–17. He had frequently dissented on Fed policy decisions that conflicted with his basic principles of sound monetary policy. In 2024, Jim Bullard joined after being president of the Federal Reserve Bank of St. Louis during 2008–23. He had brought to the Fed rigorous economic analysis supporting more systematic policies and led the Fed in its aggressive monetary tightening in 2022–23. Like Plosser, Lacker and Bullard place a primary focus on achieving low inflation, following rules and being transparent in the conduct of monetary policy. They quickly began to make constructive recommendations to their former employer.

Ongoing Concerns about the Fed's Balance Sheet and Scope

Goodfriend (2014a, 2014b) followed up on his earlier concerns about the Fed's expanded balance sheet with two provocative position papers: "The Relevance of the Federal Reserve Surplus Capital for Current Policy" and "Monetary Policy as a Carry Trade." He described the mechanics and financial and fiscal issues involved in the Fed's conduct of quantitative monetary policy at the zero bound and urged the Fed to suspend transfers of net profits to the Treasury and build surplus capital in anticipation of the cash flow losses that would occur when it raised rates and normalized policies. The subsequent rise in rates has justified his concerns and recommendations.

After rejoining the SOMC, Plosser participated in various panels at SOMC meetings and testified before Congress. He urged the Fed to address tensions placed on it by simplifying its objectives, adhering to systematic rules and constraining its monetary policy tools (Plosser 2016). He worried that there had been "mission creep" in the Fed's interpretation of its mandate, which expanded its scope of discretion. Second, Plosser (2017) urged the Fed to return to an all-Treasuries portfolio and avoid purchases of MBS and other forms of credit allocation that "opened the door to political and fiscal abuse of the central bank's portfolio" and undermined the Fed's independence. He expanded on these themes and proposed limitations on emergency lending in "Federal Reserve Independence: Is It Time for a New Treasury-Fed Accord?" (Plosser 2019, 2022).

Following the Fed's massive asset purchases in response to the COVID pandemic, Andy Levin addressed the budgetary costs and risks of the Fed's expanded balance sheet. In a thorough analysis of when the Fed purchased the assets and their yield, Levin estimated the costs to taxpayers exceeded over $1 trillion (Levin and Nelson 2023). His empirical findings validated Goodfriend's earlier concerns. Levin argued that Congress should more rigorously supervise the Fed and advocated that the Fed be subject to audits by the Government Accountability Office (GAO). While some SOMC members do not support the GAO's auditing of the Fed, all agreed that the Fed should move toward reducing its balance sheet and unwinding non-Treasury securities and be more accountable.

Lucas (2017a) provided a detailed financial assessment of the Fed's asset purchases and enlarged balance sheet and concluded that the Fed's "remittances have created hundreds of billions of dollars of budget capacity . . . the budgetary treatment obfuscates the true financial position of the government and the risks born to taxpayers." She proposed a switch to accrual accounting for the Federal Reserve in the federal budget (Lucas 2018).

Lucas took a broader view of the costs of the government's interventions during the GFC in two separate studies. She estimated that on a fair-value accounting basis, the costs to taxpayers of the government's bailouts of Fannie and Freddie and the Federal Home Loan Banks were $498 billion

(Lucas 2017b). She concluded that privatizing the GSEs would provide enormous indirect benefits (including improving fiscal transparency and reduced taxpayer costs even if the costs to the Federal Budget were high). In a broader study, Lucas quantified the magnitude of the total government credit policies and debt forgiveness in the US and other advanced economies, concluding that the total government financial subsidies of the US and advanced nations were 22% of GDP and deserved more attention (Lucas and Hong 2023).

The Fed's Evolving Interpretation of Its Dual Mandate

As described earlier, under Fed chairs Volcker and Greenspan, the Fed emphasized that its best contribution toward achieving stable low inflation and sustained healthy growth in the economy and employment was to keep inflation and inflationary expectations low. Although the Fed did not have an official inflation target, its objective was to reduce inflation to 2%, generally based on the formal targets established by other leading global central banks. They rarely referred to the dual mandate.

The Fed's first major tilt in its interpretation of its dual mandate occurred in the early 2000s when inflation dipped below 2%. Following the collapse of the dot-com bubble, the mild recession of 2001, and the trauma of 9/11, inflation dipped below 2% and the Fed feared a Japanese-style deflation. The Fed said the risks of deflation far outweighed the risks of higher inflation. As a result, the Fed kept rates at 1% even as the economy recovered and inflation rose back to 2%, and raised its rates at a measured pace, which fueled the debt-financed housing bubble and contributed to mounting inflation pressures and subsequent severe financial stresses. This marked the end of the Great Moderation.

Unlike his predecessors, Ben Bernanke frequently referred to the Fed's dual mandate when he became Fed chair in 2006. Following the GFC, the slow recovery of labor markets and low inflation led the Fed to shift its priorities toward employment. The SOMC pushed back on these asymmetric interpretations of the dual mandate and their implications for monetary policy. Amid this tilt toward labor market concerns, in January 2012, the Fed formally adopted a longer-run strategic plan. This "consensus statement" for the first time established a 2% inflation target and set a goal of maximum employment, but without a numeric target, acknowledging that employment was heavily influenced by nonmonetary factors.

The SOMC supported the Fed's adoption of an inflation target, but worried whether the Fed would stick to it. Ireland (2012a) highlighted the benefits of establishing a numeric inflation target, but noted the contradiction imposed by the Fed's maximum employment objective that was beyond the control of the Fed. Goodfriend (2012) urged the Fed to take advantage of its 2% inflation target, but pointed out that soon after this hallmark step, the Fed approved QE3 and agreed to keep rates low for several more years: "The key question is how the FOMC proposes to deal with the fluctuations of inflation and employment?" (emphasis Goodfriend's). He continued: "Lack of clarity on inflation in the [FOMC's] September 13 [2012] policy statement suggests that the Fed is willing to pursue highly accommodative monetary policy to bring unemployment down until inflation becomes the public's concern." These concerns proved prescient.

The collapse in oil prices that began mid-2014 generated a sharp transitory reduction of inflation toward zero and led many economic commentators and media to express worries about deflation. Calomiris (2014), in a position paper entitled "Phony Deflation Worries," noted that nominal GDP had continued to grow faster than estimates of potential, suggesting the remote probability of deflation, and that inflationary expectations had remained fairly closely anchored to 2%. Bordo (2015) argued that inflation had receded temporarily in response to the positive supply shock provided by the surge in oil drilling and that inflation would soon rise, suggesting that the Fed should not delay monetary policy normalization.

Soon after Janet Yellen became Fed chair in August 2014, the home page of the Fed's official website added a new feature, a Labor Market Dashboard that tracked a dozen labor market measures. There was no analogous "inflation dashboard." This clearly revealed Yellen's priority of maximizing employment and underlined the Fed's evolving interpretation of its dual mandate. Following the transitory decline in inflation caused by the collapse in oil prices in 2014–15, inflation rose back toward the Fed's target and economic performance picked up. During 2016–19, Consumer Price Index (CPI) inflation averaged 2%, and PCE inflation averaged modestly lower at 1.6%. During this period, real GDP growth persistently exceeded the Fed's estimates of longer-run potential, and the unemployment rate fell to a fifty-year low. Market- and survey-based measures of inflationary expectation remained fairly well anchored to 2%, and the Fed continued to project that inflation would rise to 2%. Nevertheless, the Fed's concerns mounted that if PCE inflation remained below 2%, the risks would grow that inflationary expectations would collapse. Such a decline in inflationary expectations combined with a low natural real rate of interest would confront the Fed with the effective lower bound (ELB), which would constrain its ability to respond to an economic downturn. These worries and presumptions skewed the Fed's interpretation of its dual mandate.

Goodfriend (2016) addressed policy concerns in "The Case (in Brief) for Unencumbering Interest Rate Policy at the Zero Bound." He argued (provocatively) that negative nominal policy rates during extreme conditions would enhance the efficiency of monetary policy and support the Fed's attainment of its dual mandate. At a subsequent SOMC meeting, Levin (2019) argued, based on earlier research with Bordo (Bordo and Levin 2017), that the Fed's toolbox for providing monetary stimulus at the ELB was inadequate and proposed central bank digital currency that could facilitate the provision of digital cash at the ELB.

The Fed's mounting worries about too-low inflation and the ELB led it to undertake its first-ever strategic review in 2019–20, which culminated in its new strategic plan announced in August 2020. The Fed's strategic plan formally established an asymmetric interpretation of its dual mandate and changed how it would respond to deviations. Most importantly, the Fed favored above-2%-average inflation, prioritized maximum inclusive employment, and formally de-emphasized preemptive monetary tightening in response to anticipated higher inflation. A month following the Fed's announced new strategy, Mickey Levy and Charles Plosser (2020) identified many flaws in the review process and plan. They were particularly critical of its flexible average inflation targeting proposal, and noted that it was only a matter of time before these flaws would be revealed. In sequels, they highlighted how the Fed's new strategy had led to misguided monetary policy (Levy and Plosser 2022, 2024).

The SOMC on Rules-Based Policies Versus Discretion

Rules-based policies rather than discretion, and avoidance of fine-tuning, had long been one of the SOMC's Core Beliefs. Some SOMC members, led by McCallum, investigated different rules and issues in rules-based policies, and often used the Taylor rule as a benchmark for assessing monetary policy. After the GFC, McCallum (2011, 2013) assessed the targeting of nominal GDP as a rule. Bordo (2016) reiterated the benefits of rules-based policies relative to the pitfalls of international central bank coordination.

Peter Ireland and Athanasios Orphanides built on the SOMC's long-standing support of a systemic approach to monetary policy, prepared numerous papers that advocated rules, and criticized the Fed's forward-guidance policies. Ireland (2012b), in "Refocusing the Fed," criticized the Fed's interest rate policies (including maturity extension), forward guidance and enlarged balance sheet, and urged the Fed to be guided by simpler rules: "The Fed could either augment or abandon altogether the forward guidance it has offered regarding the future path of the funds rate by emphasizing instead, the commitment that the FOMC has already made to its 2% inflation target. After all, unlike a path for the funds rate, which will necessarily adjust as changes in macroeconomic conditions warrant, the 2% inflation target represents an unconditional promise." Ireland emphasized that the Fed could achieve its objective "by conducting the appropriate set of open market operations to stabilize the growth of nominal variables." He detailed the benefits of nominal GDP targeting in subsequent articles.

In October 2015, in "Short-Sighted Monetary Policy and Fear of Liftoff," Orphanides (2015) criticized the Fed's "short-termism," stating "the need for a somewhat accommodative policy cannot be used to defend the current non-systematic policy and excessive emphasis on short-term employment gains." In "The Case Against the Case Against Monetary Rules," he carefully described the arguments forwarded by advocates of discretionary policy over rules and refuted each of them (Orphanides 2017). He emphasized that amid an incomplete understanding of the economy and how its structure is evolving, along with a high degree of uncertainty and potentially destabilizing shocks, systematic rules are more reliable than discretionary policy based on judgment. As part of a rules-based system, he recommended that the Fed should publish annually its evaluations of the performance of rules.

While Orphanides and Ireland highlight the benefits of systematic rules, they propose different rules. Ireland favors nominal GDP targeting. In "The Continuing Case for Nominal GDP Level Targeting," he noted that by tracking deviations of nominal GDP from its target, the Fed could diagnose troublesome trends in monetary policy and misdiagnoses of economic and inflation conditions (Ireland 2022). Ireland believes that achieving a nominal GDP target is best achieved through targeting money instruments (Ireland 2024).

Orphanides proposes a forecast-based rule based on interest rates, a modification of the Taylor rule. In "Enhancing Resilience with Natural Growth Targeting," he recommends the Fed adjust monetary policy to deviations in its projections of nominal GDP and longer-run potential growth consistent with its 2% inflation target (Orphanides 2024). The projections would be based on the Fed's Summary of Economic Projections (SEPs) that are published quarterly. This first difference model would be forward-looking and easy to track while steering the Fed toward its inflation target and avoiding the mistakes of discretionary policy.

These two approaches to rules-based policy reflect the evolution of the meaning of rules since the earlier SOMC stances. They reflect the SOMC's long-standing goals of stable low inflation while acknowledging the downside risks of the Fed's discretionary policies and judgments and the complexities of the monetary transmission channels. Both are systematic approaches that provide valuable guidelines to the Fed and are easy to track.

Fed Communications and Forecasts

The SOMC has consistently clear and transparent communications. The issue of transparency has become more pressing since the Fed started providing quarterly projections in its SEPs in 2007, and particularly since 2012, when it augmented the SEPs with the FOMC member estimates of the federal funds rate they believe would achieve their forecasts of the economy and inflation. Levy (2013) described how the Fed's SEPs were an unreliable and a problematic basis for providing forward guidance of policy. Loretta Mester (2016), then-president of the Federal Reserve Bank of Cleveland, presented a paper to the SOMC entitled "Acknowledging Uncertainty," arguing that in order to improve communications and policy deliberations, the Fed needed to come to grips with the reality that forecasting is difficult. Levy, in "The Fed's Economic Forecasts, Uncertainties, and Monetary Policy," recommended that the Fed incorporate alternative projections into its quarterly SEPs and estimates by FOMC members of how they would adjust to the different scenarios (Levy 2018). He subsequently considered hypothetical scenarios based on estimates of historical deviations of actual performance from baseline estimates (Levy 2020). Orphanides and other SOMC members called on the Fed to include information on its balance sheet in its quarterly SEPs (Hess and Orphanides 2018). Ireland (2019) underlined this point. He emphasized that the Fed's practice of focusing entirely on interest-rate policy while eschewing any mention of money draws an inappropriate distinction between monetary policy and the Fed's balance sheet, and that "all monetary policy actions have a direct impact for the size and composition of the Fed's balance sheet." He believed articulating these points would improve the Fed's communications.

Lacker teamed up with Plosser (2022) in "The Fed Should Talk about the Prescriptions of Systematic Policy Rules," arguing that a rules-based policy would improve the public's understanding of the Fed's reaction function, enhance the Fed's communications, and increase its transparency. They posited that the Fed's inexplicable policies in 2021–22 heighten the importance of a more systematic, rules-based monetary policy, and continue to be a focus of the SOMC.

The SOMC and the Pandemic Inflation

Members of the SOMC were among the earliest to accurately predict the soaring inflation that would unfold in 2021, and were prominent in signaling warnings to the Fed that high inflation would persist and be severe (Bordo and Levy 2021a, 2021b). Bordo and Levy (2020) based their predictions on their research of historical episodes in deficit spending and extreme monetary accommodation that generated excess demand, particularly during wartimes. In subsequent research, they found a consistent pattern of the Fed delaying exits from monetary ease (Bordo and Levy 2022).

At the onset of COVID-19 in March 2020, Levin (2020) presented a position paper, "Hope for the Best, Prepare for the Worst: The Federal Reserve's Monetary Toolbox for Mitigating Severe Adverse Shocks," expressing worries that the Fed was not adequately prepared for dealing with the effects of the pandemic. Bordo, Levin, and Levy (2020) emphasized the need for the Fed to improve its risk management by introducing scenario analysis into its quarterly projections to consider how it would respond to alternative outcomes.

Ireland also warned that the rise in inflation would persist based on the unprecedented surge in M2 money growth. He contrasted this with the post-GFC period, when the Fed's zero interest rates and QEs boosted bank reserves and the monetary base but not M2 (Ireland and Levy 2021). In response to the Fed's insistence in mid-2021 that the inflation was due to transitory supply shocks that involved large price increases of a small number of goods, Levy (2022) disaggregated the PCE inflation data to show that inflation had become pervasive among virtually all goods and services. Levy (2024) found the Fed's poor forecasts and judgment resulted in misguided monetary policy.

In his initial presentation as the Committee's newest member, Jim Bullard emphasized at the June 2024 SOMC meeting that the Fed should focus on its inflation target as the best foundation for achieving economic performance. He called for a national commission to study different measures of inflation. His proposal was striking in that the gap between PCE inflation and CPI inflation has widened and created thorny issues in measurement and Fed policy and communications.

Issues in Financial Regulations

Calomiris and Lucas have enhanced the SOMC's focus on finance and financial regulations. Importantly, both advocate a more systematic approach to regulations with a focus on economic efficiency and relying on cost-benefit analysis, and criticize discretionary regulations that are imposed on an ad hoc basis. Calomiris, in "What Is a Bank? What Is a Government?" argued that bank regulations and supervision have historically resulted from political maneuvering rather than clear economic reasoning (Calomiris 2024). This has resulted in economically inefficient policies that impose social costs. He recommended the establishment of rules-based regulations that reduce the unaccountable discretion of regulators and supervisors. He also advocated more accurately based capital ratios for banks and the establishment of bottom-line supervisory measures of bank weakness.

Lucas (2024) assessed the Basel III Endgame proposals for bank capital and found that they are not supported by cost-benefit analysis, and that requiring banks to evaluate their risks based on a new Fed-generated "Enhanced Risk-Based Approach" rather than their own models would be a mistake. She emphasized that the Fed should agree to conduct cost-benefit analysis of its proposed regulations, even though it is not designated as an independent government agency and required to do so. Regarding interest-rate risks of financial institutions, Lucas proposes that medium- and large-sized banks regularly report on their duration gaps (Golding and Lucas 2023). Requiring them to report on the measured gap between the duration of their liabilities and the duration of their assets and their sensitivity to interest rates would improve banks' risk management and provide important information to regulators.

The Fed's Monetary Policy Operations

The Fed's post-GFC asset purchases and enlarged balance sheet added complexities to its conduct of monetary policy, requiring the Fed to manage its short-term policy through a "floor system" rather than its traditional "corridor system."[11] Goodfriend (2015) described that the inability of the GSEs and Federal Home Loan Banks to be paid interest on their reserves at the Fed created a supply-demand imbalance in the short-term funding market, and the Fed's dominant role required in borrowing in the overnight reverse repurchase market violates a basic principle of central banking, that of minimizing interference in markets.

Jeff Lacker described how the Fed's transition from a scarce-reserves system to an ample-reserves system as a consequence of its enlarged balance sheet makes the Fed's operations too complex and has increased its presence in short-term funding markets (Lacker 2023).

Governance Issues at the Federal Reserve

In recent years, several SOMC members have addressed Fed governance issues and made recommendations that would improve the functioning of the Fed. Concerns have arisen about the lack of diversity of thinking at the Fed that has adversely affected the quality of policy deliberations. One source of the reduced diversity of thinking at the Fed has stemmed from consolidation of power at the Board of Governors and with the Fed chair, and the process of choosing new Federal Reserve Bank presidents. One metric reflecting the lack of diversity is the lack of policy dissents of FOMC members, particularly by Fed governors. Another is the lack of dispersion and skew of projections of FOMC members. Calomiris (2017a, 2017b), in "Reforming the Rules That Govern the Fed" and "Reforming and Depoliticizing the Federal Reserve," respectively, expressed the concern that the Fed has a tendency to adhere to the "latest fad in macroeconomic modeling"; he recommended changing the Fed's mandate to an inflation target and achieving it through a systematic rule in order to avoid "group think." He recommended allowing all FOMC members to vote at every FOMC meeting.

Two recent contributions by SOMC members highlight the growing concern about the Fed's expanded scope of its monetary and regulatory policies, and how poor congressional oversight has reduced the quality of the Fed's policymaking and accountability. Levin (2023) provided an overview and recommendations to strengthen the Fed's governance. Levin and Skinner (2024), in "Central Bank Undersight: Assessing the Fed's Accountability to Congress," provided a legal and economic history of Fed governance and documented how the increased scope and complexity of monetary policy and shifts in power within the Fed have undermined the balance between the Fed's independence and accountability. They pointed to the costs to taxpayers of the Fed's enlarged balance sheet and called for more effective oversight of the Fed, including enhanced reporting requirements and congressional and external reviews.

Lacker (2024), in "Governance and Diversity of the Federal Reserve," argued that the lack of dissents during the 2021–22 inflation highlights the diminished diversity of views within the FOMC since the 1960s. He focused on the process of appointing Federal Reserve Bank presidents, which he argued has shifted. The Board of Governors used to provide final-stage approval of Federal Reserve Bank presidents chosen by their respective boards of directors, but recently the Board of Governors has become a comanager of the selection process. This has changed the profile of the regional bank presidents and constrained the diversity of thinking. Lacker also discussed the changed relationship between the Fed and Congress stemming from the Fed's involvement in credit allocation and fiscal matters.

Concluding Remarks

The SOMC has had a very rich history. In its beginnings, it established itself as a distinct minority outlier associated with Milton Friedman that argued that inflation was a monetary phenomenon, and that the Fed should target money growth to achieve lower inflation. Amid upward ratcheting of inflation and the loss of policymaker credibility, the SOMC successfully promoted the importance of controlling the money supply in the public debate and in Congress. Although Paul Volcker opposed Friedman's monetarism, the SOMC and other advocates of money targeting may have had some influence on the Volcker-led Fed that temporarily shifted from targeting interest rates to targeting nonborrowed bank reserves and aggressively tightened monetary policy to successfully reduce inflation.

The SOMC continued to propose money-growth targets in the 1980s and 1990s even though it acknowledged that short-run money demand was volatile, and its monetary policy recommendations fell out of touch with the Fed, reducing its impact and following. It continued to promote inflation targeting, systematic rules-based policies over discretion, and central bank transparency and accountability. It also provided sound advice on other economic policies, including urging fiscal restraint, having a systematic approach to financial regulatory policy, and promoting economic policies that brought about prosperity. The SOMC evolved toward providing monetary policy recommendations in terms of interest rates and remained committed to sound central banking. Over time, the Fed has modified its policy deliberations and communications in some of the ways that the SOMC has recommended. Of note, several SOMC members became Fed members and were very influential in their roles. For example, Charles Plosser played a key role in developing the Fed's original longer-run strategic plan in 2012 that established the 2% inflation target.

Over time, the SOMC has strengthened itself with new members from academia and the Fed who have strengthened the Committee's analytical capabilities and enhanced the ability to provide sound, constructive advice to the Fed. Currently, three SOMC members are former Fed members, and several others are former senior Fed staffers.

In 2015, the SOMC reassessed its role and reviewed its beliefs and produced a statement on its Core Beliefs, which have many consistencies with the basic tenets of the original SOMC. The SOMC now addresses a more diverse array of issues pertaining to monetary and financial policies.

The Committee has had an excellent track record of anticipating and warning against some of the Fed's largest policy errors and undesired outcomes in modern history. Following its successes of the 1970s, the SOMC warned against the Fed's asymmetric assessment of inflation risks in the early 2000s that led it to keep interest rates too low. It identified clear flaws in the Fed's new strategic plan of 2020 soon after it was announced. And it accurately predicted the 2021–22 surge in inflation.

Of note, some SOMC members, particularly Bordo, Ireland, and Levy, continue to closely follow the monetary aggregates. Unlike the original monetarists of the SOMC, however, they acknowledge the complexities of the monetary transmission channels and the unpredictable short-run volatility of money velocity, and focus on *pronounced shifts* in money-supply growth to anticipate and predict possible outcomes. Most recently, the 40% surge in M2, combined with unprecedented deficit spending, led them to predict the 2021–22 inflation. Such an approach to assessing large outliers in money supply has been advocated by Mervyn King (2024), the ECB in its two-pillar strategy (Issing 2006), and earlier by SOMC member Bill Poole (1993).

The SOMC's current research agenda includes the Fed's upcoming strategic review, issues that would improve the Fed's governance and accountability, and continued support of systematic rules that would achieve low inflation and improvements in transparency. The SOMC looks forward to providing future constructive advice on these and other issues.

Appendix I. SOMC Members

The SOMC members and their years on the Committee are as follows:

Allan Meltzer, 1973–99, deceased 2017
Karl Brunner, 1973–89, deceased 1989
Anna Schwartz, 1973–2011, deceased 2012
Jim Meigs, 1973–78, deceased 2014

Bob Rasche, 1973–98, deceased 2016
Wilson E. Schmidt, 1973–98, deceased 1981
Beryl Sprinkel, 1975–81, deceased 2009
Jerry Jordan, 1975–80 and 1983–92 (became Fed member)
Rudolph Penner, 1977–83
Erich Heinemann, 1977–2001, deceased 2003
Robert Genetski, 1978–81
Jan Tumlir, 1980–85, deceased 1985
Burt Zwick, 1981–84
Mickey Levy, 1983–present
Bill Poole, 1984–98 and 2010
Lee Hoskins, 1992–2006, former Fed member
Charlie Plosser, 1992–2006, and 2015–present; Fed member 2006–15
Jagdish Bhagwati, 1993–95
Greg Hess, 1998–present
Ben McCallum, 2000–2015, deceased 2022
Alan Stockman, 2000–2006, deceased 2010
Marvin Goodfriend, 2008–16, deceased 2019
Michael Bordo, 2008–present
Charles Calomiris, 2008–present
Peter Ireland, 2011–present
Athanasios Orphanides, 2014–present
Deborah Lucas, 2017–present
Andrew Levin, 2019–present
Jeff Lacker, 2022–present, former Fed member
Jim Bullard, 2024–present, former Fed member

Appendix II. Guest Speakers at SOMC Meetings

September 2009: Don Kohn, member, Board of Governors of the Federal Reserve System, "Central Bank Exit Policies," and Athanasios Orphanides, governor, Central Bank of Cyprus, and member, European Central Bank, "Central Bank Exit Policies"

March 2010: Kevin Warsh, member, Board of Governors of the Federal Reserve System, "An Ode to Independence"

October 2010: Axel A. Weber, president, Deutsche Bundesbank, "Monetary Policy after the Crisis—a European Perspective"

March 2011: Charles Plosser, president, Federal Reserve Bank of Philadelphia, "EXIT"

October 2011: Thomas Hoenig, former president, Federal Reserve
  Bank of Kansas City, "Comments on Central Banking and Financial
  Regulation"

April 2012: Kevin Brady, member of Congress and vice chairman,
  Joint Economic Committee, "Remarks to the Shadow Open Market
  Committee"

November 2012: Jeffrey Lacker, president, Federal Reserve Bank of
  Richmond, "Challenges to Economic Growth"

Fall 2013: Esther George, president, Federal Reserve Bank of Kansas
  City

March 2014: Martin Feldstein, Harvard University, "Shifting Perspectives on the Dual Mandate"

November 2014: Richard Fisher, president, Federal Reserve Bank of
  Dallas, "R.I.P. QE3 . . . Or Will It?"

March 2015: John B. Taylor, Stanford University, "Getting Monetary
  Policy Back to a Rules-Based Strategy"

October 2015: Jim Bullard, president, Federal Reserve Bank of St. Louis,
  "Three Challenges to Central Bank Orthodoxies"

April 2016: Peter R. Fisher, president, Federal Reserve Bank of Dallas,
  "What's the Matter with the Fed?"

October 2016: Loretta J. Mester, president, Federal Reserve Bank of
  Cleveland, "Acknowledging Uncertainty"

May 2017: John C. Williams, president, Federal Reserve Bank of San
  Francisco, "Preparing for the Next Storm: Frameworks & Strategies
  in a Low R-Star World"

September 2017: Mervyn King, former governor, Bank of England,
  "Unwinding the Fed's Balance Sheet"

March 2018: Charles L. Evans, president, Federal Reserve Bank of Chicago,
  "Some Practical Considerations for Monetary Policy Frameworks"

October 2018: Rob Kaplan, president, Federal Reserve Bank of Dallas,
  "Q&A Session"

March 2019: Randal K. Quarles, vice chairman for supervision, Board
  of Governors of the Federal Reserve System, "Frameworks for the
  Countercyclical Capital Buffers"

September 2019: Patrick Harker, president, Federal Reserve Bank of
  Philadelphia, "An Economic Outlook"

March 2020: Jim Bullard, Charles Evans, Esther George, Loretta Mester,
  Eric Rosengren (president, Federal Reserve Bank of Boston), John
  Williams, Al Broaddus (former president, Federal Reserve Bank of

Richmond), Don Kohn, Brookings Institution, Bill Poole, John Tay-lor, Robert King, Boston University.

June 2020: Jim Bullard, president, Federal Reserve Bank of St. Louis, "The Economic Crisis and Prospects"

September 2020: Kathryn Judge, Columbia University Law School, "Why the Fed Should Issue a Policy Framework for Credit Policy"

April 2021: Rich Clarida, member, Board of Governors of the Federal Reserve System, "The Federal Reserve's New Framework and Out-come-Based Forward Guidance"

February 2022: Christina Skinner, Wharton School of the University of Pennsylvania, "Governing Monetary Policy"

June 2022: Mary Daly, president, Federal Reserve Bank of San Fran-cisco, "Policy Nimbleness Through Forward Guidance"

November 2022: John Taylor, Stanford University and Hoover Insti-tution, and Donald Kohn, Brookings Institution, panel on "How Should the Fed Address Its Current Challenge and Risks?"

October 2023: Loretta J. Mester, president, Federal Reserve Bank of Cleveland, "Monetary Policy in Word and Deed"

April 2024: Michelle W. Bowman, member, Board of Governors of the Federal Reserve System, "Risks and Uncertainties in Monetary Policy: Current and Past Considerations"

Notes

The authors thank the Money, History and Finance Workshop at Rutgers Univer-sity (September 16, 2024), and David Laidler, Jim Bullard, Peter Ireland, Andrew Levin, and Charles Plosser for their insights. We also thank Alan Chernoff for excel-lent research assistance.

1. Meltzer fashioned the SOMC after the British "shadow cabinet."

2. The SOMC website is located at https://www.shadowfed.org and the public SOMC archive is available at https://shadowfed.org/archive.

3. "Concurrent resolution expressing the sense of Congress with respect to the conduct of monetary policy." H.Con.Res. 124, 94th Cong. (1975).

4. Karl Brunner established the Konstanz Seminar on Monetary Theory and Pol-icy in 1970 to provide an alternative to Keynesian thinking. It had a tight-knit Euro-pean monetarist following that later had a significant impact on European central banking and especially the founding principles of the European Central Bank.

5. Milton Friedman also faced the same issues when he used quarterly M1 money growth to make predictions about the near-term future (Nelson 2025).

6. Theoretical advances during this period included the development of the New Keynesian and neoclassical models. Both models incorporated rational

expectations into their frameworks and evolved toward using interest rates as the monetary policy variable rather than money supply but allowed different degrees of countercyclical responses to shortfalls in aggregate demand. One innovation was the introduction of staggered wage and price contracts that allowed for both price and output adjustment (Taylor 1980). McCallum (1981) along with Stanley Fischer (1980) developed rules-based models that provided countercyclical policy responses to deviations or shortfalls of real economic conditions from desired levels, as well as deviations from desired price levels (inflation). McCallum (1981) along with Michael Parkin (1978) showed how interest rates could be used in place of money supply in a neoclassical model with rational expectations if the interest rate instrument was part of a policy package with a well-specified nominal anchor. Marvin Goodfriend (1991) developed a simple rational-expectations model in which the central bank chose the joint behavior of a monetary aggregate, the price level and the nominal interest rate. But the models differed philosophically. The New Keynesian modeling assumed market inefficiencies in response to changes in supply and demand, such as sticky wages and price adjustments, and also assumed monopolistically competitive firms with pricing power (Clarida et al. 1999). The evolution of the neoclassical model assumed that markets naturally clear and restore themselves, and more quickly adjust, and that businesses are competitive but are price-takers (Goodfriend and King 1999). As a result of these differences, the New Keynesian models allow for a short-run downward-sloping Phillips curve that supports the efficacy of countercyclical policy and the advocacy of discretionary policymaking. The market efficiencies of the neoclassical model provided a much smaller window for effective countercyclical policies and generated empirical results that reveal the costs of government intervention.

7. Earlier, William Barnett (1980) had developed the Divisia index of money that weighted the growth of each component of money supply based on a weighted index of the liquidity services provided.

8. The SFRC was composed primarily of academic economists and lawyers who favored a systematic and economically efficient approach to financial regulation. The committee successfully presented its recommendations to policymakers and at academic and business association meetings and influenced regulatory policy.

9. The site was located at http://www.somc.rochester.edu.

10. Lacker (2012) dissented from the Fed's adoption of QE3 in September 2012, arguing that efforts to increase employment were problematic for several reasons: the concept of maximum employment is beyond the scope of monetary policy; trying to maximize employment would risk higher inflation; and purchases of MBS involved credit allocation and is properly the role of fiscal policy.

11. In the traditional corridor system, the Fed establishes an upper bound (the discount rate that the Fed offers to lend funds to banks in good standing) and a lower limit (the interest rate it pays on reserves), and manages short-term rates through open market operations that adjust the supply of reserve balances so the market rate

is as close as possible to the Fed's target rate. In contrast, with an enlarged balance sheet, the Fed is incapable of managing the effective interest rate through open market operations. Instead, the floor system involves a single rate, the interest rate that the Fed sets on reserves.

References

Andersen, Leonall C. 1973. "The State of the Monetarist Debate." *Federal Reserve Bank of St. Louis Review* 55 (9): 2–9.

Barnett, William. 1980. "Economic Monetary Aggregates: An Application of Index Number and Aggregation Theory." *Journal of Econometrics* 14 (1): 11–48.

Bernanke, Ben S. 2002. "Deflation: Making Sure 'It' Doesn't Happen Here." Remarks before the National Economics Club, Washington, DC. November 21.

Bernanke, Ben S. 2008. "Federal Reserve Policies in the Financial Crisis." Remarks before the Greater Austin Chamber of Commerce, Austin, TX. December 1.

Bernanke, Ben S. 2010. "Monetary Policy and the Housing Bubble." Remarks at the Annual Meeting of the American Economic Association, Atlanta, GA. January 3.

Bernanke, Ben S. 2012. "Monetary Policy since the Onset of the Crisis." Remarks at the Federal Reserve Bank of Kansas City's Economic Symposium, Jackson Hole, WY. August 31.

Bernanke, Ben S., Thomas Laubach, Frederick S. Mishkin, and Adam S. Posen. 1998. *Inflation Targeting: Lessons from the International Experience.* Princeton University Press.

Bhagwati, Jagdish. 1993. "The Uruguay Round and Free Trade Areas." Position paper, Shadow Open Market Committee, Washington, DC. March 8.

Bordo, Michael. 2009. "The Great Contraction and the Current Crisis: Historical Parallels and Policy Lessons." Position paper, Shadow Open Market Committee, Washington, DC. April 24.

Bordo, Michael D. 2015. "US Inflation Is Not Too Low." Position paper, Shadow Open Market Committee, New York, NY. March 20.

Bordo, Michael D. 2016. "Rules Based Policies: Better Than International Central Bank Coordination and Cooperation." Position paper, Shadow Open Market Committee, New York, NY. April 29.

Bordo, Michael D. 2019. "Karl Brunner and Allan Meltzer: From Monetary Policy to Monetary History to Monetary Rules." Economics Working Paper No. 19104. Hoover Institution. March 6.

Bordo, Michael D., and Joseph G. Haubrich. 2012. "Deep Recessions, Fast Recoveries, and Financial Crises: Evidence from the American Record." Working Paper No. 18194. National Bureau of Economic Research. June.

Bordo, Michael D., Owen F. Humpage, and Anna J. Schwartz. 2015. *Strained Relations: US Foreign-Exchange Operations and Monetary Policy in the Twentieth Century.* University of Chicago Press.

Bordo, Michael, and Andrew T. Levin. 2017. "Central Bank Digital Currency and the Future of Monetary Policy." Working Paper No. 23711. National Bureau of Economic Research. August.

Bordo, Michael D., Andrew T. Levin, and Mickey D. Levy. 2020. "Incorporating Scenario Analysis into the Federal Reserve's Policy Strategy and Communications." Working Paper No. 27369. National Bureau of Economic Research. June.

Bordo, Michael D., and Mickey D. Levy. 2020. "Do Enlarged Fiscal Deficits Cause Inflation: The Historical Record." Working Paper No. 28195. National Bureau of Economic Research. December.

Bordo, Michael D., and Mickey D. Levy. 2021a. "The Short March Back to Inflation." *Wall Street Journal*, February 4.

Bordo, Michael D., and Mickey D. Levy. 2021b. "The Fed in the Sand as Inflation Threatens." *Wall Street Journal*, April 27.

Bordo, Michael D., and Mickey D. Levy. 2022. "The Fed's Delayed Exits from Monetary Ease: The Fed Rarely Learns from History." Position paper, Shadow Open Market Committee. February 11.

Bordo, Michael D., and Anna J. Schwartz. 1991. "What Has Foreign Exchange Market Intervention Since the Plaza Agreement Accomplished?" *Open Economies Review* 2 (February): 39–64.

Bordo, Michael D., and Anna J. Schwartz. 1999. "Under What Circumstances, Past and Present, Have International Rescues of Countries in Financial Distress Been Successful?" *Journal of International Money and Finance* 18 (4): 683–708.

Bordo, Michael D., and Anna J. Schwartz. 2000. "Measuring Real Economic Effects of Bailouts: Historical Perspectives on How Countries in Financial Distress Have Fared with and without Bailouts." *Carnegie-Rochester Conference Series on Public Policy* 53 (1): 81–117.

Brunner, Karl. 1968. "The Role of Money and Monetary Policy." *Federal Reserve Bank of St. Louis Review* 50 (7): 8–24.

Brunner, Karl, ed. 1969. *Targets and Indicators of Monetary Policy: Papers Presented at the Conference on Indicators and Targets of Monetary Policy, University of California, Los Angeles, April 1966.* Chandler.

Brunner, Karl. 1970. "The 'Monetarist Revolution' in Monetary Policy." *Review of World Economics (Weltwirtschaftliches Archiv)* 105 (September): 1–30.

Brunner, Karl. 1974. "Monetary Growth and Monetary Policy." Position paper, Shadow Open Market Committee, Washington, DC. March 8.

Brunner, Karl. 1979. "Testimony on Full Employment and Balanced Growth Act of 1978 before the Committee on Banking, Finance and Urban Affairs." 95th Cong. February 22. https://shadowfed.org/wp-content/uploads/somc-archive/1979_03_11.pdf.

Brunner, Karl. 1987. "Policy Coordination and the Dollar." Position paper, Shadow Open Market Committee, Washington, DC. March 8–9.

Brunner, Karl, and Allan H. Meltzer. 1964a. *Some General Features of the Federal Reserve's Approach to Policy: A Staff Analysis.* US Government Printing Office.

Brunner, Karl, and Allan H. Meltzer. 1964b. *The Federal Reserve's Attachment to the Free Reserve Concept: A Staff Analysis.* US Government Printing Office.

Brunner, Karl, and Allan H. Meltzer. 1964c. *An Alternative Approach to the Monetary Mechanism.* Report to the Subcommittee on Domestic Finance, Committee on Banking and Currency, House of Representatives. 88th Cong. August 17.

Brunner, Karl, and Allan H. Meltzer. 1964d. "Some Evidence on the Relationship of the Monetary Base to the Supply of Money." Section II of *An Alternative Approach to the Monetary Mechanism.* Report to the Subcommittee on Domestic Finance, Committee on Banking and Currency, House of Representatives. 88th Cong. August 17.

Calomiris, Charles. 2009a. "The Allocation of Regulatory Authority." Position paper, Shadow Open Market Committee, Washington, DC. April 24.

Calomiris, Charles. 2009b. "Prudential Bank Regulation: What's Broke and How to Fix It." Position paper, Shadow Open Market Committee, Washington, DC. April 24.

Calomiris, Charles W. 2014. "Phony Deflation Worries." Position paper, Shadow Open Market Committee, New York, NY. November 3.

Calomiris, Charles. 2017a. "Reforming the Rules That Govern the Fed." Position paper, Shadow Open Market Committee, New York, NY. May 5.

Calomiris, Charles W. 2017b. "Reforming and Depoliticizing the Federal Reserve." Position paper, Shadow Open Market Committee, New York, NY. September 15.

Calomiris, Charles W. 2024. "What Is a Bank? What Is a Government? Addressing the Regulatory and Supervisory Shortcomings That Plague Banking." Position paper, Shadow Open Market Committee. April 5.

Clarida, Richard, Jordi Galí, and Mark Gertler. 1999. "The Science of Monetary Policy: A New Keynesian Perspective." *Journal of Economic Literature* 37 (4): 1661–707.

Fischer, Stanley, ed. 1980. *Rational Expectations and Economic Policy.* University of Chicago Press.

Friedman, Milton. 1956. "The Quantity Theory of Money: A Restatement." In *Studies in the Quantity Theory of Money,* edited by Milton Friedman. University of Chicago Press.

Friedman, Milton. 1968. "The Role of Monetary Policy." *American Economic Review* 58 (1): 1–17.

Golding, Edward L., and Deborah J. Lucas. 2023. "Duration Gap Disclosures: A Modest Proposal to Prevent Another SVB." Position paper, Shadow Open Market Committee. October 23.

Goodfriend, Marvin. 1991. "Interest Rates and the Conduct of Monetary Policy." *Carnegie-Rochester Conference Series on Public Policy* 34 (Spring): 7–30.

Goodfriend, Marvin. 2004. "Inflation Targeting in the United States?" In *The Inflation-Targeting Debate*, edited by Ben Bernanke and Michael Woodford. University of Chicago Press.

Goodfriend, Marvin. 2009. "We Need an 'Accord' for the Federal Reserve Credit Policy." Position paper, Shadow Open Market Committee, Washington, DC. April 24.

Goodfriend, Marvin. 2012. "The Fed Should Put Its 2% Goal to Work." Position paper, Shadow Open Market Committee, New York, NY. November 20.

Goodfriend, Marvin. 2014a. "The Relevance of the Federal Reserve Surplus Capital for Current Policy." Position paper, Shadow Open Market Committee, New York, NY. March 14.

Goodfriend, Marvin. 2014b. "Monetary Policy as a Carry Trade." Position paper, Shadow Open Market Committee, New York, NY. November 3.

Goodfriend, Marvin. 2015. "The Fed Should Fix the Interest on Reserves Floor." Position paper, Shadow Open Market Committee, New York, NY. March 20.

Goodfriend, Marvin. 2016. "The Case (in Brief) for Unencumbering Interest Rate Policy at the Zero Bound." Position paper, Shadow Open Market Committee, New York, NY. October 7.

Goodfriend, Marvin, and Robert G. King. 1999. "The New Neoclassical Synthesis and the Role of Monetary Policy." In *NBER Macroeconomics Annual*, edited by Ben S. Bernanke and Julio Rotemberg. MIT Press.

Goodfriend, Marvin, and Bennett McCallum. 2009. "Exiting Credit Policy to Preserve Sound Monetary Policy." Position paper, Shadow Open Market Committee, Washington, DC. September 30.

Greenspan, Alan. 1993. "Statement before the Subcommittee on Economic Growth and Credit Formation of the Committee on Banking, Finance and Urban Affairs." 103rd Cong. July 20. https://fraser.stlouisfed.org/title/statements-speeches-alan-greenspan-452/semiannual-monetary-policy-report-congress-8489.

Greenspan, Alan. 2002. "Issues for Monetary Policy." Remarks before the Economic Club of New York, New York, NY. December 19.

Heinemann, H. Erich. 1977. "Weekly Federal Reserve Report." Position paper, Shadow Open Market Committee, Washington, DC. September 19.

Hess, Gregory D. 2002. "Is It Time for Fannie Mae and Freddie Mac to Cut the Cord?" Position paper, Shadow Open Market Committee, Washington, DC. November 17–18.

Hess, Gregory D. 2004. "Can We Avert the Next Financial Crisis?" Position paper, Shadow Open Market Committee, Washington, DC. May 3.

Hess, Gregory D. 2009. "Fannie and Freddie: The Houseguests That Just Won't Leave." Position paper, Shadow Open Market Committee, Washington, DC. September 30.

Hess, Gregory D., and Athanasios Orphanides. 2018. "Monetary Policy Normalization Should Be More Systematic and Less Wobbly." Position paper, Shadow Open Market Committee, New York, NY. March 9.

Hetzel, Robert L. 2013. "The Monetarist-Keynesian Debate and the Phillips Curve: Lessons from the Great Inflation." *Federal Reserve Bank of Richmond Economic Quarterly* 99 (2): 83–116.

Hornstein, Andreas. 2008. "Introduction to the New Keynesian Phillips Curve." In "A Special Issue on the Phillips Curve and Its Implications for Modern Monetary Policy," special issue, *Federal Reserve Bank of Richmond Economic Quarterly* 94 (4): 301–9.

Hoskins, W. Lee. 1993. "Federal Reserve Independence and Accountability." Position paper, Shadow Open Market Committee, Washington, DC. March 8.

Hoskins, Lee. 1999. "FOMC Bias." Position paper, Shadow Open Market Committee, Washington, DC. September 26–27.

Hoskins, Lee. 2000. "Monetary Policy: Credible Commitments." Position paper, Shadow Open Market Committee, Washington, DC. November 12–13.

Ireland, Peter. 2011. "What the Political System Can Do to Help the Fed." Position paper, Shadow Open Market Committee, New York, NY. October 21.

Ireland, Peter. 2012a. "Innovations to Federal Reserve Policy: Opportunities Seized and Opportunities Lost." Position paper, Shadow Open Market Committee, New York, NY. April 20.

Ireland, Peter. 2012b. "Refocusing the Fed." Position paper, Shadow Open Market Committee, New York, NY. November 20.

Ireland, Peter N. 2016. "Why Has Nominal Income Growth Been So Slow?" Position paper, Shadow Open Market Committee, New York, NY. April 29.

Ireland, Peter N. 2019. "Monetary Policy Implementation: Making Better and More Consistent Use of the Federal Reserve's Balance Sheet." Position paper, Shadow Open Market Committee, New York, NY. March 29.

Ireland, Peter N. 2022. "The Continuing Case for Nominal GDP Level Targeting." Position paper, Shadow Open Market Committee. April 29.

Ireland, Peter N. 2024. "Update on Monetary Conditions: Spring 2024." Position paper, Shadow Open Market Committee. April 5.

Ireland, Peter N., and Mickey D. Levy. 2021. "'Substantial Progress,' Transitory Versus Persistent, and the Appropriate Calibration of Monetary Policy." Position paper, Shadow Open Market Committee. October 1.

Issing, Otmar. 2006. "The ECB's Monetary Policy Strategy: Why Did We Choose a Two Pillar Approach?" Paper presented at the Fourth ECB Central Banking Conference, Frankfurt, Germany. November 10.

Johannes, James M., and Robert H. Rasche. 1982. "Forecasting Multipliers in the 80s: The More Things Change the More They Stay the Same." Position paper, Shadow Open Market Committee, Washington, DC. September 12.

Jordan, Jerry L. 1978a. "Testimony to Committee on Banking, Finance and Urban Affairs, House of Representatives, United States Congress." March 7. https://fraser.stlouisfed.org/title/monetary-policy-oversight-672/quarterly-hearings-conduct-monetary-policy-584389?page=20.

Jordan, Jerry L. 1978b. "Projections for the Economy." Position paper, Shadow Open Market Committee, Washington, DC. March 12.

Jordan, Jerry L. 1985. "Economic Outlook." Position paper, Shadow Open Market Committee, Washington, DC. March 24.

Jordan, Jerry L. 1990. "Financial Structure Reforms." Position paper, Shadow Open Market Committee, Washington, DC. October 1.

King, Mervyn. 2024. "Inflation Targets: Practice Ahead of Theory." Working Paper No. 32594. National Bureau of Economic Research. June.

Lacker, Jeffrey M. 2009. "Government Lending and Monetary Policy." *Business Economics* 44 (3): 136–42.

Lacker, Jeffrey. 2012. "Richmond Fed President Lacker Comments on FOMC Dissent." Press release, Federal Reserve Bank of Richmond. October 26.

Lacker, Jeffrey. 2023. "Some Questions About the Fed's Monetary Policy Operating Regime." Position paper, Shadow Open Market Committee, New York, NY. April 21.

Lacker, Jeffrey. 2024. "Governance and Diversity of the Federal Reserve." Position paper, Shadow Open Market Committee, April 5. Published by Mercatus Center, George Mason University, January 8.

Lacker, Jeffrey M., and Charles Plosser. 2022. "The Fed Should Talk About the Prescriptions of Systematic Policy Rules." Position paper, Shadow Open Market Committee, New York, NY. November 11.

Laidler, David. 1991. "The Quantity Theory Is Always and Everywhere Controversial—Why?" *Economic Record* 67 (4): 289–306.

Levin, Andrew. 2019. "Assessing the Federal Reserve's Toolbox for Providing Monetary Stimulus at the Effective Lower Bound." Position paper, Shadow Open Market Committee, New York, NY. September 27.

Levin, Andrew. 2020. "Hope for the Best, Prepare for the Worst: The Federal Reserve's Monetary Toolbox for Mitigating Severe Adverse Shocks." Position paper, Shadow Open Market Committee, New York, NY. March 6.

Levin, Andrew. 2023. "Quantifying the Costs and Benefits of Quantitative Easing." Position paper, Shadow Open Market Committee. June 16.

Levin, Andrew, and William R. Nelson. 2023. "The Federal Reserve's Balance Sheet: Costs to Taxpayers of Quantitative Easing." Position paper, Shadow Open Market Committee, June 16. Published by Mercatus Center, George Mason University, January 10.

Levin, Andrew T., and Christina Parajon Skinner. 2024. "Central Bank Undersight: Assessing the Fed's Accountability to Congress." Economics Working Paper No. 23120. Hoover Institution. February 8.

Levy, Mickey D. 1985. "Guidelines for Deficit Policy." Position paper, Shadow Open Market Committee, Washington, DC. March 24.

Levy, Mickey D. 1999. "Budget Surpluses and the Fiscal Policy Debate." Position paper, Shadow Open Market Committee, Washington, DC. March 7–8.

Levy, Mickey D. 2012. "The Fed's Monetary Policy: Limitations and Concerns." Position paper, Shadow Open Market Committee, New York, NY. April 20.

Levy, Mickey D. 2013. "Reconciling FOMC Forecasts and Forward Guidance." Position paper, Shadow Open Market Committee, New York, NY. September 20.

Levy, Mickey D. 2018. "The Fed's Economic Forecasts, Uncertainties, and Monetary Policy." Position paper, Shadow Open Market Committee, New York, NY. March 9.

Levy, Mickey D. 2020. "The Fed and Financial Markets: Suggestions to Improve an Unhealthy Relationship." In *Strategies for Monetary Policy*, edited by John H. Cochrane and John B. Taylor. Hoover Institution Press.

Levy, Mickey D. 2022. "Accelerating OER and Services Prices to Keep Inflation High." Position paper, Shadow Open Market Committee. February 11.

Levy, Mickey D. 2024. "The Fed: Bad Forecasts and Misguided Monetary Policy." In *Getting Monetary Policy Back on Track*, edited by Michael D. Bordo, John H. Cochrane, and John B. Taylor. Hoover Institution Press.

Levy, Mickey D., and Charles Plosser. 2020. "The Murky Future of Monetary Policy." Position paper, Shadow Open Market Committee, New York, NY. September 30.

Levy, Mickey D., and Charles Plosser. 2022. "The Murky Future of Monetary Policy." *Federal Reserve Bank of St. Louis Review* 104 (3): 178–88.

Levy, Mickey D., and Charles I. Plosser. 2024. "The Fed's Strategic Approach to Monetary Policy Needs a Reboot." Economics Working Paper No. 24018. Hoover Institution. May.

Lindsey, David, Athanasios Orphanides, and Robert H. Rasche. 2005. "The Reform of October 1979: How It Happened and Why." *Federal Reserve Bank of St. Louis Review* 87 (2): 187–235.

Lucas, Deborah. 2017a. "Fiscal Consequences of the Federal Reserve's Balance Sheet." Position paper, Shadow Open Market Committee, New York, NY. September 15.

Lucas, Deborah. 2017b. "Valuing the GSE's Government Support." Position paper, Shadow Open Market Committee, New York, NY. May 5.

Lucas, Deborah. 2018. "The Financial Crisis Bailouts: What They Cost Taxpayers Who Reaped the Direct Benefits." Position paper, Shadow Open Market Committee, New York, NY. October 19.

Lucas, Deborah. 2024. "Basel III Endgame and Bank Capital Requirements." Position paper, Shadow Open Market Committee. April 5.

Lucas, Deborah, and Gee Hee Hong. 2023. "COVID Credit Policies Around the World: Size, Scope, Costs, and Consequences." Position paper, Shadow Open Market Committee. April 21.

Lucas, Robert E., Jr. 1976. "Econometric Policy Evaluation: A Critique." *Carnegie-Rochester Conference Series on Public Policy* 1:19–46.

Mayer, Thomas. 1975. "The Case Against Credit Allocations." Position paper, Shadow Open Market Committee, Washington, DC. March 7.

McCallum, Bennett T. 1981. "Price Level Determinacy with an Interest Rate Policy Rule and Rational Expectations." *Journal of Monetary Economics* 8 (3): 319–29.

McCallum, Bennett T. 1988. "Robustness Properties of a Rule for Monetary Policy." *Carnegie-Rochester Conference Series on Public Policy* 29:173–203.

McCallum, Bennett T. 2000. "The US Deserves a Monetary Standard." Position paper, Shadow Open Market Committee, Washington, DC. November 12–13.

McCallum, Bennett T. 2001a. "Japanese Monetary Policy." Position paper, Shadow Open Market Committee, Washington, DC. April 30.

McCallum, Bennett T. 2001b. "Japanese Monetary Policy Again." Position paper, Shadow Open Market Committee, Washington, DC. October 15.

McCallum, Bennett T. 2002. "The Use of Policy Rules in Monetary Policy Analysis." Position paper, Shadow Open Market Committee, Washington, DC. November 18.

McCallum, Bennett T. 2003a. "Inflation Targeting for the United States." Position paper, Shadow Open Market Committee, Washington, DC. May 18.

McCallum, Bennett T. 2003b. "Misconceptions Regarding Rules vs. Discretion for Monetary Policy." Position paper, Shadow Open Market Committee. November 9–10.

McCallum, Bennett T. 2011. "Nominal GDP Targeting." Position paper, Shadow Open Market Committee, New York, NY. October 11.

McCallum, Bennett T. 2013. "Nominal GDP Targeting: Policy Rule or Ad-Hoc Splurge?" Position paper, Shadow Open Market Committee, New York, NY. September 20.

Meigs, James. 1975. "Implications of Possible Monetary Growth Targets." Position paper, Shadow Open Market Committee, Washington, DC. September 12.

Meltzer, Allan H. 1974. "Failures of Banks and Other Financial Institutions." Position paper, Shadow Open Market Committee, Washington, DC. September 6.

Meltzer, Allan H. 1978. "Where Do We Go from Here?" Position paper, Shadow Open Market Committee, Washington, DC. March 12.

Meltzer, Allan H. 1983. "Recent Behavior of Base Velocity." Position paper, Shadow Open Market Committee, Washington, DC. September 19.

Meltzer, Allan H. 1986. "Limits of Short-Run Stabilization Policy: Presidential Address to the Western Economic Association, July 3, 1986." *Economic Inquiry* 25 (1): 1–14.

Meltzer, Allan H. 1993. "Growth of Base Money and Nominal GDP." Position paper, Shadow Open Market Committee, Washington, DC. September 13.

Meltzer, Allan H. 1998. "A Note on Stable Velocity." Position paper, Shadow Open Market Committee, Washington, DC. March 15–16.

Meltzer, Allan H. 2000. "The Shadow Open Market Committee: Origins and Operations." *Journal of Financial Services Research* 18 (2–3): 119–28.

Meltzer, Allan H. 2005. *A History of the Federal Reserve, Vol. 1: 1913–1951*. Paperback. University of Chicago Press.

Meltzer, Allan H. 2010. *A History of the Federal Reserve, Vol. 2 (Book 1 and 2): 1951–1986*. University of Chicago Press.

Mester, Loretta. 2016. "Acknowledging Uncertainty." Position paper, Shadow Open Market Committee, New York, NY. October 7.

Nelson, Edward. 2020. *Milton Friedman and Economic Debate in the United States, Vol. 1: 1932–1972.* University of Chicago Press.

Nelson, Edward. 2025. *Milton Friedman and Economic Debate in the United States, 1973–2006, Vol. 2.* February 2 draft for forthcoming publication. http://cdevcom.win02.tmd.cloud/EdwardNelson/Chapters1to10-MFED-1973to2006.pdf.

Orphanides, Athanasios. 2002. "Monetary-Policy Rules and the Great Inflation." *American Economic Review* 92 (2): 115–20.

Orphanides, Athanasios. 2014. "European Headwind: ECB Policy and Fed Normalization." Position paper, Shadow Open Market Committee, New York, NY. November 3.

Orphanides, Athanasios. 2015. "Short-Sighted Monetary Policy and Fear of Liftoff." Position paper, Shadow Open Market Committee, New York, NY. October 2.

Orphanides, Athanasios. 2017. "The Case Against the Case Against Monetary Rules." Position paper, Shadow Open Market Committee, New York, NY. May 5.

Orphanides, Athanasios. 2024. "Enhancing Resilience with Natural Growth Targeting." Position paper, Shadow Open Market Committee. April 5.

Parkin, Michael. 1978. "A Comparison of Alternative Techniques of Monetary Control under Rational Expectations." *The Manchester School* 46 (3): 252–87.

Penner, Rudolph G. 1977. "The Federal Budget." Position paper, Shadow Open Market Committee, Washington, DC. September 19.

Plosser, Charles I. 1998. "Exaggerated Risks of Deflation." Position paper, Shadow Open Market Committee, Washington, DC. March 15–16.

Plosser, Charles I. 2003. "Deflating Fears of Deflation." Position paper, Shadow Open Market Committee, Washington, DC. November 9–10.

Plosser, Charles I. 2009. "Ensuring Sound Monetary Policy in the Aftermath of Crisis." Remarks at the US Monetary Policy Forum, "The Initiative on Global Markets," University of Chicago Booth School of Business, New York, NY. February 27.

Plosser, Charles I. 2010. "Credible Commitments and Monetary Policy after the Crisis." Speech at the Swiss National Bank Monetary Policy Conference, Zurich, Switzerland. September 24.

Plosser, Charles I. 2016. "Making the Fed More Accountable—Not More Political." Testimony before the Subcommittee on Monetary Policy and Trade of the Committee on Financial Services. 114th Cong. December 7. https://www.congress.gov/event/114th-congress/house-event/LC53442/text.

Plosser, Charles I. 2017. "Why the Fed Should Only Own Treasuries." Testimony before the Subcommittee on Monetary Policy and Trade of the Committee on Financial Services. 115th Cong. November 7. https://democrats-financialservices.house.gov/uploadedfiles/11.07.2017_charles_i._plosser_testimony.pdf.

Plosser, Charles I. 2019. "Limits to Monetary Policy and Fed Independence." Position paper, Shadow Open Market Committee, New York, NY. September 27.

Plosser, Charles I. 2022. "Federal Reserve Independence: Is It Time for a New Treasury-Fed Accord?" In *Essays in Honor of Marvin Goodfriend: Economist and Central Banker*, edited by Robert G. King and Alexander L. Wolman. Federal Reserve Bank of Richmond.

Poole, William. 1988. "US International Capital Flows in the 1980s." Position paper, Shadow Open Market Committee, Washington, DC. March 13.

Poole, William. 1991. "Choosing a Monetary Aggregate: Another Look." Position paper, Shadow Open Market Committee, Washington, DC. September 29.

Poole, William. 1993. "The Real Rate of Interest as a Guide to Monetary Policy." Position paper, Shadow Open Market Committee, Washington, DC. September 13.

Poole, William. 2001. "The Role of Government in US Capital Markets." Speech before the Institute of Governmental Affairs, University of California–Davis, Davis, CA. October 18.

Poole, William. 2009. "Exit Policies from the Financial Crisis—to What?" Position paper, Shadow Open Market Committee, Washington, DC. September 30.

Poole, William, Robert H. Rasche, and David C. Wheelock. 2013. "The Great Inflation; Did the Shadow Know Better?" In *The Great Inflation: The Rebirth of Modern Central Banking*, edited by Michael D. Bordo and Athanasios Orphanides. University of Chicago Press.

Rasche, Robert H. 1987. "Recent Behavior of M1 Velocity." Position paper, Shadow Open Market Committee, Washington, DC. September 14.

Rasche, Robert, and James Johannes. 1979. "Money Multiplier Forecasting Errors." Position paper, Shadow Open Market Committee, Washington, DC. March 11.

Romer, Christine. 2013. "Comment on 'Did the Shadow Know Better?'" In *The Great Inflation: The Rebirth of Modern Central Banking*, edited by Michael D. Bordo and Athanasios Orphanides. University of Chicago Press.

Samuelson, Paul A., and Robert M. Solow. 1960. "Analytical Aspects of Anti-Inflation Policy." *American Economic Review* 50 (2): 177–94.

Sargent, Thomas J., and Neil Wallace. 1976. "Rational Expectations and the Theory of Economic Policy." *Journal of Monetary Economics* 2 (2): 169–83.

Schmidt, Wilson E. 1975. "Fed Foreign Exchange Intervention: Some Questions." Position paper, Shadow Open Market Committee, Washington, DC. September 12.

Schwartz, Anna J. 1986. "External Debt and the Banking System." Position paper, Shadow Open Market Committee, Washington, DC. March 17.

Schwartz, Anna J. 1989. "US Monetary Authorities' Foreign Currency Purchases." Position paper, Shadow Open Market Committee, Washington, DC. September 17.

Schwartz, Anna J. 1991. "The Misuse of the Fed's Discount Window." Position paper, Shadow Open Market Committee, Washington, DC. September 29.

Schwartz, Anna J. 1992. "Foreign Exchange Market Intervention." Position paper, Shadow Open Market Committee, Washington, DC. March 8.

Schwartz, Anna J. 1995. "Trial and Error in Devising the Mexican Rescue Plan." Position paper, Shadow Open Market Committee, Washington, DC. March 6.

Schwartz, Anna J. 1996. "The Mexican Loan Repayment Sleight of Hand." Position paper, Shadow Open Market Committee, Washington, DC. March 11.

Schwartz, Anna J. 1998. "Is There Still a Need for an International Lender of Last Resort?" Position paper, Shadow Open Market Committee, Washington, DC. March 15–16.

Schwartz, Anna J. 2000. "The IMF and Its Critics." Position paper, Shadow Open Market Committee, Washington, DC. November 12–13.

Schwartz, Anna J. 2001. "The IMF Infirmary." Position paper, Shadow Open Market Committee, Washington, DC. October 14–15.

Schwartz, Anna J. 2002. "Questions Concerning Argentina, Brazil, and the IMF." Position paper, Shadow Open Market Committee, Washington, DC. November 17–18.

SOMC (Shadow Open Market Committee). 1975. "Policy Recommendations of the Shadow Open Market Committee Meeting." Washington, DC. September 12.

SOMC. 1977. "Policy Statement." March 7.

SOMC. 1994. "Policy Statement." March 7.

SOMC. 1998. "SOMC Policy Statement Summary." Press release, Shadow Open Market Committee. September 14.

SOMC. 2002a. "Policy Statement." April 15.

SOMC. 2002b. "Policy Statement." November 18.

SOMC. 2004. "Policy Statement." May 3.

Sprinkel, Beryl. 1975. "Quest for a Stabilizing Monetary Policy." Position paper, Shadow Open Market Committee, Washington, DC. March 7.

Stockman, Alan. 2000. "Learning the Right Lessons from the Current Account Deficit and Dollar Appreciation." Position paper, Shadow Open Market Committee, Washington, DC. November 13.

Stockman, Alan C. 2002. "Will the US Economy Catch the Japanese Disease?" Position paper, Shadow Open Market Committee, Washington, DC. November 17–18.

Stockman, Alan C. 2004. "Dollar Depreciation Will Not Contribute to US Inflation." Position paper, Shadow Open Market Committee, Washington, DC. May 2.

Tavlas, George S. 2023. *The Monetarists: The Making of the Chicago Monetary Tradition, 1927–1960.* University of Chicago Press.

Taylor, John B. 1980. "Aggregate Dynamics and Staggered Contracts." *Journal of Political Economy* 88 (1): 1–23.

Taylor, John B. 1993. "Discretion Versus Policy Rules in Practice." *Carnegie-Rochester Conference Series on Public Policy* 39 (December): 195–214.

Taylor, John B. 2007. "Housing and Monetary Policy." Paper presented at the Federal Reserve Bank of Kansas City's Economic Policy Symposium. Jackson Hole, WY. August.

Taylor, John B. 2011. "Review of Allan H. Meltzer's *A History of the Federal Reserve, Volume 2*, University of Chicago Press, 2009." *Journal of Monetary Economics* 58 (2): 183–89.

Tumlir, Jan. 1985. "International Trade Policy: The Two Main Tasks." Position paper, Shadow Open Market Committee, Washington, DC. March 24.

Volcker, Paul A. 1976. "The Contributions and Limitations of 'Monetary' Analysis." *Federal Reserve Bank of New York Quarterly Review*/Special Edition, 75th Anniversary.

Volcker, Paul A. 1977. "A Broader Role for the Monetary Targets." Remarks before the Toronto Bond Traders' Association, Toronto, Ontario, Canada. February 22.

David C. Wheelock*

Michael Bordo and Mickey Levy have written the definitive history of the first fifty years of the Shadow Open Market Committee. Linking their narrative to the major policy challenges of the times, the authors describe the SOMC's principal policy positions and the contributions of its individual members from the committee's formation in 1973 to the present. As long-serving SOMC members, the authors are well positioned to provide insights about SOMC policy positions and the monetary and other policies the SOMC criticized. The authors show that the SOMC held consistent guiding principles throughout its fifty-year history, including the importance of price stability, rules-based policies, and central bank independence. Bordo and Levy present a largely favorable review of SOMC policy positions and member reports, but they do point out a few missteps as well, such as the SOMC's continued advocacy of monetary aggregate targeting well into the 1980s after instability in velocity had become apparent.

The SOMC was established in 1973 by the prominent monetary economists Allan Meltzer, Karl Brunner, and Anna Schwartz to provide an ongoing critical assessment of Federal Reserve monetary policy. At the time, Fed leaders were publicly blaming high inflation on oil price shocks, government budget deficits, and monopolistic price setting by firms and labor unions—anything but monetary policy—and advocating wage and price controls to address it.[1] The stature of SOMC members and their access to members of Congress and the media brought attention to the SOMC's criticisms of the Fed and its policies. But did the SOMC's criticisms influence Fed policy? The

*The author thanks Carlos Garriga, Riccardo DiCecio, and Kevin Kliesen for comments and assistance. The views expressed herein are those of the author and not official positions of the Federal Reserve Bank of St. Louis or the Federal Reserve System.

evidence is unclear. Inflation continued to rise in waves through the 1970s and the Fed did not address it seriously until October 1979, when the Federal Open Market Committee (FOMC), under Fed chair Paul Volcker, adopted new operating procedures in a stronger effort to control inflation.

Bordo and Levy argue that the SOMC "likely influenced Fed chair Paul Volcker to shift gears in 1979 toward its successful disinflation based on reducing growth of a monetary aggregate." But, as the authors admit, Volcker was already an inflation hawk and frequent dissenter on FOMC decisions when he was president of the Federal Reserve Bank of New York. There were also many forces pushing the Fed to control inflation, including the collapsing value of the dollar in international markets. As Bordo and Levy note, Volcker's aggressive tightening was at odds with the more gradual approach to slowing of money growth advocated by the SOMC. Others have suggested that Volcker used the change in operating procedures to divert attention from actions intended to push interest rates to high levels. Wide swings in growth of monetary aggregates during the 1979–82 disinflation suggest that the Volcker-led FOMC was not following a monetarist approach even if it was committed to controlling inflation (see, e.g., Friedman 1984). Nonetheless, while the direct influence of the SOMC and its allies on the Volcker Fed is debatable, they were at least indirectly influential through their advocacy before Congress, which amended the Federal Reserve Reform Act in 1977 to require the Fed to regularly report money-supply growth targets.

After the Great Inflation, the SOMC entered something of a wilderness period in the 1980s when it continued to advocate for targeting narrow monetary aggregates long after velocity had become unstable. Bordo and Levy argue that "the SOMC overplayed its monetarist hand that had been so influential in the 1970s." Volcker transitioned the Fed's operating procedures from targeting monetary aggregates to interest rates. In 1982, the FOMC began targeting the federal funds rate—hardly the SOMC's preferred target—but the FOMC did not abandon its commitment to price stability. In that regard, the FOMC had moved into alignment with the SOMC.

As the economy recovered from the twin recessions of 1980–82 and the economy entered the Great Moderation, criticism of the Fed and its policies declined, and Alan Greenspan, who replaced Volcker as Fed chair in 1987, was hailed as the economy's "maestro" (Woodward 2001). Perhaps because there seemed to be less to criticize about monetary policy, the SOMC broadened its areas of interest to include fiscal policy, financial regulation, and exchange-rate policy. By the early 1990s the SOMC had refocused on

monetary policy when it began to call on the Fed to adopt an explicit inflation target and rules-based policies. On January 25, 2012, the Fed publicly
announced a numerical target for inflation, aligning the Fed with many other
central banks worldwide.

The SOMC has continued to provide timely and relevant policy analysis
and advocacy in recent decades, and Bordo and Levy provide a cogent summary of the SOMC's policy positions in those years. A striking aspect of the
SOMC's recent history has been the flow of members between the SOMC and
the Federal Reserve. Of the SOMC's original members, only Robert Rasche
moved to the Fed when he became research director of the Federal Reserve
Bank of St. Louis in 1998. Two other early SOMC members, Jerry Jordan, who
joined the SOMC in 1976, and William Poole, who joined the SOMC in 1984,
later became Reserve Bank presidents. More recently, the flow has mostly been
in the opposite direction. Charles Plosser, SOMC member during 1992–2006,
was the most recent SOMC member to move to the Fed when he became president of the Federal Reserve Bank of Philadelphia in 2006. Of the eleven individuals who joined the SOMC in 2000 or later, five were former Reserve Bank
presidents or senior staff members of a Reserve Bank or the Board of Governors,
and four of the ten current SOMC members are former Fed presidents or
senior staffers. The SOMC does not appear in imminent danger of being captured by the Fed. It continues to have strong academic members and those with
Fed backgrounds can undoubtedly provide perspectives that outsiders cannot.
Bordo and Levy do not discuss how potential SOMC members are identified
or recruited, or whether changes in the committee's makeup over time reflect
strategic realignments or a more haphazard approach to membership.

Perhaps no other entity within the Federal Reserve System has had a closer
relationship with the SOMC since its founding than the Federal Reserve
Bank of St. Louis. The Bank's most recent former president, James Bullard,
joined the SOMC in 2024, but the ties between the SOMC and St. Louis Fed
were especially strong in the 1970s. In many ways, the histories of the Bank's
policy positions and research focus have mirrored those of the SOMC. In
the 1970s, St. Louis Fed presidents Darryl Francis (1966–76) and Lawrence
Roos (1976–83) advocated monetarist positions in FOMC meetings and
speeches, and the Bank's economists regularly published research that supported those positions in the Bank's *Review* and in academic journals.[2]

The St. Louis Fed's monetarist tradition began with Homer Jones, who
became the Bank's research director in 1958. Jones had close ties to Milton
Friedman, having been an instructor of Friedman's at Rutgers University

when Friedman was an undergraduate student, and later a graduate student of Friedman's at the University of Chicago. Another Friedman student and original SOMC member, James Meigs, was a St. Louis Fed economist in the early 1960s. The Bank also had a close association with Karl Brunner and Allan Meltzer through Brunner's students Jerry Jordan and Anatol Balbach, both of whom were St. Louis Fed staff economists and successors of Jones as the Bank's research director. Throughout the Great Inflation era, the Bank's presidents advocated monetarist policies at FOMC meetings and in speeches like those pushed for by the SOMC, and the Bank's *Review* published supporting research. The St. Louis Fed acquired a reputation as a "maverick" within the Federal Reserve System because of its criticism of the Fed's monetary policy and its advocacy of a monetarist alternative (*Business Week* 1967).

The St. Louis Fed's close ties with the SOMC continued in subsequent decades. Like the SOMC, the St. Louis Fed's leaders continued to advocate for targeting monetary aggregates well into the 1980s. In the early 1970s, the Bank developed an empirical model for gauging the impact of monetary policy actions on economic activity that was used to generate short-run policy forecasts and prescriptions based on the growth of monetary aggregates. Early success in forecasting and apparently finding robust, stable relationships in both long- and short-run data led the Bank's economists to apply the long-run quantity-theoretic propositions of the model to short-run policy questions. When the short-run correlation between money and economic activity broke down in the 1980s, the Bank, like the SOMC, was slow to abandon monetary aggregate-based policy prescriptions. Refinements of the model in the early 1980s improved its ability to forecast output and inflation, but as the decade progressed the handwriting was on the wall and the model was eventually abandoned (Hafer and Wheelock 2001).

Just as the SOMC eventually adapted, so too did the research and policy positions of the St. Louis Fed. The close relationships between the SOMC and the St. Louis Fed continued under William Poole, who served as the Bank's president during 1998–2008, and Robert Rasche, the Bank's research director under Poole. Supported by Rasche and the Bank's research staff, Poole was a strong advocate for price stability, clear communication, and rules-based policies (e.g., Poole 1998, 1999). Poole also publicly warned of the risks that Fannie Mae and Freddie Mac posed to the financial system—a viewpoint also expressed by the SOMC (Poole 2001; Hess 2002).

James Bullard, who joined the St. Louis Fed's research staff in 1990, succeeded Poole as the Bank's president in 2008 and served until July 2023. Christopher Waller succeeded Rasche as the Bank's research director shortly thereafter and served in that position until joining the Fed's Board of Governors in 2020. Consistent with long-held SOMC positions, Bullard was a proponent of central bank independence and rules-based policy based on strong theoretical foundations (e.g., Bullard 2013, 2023a). For example, during the recent inflation episode he used a representation of a "generous" Taylor rule in public presentations to argue effectively that monetary policy was insufficiently restrictive (e.g., Bullard 2023b). In this regard, Bullard was aligned with Ben McCallum, who, in an SOMC paper, acknowledged that the Fed and central banks should not be strictly rules-driven, but that rules "[provide] a good starting place or 'benchmark' for consideration of policy settings" (McCallum 2002).

The fifty-year history of the SOMC is a testament to the energy and intellect of its founders, subsequent leaders and members, and to the significance of their work. Bordo and Levy have provided a valuable insider's guide to the history of SOMC policy positions and contributions over the group's first fifty years. The ongoing debates about monetary, fiscal, and regulatory policies will undoubtedly continue for many years to come. The SOMC is well positioned to contribute to those debates as it moves into its second fifty years. However, to be successful, it will need to attract and nurture young academic talent working in monetary economics, macroeconomics, and financial markets. Additionally, increasing its visibility through media outreach could be crucial. In today's world, leading the discussion is just as important as providing a state-of-the-art monetary framework.

Notes

1. See Bordo and Orphanides (2013) and the chapters therein for a history of the Great Inflation and alternative perspectives on what caused it. Poole et al. (2013) describe the policy views of Fed officials at the time.

2. See Hafer and Wheelock (2001, 2003) and Kliesen and Wheelock (2021) for summaries of the policy positions and research published in the *Federal Reserve Bank of St. Louis Review* in the 1970s and early 1980s.

References

Bordo, Michael D., and Athanasios Orphanides, eds. 2013. *The Great Inflation: The Rebirth of Modern Central Banking.* University of Chicago Press.

Bullard, James. 2013. "The Global Battle over Central Bank Independence." Presentation at "Federal Reserve Independence in the Aftermath of the Financial Crisis: Should We Be Worried?" panel discussion, Allied Social Science Associations annual meeting, San Diego, CA. January 4. https://www.stlouisfed.org/-/media/project/frbstl/stlouisfed/Files/PDFs/Bullard/remarks/BullardAEA2013CBIndependencePanelDiscussion4Jan2013Final.pdf.

Bullard, James. 2023a. "Credible and Incredible Disinflations." Presentation at "The Credibility of Government Policies: Conference in Honor of Guillermo Calvo," New York, NY. February 24. https://www.stlouisfed.org/-/media/project/frbstl /stlouisfed/files/pdfs/bullard/remarks/2023/bullard-calvo-columbia-24-feb -2023.pdf.

Bullard, James. 2023b. "Is Monetary Policy Sufficiently Restrictive?" *Regional Economist*, Federal Reserve Bank of St. Louis. June 1. https://www.stlouisfed.org/publications /regional-economist/2023/june/is-monetary-policy-sufficiently-restrictive.

Business Week. 1967. "Maverick in the Fed System." November 18.

Friedman, Milton. 1984. "Lessons from the 1979–82 Monetary Policy Experiment." *American Economic Review* 74 (2): 397–400.

Hafer, R. W., and David C. Wheelock. 2001. "The Rise and Fall of a Policy Rule: Monetarism at the St. Louis Fed, 1968–1986." *Federal Reserve Bank of St. Louis Review* 83 (1): 1–24.

Hafer, R. W., and David C. Wheelock. 2003. "Darryl Francis and the Making of Monetary Policy, 1966–1975." *Federal Reserve Bank of St. Louis Review* 85 (2): 1–12.

Hess, Gregory D. 2002. "Is It Time for Fannie Mae and Freddie Mac to Cut the Cord?" Position paper, Shadow Open Market Committee, Washington, DC. November 18.

Kliesen, Kevin L., and David C. Wheelock. 2021. "Managing a New Policy Framework: Paul Volcker, the St. Louis Fed, and the 1979–82 War on Inflation." *Federal Reserve Bank of St. Louis Review* 103 (1): 71–97.

McCallum, Bennett T. 2002. "The Use of Policy Rules in Monetary Policy Analysis." Position paper, Shadow Open Market Committee, Washington, DC. November 18.

Poole, William. 1998. "A Policymaker Confronts Uncertainty." *Federal Reserve Bank of St. Louis Review* 80 (5): 1–8.

Poole, William. 1999. "Synching, Not Sinking, the Markets." Paper presented at the Meeting of the Philadelphia Council for Business Economics, Philadelphia, PA. August 6.

Poole, William. 2001. "The Role of Government in US Capital Markets." Paper presented at the Institute of Government Affairs, Davis, CA. October 18.

Poole, William, Robert H. Rasche, and David C. Wheelock. 2013. "The Great Inflation: Did the Shadow Know Better?" In *The Great Inflation: The Rebirth of Modern Central Banking*, edited by Michael D. Bordo and Athanasios Orphanides. University of Chicago Press.

Woodward, Bob. 2001. *Maestro: Greenspan's Fed and the American Boom.* Simon & Schuster.

George S. Tavlas

In their superb paper, Mike Bordo and Mickey Levy provide a comprehensive analysis of the fifty-year history of the Shadow Open Market Committee. The authors affirm that during those fifty years the Fed has made three major costly monetary policy errors: the high inflation of the 1970s; the low-interest-rate policy of the early 2000s, which facilitated the debt-financed housing bubble; and the high inflation of the early 2020s. In my remarks, I will focus on the high inflation of the 1970s and the taming of inflation in the first half of the 1980s, although I will also comment on the surge of inflation of the early 2020s. In addition to the SOMC's views, I will discuss and compare the views of three economists who helped shape monetary policy during those years: Milton Friedman as well as two Fed chairs, Arthur Burns and Paul Volcker.

I start with Friedman. Friedman's role in the formation of the SOMC was pervasive, even if he was not a member. The conceptual framework that underpinned the SOMC's policy advice in the 1970s and early 1980s was developed by Friedman in the 1950s and 1960s, sometimes in collaboration with Anna Schwartz, an original member of the SOMC. That framework featured the following propositions, all based on Friedman's research findings.[1]

- Inflation is a monetary phenomenon: the key to controlling inflation is to control money growth.
- The economic system is inherently stable and reverts to the natural rate of unemployment; there is no long-run Phillips curve trade-off.
- The demand for money is a stable function of only a few variables and relatively independent of the supply of money. Friedman (1956) noted that it would be possible to approach perfect stability in the demand-for-money function by adding more and more variables to

the function. Doing so, however, would empty the function of its predictive power.

- The money stock is controllable by the central bank.
- Keynesian structural macroeconometric models are not reliable as guides to policy. Reduced form models based on money, as in the classic study by Friedman and Meiselman (1963), provide a coherent picture of the influence of money on the economy.
- The long and variable lags associated with changes in the money supply render discretionary monetary policy unstable.
- To reduce both policy uncertainty and the influence of political forces on policy formation, policy should be rules-based. Under Friedman's rule, the M2 measure of the money supply would grow by 3% to 5% annually. Friedman believed that such a rule would correspond with a roughly stable price level.
- Should money growth deviate significantly from its objective, it should be brought back to that objective in a gradual manner under the presumption that gradualist policies reduce the social costs of disinflation.

The main difference between Friedman's framework and that of the SOMC is that Friedman favored targeting M2 whereas the SOMC favored targeting the monetary base.

Enter into this picture Burns, who served as Fed chair from 1970 to 1978. Burns had been Friedman's undergraduate teacher at Rutgers in the late 1920s. It was Burns who initiated the Friedman–Schwartz collaboration on their historical work on money, beginning in 1948. Friedman thought that Burns shared his views about the importance of monetary policy. Shortly after Burns became Fed chair, Friedman wrote: "My close friend and former teacher Arthur Burns is not just another chairman. He is the right man in the right place at the right time." Friedman added that Burns was the first Fed chair to have "the right qualifications for the post" (Nelson 2020, 2:322).[2] Friedman would soon be deeply disappointed. Under Burns, the Fed permitted rapid monetary growth, which contributed to the surges in inflation to double-digit levels in the mid-1970s and the late 1970s. Monetary policy, as Bordo and Levy argue in the preceding chapter, "was in disarray." Why did Burns permit this to happen? There were three main reasons.

First, as Ed Nelson (2025) has documented, Burns arrived at the Fed holding a cost-push view of inflation. He did not believe in the effectiveness of monetary policy; nor had he ever subscribed to Friedman's advocacy of mandating the Fed to follow a strict policy rule (Nelson 2025, 147). Soon after he became Fed chair, he championed wage-price controls to tame inflation. These policies failed, and this failure was likely a reason why the SOMC was formed in 1973.

Second, as Bordo and Levy point out, Burns's decisions were often politically motivated, with the aim of ensuring President Richard Nixon's reelection—precisely the kind of situation that a policy rule aimed to avoid.

The third reason has to do with the technical advice that Burns received. The 1970s were the heyday of large-scale macroeconometric models at the Fed and elsewhere. The Fed's model, the FMP model, was developed by a team of researchers at MIT, the University of Pennsylvania, and the Board of Governors.[3] The principal architects of the model were Franco Modigliani (MIT) and Albert Ando (University of Pennsylvania), who wanted to develop a tool to resolve their inconclusive debate in the 1960s with Friedman and Meiselman on the relative importance of fiscal and monetary policies. Here is how Ando and Modigliani described the Fed's model in 1975:

> Fiscal policies, by influencing the savings-income ratio, by inserting a wedge between the rates paid by borrowers and received by lenders, by determining the size of government debts, and by a number of other means, will have important impacts on characteristics of the long-run behavior of the economy. Monetary policies, on the other hand, will not have very substantial impacts other than to determine the level of wages and prices and, perhaps, if one believed that the Phillips curve retained its importance in the long run, the level of unemployment. With a few minor exceptions, these statements all apply to the MPS model. (Ando and Modigliani 1975, 559)

For someone untrained in macroeconometric modeling, and who had been away from academic research for twenty years, Burns was susceptible to the views and advice of his staff.[4] The advice that Burns received from at least some of his technical experts reinforced his prior beliefs about the ineffectiveness of monetary policy. And so Burns got inflation wrong.

During the 1970s, Friedman and the SOMC got it right. During the first half of that decade, money-demand relationships were stable. Inflation forecasts from macroeconometric models were wide of the mark. The Great Inflation of the 1970s was largely a failure to control money growth. And the way to bring down excessive money growth for both Friedman and the SOMC was through gradual adjustment.

Enter into this picture Paul Volcker, who became Fed chair in August 1979. CPI inflation was over 12%. Base money and M2 were both growing by 8%. In its semiannual statement around that time, the SOMC continued to advocate gradualism in the reduction of base-money growth. Specifically, the SOMC stated: "To restore stability to the economy and permanently reduce inflation, the growth rate of the monetary base should now be reduced to an annual rate of 7% for the year ending August 1980" (Poole et al. 2013, appendix A, 96). In the late 1970s and early 1980s, Friedman continued to advocate gradualism in the reduction of M2 growth (see, for example, Friedman 1979).

Volcker had other ideas. In contrast to the SOMC, Volcker believed that the volatility of money velocity made monetary targeting an unreliable approach for conducting monetary policy (see Bordo and Levy). Nevertheless, and unlike Burns, Volcker appreciated the capacity of monetary policy to control inflation. But he also appreciated something else. As William Silber (2012, 134) has documented, Volcker understood the importance of endogenous expectations, which he learned from traders while he had been working on the New York Fed's trading desk in the 1950s. In 1975, when he was president of the New York Fed, he warned his Federal Open Market Committee (FOMC) colleagues not to be encouraged by projections of reduced inflation from macroeconometric models because those models "did not take adequate account of the important factor of expectations."[5] The following year, in a speech to the Boston Economic Club, Volcker argued:

> It is no historical accident that the past few years have seen the rise . . .
> of so-called rational expectations . . . in effect arguing that the ultimate
> inflationary consequences [of economic policy] will be promptly taken
> into account in today's actions. . . . Some versions . . . actually seem to
> imply that systematic demand policies will be wholly impotent to affect
> the real economy. I would not go nearly so far, but I do think . . . that
> what people think and expect . . . is a fact of economic life that we can-
> not escape. (Silber 2012, 134–35)

And so I come to a crucial difference between what Friedman and the SOMC prescribed in the early 1980s and the policy implemented under Volcker. That difference has to do with the acquisition of central bank credibility and its effect on expectations. Credibility, once earned, allows for a gradual monetary tightening because the markets trust—they expect—that, once a tightening has begun, the central bank will continue to tighten. This was plausibly the assumption underlying the gradualist approach of Friedman and the SOMC. This is precisely what happened during the past several years when inflation expectations remained near 2% in both the United States and the euro area even though actual inflation spiked upward.

Volcker's actions, in contrast, were consistent with a central bank that lacks credibility and tries to acquire it. In the early 1980s, the Fed lacked credibility. To bring down inflation expectations, Volcker believed, monetary policy had to tighten abruptly and needed to remain tight, even if it meant bringing the economy into recession. In the jargon of the literature, the Fed had to signal that it was "hard-nosed." In the absence of credibility, a central bank that embarks on a gradualist approach would not be believed. As Bordo and Levy point out, leading members of the SOMC Karl Brunner and Allan Meltzer were initially critical of Volcker's aggressive monetary tightening strategy. Brunner recognized the importance of bringing down inflation expectations and establishing credibility but thought that the Fed's erratic and unrealizable path of monetary policy had created a "murky fog" such that abrupt, aggressive tightening would not be credible and would result in a recession. Brunner and Meltzer's criticism of Volcker's policies gradually eased over the 1980s and they came around to admire Volcker's efforts.[6]

It took several years and two recessions for Volcker to establish the Fed's credibility and for long-term interest rates to come down. As Sargent and Silber (2022) noted, although inflation fell from more than 12% in 1980 to under 4% in 1984, the 10-year Treasury note averaged 11.5% in 1980 and rose to above that level in 1984. The 10-year note did not average in the single digits until 1986.

This difference in optimal monetary response to an inflationary shock plays a central role in the New Keynesian model exposited by Galí (2015) and Woodford (2003). Volcker's policy response anticipated this literature. It also anticipated the game theory literature on the importance of central bank credibility developed in the 1980s and 1990s (see, for example, Barro and Gordon 1983). This was one reason for the difference in policy prescriptions between Volcker, on the one hand, and Friedman and the SOMC, on the other.

But, as shown by Bordo and Levy, there was another reason. Both Friedman and the SOMC were misled in the 1980s by high rates of money growth. They thought that inflation would rise. In March 1983, annual Consumer Price Index (CPI) inflation had fallen to 3.6%, compared with 6.8% in March 1982.[7] Base-money growth, however, was 7% in early 1983. M1 growth was 10%. The Shadow Committee's semiannual statement in March 1983 advised: "The current inflationary policy should end. The growth of money should return to a disinflationary path. We recommend an annual growth rate of money (M1) not to exceed 5-1/2% in the year ending fourth quarter 1983" (Poole et al. 2013, appendix A, 97). It did not account for money-demand instability. Meltzer subsequently acknowledged that circumstance:

> The monetarist mistake was the failure to forecast the decline in infla-
> tion from 10.9% in 1981 to 3.2% in 1983 and 4.3% in 1984 (as reported
> at about that time). Money growth in 1983 and 1984 averaged 9%. Like
> the bondholders, we believed that the Federal Reserve was about to
> repeat the mistakes of the 1970s. It is worth noting that members of
> the Federal Open Market Committee projected an inflation rate of 6%
> to 7% in 1984. With hindsight, we recognize that we underestimated
> the increased demand for money per unit of income. Our error came
> mainly from velocity or money demand, not from the Phillips curve
> term. (Meltzer 2000, 126–27)

In contrast, Volcker emphasized high interest rates as the indicator of policy tightness, not money growth. Once credibility was earned, the Fed main-tained it—and built on it—by following, if implicitly, a Taylor rule during the Great Moderation of the mid-1980s to the early 2000s.

My final comments concern the inflation surge associated with the COVID-19 pandemic. Bordo and Levy show that SOMC members accurately pre-dicted that surge. Ireland (2022), for example, warned that the rise in inflation would persist based on the unprecedented surge in M2 growth. In this regard, an important issue that emerged from the recent inflation was the relative con-tributions of demand and supply factors—different policy responses would be warranted if the surge in inflation had been due to supply factors rather than demand factors. Ireland's (2022) view that M2 growth would play a leading role was confirmed by Hall et al. (2023), who found that, of the cumulative rise in US inflation in the twenty-four months through April 2022, 7.0 percentage points was due to the rise in M2 and 8.5 percentage points to the rise in govern-ment spending as a share of GDP; supply chain disruptions, caused by COVID and higher oil prices, contributed 1.9 percentage points. Hall et al. (2023) also found that the situation in the euro area had been different: during the same period, supply factors dominated, accounting for 9.5 percentage points of the cumulative rise in inflation in the twenty-four months through April 2022; the rise in euro-area M2 accounted for only 0.4 of a percentage point.[8]

What are the conclusions? In the 1970s, a money-supply rule would have prevented the steep rise in inflation and its entrenchment. Friedman and the SOMC got it right. What Friedman and the SOMC also got right was the first-order issue that monetary policy is an important policy tool—and that a Taylor-type rule can work very well—at a time when the profession downgraded the importance of monetary policy. In the early 1980s, a monetary growth rule would not have worked. Money demand was unstable. The Fed not only had to bring down inflation, but had to convince the markets that it was hard-nosed. Volcker got it right. Once that was done, policy that was consistent with a Taylor rule proved to be effective. The mantle of policy rules had passed from Milton Friedman to John Taylor.

Notes

1. For discussions of Friedman's development of these propositions, see Nelson (2020) and Tavlas (2023). The above listing is consistent with the six principles of monetarism identified by Bordo and Levy. It is also consistent with the more detailed listing presented in Poole et al. (2013).

2. Nelson reproduced the above remarks from a *Newsweek* column by Friedman published on February 2, 1970.

3. The letters "FMP" represent the three institutions that developed the model: the Federal Reserve, MIT, and the University of Pennsylvania. Backhouse and Cherrier (2019, 426, fn. 3) point out that the model was also called the MPS model, where the letter "S" denotes Social Science Research Council. Doctrinal historians, however, refer to the model as the FMP model. See Backhouse and Cherrier (2019) and Rancan (2019). In its initial stages, the model was known as the FMP model also at the Board—see de Menil and Enzler (1972, 277–308).

4. For a recent discussion of the role of the Fed staff on decision making, see Kuvvet (2022).

5. Volcker made those remarks at his first FOMC meeting on August 19, 1975.

6. Reflecting, in part, Volcker's "hard-nosed" policy, Nelson (2025, 147) reported that "Friedman was very far from a friendly commentator with regard to the Volcker Federal Reserve."

7. Monthly (year-on-year) inflation would rise to a range between 3.9% and 4.8% in 1984, before falling again in 1985.

8. For both the United States and the euro area, Hall et al. (2023) found that output growth below potential contributed negatively to inflation in the early 2020s.

References

Ando, Albert, and Franco Modigliani. 1975. "Some Reflections on Describing Structures of Financial Sectors." In *The Brookings Model: Perspective and Recent Developments*, edited by Gary Fromm and Lawrence R. Klein. North-Holland.

Backhouse, Roger, and Beatrice Cherrier. 2019. "The Ordinary Business of Macro-econometric Modeling: Working on the Fed-MIT-Penn Model, 1964–1974." *History of Political Economy* 51 (3): 425–47.

Barro, Robert J., and David B. Gordon. 1983. "Rules, Discretion and Reputation in a Model of Monetary Policy." *Journal of Monetary Economics* 12 (1): 101–21.

De Menil, George, and Jared J. Enzler. 1972. "Prices and Wages in the FR-MIT-PENN Econometric Model." In *The Econometrics of Price Determination*, edited by Otto Eckstein. Board of Governors of the Federal Reserve System.

Friedman, Milton. 1956. "The Quantity Theory of Money: A Restatement." In *Studies in the Quantity Theory of Money*, edited by Milton Friedman. University of Chicago Press.

Friedman, Milton. 1979. "The Fed: At It Again." *Newsweek*, February 19.

Friedman, Milton, and David Meiselman. 1963. "The Relative Stability of Monetary Velocity and the Investment Multiplier in the United States, 1897–1958." In *Stabilization Policies*, edited by the Commission on Money and Credit. Prentice Hall.

Galí, Jordi. 2015. *Monetary Policy, Inflation, and the Business Cycle.* 2nd Ed. Princeton University Press.

Hall, Stephen G., George S. Tavlas, and Yongli Wang. 2023. "Drivers and Spillover Effects of Inflation: The United States, the Euro Area, and the United Kingdom." *Journal of International Money and Finance* 131 (March): article 102776.

Ireland, Peter. 2022. "The Continuing Case for Nominal GDP Level Targeting." Position paper, Shadow Open Market Committee not used for 2021 on April 29.

Kuvvet, Emre. 2022. "How Politicized Is the Federal Reserve?" *Wall Street Journal*, March 7.

Meltzer, Allan H. 2000. "The Shadow Open Market Committee: Origins and Operations." *Journal of Financial Services Research* 18 (2–3): 119–28.

Nelson, Edward. 2020. *Milton Friedman and Economic Debate in the United States, 1932–1972, Vols. 1 and 2.* University of Chicago Press.

Nelson, Edward. 2025. *Milton Friedman and Economic Debate in the United States, 1973–2006, Vols. 1 and 2.* February 2 draft for forthcoming publication. University of Chicago Press. http://cdevcom.win02.tmd.cloud/EdwardNelson/Chapters1to10-MFED-1973to2006.pdf.

Poole, William, Robert H. Rasche, and David C. Wheelock. 2013. "The Great Inflation: Did the Shadow Know Better?" In *The Great Inflation: The Rebirth of Modern Central Banking*, edited by Michael D. Bordo and Athanasios Orphanides. University of Chicago Press.

Rancan, Antonella. 2019. "Empirical Macroeconomics in a Policy Context: The Fed-MIT-Penn Model Versus the St. Louis Model, 1965–75." *History of Political Economy* 51 (3): 449–70.

Sargent, Thomas J., and William L. Silber. 2022. "The Market Is Too Serene about Inflation." *Wall Street Journal*, January 11.

Silber, William L. 2012. *Volcker: The Triumph of Persistence.* Bloomsbury Press.

Tavlas, George S. 2023. *The Monetarists: The Making of the Chicago Monetary Tradition, 1927–1960.* University of Chicago Press.

Woodford, Michael. 2003. *Interest and Prices: Foundations of a Theory of Monetary Policy.* Princeton University Press.

GREGORY D. HESS: Thank you very much. Mike [Bordo] and Mickey [Levy] would like us to give them thirty seconds for some responses, and then we'll take some questions.

MICHAEL D. BORDO: These were great comments, Dave [Wheelock], and we really appreciate them. I completely agree with them. Indeed, I was a visitor at the St. Louis Fed in 1981 and observed its monetarism firsthand. I think what happened in the 1970s with the monetarists and the Great Inflation can be viewed as an analogy to D-Day in June 1944 in World War II. General Dwight Eisenhower as supreme commander of the Allied Forces can be thought of as similar to Milton Friedman, as leader of the monetarist campaign against the inflationary policies of the Fed. Eisenhower had some very brilliant generals who led the invasion of France: Generals Patton and Montgomery. They are analogous to the SOMC and the St. Louis Fed, who led the charge against inflation. The SOMC and St. Louis were very much intertwined; Homer Jones, who started his career as an instructor at Rutgers, my home university, was a teacher of Milton Friedman. So, also, was Homer's foe in the '70s, Arthur Burns, who also taught Jones at Rutgers. Both Jerry Jordan and Ted Balbach, research directors at St. Louis, were students of Karl Brunner.

HESS: Mickey, please.

MICKEY D. LEVY: Very quickly, the excellent contributions by David Wheelock and George Tavlas focused primarily on the 1970s. I want to emphasize that having gone through over 550 papers written by Shadow members over the last fifty years, it's really a very rich committee that focuses on a diverse array of monetary issues today and is really quite relevant.

The other point, Greg, is that [Paul] Volcker followed through with aggressive monetary tightening in the late 1970s. He was extraordinarily worried, not just about the Fed's credibility, but also the government's. This concern led him to take very aggressive action. This provides a lesson for today. In the Fed's new strategic plan of 2020 and the Fed's research leading up to it, the emphasis was on the Fed's ability to manage inflationary expectations through forward guidance.

This was one factor that led them to discard the need for preemptive tightening. In this regard, Volcker's lesson still resonates—that is, forward guidance may be used to manage expectations, but you better back it up with action.

HESS: Let's go with a couple questions, if there are any. Are there any questions at this point?

I'll go with Andy, please, I saw Andy's hand earlier, please, Andy Levin. We have a microphone.

ANDREW T. LEVIN: Well, first of all, thanks so much, really awesome presentation, and thanks to David and George for the discussion. I just want to make three factual points.

First, as George has carefully explained, the Federal Reserve Board's structural macro model was developed in the late 1960s and early 1970s. That model was still being used twenty-five years later when I joined the Fed Board staff in the early 1990s. By that time, it was simply referred to as the "MPS" model.

At that point, Peter Tinsley and Flint Brayton and Dave Reifschneider were developing the FRB/US model, which continues to serve as the Fed Board's primary macro model nearly thirty years later. So, perhaps the time is now getting ripe for another fresh vintage of macro modeling at the Fed?

Second, Mickey and Mike flagged the possibility that the SOMC was a bit too alarmist during the second half of the 1980s. However, the Philadelphia Fed's survey of professional forecasters shows how it took a long time for the Fed to regain credibility regarding its commitment to price stability. In fact, long-run inflation expectations were still at around 4% in 1991 and didn't settle at around 2.5% until the mid-to-late 1990s. Perhaps it could have been helpful if the Fed had adopted a numerical inflation target in the 1980s rather than waiting until 2012.

Third, it's important to note the Fed officials were still far too optimistic throughout 2021 and much of 2022. As of December 2021, the FOMC's [Federal Open Market Committee's] median forecast for the federal funds rate at the end of 2022 was only 0.9%. Throughout 2021 and early 2022, Fed officials were still expecting that interest rates would only edge up slowly, similar to the Fed's policy path over the previous decade. And that's the message that was being conveyed to financial markets and to institutions like Silicon Valley Bank. It wasn't until late 2022 that Fed officials started clearly communicating that a lot more tightening would be needed.

HESS: Great points, Andy. Please, Bob.

ROBERT G. KING: I'd like to make two comments on expectations through the lens of two things: first, the FOMC documents, and second, the simple New Keynesian model stressing imperfect credibility that I developed with Marvin Goodfriend. Now at the time that we did that, Marvin also was quite insistent that we should say that the Fed was not managing money, that managing money was just a screen, that it was an excuse or a way of raising nominal interest rates extremely aggressively.

Now, not everybody agrees with that. Immediately after the conference, we had a high-energy—perhaps irate—discussion with Robert Lucas about that. And I think it's still an open question in terms of that period: How much did the Fed really believe in the monetarist experiment, and how much did they just raise rates?

JERRY L. JORDAN [SOMC MEMBER, 1975–80 AND 1983–92]: Related to these comments, I want to suggest a proposition and get the panel to respond Yes or No regarding Volcker and expectations in that period. The proposition is, without the strong, unwavering support of the president throughout the early 1980s, Volcker could not have prevailed.

HESS: Jerry, do you want a response to that?

LEVY: Yes, absolutely. You're right, I mean, it was really quite striking that— so Volcker was nominated by [President Jimmy] Carter, and then President [Ronald] Reagan fully supported Volcker and his cold-turkey policies, even though it created a recession. And if you remember back then, there were two back-to-back recessions, and Reagan supported Volcker and the Fed through the whole episode.

HESS: I would tend to agree that President Reagan did have a very strong commitment to get inflation out of the system. He, of course, moved on to a different Fed chairman after it was delivered.

JACK KRUPANSKY [RETIRED TECHNOLOGIST AND FREELANCE CONSULTANT]: Hi, my name is Jack Krupansky. I've been following the Shadow, or shadowing the Shadow, for about twenty-five years now.

One question about two things: Is the output gap effectively obsolete? And if you look at both the output gap and the dual mandate of stable prices and full employment, do they really factor it in at all? Should they, from the committee's perspective, factor it in much at all in the conduct of monetary policy itself?

Or are they both more consequences rather than factors that you actually plug into what your rule should be?

LEVY: Jack, you're bringing up a great question, because the gap between actual real GDP and potential is based on an estimate of potential, which Shadow member Athanasios Orphanides has shown is often adjusted after the fact to make the models look good.

And then the other angle on that, when you look at gaps: When we talk about the Fed's dual mandate of 2% inflation and maximum inclusive employment, nobody knows what "maximum inclusive employment" is, but it's generally agreed that it's beyond the scope of the Fed to achieve it. But it's part of its mandate.

HESS: And with that, I'm sure this topic will come up again. Thank you very much, everyone, for this great first session.

Monetarism in Europe and
the United Kingdom

Introduction

Charles I. Plosser

Good morning, everyone, and let me pass my own welcome to everyone here today on this occasion. I particularly want to thank John Taylor and Hoover for their support and willingness to help us with this celebration. I think next to [Mickey] Levy, I'm probably the longest-running member of the SOMC that's still around and actively involved, although it was divided up into two stints, call it Before and After: before I joined the Fed and then after I joined the Fed.

And so I'm really privileged to be here. And thanks to all of you for being here as well. This next section is going to be particularly interesting, I think. Condi [Rice] talked to us this morning about the international aspects of economic policymaking and even of monetary policy.

And so this next section, I think, directly addresses the importance of those international considerations. We are fortunate to have with us this morning a group of central bankers who represent international economies and have all been involved over an extended length of time in the development of monetary policy in Europe and other countries.

Their knowledge and history of that involvement and that practice is really important, and hopefully we will hear some about those involvements as well. We have Georg Rich from the Swiss National Bank, Switzerland's central bank. Georg Rich, director of research for the Swiss National Bank for over twenty-five years, was deeply involved in the evolution of monetary policy in Switzerland for many of those years.

And he knew personally, for a long time, Karl Brunner and Allan [Meltzer], and has his own perspective about how that [European monetary policy] evolved over time. We are also pleased to have with us Charles Goodhart, who is probably one of the most influential and knowledgeable monetary economists in the UK. His career extended both to academia as well as work at the Bank of England over many, many years, and so he has a tremendous perspective on the evolution of policy in the UK.

We also have with us Otmar Issing. Otmar was a part of the Bundesbank for many, many years and was deeply involved in the development and practices at the ECB [European Central Bank], as the ECB was founded and as it evolved as an independent central bank. And finally, we have with us Axel Weber, who also spent time as president of the Bundesbank in Germany and on the governing council of the ECB for many years.

So we have four European economists deeply involved in the evolution of monetary policy in Europe. And it's going to be fascinating to hear some of their perspectives about that development, and how it has tied to the developments of monetary policy in the United States. And even each of them have had involvement at one point or another with the SOMC.

So we are very fortunate. We're going to start off, Georg, with your remarks, and we'll go from there. Thank you.

3

The Genesis and Performance of Swiss Monetary Targeting

Georg Rich

Introduction

This paper was presented as part of a panel devoted to a discussion of the influence of the Shadow Open Market Committee (SOMC) and monetarism in the United Kingdom and Europe. As a former official of the Swiss National Bank (SNB), Switzerland's central bank, I wanted to add a Swiss perspective. Monetarism certainly influenced the policy strategy of the SNB. Moreover, Karl Brunner, one of the founders of the SOMC, though not an official advisor to the SNB, maintained close relations with the central bank's research staff and made his mark on Swiss monetary policy in indirect ways.

Adoption of a Money Stock Target

In January 1973, Swiss authorities decided, reluctantly, to adopt a floating exchange rate after they had been firm supporters of the gold standard for a long time. With hindsight, the shift to floating was a major turning point in Swiss monetary policy.[1] It allowed the SNB to gain full control of the money supply and to direct monetary policy at domestic objectives, with price stability serving as the overriding goal.

The SNB at first did not fully realize that floating created a new environment for monetary policy. Its approach remained business as usual. During the period of fixed exchange rates, it had relied on regulatory measures such as restrictions on capital inflows and credit controls as instruments for fighting inflation. It did not occur to the SNB's Governing Board that floating had opened the opportunity for achieving price stability through strict control of the money supply. In July 1974, the banks, which despised credit controls, pointed out to the Board that they considered credit controls to be "superfluous" since "the SNB had gotten a grip on the money supply."[2] The Board in turn decided to charge the SNB's economists with studying this issue.

Although the Board agreed that strict control of the money supply was a viable alternative, it was concerned that abolishing credit controls would lead to a sharp increase in interest rates (SNB *MG* 9/19/1974, 1333).

Despite reservations about lifting credit controls, SNB chair Fritz Leutwiler became increasingly convinced that management of the money supply was the key to fighting inflation. He cited a study by the German Council of Economic Experts (a body of academics advising the German government) that recommended the money supply be increased in line with real growth of the economy and an inflation rate the central bank considered to be unavoidable (SNB *MG* 9/26/1974, 1363–64). In the meantime, the SNB staff, comprising economists trained or influenced by Karl Brunner, worked out a proposal for a policy approach based on targets for the money supply.

Since Leutwiler realized that such an approach would have to be rooted in economic analysis, he decided to establish a research department, which was to play a key role in the conception and implementation of Swiss monetary policy.[3] Furthermore, Leutwiler was aware that in a democratic country an independent central bank such as the SNB had to explain its policy decisions and actions to the public. For this reason, he also set up a media office. The Board in turn began to hold regular press conferences, with the first taking place in November 1974 (SNB *MG* 11/14/1974, 1729–31).

The Board discussed the possibility of setting monetary targets for the first time in October 1974, based on a report by the staff (SNB *MG* 10/31/1974, 1578). After subsequent discussions, it announced a growth target for the money stock M1 (currency, sight deposits, and deposits in transactions accounts in the hands of the nonbank public) for 1975 at the beginning of that year (SNB *MG* 12/5/1974, 1913–15; 1/9/1975, 68–69). Credit controls were abolished a few months later since they were no longer needed.

Setting the Targets and Managing the Money Supply
From 1976 to 1978, the SNB continued to fix annual targets for M1. In 1979, it abstained from setting a monetary target, for reasons to be discussed below. In 1980, it switched to an annual growth target for the monetary base (money created by the SNB consisting of currency in the hands of the public and reserves of the banks held at the SNB), a practice it continued to pursue in the period from 1981 to 1990 (Rich 2007, 291). At the end of 1990, it adopted a medium-term approach by setting growth paths for the monetary base for five-year periods. At the end of 1999, it abandoned monetary targeting altogether and shifted to an approach based largely on inflation forecasts.

In principle, the SNB adopted the prescription offered by Milton Friedman and strove to expand the money supply by accommodating potential growth in real GDP, estimated to be slightly less than 2% per year, and consumer price inflation of 0% to 1%, the SNB's inflation target (in its official announcements, the SNB was somewhat opaque in quantifying precisely its inflation target). The annual expansion in the monetary base required for meeting these objectives was initially estimated to be 2% to 3% (unitary income elasticity of monetary base). However, this turned out to be too high, and the SNB gradually reduced the required trend growth in the monetary base to less than 2% in the 1980s and 1990s (Rich 2007, 304–5).[4]

In contrast to calculating the required trend growth in the monetary base, there was no set procedure for fixing the annual targets. The SNB aimed at reducing annual growth in the monetary base and M1 gradually from 6% in 1975 to 2% in 1990. In practice, the slowdown in base-money growth was less gradual than indicated by the targets, for reasons to be discussed below. However, from about 1983 onward, the SNB largely succeeded in steadying the expansion in the monetary base (figure 3.1). After considerable experimentation, the SNB at the end of 1982 adopted a procedure for determining the annual monetary targets, which it continued to follow in the subsequent years.[5] It started out by forecasting real GDP growth and consumer price inflation in the subsequent year. From these forecasts and its estimated money-demand

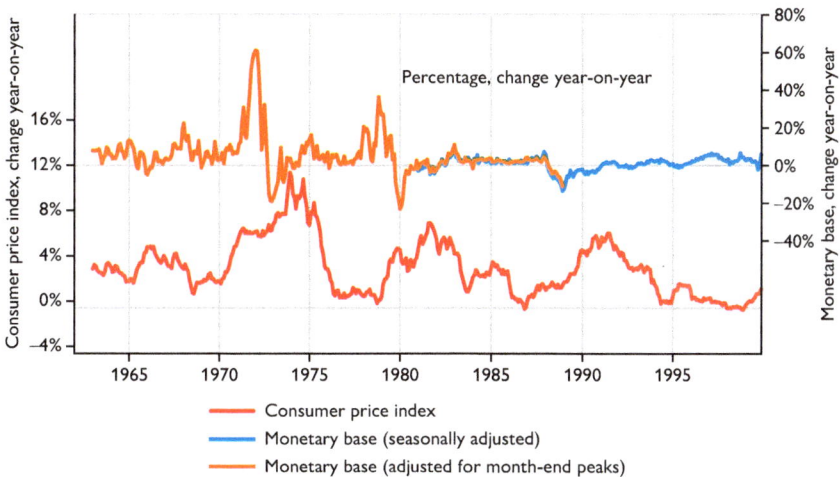

Figure 3.1. Consumer prices and monetary base.

Source: Swiss National Bank, Data Portal.

function, it calculated the activity-induced change in money demand (i.e., the change in demand for base money prompted by the estimated change in real GDP and the price level). In an inflationary environment, it was likely that the expected activity-induced increase in base-money demand was higher than the 2% to 3% consistent with price stability in the longer run. Therefore, the SNB had to decide how quickly it endeavored to reduce base-money growth to the desired long-run path. If it set a target below the expected increase in activity-induced money demand, interest rates had to rise to maintain equilibrium in the market for base money. The boost in interest rates was required to curb real growth and to push inflation down to the desired level.[6]

The then available econometric evidence suggests that both the demand for base money and M1 were negatively related to interest rates. In the case of the monetary base, it was mostly the demand for large-denomination banknotes, serving mainly as a store of value, that was responsible for the sensitivity to interest rates. The interest sensitivity of the demand for base money implies a positive relationship between the income velocity of that aggregate and interest rates. Figure 3.2 shows that there was a positive relationship between the deviations in the base-money velocity from its trend growth and the three-month interest rate in the Swiss franc money market.

Relying on monetary targets provided an important advantage over a policy approach based solely on inflation forecasts. As indicated above, to set the monetary target, the SNB required forecasts for real growth and inflation one year ahead. Had it relied on inflation forecasts alone, it would have been

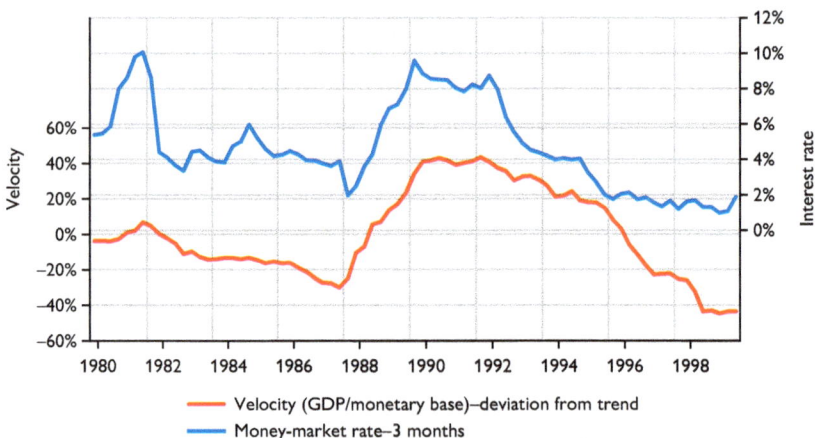

Figure 3.2. Velocity and interest rate.

Source: Swiss National Bank, Data Portal.

compelled to predict price movements three years ahead, as the SNB is doing now, due to the long lags in the effects of monetary policy. The then available forecasting models did not yield sensible results for the longer run because, for obvious reasons, they were estimated largely from data derived from the period of fixed exchange rates. Generating one-year-ahead forecasts was easier because the SNB could draw on a variety of sources for that purpose.[7]

Tight control of money allowed the SNB to reduce inflation to low levels. Figure 3.1 shows that the SNB managed to stabilize growth in the monetary base slightly above zero from the early 1980s onward. Even though Swiss inflation was lower than that of most other countries, the SNB's performance was less than stellar. The same chart reveals that inflation accelerated again temporarily in the late 1970s and 1980s. Why did the SNB allow inflation to rise despite its commitment to monetary targeting? Several problems arose from the SNB's targeting approach.

Excessive Movements in the Exchange Rate

After the switch to floating, the rise in the Swiss franc exchange rate both in nominal and real terms did not come as a surprise (figure 3.3) since the currency had been strongly undervalued. However, in the summer of 1978 the exchange rate reached heights that could no longer be explained by fundamentals. To avert a catastrophic slump in the export sector, the SNB was forced to act. It set a floor underneath the Swiss franc price of the deutsche

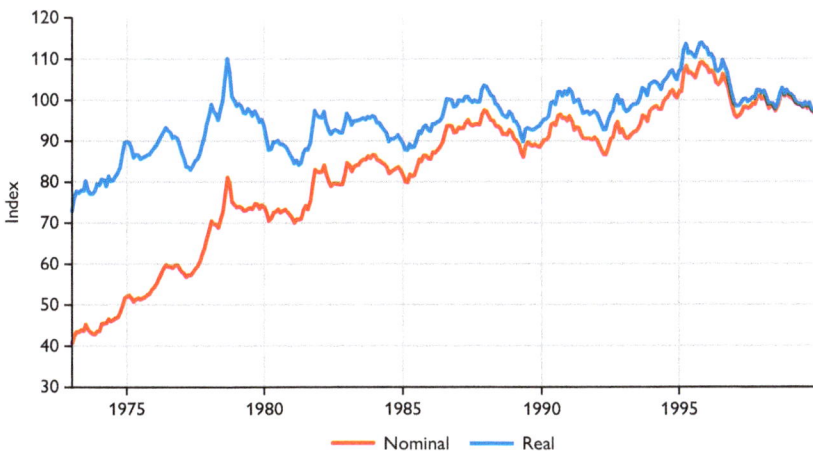

Figure 3.3. Nominal and real effective exchange rate of Swiss franc.

Source: Swiss National Bank, Data Portal.

mark and intervened heavily in the foreign exchange market. As a result, the
monetary base exploded again (figure 3.1). The SNB temporarily abandoned
its money stock target and abstained from setting such a target for 1979. At
the end of 1979, it decided to return to monetary targeting. It should be noted
that the adoption of a temporary exchange-rate floor was not regarded as a
breach of its commitment to price stability. After announcing its monetarist
strategy at the end of 1974, the SNB had already emphasized that its target
was *contingent* on various unexpected developments—in particular, excessive
movements in the exchange rate.

Despite the return to monetary targeting, the expansionary stance in
the late 1970s led to a renewed increase in inflation. Various observers
(Schiltknecht 1989; Baltensperger and Kugler 2017; Kugler and Rich 2002)
have argued that the SNB was too tardy in removing the monetary overhang
created by its interventions. As a matter of fact, the economics staff pleaded
for a speedier return to monetary normality than the Board (SNB *MG*
3/1/1979, 247–50; 6/21/1979, 643–46; 8/30/1979, 876–77; 11/22/1979,
1214). The latter insisted on a cautious procedure because of concerns about
a return of the troubles in the foreign exchange market. In my view, the overly
cautious approach to removing the monetary overhang was not the only factor explaining the return of inflation, as I show below.

After the return to monetary targeting, the authorities gradually eliminated all the restrictions on capital inflows from abroad that had been inher-
ited from the fixed-exchange-rate period and maintained to curb the Swiss
franc appreciation. Interestingly, the shift to market-based policy instruments
was reflected in the length of the SNB's Board minutes. While in the 1960s
and 1970s the length of the minutes typically amounted to about two thousand pages per year, that number fell to less than one thousand in the 1980s.

Steady Money Growth Not an Optimum Strategy

For the years 1980 and 1981, the SNB set a target for base-money growth
of 4% each. In hindsight, these targets were likely to be too high. Inflation
had fallen to nearly zero but was rising again, while economic activity was
recovering. Inflation continued to accelerate throughout 1980 and 1981.
Considering the dire inflation outlook, the Board, following the advice of
the research department, tightened monetary policy at the beginning of 1981
and allowed base-money growth to drop below 4%, turning slightly negative
for the whole year (SNB *MG* 5/7/1981, 566–70; 7/30/1981, 948–50). The
Board probably would have been more successful in curbing inflation had it
aimed at lower or even zero base-money growth as early as 1980. However,

this would have been incompatible with its professed aim of reducing money growth gradually. For 1982 the Board set a target of 3%, which it was largely to achieve (SNB *MG* 12/3/1981, 1513–30; the research department proposed an even higher target of 4% for that year).

The episode of 1980/81 revealed a fundamental problem of monetary targeting. Steady money growth was not a sufficiently effective buffer against cyclical and other shocks to inflation. The reason lay in the interest sensitivity of the targeted aggregate. In principle, in a cyclical expansion the activity-induced demand for money rose more quickly than the supply, as determined by the target. As a result, interest rates rose and mitigated the cyclical expansion. In the Swiss case, the interest movements triggered by steady money growth were not strong enough to soften the impact on inflation of a cyclical expansion in economic activity.[8]

This drawback of a policy of steady money growth prompted the SNB to switch to a medium-term approach at the end of 1990. Although that approach was quite successful, it created several new problems for the SNB.[9] A multi-year target was more difficult to communicate to the public than its annual analogue. Furthermore, and more importantly, the SNB at first did not realize that it had lost a key advantage of annual targets after it had adopted the multiyear approach. If economic circumstances called for major deviations from the multiyear target line, the SNB was all at sea in trying to determine the size of such deviations. No matter how the SNB looked at the problem, it could not help relying on inflation forecasts with a horizon of more than one year to determine its policy course. Thus, the multiyear strategy involved a strong dose of inflation targeting, although money continued to play an important role. In my view, these considerations were mainly responsible for the SNB's decision at the end of 1999 to abandon monetary targeting and to shift to an approach based on three-year inflation forecasts and an inflation objective of 0% to 2%. Another reason was instabilities in the demand for base money appearing toward the end of the 1990s. Despite the shift in strategy, the SNB emphasized that money continued to serve as an important indicator for properly gauging monetary policy.[10]

Notes

1. On this point, see Baltensperger and Kugler (2017), Bernholz (2007), Peytrignet (2007), and Rich (2007).

2. SNB, Minutes of the Governing Board July 11, 1974, 950, henceforth cited as SNB *MG* 7/11/1974, 950, translation mine. The SNB Board meets weekly. There is a curfew of thirty years on disclosing the Board minutes to the public.

3. Karl Brunner taught at the University of Bern in addition to holding a professorship in the US. For more detail, see Bernholz (2007, 174–75). I joined the research department in 1977.

4. In the 1990s, even 1% would have been sufficient. The SNB underestimated the effect of innovations in the payments system on the demand for banknotes.

5. See the proposal of the research staff on the target for 1983 and the Board discussion. This was the first time I wrote the proposal (SNB *MG* 12/2/1982, 1073–83).

6. In setting the target the SNB assumed that the increase in interest rates would begin to affect economic activity only after a year.

7. See Rich (2007, 292) for a table comparing the SNB's forecasts with the actual outcomes.

8. Ben Friedman et al. (1977) had already pointed to this problem.

9. See Rich (2007, 313–23), Peytrignet (2007, 245–54), and Baltensperger and Kugler (2017, 116–19) for detailed discussions.

10. Since I was involved both in developing the multiyear targeting approach and the subsequent policy based on three-year inflation forecasts, this paragraph embraces a good dose of self-criticism.

References

Baltensperger, Ernst, and Peter Kugler. 2017. *Swiss Monetary History since the Early 19th Century*. Cambridge University Press.

Bernholz, Peter. 2007. "From 1945 to 1982: The Transition from Inward Exchange Controls to Money Supply Management under Floating Exchange Rates." In *The Swiss National Bank 1907–2007*, edited by Swiss National Bank. Swiss National Bank.

Friedman, Benjamin M., James Duesenberry, and William Poole. 1977. "The Inefficiency of Short-Run Monetary Targets for Monetary Policy." *Brookings Papers on Economic Activity* 1977 (2): 293–346.

Kugler, Peter, and Georg Rich. 2002. "Monetary Policy under Low Interest Rates: The Experience of Switzerland in the Late 1970s." *Swiss Journal of Economics and Statistics* 138 (3): 241–69.

Peytrignet, Michel. 2007. "The Money Supply as an Intermediate Monetary Target." In *The Swiss National Bank 1907–2007*, edited by Swiss National Bank. Swiss National Bank.

Rich, Georg. 2007. "Swiss Monetary Targeting 1974–1996: The Role of Internal Policy Analysis." *Swiss Journal of Economics and Statistics* 143 (3): 283–329.

Schiltknecht, Kurt. 1989. "Geldmengenpolitik und Wechselkurs—der schweizerische Weg." In *Geldwertsicherung und Wechselkursstabilität: Essays in Honour of Helmut Schlesinger*, edited by Norbert Bub, Dieter Duwedag, and Rudolf Richter. Knapp.

SNB (Swiss National Bank). Various dates. Minutes of the Governing Board. Unpublished.

4

Central Bank Watch 2024/2025

Monetary Policy Normalization Ahead

Axel A. Weber

This chapter builds on Otmar Issing's essay (2025, in this volume). Throughout my early career, I was greatly influenced by my experiences at the University of Konstanz, and later on by listening to Allan Meltzer, Karl Brunner, and many other significant figures here today.

When I joined the Bundesbank as president, the monetary strategy was already well established, as Otmar mentions in his chapter. I'd like to expand on this, as the policy angle of my academic career began around 1998 in Frankfurt, where Otmar and I initiated what is still today known as the ECB Watchers Conference. That conference created an open platform for dialogue, where both critics from academia and financial markets were encouraged to share their perspectives on the European Central Bank's (ECB) policies. Given that monetary policy impacts financial markets so heavily, it was essential to engage with both fields.

Until 2004, when I became Bundesbank president, Otmar and I co-organized those conferences. Later, the University of Frankfurt continued hosting them, and I have recently returned to head the Center for Financial Studies after Otmar. Volker Wieland has maintained this conference over the years, and now, on its twenty-fifth anniversary, the ECB still participates—an engagement that I find beneficial. However, observing from the outside, I believe the character of this and other central banking conferences has evolved.

Following my role at the Bundesbank, where I played a central role in managing the Great Financial Crisis in Germany, I led the Swiss commercial bank UBS Group AG for a decade. During the Great Financial Crisis, central banks intervened with massive financial assistance to the financial sector.

As a consequence, financial market participants were increasingly excluded from major central bank conferences like Jackson Hole and Sintra. This exclusion stemmed from policymakers' concerns that the public would criticize their close ties to financial market participants in the light of the substantial bailouts provided. Consequently, I found that these debates became more one-sided.

Additionally, as Otmar notes, the lack of focus on monetary aggregates carried certain disadvantages. The correlation between liquidity in global markets and stock market performance was not identified early enough. In my view, central banks started utilizing both interest rates and balance sheets as instruments, but just as balance sheets expanded significantly, central banks ceased closely monitoring these metrics, which later presented challenges.

In the 2000s, and particularly after the financial crisis, central banks adopted the monetary policy strategy of average inflation targeting. In my opinion, this was an inadequately designed monetary policy framework, effectively amounting to price-level targeting without actually monitoring the evolution of the price level. As a result, central banks faced delays in recognizing and responding to substantial changes in inflation trends.

Figure 4.1 presents data regarding the US Consumer Price Index (CPI) post-2014, after the financial crisis. The orange straight line represents a consistent 2% inflation target. While initially below the target, inflation largely aligned with this trend until the COVID-19 pandemic. However, during the

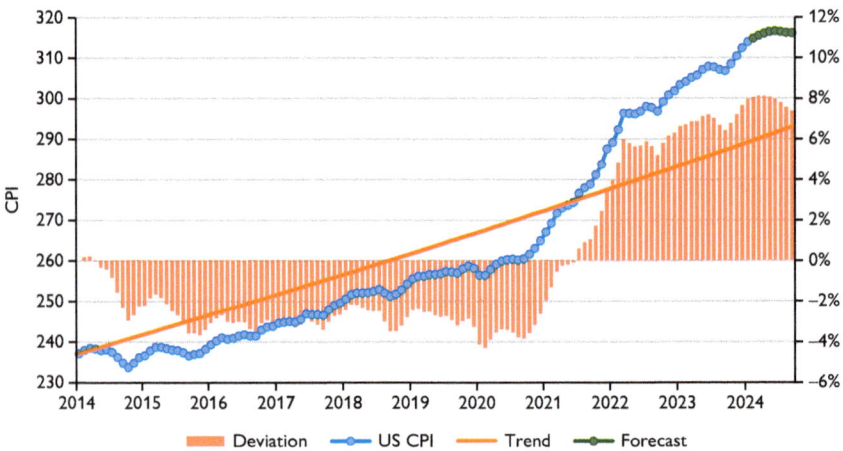

Figure 4.1. US Consumer Price Index, 2% inflation trend and postpandemic trend breaks (2014–24).

Source: Author's calculations.

pandemic, fiscal stimulus—amplified by extremely accommodative monetary policy—caused a sharp rise in the price level, a rise of approximately three times the previous average rate. Central banks took more than a year to adjust their policies, leading to an eighteen-month period of escalating prices before they intervened by raising interest rates and shrinking balance sheets.

Furthermore, central banks compounded their initial delays with a communications strategy—often labeled "team transitory"—that downplayed inflation concerns. Additionally, their promise to taper balance sheet policies before raising rates led to further delays in tightening, making things worse.

Looking at figure 4.2 for the ECB, we observe that average inflation prior to the pandemic ran below target and was close to 1%. But during the postpandemic period, European inflation also massively exceeded 2%, leading to a substantial loss in purchasing power as the price level trended higher. Today, although inflation rates are back around 2%, the loss of purchasing power remains substantial due to these cumulative price increases. This gap has triggered demands for second-round wage increases and producer price adjustments as households and businesses seek to compensate for the lost purchasing power and increased costs.

In the broader context, central banks implemented the most rapid, extensive, and synchronized rate hikes seen in postwar history. Coupled with notable balance sheet reductions, this strategy has had a significant impact on

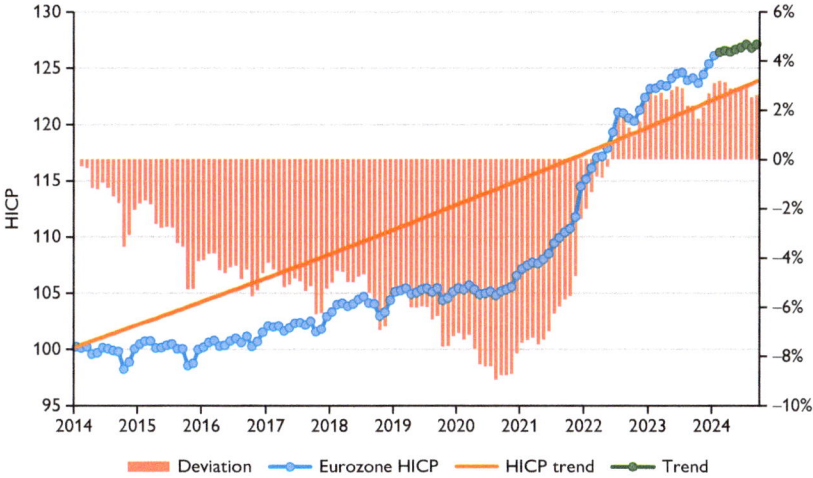

Figure 4.2. Eurozone Harmonized Index of Consumer Prices (HICP), 2% inflation trend and postpandemic trend breaks (2014–24).

Source: Author's calculations.

markets and the economy. While the ECB projects a gradual balance sheet reduction over the coming years, central banks will remain deeply involved in economic activity, reflecting a departure from pre-crisis norms.

In conclusion, while central banks recently regained control of inflation, they face the challenge of addressing the persistent erosion of purchasing power. I'm concerned that central banks still today place too much emphasis on their inflation forecasting models—assuming a return to 2% inflation. This might be overly optimistic, as they rely heavily on model assumptions rather than actual data. I am concerned that central banks might repeat past mistakes by adhering to these projections without adequately factoring in underlying market conditions and price dynamics.

Reference

Issing, Otmar. 2025. "Bundesbank and ECB—Monetarist Strategies?" In *Fifty Years of the Shadow Open Market Committee: A Retrospective on Its Role in Monetary Policy* edited by Michael D. Bordo, Jeffrey M. Lacker, Mickey D. Levy, and John B. Taylor. Hoover Institution Press.

5

European Experience of Monetarism and the SOMC

Charles Goodhart

One of the reasons for the growing influence of monetarism in Europe and in the United Kingdom during the 1970s and early 1980s was our own historical experience. Thus, figure 5.1 shows the path of inflation for Germany in red, the United States in orange, and the UK in blue from 1970 through, more or less, to the present.

In the 1970s, there were two very severe energy shocks, first in 1973–74, followed by the Iran shock in 1979. Although the shocks were more or less similar across countries, there was massive difference in the inflation feed-through into these countries. Actually, note the very considerable difference with the last energy shock after Vladimir Putin's invasion of Ukraine, where, although the energy effect and shock was massively different between Europe and the US—that is, much worse in Europe than in the US—the inflation outcome was more or less the same.

So in the 1970s: similar energy shock, differing inflation outcomes. In the period 2021–24: very different energy shocks, very similar inflation outcomes. On this occasion, I am not going to talk about the recent similarity in inflation, but I do want to go back to the point that the inflation outcomes were very different in the 1970s. Why were these outcomes so different?

In figure 5.2, in red, you will see the paths of the money supply for the US on top, the UK in the middle, and Germany at the bottom. What appears quite clearly, in fact, is that the UK monetary growth was far higher and much more variable; the United States was more or less in the middle; and Germany had a much slower and more stable monetary growth over this particular time period. These differences in monetary growth matched differences in inflation and interest rate outcomes rather closely.

This relationship between monetary experience and inflation outcomes at the time played a large role in encouraging people to believe in the importance of monetary growth and monetarism. It was not just Milton Friedman's

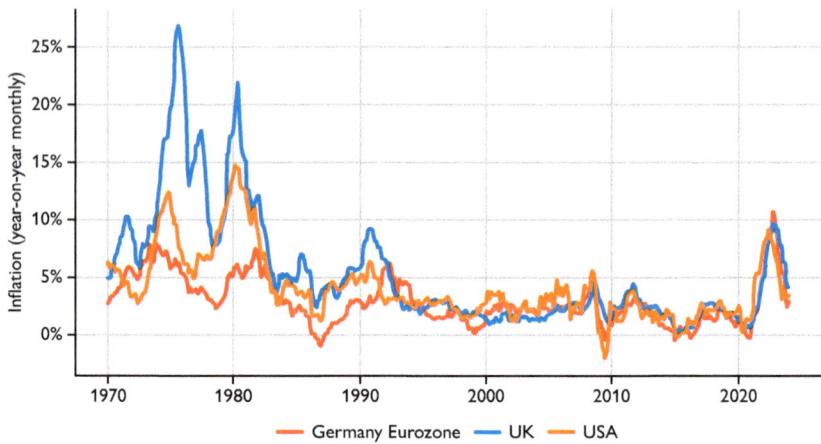

Figure 5.1. Inflation rates over time.

Source: Jongrim Ha (2024), World Bank, and Federal Reserve Bank of St. Louis.

analysis, it was the practical experience of differing countries at the time of the energy shocks and the crises of the 1970s that played a massively large role. It is practical experience that is so important to central bankers.

The next thing I wanted to do as part of the discussion about the effect of the Shadow Open Market Committee on ideas in various countries abroad was a literature search—a search of references to the SOMC in the main newspapers in Europe. Such references were rather less than I had expected, given how famous and influential all the members of the SOMC have been. In the UK, there were quite a lot of references, almost all of them in the *Financial Times*; several were in the *Times*, where Peter Jay and Tim Congdon, who is still going strong along monetarist lines, were running its economics editorials for a long time. Very rarely, oddly enough, in the *Telegraph*; quite a lot in the news agencies.

In Germany there were a few references, in all the main papers. Switzerland had several references, mostly in the news agencies. In France, there were a couple in Agence France-Presse and *Le Monde*, and Spain had one in *Cinco Días*. Several of the reports related to the famous individual members of the SOMC, Allan Meltzer and Karl Brunner.

One of the reasons, I think, why there was relatively little discussion of the SOMC in the media in Europe is that the SOMC, unsurprisingly, focused almost entirely on what was happening in the US, while we, in our various countries in Europe, necessarily focused on our own monetary developments and what was likely to happen to ourselves.

USA M3 growth and central bank rates (1970–80)

M3 growth USA   CB rate USA

UK M3 growth and central bank rates (1970–80)

M3 growth UK   CB rate UK

Germany M3 growth and central bank rates (1970–80)

M3 growth Germany   CB rate Germany

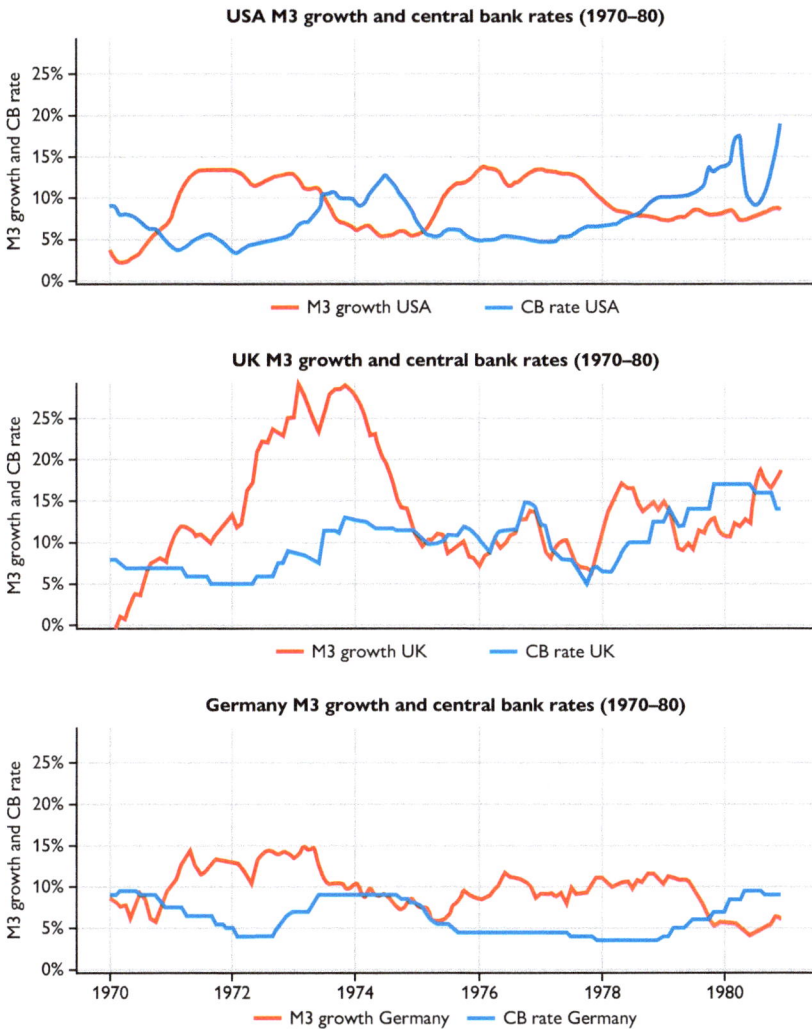

Figure 5.2. US, UK, and German M3 growth and central bank rates, 1970–80.

Source: Federal Reserve Bank of St. Louis.

And most of us had our own somewhat specific equivalence of the SOMC. For example, in the UK, there was a very influential writer, Gordon Pepper, who wrote monthly in Greenwell's *Monetary Bulletin*, which I think was read continuously by Margaret Thatcher. And Brian Griffiths followed monetarism, and again was very close to Thatcher.

Alan Walters, although he was very strongly supportive of Thatcher, was not quite such a steadfast monetarist. In particular, he and Alfred Sherman, of the Centre for Policy Studies, invited their colleague Jürg Niehans over to the UK to comment on British monetary policy in 1981.

And Niehans surprised everybody by claiming that British monetary policy wasn't too weak because we had very fast broad monetary growth; it was too tight because M1 was growing very, very slowly. And again, one of the problems that monetarism has had was that there have been very different monetary aggregates—monetary base, M0, M1, M2, M3, Divisia money, etc., etc. And they frequently point in differing directions.

Let me end by commenting on one extraordinary event that occurred in the UK in which Karl Brunner played a major role. In 1981, a directly restrictive policy that I had been involved in introducing, called the Corset, was removed from the commercial banks.

There was, as a result, a surge in the monetary growth, which was far in excess of the medium-term financial strategy that the Conservatives had just introduced; it appeared to blow a hole in it. I had warned both the governor, Gordon Richardson, and his deputy, Kit McMahon, and indeed, the executive director (home finance), John Fforde, that they ought to go to Thatcher, explain what had happened, and say what they were going to do about it.

But it was August and they were all on holiday, and they didn't feel that they wanted to do it anyhow, so they didn't. Meanwhile Mrs. T, who was on holiday in Switzerland, spending time with a Conservative MP who had a holiday home there, suddenly found there was this horrible shock to her medium-term financial strategy.

Then the Conservative MP in whose house she was staying said: "You ought to go and talk to Fritz Leutwiler," which she did. And Leutwiler said: "You ought to go and talk with Karl Brunner." And what then occurred was that Thatcher required the Bank of England to organize a group, including Karl Brunner and Hermann-Josef Dudler from the Deutsche Bundesbank, to visit the UK to talk both to her, Mrs. Thatcher, and to the Bank. I had to play the role of travel agent in arranging this, which was one of the more extraordinary activities of my life.

And they spent a long time talking to Thatcher; so long that they didn't really have much time to visit the Bank of England. It was a fascinating occasion. But in the longer run I don't think it had that much effect on British monetary policy because, as everybody has been saying, the monetary aggregates, or rather their velocity, then became relatively unstable.

Then we all moved gently toward first of all being much more concerned directly with interest rates, and then ultimately to inflation targeting. But that's another story to discuss on another occasion. Let me leave it at that.

6

Bundesbank and ECB—Monetarist Strategies?

Otmar Issing

The Bundesbank's Monetary Target

In 1975, the Deutsche Bundesbank announced a money-supply target for the first time. With a number of technical modifications, it stuck to this strategy until the deutsche mark was replaced by the euro on January 1, 1999. From the outset, the Bundesbank declared that it would not align its monetary policy strictly with the annual money-supply target and described its strategy as "pragmatic monetarism" (Issing et al. 2006). This immediately brought criticism from "true" monetarists such as Karl Brunner and Manfred J. M. Neumann, who, in short, denied that the Bundesbank's monetary policy strategy and practice even deserved the name "monetarist."

Despite this criticism, the Bundesbank was widely regarded as a representative of monetarism, at least in terms of its categorization. A number of authors from the Anglo-Saxon world "accused" the Bundesbank of actually pursuing a policy of inflation control under the guise of the money-supply target.

The ECB's Monetary Policy Strategy

When I was appointed to the executive board of the European Central Bank (ECB), I was given responsibility for the Directorates General Economics and Research. The first president of the ECB, Wim Duisenberg, gave me complete freedom and assured me of his unconditional support.

The most important task, and at the same time the greatest challenge, was to develop the monetary policy strategy of the new central bank for a new currency, the euro. There was not much time. In seven months, a new era was to begin with the introduction of the euro. At first, the matter seemed quite simple. Over the last two years, I had argued in several articles that the ECB should decide on a money-supply target. The decisive argument was that this choice would transfer the credibility of the Bundesbank, which was recognized throughout the world as an anchor of price stability, to the new institution, the ECB.

Having moved from the position of chief economist at the Bundesbank to the same position at the ECB, what was for me so far a theoretical question became a problem of concrete monetary policy and the corresponding responsibility.

First of all, I abandoned the idea of a money-supply target. The Bundesbank had missed its monetary target roughly half the time. This was also the case during my term in office. This forced me to explain to the public the reasons and justifications for why we were sticking to the money-supply strategy and were convinced that we would reach the target again in the foreseeable future—which is what happened. The probability that the development of the money supply after the currency changeover to the euro could be extremely volatile, possibly even erratic, should not be underestimated. How could it then succeed, as in the case of the deutsche mark, in convincingly explaining the deviation combined with the assurance that the development of the money supply would swing back to the level of the agreed target? There was a great danger that the ECB would have to admit that its strategy had failed shortly after assuming monetary policy responsibility. That would have been a catastrophe for a new central bank that was already surrounded by mistrust. For me, this ruled out a money-supply strategy for the ECB.

In the next step, I formed a group of excellent economists from the Directorates General Economics and Research to discuss the problem of the ECB's future monetary policy strategy. To the surprise of my colleagues, who were familiar with my previous publications, I opened the first meeting by stating: "There will be no ECB money-supply target, not even in the pragmatic Bundesbank variant. But 'money,' understood from the outset in the broadest sense as a term for monetary factors, should play a prominent role. Let us develop a strategy that meets these conditions."

It was also necessary to take into account the extreme degree of uncertainty associated with the introduction of a new currency. The euro area was only created when the decision was made about the eleven participating states on May 2, 1998. It would therefore take a considerable time, well after the launch of the euro, before reliable data would be available. Accordingly, it was also necessary to develop completely new models and projections for the new currency area.

As a result of our discussion I proposed a monetary policy strategy to the Board and Governing Council, which was adopted by the Council on October 13, 1998, and announced publicly on the same day (Issing 2008). The soon-to-be-named "Two-Pillar Strategy" is based on the following two elements:

1. The monetary analysis, which initially included a reference value for the growth of the M3 aggregate and was expanded over time into a comprehensive analysis of the monetary and financial sectors.
2. The economic analysis. The economic pillar was based on an assessment of a wide range of indicators from the real sector relevant for the outlook of price stability in the euro area.

The essence of the two-pillar approach is that the information produced under one methodological perspective is always cross-checked against information and analysis produced by the other. It provides an effective insurance against the uncertainties and complexities of the economic environment, guaranteeing the robustness of monetary policy decisions and reducing the risks of policy errors. The effort to analyze and reconcile results from different perspectives stimulates deeper analysis and ultimately leads to a better understanding of the economic situation.

A key element of this strategy is the medium-term orientation, which means that the conduct of monetary policy is focused on maintaining price stability over the medium term. Two aspects are relevant. From an ex post, accountability point of view, it acknowledges the existence of short-term volatility in prices, resulting from shocks that cannot be fully anticipated. Quite obviously, monetary policy cannot be held responsible for short-run deviations from price stability that it cannot control. From an ex ante, forward-looking point of view, the medium-term orientation reflects the lags and uncertainties facing the central bank, recognizing that monetary policy would be ill-suited to actively fine-tune short-term economic developments. Furthermore, a medium-term perspective is important in order to permit a gradualist and measured response to some kind of economic disturbances—such as supply shocks—thereby avoiding introducing unnecessary volatility into the real economy. In this way, it embodies concern for, and contributes to, the stabilization of output in the economy.

It is obvious that these elements were of particular importance in the case of a new currency.[1]

ECB—A Monetarist Strategy?

Although the two-pillar strategy was even further removed from the ideas of Milton Friedman or Karl Brunner than the pragmatic approach of the Bundesbank, the ECB was widely seen as a kind of last bastion of monetarism. This assessment also applied to those national central bank presidents who had more or less since long stopped paying attention to money-supply developments in their central banks. Incidentally, another group of central bank presidents was disappointed that I had not proposed a money-supply strategy. It was precisely because of this fundamental difference of opinion that the separation into monetary and economic analysis proved to be an almost perfect framework for a structured discussion, which ultimately led to a common denominator for monetary policy decisions through cross-checking.

In the media, and not least in the Anglo-Saxon-dominated mainstream, the ECB was seen as the last representative of a hopelessly discredited monetarism. As this conference is under the motto "Fifty Years of the Shadow Open Market Committee," I would like to briefly address the discussion with the ECB watchers. From the very beginning, in the tradition of the Bundesbank critics, they were negative about the ECB's strategy and above all about the importance of monetary analysis. The first verdict was extremely negative. In a report under the title *The ECB: Safe at Any Speed?* (Begg et al. 1998), the verdict—before the launch of the Euro!—was clear and scathing: "At present, it is both weak and unprepared"—as if we at the bank had decided on the early beginning of monetary union.

The comment from a 2004 report (Galí et al. 2004, 33) is telling: "In its policy choices the ECB has not given much attention to monetary growth rates so far. Rather, this has been a rhetorical means to borrow the reputation of the Bundesbank as the guarantor of a stable European monetary policy. With the ECB now able to walk by itself, it no longer needs the Bundesbank monetary crutch. We have carefully examined in this chapter whether there can be some special role for monitoring the growth rate of a monetary aggregate—assuming that the ECB surely should and does monitor medium-term inflationary trends—and we did not find any. We therefore view the new strategy as slowly adjusting the original monetary pillar towards a clarification of what the ECB really means by its still opaque 'medium-term' orientation of its inflation policy goals."

By and large, this is the tone with which the ECB's strategy has been criticized by the majority of macroeconomists, not to mention the media.

Monetary Policy Without Money?

For me, as the "inventor" of the two-pillar strategy, it was a constant challenge to explain this approach and defend it against sometimes fierce criticism.[2] This also came from other central banks and was primarily about the importance that the ECB gave to monetary analysis. I discussed the reasons for our decision in detail with these colleagues and did not ignore problems. I regularly ended such discussions with the comment: "Let's leave the criticism of the ECB strategy aside for now. How does your central bank deal with the problem—by simply ignoring developments of money and credit? As a result, monetary policy without any consideration of monetary factors?"[3]

Monetarism seemed to be discredited by the collapse of the quantity-theoretic relationship between money supply and prices. This is what numerous authors have pointed out for developments in the 2010s.[4] This is certainly a warning for the central bank not to opt for a strict money-supply strategy. But is this an argument to exclude money from the analysis of inflation, as this is the practice now at most central banks? The neglect of monetary developments evidently went so far that even high growth rates of the various monetary aggregates were seen as unproblematic. "I do think it would have been sensitive to ask in 2020 and 2021: if broad money is growing at 25% . . . a year, what is going on here? In the past decade, central banks have unfortunately abandoned reporting on and monitoring the broad monetary aggregates" (King 2024).[5]

At its core, the decisive factor here is the assessment of inflation targeting. As this strategy defined and referred to as "state of the art" is now being practiced by all major central banks after the ECB joined this camp, it is an approach of "monetary policy without money." But this weakness goes even further. "No model of inflation targeting exists so far which integrates the risks from the banking system and financial markets with all their dynamics, non-linearities and overall complexity. Central banks should agree that the search for an 'optimal' monetary policy regime has not come to an end and inflation targeting might entail risks and shortcomings. From this perspective, one could argue that a situation in which central banks follow the same strategy might also bring systemic risks and that there are benefits to a more diversified and robust approach" (Issing 2020).

These weaknesses of the theory of inflation targeting have been shown again in the recent phase of high inflation. Based on the reactions of the relevant representatives so far, one must expect that they see the "solution" in refining the models, resulting in increasing complexity (see King 2024). Based on previous experience, it is difficult to imagine that this path will lead to success.

Is Monetarism Dead?

The Bundesbank's "pragmatic" money-supply strategy was accused by leading monetarists of not being a "monetarist" approach, while the majority of criticism from the other side placed the Bundesbank in this camp. As shown, the discrepancy is even more striking when assessing the ECB's strategy.

In short, it seems as if any approach in which the development of the money supply plays a role is classified as "monetarist" and thus relegated to the dustbin of disproven ideas. This is especially true of the quantity theory. But shouldn't centuries of experience advise a more cautious assessment? Shouldn't research, for example, also devote more attention to the question of how to define the money supply relevant for the relationship to inflation during times of rapid growth in electronic means of payment?

Whatever one may call "monetarism" today, one cannot simply ignore the importance of the development of the money supply for inflation. Mervyn King (2002) once summed it up succinctly: "No money—no inflation."

Over one hundred years ago, Joseph Schumpeter (1918, 116) warned: "And all the defects of metallism and the quantity theory, which I have certainly not defended . . . do not change the fact that in the theories so often condemned under these titles there is a great deal of sound insight, a great deal of practical wisdom—which even today is a more reliable guide than much of what the writings of the day offer. Above all, there is seriousness and sincerity in them, which we urgently need." (Translation mine.)

Notes

1. The process of this discussion and decision making is documented in detail in a book that was published soon after the launch. The book also discusses the definition of price stability in detail (Issing et al. 2001). A crucial element of the strategy was also the statement that the ECB interprets price stability as an annual average increase in the Harmonized Index of Consumer Prices of below 2%. At the first review of the strategy in 2003, the ECB stated that it would pursue a course of keeping the increase "close to, but below, 2%." The definition of "below 2%" was mainly due to the special situation of price developments before the launch of the euro. At the next review in 2020, the ECB announced a symmetric inflation target of 2%.

2. Incidentally, the term "two-pillar" was not mine at all. It was created spontaneously during a press conference of the president.

3. For example, I have heard numerous speeches by Alan Greenspan on the US Fed's monetary (!) policy in which not only did the term "money" not appear, but no nominal quantities were mentioned at all.

4. To use Friedman's words, at that time money was not "chasing" goods but assets. Was it not reckless to ignore the danger posed by this?

5. One could think of the man who considers himself fit to drive after a glass of beer and then believes that this also applies when completely drunk. By the way, the ECB still reports on the development of money and credit.

References

Begg, David K., Paul de Grauwe, Francesco Giavazzi, Harald Uhlig, and Charles Wyplosz. 1998. *The ECB: Safe at Any Speed?* Centre for Economic Policy Research.

Galí, Jordi, Stefan Gerlach, Julio Rotemberg, Harald Uhlig, and Michael Woodford. 2004. *The Monetary Policy Strategy of the ECB Reconsidered.* Centre for Economic Policy Research.

Issing, Otmar. 2008. *The Birth of the Euro.* Cambridge University Press.

Issing, Otmar. 2020. "Encompassing Monetary Strategy Review." White Paper No. 68, Sustainable Architecture for Finance in Europe, Leibniz Institute for Financial Research. June.

Issing, Otmar, Vitor Gaspar, Ignazio Angeloni, and Oreste Tristani. 2001. *Monetary Policy in the Euro Area.* Cambridge University Press.

Issing, Otmar, Vítor Gaspar, Oreste Tristani, and David Vestin. 2006. *Imperfect Knowledge and Monetary Policy.* Cambridge University Press.

King, Mervyn. 2002. "No Money, No Inflation: The Role of Money in the Economy." Lecture at the First Economic Policy Forum, Banque de France, Paris, France. March 13.

King, Mervyn. 2024. "Inflation Targets: Practice Ahead of Theory." Paper prepared for "The Quest for Nominal Stability" conference, Sveriges Riksbank, Stockholm, Sweden. May 24.

Schumpeter, Joseph. 1918. "Das Sozialprodukt und die Rechenpfennige. Glossen und Beiträge zur Geldtheorie von heute (The National Product and Counting Pennies: Glosses and Contributions to the Monetary Theory of Today)." *Archiv für Sozialwissenschaft und Sozialpolitik (Archives for Social Science and Social Policy)* 44 (3).

CHARLES I. PLOSSER: We have some time for a few questions, but I'd like to remind everybody to wait for a microphone and tell us who you are. So, questions? Comments?

MATTHEW KLEIN: My name is Matthew Klein. I'm curious for everyone's perspective, particularly Georg's, about the Swiss National Bank's experience over the past few years. Where they mostly avoided the pandemic-related inflation that the other major economies did. They didn't raise interest rates nearly as much, but they also used much more balance sheet capacity to manage the exchange rate.

I'm curious maybe if everyone could talk about how that worked and what lessons there might be for the other major economies. Thank you.

PLOSSER: Would you like to respond?

GEORG RICH: Well, are you talking about the most recent period? Yeah, well, I think the Swiss National Bank tightened earlier than most central banks, and the result was that inflation rose to 3.5%, whereas everywhere else, I mean, they rose to 10%.

And the exchange rate, of course, served to insulate the domestic economy from these high foreign inflation rates. So I think we are very fortunate in that regard.

MICHAEL D. BORDO: My comment is for Georg, Otmar [Issing], and Axel [Weber]. If you delve into the history of the SNB [Swiss National Bank], as I did once with Harold James for its one-hundred-year anniversary in 2007, or of the DBB [Deutsche Bundesbank] as Otmar wrote in the NBER "Great

Inflation" conference volume in 2013, the guiding concept for monetary policy always was to maintain price stability—they followed the "'stability culture."' This was the case long before the monetarists Milton [Friedman], Anna
[Schwartz], Karl [Brunner], and Allan [Meltzer] came along. So the evidence
on inflation across countries, showing that Switzerland and Germany were
below the other advanced countries during the Great Inflation of the 1970s,
held long before that time. Would you please be so kind and elaborate on this.

RICH: Well, the Swiss, until 1973, were really staunch believers in the gold
standard. And if you believe that the gold standard is a great source of stability, then you may be right, but I'm somewhat skeptical about that.

PLOSSER: Otmar, Charles.

OTMAR ISSING: Charlie, my pleasure. I think on the German history, one
should be aware of the fact that we had two devastating events, money was
totally destroyed in 1923 and in 1948.
    So these two episodes from which one generation suffered left a deep
imprint on German thinking on the importance of price stability. And the
special role of the D-mark was also due to the fact that it was the first kind of
national confidence, because anything else was destroyed by the Nazi past.
    And then came the '70s and '80s, in which, basically, the Bundesbank
dominated the monetary policy in Europe. Strictly for those central banks
who had fixed their exchange rate to the D-mark like the Dutch central bank.
Those central banks that did not follow the pace of the Bundesbank in the
disinflation process, like the French, had to devalue their currency. This experience laid the basis for finally agreeing on the introduction of the euro as a
common currency.
    But unfortunately, I think overoptimistic views that all euro-area countries
would give the same importance to price stability has not come true. We still
see differences, so to say, in this kind of stability culture.

AXEL A. WEBER: Charles, if I may add one aspect, having lived in Switzerland
for ten years. The exchange rate has played a key role in the conduct of monetary policy by the Swiss National Bank. They have intervened massively in
the foreign exchange market. But they couldn't prevent a more than 20%
appreciation of the Swiss franc, and that has cushioned domestic inflation
against the stronger inflation abroad. And the Swiss National Bank, like the

Bundesbank in the old days, never considered very low inflation in the range between zero and 2% as a problem. I think that this pragmatism about inflation being consistent with price stability if it was in a range of zero to 2% has helped Switzerland as a small open economy with a strong currency to import less global inflation. A small, open economy can never isolate itself completely from global inflation, as Georg was saying, but the exchange rate appreciation helped cushion the Swiss economy against the inflation shock.

PLOSSER: Thank you, Axel. Any other questions or comments?

JACK KRUPANSKY: Hi, Jack Krupansky again—maybe this question actually is for the US Fed, but since the topic here is Europe, and it was on the charts here: How do you square the three concepts of the rate of inflation, the heightened price levels, and then this vaguer concept of price stability, which the unions may treat as, "Hey, price stability means we get to raise our wages a lot more than inflation." So do Europe and the UK have a plan for how they're going to deal with those heightened prices? And if you look at the US, we just had this port strike and people celebrated how short the port strike was, but they ignore the fact that there's this heightened wage cost that is probably going to percolate through the system in the next year or so, and whether the Fed has a plan for that. How does Europe want to deal with those heightened wages and heightened price levels?

WEBER: Well, I think that European data on wages, and in particular real wages, show that real wages declined massively during this inflation boom. And as soon as inflation started coming down, wage negotiations kicked in and more than recovered the previous loss in purchasing power. We have countries like the Netherlands, where currently wage increases are trending at 7%. The unions in some eurozone countries have not only made up for the accumulated purchasing power loss they suffered from the inflation increase; we are actually at a point where the real wage improvements relative to pre-pandemic levels have more than caught up by now.

The real concern for central banks, then, should be the emergence of second-round effects. Central banks, in my view, should not yet declare victory over inflation, since I believe the period of elevated inflation is not over. The lingering effects from wage increases and cost pass-throughs could lead to future inflation data not looking quite as favorable. I do think that declaring victory too early could undermine central bank credibility if the real wage increases we're now seeing in some of the European economies would reignite inflation in the future.

ISSING: I fully agree with you, Axel, claiming victory over inflation is premature; this neglect of risks might lead to another phase of rising inflation. But my point is the following.

Unions ask compensation for inflation. I think we have to separate two things. This period of inflation driven by commodity price increases implied a huge term of trade loss for the economy. And for this part no compensation should be accepted because this is a welfare loss that has to be borne by the whole country, by all groups.

No group can be excluded from this process. If the unions still ask compensation for this inflation part, then we will have a continuing process of rising inflation correlated with rising unemployment; these two things, then, unfortunately, may come together.

CHARLES GOODHART: And not only that, we've got a fiscal problem as well with public sector deficits and debt ratios, which are out of hand in many cases and quite unsustainable in several countries.

PLOSSER: I think we are out of time for this session, and I want to thank all our participants for their comments and observations and the audience for their questions.

The Search for a Nominal Anchor

Introduction

Kevin Warsh

Welcome to a new discussion, "The Search for a Nominal Anchor." It's an honor to be here moderating this panel. I've long been a friend of and admirer of the work of Greg [Hess], Peter [Ireland], and Bob [Hetzel]. "The Search for a Nominal Anchor" is a good title. I don't know which of our organizers entitled it, but I take the language as important and consequential.

It's a *search* for an anchor because we're on an expedition, as if the nominal anchor itself might be hiding in plain sight, or missing altogether.

There is a tendency when economists get together to think back to some bygone era when policy was somehow perfected. That era never existed. That's the myth of "the good old days." If only we could go back to a time when we were good at counting money, right? And when the conduct of monetary policy was easy? That day didn't exist.

So what we're going to try to do over the course of the next forty-five minutes to an hour is do a bit of history—with one eye on lessons learned and another eye on what can be done to improve policymaking going forward.

And I will start our discussion with a line from [Friedrich] Hayek that some of you might know. He said: "If old truths are to retain their hold on men's minds, they must be restated in the language and concepts of successive generations."

Well, that's our deliverable. At the end of the day, we want to sow the seeds for making Hayek's words a reality.

Before I turn the podium over to Peter to start with some history, I will reiterate what Condi [Rice] said at the outset of the discussion about the environment in which the broad contour of economic policymaking is happening.

I will state it less diplomatically than Condi did: We have two hot wars and one larger cold war. The world, in a geopolitical, national-security sense, is, as our former colleague and dearest friend George Schultz said, at a hinge point in history. So if there were ever a moment where economic policy, including the conduct of monetary policy, needed a stronger ballast, it would be now.

If we continue to make grave errors in the conduct of economic policy, it will only make those geopolitical challenges harder, the world less prosperous, and the environment more dangerous.

The goal of this panel is to ask the right questions, including whether we have a reliable theoretical and empirical model for inflation.

We won't come out of today's discussion with easy answers. But if we are asking the big questions, we should be able to agree that the answer to this question has little to do with the latest data from the US government—especially when rounding to a hundredth of a decimal point whether the US is on track or off track to a 2% inflation target.

Looking so far to the right of the decimal point strikes me as indicative of a policy that is decidedly off track. I worry that policymakers are not asking the right questions. A preoccupation with whether the next move is 0, 25, or 50 basis points? Or a preoccupation with Fed forecasts of what policy will look like in eighteen months' time? Each strikes me as a task far less important than the critical task this group has been called together to do.

So in some sense, we need to think anew about fundamental questions. What is inflation? What causes it? Is the central bank responsible for it or just a bystander? And how should inflation be measured? It is, as I said a moment ago, not obvious that key policymakers have the right empirical or theoretical framework for answering these questions. But it's high time we establish more robust frameworks, especially given the policy mistakes and the inflation damage of this recent period.

In some broad sense, we have to begin with one question: Is America's inflation problem a result of Americans earning too much and living too well—or is it because our government is living too well, spending and printing too much? Some in our profession can try to dodge the essential inflation question and turn to DSGE [dynamic stochastic general equilibrium] models like FRB/US and other output gap models. But in so doing, it strikes me we're unlikely to make much progress.

A second point of emphasis from your moderator is whether policymakers are ready to consider the benefits to a new, reformed inflation framework.

I have a bit of an old-fashioned view: Monetary policy has something to do with money. This ought not be a dirty word in the world of central banks. But if one were to do a search of FOMC [Federal Open Market Committee] transcripts, the paucity of references to money speaks volumes about what most policymakers think about money and its relevance to the Fed.

If Milton Friedman were here, I think he would be inspired by the Hayek quote I referenced. Milton would not have returned as if by rote to his views of thirty or forty years ago. Instead, I'd suggest he'd be thinking anew about the role of money on inflation in the modern world.

Finally, before I turn it over to my panelists: Absent finding a nominal anchor, absent developing a rigorous new framework, I'm afraid our profession is left with some puzzling contradictions. Contradictions that might be glossed over at a time that the financial markets are at new all-time highs, but contradictions with which policymakers should rightly wrestle.

Is it right for a central bank to take credit for a soft landing if it does not take responsibility for the inflation surge that preceded it? Is it right for a central bank that had announced in August of 2020 a brand-new framework for inflation—so-called flexible average inflation targeting—to leave it in limbo? After all, it's never been renounced or replaced. And is it right for the Fed to say that they'll revisit that framework in a year or eighteen months' time? Or should the Fed treat the failures of its 2020 framework to be the first order of business?

Another contradiction: The Fed talks often about "data dependence." It's a piety thrown around. I think there are only two problems with it: the data and the dependence. The data being released by the Bureau of Labor Statistics and other statistical agencies are lagging indicators, revealing only a bit of where the economy once was. They are not forward indicators as to where the economy is going. Nor is the data a great contemporaneous indicator.

A final puzzling contradiction: Absent finding a new framework or a new nominal anchor, we should better judge the role of the new policy tool created in the darkest days of the Global Financial Crisis. That is, quantitative easing (QE). At the time, we policymakers described QE as a key, complementary tool in the conduct of monetary policy. We at the Fed cut interest rates to zero. We had run out of other tools. And we said we needed monetary policy to be looser. So we started buying the bonds and mortgages of other parts of the US government.

But now, as we fast-forward, the Fed retains a $7 trillion-plus balance sheet. And we are told by policymakers, curiously, that the asset purchases have nothing to do with monetary policy. I find it a puzzling contradiction. Either it is monetary policy or it's not.

And if it is monetary policy, the Fed is loosening conditions with the policy rate but seemingly tightening policy by shrinking its balance sheet. What is the theoretical or empirical model to incorporate these crosscurrents? Or is it only monetary policy when we want it to be?

These are some of the questions, none of the answers.

I'm going to turn first to our panelists to give us a bit of a history and see if we can't move the discussion forward. So let me introduce Peter and welcome him to the podium.

7

Money in the Search for a Nominal Anchor

Peter N. Ireland

Introduction

Founded by Karl Brunner and Allan Meltzer, the Shadow Open Market Committee first met on September 14, 1973. At the time, inflation as measured by the Consumer Price Index had reached 7.4%.[1] The SOMC's principal objective from the start, Meltzer (2000, 120) recalls, was to reject the price and wage controls favored by President Richard Nixon, "large parts of the business community, the Congress, many economists, and parts of his own government," and to "show that better policy choices were available and that inflation could be controlled at acceptable cost, if the Federal Reserve controlled money growth."

Despite the SOMC's best efforts, things would get much worse before they got any better. Inflation peaked at 12.2% in November 1975 and, after falling back to 5.0% in December 1976, spiked higher again, reaching 14.6% in March 1980. And while inflation did come down substantially from 1980 through 1983 under Federal Reserve Chair Paul Volcker, it was not until the early 1990s, under Chair Alan Greenspan, that inflation finally stabilized at levels below 3.0%.

Throughout this extended period, the SOMC consistently advocated for a monetary policy strategy focused on controlling inflation. In doing so, Brunner, Meltzer, and other SOMC members relied on a set of arguments that, while unpopular at the time, have since become widely accepted by academic economists and Federal Reserve policymakers alike. More specifically, however, the SOMC also consistently favored an operational approach that emphasized the use of the monetary base instead of the federal funds rate as the monetary policy instrument and the growth rate of a broader monetary aggregate as an intermediate target. These elements of SOMC doctrine have never received much endorsement, either among academics or at the Fed.

After reviewing these points of convergence and divergence between the SOMC and the mainstream, this paper describes how the SOMC's preferred money-based strategy and Committee members' arguments for it evolved over time. It then shows that these arguments still apply with force today. Had policymakers paid more attention to the behavior of the monetary base and the broader monetary aggregates, the return to high inflation in 2021— what Levy (2024, 261) calls the "biggest monetary policy error" since the 1970s—would likely have been avoided. And if policymakers pay more attention to the monetary base and the broader monetary aggregates, the way back to price stability will become much clearer, too.

The SOMC and the Mainstream: Points of Convergence

Poole, Rasche, and Wheelock (2013, 64–71) identify nine core principles that underlie the SOMC's preferred monetary policymaking framework. These are the beliefs that:

1. Inflation is a monetary phenomenon.
2. The market system is inherently stable and economic growth reverts to a natural rate.
3. Monetary policy should focus on price stability.
4. Adverse supply shocks reduce potential output.
5. The cost of disinflation reflects the monetary authority's credibility.
6. Policy should be rules-based and transparent.
7. Money-market (nominal interest rate) targeting is flawed.
8. Money demand is stable.
9. The money stock is controllable.

Poole et al. (2013) and Romer (2013) agree that, while unpopular at the time of the SOMC's founding, principles 1 through 6 have since become generally accepted by academic economists and Federal Reserve policymakers alike. Ireland (forthcoming-a) likewise shows how these principles emerged from developments in macroeconomic theory during the 1960s through the 1990s and were eventually reflected in the Federal Open Market Committee's (FOMC) (2012) "Statement on Longer-Run Goals and Monetary Policy Strategy."

The assertion that "inflation is a monetary phenomenon" echoes, of course, Milton Friedman's (1968, 39) famous dictum that "inflation is always and everywhere a monetary phenomenon." As Karl Brunner emphasizes in a position paper for the SOMC's September 1979 meeting, this view was not widely shared during the 1970s. Brunner (1979b, 9) quotes Arthur Okun to illustrate this point:

> A prevalent view asserts that the "inflation of the seventies is a new and different phenomenon." It follows that it "cannot be diagnosed correctly with old theories or treated effectively with old prescriptions" (Arthur Okun, 1979). The "new phenomenon" requires a correspondingly new diversified approach. This would include "enough fiscal-monetary discipline to provide a safety margin against excess demand, a coordinated federal initiative to reduce private costs and constructive measures to obtain price-wage restraint."

That is, monetary policy plays at most a supporting role in the fight against inflation. More important tools include tax and regulatory policies that directly reduce firms' costs of production and the promotion of "voluntary" wage and price controls. In the policy statement prepared for the same SOMC meeting, Allan Meltzer (1979, 4) offers a very different view, putting monetary policy at the heart of an anti-inflationary program:

> For several years, the Committee has urged the Federal Reserve to adopt a policy of steady, pre-announced reductions in money growth. If this policy had been adopted and maintained for the past three years, we would enter the 1980's with low inflation, low market interest rates and less uncertainty about the future.

In announcing the Federal Reserve's explicit 2% target for inflation, the FOMC's (2012) own "Statement on Longer-Run Goals and Monetary Policy Strategy" comes much closer to Meltzer's position than to Okun's:

> The inflation rate over the longer run is primarily determined by monetary policy, and hence the Committee has the ability to specify a longer-run goal for inflation. The Committee judges that inflation at the rate of 2 percent, as measured by the annual change in the price index for personal consumption expenditures, is most consistent over the longer run with the Federal Reserve's statutory mandate.

Notably, however, the FOMC's statement omits any reference to "money growth" from its description of monetary policy goals and strategy.

Brunner (1970) and Mayer (1978) both list stability of the free-market economy as a core monetarist principle. Public debate over this belief erupted early on in SOMC history when, in response to questioning from Senator William Proxmire, Fed chair Arthur Burns (1973, 792) wrote:

> Neither historical evidence nor the thrust of explorations in business cycle theory over a long century gives support to the notion that our economy is inherently stable. On the contrary, experience has demonstrated repeatedly that blind reliance on the self-correcting properties of our economic system can lead to serious trouble. Discretionary economic policy, while it has at times led to mistakes, has more often proved reasonably successful. The disappearance of business depressions, which in earlier times spelled mass unemployment for workers and mass bankruptcies for businessmen, is largely attributable to the stabilization policies of the last 30 years.

In his position paper for the SOMC meeting held the following spring, Brunner (1974a, 19–20) responded with a "short critique" that begins:

> The Federal Reserve's fundamental thesis of an inherently unstable process generating on its own major fluctuation may be very plausible, just as plausible as the rotation of the sun around the earth. It is quite probable that this thesis guided much of the Chairman's previous activities at the National Bureau of Economic Research. Still, all the time series collected yield no relevant evidence favoring this thesis against the rival view of a fundamentally stable process.

As evidence to support the stability hypothesis instead, Brunner goes on to cite Friedman and Anna Schwartz's (1963) *A Monetary History of the United States*, related work by Friedman (1964) on serial correlation in the amplitude of business cycle expansions and contractions, and his own research (Brunner et al. 1973) on the effects of monetary and fiscal policies on inflation in Italy, Germany, and the US.

As Hetzel (2024) explains, disagreements over the inherent stability or instability of the free-market economy continue to underlie debates among economists, both in academia and at the Fed, even if participants in those debates don't explicitly recognize that source. But as Hetzel emphasizes as well, New Keynesian models such as those in Ireland (1996) and Goodfriend and King (1997) provide a contemporary restatement of the monetarist principle of stability, through what Blanchard and Galí (2007) call "the divine coincidence": their implication that a monetary policy directed at stabilizing the aggregate nominal price level simultaneously allows the economy to adjust efficiently to nonmonetary shocks. As noted by Ireland (forthcoming-a), the FOMC's (2012) Statement on Longer-Run Goals and Monetary Policy Strategy recognizes that the divine coincidence can often apply in practice as well as theory, when it states:

> In setting monetary policy, the Committee seeks to mitigate deviations of inflation from its longer-run goal and deviations of employment from the Committee's assessments of its maximum level. These objectives are generally complementary.

Once again, however, it is noteworthy that, just as the FOMC's statement makes no reference to "money," most New Keynesian models describe monetary policy, even under the divine coincidence, exclusively in terms of interest rates, assigning little or no role to money supply and demand.[2]

By emphasizing that monetary policy should focus on price stability, the SOMC also rejected the notion of an exploitable Phillips curve that the Fed could use to achieve lower unemployment in exchange for higher inflation. In his statement to the House Banking Committee, also presented at the March 1979 SOMC meeting, Karl Brunner (1979a, 126) argues:

> The choice is not between lower unemployment and higher inflation on the one side or higher unemployment and lower inflation on the other side. Our choice lies between a temporary increase of unemployment in the present above its normal level in conjunction with a return to the normal level and no inflation in the future on one side, or, on the other side, permanent inflation with intermittent spurts of unemployment beyond its normal level augmented very likely by an increase in the normal level.

This view contrasts sharply with Samuelson and Solow's (1960, 192) description of the Phillips curve as showing "the menu of choice between different degrees of unemployment and price stability." But it resembles quite closely the position that underlies the inflation targeting strategies advocated by many economists and implemented by many central banks around the world today, as Bernanke et al. (1999, 16) explain, in terms that echo Brunner's (1979a):

> Thirty years ago, policy-makers and most economists supported "activist" monetary policies, which were defined as policies whose purpose was to keep output and unemployment close to their "full employment" levels at all times. Supporters of activism believed that there was a long-run tradeoff between inflation and unemployment known as the Phillips curve. . . . To many economists and policy-makers, it seemed possible that actively managed monetary (and fiscal) policies could be used to maintain maximum employment pretty much all the time. That happy outcome was not to be. . . . In short, the activist monetary policies of the 1960s and 1970s not only failed to deliver their promised benefits, they helped to generate inflationary pressures that could be subdued only at high economic cost.

Likewise, that adverse supply shocks decrease potential as well as actual output was first noted by Brunner at the September 1975 SOMC meeting, in reaction to the severe and prolonged recession of 1973–75. Brunner's (1975b) position paper cites an earlier report by Norman Bowsher (1975, 2), which breaks the downturn into two stages:

> The first stage, which began in the late fall of 1973, was largely a response to constraints placed on aggregate supply. The second stage, which began in the early fall of 1974, reflected, in addition, a reduction in the growth of demand for goods and services.

The supply shocks that triggered stage one include, in Bowsher's view, higher oil prices, poor weather conditions, and the adverse effects of price controls. Brunner (1975b, 15) builds on Bowsher's assessment by making a distinction of his own, with key implications for monetary policymaking:

> The distinction between a "real shock decline" in output and a "cyclic decline" in output seems to me important for rational policy making. The latter creates an "output gap" really absent from the former. A disregard of the two distinct processes thus magnifies estimates of the "potential gap" to be removed by expansionary policies. An inadequate analysis of the decline in output observed since November 1973 thus

reenforces the danger of inflationary financial responses on the part of policy-makers.

Brunner (1975b, 18) goes on to contrast his own views with those of the "Keynesian establishment," summarized in a newspaper article by Soma Golden (1975) that quotes Walter Heller and Franco Modigliani in arguing for a policy of sustained low interest rates in the face of persistent economic weakness.

The SOMC's (1976, 3) September 1976 policy statement echoes Brunner's earlier concerns, stating that "monetary policy can contribute to cyclical recovery but can do little to replace capacity lost in the shocks of recent years." That statement, controversial at the time, gradually found support, first, in the development of real business cycle models by Finn Kydland and Edward Prescott (1982) and John Long and Charles Plosser (1983) in the 1980s and then, by extension, in New Keynesian models where, as noted above, the divine coincidence applies. In all of these models, potential output, instead of following a smoothly evolving trend, fluctuates at high frequencies as shocks hit the economy from the supply side, and monetary policy should allow actual output to fluctuate, too, in order to track those movements in potential. As Galí (2015, 103) explains:

> Stabilizing output is not desirable in and of itself. Instead, output should vary one-for-one with the natural level of output. . . . There is no reason, in principle, why the natural level of output should be constant or take the form of a smooth trend, because all kinds of real shocks are a potential source of variation in its level. In that context, policies that stress output stability (possibly around a smooth trend) may generate potentially large deviations of output from its natural level and, thus, be suboptimal.

Ireland (forthcoming-a) discusses how, similarly, real business cycle and New Keynesian theories helped shape the FOMC's (2012) monetary policy strategy statement.

The idea that the costs of disinflation depend on the credibility of the central bank's commitment to price stability was first raised by Brunner (1974b) in his position paper for the September 1974 SOMC meeting. There, Brunner responds to comments by James Tobin on the SOMC's earlier recommendation to end inflation through a program of gradual reductions in money growth. Tobin (1974, 228–29) summarizes a pair of simulations, based on two alternative estimates of the Phillips curve slope parameter, both indicating that the SOMC's prescribed policy would require a prolonged period of high unemployment. In the more pessimistic case, "unemployment rises steadily for eight years" in exchange for modest reductions in inflation. Brunner (1974b, 10) provides a very early reference to the Lucas (1976) critique in his counterargument:

The Phillips curve models showed in the recent past repeatedly deviations from observations sufficiently large to question the relevance of the longer-run simulation exercised by Tobin. But these longer-range simulations are really made quite dubious and probably quite irrelevant by a property of economic systems recently emphasized by Robert Lucas at a Carnegie-Rochester Conference. . . . The structural properties and response patterns of an economic system are not invariant to different policies and policy patterns. The mechanical simulation of a policy program substantially different from policy patterns prevailing over the sample period used to estimate the model yields thus little information about the consequences of the program proposed. In particular, the simulations of a model estimated over a period of accelerating inflation probably exaggerates the longer-run unemployment effects of an anti-inflationary program.[3]

Brunner (1982, 10–11) restates these ideas even more bluntly:

First and foremost, we need to emphasize that a necessary and sufficient condition for lower inflation is a correspondingly lower rate of monetary growth. We deny on the other hand that a recession of sufficient length and depth is a necessary condition of an anti-inflationary program. Whether or not the monetary retardation required for our purposes translates into a recession depends crucially on the credibility of the policies pursued.

Brunner (1982, 11) concludes by quoting Goodfriend (1981, 13): "The policy will work well only if the monetary authority establishes a commitment to bring money growth down that is credible to the financial markets and the public in general."

Today, the important roles played by expectations and credibility in determining the costs of disinflation are widely acknowledged. For example, in outlining his strategy for bringing US inflation back down after its 2021 surge, Federal Reserve Chair Jerome Powell (2022, 3–5) lists as two of the three "important lessons" learned from the experience of the "high and volatile inflation of the 1970s . . . that the public's expectations . . . can play an important role" and that "the employment costs of bringing down inflation are likely to increase . . . as high inflation becomes more entrenched in wage and price setting." Powell (2022, 2) departs, however, from SOMC prescriptions by describing the Fed's disinflationary strategy in terms of higher settings for interest rates, rather than lower rates of money growth.

Finally, the SOMC preferred a transparent and rules-based approach to monetary policymaking, strongly and from the very start, through its advocacy of a strategy based on preannounced targets for money growth. The policy statement approved at the Committee's first meeting in September 1973 reads quite simply:

We believe the objective of monetary policy over the next year should be to reduce the rate of inflation. To accomplish this, the growth rate of money for the next six months should be at a steady rate of about 5½%. (SOMC 1973, 7)

As actual rates of money growth and inflation continued to rise, the Committee extended the horizon over which its preannounced plans for money growth applied. The Committee's policy statement prescribes 6% money growth for 1978, then continues:

We recommend reduction in the average rate of monetary expansion by 1% a year until a noninflationary rate of monetary expansion is achieved. The Federal Reserve should publicly commit monetary policy to this stabilizing long-term monetary course in order to fulfill its legal responsibilities under the Federal Reserve Reform Act of 1977. (SOMC 1978a, 3–4)

And the SOMC continued to emphasize the advantages of a rules-based approach to policymaking, even after lower rates of inflation were achieved under Federal Reserve Chairs Paul Volcker and Alan Greenspan. On the

occasion of its twenty-fifth anniversary, the SOMC (1998, 7) emphasized
that at the Fed,

> decisions remain ad hoc. Once memories of the costs of inflation fade,
> or there is a change in membership and leadership, the Federal Reserve
> might return to past policies. . . . To avoid a return to these mistaken
> policies, we will continue to urge the Federal Reserve to develop and
> adopt systematic rules for monetary policy.

As many of the essays collected in Bordo et al. (2024) make clear, John
Taylor's (1993) article, "Discretion Versus Policy Rules in Practice," played
a huge role in convincing economists and financial market participants that
Federal Reserve policy can, and should, be made with reference to a benchmark prescribed by a relatively simple rule. But while the Federal Reserve's
March 2024 semiannual report to Congress presents the interest rate settings
prescribed by the Taylor (1993) rule and several variants, it also argues:

> As benchmarks for monetary policy, simple policy rules have impor-
> tant limitations. One of these limitations is that the simple policy rules
> mechanically respond to only a small set of economic variables and
> thus necessarily abstract from many of the factors the FOMC consid-
> ers when it assesses the appropriate setting of the policy rate. (Board of
> Governors 2024, 42)

Brunner (1983, 9–10) anticipates and provides the other side of this argument, from the SOMC viewpoint:

> The idea that central banks should "look at everything" and "flexibly
> adjust to circumstances" still finds much sympathy and has an intui-
> tive appeal. But, of course, nobody can look at everything. Attention
> is unavoidably selective and guided by some prior conception. . . . The
> consequences of a strategy of "flexible adjustment to prevailing cir-
> cumstances" are highly sensitive to the reliability of the policymakers'
> detailed knowledge of the economy's response structure. . . . But in spite
> of all the claims to such knowledge, implicitly raised by advocates of
> activist policymaking, we do not possess the required degree of knowl-
> edge. The pursuit of flexible adjustments . . . becomes thus a speculative
> game. Attempts to offset shocks are translated with substantial likeli-
> hood into effects reinforcing the shocks operating on the economy.

A noteworthy gap remains, therefore, between the SOMC's and the Federal Reserve's confidence in the use of monetary policy rules. Even deeper disagreements appear, however, over the appropriate roles of interest rates versus the money stock as instruments, indicators, and targets for successful monetary policymaking.

The SOMC and the Mainstream: Points of Departure

The biggest departure of the SOMC's framework from conventional wisdom, both past and present, comes through the principle that comes seventh on the Poole et al. (2013) list: that interest rate targeting is fundamentally flawed. The SOMC's strong preference, from the very start in 1973, for money growth over interest rates as indicators of the stance of monetary policy was presaged by Brunner and Meltzer's (1968) explanation for the Great Depression, which differs from that in Friedman and Schwartz (1963). Friedman and Schwartz blame the Fed's inaction, which allowed the broad money stock and the price level to decline by more than one-third from 1929 through 1933, on an intellectual vacuum at the Fed left by the death of Benjamin Strong. Brunner and Meltzer argue, instead, that Federal Reserve officials as a group misinterpreted very low interest rates as a sign of sufficient monetary ease and ignored the contraction in the money stock as a sign of extraordinary monetary tightness.

Brunner and Meltzer (1968, 348) therefore see the Great Depression as exceptional only in its length and severity and not in its fundamental cause. In their view, it appears as just one case among many in which the "use of short-term interest rates as an indicator of monetary policy explains why the Federal Reserve regards its policy as countercyclical despite the fact that the monetary base and the money supply (currency plus demand deposits) grow at a greater rate during periods of economic expansion and a lower rate during recessions." Brunner (1975a, 12) elaborates on this point in his March 1975 SOMC position paper:

An interest target policy misleads monetary authorities and many spectators to believe that expansive (or restrictive) actions have been initiated when nothing has been done or even worse, when actually restrictive measures have been introduced. A decline in interest rates resulting from falling credit demand possesses no expansionary meaning and simply reflects one aspect of the ongoing deflationary process. Its interpretation as an expansive action by the Fed is a dangerous illusion obstructing the useful application of actually expansive policies.

The SOMC also argued frequently that interest rate targeting procedures made it difficult for the Fed to begin lowering interest rates as business activity weakened at the onset of recessions and to begin raising interest rates to prevent inflation from rising at the start of economic recoveries. Inertia around business cycle turning points was followed by overreaction later on, generating a "stop-go" pattern of monetary policy that amplified fluctuations instead of stabilizing the economy. As William Poole (1990, 63) explains, the problem of interest rate smoothing is both economic and political:

> The problem the Fed faces in keeping money growth on track is one of its own making – its policy of maintaining the federal funds rate in a very narrow band. . . . The narrow fed funds band has both economic and political disadvantages. The economic problem is that when economic conditions change the Fed sometimes has difficulty in adjusting the rate quickly enough to keep money growth from becoming procyclical. . . . The political problem . . . is that everyone knows that the Fed is directly and immediately responsible for changes in the federal funds rate and almost as directly responsible for money market rates tied closely to the funds rate. . . . People damaged by a rate change have a perfectly natural reaction = "why me?" . . . The Fed has no way to answer such a question because the timing of the Fed's rate changes in inherently arbitrary.

Critics of the SOMC's preferred alternative to federal funds rate targeting—setting preannounced targets for the growth rate of the monetary base instead—often argue that this change would allow for harmful and avoidable volatility in market rates of interest. Brunner (1981, 78) acknowledges, but then downplays the relevance of, these concerns:

> Under a policy of monetary control ongoing shocks are unavoidably absorbed and reflected by interest rates. This will indeed produce some volatility. But the nature of this volatility need be more carefully examined. Transitory shocks will be reflected by a volatile pattern of shortest and short rates with little, if any, spillover to intermediate or long term rates. Permanent shocks also affect interest rates and contribute to generate movements over the whole term structure. The crucial condition requiring our attention at this point is the fact that these movements in interest rates generated by permanent shocks operating beyond the money market cannot be removed by an interest target policy. The

latter converts these shocks into permanent accelerations (or decelerations) via monetary accommodation into corresponding accelerations (or decelerations) in the price-level and matching adjustments in the level of nominal interest rates. The uncertainty about the timing and magnitude of monetary accommodation, augmented by the uncertainty of a change in policy, tends however to produce a larger volatility of interest rates in response to permanent shocks under an interest targeting regime than under a regime of monetary control. The social cost of volatile short rates reflecting ongoing transitory shocks seems in my judgment small compared to the social cost imposed on the economy by the alternative policy.

As noted above and as Hetzel (2024) explains in more detail, New Keynesian models such as that in Goodfriend and King (1997) provide contemporary restatements of the traditional monetarist principles on the stability of the free-market economy, the primary importance of monetary policy is stabilizing the aggregate nominal price level, and the distinction between shocks to aggregate supply, which affect both the actual and natural rates of output, and shocks to aggregate demand, which lead to gaps between the actual and natural levels of output. Hetzel (2024, 4) also explains how, by using a monetary policy rule under which the nominal interest rate tracks movements in the equilibrium real interest rate—the real interest rate that would prevail in the model's real business cycle core—the central bank can optimally turn "over the determination of real variables to the unfettered operation of the price system" and thereby maintain "the output gap . . . equal to zero." Galí (2015, 103) emphasizes this point as well: Optimal monetary policy in the New Keynesian model implies that nominal interest rate must track movements in the natural real rate of interest.

While Brunner, Meltzer, and other SOMC members would surely appreciate the elegance of this theoretical result as well as the monetarist arguments for it, they might still express doubts about the ability of the Federal Reserve, in practice, to measure and track precisely movements in the equilibrium real rate. Some indication of this is given by the SOMC's response to congressional testimony by Fed chair Alan Greenspan (1993, 11), which anticipates the New Keynesian proposition by arguing that

One important guidepost is real interest rates, which have a key bearing on longer-run spending decisions and inflation prospects. In assessing

real rates, the central issue is their relationship to an equilibrium interest rate, specifically the real interest rate level that, if maintained, would
keep the economy at its production potential over time. Rates persist-
ing above that level, history tells us, tend to be associated with slack,
disinflation, and economic stagnation – below that level with eventual
resource bottlenecks and rising inflation, which ultimately engenders
economic contraction. Maintaining the real rate around its equilibrium
level should have a stabilizing effect on the economy, directing production towards its long-term potential.

The SOMC (1993, 4) policy statement that followed counters with

Analysts have no reliable way to estimate the equilibrium real interest
rate, and they cannot measure accurately or in a timely way changes in
real interest rates or changes in anticipated inflation. Hence they cannot
be certain whether real interest rates are moving toward or away from
the equilibrium real interest rate.

An SOMC position paper by William Poole (1993, 85–86) elaborates, before
concluding:

At the present state of knowledge, there is no possibility that the Fed
will be able to announce an informative quantitative target for the real
interest rate that will provide useful information to the market. . . . The
Fed should, I believe, reinforce the message of the value of monetary
aggregates targets . . . and should downplay the usefulness of the real
interest rate as a guide to policy.

The SOMC's arguments against using an interest rate rule to track movements in the equilibrium real rate anticipate the difficulties that Powell
(2018, 4) describes with reference to "the stars":

For example, u^* (pronounced "u star") is the natural rate of unemployment, r^* ("r star") is the neutral real rate of interest, and π^* ("pi star") is
the inflation objective. According to the conventional thinking, policymakers should navigate by these stars. . . . Guiding policy by the stars in
practice, however, has been quite challenging of late because our best
assessments of the location of the stars have been changing significantly.

In contrast to Poole (1993), however, Powell (2018, 11) ultimately expresses confidence in the Fed's ability to "visualize and manage" the "risks from misperceiving the stars."

It seems quite fair to say, therefore, that the SOMC's various objections to interest rate targeting have had little or no long-run impact on the consensus of academic economists or on the implementation of monetary policy by the Fed. Thomas Sargent and Neil Wallace's (1975) early result, showing that under the rational-expectations hypothesis, a monetary policy that pegs the nominal interest rate fails to pin down a determinate price level, might be interpreted as supporting the SOMC's arguments linking interest rate targeting to nominal instability. But Bennett McCallum (1981), who would later join the SOMC, qualifies this result importantly by showing that price-level determinacy under an interest rate rule is restored when the rule includes a term through which the interest rate target responds to changes in the money stock or the price level.[4] Building on this insight, Clarida et al. (2000) compare interest rate rules estimated with data pre- and post-1979 to blame macroeconomic volatility during the earlier period on the Fed's insufficient willingness to adjust its interest rate targets in response to changes in inflation and to give credit for the greater macroeconomic stability during the later period to the Fed's more vigorous interest rate response to inflation. Their results reinforce Taylor's (1993, 1999) arguments that successful monetary policy can be implemented with an interest rate instrument, provided the interest rate rule prescribes a sufficiently strong response to inflation. The SOMC, via a position paper by Robert Rasche (1992, 98), recognizes this point as well:

The singular distinction between the present funds rate operating procedure and that of the 1970s is that the current FOMC appears to be much more aggressive about implementing changes in the funds rate target, and hence the operating procedure is not characterized by the inertia of the 1970s.

Meanwhile, though from 1979 through 1982 the Federal Reserve briefly but publicly abandoned strict interest rate targeting in favor of procedures focused on bank reserves, Cook (1989) and Gilbert (1994) argue that, even during this period, many policy actions were nevertheless directed toward influencing the federal funds rate. And, as discussed in Thornton (2006), the Fed in 1982 returned to federal funds rate targeting, a practice it continues today.

Similarly, there has been absolutely no convergence between the SOMC and the mainstream on the issue of money-demand stability. Instead, two highly influential papers from the same volume of the *American Economic Review*—Bernanke and Blinder (1992) and Friedman and Kuttner (1992)— argue that money-demand equations and other statistical relationships link- ing the monetary aggregates to key macroeconomic variables break down when estimated with data starting in the early 1980s. Those same studies find, by contrast, that the federal funds rate and other short-term interest rates have much stronger predictive power for income and prices, especially in the post-1980s data. Research on money demand, both inside and outside the Fed, has largely ceased since the publication of the fourth and last edition of David Laidler's (1993) volume surveying the field.

Most recently and as discussed in more detail below, the monetary base expanded dramatically during and after the Great Financial Crisis and Great Recession of 2008–9 without kindling a noticeable acceleration in nomi- nal income growth, leading many observers to conclude that whatever links between money, income, and prices may have been seen in the past have now disappeared altogether. Federal Reserve Chair Jerome Powell's response to Senator John Kennedy in congressional testimony summarizes quite nicely the beliefs of most economists and central bankers today:

> Well, when you and I studied economics a million years ago, M2 and monetary aggregates seemed to have a relationship to economic growth. Right now, I would say the growth of M2, which is quite sub- stantial, does not really have important implications for the economic outlook. M2 was removed some years ago from the standard list of leading indicators, and just that classic relationship between monetary aggregates and economic growth and the size of the economy, it just no longer holds. We have had big growth of monetary aggregates at various times without inflation, so [it's] something we have to unlearn, I guess.[5]

Against this backdrop, whether the money stock can be accurately controlled, as the last Poole et al. (2013) SOMC principle asserts, becomes irrelevant: The Fed wouldn't want to control the money stock, even if it could do so perfectly.

Thus, Poole et al. (2013, 71) conclude their review by noting that while "many aspects of the SOMC policy framework are now widely accepted," "today there are few proponents of money supply rules." And in commenting on their paper, Christina Romer (2013, 108) admits that "reading the authors' chapter, I was struck by the overwhelming sense that 1970s monetarism would have been very sensible if it weren't for all this silly stuff about money." It remains necessary, therefore, to work harder to make sense of the SOMC's money-based operational approach and to ask again if this approach has any relevance for monetary policymaking today.

The SOMC's Money-Based Operational Approach

Throughout the 1970s, the SOMC urged the Federal Reserve to gradually reduce the rate of money growth along a preannounced path until it reached a level consistent with price stability. The SOMC's (1978a, 3) policy rule for this period is described most succinctly in its March 1978 policy statement: "We recommend reductions of 1% per year in the average rate of monetary expansion until a noninflationary rate . . . is achieved." But the rationale for the general approach—involving a gradual, preannounced deceleration of money growth—is spelled out clearly from the start, in SOMC (1973, 9–10):

> There are costs of maintaining inflation and costs of ending inflation, but there is no way to end inflation easily or without cost. Sharp and sudden swings between extremes, attempts to break expectations, false promises, ringing statements of commitment to anti-inflationary policy and controls have not succeeded during the past eight years. Less dramatic policies will cost less and will, perhaps, be more effective. They are unlikely to be less effective.

A number of the SOMC's core beliefs listed by Poole et al. (2013) underlie this view: that inflation is a monetary phenomenon, that monetary policy should focus on price stability, that the cost of disinflation reflects the monetary authority's credibility, and that policy should be rules-based and transparent. But the SOMC rule also reflects the view that money growth serves more reliably than interest rates in indicating the stance of monetary policy— a theme that, again, can be traced back to Brunner and Meltzer (1968).

Poole et al. (2013, 94–104) and Romer (2013, 111–12) observe that the specific numerical targets for money growth recommended in SOMC policy statements fluctuate noticeably from meeting to meeting. For instance, in September 1973 the SOMC recommended 5.5% money growth; in September 1976 the target fell to 4%; and in March 1978 it rose to 6%. These fluctuations, however, do not represent discretionary deviations from the

SOMC's preferred rule. Instead, they reflect the Committee's consistent application of the same rule—a deliberate but graduate moderation in the rate of money growth—starting from initial conditions that shifted over time as the Fed by contrast continued to allow for volatility in the rates of money growth and inflation. Meltzer (2000, 124) explains:

> Problems arose very early in our experience. First, the Federal Reserve did not follow our recommendations. As proponents of gradualism, we had to either propose a large correction or rebase our recommendation in light of what had happened. We almost always chose the latter course.

Similarly, from 1973 through 1978, the SOMC's money-growth targets typically refer to M1, although policy statements and position papers occasionally cite growth-rate figures for the monetary base as well. Rather than arbitrary oscillations between different measures of money, this reflects consistent application of a monetary policy framework that uses the base as its instrument and M1 growth as an intermediate target. As Brunner explains, "The monetary base effectively summarizes the behavior of the monetary authorities" (Brunner 1974a, 4). This central bank behavior—as reflected in the monetary base—"is clearly visible" in M1 even "within shorter horizons," but "dominates beyond the shorter horizons the evolution" (7) of M1 growth. The SOMC's statistical work supporting this approach, initiated by Brunner (1974a), continues with Johannes and Rasche (1980a, 1980b).[6]

Beginning in the fall of 1978, however, the SOMC shifted its emphasis away from M1 and toward the monetary base. This shift reflects concerns that regulatory changes and financial innovations could potentially make variations in M1 growth misleading signals of the monetary policy stance (SOMC 1978b, 4). At that time, growth in the dollar volume of funds held by the public in newly introduced, interest-bearing but still highly liquid assets—especially negotiable order of withdrawal (NOW) accounts and money-market mutual fund shares—began to blur the distinction between checking and savings deposits reflected traditionally by the definitions of M1 and M2. In response to those same changes, in fact, the Federal Reserve soon redefined its monetary aggregates as described by Simpson (1980), introducing two variants of M1, labeled M1-A and M1-B, with NOW accounts included in the latter but not the former, in addition to modifying the range of assets included in M2 and M3. Addressing the problem, Brunner (1982, 16)

concludes: "in the context of unresolved or unattended measurement problems for both M1 and M2 . . . monetary policymakers should provisionally
target the monetary base."

The SOMC's search for a replacement of M1 as a suitable intermediate target for policy continued into the 1990s. For a brief period in 1990 and 1991,
SOMC policy statements set recommended growth rates for M2, comparing these to the Federal Reserve's own announced targets (Poole et al. 2013,
100–101). But continuing financial innovations, discussed by Duca (2000),
Bachmeier and Swanson (2005), and Carlson et al. (2000), began to distort
the M2 figures as well. In response, William Poole (1991) argues, first, for a
modification he calls "M2-ST" (pronounced "M2 minus ST") that subtracts
small time deposits from M2. Poole (1992) then calls for a further modification, also suggested by Motley (1988), that adds institutional money-
market mutual fund shares and names this preferred monetary aggregate
"MZM" for "money zero maturity." Poole (1994, 104) traces the organizing
principle behind MZM back to the empirical definition of money suggested
by Friedman and Schwartz (1963): "currency plus all assets convertible on
demand and at par (that is, without penalty)."

Thus, while the SOMC consistently favored a policy with the monetary
base as its instrument, the Committee struggled to find an appropriate
broader monetary aggregate for use as an intermediate target, switching over
time from M1 to M2 and then MZM. Robert Rasche (1992, 97) laments,
"at a quick glance, the behavior of various monetary aggregates in the recent
past is quite bewildering." This problem—of finding the "right" monetary
aggregate—will be returned to below.

Though it was cast in terms of the monetary base more frequently than
a broader monetary aggregate, the SOMC's preferred monetary policy rule
resembles Friedman's (1960) more closely than Taylor's (1993), not only
because it focuses on the money stock instead of the interest rate but also
because, apart from issues relating to the transition from inflationary initial
conditions to price stability in steady state, it eschews any feedback from
economic conditions to its prescribed policy actions. The SOMC's arguments against the use of a more activist feedback rule echo Friedman's as
well. Friedman (1960, 87) emphasizes that because "monetary changes have
their effect after a considerable lag and over a long period and that the lag
is rather variable," departures from his constant money growth rate rule are
more likely to be destabilizing than stabilizing. Similarly, SOMC members
frequently argued that policymakers lack the timely information and detailed

knowledge of the economy's structure that would allow them to successfully implement more activist policies.

Brunner (1982, 16–17) uses the incomplete-information argument to explain why monetary policy should focus on controlling money growth, instead of nominal income or the price level directly:

> Monetary control is not exercised for its own sake. It is an instrument used to influence the behavior of the price level or of the nominal gross national product. A strategy of monetary control manipulates an intermediate magnitude as a means to influence the behavior of an ultimate target. It is claimed on occasion that this intermediate targeting is inefficient. A "final targeting" is offered as a more efficient strategy. Monetary policy should directly control the nominal gross national product. Analytic elaborations of this idea that postulate a direct control of nominal GNP by the authorities, in the sense of a special action that can immediately fix this magnitude, are hardly worth any discussion. A more relevant approach argues that an economic structure, defined by a model, implies a unique relation between policy instruments and nominal GNP. No intermediate target is needed. On the contrary, it can be shown that, given the model, the use of intermediate targeting is in general an inferior procedure. This argument depends however crucially on the assumption of full and reliable information expressed by the model. This assumption still belongs at this stage to never-never land. Controlling GNP on the basis of misconceived beliefs about the details of the economy's response structure involves substantial risks of a destabilizing activist policy pattern.

The SOMC's September 1983 policy statement makes the same point more concisely:

> Targets for nominal GNP growth have been proposed as an alternative to monetary targets. The idea is that the Federal Reserve would adjust the growth of money to achieve targets for GNP growth. We find no merit in proposals of this kind. They would increase economic instability and make money growth even more unstable than under current procedures. (SOMC 1983, 3)

Likewise, Brunner (1984) compares a "price rule" that adjusts the growth rate of the money supply to target the price level with a "quantity rule" that simply fixes the growth rate of money. He concedes (15) that while a quantity rule "avoids potential risks," it also "sacrifices potential gains of performance." But he also emphasizes that the "risks are real and the potential gains in the absence of adequate knowledge somewhat illusory."

Eventually, however, even the SOMC gave up on constant money growth rate rules. The September 1991 policy statement explains:

> For many years, we advocated and cited growth of the monetary base as the most reliable measure of Federal Reserve actions. In spring 1990, we realized that growth of the base was distorted by large increases in currency to meet demands for a relatively stable and generally acceptable money in Eastern Europe and Latin America. These distortions continue to affect the level of the monetary base but no longer substantially affect its current growth rate. Our calculations show that the annual growth of the monetary base for the year to date has remained in a range of 5 percent to 6 percent after correcting for past distortions. . . . The Federal Reserve should maintain growth of the monetary base within this range next year, excluding changes in demand for U.S. currency from the Soviet republics, Eastern Europe, Latin America or elsewhere, which should be accommodated. (SOMC 1991, 5)

Two years later, Allan Meltzer (1993) presented an SOMC position paper that introduced a simple formula for computing a target rate of growth for the monetary base, adaptively correcting for all changes in base velocity, not just those caused by increases in foreign holdings of US currency, and adjusting for changes in real GDP growth as well. According to this new rule, year-over-year growth of the monetary base gets set equal to 2% plus the three-year average of real GDP growth minus the three-year average of base velocity growth. The rule is thereby constructed to achieve 2% inflation on average but also seeks to achieve modest stabilization objectives. According to Meltzer (1987, 12–13):

> The three year moving average gives time to learn whether shocks are permanent or transitory. It provides for faster money growth relative to output in a cyclical recession and slower money growth relative to output in a cyclical expansion. Money growth adjusts to maintained changes in the growth rate of output or in the growth rate of monetary velocity. The rule does not rely on forecasts. Unlike a rule prescribing a fixed rate of money growth, the proposed rule keeps the expected price level constant.

Personnel changes also affected the nature and range of policy rules consulted by the SOMC. In November 1999, Allan Meltzer retired both as member and chair of the Committee. Charles Plosser and Anna Schwartz became cochairs, and Bennett McCallum joined as a new member. Not surprisingly, starting in November 2002, SOMC policy statements began referring to the prescriptions of the monetary policy rule proposed by McCallum (1987, 1988).[7] Like Meltzer's, the McCallum rule provides a target for the growth rate of the monetary base that adjusts, adaptively, to past changes in base velocity. Slightly different from Meltzer's, the McCallum rule prescribes a quarter-to-quarter growth rate for the monetary base and uses a four-year average of base velocity to adjust for shifts in currency and reserves demand. A more substantial distinction between the two rules comes, however, through McCallum's inclusion of an additional feedback term through which the prescribed rate of base growth would increase or decrease as nominal income fell below or rose above a target level. McCallum's (1988) experiments using a range of small-scale macroeconomic models led him to prefer a rule that placed a modest but still significant weight on this additional feedback term, marking a further departure from the constant money growth rule.

Beginning in November 2002, the SOMC's policy statements (e.g., SOMC 2002) also began referring to the settings for the federal funds rate prescribed by the Taylor (1993) rule. This might be regarded as surprising, given the SOMC's long-standing objections to the Federal Reserve's interest-rate targeting procedures. As noted above, however, McCallum's (1981, 1986) earlier research suggested that the problem with those procedures was not so much that they used an interest rate instrument but that they failed to adjust the interest rate instrument with sufficient speed and vigor in response to changes in inflation—a critical distinction recognized later by Rasche (1992) and illustrated in more detail by Clarida et al. (2000). In fact, the Taylor rule embodies what Woodford (2003, 40) calls the "Taylor principle," that is, the guideline that the interest rate must rise more than proportionally to a change in inflation to preserve the stability of inflation around its long-run target. McCallum's (2006) SOMC position paper uses both his own rule and Taylor's to evaluate Federal Reserve policy under Chair Alan Greenspan. With studies like his, the SOMC continued to argue for the usefulness of policy rules for the monetary base, even as it recognized the value of the Taylor rule as well.

Evidence of Money's Continued Relevance Today

Problems with the SOMC's reliance on M1 both as an indicator of the Fed's monetary policy stance and as an intermediate target within the Committee's preferred strategic framework arose in the early 1980s when financial innovations and regulatory changes blurred the distinction between non-interest-bearing demand deposits in M1 and interest-bearing savings deposits in M2. These problems intensified in 1983 and 1984, when observations of extremely rapid M1 growth led the SOMC to warn of a return to higher rates of inflation that, fortunately, never materialized. Meltzer (2000, 126) recounts:

The monetarist mistake was the failure to forecast the decline in inflation from 10.9% in 1981 to 3.2% in 1983 and 4.3% in 1984. . . . Money growth in 1983 and 1984 averaged 9%.

Milton Friedman (1984, 400) makes the same "monetarist mistake" in expressing these concerns:

The increased rate of monetary growth in the 1981–83 biennium suggests that we have passed the trough in inflation and that inflation will be decidedly higher from 1983 to 1985 than it was from 1981 to 1983.

As Laidler (2024, 1065) emphasizes, "This widely publicized and erroneous prediction of the imminent reappearance of double digit inflation . . . did much to undermine the empirical case for basing monetary policy on control of the money supply, even among interested lay observers."

Around this same time, however, Barnett (1980) demonstrated how economic aggregation and statistical index number theory could be used to construct more accurate measures of the money supply in circumstances—exactly like those that have prevailed in the US since the early 1980s—in which consumers derive liquidity services from a range of assets that pay interest at different rates and substitute imperfectly for one another in their portfolios. Barnett's preferred "Divisia" monetary aggregates assign different weights to these different assets based on the spreads between the interest rate on an illiquid "benchmark" asset and the interest rates paid on the liquid assets themselves.

Belongia and Ireland (2016, 1228–29) compare the growth rates of the Federal Reserve's official "simple-sum" M1 and M2 aggregates to the corresponding Divisia aggregates. Most notably, the Divisia aggregates signal a much sharper monetary contraction, not only during the 1983–84 episode but throughout the years of the Volcker disinflation. Barnett (2011, 102–11) discusses this episode, concluding (111) that "Friedman's error resulted from his use of the Fed's official simple-sum monetary aggregates, which greatly distorted what had happened to the economy's monetary service flow."

Chrystal and MacDonald (1994, 76) coin the term "Barnett critique" to refer to the broader set of findings suggesting that "problems with tests of money in the economy in recent years may be more due to bad measurement theory rather than to an instability in the link between the true money and the economy." Belongia (1996), Hendrickson (2014), and Belongia and Ireland (2016) provide illustrations of this critique, by showing that results from Bernanke and Blinder (1992), Friedman and Kuttner (1992), and related studies suggesting instability in money demand and weakness in other statistical relationships between the money stock and measures of aggregate prices and income are frequently reversed when Divisia aggregates replace simple sums in their analyses.

More recently, the usefulness of quantity-theoretic approaches to monetary policy evaluation appears to have been cast in strong doubt by the experience during and after the Great Financial Crisis and Great Recession of 2007–9 when, as noted above, the monetary base increased by a factor of four without generating anything close to a proportional increase in nominal income or the price level. However, a quick look at the data together with a small amount of reflection reveal that this conclusion is not as immediate and obvious as many seem to think.

First, as the top panel of figure 7.1 shows, a substantial fraction of this increase in the monetary base occurred during a very narrow interval at the height of the financial crisis in late 2008. As emphasized by Walter and Haltom (2009) and Ireland (2019), the Federal Reserve began paying interest on bank reserves during this time, precisely so that the huge increase in reserves required by the expansion of its emergency lending programs following the failure of Lehman Brothers and AIG would *not* put further downward pressure on the federal funds rate and thereby add to inflationary pressures. The approximate doubling of the monetary base in 2008 is, therefore, best interpreted as reflecting rightward shifts in both the demand for and supply of bank reserves that left the stance of monetary policy approximately unchanged.

It remains true that the monetary base expanded rapidly again as the Fed implemented two more waves of quantitative easing from 2009 through 2014. Allowing for the subsequent years of "quantitative tightening," however, the base just about doubled, from $1.7 trillion in January 2009 to $3.3 trillion in January 2019.[8] In absolute terms this increase appears large, but it occurred over a period spanning an entire decade, long enough for the power of compounding to kick in. When expressed as an annualized growth rate, the increase amounts just slightly less than 7% on average over 2009–19:

Board of Governors monetary base

Simple-sum M2

Divisia M2

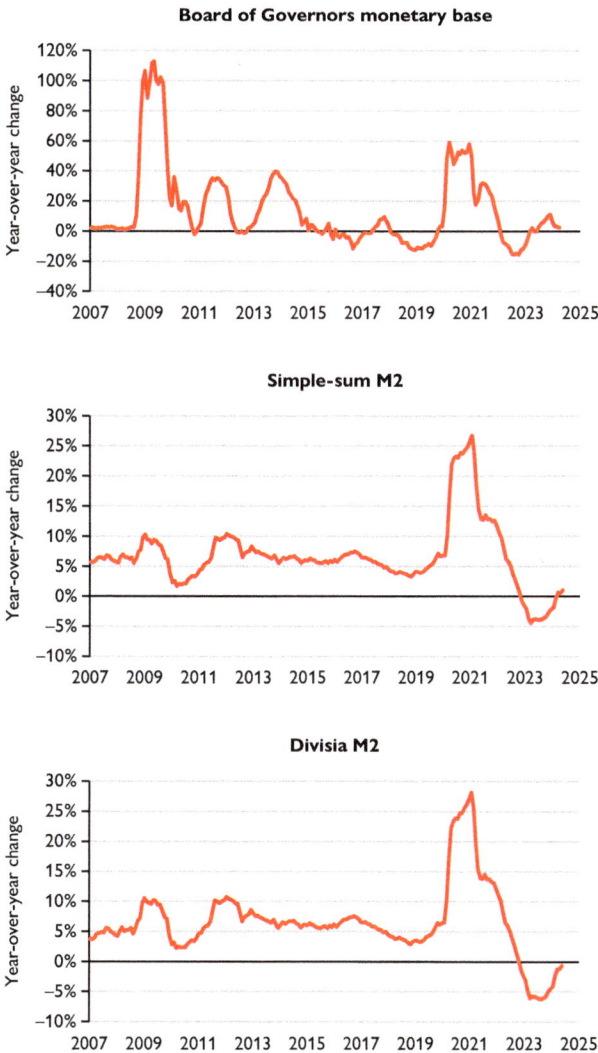

Figure 7.1. Monetary base and M2 growth.

Source: Federal Reserve Bank of St. Louis (FRED) and Center for Financial Stability (CFS).

somewhat rapid, to be sure, but as Belongia and Ireland (2024) emphasize, not out of line with postwar historical experience, and certainly quite far from hyperinflationary.

Further evidence that the 2008 increase in the supply of base money was largely "sterilized," as Walter and Haltom (2009, 2) put it, by a corresponding shift in the demand for reserves appears in the remaining two panels of figure 7.1, which reveal that neither simple-sum nor Divisia M2 growth accelerated persistently between 2008 and 2019. By contrast, M2 growth did surge during the period of zero interest rates and quantitative easing in 2020–21, presaging the unwanted inflation that followed. Reynard (2023) examines these and several other episodes of central bank balance sheet expansion in the US, Japan, and Argentina and finds that consistently, rapid growth of base money gets followed by more rapid inflation only when broad money growth accelerates as well.

These observations point to the need, first, to measure the money stock as accurately as possible and, second, to control for slow-moving trends in money demand when looking for quantity-theoretic links between money growth and nominal spending. As noted above, the SOMC gradually reached the same conclusions post-1980, through Poole's (1991, 1992, 1994) work developing the MZM aggregate as an alternative to the Federal Reserve's M1 and M2 and through Meltzer's (1987, 1993) and McCallum's (1987, 1988, 2006) work with monetary policy rules that adapt to shifts in base velocity. These ideas have been used, most recently, by Belongia and Ireland (2015, 2017, 2022) and Ireland (2023, 2024, forthcoming-b) to confirm the continued relevance of measures of money within a strategic framework directed at achieving and maintaining aggregate price stability.[9]

This work extends the P-star model, which was developed by researchers at the Federal Reserve in the late 1980s at the request of then-chair Alan Greenspan and presented to an academic audience via an article in the *American Economic Review* by Jeffrey Hallman, Richard Porter, and David Small (1991). As emphasized by Ireland (2023), these facts are not just trivia. They serve as reminders that empirical work exploring quantity-theoretic linkages between monetary aggregates and the price level *were* once of at least some interest to top policymakers and their advisors at the Fed and to academic economists as well.

The original P-star model takes as its starting point the equation of exchange

$$M_t V_t = P_t Y_t \tag{1}$$

In (1), M_t denotes the money stock, V_t monetary velocity, P_t the aggregate nominal price level, and Y_t real GDP. Of course, (1) holds as an identity, by virtue of the definition of velocity as nominal GDP $P_t Y_t$ divided by the money stock M_t. The P-star model gives the equation testable implications and predictive power, however, by making assumptions about the behavior of velocity and real GDP. To accomplish this, Hallman et al. rewrite (1) to define the variable—"P-star"—that gives their model its name:

$$P_t^* = \frac{M_t V_t^*}{Y_t^*} \qquad (2)$$

In (2), V_t^* and Y_t^* denote the "natural," "equilibrium," or "trend" levels to which velocity and real GDP are expected to return in the long run. Both can vary over time, V_t^* because of persistent shifts in the demand for money relative to other assets, including those resulting from financial innovations and regulatory changes like those that affected M1 velocity in the early 1980s and M2 velocity in the early 1990s, and Y_t^* because of technological changes that generate fluctuations in the rate of long-run economic growth. The variable P_t^* then has the interpretation as the level to which aggregate prices will converge, given the current level of the money stock, as velocity and real GDP return to their own long-run levels.

Consistent with the quantity theory of money, therefore, the P-star model allows increases in the money supply to be held temporarily as excess cash balances, thereby lowering velocity, or to temporarily stimulate spending, thereby increasing real GDP, in the short run. The model implies, however, that as these effects wear off in the long run, any change in the money stock will be matched by a proportional change in the aggregate price level.[10]

Hallman et al. (1991) test the P-star model with the regression equation:

$$\Delta\pi_t = \alpha + \beta_1\Delta\pi_{t-1} + \beta_2\Delta\pi_{t-2} + \beta_3\Delta\pi_{t-3} + \beta_4\Delta\pi_{t-4} + \gamma\left(p_{t-1}^* - p_{t-1}\right) + \varepsilon_t \quad (3)$$

In this regression equation, $\pi_t = 400\left[\ln\left(P_t\right) - \ln\left(P_{t-1}\right)\right]$ denotes the quarterly inflation rate, expressed in annualized percentage-point terms; $\Delta\pi_t = \pi_t - \pi_{t-1}$ denotes the corresponding change in inflation; the lagged "price gap" variable $p_{t-1}^* - p_{t-1} = 100\left[\ln\left(P_{t-1}^*\right) - \ln\left(P_{t-1}\right)\right]$ is the percentage-point deviation of the equilibrium price level from the actual price level; and the regression error ε_t is assumed to be uncorrelated with its own lagged values as well as with the other right-hand-side variables in (3).

In (3), a positive and statistically significant estimate of the coefficient γ confirms the model's quantity-theoretic implication that inflation will accelerate when the price gap is positive, as P_t rises to meet P_t^*. Likewise, inflation will decelerate when the price gap is negative. The past changes in inflation included on the right-hand side of (3) allow the convergence of P_t to P_t^* to take place smoothly and with a longer lag. A positive and statistically significant estimate of γ, therefore, implies that the P-star price gap is a useful indicator of the effects that past money growth will have on future inflation.

Belongia and Ireland (2015, 2017) modify the P-star model to apply to nominal GDP growth instead of inflation and to account for the larger movements in monetary velocity seen in the US since 1980. The modification starts by rewriting the equation of exchange (1) as

$$M_t V_t = Q_t \qquad (4)$$

Starting from (1), (4) simply replaces the aggregate price level of real GDP on the right-hand side by their product, nominal GDP: $Q_t = P_t Y_t$. Next, the variable "Q-star" gets defined analogously to P-star as

$$Q_t^* = M_t V_t^* \qquad (5)$$

In (5) as in (2), V_t^* represents the equilibrium level of velocity. Therefore, Q_t^* is the equilibrium level of nominal GDP implied by the current level of the money stock, to which nominal GDP should converge as velocity returns to its own long-run level.

Comparing (2) and (5) reveals one key advantage of nominal GDP growth over inflation targeting when implemented with reference to the P-star model: Nominal GDP targeting does not require an estimate of the natural rate of output Y_t^*.[11] On the other hand, (5) still requires an estimate of velocity's trend value V_t^*. Hallman et al. (1991) selected M2 as their measure of money and took V_t^* to be a constant, since M2 velocity fluctuated around a constant long-run value in quarterly data from 1955 through 1988. This modeling choice, though quite convenient at the time, proved unfortunate when, in the early 1990s, the financial innovations discussed by Duca (2000), Bachmeier and Swanson (2005), and Carlson et al. (2000) caused M2 velocity to move sharply higher. As discussed further by Orphanides and Porter (2000), this shift in velocity threw the original P-star model's forecasts off track almost immediately after the publication of the Hallman et al. article.

Belongia and Ireland (2015, 2017) show, however, that movements in equilibrium velocity can be tracked closely by estimates provided by a one-sided version of the Hodrick–Prescott time-series filter (Hodrick and Prescott 1997) described by James Stock and Mark Watson (1999). Essentially, this version of the HP filter uses a long moving average of past values of velocity itself to compute a time-varying estimate of V_t^* similar to those used in Meltzer's (1987, 1993) and McCallum's (1987, 1988, 2006) rules for adjusting a target for monetary base growth for velocity shifts. Importantly, the one-sided filter's use of past data alone means that the model's estimates of V_t^* and Q_t^* can be updated with information available to policymakers in real time.

Figure 7.2 plots the velocities of both simple-sum and Divisia M2, as well as two measures of the monetary base.[12] The first measure—the St. Louis adjusted monetary base—is the one preferred by Meltzer (1993) and McCallum (2006). As its name suggests, this measure was constructed at the Federal Reserve Bank of St. Louis and adjusts for changes in reserve requirements as well as for the retail deposit sweep programs used by banks starting in the mid-1990s to minimize their required reserves.[13] Unfortunately, the St. Louis Fed discontinued this series in the fourth quarter of 2019. Hence, figure 7.2 also plots the velocity of the monetary base as computed by the Federal Reserve Board over the period since 2009. Unlike the St. Louis measure, the Board's base series is not adjusted for changes in reserve requirements, nor is it seasonally adjusted. The graph in figure 7.2 reveals, however, that base velocity computed with the Board's measure since 2009 does not appear to contain important seasonal fluctuations.

Each panel of figure 7.2 compares velocity V_t to the corresponding estimate of V_t^* obtained from the one-sided HP filter.[14] In every case—including, impressively, for the St. Louis base series, which shows a massive decline in velocity in 2008—movements in V_t^* adapt quickly to changes in velocity itself, raising hopes that, after accounting for movements in trend velocity, the P-star model will remain a useful guide, either in using a broad monetary aggregate like M2 as an intermediate target to achieve a desired path for nominal GDP as suggested by Brunner (1982), or in using the monetary base to directly target nominal GDP as suggested by McCallum (1987, 1988, 2006).

To test this hypothesis, the original P-star regression (3) can be replaced by:

$$\Delta g_t = \alpha + \beta_1 \Delta g_{t-1} + \beta_2 \Delta g_{t-2} + \beta_3 \Delta g_{t-3} + \beta_4 \Delta g_{t-4} + \gamma \left(q_{t-1}^* - q_{t-1} \right) + \varepsilon_t \quad (6)$$

In (6), $g_t = 400 \left[\ln \left(Q_t \right) - \ln \left(Q_{t-1} \right) \right]$ denotes the quarterly growth rate of nominal GDP, expressed in annualized percentage-point terms; $\Delta g_t = g_t - g_{t-1}$ denotes the corresponding change in nominal GDP growth; and the lagged

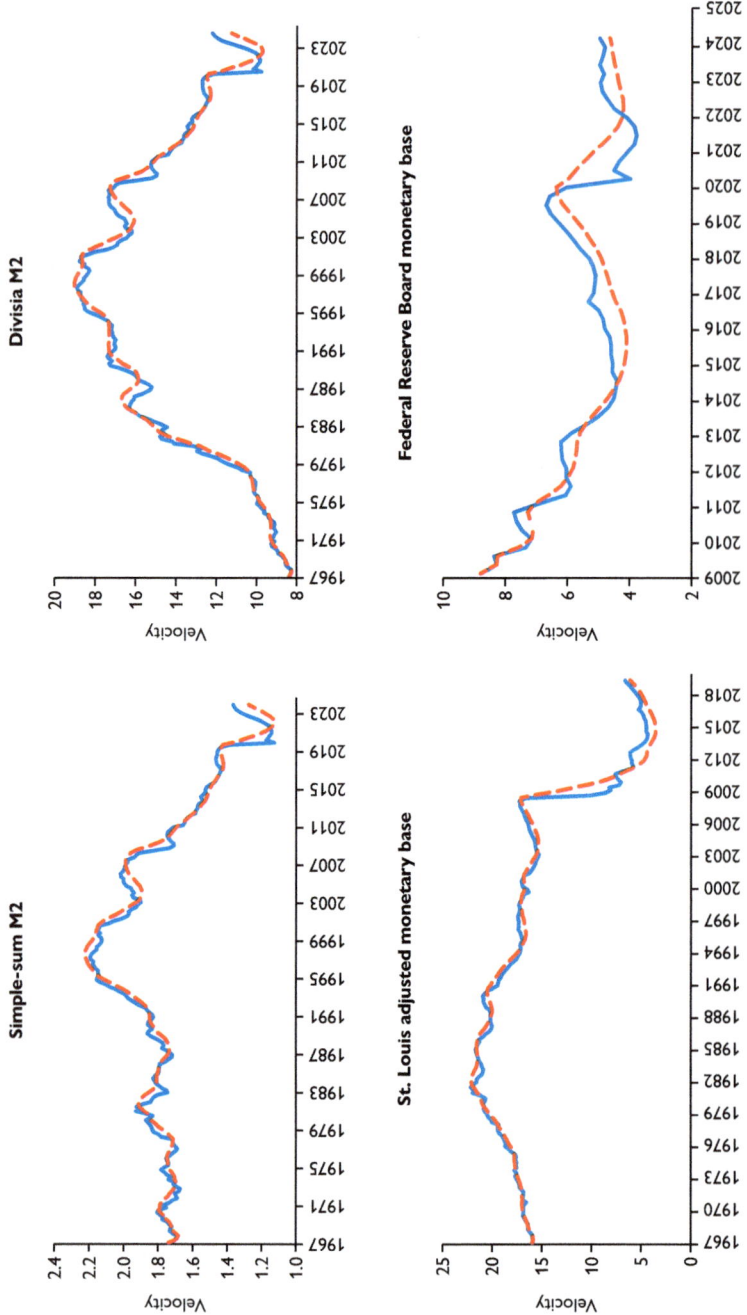

Figure 7.2. Velocities of broad and base money.

Note: Each panel shows the velocity of the indicated monetary aggregate (solid blue line) together with its equilibrium value (dashed red line), estimated using the one-sided Hodrick–Prescott filter.

Source: FRED, CFS, and author's calculations.

"nominal GDP gap" $q_{t-1}^{*} - q_{t-1} = 100 \left[\ln\left(Q_{t-1}^{*}\right) - \ln\left(Q_{t-1}\right) \right]$ is computed as the percentage-point deviation between the equilibrium and actual levels of nominal GDP. Just as before, a positive and statistically significant estimate of the coefficient γ from (6) implies that the Fed could use its influence over M2 or its direct control of the monetary base to successfully stabilize nominal income and spending. In particular, the Fed could stimulate M2 growth or directly increase the growth rate of the monetary base to increase Q_t^{*} via (5) and thereby put upward pressure on nominal GDP growth through (6). Likewise, it could act to slow the rate of M2 or monetary base growth, reducing Q_t^{*} and putting downward pressure on nominal GDP growth.

Table 7.1 displays results when (6) is estimated with quarterly data on simple-sum and Divisia M2. The longest sample period starts in 1967 Q1, as determined by the availability of data on Divisia M2, and ends in 2024 Q2. From that long sample, both estimates of the key parameter γ are large, associating a 1-percentage-point nominal GDP gap with an acceleration of nominal GDP growth, one quarter later, of more than half a percentage point. These estimates are both highly significant as well: p values less than 0.01 reject the null hypothesis that the coefficient equals zero with an extremely high degree of confidence.

Since, as noted above, the predictive power of broad money growth is widely believed to have weakened after 1980, table 7.1 also reports estimates of (6) from subsamples of data before and after 1980. Indeed, estimates of γ do decline from around 0.90 before 1980 to about 0.55 after. But even the post-1980 estimates associate the lagged nominal GDP gap with a sizable acceleration in nominal GDP growth. And estimates from both subsamples remain highly significant.

Finally, table 7.1 zooms in on two recent periods: the first starting in 1980 and running through 2007, and the second covering the period since 2008, when the Federal Reserve's target for the federal funds rate has been repeatedly constrained by the zero lower interest rate bound. The estimates of γ of across these two subsamples show that the effects of broad money growth on nominal GDP have actually become *stronger* since 2008. And while the Barnett critique favoring the use of Divisia over simple-sum monetary aggregates has often been found to be important, none of the results here appears sensitive to the choice between simple-sum and Divisia M2.

Table 7.2 focuses on estimates of (6) using the two measures of the monetary base. As noted above, base velocity moved sharply lower in 2008, when the Fed began paying interest on bank reserves. Not surprisingly, therefore,

Table 7.1. Estimated p-star forecasting equations for nominal GDP using broad money. Dependent variable: Changes in nominal GDP growth Δg_t

	1967 Q1–2024 Q2					
	Simple–Sum M2			Divisia M2		
	estimate	t stat	p value	estimate	t stat	p value
constant	−0.02	−0.08	0.94	−0.01	−0.03	0.98
Δg_{t-1}	−0.84	−13.69	0.00	−0.85	−13.94	0.00
Δg_{t-2}	−0.57	−7.35	0.00	−0.59	−7.63	0.00
Δg_{t-3}	−0.35	−4.58	0.00	−0.37	−4.85	0.00
Δg_{t-4}	−0.17	−2.87	0.00	−0.18	−3.03	0.00
$q^*_{t-1} - q_{t-1}$	0.61	6.20	0.00	0.54	6.21	0.00

	1967 Q1–1979 Q4					
	Simple–Sum M2			Divisia M2		
	estimate	t stat	p value	estimate	t stat	p value
constant	0.17	0.31	0.76	0.44	0.77	0.45
Δg_{t-1}	−0.93	−6.57	0.00	−0.94	−6.74	0.00
Δg_{t-2}	−0.72	−4.25	0.00	−0.74	−4.45	0.00
Δg_{t-3}	−0.61	−3.61	0.00	−0.64	−3.82	0.00
Δg_{t-4}	−0.21	−1.55	0.13	−0.23	−1.65	0.11
$q^*_{t-1} - q_{t-1}$	0.86	2.82	0.01	0.90	3.02	0.00

	1980 Q1–2024 Q2					
	Simple–Sum M2			Divisia M2		
	estimate	t stat	p value	estimate	t stat	p value
constant	−0.03	−0.09	0.93	−0.19	−0.54	0.59
Δg_{t-1}	−0.83	−11.92	0.00	−0.84	−12.07	0.00
Δg_{t-2}	−0.52	−5.86	0.00	−0.54	−6.07	0.00
Δg_{t-3}	−0.28	−3.16	0.00	−0.29	−3.36	0.00
Δg_{t-4}	−0.16	−2.30	0.02	−0.16	−2.40	0.02
$q^*_{t-1} - q_{t-1}$	0.58	5.47	0.00	0.52	5.40	0.00

1980 Q1–2007 Q4					
	Simple–Sum M2			Divisia M2		
	estimate	t stat	p value	estimate	t stat	p value
constant	−0.05	−0.20	0.84	−0.19	−0.81	0.42
Δg_{t-1}	−0.51	−5.81	0.00	−0.52	−5.94	0.00
Δg_{t-2}	−0.06	−0.61	0.55	−0.08	−0.83	0.41
Δg_{t-3}	0.03	0.38	0.71	0.01	0.16	0.88
Δg_{t-4}	−0.03	−0.38	0.70	−0.03	−0.40	0.69
$q^*_{t-1} - q_{t-1}$	0.34	2.89	0.00	0.27	2.87	0.01

2008 Q1–2024 Q2					
	Simple–Sum M2			Divisia M2		
	estimate	t stat	p value	estimate	t stat	p value
constant	1.25	1.34	0.19	1.29	1.38	0.17
Δg_{t-1}	−0.94	−8.06	0.00	−0.95	−8.08	0.00
Δg_{t-2}	−0.70	−4.51	0.00	−0.71	−4.56	0.00
Δg_{t-3}	−0.44	−2.86	0.01	−0.45	−2.91	0.01
Δg_{t-4}	−0.24	−2.12	0.04	−0.25	−2.16	0.04
$q^*_{t-1} - q_{t-1}$	0.72	3.74	0.00	0.66	3.65	0.00

the parameter value $\gamma = 0.04$ appears small when estimated with quarterly data on the St. Louis monetary base running from 1967 Q1 through 2019 Q3.[15] But even in this case, the p value for testing the null hypothesis that this key coefficient equals zero falls below 0.10, rejecting that hypothesis with 90% confidence.

Stronger results reemerge when (6) is estimated with data over separate subsamples, using the St. Louis base measure for periods running from 1967 Q1 through 1979 Q4 and from 1980 Q1 through 2007 Q4, and using the Federal Reserve Board's measure for a period running from 2009 Q1 through 2024 Q2—thereby allowing for a one-year transition period during which banks adjusted their demand for reserves in response to the Fed's decision to pay interest on reserves. Once more, the estimated value of γ falls after 1980, but remains sizable in both recent periods, associating a 1-percentage-point increase in the nominal GDP gap with a quarter percentage-point acceleration in nominal GDP growth one quarter later. And in each of the three subsamples, the estimate of γ retains a high degree of statistical significance.

These results confirm that, while a constant money growth rate rule like that prescribed by the SOMC from the earliest years of its existence is no longer desirable, a modified rule like Meltzer's (1987, 1993) or McCallum's (1987, 1988, 2006) can still serve as a useful alternative to Taylor's (1993), as a benchmark that uses information in measures of the money stock to

Table 7.2. Estimated p-star forecasting equations for nominal GDP using base money. Dependent variable: Changes in nominal GDP growth Δg_t

	St. Louis Adjusted Base			St. Louis Adjusted Base		
	1967 Q1–2019 Q3			1967 Q1–1979 Q4		
	estimate	t stat	p value	estimate	t stat	p value
constant	0.00	0.00	1.00	0.45	0.74	0.46
Δg_{t-1}	−0.62	−8.89	0.00	−0.81	−5.36	0.00
Δg_{t-2}	−0.38	−4.78	0.00	−0.57	−3.14	0.00
Δg_{t-3}	−0.28	−3.57	0.00	−0.47	−2.64	0.01
Δg_{t-4}	−0.07	−1.04	0.30	−0.13	−0.90	0.37
$q^*_{t-1} - q_{t-1}$	0.04	1.77	0.08	1.29	2.28	0.03

	St. Louis Adjusted Base			Board of Governors Base		
	1980 Q1–2007 Q4			2009 Q1–2024 Q2		
	estimate	t stat	p value	estimate	t stat	p value
constant	−0.07	−0.29	0.77	0.75	0.75	0.45
Δg_{t-1}	−0.51	−5.81	0.00	−0.99	−8.05	0.00
Δg_{t-2}	−0.09	−0.86	0.39	−0.79	−4.79	0.00
Δg_{t-3}	0.00	0.02	0.99	−0.53	−3.22	0.00
Δg_{t-4}	−0.04	−0.56	0.57	−0.29	−2.38	0.02
$q^*_{t-1} - q_{t-1}$	0.26	2.47	0.02	0.27	3.31	0.00

evaluate the stance—neutral, overly accommodative, or overly restrictive—of the Federal Reserve's monetary policies.

Conclusion: A Final Case Study

A final case study highlights the continued usefulness of the SOMC's preferred approach to monetary policy analysis and evaluation using the monetary base and the broader monetary aggregates. The top left-hand panel of figure 7.3 plots year-over-year growth in nominal GDP since 2009. The graph shows the extended period of moderate and stable nominal GDP growth extending from 2011 through 2019, the sharp decline in nominal spending during the 2020 economic closures, and the even more dramatic acceleration in nominal GDP growth reflecting the unwanted rise in inflation since 2021.

Most recently, nominal GDP growth has been trending downward. But will this trend continue? To help answer this question, the remaining panels of figure 7.3 plot the three measures of the nominal GDP gap used, above, in estimating (6) over periods running through the present: based on simple-sum and Divisia M2 and the Board's measure of the monetary base. Negative values for all three measures show how monetary policy put downward pressure on nominal GDP growth from 2011 through 2019. That the federal funds rate target remained in a range near zero for much of this period should bring back to mind the SOMC's warning that interest rates can be misleading indicators of the monetary policy stance. Strongly positive measures for all three money-based gap measures show, too, how excess money growth propelled nominal GDP growth and inflation higher in 2020 and 2021—dynamics reminiscent of SOMC descriptions of monetary policy during the 1970s, which emphasized how, by holding interest rates too low for too long during the early stages of economic recovery, the Fed generated procyclical fluctuations in money growth and fueled inflation's rise.

Most recently, however, all three gap measures have moved back into negative territory. These readings confirm that the interest rate increases implemented by the FOMC in 2022 and 2023 *have* worked, as intended, to greatly reduce inflationary pressures. Recent patterns in money growth help assure us that Federal Reserve policy is now consistent with a return of nominal income growth and inflation to more normal levels. In doing so, they also confirm the continued relevance of the SOMC's arguments for a money-based operational strategy.

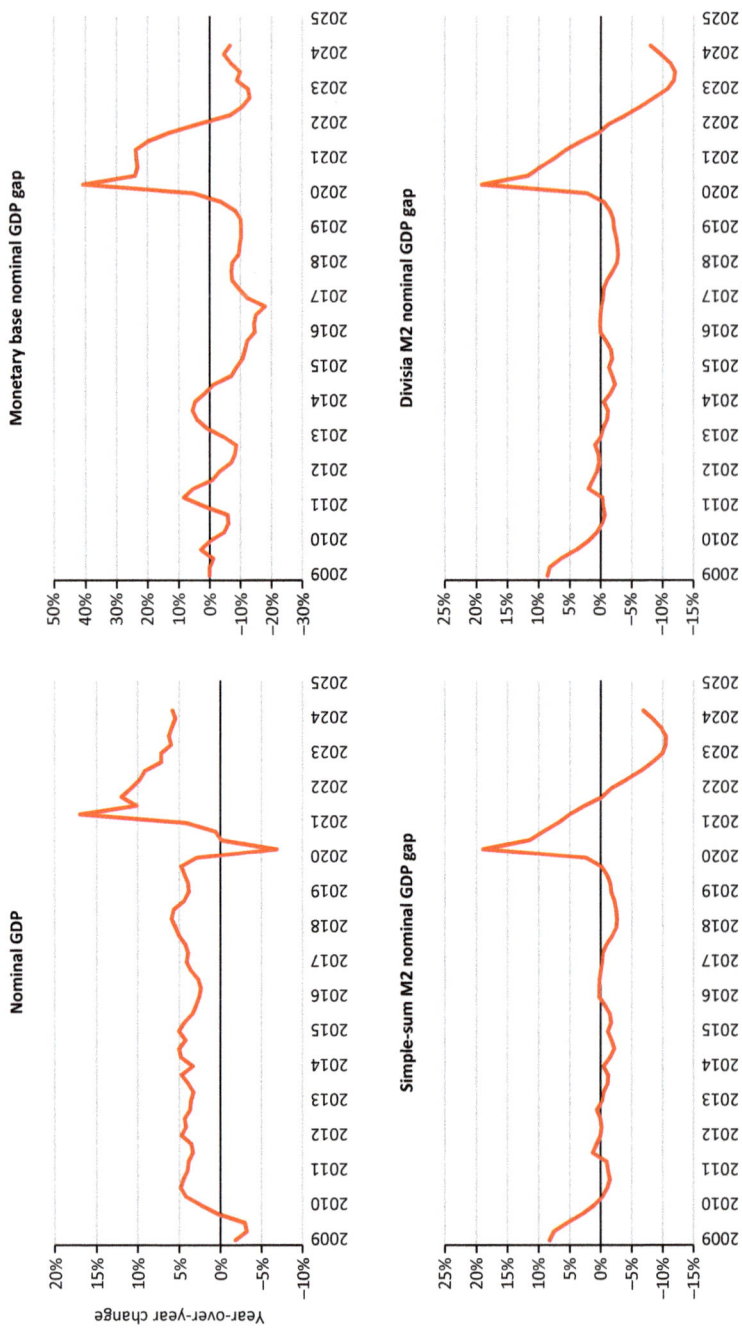

Figure 7.3. Nominal GDP growth and money-based nominal GDP gaps.

Source: FRED, CFS, and author's calculations.

Notes

1. All data used in this study come from the Federal Reserve Bank of St. Louis's FRED database at https://fred.stlouisfed.org/, except those for the Divisia monetary aggregates, which are described by Barnett et al. (2013) and are available from the Center for Financial Stability at https://centerforfinancialstability.org/amfm_data.php.

2. For further discussions of this point, see Ireland (2004), Leeper and Roush (2003), Nelson (2008), and Belongia and Ireland (2021).

3. The omitted text from this quote, indicated with ellipses, states mistakenly that Lucas's paper was presented at the November 1973 Carnegie-Rochester Conference on price and wage controls, when in fact it was presented at the April 1973 conference on the Phillips curve (see Brunner and Meltzer 1976).

4. McCallum (1986) also credits Parkin (1978) with this insight.

5. *Semiannual Monetary Policy Report to Congress: Hearing before the Comm. on Banking, Housing, and Urban Affairs,* US Senate, 117th Cong., 24 (February 23, 2021) (testimony of Jerome Powell).

6. James Johannes and Robert Rasche regularly provided money multiplier forecasts to support SOMC discussions via position papers throughout the early to mid-1980s. Their research on this topic culminates in a monograph: Rasche and Johannes (1987).

7. See, for example, SOMC (2002, 1–3; 2003, 2–3).

8. These figures refer to the monetary base as reported by the Federal Reserve Board of Governors. The SOMC typically referred to an alternative measure of the monetary base, adjusted for changes in reserve requirements by the St. Louis Federal Reserve Bank. Both of these measures of the monetary base are examined in more detail below, but since the St. Louis Fed discontinued its series in 2019, the graph in figure 7.1—running through 2024—uses the Board of Governors' measure instead.

9. Much of the analysis that follows draws on and extends that from Ireland (2024c).

10. Humphrey (1989) discusses the P-star model's quantity-theoretic foundations in more detail.

11. For a broader discussion of the problems monetary policymakers face when estimating the natural rate of output, see Orphanides (2001) and Orphanides and van Norden (2002).

12. When comparing the four panels of figure 7.2, it is important to note that while simple-sum M2 and both measures of the monetary base are expressed in units of dollars, Divisia M2 is an index number, normalized to equal 100 in the base year of 1967. Thus, unlike the numerical values of base and simple-sum M2 velocity, which measure the dollar value of nominal GDP relative to the dollar value of the money stock, the numerical values of Divisia M2 velocity has no special meaning. Instead, the percentage changes in Divisia M2 velocity should be compared to those

in simple-sum and base velocity: All measure the growth rates of nominal GDP relative to the corresponding measure of the money stock.

13. The St. Louis adjusted base series is described by Anderson and Rasche with Loesel (2003). Deposit sweep programs are discussed by Anderson and Rasche (2001).

14. Applying the filter requires choosing a value for the parameter λ that governs the relative volatilities of the cyclical and trend components; the setting $\lambda = 1600$ used here is the one recommended for quarterly data by Hodrick and Prescott (1997).

15. As also noted above, the St. Louis Fed discontinued its series for the adjusted monetary base, so that samples of data using this series must end no later than 2019 Q3.

References

Anderson, Richard G., and Robert H. Rasche. 2001. "Retail Sweep Programs and Bank Reserves, 1994–1999." *Federal Reserve Bank of St. Louis Review* 83 (1): 51–72.

Anderson, Richard G., and Robert H. Rasche, with Jeffrey Loesel. 2003. "A Reconstruction of the Federal Reserve Bank of St. Louis Adjusted Monetary Base and Reserves." *Federal Reserve Bank of St. Louis Review* 85 (5): 39–69.

Bachmeier, Lance J., and Norman R. Swanson. 2005. "Predicting Inflation: Does the Quantity Theory Help?" *Economic Inquiry* 43 (3): 570–85.

Barnett, William A. 1980. "Economic Monetary Aggregates: An Application of Index Number and Aggregation Theory." *Journal of Econometrics* 14 (1): 11–48.

Barnett, William A. 2011. *Getting It Wrong: How Faulty Monetary Statistics Undermine the Fed, the Financial System, and the Economy.* MIT Press.

Barnett, William A., Jia Liu, Ryan S. Mattson, and Jeff van den Noort. 2013. "The New CFS Divisia Monetary Aggregates: Design, Construction, and Data Sources." *Open Economies Review* 24 (1): 101–24.

Belongia, Michael T. 1996. "Measurement Matters: Recent Results from Monetary Economics Reexamined." *Journal of Political Economy* 104 (5): 1065–83.

Belongia, Michael T., and Peter N. Ireland. 2015. "A 'Working' Solution to the Question of Nominal GDP Targeting." *Macroeconomic Dynamics* 19 (3): 508–34.

Belongia, Michael T., and Peter N. Ireland. 2016. "Money and Output: Friedman and Schwartz Revisited." *Journal of Money, Credit and Banking* 48 (6): 1223–66.

Belongia, Michael T., and Peter N. Ireland. 2017. "Circumventing the Zero Lower Bound with Monetary Policy Rules Based on Money." *Journal of Macroeconomics* 54 (Part A): 42–58.

Belongia, Michael T., and Peter N. Ireland. 2021. "A Classical View of the Business Cycle." *Journal of Money, Credit and Banking* 53 (2–3): 333–66.

Belongia, Michael T., and Peter N. Ireland. 2022. "Strengthening the Second Pillar: A Greater Role for Money in the ECB's Strategy." *Applied Economics* 54 (1): 99–114.

Belongia, Michael T., and Peter N. Ireland. 2024. "The Transmission of Monetary Policy Shocks through the Markets for Reserves and Money." *Journal of Macroeconomics* 80 (June): article 103590.

Bernanke, Ben S., and Alan S. Blinder. 1992. "The Federal Funds Rate and the Chan-
nels of Monetary Transmission." *American Economic Review* 82 (4): 901–21.
Bernanke, Ben S., Thomas Laubach, Frederic S. Mishkin, and Adam S. Posen. 1999.
Inflation Targeting: Lessons from the International Experience. Princeton University
Press.
Blanchard, Olivier, and Jordi Galí. 2007. "Real Wage Rigidities and the New Keynes-
ian Model." *Journal of Money, Credit and Banking* 39 (Supplement 1): 35–65.
Board of Governors (Board of Governors of the Federal Reserve System). 2024.
"Monetary Policy Report." March 1.
Bordo, Michael D., John H. Cochrane, and John B. Taylor, eds. 2024. *Getting Mon-
etary Policy Back on Track.* Hoover Institution Press.
Bowsher, Norman N. 1975. "Two Stages to the Current Recession." *Federal Reserve
Bank of St. Louis Review* 57 (6): 2–8.
Brunner, Karl. 1970. "The 'Monetarist Revolution' in Monetary Policy." *Review of
World Economics* (*Weltwirtschaftliches Archiv*) 105 (September): 1–30.
Brunner, Karl. 1974a. "Monetary Growth and Monetary Policy." Position paper,
Shadow Open Market Committee, Washington, DC. March 8.
Brunner, Karl. 1974b. "Assessment of Monetary Policy." Position paper, Shadow
Open Market Committee, Washington, DC. September 6.
Brunner, Karl. 1975a. "Monetary Policy and the Economic Decline." Position paper,
Shadow Open Market Committee, Washington, DC. March 7.
Brunner, Karl. 1975b. "Monetary Policy, Economic Policy and Inflation." Position
paper, Shadow Open Market Committee, Washington, DC. September 12.
Brunner, Karl. 1979a. "Statement Prepared for the Hearings on the Conduct of
Monetary Policy, Held Pursuant to the Full Employment and Balanced Growth
Act of 1978." Statement before the Committee on Banking, Finance and Urban
Affairs. 96th Cong. 1st session. February 22. https://fraser.stlouisfed.org/title
/monetary-policy-oversight-672/conduct-monetary-policy-pursuant-full
-employment-balanced-growth-act-1978-pl-95-523-22443?page=13.
Brunner, Karl. 1979b. "SOMC Position Paper, September 1979." Position paper,
Shadow Open Market Committee, Washington, DC. September 17.
Brunner, Karl. 1981. "Policymaking, Accountability, and the Social Responsibility
of the Fed." Position paper, Shadow Open Market Committee, Washington, DC.
March 15.
Brunner, Karl. 1982. "The Voices of 'Failure' and the Failure of Monetary Policy-
Making." Position paper, Shadow Open Market Committee, Washington, DC.
September 12.
Brunner, Karl. 1983. "Monetary Policy as a Random Walk Through History." Position
paper, Shadow Open Market Committee, Washington, DC. March 6.
Brunner, Karl. 1984. "From the 'Upper Tail Theory of Inflation' to the 'Lower Tail
Theory of Deflation.'" Position paper, Shadow Open Market Committee, Wash-
ington, DC. September 30.

Brunner, Karl, Michele Fratianni, Jerry L. Jordan, Allan H. Meltzer, and Manfred J. M. Neumann. 1973. "Fiscal and Monetary Policies in Moderate Inflation: Case Studies of Three Countries." *Journal of Money, Credit and Banking* 5 (1, part 2): 313–53.

Brunner, Karl, and Allan Meltzer. 1968. "What Did We Learn from the Monetary Experience of the United States in the Great Depression?" *Canadian Journal of Economics* 1 (2): 334–48.

Brunner, Karl, and Allan Meltzer. 1976. "The Phillips Curve." *Carnegie-Rochester Conference Series on Public Policy* 1:1–18.

Burns, Arthur F. 1973. "Money Supply in the Conduct of Monetary Policy." *Federal Reserve Bulletin* 59 (11): 791–98.

Carlson, John B., Dennis L. Hoffman, Benjamin D. Keen, and Robert H. Rasche. 2000. "Results of a Study of the Stability of Cointegrating Relations Comprised of Broad Monetary Aggregates." *Journal of Monetary Economics* 46 (2): 345–83.

Chrystal, K. Alec, and Ronald MacDonald. 1994. "Empirical Evidence on the Recent Behavior and Usefulness of Simple-Sum and Weighted Measures of the Money Stock." *Federal Reserve Bank of St. Louis Review* 76 (2): 73–109.

Clarida, Richard, Jordi Galí, and Mark Gertler. 2000. "Monetary Policy Rules and Macroeconomic Stability: Evidence and Some Theory." *Quarterly Journal of Economics* 115 (1): 147–80.

Cook, Timothy. 1989. "Determinants of the Federal Funds Rate: 1979–1982." *Federal Reserve Bank of Richmond Economic Review* 75 (January/February): 3–19.

Duca, John V. 2000. "Financial Technology Shocks and the Case of the Missing M2." *Journal of Money, Credit and Banking* 32 (4, part 1): 820–39.

FOMC (Federal Open Market Committee). 2012. "Statement on Longer-Run Goals and Monetary Policy Strategy." January 24.

Friedman, Benjamin M., and Kenneth N. Kuttner. 1992. "Money, Income, Prices, and Interest Rates." *American Economic Review* 82 (3): 472–92.

Friedman, Milton. 1960. *A Program for Monetary Stability.* Fordham University Press.

Friedman, Milton. 1964. "The Monetary Studies of the National Bureau." In "Reports on Selected Bureau Programs," in *The National Bureau Enters Its Forty-fifth Year,* edited by the National Bureau of Economic Research. NBER.

Friedman, Milton. 1968. "Inflation: Causes and Consequences." In *Dollars and Deficits: Living with America's Economic Problems.* Prentice-Hall.

Friedman, Milton. 1984. "Lessons from the 1979–82 Monetary Policy Experiment." *American Economic Review* 74 (2): 397–400.

Friedman, Milton, and Anna Schwartz. 1963. *A Monetary History of the United States, 1867–1960.* Princeton University Press.

Galí, Jordi. 2015. *Monetary Policy, Inflation, and the Business Cycle.* 2nd Ed. Princeton University Press.

Gilbert, R. Alton. 1994. "A Case Study in Monetary Control: 1980–82." *Federal Reserve Bank of St. Louis Review* 76 (5): 35–58.

Golden, Soma. 1975. "Critics Urge Fed to Hold Down Rates." *New York Times,* July 14.

Goodfriend, Marvin. 1981. "A Prescription for Monetary Policy 1981." *Federal Reserve Bank of Richmond Economic Review* 67 (November/December): 11–18.

Goodfriend, Marvin, and Robert G. King. 1997. "The New Neoclassical Synthesis and the Role of Monetary Policy." In *NBER Macroeconomics Annual 1997,* edited by Ben S. Bernanke and Julio Rotemberg. MIT Press.

Greenspan, Alan. 1993. "Statement before the Subcommittee on Economic Growth and Credit Formation of the Committee on Banking, Finance and Urban Affairs." 103rd Cong. July 20. https://fraser.stlouisfed.org/title/statements-speeches -alan-greenspan-452/semiannual-monetary-policy-report-congress-8489.

Hallman, Jeffrey J., Richard D. Porter, and David H. Small. 1991. "Is the Price Level Tied to the M2 Monetary Aggregate in the Long Run?" *American Economic Review* 81 (4): 841–58.

Hendrickson, Joshua R. 2014. "Redundancy or Mismeasurement? A Reappraisal of Money." *Macroeconomic Dynamics* 18 (7): 1437–65.

Hetzel, Robert L. 2024. "Making Monetarist Principles Relevant Again through a Re-exposition of the Quantity Theory." Unpublished manuscript. April 29.

Hodrick, Robert J., and Edward C. Prescott. 1997. "Postwar US Business Cycles: An Empirical Investigation." *Journal of Money, Credit and Banking* 29 (1): 1–16.

Humphrey, Thomas M. 1989. "Precursors of the P-star Model." *Federal Reserve Bank of Richmond Economic Review* 75 (July/August): 3–9.

Ireland, Peter N. 1996. "The Role of Countercyclical Monetary Policy." *Journal of Political Economy* 104 (4): 704–23.

Ireland, Peter N. 2004. "Money's Role in the Monetary Business Cycle." *Journal of Money, Credit and Banking* 36 (6): 969–83.

Ireland, Peter N. 2019. "Interest on Reserves: History and Rationale, Complications and Risks." *Cato Journal* 39 (2): 327–37.

Ireland, Peter N. 2023. "US Monetary Policy, 2020–23: Putting the Quantity Theory to the Test." *Journal of Applied Corporate Finance* 35 (3): 42–48.

Ireland, Peter N. 2024. "Targeting Nominal GDP Through Monetary Control." Policy brief, Mercatus Center at George Mason University. December 10.

Ireland, Peter N. Forthcoming-a. "The Devolution of Federal Reserve Monetary Policy Strategy, 2012–24." *Southern Economic Journal.* https://doi.org/10.1002 /soej.12730.

Ireland, Peter N. Forthcoming-b. "Money Growth and Inflation in the Euro Area, United Kingdom, and United States: Measurement Issues and Recent Results." *Macroeconomic Dynamics.* https://doi.org/10.1017/S1365100524000282.

Johannes, James M., and Robert H. Rasche. 1980a. "Money Multiplier Forecasts." Position paper, Shadow Open Market Committee, Washington, DC. February 3.

Johannes, James M., and Robert H. Rasche. 1980b. "The Construction and Fore-casting of Money Multipliers for the New Monetary Aggregates." Position paper, Shadow Open Market Committee, Washington, DC. September 21.

Kydland, Finn E., and Edward C. Prescott. 1982. "Time to Build and Aggregate Fluctuations." *Econometrica* 50 (6): 1345–70.

Laidler, David E. W. 1993. *The Demand for Money: Theories, Evidence, and Problems.* 4th Ed. HarperCollins College Publishers.

Laidler, David. 2024. "Lucas (1972): A Personal View from the Wrong Side of the Subsequent Fifty Years." *European Journal of the History of Economic Thought* 31 (6): 1058–76.

Leeper, Eric M., and Jennifer E. Roush. 2003. "Putting 'M' Back in Monetary Policy." *Journal of Money, Credit and Banking* 35 (6, part 2): 1217–56.

Levy, Mickey D. 2024. "The Fed: Bad Forecasts and Misguided Monetary Policy." In *Getting Monetary Policy Back on Track*, edited by Michael D. Bordo, John H. Cochrane, and John B. Taylor. Hoover Institution Press.

Long, John B., Jr., and Charles I. Plosser. 1983. "Real Business Cycles." *Journal of Political Economy* 91 (1): 39–69.

Lucas, Robert E., Jr. 1976. "Econometric Policy Evaluation: A Critique." *Carnegie-Rochester Conference Series on Public Policy* 1:19–46.

Mayer, Thomas. 1978. "The Structure of Monetarism (I)." In *The Structure of Monetarism*, edited by Thomas Mayer. W. W. Norton & Company.

McCallum, Bennett T. 1981. "Price Level Determinacy with an Interest Rate Policy Rule and Rational Expectations." *Journal of Monetary Economics* 8 (3): 319–29.

McCallum, Bennett T. 1986. "Some Issues Concerning Interest Rate Pegging, Price Level Determinacy, and the Real Bills Doctrine." *Journal of Monetary Economics* 17 (1): 135–60.

McCallum, Bennett T. 1987. "The Case for Rules in the Conduct of Monetary Policy: A Concrete Example." *Federal Reserve Bank of Richmond Economic Review* 73 (September/October): 10–18.

McCallum, Bennett T. 1988. "Robustness Properties of a Rule for Monetary Policy." *Carnegie-Rochester Conference Series on Public Policy* 29:173–204.

McCallum, Bennett T. 2006. "Policy-Rule Retrospective on the Greenspan Era." Position paper, Shadow Open Market Committee, Washington, DC. May 8.

Meltzer, Allan. 1979. "Draft of Proposed Statement, SOMC." Policy Statement, Shadow Open Market Committee. September 17.

Meltzer, Allan H. 1987. "Limits of Short-Run Stabilization Policy: Presidential Address to the Western Economic Association, July 3, 1986." *Economic Inquiry* 25 (1): 1–14.

Meltzer, Allan H. 1993. "Growth of Base Money and Nominal GDP." Position paper, Shadow Open Market Committee, Washington, DC. September 13.

Meltzer, Allan H. 2000. "The Shadow Open Market Committee: Origins and Operations." *Journal of Financial Services Research* 18 (2–3): 119–28.

Motley, Brian. 1988. "Should M2 Be Redefined?" *Federal Reserve Bank of San Francisco Economic Review*, no. 1 (Winter): 33–51.

Nelson, Edward. 2008. "Why Money Growth Determines Inflation in the Long Run: Answering the Woodford Critique." *Journal of Money, Credit and Banking* 40 (8): 1791–814.

Okun, Arthur. 1979. "Sticks with Two Short Ends." *Challenge* 22 (3): 47–51.

Orphanides, Athanasios. 2001. "Monetary Policy Rules Based on Real-Time Data." *American Economic Review* 91 (4): 964–85.

Orphanides, Athanasios, and Richard D. Porter. 2000. "*P** Revisited: Money-Based Inflation Forecasts with a Changing Equilibrium Velocity." *Journal of Economics and Business* 52 (1–2): 87–100.

Orphanides, Athanasios, and Simon van Norden. 2002. "The Unreliability of Output-Gap Estimates in Real Time." *Review of Economics and Statistics* 84 (4): 569–83.

Parkin, Michael. 1978. "A Comparison of Alternative Techniques of Monetary Control Under Rational Expectations." *Manchester School* 46 (3): 252–87.

Poole, William. 1990. "Monetary Policy After Oil Shock III." Position paper, Shadow Open Market Committee, Washington, DC. October 1.

Poole, William. 1991. "Choosing a Monetary Aggregate: Another Look." Position paper, Shadow Open Market Committee, Washington, DC. September 29.

Poole, William. 1992. "Where Do We Stand in the Battle Against Inflation?" Position paper, Shadow Open Market Committee, Washington, DC. March 8.

Poole, William. 1993. "The Real Rate of Interest as a Guide to Monetary Policy." Position paper, Shadow Open Market Committee, Washington, DC. September 13.

Poole, William. 1994. "Monetary Aggregates Targeting in a Low-Inflation Economy." In *Goals, Guidelines, and Constraints Facing Monetary Policymakers*, edited by Jeffrey C. Fuhrer. Federal Reserve Bank of Boston.

Poole, William, Robert H. Rasche, and David C. Wheelock. 2013. "The Great Inflation: Did the Shadow Know Better?" In *The Great Inflation: The Rebirth of Modern Central Banking*, edited by Michael D. Bordo and Athanasios Orphanides. University of Chicago Press.

Powell, Jerome H. 2018. "Monetary Policy in a Changing Economy." Remarks presented at the Federal Reserve Bank of Kansas City's Economic Policy Symposium, "Changing Market Structure and Implications for Monetary Policy." Jackson Hole, WY. August 24.

Powell, Jerome H. 2022. "Monetary Policy and Price Stability." Remarks presented at the Federal Reserve Bank of Kansas City's Economic Policy Symposium, "Reassessing Constraints on the Economy and Policy." Jackson Hole, WY. August 26.

Rasche, Robert H. 1992. "Monetary Aggregates and Monetary Policy." Position paper, Shadow Open Market Committee, Washington, DC. September 13.

Rasche, Robert H., and James M. Johannes. 1987. *Controlling the Growth of Monetary Aggregates*. Kluwer Academic Publishers.

Reynard, Samuel. 2023. "Central Bank Balance Sheet, Money and Inflation." *Economics Letters* 224 (March): article 111028.

Romer, Christina D. 2013. "Comment on 'The Great Inflation: Did the Shadow Know Better?'" In *The Great Inflation: The Rebirth of Modern Central Banking*, edited by Michael D. Bordo and Athanasios Orphanides. University of Chicago Press.

Samuelson, Paul A., and Robert M. Solow. 1960. "Analytical Aspects of Anti-Inflation Policy." *American Economic Review* 50 (2): 177–94.

Sargent, Thomas J. and Neil Wallace. 1975. "'Rational' Expectations, the Optimal Monetary Instrument, and the Optimal Money Supply Rule." *Journal of Political Economy* 83 (2): 241–54.

Simpson, Thomas D. 1980. "The Redefined Monetary Aggregates." *Federal Reserve Bulletin* 66 (2): 97–114.

SOMC (Shadow Open Market Committee). 1973. "Statement on Monetary Policy." September 14.

SOMC. 1976. "Draft: Policy Statement." September 13.

SOMC. 1978a. "Policy Statement." March 13.

SOMC. 1978b. "Policy Statement." September 11.

SOMC. 1983. "Policy Statement." September 19.

SOMC. 1991. "Policy Statement." September 29–30.

SOMC. 1993. "Policy Statement." September 12–13.

SOMC. 1998. "Policy Statement." September 14.

SOMC. 2002. "Policy Statement." November 18.

SOMC. 2003. "Policy Statement." May 19.

Stock, James H., and Mark W. Watson. 1999. "Forecasting Inflation." *Journal of Monetary Economics* 44 (2): 293–335.

Taylor, John B. 1993. "Discretion Versus Policy Rules in Practice." *Carnegie-Rochester Conference Series on Public Policy* 39 (December): 195–214.

Taylor, John B. 1999. "A Historical Analysis of Monetary Policy Rules." In *Monetary Policy Rules*, edited by John B. Taylor. University of Chicago Press.

Thornton, Daniel L. 2006. "When Did the FOMC Begin Targeting the Federal Funds Rate? What the Verbatim Transcripts Tell Us." *Journal of Money, Credit and Banking* 38 (8): 2039–71.

Tobin, James. 1974. "Monetary Policy in 1974 and Beyond." *Brookings Papers on Economic Activity* 1974 (1): 219–32.

Walter, John R., and Renee Haltom. 2009. "The Effect of Interest on Reserves on Monetary Policy." Economic Brief No. EB09-12. Federal Reserve Bank of Richmond. December.

Woodford, Michael. 2003. *Interest and Prices: Foundations of a Theory of Monetary Policy*. Princeton University Press.

8

The Nominal Anchor, *In Originali*, and the Fed

Gregory D. Hess*

The "Nominal Anchor" Concept, In Originali

What is our understanding of the term "nominal anchor"? The first reference to "nominal anchor" in the economics literature appears in Barro (1979).[1] Based on my conversations with other economists, it is surprising that the term does not appear earlier. The topic of Robert Barro's paper was the gold standard or, more broadly, commodity-based money. He writes:

> Since the "central bank" supports the nominal price of a reserve commodity such as gold under these systems, the determination of the absolute price level amounts to the determination of the relative price of the reserve commodity. In this sense the absolute price level becomes a determinate quantity that is amenable to usual supply and demand analyses, as applied to such things as gold production and nonmonetary uses of gold. Although changes in the ratio of "money" to its commodity backing or shifts in velocity can influence the price level, the system possesses an important *nominal anchor* [emphasis mine] in the fixed price of the reserve commodity. (Barro 1979, 13)

"Nominal anchor" has subsequently become a weighty metaphor in the systematic design of monetary policy—an anchor, denoted in nominal terms, prices a key resource that is an irreplaceable component of a system that tethers the nominal anchor to a policy objective of importance. Consequently, a presumably sound nominal anchor that is not embedded in a corresponding

*Many thanks to Mickey Levy and Athanasios Orphanides for their comments and insights. The views expressed are those of the author and do not necessarily reflect views of IES Global or any of its affiliates.

able system turns out to be no anchor at all, as it simply cannot stop the vari-able of importance, the price level, from arbitrarily drifting from its target.

Barro continues by contrasting the gold standard's system of possessing a nominal anchor to a fiat currency standard where, in his belief, a nominal anchor is lacking:

By way of contrast the absolute price level is determinate under a fiat (government-issue) currency system only up to the determination of the quantity of the fiat currency. Analysis of the price level involves, as its major element, a theory of government behaviour with respect to the quantity of money. In particular, there is no obvious nominal anchor that prescribes some *likely limits* [emphasis mine] to changes in the absolute price level. (Barro 1979, 13)

Barro concludes the article by noting that:

In this context the choice among different monetary constitutions – such as the gold standard, a commodity-reserve standard, or a fiat standard with fixed rules for setting the quantity of money (possibly in relation to stabilising a specified price index) – may be less important than the decision to adopt some monetary constitution. On the other hand, the gold standard actually prevailed for a substantial period (even if from an "historical accident," rather than a constitutional choice pro-cess), whereas the world has yet to see a fiat currency system that has obvious "stability" properties. (Barro 1979, 31)

Again, based on Barro's original definition, a policy variable alone cannot be a nominal anchor if it is not embedded in a coherent, effective, and constrained policy process in place to deliver the desired outcome. In other words, a pro-posed nominal anchor without an effective and systematic policy chain is just a disconnected lump of metal laying at the bottom of the ocean floor.

Barro (1982) follows up on this topic in a subsequent paper that focuses on the US inflation experience at that time:

What is certainly clear is that before 1971 most economists underesti-mated the extent to which the international system of fixed exchange rates with some role for gold served, although imperfectly, to restrain growth in the world money supply and thereby the world price level. Since the move in 1971 toward flexible exchange rates and the complete divorce of United States monetary management from the objective of a pegged gold price, it is clear that the nominal anchor for the monetary system—weak as it was earlier—is now entirely absent. Future monetary growth and long-run inflation appear now to depend entirely on the year-to-year "discretion" of the monetary authority, that is, the Federal Reserve. (Barro 1982, 105)

Based on these early contributions, the presence of a nominal anchor includes not just an ability to deliver price stability, but also a framework for delivering the price stability goal and routinizing and constraining policy actions to be free from political decision making and discretion. That is, not only must the nominal anchor be able to achieve its price stability goal, but it must also be part of a system that has intrinsically embedded and operationally automated constraints to do so. Metaphorically, no (dependable systematic policy) chain, no gain (from a presumed nominal anchor).

The Federal Reserve's "Nominal Anchor"

The Federal Reserve's website devoted to "Monetary Policy Principles and Practice: Historical Approaches to Monetary Policy" proudly advocates the importance of a "nominal anchor" as a linchpin in the conduct of monetary policy. It states:

Historically, in efforts to ensure that central banks managed financial conditions in a way consistent with achieving low and stable inflation over time, various *nominal anchors* [emphasis in the original] have been adopted or proposed in the United States and other countries. *A nominal anchor is a variable--such as the price of a particular commodity, an exchange rate, or the money supply--that is thought to bear a stable relationship to the price level or the rate of inflation over some period of time* [emphasis mine]. The adoption of a nominal anchor is intended to help households and businesses form expectations about the conduct of monetary policy and future inflation; stable inflation expectations can, in turn, help stabilize actual inflation. (Board of Governors 2018)

The document goes on to say:

Today the nominal anchor in the United States is the Federal Open Market Committee's (FOMC) explicit objective of achieving inflation at the rate of 2 percent per year over the longer run. This goal is supported by a policy strategy by which the FOMC responds to economic developments in a way that systematically aims to return inflation to 2 percent over time. By aiming to achieve low and stable inflation (as opposed to maintaining a particular price of gold or foreign exchange or a particular growth rate of the money supply), the FOMC has the flexibility to adapt its strategy as its understanding of the economy improves and as economic relationships evolve. The FOMC's strong commitment to its inflation objective helps crystalize the public's longer-run inflation expectations around that objective, which, in turn, helps keep actual inflation near 2 percent. This commitment further gives the FOMC room to support employment and makes monetary policy a more potent force for stabilizing the economy overall. (Board of Governors 2018)

Interestingly, the Fed's nominal anchor declaration stipulates that its long-run inflation goal will be twinned with a flexible monetary policy strategy that will systematically return inflation to its nominal anchor. In other words, the Fed's policy actions will be strategically constrained in a flexible way to deliver inflation systematically to its long-run value of 2%. In turn, the nominal anchor will make the job of hitting the target easier, which is presumably where the benefits of the Fed's well-used expression "anchored inflation expectations" derives. Critically, this leaves the existence and actual implementation of the Fed's flexible policy actions as the determining factor as to whether 2% is just a smart long-run policy goal or truly part of a "nominal anchor" system as Barro originally conceived.

Put another way, Barro's 1979 concept of a "nominal anchor" was intended to be comprehensive—it envisioned placing the right constraints on the monetary policy process that eliminated discretion and provides systematic and automated policy responses (i.e., a form of rules that delivered price stability).[2] Barro believed that a nominal anchor must have an effective and systematic chain to deliver price stability. The Fed's use of the term "nominal anchor" is different, narrower, and altered from Barro's concept—it equates the nominal anchor as a long-term inflation goal, and then asserts a flexible, and likely "data dependent," policy response that will systematically bring inflation to its 2% goal in the long run. As such, the crucial question for the Fed's nominal anchor is whether it can be systemically depended upon to deliver price stability or not. The evidence, so far, is decidedly mixed.

The Fed's Nominal Anchor Following the Postpandemic Recession?

Since the FOMC adopted its 2% long-run inflation nominal anchor in 2012 until the end of the pandemic recession in April of 2020, inflation—year-over-year percentage change, personal consumption expenditures (PCE) price deflator excluding food and energy—averaged below 2% per year (see figure 8.1). As shown (right scale), inflation was 0.93% in March of 2020, and did not rise above 2% until March of 2021, when it was 2.26%. That's quite a remarkable achievement for the nominal anchor, even while recognizing the arguments of economists concerned that inflation ran below a 2.0% average during this extended time period.

Unfortunately, inflation thereafter rose unabated from March of 2021 until February of 2022—eleven months—when it crested at 5.57%. Though not shown, PCE inflation's rise, including food and energy, was steeper, higher, and of longer duration (peaking at 7.12% in June of 2022 as a year-over-year percentage change). Quite surprisingly, and not in a good way, facing a persistent surge of inflation almost a year in duration, the FOMC did not raise the federal funds rate until March 17, 2022.

Why did the Fed's nominal anchor as a system wobble during this time period? There are two noncompeting explanations. The first is that while the Fed's nominal anchor suggested that an important and critical constraint on policy was in place for it to systematically return inflation to 2%, there were too many additional constraints on policy that conflicted with this primary

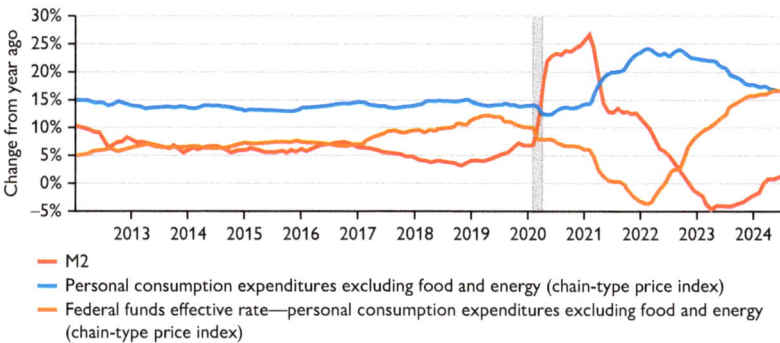

— M2
— Personal consumption expenditures excluding food and energy (chain-type price index)
— Federal funds effective rate—personal consumption expenditures excluding food and energy (chain-type price index)

Figure 8.1. M2 growth, inflation, and the federal funds rate.

Source: Board of Governors and US Bureau of Economic Analysis, via Federal Reserve Bank of St. Louis (FRED).

goal. My SOMC colleague Athanasios Orphanides (2023) provides substantial evidence that the recent postpandemic inflation episode can be attributed to inappropriate constraints contained in the Fed's forward guidance in (a) the Fed's management of its policy rate in response to economic data as well as (b) the sequencing of its balance sheet decisions relative to changes in its policy rate. Together these resulted in a "forward guidance trap":[3]

> Two elements in the Fed's implementation of forward guidance induced a significant delay in the policy response to an unexpected increase in inflation: First, a decision to move from forecast-based to outcome-based forward guidance; and second, an implicit commitment to a gradual reduction of net asset purchases (tapering), and to raising policy rates only after net asset purchases ended. (Orphanides 2023, 7)

With regards to the first element, Orphanides identifies this shift by contrasting the FOMC statement released on July 29, 2020, with the subsequent one released on September 16, 2020. In the former, the Fed provided forward guidance based on the outlook of the economy, while in the latter it introduced outcome-based language explicitly derived from its August 2020 adopted "New Framework." He concludes:

> With this change, the Fed communicated a shift towards a myopic approach to policy. This decision alone virtually ensured a policy error in case the inflation outlook deteriorated abruptly. (Orphanides 2023, 7)

Orphanides further argues that in managing its balance sheet, the Fed's prior protocol from the Great Financial Crisis suggested that it would not raise short-term interest rates until it had finished its planned net asset purchases. Furthermore, and again based on the Fed's post–Great Financial Crisis experience (e.g., the "Taper Tantrum" of 2013), quick changes to planned adjustments to the balance sheet were to be avoided. These constraints and guidance inappropriately predetermined the sequence of balance sheet actions prior to conducting interest rate tightening, and made the Fed fall further behind in addressing the secular rise in inflation in the last quarter of 2021 and the first quarter of 2022. Taken together, this led the Fed to lose the "flexibility to adapt its strategy as its understanding of the economy [improved]," as in the Fed's quote above, that it needed to pursue a systematic path to price stability.[4]

The second explanation for the recent wobbliness of the nominal anchor is that the Fed made an incorrect call in its initial determination that the rise in inflation was purely "transitory." There is compelling ex ante and ex post evidence that this was incorrect. First, not only was the observed inflation rate (figure 8.1, right scale) continuously rising and in excess of 2% from March 2021 to February 2022, but standard measures of monetary policy—e.g., the annual growth in M2 (figure 8.1, left scale) surging above 20% and measures of the real federal funds rate below –5% (figure 8.1, right scale)—pointed to enormous monetary thrust that theory and history inform us drive large increases in the observed rate of inflation. Indeed, as inflation continued to rise above 2% and higher from March of 2021 onward for almost a year, the real federal funds rate continued to decrease, bottoming out at –5.5% in February of 2022.

Second, the theoretical distinction that economists make between "transitory" or "permanent" relies on statistical inference. Given the well-documented persistent and "sticky" characteristics of US inflation, it would appear to be, ex ante, a risky and historically contrarian bet for the Fed to place full weight on the "transitory" inference.[5] Moreover, even if the Fed believed the rise in inflation to be ephemeral, my former SOMC colleague Marvin Goodfriend's (1993) seminal work on inflation scares would have been a worthwhile reread:

> Inflation scares present the Fed with a fundamental dilemma the resolution of which has decided the course of monetary policy in the postwar period. Prior to the 1980s, the Fed generated an upward trend in the inflation rate by reacting to inflation scares with a delay. The more prompt and even preemptive reactions since the late 1970s have been a hallmark of the recent disinflation.

Surprisingly, this time-honored advice was ignored by the Fed.

In summary, the Fed's nominal anchor system was meaningfully destabilized during the postpandemic inflation episode for two reasons: (a) its Great Delay in tightening policy due to the "forward guidance trap" identified by Orphanides (2023) added undue constraints to the pursuit of price stability; and (b) its Great Denial, that the significant rise in inflation in 2021–22 warranted immediate action, demonstrated a fundamental lack of policy constraint needed for price stability.

Concluding Thoughts

Barro's (1979) concept of a nominal anchor is comprehensive, requiring the appropriate constraints on monetary policy to insure automatic, systematic, and nondiscretionary policy responses to insure price stability. Such rule-like behavior advocated by Barro is a core tenet of the Shadow Open Market Committee's view and is also embodied in descendants of the Taylor (1993) interest rate rule.[6] Unfortunately, during the recent postpandemic inflation episode, the Fed's forward guidance on its balance sheet imposed the wrong constraints on policy, while its initial "transitory" call on inflation reveals that it failed to impose sufficient constraint against discretionary decision making. As a result, for a significant time, these decisions unnecessarily called the efficacy and existence of the Fed's nominal anchor into question.

One can only hope that these fundamental issues for comprehensively establishing a nominal anchor will be fully addressed in the Fed's upcoming review of its 2020 Statement on Longer-Run Goals and Monetary Policy Strategy.

Notes

1. The original reference is based on a review of the economics literature using standard sources such as FRASER and others, and separately "blind" evaluated by Edward Nelson. Additional verification of Barro's coining of the concept can be found in footnote #16 in McCallum (1984), as well as in footnote #2 in Hoehn (1981). Should there exist uses of "nominal anchor" prior to Barro (1979), I simply apologize in advance. That said, Barro's definition and insights remain compelling for understanding and contrasting monetary systems.

2. It should come as no surprise that Barro's work on "nominal anchors" evolved into positive theories that advocated for rules rather than discretion in monetary policy—e.g., see Barro and Gordon (1983).

3. Governor Christopher Waller (2022) also thoughtfully evaluates how forward guidance may have placed additional constraints on normalizing monetary policy postpandemic.

4. There also remains the possibility that the adoption of the FOMC's New Framework in August of 2020, which introduced a significant and official asymmetry in determining monetary policy, shifted perceptions of the Fed's intermediate target for inflation and destabilized medium-term inflation expectations during the postpandemic recovery. In turn, this may have weakened the feedback mechanism (emphasized by the Fed in an earlier quote above) of the nominal anchor on inflation.

5. This is particularly true given the potentially large magnitude of the shock as observed in the growth of the money supply. In addition to the M2 growth

noted above, monetary base growth rates exceeded 40% on an annual basis from April of 2020 to March of 2021. In practical terms, a large transitory shock to the price level may have a substantially different and destabilizing impact on inflation dynamics, the predictability of the long-run price level, and the effectiveness of the nominal anchor than a small transitory shock to the price level, ceteris paribus. A primary reason is that the Fed's 2% inflation anchor allows for "base-drift" in the price level, so that long-run prices become nonstationary. These effects can be even more destabilizing for the predictability of the long-run price level when one-sided deviations are explicitly tolerated, as the Fed's 2020 New Framework incorporates. My SOMC colleague Mickey Levy (2021) argued during this critical time period that the Fed's assessment that the high inflation of 2021 was due to a transitory supply shock was inconsistent with the fastest acceleration of nominal GDP in modern history and the widespread distribution of accelerating price increases.

6. Indeed, my SOMC colleague Mike Bordo coauthored an important piece with Finn Kydland (1995) that provides compelling evidence that the gold standard itself, upon which Barro (1979) identifies the nominal anchor, can be interpreted as rule-like behavior.

References

Barro, Robert J. 1979. "Money and the Price Level under the Gold Standard." *Economic Journal* 89 (353): 13–33.

Barro, Robert J. 1982. "United States Inflation and the Choice of Monetary Standard." In *Inflation: Causes and Effects*, edited by Robert E. Hall. University of Chicago Press.

Barro, Robert J., and David B. Gordon. 1983. "A Positive Theory of Monetary Policy in a Natural Rate Model." *Journal of Political Economy* 91 (4): 589–610.

Board of Governors (Board of Governors of the Federal Reserve System). 2018. "Historical Approaches to Monetary Policy." Monetary Policy Principles and Practice, Monetary Policy, Board of Governors of the Federal Reserve System. Last updated March 8. https://www.federalreserve.gov/monetarypolicy/historical-approaches-to-monetary-policy.htm.

Bordo, Michael D., and Finn E. Kydland. 1995. "The Gold Standard as a Rule: An Essay in Exploration." *Explorations in Economic History* 32 (4): 423–64.

Goodfriend, Marvin. 1993. "Interest Rate Policy and the Inflation Scare Problem: 1979–1992." *Federal Reserve Bank of Richmond Economic Quarterly* 79 (1): 1–23.

Hoehn, James G. 1981. "Back to Gold?" *Voice of the Federal Reserve Bank of Dallas* (March): 1–11.

Levy, Mickey. 2021. "Inflation: Some Temporary Factors, but Underlying Pressures Mount." Paper presented at the Shadow Open Market Committee Conference, Chapman University, Orange, CA. June 19.

McCallum, Bennett T. 1984. "Credibility and Monetary Policy." Paper prepared for the Federal Reserve Bank of Kansas City's Economic Policy Symposium, "Price Stability and Public Policy." Jackson Hole, WY. August 1–3.

Orphanides, Athanasios. 2023. "The Forward Guidance Trap." Working Paper No. 2023-E-6. Institute for Money and Economic Studies, Bank of Japan, October.

Taylor, John B. 1993. "Discretion Versus Policy Rules in Practice." *Carnegie-Rochester Conference Series on Public Policy* 39 (December): 195–214.

Waller, Christopher J. 2022. "Lessons Learned on Normalizing Monetary Policy." Speech at the "Monetary Policy at a Crossroads" panel discussion at the Dallas Society for Computational Economics. Dallas, TX. June 18.

9

In Search of a Stable Nominal Anchor

Robert L. Hetzel

The period following the 2024 elections will undoubtedly pose threats both to the independence of the Federal Reserve System and to price stability. It is important to evaluate those threats in advance and to ask both how the Fed should defend its independence and what kind of defense it should offer for a policy of price stability. The first section of this paper offers conjectures on the likelihood of specific threats. It then asks what consequences would ensue if they resulted in limiting Fed independence and its ability to maintain price stability. The concern is that a revival of inflation would endanger the free-market system. The second section presents a specific scenario foretelling that a policy of price stability could be threatened in a crisis when financial markets become concerned that a dysfunctional political system cannot deal with a structural budget deficit.

The third section starts a discussion of what strategy for monetary policy the Fed should implement in order to provide a stable nominal anchor (price stability). Moreover, how should it communicate that strategy to the public? The paper pursues these questions by first reviewing the periods over which the Fed has either provided or restored a stable nominal anchor, specifically, price stability. As an empirical matter, is nominal stability consistent with stability in the real economy—that is, with the other part of the dual mandate, namely "maximum employment"? If so, what rule, understood as the underlying consistency in the implementation of monetary policy, produced that result? What model of the economy allows such a rule to stabilize both the price level and the real economy? How should the Federal Open Market Committee (FOMC) communicate in a way that makes transparency a cornerstone of accountability? Finally, how does that transparency and accountability defend its independence?

Likely Threats to Fed Independence and Its Maintenance of Price Stability

How did the Fed initiate the Great Inflation that lasted from the mid-1960s until the early 1980s (Hetzel 2008)? Could it happen again? The pressure on the Fed to inflate began with the replacement of the Kennedy administration, which did not want a dollar crisis while it was dealing with the Cuban Missile Crisis, by the Johnson administration, which reset national priorities to achieve 4% unemployment. The Keynesian Walter Heller Council of Economic Advisers (CEA) considered the optimal policy one of fiscal stimulus with low interest rates. With his populist temperament, Lyndon Johnson naturally also favored "low" interest rates.

John F. Kennedy had proposed a tax cut in 1963 "to get the country moving again." When Johnson succeeded Kennedy after the latter's assassination, he pushed Congress to pass the tax cut, which passed in spring 1964. The FOMC chair William McChesney Martin had threatened to raise interest rates but had then been met with a barrage of criticism for "thwarting the will of Congress," which had passed the tax cut to stimulate the economy and lower the unemployment rate. Martin hesitated and in 1964 the change began from low rates of money growth producing price stability to high rates of money growth producing inflation.

The comparable situation in 2025 would be the extension of the Tax Cuts and Jobs Act of 2017 (TCJA), which when passed was set to expire in 2025. Although derided by populists as "a tax cut for the rich," its provisions are widely popular.[1] The standard deduction doubled under the TCJA so that 90% of taxpayers now claim it. It doubled the child tax credit and raised the deduction for state and local taxes.[2] York (2024) wrote: "If Congress fully extends the individual, estate, and business provisions, federal tax revenues would fall by more than $4 trillion."

As a candidate in 2024, President Trump claimed that higher tariffs would raise federal revenues. However, the effect on the deficit is unclear. Fewer imports would give foreigners fewer dollars to spend and would reduce US exports. Assuming that the tariffs would set off a trade war when other countries imposed retaliatory tariffs, US exports would decline further, risking a recession. In calculating the taxes paid by US households, it is also important to realize that the tariffs themselves are a tax. Clausing and Lovely (2024) of the Peterson Institute wrote: "We find that imposing a 20 percent across-the-board tariff combined with a 60 percent tariff on China would cost a typical US household in the middle income distribution more than $2,600 a year."

An extension of the TCJA would take place in the context of an unsustainable deficit. The Committee for a Responsible Federal Budget (2024) wrote:

As deficits remain high, debt continues to rise. Federal debt held by the public rose from 96 percent of GDP in FY 2023 to 98 percent in 2024, according to the BEA's latest GDP estimates and revisions. Debt as a percentage of GDP has grown 19 percentage points from 79 percent in 2019 and will continue to grow rapidly, reaching roughly 120 percent of GDP by the end of the decade. Deficits are projected to remain high in FY 2025 and throughout the next decade, rising to $2.9 trillion by 2034. The gap between revenue and spending is large and growing, and a substantial policy change will be needed to put the nation's finances on a sustainable path.

What challenges would the Fed confront to its independence, assuming that an extension of the TCJA caused financial markets to raise Treasury bond rates—both out of a realization that the federal deficit is unsustainable given the lack of political will to deal with it, and also because of a rise in expected inflation? What if the inflation scare was accompanied by at least a growth recession, which in itself would raise the deficit, due to a world trade war? A plausible answer to these questions must take account of the populist political environment likely to prevail.

An overview of the populist threat to the Fed from the new administration was offered by Meyer (2024).

[Vice President J. D.] Vance singled out his concern that financial capital could thwart Trump's agenda, citing BoE's [Bank of England's] demonstrated capacity and willingness to depose UK PM [Elizabeth] Truss: "So I really worry . . . do the bond markets. . . try to take down the Trump presidency by spiking bond rates?"[3]

A yield spike could arrest progress, Vance fears: "the most important and the most impactful way they could try to take down Trump's presidency is by spiking the interest rates." He suspected BoE's moves against PM Truss were "maybe intentional." The presumed enemy was identified by Vance as "international investors," globalization beneficiaries, China-trade advocates, and the military-industrial complex, who will "try to take him down in a very big way." . . . If Republicans suspect the Fed is a part of any scheme they might be apt to re-open the

Federal Reserve Act and remove discretionary powers. Vance appealed to populist logic: Monetary policy "should fundamentally be a political decision: Agree or disagree, we should have elected leaders having input about the most important decisions confronting our country."

. . . Calling to mind Truss's misgivings about the power the central bank has over financial markets, effectively giving central bankers veto power over fiscal policy, Vance agreed with Trump on "it's kind of weird that you have so many bureaucrats making so many important decisions." . . . "The criticism of the Federal Reserve that makes the most sense to me is that it gives massive corporations a lower cost of money than the average American." He says he has "kind of come around to the Ron Paul argument."[4]

The populist sentiment reflected in the comments above of J. D. Vance is widespread as evidenced in the comments by Robert Reich, who was secretary of labor in the Clinton administration, and has spread to progressive liberals. Reich (2024) wrote of interviews he conducted in 2015, which foresaw the populist discontent of the 2024 presidential election:

When I did my interviews, the overall economy was doing well in terms of the standard measures of employment and growth. But those indicators didn't reflect the economic insecurity most Americans felt and continue to feel, nor did they show the seeming unfairness most people experienced.

The indicators didn't reveal the linkages many Americans saw, and still see, between wealth and power, crony capitalism and stagnant real wages, soaring CEO pay and their own loss of status, the emergence of a billionaire class and the undermining of democracy, and globalization and the loss of their communities.

The standard measures didn't show the frustration of American workers without college degrees, who for decades have had to work harder with very little to show for it, and whose lifespans have shrunk.

It is important to understand the reason for the popularity of populist sentiment especially to understand how persistent it is likely to be. Specifically, why do so many people see a market economy as a zero-sum game with the wealthy benefiting at the expense of the average household? One answer is the nature of innovation. The only form of market organization that produces secular increases in wealth is the free market. However, in the early 1980s, the distribution of that increase in wealth changed from "lifting all boats" to disadvantaging those with a high-school education in favor of those with a college education.

Economists use the term "skill-biased technological innovation." Powered by the adoption of computers, the economy changed in nature from a manufacturing economy to a services economy. The change disadvantaged workers performing routine tasks in favor of workers with analytical skills. A manifestation of this change was the rise in the college wage premium.[5]

A facet of the change to a knowledge-based economy is "agglomeration externalities." That is, the high-tech start-ups concentrate in particular geographic locations where there is a broad pool of educated workers, such as Silicon Valley. That concentration disadvantages rural areas. Unlike during the change in the US from an agricultural economy to an urban economy, rural workers face difficulty migrating to urban areas to work in the service sector. The reason is that low-density zoning regulations restrict the ability of the supply of housing to expand in line with the demand for housing. The result is very high housing prices in urban areas. Moreover, the high price of housing due to zoning regulations in the suburbs favors the increase over time in inequality.[6]

A characteristic of the populist view of the world, with its zero-sum assumption about wealth distribution, is the belief that the powerful wealthy owe their wealth to the exploitation of the less powerful poor. Within this worldview, corporations are personified as a source of the exploitation. They power inflation through price rises imposed to increase profits. Presumably, increases in inflation correspond to increases in the greediness of the owners of the corporation, the stockholders. Figure 9.1 shows the share of corporate

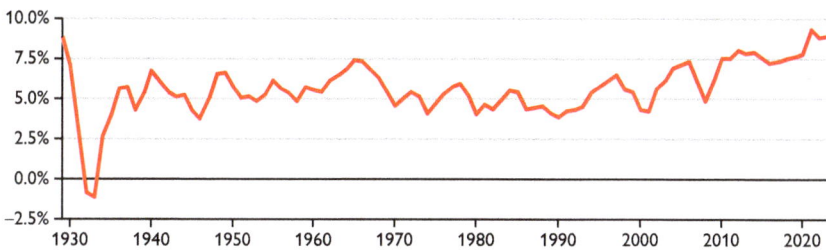

Figure 9.1. Shares of corporate profits in gross domestic income.

Source: US Bureau of Economic Analysis, via Federal Reserve Bank of St. Louis (FRED).

profits in GDP. As shown, periods of economic recovery are most commonly associated with increases in the share of profits in GDP.

The period after the 2008–9 recession exhibits a historically high share. The extended period of low interest rates as evidenced by a funds rate at the zero lower bound (ZLB) undoubtedly spurred corporate profits because of the low cost of bond financing. The increased share following the brief pandemic recession, with a peak in February 2020 and a trough in April 2020, likely came from the strong growth in aggregate nominal demand due to highly stimulative fiscal and monetary policy interacting with the supply constraints due to the COVID-19 pandemic. Stimulative monetary and fiscal policy raised both inflation and profits. The association of the 2021–22 inflation with the increased share of corporate profits feeds the populist narrative. The association, however, was not due to corporate greed but rather due to the common cause of the interaction of a highly stimulative monetary and fiscal policy with COVID supply constraints.

In addition, another association must have fed the populist narrative that helped Donald Trump. Carla Norrlöf (*PS* Commentators, 2024) noted: "Exit polls indicate that 52% of voters trust Trump more to handle the economy, a perspective likely bolstered by positive income growth across all income groups during his previous tenure." By coincidence, the economy finally began to grow strongly during the recovery starting in 2016, which caused the FOMC to initiate sustained increases in the funds rate. The year 2016 was the first of the Trump administration.

The remainder of the paper argues that to deal with populist pressures in the next four years the FOMC will need to affirm its commitment to the "stable prices" part of its mandate. Moreover, as an essential part of dealing with those pressures, the FOMC must abandon the language of discretion and replace it with a rules-based language for communicating with the public. At present, the Fed favors the language of discretion because it believes that it conveys the message to the public that monetary policy possesses the flexibility to respond to the economy's most pressing problem. It purports to be the economy's risk mitigator. But what if the political consensus is that the chief risk to the economy is high interest rates and their adverse effect on unemployment? Does not the Fed's maximum-employment mandate outweigh in importance the stable-nominal-anchor mandate? An affirmative answer to this question can only lead to fiscal dominance, inflation, and the end of Fed independence.

The next section begins the argument by pointing out that in addition to the dual mandate the Fed possesses a mandate for financial stability. A loss of Fed credibility accompanied by an increase in expected inflation could set off a run on the uninsured deposits of regional banks to the too-big-to-fail banks. The underlying cause of such a run would be that many regional banks hold long-term Treasury securities whose value declines as interest rates rise. An increase in expected inflation produces an increase in interest rates and a decline in the value of Treasury securities. The quandary for the Fed is that an increase in the funds rate could exacerbate the run by increasing market interest rates.

The Fed Between a Rock and a Hard Place

How can the Fed defend its independence faced with populist pressures? To make the question more specific, consider an inflation scare, precipitated by a loss in confidence in financial markets, that the political system will deal with an unsustainable deficit. How could the FOMC defend an increase in the funds rate either to forestall an increase in the market's expectation of inflation or to reverse an actual increase? The FOMC will have to start with a defense of the dual mandate. However, that is where the problem emerges.

Although the FOMC talks about a dual mandate, in reality its behavior is determined by a triple mandate, with financial stability as the third mandate. At least since 1984, with the bailout of Continental Illinois Bank and its holding company, the cornerstone of Fed policy has been "too big to fail" (TBTF). As made evident by the bailout of Bear Stearns in March 2008, which was an investment bank and a minor player, the policy is actually "too indebted to fail" (TITF). The Fed does not make explicit to the public its interpretation of its unlegislated financial stability mandate because of the political sensitivity of its de facto policy of bailing out big banks, the TBTF bedrock.

The bailout of Silicon Valley Bank (SVB) in March 2023, followed by an outflow of funds from the regional banks to the TBTF banks—and the Fed's and the regulators' reaction of informally communicating that all bank deposits would be protected—illustrates the bind that the Fed has gotten itself into with its pervasive financial safety net. Congress has not granted the Fed the authority to bail out the large banks, much less guarantee the safety of all bank deposits. The living will provision of the Dodd–Frank Act reflects the opposition by Congress to such bailouts.

The run on SVB, followed by First Republic, revealed the potential insolvency of many of the regional banks. The problem arose because they had purchased long-term Treasury bonds during the period of low interest rates that started with the FOMC's ZLB policy of maintaining the funds rate near zero at its December 2008 meeting. With the rise in the funds rate that began in March 2022, and the concomitant rise in long-term interest rates, these bonds lost value, potentially threatening the solvency of the banks heavily invested in them. Given the size limits on insured deposits by the FOMC, depositors holding large amounts of bank deposits such as businesses needing to meet a payroll had an incentive to transfer their funds to the TBTF banks. The affected community banks of course would then protest to their congressmen about the unfairness of the way that TBTF favored the large banks.

If a similar rise in long-term bond rates happens again with a loss of confidence in the ability of the political system to eliminate a structural deficit, how does the FOMC respond? Its informal financial stability mandate would militate against an increase in the funds rate even if inflationary expectations rise given the fear of an out-of-control deficit. Is the FOMC then trading off among its multiple objectives, hopefully, in a way that allows only a controlled increase in actual and expected inflation? The contention here is that the FOMC should concentrate on a policy of maintaining price stability implemented in the way pioneered in the Volcker–Greenspan era.

However, the FOMC would have to engage in an unprecedented debate over whether to articulate the underlying consistency in policy. Movement away from the language of discretion would represent a profound cultural change. Unfortunately, the challenge is great because the FOMC possesses no procedures for maintaining an institutional memory. Nowhere in the Fed is there a group devoted to the study of Fed history. As a matter of political economy, the advantage is that the FOMC never has to admit that it has in the past made mistakes and destabilized the economy. The disadvantage is that there is no organized way of learning from past mistakes.

The FOMC has no choice but to start the first discussion in its history of how to communicate in terms of a rules-based monetary policy. If it allows actual and expected inflation to rise, the obvious assumption will be that fiscal dominance has replaced Fed independence. With that assumption, the administration can take advantage of the same-party control in both branches of Congress to change the Federal Reserve Act to institutionalize a role for the administration in the conduct of monetary policy.

The next section discusses how the language of discretion obscures the necessary debate over how to identify the underlying consistency in policy and then to articulate it to the public in the form of a rule. Only by communicating using the language of rules can the FOMC defend a concentration on price stability even if it requires raising the funds rate in response to an inflation scare.

Making FOMC Communication Consistent with Transparency and Accountability

As monetary policy becomes more and more complex with complications like interest on reserves, quantitative easing and tightening, a ballooning asset portfolio, a repurchase facility and a reverse repurchase overnight facility, and so on, it becomes more and more of a black box for the American public. The public needs to have a simple answer to the question: "What does the FOMC control and how does it exercise that control?" That answer also needs to be put into the language of economics so that it can be debated by the academic community. Such transparency is required for accountability.

The standard Fed answer to the above question is: "We pursue the dual mandate of 'maximum employment' and 'stable prices.' Success requires flexibility to respond to the more pressing of the two components of the dual mandate. Because of the uncertainty about the evolution of the economy and future unanticipated shocks, the stance of monetary policy must be left free to change based on changes in the priority to assign to the different parts of the dual mandate." Left unstated in this response is the FOMC's understanding of the structure of the economy that determines how its policy actions exercise the desired control.

The FOMC's public communication concentrates on the complex exercise of forecasting the near-term behavior of the economy and then moving the FOMC's instrument, the funds rate, in a commonsense way to deal with whichever part of the dual mandate—maximum employment or stable prices—is the more pressing. The underlying assumption seems to be that because FOMC participants can talk knowledgeably about the behavior of the economy they must understand its structure. Given that understanding of the structure of the economy, they can then predict reliably how their policy actions with the funds rate will influence the behavior of the "agents" in the economy (firms and households).

Given that knowledge of the structure of the economy, the FOMC should be able to explain how, if it is taking policy actions period by period based on the contemporaneous behavior of the economy, it deals with the long-and-variable-lag critique of Milton Friedman (1960). Another way to phrase the issue is to note that for monetary policy to be stabilizing, the FOMC must solve the issue of simultaneity bias, the identification problem. That is, the behavior of the FOMC affects the economy, and the behavior of the economy affects the FOMC. For policy to be stabilizing, the FOMC must sort out the one-way causation from its actions to the behavior of the economy.

Economists who have dealt with the problem of sorting out the one-way causation of monetary policy actions have used a model with a reaction function. A model makes explicit how the price system transmits monetary policy to the economy. Understanding the role of the price system is essential in the absence of a wartime command and control economy. To achieve the goal of the maximum-employment component of the dual mandate, the FOMC must somehow cause the collective spending of an almost innumerable number of households and firms to just equal contemporaneous potential output. To achieve the goal of stable prices, the FOMC must somehow manage the collective price setting of an almost innumerable number of firms setting relative prices in dollar terms so that the individual changes average out to zero.

To achieve this dual feat, monetary policy must rely on a combination of the way in which the price system coordinates the behavior of agents and the way in which monetary policy coordinates their expectations. A model explains how the price system works and how expectations are formed. Because individual policy actions cannot shape expectations, the model must use a reaction function that imposes the consistency on policy required to control expectations. The question then is how does the FOMC square this reality with its language of discretion? Although the FOMC never addresses this question, the answer must be that the FOMC communicates on two tracks.

One track is to the public. The absence of any reference to the stabilizing properties of the price system conveys the message that the FOMC alone is offsetting instability in the economy. Implicitly, the message is that interference with Fed independence would limit its ability to stabilize the economy. The other track is conveyed implicitly to markets and communicates the consistency in monetary policy. The FOMC reconciles the two by not making its reaction function explicit. That is, the FOMC does not make explicit the consistency in its behavior by communicating clearly not only how it responds to current information on the economy but also the consistency in how it responds to incoming new information on the economy.

Commentary by Ben Bernanke when he was a governor in the Alan Greenspan FOMC suggests that the FOMC understands the need to convey the consistency in its policy. Bernanke (2005) said:

> The Fed controls very short-term interest rates quite effectively, but the long-term rates that really matter for the economy depend not on the current short-term rate but on the whole trajectory of future short-term rates expected by market participants. Thus, to affect long-term rates, the FOMC must somehow signal to the financial markets its plans for setting future short-term rates. . . . FOMC talk probably has the greatest influence on expectations of short-term rates a year or so into the future, as beyond that point the FOMC has very little, if any, advantage over market participants in forecasting the economy or even its own policy actions. . . . First, to the extent practical, the FOMC strives to be consistent in how it responds to particular configurations of economic conditions and transparent in explaining the reasons for its response. By building a consistent track record, the FOMC increases its own predictability as well as public confidence in its policies. Second, more generally, comments by FOMC officials about the Committee's general policy framework, including the Committee's economic objectives and members' views about the channels of monetary policy transmission and the structure of the economy, help the public deduce how policy is likely to respond to future economic circumstances.

Commentary by Stanley Fischer when he was vice chair of the Board of Governors in the Janet Yellen FOMC reinforces Bernanke's statement. Fischer (2017a, 1) said:

> It has been increasingly acknowledged that monetary policy implementation relies importantly on the management of market expectations. . . . Clarity about the central bank's reaction function . . . helps meet the central bank's policy targets, with the result that the markets are working in alignment with the policymaker's goals. . . . Clear communication of the Federal Open Market Committee's (FOMC's) views on the economic outlook and the likely evolution of policy is essential in managing the market's expectations.

Fischer's commentary suggests that a model of how monetary policy affects the economy would possess forward-looking agents. When he talked about the Board of Governors' staff model, FRB/US, Fischer (2017b, 6–7) said:

An increase in the federal funds rate affects expectations of future values of that rate, which in turn affect interest rates on longer-term bonds, equity prices, and the exchange value of the U.S. dollar. Households and firms are forward looking. . . . [They] set out a plan—a contingency plan—for consumption, savings, and employment for the future. . . . So the expectations of decisionmakers, be they households, firms, or investors, are at the center of how monetary policy works—both in the real world and in FRB/US.

However, neither Bernanke nor Fischer took the next step to sketch out the kind of model that would formalize their views. Such a model would contain a reaction function—a "contingency plan" in Fischer's words.

To take this next step, Bernanke and Fischer would have had to answer the fundamental question of "What does the FOMC control and how does it exercise that control?" As discussed in the next section, monetary policy in the post–1951 Treasury-Fed Accord period has been organized around two basic choices. One choice characteristic of the 1970s assumed that inflation was a nonmonetary phenomenon powered by the market power of corporations and unions. Consequently, the FOMC's intermediate target was slack in the economy. Monetary policy had to manipulate that slack in a discretionary way to balance off the need to control inflation through socially costly increases in inflation (Burns 1979; Nelson 2005). The heart of monetary policy was the empirical trade-offs given by the Phillips curve.

The other choice, characteristic of the Volcker–Greenspan decades, was that inflation was a monetary phenomenon. As such, the FOMC needed procedures for disciplining the amount of liquidity that investors demanded in their portfolio to be consistent with price stability and by following procedures that allowed the price system to keep output growing at potential. With an interest-rate target, banks would accommodate the required increase in deposits and the Fed would meet the associated reserves demand as a consequence of maintaining its funds rate target. The price system was responsible for eliminating slack in the economy. Note that monetary control need not involve targets for money or bank reserves. The heart of monetary policy was a rule that provided a stable nominal anchor in the form of the expectation of price stability and that allowed the price system to determine real variables through procedures that caused the funds rate to track the natural rate of interest.

The Empirical Generalizations about Monetary Policy That a Model Must Explain

A model must use the empirical generalizations about the behavior of monetary policy over time and be able to predict how the changes either stabilized or destabilized the economy. Since the 1951 Treasury-Fed Accord, there has existed a baseline monetary policy invented by William McChesney Martin and his assistant Winfield Riefler (Hetzel 2008, 2012, 2022). Martin termed it "leaning against the wind" (LAW).

Prior to the 1951 Accord, at times when the Fed was not under the control of the Treasury, the guiding principle for monetary policy had been real bills. The policy departed from the quasi-automatic operation of the gold standard prior to World War I in that it was activist. Policy assumed that recession and deflation resulted from the collapse of prior speculative excess. The organizing principle was then to preempt speculative excess. In effect, by attempting to squash the rise in asset prices (house and equity prices) associated with optimism about the economy, the Fed became a doomsday machine.

However, the policy of real bills was discredited by a failure of recession and deflation to follow World War II despite the fact that the credit structure had been built on bank holdings of government debt rather than on real bills. The spirit of LAW that replaced it entailed offsetting unsustainable strength in the growth of real output by increases in market interest rates (the three-month Treasury bill rate).[7] Because the FOMC had no measure of potential output, policy deliberation focused on whether the economy's rate of resource utilization (declines in the unemployment rate) was increasing to an unsustainable degree. Converse statements hold for unsustainable weakness in the growth of real output.

Based on the productive power in the US economy in World War II, despite the Depression, Martin and early policymakers like Allan Sproul, president of the New York Fed, supported a free-market economy. Averse to the price controls imposed during World War II and the Korean War, they directed policy toward the goal of price stability. Price stability replaced asset-price stability. The conservative Eisenhower administration supported the Fed. Early policymakers continued to view the transmission of monetary policy from the vantage point of its influence on conditions in the credit market. The idea was that if the economy grew at an unsustainable pace, excess credit creation would create inflation. The traumatic experience of being forced to monetize sales to it by banks during the Korean War–era inflation, because of the rate ceiling set on long-term Treasuries, caused the Fed to assume responsibility for excessive growth in bank reserves.

The baseline LAW policy has assumed two variants since its inception. Hetzel (2012) terms one variant "LAW with credibility" or, alternatively, "LAW with preemptive moves in the funds rate." The other variant is termed "LAW with trade-offs" or, alternatively, "LAW with cyclical inertia in the funds rate." By itself, LAW lacks a guide for when to terminate persistent increases or reductions in the funds rate. The issue arises because of the lags in the implementation of monetary policy highlighted by Friedman (1960). The variant known as LAW with credibility corresponded to primacy attached to the maintenance of price stability; LAW with trade-offs corresponded to primacy attached to juggling low unemployment with a low rate of inflation, with each considered as independent goals. The alternations between these two variants constitute the "experiments" policy has furnished. They can be considered experiments in the sense that they corresponded to changes in the understanding of the appropriate role of monetary policy held by policymakers—an understanding not necessarily confirmed by the results.

In the 1950s, Martin moved to LAW with credibility, but only through experience. In 1956, Consumer Price Index inflation rose from price stability to 3%. Martin concluded that the slowness in raising market interest rates after the first post-Accord recession (peak July 1953, trough May 1954) produced the rise in inflation. Martin then turned to LAW with preemptive increases in the funds rate to prevent the emergence of inflation. However, the preemptive moves in the policy rate were asymmetric and did not carry over to preemptive decreases when the economy weakened.

Martin intended to carry the policy through in the recovery from the early 1960s recession (peak April 1960, trough February 1961). As noted above, the Heller CEA under President Johnson opposed increases in the policy rate until the unemployment rate was clearly on track to reach 4%. When inflation emerged in 1966, Martin and Treasury Secretary Henry Fowler agreed to urge President Johnson to advocate for a tax surcharge to restore a balanced budget. It passed in June 1968 and the Fed lowered regional Reserve Bank discount rates. Only in 1969 did Martin realize his mistake in failing to raise interest rates significantly earlier and aggressively raise the policy rate. However, his term ended in February 1970, and Arthur Burns took over as FOMC chair.

The combination of 6% inflation with 6% unemployment in 1970—given the belief that 4% inflation constituted full employment—convinced Burns and most FOMC participants that inflation was powered by cost-push pressures; that is, by upward shifts in the Phillips curve. Price stability would presumably then require rightward movement along the Phillips curve, which meant socially costly increases in the unemployment rate. Judging how much unemployment would be politically acceptable required a policy of ongoing discretion (Burns 1979). Burns repeatedly held off increases in the funds rate as part of bargaining with the administration over incomes policies, which reputedly would lessen the costly trade-off required to maintain price stability. Inflation rose over the decade of the 1970s, reaching low double digits in 1981.

By August 1979, when Paul Volcker replaced G. William Miller as FOMC chair, the United States had lost a stable nominal anchor. That is, expected inflation rose along with increases in actual inflation and also in response to monetary policy, which as extrapolated by financial markets from the go-stop policies of the 1970s was considered expansionary and ultimately inflationary. After an initial false start when the Volcker FOMC signed on to the Carter credit controls announced in March 1980, the Volcker FOMC pursued a policy of disinflation, which lowered inflation to 4% by the end of Volcker's FOMC chairmanship in July 1987.

The Volcker disinflation was guided by the goal of restoring the expectation of price stability. The bond-market vigilantes who had been burned by the 1970s' inflation imposed a discipline on this policy, which prevented any attempt to exploit a Phillips curve trade-off. Whenever the economy began to grow strongly, they created an inflation scare in the form of an increase in bond rates. The FOMC responded by raising the funds rate, effectively restoring the early Martin policy of LAW with credibility through preemptive increases in the funds rate intended to forestall an increase in inflation.

When he became FOMC chair, Alan Greenspan followed this policy. When the FOMC raised the funds rate in 1994 with no evidence of inflation and without causing a recession, the Fed finally restored a stable nominal anchor by anchoring the expectation of price stability. Given the retreat of the bond-market vigilantes, signs of overheating in labor markets became guides to preemptive increases in the funds rate.

For a detailed history of monetary policy following the Greenspan chairmanship, see Hetzel (2022). Very briefly, in the 2008–9 recession, Bernanke abandoned LAW with credibility, in that the FOMC was slow to lower the funds rate after its May 2008 meeting because of high headline inflation caused by a worldwide commodity price shock due to integration of the BRICs (Brazil, Russia, India, and China) into the world economy. Despite a weakening economy, the FOMC remained focused on a fear that high headline inflation would raise the inflationary expectations of the public.

To be stabilizing, LAW needs to be implemented symmetrically with reductions in the funds rate initiated promptly in response to sustained weakness in the economy. Hetzel (2022, ch. 3) shows that with the establishment of the Fed, a consistent indicator for recession is inertia introduced into reduction in money-market interest rates (later the funds rate) when the economy weakens. In 2008, a complicating factor was the reduction in the natural rate of interest to a negative value, especially after the turmoil in financial markets following the Lehman bankruptcy on September 15. The combination of high unemployment and disinflation in the Great Recession signaled that monetary policy was contractionary.

The economy recovered after the Fed initiated quantitative easing (QE) in early 2009. Through a portfolio balance effect, QE counterbalanced the depressing effect of the negative natural rate of interest. In December 2016, when a weak economy again began to grow strongly, FOMC chair Yellen led the FOMC in raising the funds rate despite growth in inflation consistent with price stability. In doing so, she restored LAW with credibility. Although bank reserves grew strongly with QE, M2 grew moderately and steadily. With procedures that track the natural rate of interest, money is not a source of disturbances and offers no predictive power for the economy.

With the clear emergence of the pandemic in March 2020, the Powell FOMC began to engage in a highly expansionary monetary policy. It kept the funds rate at the ZLB while monetizing large amounts of the government pandemic payments. Although the pandemic was a negative supply shock reducing potential real output, the FOMC decided to stimulate aggregate nominal demand. The result was inflation. The policy of flexible average inflation targeting (FAIT) informed markets that the FOMC would maintain the funds rate until inflation emerged. Assuming the existence of a Phillips curve flat down to at least an unemployment rate as low as the prepandemic level of 3.5%, the FOMC assumed that the inflation that began in early 2021 was transitory and would disappear without the need for the funds rate to rise off the ZLB. The result was a Friedman helicopter drop of money. There was a quantitative difference but not a qualitative difference from the money creation in countries like Zimbabwe and Venezuela. The result was inflation.

Choosing a Model Capable of Predicting the Effect of Changes in Monetary Policy

What model can explain the Great Moderation in the Volcker–Greenspan era, which featured the coexistence of moderate unemployment with the move to price stability and then its maintenance? The answer has to be that a stable nominal anchor allows the stabilizing properties of the price system to work. To allocate their own resources (time and capital) optimally, individuals must distinguish between nominal (dollar) and real (relative) prices. Price stability allows them to do so. In the spirit of Adam Smith, the price system then ensures the efficient allocation of resources for the economy. Robert Lucas (1981) formalized this insight.

The NK models of Kosuke Aoki (2001) and Marvin Goodfriend and Robert King (1997) together explain how a credible rule for price stability allows the operation of the price system to maintain full employment. Aoki divides firms into those in the sticky-price sector, which set prices for multiple periods, and those in the flexible-price sector, which set prices in auction markets. The FOMC needs to stabilize prices in the sticky-price sector because inflation distorts relative prices with sticky prices and causes a misallocation of resources. Monetary policy should let price increases in the flexible-price sector pass through to headline inflation because they do not distort relative prices. A credible rule that coordinates the price setting of firms in the sticky-price sector and controls underlying inflation leaves the FOMC free to pursue operating procedures that give the price system free rein to ensure the full employment of resources. As demonstrated in the Goodfriend–King model, price stability is optimal because it turns over the determination of real variables (output and employment) to the real business cycle core of the economy.

The issue then is to explain how the LAW-with-credibility procedures of the Volcker–Greenspan era give empirical content to the Aoki and Goodfriend–King models of the economy. Those procedures can be characterized as a difference Taylor rule. The reason is that they stabilize the economy's rate of resource utilization. The price system is left free to eliminate slack in the economy. The rate of growth of potential real output then determines the rate of growth of real output. Labor markets are left free to determine the natural rate of unemployment through the matching of workers seeking employment and firms seeking workers. The FOMC is not using a gap Taylor rule to balance off the twin objectives for low inflation and low unemployment as with LAW with trade-offs and its focus on the Phillips curve.

How does the LAW-with-credibility rule followed in the Volcker–Greenspan era allow the price system to work to eliminate slack in the economy and keep real output growing at potential? The reason the rule works is that sustained growth above potential (sustained reductions in the economy's rate of resource utilization) signals to the FOMC that the real rate of interest lies below the natural rate of interest. The LAW procedures then indicate that the real rate of interest must rise. Accordingly, the natural rate of interest works to distribute aggregate demand intertemporally so that contemporaneous aggregate demand remains equal to potential output. Sustained growth above potential indicates that the real rate of interest needs to increase to offset the optimism about the future that makes households try to move consumption from the future to the present to smooth consumption (Goodfriend 2004).

An example can help explain how the rule shapes the expectations of financial markets so as to allow the price system to stabilize the economy. Assume that the FOMC determines that the economy's rate of resource utilization is increasing at an unsustainable rate. The FOMC will raise the funds rate. However, in the absence of a structural model of the economy that reveals the natural values of real variables like the natural rate of interest, the FOMC does not know the magnitude of the required increase. In practice, the FOMC will raise the funds rate typically by one quarter of a percentage point. Is the FOMC not then likely behind the curve, in that the natural rate of interest could be much higher than the existing funds rate plus a quarter of a percentage point?

The answer is that the transmission of monetary policy occurs through the yield curve and shifts in the yield curve are not constrained in any way. Just because the funds rate is moved up by a quarter of a percentage point does not mean the yield curve will rise by a quarter of a percentage point. Markets understand that the objective of the rule is to stabilize the economy's rate of resource utilization. It is the North Star that conditions how participants in financial markets move the yield curve based on their forecasts of what shift in the yield curve will be required to stabilize the rate of growth of real output. As a consequence, the yield curve responds continually to incoming, new information on the economy to offset unsustainable weakness or strength in economic growth. Deviations of the real term structure of interest rates from its natural level are continually self-correcting and prevent significant departures from the full employment of resources. It is this tracking of the natural rate of interest by the yield curve through continuous adjustment of the latter that obviates the Friedman long-and-variable-lag critique.

In the Barsky et al. (2014) exposition of the NK model, the output gap stays at zero so long as the contemporaneous and expected future difference between the real rate of interest and the natural rate of interest remains at zero. The spirit of this condition is captured by the behavior of the yield curve described above. In the NK model, also, inflation equals expected inflation plus a markup, which is kept at zero if the output gap is kept at zero. Price stability is then obtained with a rule that maintains the expectation of price stability and that lets the price system work. How does that rule provide for the required monetary control assuming that inflation is a monetary phenomenon?

With the interest rate as the policy variable, a necessary condition for monetary control is that the interest-rate target maintain equilibrium in the bond market. In that way, the FOMC does not need to monetize excess supplies by buying bonds or demonetize excess demands by selling bonds. Both would create erratic changes in the money stock and destabilize the price level. Procedures that keep the real rate of interest equal to the natural rate of interest and thus maintain equilibrium in the goods market ensure this necessary condition. (Don Patinkin [1965] explained how excess demand in the goods market creates excess supply in the bond market.) Phrased alternatively, these procedures avoid the macroeconomic equivalent of price fixing.

The necessary rule that provides for the monetary control required for price stability then comprises two parts. The rule must allow the price system to work to maintain equilibrium in the goods market and consequently in the bond market. The rule must also maintain the expectation of price stability. Banks accommodate changes in the demand for money by the public while the FOMC accommodates the associated demand for reserves creation as a consequence of maintaining its funds rate target. In this way, the rule disciplines the demand for money and its growth to remain consistent with price stability.

What about Friedman's monetarism, which emphasized the control of the monetary aggregates through bank-reserves targets and which advocated steady money growth in M2? What about the fact that these monetary aggregates do not appear in the NK model? The first thing to note is that the NK model, say, of Goodfriend–King abstracts from monetary disorder. It is a template for how to conduct monetary policy without monetary disorder. Because money is not then a source of disturbances, it need not appear in the model.

The second thing to note is that M1 and M2 are empirical measures of the liquidity in the public's asset portfolio. As such, M1 in 1982 and M2 in 1992 ceased being useful measures of the desired theoretical concept. Consider how changes in computer technology and large movements in money-market interest rates in the early 1980s robbed M1 of its predictive power for nominal and real output. The former facilitated a flow of funds between relatively illiquid money-market instruments and liquid bank deposits. Consider weakness in the economy, which causes a decline in money-market interest rates. Banks, however, only reduce the interest paid on their deposits with a long lag. The resulting flow of funds from money-market instruments used for savings purposes into bank deposits increases M1 but without a commensurate increase in the liquidity represented by M1. As a result, the behavior of M1 ceased being procyclical and instead became countercyclical. It then offered misleading information on the desirable changes in the funds rate.

Modeling a Rule after the Volcker–Greenspan Policy of Restoring Price Stability

The rule that would implement the underlying policy that restored price stability in the Volcker–Greenspan era is termed here "LAW with credibility." In short, the rule provides for a stable nominal anchor in the form of the expectation of price stability. The FOMC's operating procedures then allow the price system to determine real variables like output and employment through procedures that cause the funds rate to track the natural rate of interest. These procedures require ongoing judgment at FOMC meetings because of the long lags from monetary policy to the behavior of inflation. There needs to be some intuitively obvious measure that financial markets and the public can use on an ongoing basis to ensure the FOMC's adherence to the rule.

A price-stability rule requires that the rate of growth of nominal output must align with the rate of growth of potential real output. However, neither variable is available in real time. Athanasios Orphanides gets around this problem with what he calls "a natural growth rule" in which he uses forecasts in place of actual values. Orphanides (2024, 9) characterized the rule:

> In real time, the natural growth rule employs short-term forecasts to check whether nominal income grows in line with the economy's natural growth rate. . . . According to this rule, the change of the federal funds rate from the previous quarter can be guided by the difference between the projected growth of nominal income, n, and the natural growth rate, $n*$, defined as the sum of the Fed's inflation goal, $\pi*$,

and the growth rate of real potential GDP, $g*$. The rule takes the first-difference form:

$$\Delta i = \theta(n - n*)$$

where Δi is the rule's prescription for the quarterly change of the funds rate from the previous quarter, and θ is a parameter governing how responsive policy should be to the projected imbalance.

Orphanides's rule works well over the period of relative price stability that started in 1992. It also flags the two exceptions. First, it flags the disinflation that occurred with the 2008–9 recession. Despite an increase in the unemployment rate from 4.4% in May 2007 to 7.3% in December 2008, the FOMC reduced the funds rate to the ZLB only at its December 2008 meeting. Second, the Orphanides rule flags the 2021–22 inflation. Although forecasted nominal GDP growth began to rise significantly in 2020 Q4, the FOMC did not begin to raise the funds rate off the ZLB until March 2022. Quarterly annualized nominal GDP growth went from 4.0% in 2019 Q4 to 7.3% in 2020 Q4 and peaked at 15.1% in 2021 Q4.

To see how an explicit rule would work, one can ask how the FOMC's public communication would change. At present, the FOMC uses the quarterly forecasts in the Summary of Economic Projections (SEP) to communicate with the public and with markets. Assuming that it is possible to deduce from the SEP an FOMC consensus, the SEP does communicate to markets information on how the FOMC is likely to move the funds rate for its given forecast of the economy. However, that information is far from revealing as regards the consistency in how it will change its projected funds rate path in response to new information on the economy, that is, a reaction function.

Consider first the deficiencies in the current SEP and how they would be corrected by an FOMC-consensus SEP as a first step toward articulation of a rule. The SEP contains forecasts for a variety of variables: real GDP, inflation (PCE, or personal consumption expenditures deflator, and core PCE), and the unemployment rate. It also presents a path for the funds rate. The current SEP is a mélange of the views of the individual participants in FOMC meetings. There is no way to connect the forecasts of the individual variables with a particular author.

The only criterion that the authors receive for their forecasts is that they should be "optimal." Optimal means that all participants will forecast a long-run inflation rate of 2%. However, the SEP offers no information on the consistency that the FOMC participants must impose on the individual policy actions to achieve that goal. It does contain their forecasted path for the funds rate. However, the SEP reveals no information on how the FOMC would respond if the forecasted variables come in differently than those contained in the SEP. That is, it does not reveal a reaction function.

Explicitness about the rule that ensures long-run price stability could begin with an FOMC-consensus SEP. The Tealbook Part A forecast of the economy is the benchmark that FOMC participants use in that they either agree with it or shade their differences in a way that supports their choice of the funds that differs from option B in the Tealbook Part B. Option C is for an increase in the funds rate and option A is for a reduction in the funds rate. In the second part of FOMC meetings, the chair finds common ground to support FOMC agreement on which option to choose, A, B, or C. With the LAW-with-credibility rule, the Tealbook would format its forecasts around values that give content to Orphanides's formula shown above, $\Delta i = \theta(n - n*)$, which is the prescription for policy that aligns the rate of growth of nominal output with the rate of growth of potential real output. The Committee would modify the arguments of the right-hand side based on the judgment of the participants.

At the post-FOMC meeting press conference, the FOMC chair would present the FOMC consensus over the chosen funds rate target based on its forecasts of the right-hand-side variables in the formula. The funds rate chosen would be consistent with elimination of the difference between nominal GDP growth and potential real GDP growth. Fed accountability would be encouraged because reporters at the chair's press conference would ask the chair to defend differences between the Committee's forecast and publicly available forecasts such as those contained in the blue chip forecasts.

Concluding Comment

If the FOMC decides to commit to the maintenance of price stability, it will need to accompany that decision by a rule. The conservative choice would be to institutionalize the consistency that restored price stability in the Volcker–Greenspan era. That is, it would give content to "LAW with credibility" (LAW with preemptive changes in the funds rate). The need for an announced rule is that preemptive increases in the funds rate occur without the emergence of inflation. In the fraught environment likely to obtain in the future, explanation of the rationale for the rule will be required to head off the 1970s-era criticism that funds rate increases are intended to slow the growth of the economy and are therefore controlling inflation on the "backs of workers." The FOMC will have to acknowledge that it is relying on the stabilizing properties of the price system to maintain full employment.

Communication in terms of a rule would require a change in the culture of the FOMC. The FOMC would have to acknowledge that its role is to provide for a stable nominal anchor in the form of price stability. The resulting price stability will then allow the stabilizing properties of the price system to work to maintain the full employment of resources. Fed independence is a prerequisite for the consistent implementation of such a rule and should be defended on that basis.

Notes

1. The top marginal tax rate went from 39.6% to 37%, which applies to income for joint filers making $771,550 as opposed to $615,100 before TCJA (York et al. 2024).

2. Figures from Lee (2024).

3. Elizabeth Truss was the prime minister in the UK over the brief six-week period from September 2022 to October 2022. She had to resign when her proposed tax cut initiated a spike in interest rates. Serhan (2022) wrote: "Her signature package of £45 billion ($50.6 billion) in unfunded tax cuts, which disproportionately favored the country's wealthiest, succeeded only in crashing the pound, spooking the markets, and undermining Britain's credibility around the world."

4. Wikipedia (2025) wrote: "*End the Fed* is a 2009 book by Congressman Ron Paul of Texas. The book debuted at number six on the *New York Times* Best Seller list and advocates the abolition of the United States Federal Reserve System 'because it is immoral, unconstitutional, impractical, promotes bad economics, and undermines liberty.' The book argues that the booms, bubbles and busts of the business cycle are caused by the Federal Reserve's actions. . . . In *End the Fed*, Paul argues that the Federal Reserve was created to bail out banks when they got into trouble. He says that this is bad for competition in banking, as it strengthens the big banks."

5. James (2012) wrote: "The college wage premium is calculated as the ratio of the median hourly wage for those holding a bachelor's degree and the median hourly wage for those who have only completed high school. . . . These data show that the college wage premium increased rapidly through the 1980s and early part of the 1990s, rising from 40 percent to upwards of 70 percent. Since the late 1990s, the premium has experienced a much slower rate of growth, drifting at times below and above 80 percent. Importantly though, the premium has persisted at historically high levels through the 2000s, becoming an enduring feature of the U.S. wage structure." Deming (2023) wrote: "The U.S. college wage premium doubles over the life cycle, from 27 percent at age 25 to 60 percent at age 55. Using a panel survey of workers

followed through age 60, I show that growth in the college wage premium is primarily explained by occupational sorting. Shortly after graduating, workers with college degrees shift into professional, nonroutine occupations with much greater returns to tenure. . . . College acts as a gateway to professional occupations, which offer more opportunity for wage growth through on-the-job learning."

6. Fogli and Guerrieri (2019) explained how the housing segregation by income that excludes poor families from the suburbs and their superior schools perpetuates inequality: "Since the '80s the US has experienced not only a steady increase in income inequality, but also a contemporaneous increase in residential segregation by income. Using US census data, we first document a positive correlation between inequality and segregation at the MSA level between 1980 and 2010. . . . Segregation and inequality amplify each other because of a local spillover that affect the returns to education. . . . [When] an unexpected permanent skill premium shock hits the economy . . . segregation contributes to 28% of the subsequent increase in inequality."

7. The FOMC's publicly announced target of free reserves (excess reserves minus borrowed reserves) allowed the Fed to tell the Treasury that it did not control interest rates (and should never again become a residual buyer of the Treasuries the Treasury failed to sell in its offerings to the public). In effect, free reserves controlled market interest rates as determined by the discount rate plus an amount that corresponded to the amount of free reserves.

References

Aoki, Kosuke. 2001. "Optimal Monetary Policy Responses to Relative-Price Changes." *Journal of Monetary Economics* 48 (1): 55–80.

Barsky, Robert Alejandro Justiniano, and Leonardo Melosi. 2014. "The Natural Rate of Interest and Its Usefulness for Monetary Policy." *American Economic Review: Papers and Proceedings* 104 (5): 37–43.

Bernanke, Ben S. 2005. "Implementing Monetary Policy." Remarks at the Redefining Investment Strategy Education Symposium, Dayton, Ohio. March 30.

Burns, Arthur. 1979. "The Anguish of Central Banking." Lecture at the Per Jacobsson Foundation, Belgrade, Yugoslavia. September 30.

Clausing, Kimberly, and Mary E. Lovely. 2024. "Trump's Bigger Tariff Proposals Would Cost the Typical American Household over $2,600 a Year." Peterson Institute for International Economics. August 21. https://www.piie.com/research/piie-charts/2024/trumps-bigger-tariff-proposals-would-cost-typical-american-household-over.

Committee for a Responsible Federal Budget. 2024. "FY 2024 Ends with $1.8 Trillion Deficit." *The Bottom Line* (blog). November 6. https://www.crfb.org/blogs/fy-2024-ends-18-trillion-deficit.

Deming, David. 2023. "Why Do Wages Grow Faster for Educated Workers?" Faculty Research Working Paper No. RWP23-017. Harvard Kennedy School. June.

Fischer, Stanley. 2017a. "Monetary Policy Expectations and Surprises." Speech at the Columbia University School of International and Public Affairs, New York, NY. April 17.

Fischer, Stanley. 2017b. "I'd Rather Have Bob Solow than an Econometric Model, But. . . ." Remarks at the Warwick Economics Summit, Coventry, United Kingdom. February 11.

Fogli, Alessandra, and Veronica Guerrieri. 2019. "The End of the American Dream? Inequality and Segregation in US Cities." Working Paper No. 26143. National Bureau of Economic Research. August.

Friedman, Milton. 1960. *A Program for Monetary Stability.* Fordham University Press.

Goodfriend, Marvin S. 2004. "Monetary Policy in the New Neoclassical Synthesis: A Primer." *Federal Reserve Bank of Richmond Economic Quarterly* 90 (3): 21–45.

Goodfriend, Marvin, and Robert G. King. 1997. "The New Neoclassical Synthesis." In *NBER Macroeconomics Annual,* edited by Ben S. Bernanke and Julio Rotemberg. NBER.

Hetzel, Robert L. 2008. *The Monetary Policy of the Federal Reserve: A History.* Cambridge University Press.

Hetzel, Robert L. 2012. *The Great Recession: Market Failure or Policy Failure?* Cambridge University Press.

Hetzel, Robert L. 2022. *The Federal Reserve. A New History.* University of Chicago Press.

James, Jonathan. 2012. "The College Wage Premium." *Economic Commentary,* no. 2012-10 (August 8).

Lee, Medora. 2024. "Higher Tax Rates, Smaller Child Tax Credit and Other Changes Await as Trump Tax Cuts End." *USA Today,* July 23.

Lucas, Robert E., Jr. 1981. "Expectations and the Neutrality of Money (1972)." In *Studies in Business-Cycle Theory.* MIT Press.

Meyer, Larry. 2024. "Fed Balance Sheet Watch: Transition to Endgame." Monetary Policy Analytics, *LHMeyer* newsletter, LHM. October 28.

Nelson, Edward. 2005. "The Great Inflation of the Seventies: What Really Happened?" *Topics in Macroeconomics* 5 (1): article 3. https://doi.org/10.2202 /1534-6013.1297.

Orphanides, Athanasios. 2024. "Enhancing Resilience with Natural Growth Targeting." Draft prepared for the AIER Fed Framework Review Workshop, Florida Atlantic University, Boca Raton, FL. January 20.

Patinkin, Don. 1965. *Money, Interest, and Prices.* Harper & Row.

PS Commentators. 2024. "*PS* Roundtable: The Return of Trump." *PS* Longer Reads, *Project Syndicate,* November 8. https://www.project-syndicate.org/onpoint /trump-return-ps-commentators-explain-what-it-means-by-ps-editors-2024-11.

Reich, Robert. 2024. "How to Root Out Trumpism." Substack.com. November 11.

Serhan, Yasmeen. 2022. "Liz Truss Has Resigned. Here's How She Lost Control." *Time,* October 20.

Wikipedia. 2025. "End the Fed." January 19. https://en.wikipedia.org/w/index
.php?title=End_the_Fed&direction=prev&oldid=1274490746.
York, Erica. 2024. "How 2026 Tax Brackets Would Change if the TCJA
Expires." Tax Foundation (blog). October 24. https://taxfoundation.org
/blog/2026-tax-brackets-tax-cuts-and-jobs-act-expires/.
York, Erica, Alex Durante, Huaqun Li, Garrett Watson, and Will McBride. 2024.
"Options for Navigating the 2025 Tax Cuts and Jobs Act Expirations." Research,
Federal Taxes, Tax Foundation. May 7. https://taxfoundation.org/research/all
/federal/2025-tax-reform-options-tax-cuts-and-jobs-act/.

KEVIN WARSH: Great, thank you, Greg [Hess]. We've got time for a few questions before Chris [Waller] leads us at lunch at noon. Let me call on folks. I see Andy over here.

Can we pass a microphone in the front?

ANDREW T. LEVIN: Great session. It's important to ensure that the history gets preserved accurately. So, the Fed finally initiated its first rate hike in March 2022. By how much? A quarter of a percentage point. And there was only a single dissenting vote: Jim Bullard. The FOMC [Federal Open Market Committee] press release indicates that Jim "preferred to raise the target rate by half a percentage point."

So the FOMC's first rate hike definitely didn't convey the idea that "Oh, we're really behind the curve here." In fact, over the next six months there was a protracted period where Fed officials were describing these adjustments as simply bringing policy back to a neutral stance. At the March 2022 meeting, the FOMC's median projection was that the federal funds rate would be 1.9% at the end of 2022, then reach a peak at around 2.5% before declining a little bit.

So I'd like to ask Kevin, as the chair of this session, what steps would be helpful for mitigating the problem of groupthink at the Fed? Because it seems like groupthink is really the deeper problem that lies underneath all of these other problems.

WARSH: It's a good question. I'll try to give a brief answer. First, there has to be a genuine openness intellectually to ideas that would otherwise be thought heretical. The notion of money as relevant to monetary policy is an idea that had fallen so far out of favor. Any discussion around the Fed table about M2 growth, I suspect, might be met by people that would avert their eyes.

But policymakers must be justifiably humble, not just rhetorically humble but justifiably humble, about their forecasting abilities and about the reliability of their workhorse models like FRB/US. Otherwise, it will be very difficult to prepare for the future. If most policymakers are too sure about the causes and consequences of inflation, others have to be encouraged to step up.

Second, there has to be an understanding about the dangers of forward guidance. Human nature infects central bankers, too. The more policymakers reveal their forecasts/dots for the next several meetings, the more they will resist being proven wrong.

Hence, policymakers crowd out ideas that might be at odds with the forecasts they gave. Around the time that I departed the Fed, it came to be understood that being hugely transparent was an unvarnished good.

The essential part of central bank forward guidance is to demonstrate the policymakers' reaction function to different events. But the moment that you give your forecast, we all tend to lock ourselves in. We tend to be resistant to change. We tend to herd in our behavior.

And Andy, as you know, one negative consequence of the last decade of Fed forecasts is policymakers' forecasts are largely the same. The growth forecasts and inflation forecasts from the Fed staff happen to mirror very similarly the forecasts from the other nineteen participants around the table.

Who wants to break from the center with a disparate view? Who wants to do that? In which case, when you're wrong, you're horribly wrong, and alone.

Don Kohn and I used to have a lot of intellectual fights when we were at the Fed back in the day. But they were useful family fights. We would debate whether the job of the FOMC is to minimize deviations in output and employment from its objectives. Or is it the job of the FOMC to minimize very significant deviations in output and employment? Is the Fed well placed to effectively be in the fine-tuning business? Or should the Fed be in the business principally of avoiding very big mistakes?

Andy, in my view, when everybody around the FOMC speaks so frequently about their dots and forecasts, it tends to exacerbate the risks. When the Fed makes a mistake, it'll be a doozy. And it proved to be.

ROBERT L. HETZEL: One problem is that people are human and the stakes are so high; you just can't say, "I screwed up. I caused the Great Recession." Why did Ben Bernanke write a paper in the *AER* [*American Economic Review*] where he only talks about credit policy? He never talks about monetary policy. Well, so that makes it very hard to learn, because the Fed just rationalizes whatever it's done, right or wrong, and then it goes, Yeah, the economy's evolving, we don't really have a good way of learning.

So if you had a rule, then that would force you to move away from rationalizing what you did, but actually defend what you did in terms of that rule, and that would be a lot harder.

WARSH: Great, let's turn to other questions. John, right behind you.

JOHN H. COCHRANE: This is great, thank you.

I feel like I am at a memorial service for a friend who died in 1982, and the eulogy starts with, "Wait, the body is moaning in the casket, maybe he isn't dead after all!" The body, of course, is monetarism.

To Peter Ireland the moan from the casket is that M2 went up before the recent inflation. But the Fed does not control M2. And for the quantity of money to control the price level, the Fed must control the supply of money.

There are no reserve requirements. The interest rate on money is either zero or equal to the interest rate on bonds. We're in a perpetual liquidity trap. So it seems pretty obvious that today the price level determines M2, not the other way around. M2 is completely endogenous.

That leads to my larger question. What do we even mean by "nominal anchor" anyway?

I sense two definitions. One presumes that the Fed can control inflation, but asks what is in the Fed's procedures to make it pay attention to inflation and keep it under control? The other, and the one that Robert Barro had in mind, is a property of an economic model. What is the key ingredient of an economic model that allows that model to determine the price level? Here we have a problem: The Fed does not control the money supply. So even if money does, in principle, determine the price level, the Fed is not doing it. We do not have a gold standard either; that, in principle, could determine the price level, but not today. Even if the Fed determined the money supply, when velocity is interest elastic, there are multiple equilibria, so money-supply control doesn't determine the price level. Interest rate targets lead to multiple equilibria. Our Fed does not engage in off-equilibrium threats to kill the economy to eliminate multiple equilibria, so that doesn't determine the price level.

As you know, I think there's only one answer remaining. But I'm curious what your view is of the subject of this question, at least the economic one. What is the nominal anchor? What economic mechanism does determine the price level?

WARSH: Peter, in the interest of time, maybe you answer the first two questions, and the other sounds like the next meeting of the SOMC.

PETER N. IRELAND: Two quick answers to the question. One is, is there any information content in the monetary aggregates? Monetarist analysis has almost always been reduced form, and this is reduced-form evidence. And you ask, does that reduced-form evidence provide any signal about whether monetary policy conducted not in an attempt to target M2, but holding interest rates at zero while you're conducting quantitative easing—is it inappropriately overly accommodative?

Now, you're right, velocity moves around; I admitted as much. If your narrow definition of monetarism is that we follow a constant money-growth rule, my point was that that's dead, and rightly so. I still think that there's a legitimate question of what you glean from information about M2 against the backdrop of tremendous uncertainty about whether the Fed was overdoing it or whether to pull back would risk falling back into a terrible recession.

The second answer to the question, is, just because the Fed Reserve has a monetary system where it cannot control M2, one could conceive of a monetary policy system where it could exercise more control over M2. And would that be better or worse than what we have right now?

It's important to remember that Milton Friedman never argued that the constant money-growth rule would be the optimal policy in any specific model. What he argued was a monetary policy dedicated to holding M2 growth constant would have been better than what we experienced during the Great Depression, and better than what we experienced during the 1970s.

It so happens I still agree with that. And then you ask, about the cry out in the coffin. That cry asks, are we happy with what happened in 2020? As Kevin suggested in his introduction, a lot of people want to say, "Well, sure, that happened, but now we're back to 2% inflation, so now let's just move on." But that's not really what I want.

WARSH: Great, we have time for one final question. I saw a hand over here.

ROBERT G. KING: So I wanted to praise Greg Hess's archaeological work.

GREGORY D. HESS: Thank you.

KING: I remember Barro giving a version of that paper and some related seminars at Rochester.

And I think it's very important to recognize that what he was talking about was determining the price level. The current system we have in the United States of an inflation target, taken narrowly, does not determine the price level. It determines a rate of change of the price level.

And Barro was actually very interested in what the behavior of the price level would be under a constant money-growth rule, because it was a period in which the US was looking forward optimistically to a deflation, excuse me, a disinflation. A disinflation would cut the nominal interest rate, increase the real demand for money, and potentially cause havoc with analysis based on constant money-growth rule.

Now, the final observation I'd make, given that that's ancient history, is to look at the recent years. I think there's significant evidence that during the recent period, some measures of market expectations for long-term inflation have gone up not hugely, but a percent. And some other shorter-term measures of expected inflation have gone up much more.

Now, that's understandable if the world's partly transitory and partly permanent. And what seems a success for the Powell Fed so far is that they've gotten those longer-term numbers to come down. And yet it also suggests that there was some significant uncertainty in the public mind about that inflation targeting system.

WARSH: Greg, a final word, and then we're going to call it.

HESS: Thank you, let's have lunch.

WARSH: Thank you.

Keynote Speech

Thoughts on the Economy
and Policy Rules at the Federal
Open Market Committee

Introduction

Athanasios Orphanides

Let me start by thanking John Taylor in particular, and the Hoover Institution more generally, for organizing and hosting this wonderful event. It's a great pleasure for me to introduce as our lunch speaker Chris Waller, governor of the Federal Reserve. We all know Chris, and I'm not going to go through his CV; I will just mention two things.

Number one, he only started his term as governor in December of 2020, so he's not responsible in any way for the August 2020 policy strategy that the Fed is currently operating by. So this is one element I want to mention. The second element I want to mention is something I really appreciate for people in the Fed System.

Chris has been one of the dedicated civil servants operating the Fed System for many years. And I think as a nation in the United States, we're very lucky that we have so many people like Chris trying to run the country's monetary policy and do a good job.

Chris, the floor is yours.

10

Thoughts on the Economy and Policy Rules at the Federal Open Market Committee

Christopher J. Waller*

In support of the theme of the conference, I have some thoughts on the Shadow Open Market Committee's contributions to the policy debate, in particular its advocacy for policy rules. But before I get to that, I want to offer my views on the economic outlook and its implications for monetary policy. Afterward, I will discuss the role that policy rules play in my decision making and in the deliberations of the Federal Open Market Committee (FOMC).

In the three weeks or so since the FOMC meeting on September 17–18, 2024, data we have received has been uneven, as it sometimes has been over the past year. I continue to judge that the US economy is on a solid footing, with employment near the FOMC's maximum employment objective and inflation in the vicinity of our target, even though the latest inflation data was disappointing.

Real GDP grew at a 2.2% annual rate in the first half of 2024, and I expect it to grow a bit faster in the third quarter. The blue chip consensus of private-sector forecasters predicts 2.3%, while the Federal Reserve Bank of Atlanta's GDPNow model, based on up-to-the-moment data, is predicting real growth of 3.2%.

Earlier, there were concerns that GDP in the first half of 2024 was overstating the strength of the economy, since gross domestic income (GDI) was estimated to have grown a mere 1.3% in the first half of 2024, suggesting a big downward revision to GDP was coming. But revisions received after our

*This chapter derives from a speech given at the Shadow Open Market Committee Conference on October 14, 2024, and has been edited for publication. The original speech may be found at https://www.federalreserve.gov/newsevents/speech/waller20241014a.htm.

September FOMC meeting showed the opposite—GDI growth was revised up substantially, to 3.2%. This change in turn led to an upward revision in the personal saving rate of about 2 percentage points in the second quarter, leaving it at 5.2% in June. This revision suggests that household resources for future consumption are actually in good shape, although data and anecdotal evidence suggest lower-income groups are struggling. These revisions are a sign that the economy is much stronger than previously thought, with little indication of a major slowdown in economic activity.

That outlook is supported by consumer spending that has been and continues to be strong. Though the growth in personal consumption expenditures (PCE) has moderated since the second half of 2023, it has continued at an average pace of close to 2.5% so far this year. Also, my business contacts believe that there is considerable pent-up demand for durable goods, home improvements, and other big-ticket items, demand that built up due to high interest rates for credit cards and home equity loans. Now that rates have started to come down and are expected to come down more, consumers will be eager to make those purchases. For business spending, purchasing managers for manufacturing firms describe ongoing weakness in that sector, but those for the large majority of businesses outside of manufacturing continue to report a solid expansion of activity.

Now let's talk about the labor market. During the summer of 2024, it appeared that the labor market was cooling too quickly. Low numbers for job creation and a jump in the unemployment rate from 4.1% in June to 4.3% in July 2024 raised risks that the labor market was deteriorating. To remind you of how bad the markets viewed the July data, some Fed watchers were calling for an emergency FOMC meeting to discuss a rate cut. While the unemployment rate ticked down in August, job growth was once again well below expectations. Many were arguing that the labor market was on the verge of a serious deterioration and that the Fed was behind the curve even after a 50-basis-point cut in the policy rate at the September FOMC meeting.

Then we got the September 2024 employment report. Job creation in September was unexpectedly strong at 254,000, and the unemployment rate fell back down to 4.1%, which is where it was in June. The report also showed big upward revisions to payroll gains for the previous two months. Together, the message was loud and clear: While job creation has moderated and the unemployment rate has risen over the past year, the labor market remains quite healthy.

Along with other new data on the labor market, the evidence is that labor supply and demand have come into balance. The number of job vacancies, a sign of strength in the labor market, has fallen gradually since the beginning of the year. The ratio of vacancies to unemployed is at 1.2, about the level in 2019, which was a pretty strong labor market. To put this number into perspective, recent research has shown that this ratio has been above 1 only three times since 1960.[1] The quits rate, another sign of labor market strength, has fallen lower than it was in 2019, a decrease that partly reflects that the hiring rate has fallen as labor supply and demand have come into better balance.

In sum, based on payrolls, the unemployment rate, and job revisions, there has been a very gradual moderation in labor demand relative to supply, but not a deterioration. The stability of the labor market, as reflected in these two measures as well as the other metrics I mentioned, bolsters my confidence that we can achieve further progress toward the FOMC's inflation goal while supporting a healthy labor market that adds jobs and boosts wages and living standards for workers.

I will be looking for more evidence to support this outlook in the weeks and months to come. But unfortunately, it won't be easy to interpret the October jobs report to be released just before the November 6–7, 2024, FOMC meeting. This report will most likely show a significant but temporary loss of jobs from the two recent hurricanes and the strike at Boeing. I expect these factors may reduce employment growth by more than 100,000 this month, and there may be a small effect on the unemployment rate, but I'm not sure it will be that visible. Since the jobs report will come during the usual blackout period for policymakers commenting on the economy, you won't have any of us trying to put this low reading into perspective, though I hope others will.

Looking ahead, I expect payroll gains to moderate from their current pace but continue at a solid rate. The unemployment rate may drift a bit higher but is likely to remain quite low in historical terms. While I believe the labor market is on a solid footing, I will continue to watch the full range of data for signs of weakness.

Meanwhile, inflation, after showing considerable progress for several months toward the FOMC's 2% target, likely moved up in September. The Consumer Price Index (CPI) grew 0.2% over the past month, 2.1% over the past three months, 1.6% over six months, and 2.4% in the past year. Oil prices fell over most of the summer but then more recently have surged. Excluding energy and also food prices that likewise tend to be volatile, and just as it did in August, core CPI inflation printed at 0.3% in September and 3.3% over the past year.

Private-sector forecasts are predicting that PCE inflation, the FOMC's preferred measure, will also move up in September. Core PCE prices are expected to have risen around 0.25% last month. While not a welcome development, if the monthly core PCE inflation number comes in at around this level, that means that over the last five months it is still running very close to 2% on an annualized basis. We have made a lot of progress on inflation over the course of the last year and half, but that progress has clearly been uneven—at times it feels like being on a roller coaster. Whether or not the September inflation reading is just noise or if it signals ongoing increases is yet to be seen. I will be watching the data carefully to see how persistent this recent uptick is.

The FOMC's inflation goal is an average of 2% over the longer run and there are some good reasons to think that price increases will be modest going forward. I am hearing reports from firms that their pricing power seems to have waned as consumers have become more sensitive to price changes. There has also been a steady slowing in the growth of labor compensation. It is true that average hourly earnings growth in September 2024 ticked up to 4% over the past year. And though it might seem like wage increases of 4% a year would put upward pressure on inflation that is near 2%, that might not be true if one considers productivity, which has grown at an average annual rate of 2.9% for the past five quarters. Some of this strength was making up for productivity that shrank due to the COVID-19 pandemic, but the longer it continues—up 2.5% for the second quarter—the better productivity supports wage growth of 4%, or even higher, without driving up inflation. All that said, I will be watching all the data related to inflation closely.

With the labor market in rough balance, employment near its maximum level, and inflation generally running close to our target over the past several months, I want to do what I can as a policymaker to keep the economy on this path. For me, the central question is how much and how fast to reduce the target for the federal funds rate, which I believe is currently set at a restrictive level. To help answer questions like this, I often look at various monetary policy rules to assess the appropriate setting of policy. Policy rules have long been of serious interest to the Shadow Open Market Committee. So before I turn to my views on the future path of policy, I thought I would talk about monetary policy rules versus discretion and begin with some background about the use of rules at the FOMC.

For a brief overview of the history of the advent of rules at the Board, I have been directed to the second chapter of *The Taylor Rule and the Transformation of Monetary Policy* written by George Kahn, and I have also consulted the memories of longtime members of the Board staff.[2] Rules came along in the 1990s as the Fed was moving away from monetary targeting, focusing more on interest-rate policy, and taking its first major steps toward increased transparency. There was immediate interest in Taylor-type rules among Fed staff, and even some contributions of research.[3] There was a presentation to the FOMC on rules in 1995, and that was the same year that John Taylor's Bay Area colleague, Janet Yellen, was apparently the first policymaker to mention the Taylor rule at an FOMC meeting. While FOMC decisions mimicked a Taylor rule much of the time under Chairman Alan Greenspan, he was famously an advocate of "constructive ambiguity" in communication, and he and other central bankers since have resisted the suggestion that decisions could be handed over to strict rules. Today, of course, a number of rules-based analyses are included in the material submitted to policymakers ahead of every FOMC meeting, and we publish the policy prescriptions of different rules as part of the Board's semiannual Monetary Policy Report. Rules have become part of the furniture in modern policymaking.

Taylor rules relate the level of the policy interest rate to a limited number of other economic variables, most often including the deviation of inflation from a target value and a measure of resource use in the economy relative to some long-run trend.[4] There are numerous forms of the Taylor rule, but they generally fall into two categories.

The first of these, an inertial rule, has the property that the policy rate changes only slowly over time. I tend to think of it as an approach that captures the reaction function of a policymaker in a stable economy where the forces that would tend to change the economy and policy build over time. When change does occur, a gradual response may give policymakers time to assess the true state of the economy and the possible effects of their decision. One example I can use is the steadfastness of policymakers in the latter part of 2023, when inflation fell more rapidly than was widely expected, and again in early 2024, when it briefly escalated. The FOMC did not change course either time, an approach validated by inertial rules.

A non-inertial rule, on the other hand, allows and in fact calls for relatively quick adjustments to policy. The guidance from these rules is more useful when there is a turning point in the economy, and policymakers need to stay ahead of events. One saw these non-inertial rules prescribe a sharper rise in the policy rate above the effective lower bound starting in 2021 as inflation began climbing above the FOMC's 2% target. Non-inertial rules are also more useful in the face of major shocks to the economy such as the 2008 financial crisis and the start of the pandemic.

The great promise of rules is that they provide a simple and reliable guide to policy, but what should one do when different rules recommend different policy actions given the same economic conditions? Right now, inertial rules tell us to move slowly in reducing policy rates toward a neutral stance that neither restricts nor stimulates the economy. On the other hand, non-inertial rules tell us to cut the policy rate more aggressively, subject to the caveat that one is certain of the values of all the "star" variables: U^*, Y^*, and r^*. I think the answer is that while rules are valuable in helping analyze policy options, they have limitations. Among these are the limits of the data considered, which is typically narrower than the range of data that policymakers use to make decisions, and also the fact that simple policy rules do not take into account risk management, which is often a critical consideration in policy decisions. So, while policy rules serve as a good check on discretionary policy, there are times when discretion is needed. As a result, I prefer to think of them as "policy rules of thumb."

Turning to my view for the path for policy, let me discuss three scenarios that I have had in mind to manage the risks of upcoming decisions in the medium term.

The first scenario is one where the overall strong economic developments that I have described here continue, with inflation nearing the FOMC's target and the unemployment rate moving up only slightly. This scenario implies to me that we can proceed with moving policy toward a neutral stance at a deliberate pace. This path would be based on the judgment that the risks to both sides of our dual mandate are balanced. In this circumstance, our job is to keep inflation near 2% and not slow the economy unnecessarily.

Another scenario, less likely in light of recent data, is that inflation falls materially below 2% for some time, and/or the labor market significantly deteriorates. The message here is that demand is falling and the FOMC may suddenly be behind the curve, and that message would argue for moving to neutral more quickly by front-loading cuts to the policy rate.

The third scenario applies if inflation unexpectedly escalates either because of stronger-than-expected consumer demand or wage pressure, or because of some shock to supply that pushes up inflation. As we learned in the recovery from the pandemic recession, when demand was stronger and supply weaker than initially expected, such surprises do occur. In this circumstance, as long as the labor market isn't deteriorating, we can pause rate cuts until progress resumes and uncertainty diminishes.

Most recently, we have seen upward revisions to GDI, an increase in job vacancies, high GDP growth forecasts, a strong jobs report, and a hotter-than-expected CPI report. This data is signaling that the economy may not be slowing as much as desired. While we do not want to overreact to this data or look through it, I view the totality of the data as saying monetary policy should proceed with more caution on the pace of rate cuts than was needed at the September meeting. I will be watching to see whether data due out before our next meeting, on inflation, the labor market, and economic activity confirms or undercuts my inclination to be more cautious about loosening monetary policy.

Whatever happens in the near term, my baseline still calls for reducing the policy rate gradually over the next year. The median rate for FOMC participants at the end of 2025 is 3.4%, so most of my colleagues likewise expect to reduce the policy rate over the next year. There is less certainty about the final destination. The median estimated longer-run level of the federal funds rate in the Committee's Summary of Economic Projections (SEP) is 2.9%, but with quite a wide dispersion, ranging from 2.4% to 3.8%. While much attention is given to the size of cuts over the next meeting or two, I think the larger message of the SEP is that there is a considerable extent of policy restrictiveness to remove, and if the economy continues in its current sweet spot, this will happen gradually.

Thank you again, for the opportunity to be part of the conference, and for allowing me to share some thoughts relevant to monetary policy rules and my day job back in Washington. The Shadow Committee has elevated the public debate about monetary policy. May it continue to play that role for many years to come.

Notes

1. See Benigno and Eggertsson (2024).

2. See Koenig et al. (2012). I was assisted in this brief history by Board economists James Clouse and Edward Nelson.

3. See Henderson and McKibbin (1993).

4. For a variety of Taylor rules and their implication for policy, see the Monetary Policy Report, available on the Board's website at https://www.federalreserve.gov/monetarypolicy/publications/mpr_default.htm.

References

Benigno, Pierpaolo, and Gauti B. Eggertsson. 2024. "Revisiting the Phillips and Beveridge Curves: Insights from the 2020s Inflation Surge." Paper presented at the Federal Reserve Bank of Kansas City's Economic Policy Symposium, "Reassessing the Effectiveness and Transmission of Monetary Policy." Jackson Hole, WY. August 23.

Henderson, Dale W., and Warwick J. McKibbin. 1993. "A Comparison of Some Basic Monetary Policy Regimes for Open Economies: Implications of Different Degrees of Instrument Adjustment and Wage Persistence." *Carnegie-Rochester Conference Series on Public Policy* 39 (December): 221–317.

Koenig, Evan F., Robert Leeson, and George A. Kahn, eds. 2012. *The Taylor Rule and the Transformation of Monetary Policy.* Hoover Institution Press.

ATHANASIOS ORPHANIDES: Thank you, Chris [Waller]. So this was a wonderful talk before our main course is served. But thank you also for agreeing to take a few questions. And I'm going to start with a couple of them.

CHRISTOPHER J. WALLER: With all the sharks in the room.

ORPHANIDES: Yep, well, I'm going to ease things. I do not consider myself a shark in this setting, but I do want to start with the issue that you mentioned that, the economy is stronger than you thought, and this raises some questions about the stars. So first, perhaps policy has not been as restrictive as the Fed previously thought over the past couple of years.

Second, and you gave some data on productivity, perhaps productivity trends have started to shift. Both of those considerations have major implications about what the neutral rate is and would shape what the outlook for rates is. Based on the three scenarios you have, can you tell us a little bit about how you think about this?

How have recent data, the last years of data, influenced your thinking of the uncertain stars?

WALLER: Right, so let me just start with productivity. So we've seen a reasonable number of quarters with 2%-plus productivity growth. But you've got to remember, we had three quarters of negative productivity growth.

So the level of productivity was here. It drops. It comes up. Okay, it's going to look like it's growing really fast. If you look from the first quarter of 2021 to now and look at the annualized growth and productivity, it's 1.7%, pretty much what it was for the previous twenty years.

So I hope this continues. But right now, a lot of what I think we're seeing is just a rebound from a bunch of quarters of negative productivity growth. But for the good of the economy, that's what I would really like to see is this continue on. Now, in terms of r-star, I sometimes feel like this is, we could sit here and argue about this all day long and get absolutely nowhere.

But at the end of the day, you kind of have to have some idea of what it might be to go forward. Now, I gave a speech in Iceland back in May, where I talked about r-star and where I thought were the causes of the long-run decline in r-star, and then asked a simple question.

Given that these are the causes of this long-run decline in the real return on safe, liquid government debt, what are the factors that would reverse that and drive up r-star? Now, for me, the biggest concern I have would just be the unsustainability of fiscal policy. If the supply of Treasuries starts growing faster than the supply of demand, or the demand for these Treasuries, there's only one thing that tends to happen.

Prices tend to fall and yields tend to rise. So for me, the biggest threat to r-star down the road is unsustainable fiscal policy.

ORPHANIDES: Yeah, thank you for that. I'm going to pile on for the r-star issue, but with a new angle. In your remarks, you focused virtually exclusively on interest rate policy.

And the policy rules that you mentioned are all interest rate rules. But of course, since the Global Financial Crisis, and with the effective lower bound constraints to policy, the Fed has been relying on balance sheet policies as well. Both to provide tremendous additional accommodation after the Global Financial Crisis and then with the pandemic, and also to restrict monetary policy by shrinking its balance sheet.

And one of the questions this brings is: How do you see the new normal on the balance sheet? I feel like the Fed has not been communicating as much about that as about interest rates. But of course, we need to have some information about what the new-normal balance sheet size is in order to determine how it relates to the neutral rate.

Since the two are linked, two tools can provide accommodation. If you fix the normal at a different level on the balance sheet, you're going to have consequentially a different estimate of the neutral rate at the same time. How do you think about this?

WALLER: Right, so the first thing I'd make on the balance sheet is, we want to make a distinction between the size and the composition of your assets and liabilities.

If our balance sheet was the current size and it was all currency, you wouldn't be talking about r-star or anything like that. So the size is not the issue. It's like, what are you buying? What are you holding that somehow is affecting market rates? So I think that's the first question.

Not the size, but what are you holding that somehow does this? Now, I've said this, and if somebody can prove me wrong, let me know, because I've been saying this for years. There is no economic theory for how large the central bank balance sheet should be. And we have examples in the world of central bank balance sheets that are 100% of GDP and they're running very low inflation.

They don't seem to be causing any problems. Switzerland, where'd you go? So it's not obvious just from looking around the world that the size of a central bank's balance sheet drives the performance or outcome of a lot of these variables. Now, in terms of the balance sheet, a lot of what we did was, when you're at the zero lower bound, you're trying to put downward pressure on longer-term rates.

You go out, you buy, you try to push up the price, drive down the yields. How big of an effect is that? Various estimates have about a trillion dollars of purchases, might give you 25 basis points. So it has potentially some effect. It's not clear it has a really big effect.

So if you take a trillion dollars out, it can't have really a potentially big effect either. Now, a lot of times when I talked at the US Monetary Policy Forum, back on February 1, about the arguments I made—I personally think a lot of this is like putting out a fire.

You have a bad economic outcome, you pour water on the fire, and then when the fire's out, you drain the water away. And when the water drains away, the fire doesn't restart. And that's the asymmetry of policy actions at a time. They do certain things in one direction that don't necessarily have the same effect going the other way.

So I think right now, a lot of what we're doing in shrinking the balance sheet, we're just draining all this liquidity that we put in the system. And if we tell the markets, like we did in 2022, roughly how much you're going to take out, at what pace you can price it in immediately.

If you go back to when we put this out, long-term Treasury went up about 37 basis points based on about a $1.7 trillion expectation. Sounds about what the estimates were.

ORPHANIDES: Okay, and we do have a few more minutes for questions from the sharks in the audience.

Who would like to identify themselves as a shark in the audience? Yes, please.

DAVID BECKWORTH [RESEARCH FELLOW, MERCATUS CENTER]: David Beckworth. So, back when this disinflation began, or when the attempts to create it began, you had a paper that came out that said that you could do this without creating a lot of unemployment.

WALLER: Yep.

BECKWORTH: And some prominent names pushed back against you.

WALLER: Yep.

BECKWORTH: Colorful claims, yes. So how do you feel now?

WALLER: Vindicated.

I mean, no, in May of '22, I gave this speech wherever by using Beveridge curve analysis, which, trust me, at the time, most media didn't even know what it was. Now, they all know.

It was this argument that we're on this very steep portion. The Beveridge curve is a very nonlinear function from a theoretical model. And I was just arguing, we're on this vertical portion of this thing. And as long as the involuntary separation rate didn't go up, you could just slide right down this Beveridge curve by putting downward pressure on demand and labor demand, and it would show up through reduced vacancies.

In that May '22 speech, I said, if we get back to where we were in 2019 in terms of the vacancy rate and jobs ratio, unemployment would go to 4.4%. I was wrong. It went to 4.1%. So, I mean, that was what I claimed, that's good theory. Good data work leads to good policymaking.

So, in that sense, that is what happened. But now, you've come down the steep part. Now, you're looking at the flat part. So if you continue to have this reduction in demand and labor demand, you're going to start moving, and you'll see I have to stick with my own model.

You're going to start seeing more unemployment, and that's suddenly why we're worried. I'm sitting here saying: We're in the sweet spot right now, we have got to keep it there, that's our job. Go ahead, you've got the mic.

LORENZO GIORGIANNI: Thank you. Lorenzo Giorgianni with Tudor. I am going to put you on the spot a bit.

So in the speech, you highlighted a model scenario, which envisages "deliberate" cuts. You used the word "gradual" many times in your speech. Are you now endorsing quarterly cuts, meaning, we're skipping November?

WALLER: I didn't say any more *quarterly*.

GIORGIANNI: Okay.

WALLER: I don't think I said the word in my speech.

GIORGIANNI: No, that's why I'm asking whether you can clarify what "gradually," "deliberate," means.

WALLER: Eh, it's in the eye of the beholder. That's for you guys to figure out.

GIORGIANNI: That's fine. Second point, if in fact that means quarterly, and so the idea is to skip November, there is a considerable risk, I would say a 50% risk, that on the day of the meeting you will have seen on the screens in Bloomberg markets moving 25 to 30 basis points up in yields with a significant tightening of financial conditions depending on the election outcome.

In the speech you highlight a number of economic considerations that guide the decisions of the Fed. How would you weigh in the financial-conditions side of it, which might actually tighten sharply on the day of the meeting?

WALLER: Yeah, I mean, as far as I know, no policy rule in this audience would say you react to the election.

I just don't see what it is. It would have to show up at some point in the form of inflation, unemployment, GDP growth. That's what goes into a policy rule, not the election per se. What you were just describing would be something to say, we're going to use discretion, and, okay, we're going to move the policy rate because of this one event, the day before that to me would be problematic.

So I don't see myself—I can't speak for anybody else, but I don't see us doing anything in response to the election in and of itself.

ORPHANIDES: Thanks, Chris. So I'm going to take two questions before you answer. So first, yes, and then the second.

DAVID ZERVOS [CHIEF MARKET STRATEGIST FOR JEFFERIES LLC]: I love your reference to constructive ambiguity, but I remember [Alan] Greenspan having a slightly different take on it, which was purposeful obfuscation, which I thought was a more accurate term, at least these days.

In the spirit of Athanasios's question, it does seem that almost to a person at the Federal Reserve or on the FOMC [Federal Open Market Committee], there's a minimization of the importance of the balance sheet at this current point in time. And your answer of water that puts out a fire but then sort of drains away, or your metaphor, seems to be very consistent with that.

I wonder in your risk-management exercises, and how you think about the balance sheet, you often step back and say, Well, maybe we're all wrong on that. Maybe the balance sheet actually was the reason policy wasn't that restrictive over the last few years. That the balance sheet exerted additional pressure, positive pressure on the economy, even as we were raising rates, and that all of these new balance sheet tools actually have enormous impacts on financial markets and the economy.

And we're really underestimating how restrictive we were and are. And that as we take that away, we really have a lot of risks to consider, that we do that in a careful way and not too quickly, like we saw back in 2017 and 2018, when we did it a little quickly and things got messy.

I just wonder how, how does that risk management of not understanding—and I'm a big believer in not understanding exactly how balance sheets work and how money and monetary policy works and how we bring money back into the debate on policy because we've left it aside. And it seems to have been a big part of everything that we've seen in the last fifteen years has been balance-sheet-related.

So how do you think about that?

ORPHANIDES: Let's take the second question as well.

JACK KRUPANSKY: Hi, my name is Jack Krupansky. What do you say to people who look at the persistently elevated prices, so that even if the rate of inflation is low, some people may look at the high price level and say, "That's not really price stability"?

Is that the Fed's job to do something, or is that somebody else's job to do something about those elevated prices?

WALLER: Yeah, when I gave a talk at [the] Brookings [Institution], last January I think, the idea that you have a permanently elevated price level because of temporary supply shocks just sounds wrong.

I mean, if they're temporary, they go away. Prices should readjust back down to the previous price level. So to me, that's always been a signal. There had to have been a lot of demand involved in this inflation that drove it up instead of, it's just all supply now. It is true.

I mean, our job is not to be price-level targeters. That is not our objective. We look like we did. We saw some graphs earlier in the conference today that looked like, for long periods of time, the Fed was on a pretty good price-level-targeting path, and then it veered off by various points in time.

Now, in terms of the high prices—that's, again, one of the distinctions, price level effects versus inflation effects longer-term. I get it. I go to the grocery store too, right? And there's stuff that I buy that I look at and go, "I'm not paying that." I can afford to, it's not that I can, I just refuse to.

So I am—I understand where people who have a harder time being able to afford it have to be really angry about this. But the price level is what it is. It's going to be very hard to try to say "I want to go back to 2019 prices" without doing some pretty dramatic, drastic monetary tightening.

And I don't know if people would really want to see, say, interest rates of 12% or 14% to get it back to 2019 levels. So that's kind of the problem you have with it right now. On the balance sheet, let me turn back to that. I mean, right now, the thing we worry about mainly is, is there sufficient liquidity in the financial markets to function properly?

And we've slowed down the pace because we didn't want to drain it too fast and then suddenly get some financial market dislocations like we saw back in 2019. So we've kind of slowed down the pace. We're watching price signals as well as quantity, and we're going to slowly keep trying to rein it as far in, but we're going to end up with an ample-reserves.

We're going to have a floor system for reserves that automatically means you're going to have a much bigger balance sheet than you would if you were in a scarce-reserves regime at some point.

JOHN H. COCHRANE: This inflation reminded us of an old lesson: The price level rise hits the least fortunate harder. They certainly respond that way in political surveys: They are much madder about higher prices than unemployment. Now, traditionally, the Fed has had hawks who worry about inflation and doves who worry about unemployment. I wonder if some of your doves are as a result becoming hawks.

ORPHANIDES: And the last question.

WALLER: I can't answer my other colleagues?

ORPHANIDES: Give me a second, Chris. Let's have the last question as well and then you respond.

COLBY SMITH: Colby Smith with the *Financial Times*. I just wanted to ask about the third scenario that you sketched out in your speech about inflation potentially reaccelerating or perhaps taking a bit longer to come back to target, and that potentially preempting the conversation about a pause, let's say. How much weight do you put on that potential outcome?

WALLER: That's what you have to—that's kind of what you have to sort out. Earlier this spring, we saw this happen. We saw this rebound, and we had six months of very low inflation readings, and then unexpectedly, in January, this thing just blows up. First thought: It's January, it's a seasonal, there's something, it's not going to continue.

And then we got it again in February, and then we got it again in March, and then by May, it's back down again. So this has been kind of a weird time for any policymaker, because the data has been this kind of volatile. But I want to just point out that since March of '23, at the March SEP [Summary of Economic Projections] 2023, we projected three cuts for this year.

And that thing hardly moved from March, June, September, December, January, March. Meanwhile, we went through a banking crisis when people said "stop raising rates." Then we saw six months of super-low inflation and people were calling for cutting rates. We didn't.

And then it rebounded and there were even calls to start raising rates again, and we didn't. So we did not overreact to these kinds of wild swings in terms of how we set policy. We never changed the policy rate during that whole period. And the SEP, if you go back and look, was three cuts for 2024 all the way through.

So I don't think of us as being overreactive in the data, because if you did, you'd see it in the SEP or you'd see it in our actual policy actions.

ORPHANIDES: So please join me in thanking Chris.

The Fed's Evolving Mandate

Introduction

Steven J. Davis

My name is Steven Davis. I'm a senior fellow at the Hoover Institution. I have the delightful and easy task of moderating these three distinguished gentlemen with deep careers in central banking. All three of them have made important analytical contributions to monetary policy, and central banking as well.

We will kick off with Jim Bullard, dean of the Purdue University Business School and former president of the Federal Reserve Bank of St. Louis. After Jim, we'll turn to Andy Levin of Dartmouth College. Although Andy has asked that if Jim hits it out of the park, he'd like to go last. Athanasios Orphanides, currently at MIT, will round it up. Jim, it's all yours.

11
The Federal Reserve's Evolving Interpretation and Implementation of Its Mandate

Athanasios Orphanides

Introduction

The Shadow Open Market Committee (SOMC) was founded in 1973 to help improve monetary policy at a critical time.[1] The Federal Reserve had failed. The United States was experiencing the third major inflation episode since the founding of the Fed in 1913 (figure 11.1), the first during peacetime. In his welcoming statement at the inaugural meeting of the SOMC, on September 14, 1973, Allan Meltzer noted that "recent economic policy had produced some of the poorest results in many years," and that "inflation is at the highest rate in peacetime history and shows no sign of ending" (SOMC 1973). It took another six years for the Fed to act. In October 1979, the Fed abandoned the policy strategy that led to the Great Inflation. During the 1980s, it largely restored price stability and succeeded in fostering growth and prosperity.

The Federal Reserve's checkered record in defending price stability has improved since the founding of the SOMC half a century ago. But more recently, Fed policy strategy shifted again, resulting in the recent inflation spike that evoked the malaise of the 1970s. Despite some policy improvement, notably the adoption of a quantitative definition for price stability in 2012, the Fed's monetary policy strategy proved insufficiently resilient once again.

This study presents a brief history of the evolution of the Fed's interpretation of its mandate and examines how this evolution shaped policy strategy and economic outcomes over time. Throughout its history, the Fed has operated with a muddled statutory mandate that has not explicitly recognized price stability as the primary goal of monetary policy. At present, the

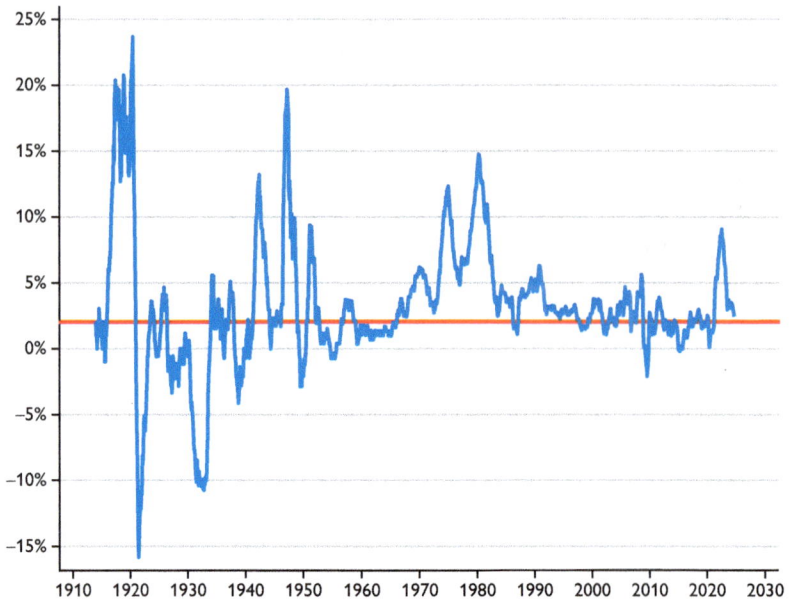

Figure 11.1. The Federal Reserve's record in maintaining price stability.

Note: Percent change of Consumer Price Index (CPI) for all urban consumers, year-on-year, monthly.

Source: US Bureau of Labor Statistics and author's calculations.

pertinent legislation mentions three goals that cannot be simultaneously attained: maximum employment, stable prices, and moderate long-term interest rates.

A muddled mandate requires operational interpretation before a policy strategy can be adopted toward attaining it. The Fed's policy success has varied over time with the interpretation of its mandate and associated policy strategy. At times, such as the 1950s, 1980s, and 1990s, the Fed adopted a modest interpretation of its mandate and succeeded in fostering growth and prosperity. But at other times, such as the 1970s, as well as the recent past, the Fed interpreted its mandate in an overambitious fashion, placing excessive emphasis on achieving the elusive goal of maximum employment. Sooner or later, episodes of high inflation followed.

A key lesson from the historical record is that successful policy is associated with a policy strategy that recognizes price stability as the Fed's primary operational objective.[2] Price stability is essential for a well-functioning monetary system that fosters good economic performance over time. An act of

Congress that clarifies the Fed's statutory mandate would reduce the scope for unhelpful discretion, improve accountability, and facilitate an improvement in the Fed's policy strategy (Orphanides 2014; Levin and Skinner 2024). Legislation along these lines has been proposed in the past but failed.[3] But legislative change is not required for policy improvement. Current legislation affords the Fed broad discretion on how to interpret its mandate, and the authority to adopt a strategy best suited to deliver good policy outcomes over time. The Fed can improve its policy by reverting to a more modest interpretation of its current statutory mandate, recognizing price stability as a primary operational objective and correcting the undue emphasis it currently places on the goal of maximum employment.

The Federal Reserve's Statutory Mandate: 1913, 1946, and 1977

The evolution of the Fed's statutory mandate since 1913 can be briefly described by focusing on three legislative acts: the Federal Reserve Act that established the Fed in 1913; the Employment Act of 1946 that declared national policy goals; and the Federal Reserve Reform Act of 1977 that added the current statement of monetary policy objectives in the Federal Reserve Act. Key provisions are collected in table 11.1.

Unlike modern central banking law, the Federal Reserve Act made no mention of price stability, economic growth, or employment as policy goals.

Table 11.1. Evolution of the Federal Reserve's statutory mandate

1913	"[Rates of discount] shall be fixed with a view of accommodating commerce and business."
	Federal Reserve Act of 1913, Pub. L. 63-43, 38 Stat. 251, Section 14(d)
1946	"The Congress hereby declares that it is the continuing policy and responsibility of the Federal Government to use all practicable means . . . to promote maximum employment, production and purchasing power."
	Employment Act of 1946, Pub. L. 79-304, 60 Stat. 23, Section 2
1977	"The Board of Governors of the Federal Reserve System and the Federal Open Market Committee shall maintain long run growth of the monetary and credit aggregates commensurate with the economy's long run potential to increase production, so as to promote effectively the goals of maximum employment, stable prices, and moderate long-term interest rates."
	Federal Reserve Reform Act of 1977, Pub. L. 95-188, 91 Stat. 1387, Section 2A

The Fed was founded in 1913 in response to the panic of 1907. The resulting legislation was meant to create a decentralized reserve system with the
authority to address such panics and provide a safer banking and monetary
system. To that end, the Fed would furnish an "elastic currency," as noted in
the preamble to the Act:

> An Act to provide for the Establishment of Federal Reserve Banks, to
> Furnish an Elastic Currency, to Afford Means of Rediscounting Com-
> mercial Paper, to Establish a More Effective Supervision of Banking in
> the United States, and for Other Purposes.[4]

The Act came closest to describing a macroeconomic policy goal in Section
14(d). Reserve Banks were granted numerous powers, including to purchase
and sell assets in open markets and to engage in credit operations. The Act
instructed the Fed to set the rates of discount in such operations "with a view
of accommodating commerce and business."

In effect, the law afforded the Fed remarkably broad discretion in interpreting its mandate and formulating its policy strategy. The most important
function of the Federal Reserve in the very first years of its operations was to
facilitate government finance during World War I. The result was high inflation, the first inflationary episode in figure 11.1.

The Employment Act of 1946 was enacted after the end of World War II,
aiming to protect the United States from the disastrous economic outcomes
experienced during the Great Depression. It marked a major shift in national
policy objectives, affecting all government institutions, including the Federal
Reserve. Section 2 was the declaration of policy:

> The Congress hereby declares that it is the continuing policy and respon-
> sibility of the Federal Government to use all practicable means . . . to coor-
> dinate and utilize all its plans, functions and resources for the purposes of
> creating and maintaining, in a manner calculated to foster and promote
> free competitive enterprise and the general welfare, conditions under
> which there will be afforded useful employment opportunities, includ-
> ing self-employment, for those able, willing, and seeking to work, and to
> promote maximum employment, production and purchasing power.[5]

The Employment Act introduced the concept of "maximum employment"
as a policy objective for the Fed. The law could be read as elevating the status

of "maximum employment" as the predominant policy goal but was open to alternative interpretations. The law also demanded promoting "maximum purchasing power," which could be read as an implicit reference to "price stability" as a policy goal. The meaning of "maximum" was not defined in a practicable manner. A literal interpretation of this language would be a recipe for trouble. It would not be feasible to attain the stated goals simultaneously. In effect, the Fed retained considerable discretion in interpreting its mandate and formulating its policy strategy.

The Fed's current statutory mandate reflects an amendment to the Federal Reserve Act introduced with the Federal Reserve Reform Act of 1977. The 1977 Act added section 2A to the Federal Reserve Act:

> The Board of Governors of the Federal Reserve System and the Federal Open Market Committee shall maintain long run growth of the monetary and credit aggregates commensurate with the economy's long run potential to increase production, so as to promote effectively the goals of maximum employment, stable prices, and moderate long-term interest rates.[6]

With this amendment, the list of three objectives, "maximum employment, production and purchasing power," was replaced with a new, similarly unhelpful list, "maximum employment, stable prices, and moderate long-term interest rates."

The introduction of "stable prices" as an explicit policy objective reflected frustration with the Fed's failure to maintain price stability over the previous decade. The amendment provided useful guidance on policy strategy, instructing the Fed to maintain "long run" growth of money and credit "commensurate with the economy's long run potential to increase production." On the other hand, the amendment retained "maximum employment" as a policy goal and introduced "moderate long-term interest rates" as an additional policy goal for the Fed, without defining the meaning of either "maximum" or "moderate." In effect, the 1977 amendment kept the Fed's statutory mandate as muddled as it had been earlier. Once again, the implied guidance was that the Fed was expected to use its discretionary authority to interpret its statutory mandate in a sensible manner.

In summary, throughout its history, the Fed has operated with a statutory mandate that has not explicitly recognized price stability as the primary goal of monetary policy. The muddled formulation, describing multiple and potentially incompatible goals, has afforded the Fed broad discretion regarding how to interpret its mandate and how to employ its considerable powers to attain it.

Evolution of the Interpretation of the Mandate and Policy Strategy

In light of the unhelpful formulation of the Fed's statutory mandate, the Fed's success in delivering price stability and fostering the good economic performance that is associated with it has rested on the interpretation of the mandate and implementation of its policy strategy. This section briefly reviews the evolution of the Fed's interpretation of its mandate over time and relates this evolution to subsequent developments in inflation.

As already mentioned, when the Fed was founded in 1913, the Federal Reserve Act did not offer much guidance on macroeconomic policy goals. The Fed's first major task was to help finance World War I. Yet, within a decade of its founding, the Fed had developed into a modern central bank and had adopted an activist, preemptive policy framework that aimed to control business cycle fluctuations. But the Fed opposed proposals that would have explicitly recognized stable prices as a policy goal.[7] The Fed's policy approach appeared successful for a time, but subsequently failed, leading to the economic disaster of the Great Depression.[8]

How did the Fed interpret its mandate during the 1930s? The Fed's 1939 publication of *The Federal Reserve System: Its Purposes and Functions* makes for interesting reading:

> The purpose of Federal Reserve functions, like that of Governmental functions in general, is the public good. Federal Reserve policy can not be adequately understood, therefore, merely in terms of how much the Federal Reserve authorities have the power to do and how much they have not the power to do. It must be understood in the light of its objective—which is to maintain monetary conditions favorable for an active and sound use of the country's productive facilities, full employment, and a rate of consumption reflecting widely diffused well-being. (Board of Governors 1939, 28)

"Widely diffused well-being" makes us wince. A charitable reading is that, despite what we now know about Fed policy during the Great Depression, the Fed's intentions were noble. But good intentions do not imply good policy. Another notable element in this description is the omission of any reference to price stability, which highlights the continued lack of appreciation of the critical nature of preserving price stability as an operational objective for monetary policy.

The Employment Act of 1946 prompted the Fed to modify the way it described its goals. The second edition of *The Federal Reserve System: Its Purposes and Functions,* published in 1947, provides the following description:

> The principal purpose of the Federal Reserve is to regulate the supply, availability, and cost of money with a view to contributing to the maintenance of a high level of employment, stable values, and a rising standard of living. (Board of Governors 1947, 1)

This relates to the formulation of the three objectives in the Employment Act but with some important differences. While referring to all three goals mentioned in the Employment Act in some way, the Fed avoided the adjective "maximum," which had not been defined in a practicable manner. The Fed attempted to explain the wording in the Act in more reasonable terms. Note the reference to a "high level" of employment as a policy objective, instead of maximum employment, and the usage of "stable values, and a rising standard of living" instead of maximum production and maximum purchasing power. The use of "stable values" suggests that the Fed interpreted the reference to maximum purchasing power in the Employment Act of 1946 as an implicit reference to the goal of "stable prices," which subsequently became explicit in 1977.

The 1947 edition of *Purposes and Functions* was also refreshingly transparent about the causes of high inflation earlier in the 1940s. It explained, in plain terms, that similar to the first inflation episode after the founding of the Fed, the second episode could also be attributed to the Fed's role in facilitating war finance:

> In time of war the duty of the Federal Reserve, as of everyone, is to support the country's war effort. The Federal Reserve provides machinery for aiding the Government to finance the enormous expenditures necessitated by war. . . .
> . . . Prevention of inflation had to become secondary to providing the sinews of war. (Board of Governors 1947, 105–7)

Fed policy improved considerably in the 1950s. The improvement, however, was not prompted by the change in the Fed's statutory mandate in 1946.

Rather, it reflected a fundamental change in the *interpretation* of the mandate toward recognition of the primacy of price stability as an operational policy objective. Under Chair William McChesney Martin, price stability was described as a necessary condition for the achievement of favorable growth and employment outcomes and the fulfilment of the Fed's statutory mandate as described in the Employment Act.[9]

The evolving interpretation of the (unchanged) statutory mandate can be seen by comparing the 1954 edition of *Purposes and Functions* to the 1947 edition. The revised edition provided the following description:

> The basic function of the Federal Reserve System is to make possible a flow of credit and money that will foster orderly economic growth and a stable dollar. An efficient monetary mechanism is indispensable to the steady development of the nation's resources and a rising standard of living. (Board of Governors 1954, 1)

Note, in particular, that no reference to either "maximum" or "high" employment is made. Instead, the focus is on "orderly economic growth." Similar to the use of "stable values" in 1947, the reference to "a stable dollar" in 1954 reflected the goal of price stability.

Aiming to deliver "orderly economic growth" implied a more robust policy strategy for the Fed, relative to the activist pursuit of level targets of real economic activity (such as the output gap, or the unemployment gap).

Statements by Chair Martin, in speeches and congressional testimony, confirm that this evolved interpretation of the mandate and policy strategy was seen as consistent with the Employment Act. The testimony provided in 1957 at the Senate hearings on the Investigation of the Financial Condition of the United States is illuminating. Regarding Fed goals and the Employment Act, Chair Martin's responses included the following (Martin 1957):

> The objectives expressed in section 2 of the Full Employment Act of 1946 have been, in fact, the aims and goals of the Federal Reserve System since early in its history. . . .
> The goal of price stability, now implicit in the Employment Act, can be made explicit by a straightforward declaration and directive to all agencies of the Government that anti-inflationary actions are to be taken promptly whenever the cost of living begins to rise. . . . (1256–57)

... The only possible means of attaining the objectives of the Employment Act, in my judgment, are to resist inflation. (1301)

It took another twenty years before Chair Martin's recommendation to
make price stability an explicit goal was adopted. This did not prevent the
Fed from recognizing price stability as the primary operational objective for
attaining the objectives of the Employment Act.

Unfortunately, by the end of Chair Martin's tenure, and especially following Arthur Burns's appointment as Fed chair in 1970, the Fed shifted toward
a more literal interpretation of its mandate, placing higher priority on maximum employment. While price stability was recognized as desirable, it was
no longer seen as the primary operational objective for monetary policy.
The associated change in policy strategy could be understood as an attempt
to improve on the more modest approach that prevailed during the 1950s.
Perceived advances in economic theory and policy that had been popular in
academic circles, akin to the modern optimal control approach to monetary
policy, influenced policy design.

Indeed, the activist approach that characterized policy during this period
can be successful, in theory, under the assumption of perfect knowledge of the
structure of the economy. The fragility of optimal control methods and the
lack of robustness to structural change in the economy was not well understood at the time. Limits to knowledge were downplayed. In the event, the Fed
was unable to detect structural change in real time, exposing the fragility of its
approach. During most of the 1970s, the Fed attempted to stabilize the unemployment rate at levels that it subsequently recognized were overly optimistic.
The delay in understanding the changing structure of employment—coupled
with the Fed's excessive emphasis on the maximum-employment side of its
statutory mandate—led to high inflation, despite the Fed's continued recognition of price stability as a desirable goal.[10] The Fed could have largely avoided
the Great Inflation if it had retained the more modest interpretation of its
mandate that characterized Fed policy in the 1950s and treated price stability
as the primary operational policy goal.[11]

Arthur Burns acknowledged the origins of the policy error in his 1979
Per Jacobsson Lecture. However, he failed to grasp the significance of the
overambitious interpretation of the Fed's mandate and its associated policy
strategy. Burns noted that the natural rate of unemployment had increased
significantly during the 1970s and explained how this led to a rise in inflation.

He then suggested that the Fed could have checked inflation, but implied that its statutory mandate constrained policy action:

> Viewed in the abstract, the Federal Reserve System had the power to abort the inflation at its incipient stage fifteen years ago or at any later point, and it has the power to end it today. . . .
>
> The Employment Act of 1946 prescribes that "it is the continuing policy and responsibility of the Federal Government to . . . utilize all its plans, functions, and resources . . . to promote maximum employment." The Federal Reserve is subject to this provision of law, and that has limited its practical scope for restrictive actions. (Burns 1979, 15)

Burns's account of the inflationary episode rested on the interpretation of the mandate that the Fed had adopted during his tenure, specifically the counterproductive, excessive emphasis given to maximum employment. The Fed had the discretion to revert to the earlier interpretation of its mandate and the associated robust policy strategy. Doing so would have improved economic outcomes and fulfilled the Fed's statutory mandate better.

Indeed, when Arthur Burns delivered his address in September of 1979, Fed staff was already preparing the policy reform introduced by Chair Paul Volcker in October of 1979 (Lindsey et al. 2005). The law had not changed between September and October of 1979. What changed was the interpretation of the Fed's mandate.

In the aftermath of the Great Inflation, a revised interpretation of the mandate and a change in policy strategy were essential for the restoration of monetary stability. The revised interpretation was reflected in the 1984 edition of *Purposes and Functions*:

> The Federal Reserve contributes to the attainment of the nation's economic and financial goals through its ability to influence money and credit in the economy. As the nation's central bank, it attempts to ensure that growth in money and credit over the long run is sufficient to encourage growth in the economy in line with its potential and with reasonable price stability. (Board of Governors 1984, 1)

Note that, similar to the "orderly economic growth" clause in the 1954 edition, the 1984 edition focused on growth "in line with its potential." This was an important marker reflecting a preference for policy robustness, in contrast to the overambitious approach aiming for maximum employment. The focus on the growth rate of output (instead of level targets relating to maximum production or maximum employment) is a common characteristic of robust policy rules.[12]

It is also noteworthy that this shift in interpretation had nothing to do with the actual change in the Fed's statutory mandate in 1977. Recall that the 1977 amendment had replaced the list of three objectives, "maximum employment, production and purchasing power," with the new list, "maximum employment, stable prices, and moderate long-term interest rates." While "maximum employment" is common to both the old and new list, no reference to "maximum employment" appears either in the 1954 or 1984 descriptions of Fed goals and policy strategy. Attempting to achieve "maximum employment" was recognized as inconsistent with the design of a robust monetary policy strategy that could deliver good economic outcomes over time.

During the 1980s and 1990s, under both Chairs Volcker and Greenspan, the Fed avoided the trap of focusing directly on maximum employment. The Fed effectively treated price stability as its primary mandate and communicated that achieving and maintaining price stability is the best way for the central bank to contribute to maximum sustainable growth and employment over time. Chair Greenspan summarized the Fed's policy strategy as

a strategy for policy directed at maximizing the probabilities of achieving over time our goals of price stability and the maximum sustainable economic growth that we associate with it. (Greenspan 2004, 37)

By adopting this modest interpretation of the Fed's statutory mandate, and implementing a policy strategy that recognized the primacy of price stability, the Fed successfully supported economic growth and prosperity into the 2000s.

The Great Moderation era ended abruptly with the Global Financial Crisis. One consequence of that crisis was an increase of the unemployment rate to levels not seen since the Great Depression. The unemployment rate rose to 10% in October 2009 and stayed stubbornly high for several quarters. The salience of high unemployment appears to have influenced the Fed toward a more literal interpretation of its mandate: Once again, the Fed raised the prominence of maximum employment as an explicit policy goal. References to "sustainable economic growth" in Federal Open Market Committee (FOMC) statements were eventually replaced with references to "maximum employment." Compare, for example, the FOMC statement issued on January 28, 2009, to that issued on November 3, 2010:[13]

> The Federal Reserve will employ all available tools to promote the resumption of sustainable economic growth and to preserve price stability. (FOMC 2009)
> Consistent with its statutory mandate, the Committee seeks to foster maximum employment and price stability. (FOMC 2010)

This shift occurred in the context of an ongoing discussion at the Fed that had started long before the crisis, aiming to improve the communication of the Fed's definition of price stability. This reflected the recognition that a clearer definition of price stability could facilitate better anchoring of inflation expectations, thereby improving the effectiveness of monetary policy in delivering price stability and economic stability over time.[14]

On January 24, 2012, the FOMC adopted a "Statement on Longer-Run Goals and Monetary Policy Strategy" (the "consensus statement"; FOMC 2012). The consensus statement was a milestone for the Fed.[15] It announced the adoption of a 2% inflation target as the definition of price stability. In parallel, however, while recognizing that "maximum employment" could not be described in similarly precise terms, the consensus statement pointed to participants' estimates of "the longer-run normal rate of unemployment" as a guide. Furthermore, it described a "balanced approach" in resolving conflicts in policy when inflation deviated from 2% and unemployment deviated from the Committee's assessment of maximum employment. This effectively placed "maximum employment" on equal footing with "price stability" in the Fed's monetary policy strategy, inviting the possibility of policy mistakes similar to those that characterized the 1970s (Orphanides 2014).

The inflationary risk emanating from interpreting the mandate in an overambitious manner was magnified following a review of the consensus statement in 2020. The revised statement (FOMC 2020), released on August 27, 2020, elevated the prominence of maximum employment further. The ordering of discussion of the Fed's multiple goals was switched so that the goal of "maximum employment" would be discussed first. The goal of "stable prices" was relegated to second place, while discussion of the goal of "moderate long-term interest rates" continued to be absent. More importantly, the revised statement introduced an asymmetric focus on "shortfalls of employment from its maximum level" and an asymmetric tolerance for overshooting the

2% inflation goal. This set the stage for a policy error that contributed to the spike in inflation soon after.[16]

Similar to the events of the 1970s, the Fed's recent inflationary error could be attributed to the overambitious manner in which it interpreted its mandate, placing excessive emphasis on maximum employment. This implied a policy strategy that was not resilient to unexpected developments. The problem became apparent during the very first episode requiring policy tightening after the adoption of the revised strategy. During 2021, inflation rose faster than had been anticipated, a forecast error (Levy 2024). However, the Fed continued to ease policy until March 2022. This policy easing was implemented by keeping the federal funds rate near zero, thereby guiding short-term real-interest rates to lower negative levels, and by expanding the Fed's balance sheet through bond purchases, thereby exerting downward pressure on longer-term interest rates. Despite inflation and the Fed's inflation forecasts having exceeded the Fed's 2% target, the Fed continued to cite insufficient progress toward maximum employment to explain its policy.[17]

Unlike in the 1970s, the Fed recognized its error before inflation rose to double digits and normalized policy more quickly. This avoided a protracted disanchoring of inflation expectations and contained the economic cost of the Fed's inflation error.

Conclusion

The Fed has been operating with a muddled statutory mandate that has not explicitly recognized price stability as the primary goal of monetary policy. By necessity, the Fed has had to provide an operational interpretation to formulate monetary policy. The Fed's success in maintaining price stability and fostering the good economic performance that is associated with it has largely depended on how it interpreted its mandate and implemented its policy strategy.

During the 1950s, 1980s, and 1990s, the Fed adopted a modest interpretation of its mandate that succeeded in fostering growth and prosperity. In contrast, in the 1970s and in the recent past, the Fed interpreted its mandate in an overambitious fashion by placing undue emphasis on the elusive goal of maximum employment. On both occasions, the Fed's strategy proved insufficiently resilient and high inflation followed. While the Fed's track record on price stability has improved over the past fifty years, the recent inflation surge serves as a reminder of the inevitable policy errors that can occur when the Fed loses sight of the primacy of price stability.

An act of Congress explicitly recognizing price stability as the Fed's primary goal could mitigate the risk of policy error. However, improvement is possible even without legislative change. Current law affords the Fed broad discretion in interpreting its mandate, and the authority to adopt a strategy best suited for delivering good economic outcomes over time. The Fed could enhance its policy strategy by reverting to a more modest interpretation of its statutory mandate, recognizing price stability as the primary operational objective and correcting the undue emphasis it currently places on the goal of maximum employment. To become a more successful central bank, the Fed must resist the temptation to overreach and recognize that price stability is a precondition for maximizing economic growth and fostering prosperity.

Notes

1. Michael Bordo and Mickey Levy (2025, in this volume) document the history of the SOMC.

2. The SOMC has consistently advocated the primacy of price stability. According to the SOMC's "core beliefs": "Price stability is the best contribution that monetary policy can make to overall macroeconomic performance and for this reason should be the primary objective of the central bank" (SOMC 2014, 2).

3. An example is the zero-inflation resolution, proposed in 1989. It would have clarified the Fed's mandate and found support at the Fed. As Chair Alan Greenspan testified: "The Zero-Inflation Resolution represents a constructive effort to provide congressional guidance to the Federal Reserve. If passed, it would further clarify the intent of Congress and the president as expressed in prior legislation. Legislative direction as to the appropriate goals for macroeconomic policy in general and monetary policy in particular have been provided before. Unfortunately, the instructions have defined multiple objectives for policy, which have not always been entirely consistent—at least over the near term. The current resolution is laudable, in part because it directs monetary policy toward a single goal, price stability, that monetary policy is uniquely suited to pursue" (Greenspan 1989, 4–5).

4. Federal Reserve Act of 1913, Pub. L. 63-43, 38 Stat. 251, 1.

5. Employment Act of 1946, Pub. L. 79-304, 60 Stat. 23, 1.

6. Federal Reserve Reform Act of 1977, Pub. L. 95-188, 91 Stat. 1387, 1.

7. The implementation of preemptive policy was facilitated by important advances in data collection and policy analysis, including detrending methods that could be used to assess the "normal" level of economic activity. See Meltzer (2003) and Orphanides (2003) for additional information on the Fed's policy strategy at the time.

8. Friedman and Schwartz (1963) and Meltzer (2003) document the contribution of Fed policy errors.

9. Romer and Romer (2002) characterize policy in the 1950s as remarkably similar to that of the 1990s; both shared an overarching concern about inflation.

10. López-Salido et al. (2024) document the Fed's consistent recognition of the desirability of price stability, including in periods when it failed to defend it.

11. Orphanides and Williams (2013) provide a narrative history of this episode and show how the Great Inflation would have been avoided had a more robust policy approach been in place.

12. Examples with an interest rate instrument include the speed-limit/timeless-perspective policies in Walsh (2003) and Woodford (2003), natural growth targeting in Orphanides (2003, 2025), and the lean-against-the-wind approach in Hetzel (2022, 2025, in this volume).

13. A reference to "maximum employment" was first included in the September 21, 2010, FOMC statement. A reference to "sustainable economic growth" was last included in the August 12, 2009, statement.

14. The critical role of inflation expectations had already been recognized and reflected in policy strategy during the Volcker–Greenspan era, but Chairs Volcker and Greenspan opposed a precise numerical definition of price stability. By contrast, Chairs Ben Bernanke and Janet Yellen had both expressed support for a numerical definition of price stability long before their appointments as Fed chairs.

15. Lacker (2020) and Orphanides (2019) provide accounts of the deliberations leading to the consensus statement.

16. See Bordo et al. (2023, 2024), Eggertsson and Kohn (2023), Ireland (2025), and Orphanides (2024, 2025) for analysis of this policy error, including the role of the 2020 consensus statement.

17. For example, following the December 15, 2021, FOMC decision to keep its target range for the federal funds rate unchanged at 0% to 0.25%, Chair Jerome Powell explained: "With inflation having exceeded 2 percent for some time, the Committee expects it will be appropriate to maintain this target range until labor market conditions have reached levels consistent with the Committee's assessments of maximum employment" (FOMC 2021).

References

Board of Governors (Board of Governors of the Federal Reserve System). 1939. *The Federal Reserve System: Its Purposes and Functions.*

Board of Governors. 1947. *The Federal Reserve System: Its Purposes and Functions.* 2nd Ed.

Board of Governors. 1954. *The Federal Reserve System: Its Purposes and Functions.* 3rd Ed.

Board of Governors. 1984. *The Federal Reserve System: Its Purposes and Functions.* 7th Ed.

Bordo, Michael D., John H. Cochrane, and John B. Taylor, eds. 2023. *How Monetary Policy Got Behind the Curve—and How to Get Back.* Hoover Institution Press.

Bordo, Michael D., John H. Cochrane, and John B. Taylor, eds. 2024. *Getting Monetary Policy Back on Track*. Hoover Institution Press.

Bordo, Michael D., and Mickey D. Levy. 2025. "The Fifty-Year History of the SOMC and the Evolution of Monetary Policy." In *Fifty Years of the Shadow Open Market Committee: A Retrospective on Its Role in Monetary Policy*, edited by Michael D. Bordo, Jeffrey M. Lacker, Mickey D. Levy, and John B. Taylor. Hoover Institution Press.

Burns, Arthur. 1979. "The Anguish of Central Banking." Lecture at the Per Jacobsson Foundation, Belgrade, Yugoslavia. September 30.

Eggertsson, Gauti B., and Donald Kohn. 2023. "The Inflation Surge of the 2020s: The Role of Monetary Policy." Working Paper No. 87. Hutchins Center, Brookings Institution. August.

FOMC (Federal Open Market Committee). 2009. "FOMC Statement." Press release. January 28.

FOMC. 2010. "FOMC Statement." Press release. November 3.

FOMC. 2012. "Statement on Longer-Run Goals and Monetary Policy Strategy." January 24.

FOMC. 2020. "Statement on Longer-Run Goals and Monetary Policy Strategy." August 27.

FOMC. 2021. "Chair Powell's Press Conference." December 15. Transcript at https://www.federalreserve.gov/mediacenter/files/FOMCpresconf20211215.pdf.

Friedman, Milton, and Anna Schwartz. 1963. *A Monetary History of the United States, 1867–1960*. Princeton University Press.

Greenspan, Alan. 1989. "Statement Before the Subcommittee on Domestic Monetary Policy of the Committee on Banking, Finance and Urban Affairs." 101st Cong. October 25.

Greenspan, Alan. 2004. "Risk and Uncertainty in Monetary Policy." *American Economic Review* 94 (2): 33–40.

Hetzel, Robert. L. 2022. *The Federal Reserve: A New History*. University of Chicago Press.

Hetzel, Robert L. 2025. "In Search of a Stable Nominal Anchor." In *Fifty Years of the Shadow Open Market Committee: A Retrospective on Its Role in Monetary Policy*, edited by Michael D. Bordo, Jeffrey M. Lacker, Mickey D. Levy, and John B. Taylor. Hoover Institution Press.

Ireland, Peter N. 2025. "The Devolution of Federal Reserve Monetary Policy Strategy, 2012–24." *Southern Economic Journal* 91 (4): 1247–64. https://doi.org/10.1002/soej.12730.

Lacker, Jeffrey. M. 2020. "A Look Back at the Consensus Statement." *Cato Journal* 40 (2): 285–319.

Levin, Andrew T., and Christina Parajon Skinner. 2024. "Central Bank Undersight: Assessing the Fed's Accountability to Congress." Economics Working Paper No. 23120. Hoover Institution. February 8.

Levy, Mickey D. 2024. "The Fed: Bad Forecasts and Misguided Monetary Policy." In *Getting Monetary Policy Back on Track*, edited by Michael D. Bordo, John H. Cochrane, and John B. Taylor. Hoover Institution Press.

Lindsey, David, Athanasios Orphanides, and Robert H. Rasche. 2005. "The Reform of October 1979: How It Happened and Why." *Federal Reserve Bank of St. Louis Review* 87 (2): 187–235.

López-Salido, David, Emily J. Markowitz, and Edward Nelson. 2024. "Continuity and Change in the Federal Reserve's Perspective on Price Stability." Working Paper No. 2024-041, Finance and Economics Discussion Series. Board of Governors of the Federal Reserve System. May 30. https://www.federalreserve.gov /econres/feds/files/2024041pap.pdf.

Martin, William McChesney. 1957. Testimony, "Investigation of the Financial Condition of the United States, Hearings before the Committee on Finance." 85th Cong. 1st session. August 13. https://fraser.stlouisfed.org/title/investigation -financial-condition-united-states-1088/part-3-1281.

Meltzer, Allan H. 2003. *A History of the Federal Reserve, Vol. 1: 1913–1951*. University of Chicago Press.

Orphanides, Athanasios. 2003. "Historical Monetary Policy Analysis and the Taylor Rule." *Journal of Monetary Economics* 50 (5): 983–1022.

Orphanides, Athanasios. 2014. "The Need for a Price Stability Mandate." *Cato Journal* 34 (2): 265–79.

Orphanides, Athanasios. 2019. "Monetary Policy Strategy and Its Communication." In *Challenges for Monetary Policy: A Symposium Sponsored by the Federal Reserve Bank of Kansas City, Jackson Hole, Wyoming, Aug. 22–24, 2019*, edited by Richard A. Babson. Federal Reserve Bank of Kansas City. https://www.kansascityfed .org/documents/6954/Orphanides_Jh2019.pdf.

Orphanides, Athanasios. 2024. "The Forward Guidance Trap." *Monetary and Economic Studies* 42 (November): 71–92.

Orphanides, Athanasios. 2025. "Enhancing Resilience with Natural Growth Targeting." *Southern Economic Journal* 91 (4): 1420–39. https://doi.org/10.1002/ soej.12752.

Orphanides, Athanasios, and John C. Williams. 2013. "Monetary Policy Mistakes and the Evolution of Inflation Expectations." In *The Great Inflation: The Rebirth of Modern Central Banking*, edited by Michael D. Bordo and Athanasios Orphanides. University of Chicago Press.

Romer, Christina, and David Romer. 2002. "A Rehabilitation of Monetary Policy in the 1950's." *American Economic Review* 92 (2): 121–27.

SOMC (Shadow Open Market Committee). 1973. "Minutes of the Meeting of the Shadow Open Market Committee." September 14. https://shadowfed.org /wp-content/uploads/somc-archive/1973_09_14.pdf.

SOMC. 2014. "The SOMC and Its Core Beliefs." Shadow Open Market Committee, New York, NY. November 3. https://shadowfed.org/wp-content/uploads/ somc-archive/SOMC-CoreBeliefs2014.pdf.

Walsh, Carl. 2003. "Speed Limit Policies: The Output Gap and Optimal Monetary Policy." *American Economic Review* 93 (1): 265–78.

Woodford, Michael. 2003. *Interest and Prices*. Princeton University Press.

12
Strengthening the Federal Reserve's Accountability to the US Congress*

Andrew T. Levin and Christina Parajon Skinner

The US Constitution specifically vests Congress with the duty to regulate the value of money. In the modern era, Congress has delegated this duty to the Federal Reserve, giving the Fed a broad mandate to foster maximum employment and price stability and granting it wide discretion in conducting monetary policy. While Congress certainly has the power to delegate this crucial duty to the Fed, the Constitution does not permit Congress to abdicate responsibility for overseeing this task. In effect, allowing the Fed to function as a "fourth branch" of government is not constitutionally permissible.

In an article for the *Vanderbilt Law Review*, our analysis indicates that the current regime of congressional oversight is more properly characterized as "undersight" (Levin and Skinner 2024). We analyze Congress's delegation of monetary powers to the Fed, highlight the shortcomings in the current regimen of congressional oversight, and identify options for strengthening the Fed's public accountability while protecting its independence from political interference. The remainder of this chapter provides a synopsis of our analysis.

- Congress has exempted the Fed from almost all the mechanisms for congressional oversight of other independent agencies, including the Commodity Futures Trading Commission, the Federal Deposit Insurance Corporation, and the Securities and Exchange Commission.

*This chapter was originally published in September 2024 as a policy brief by the Mercatus Center at George Mason University.

- The Fed's monetary policy reports to Congress do not provide cost-benefit analysis of its programs and do not provide any assessments of potential risks associated with its policies.
- The Fed is authorized to issue interest-bearing obligations that are not subject to the federal debt ceiling.
- The Fed sets its own accounting rules, in contrast to other federal entities that are subject to GAAP (generally accepted accounting principles).
- The Fed's monetary policy framework and programs are exempt from review by the Government Accountability Office (GAO), which conducts periodic performance audits of all federal offices and agencies.
- The Fed's inspector general (IG) is a Fed employee, whereas a fully independent IG is in place at other major government entities (i.e., offices and agencies with operating budgets exceeding $5 billion).

Many of the congressional decisions that led to the adoption of this light-touch oversight were made in the 1970s and now appear anachronistic. In particular, Congress designed the Fed's monetary policymaking body, the Federal Open Market Committee (FOMC), to ensure that its policy decisions would be thoroughly debated by individually accountable experts with diverse points of view. In recent years, however, FOMC voting patterns suggest that the Fed's internal governance has shifted to expand the power of the Fed chair and to diminish the independence of other Fed officials. There has been a dearth of FOMC dissents over the past few years, and the FOMC acts like a corporate board whose members speak with one voice. The scarcity of dissenting views has likely hampered Congress's ability to raise important and sufficiently specific questions about the Fed's monetary policy programs and operations.

The Fed did not consult with Congress before overhauling its monetary policy framework in 2020. That framework likely contributed to the Fed's passivity when inflation surged in 2021, but there were no dissenting FOMC votes regarding the framework revision or the subsequent policy inertia. Moreover, the Fed's asset purchase program in 2020–22 has subsequently led to unprecedented operating losses and to the suspension of its remittances to the US Treasury. Indeed, this program's total cost to taxpayers is now projected to be about $1.6 trillion, but the Fed has never provided Congress with any cost-benefit analysis for the program.

The Fed is not the first agency in US history to outpace appropriate congressional oversight. Congress established national security agencies shortly after World War II but did not institute mechanisms for meaningful oversight of those agencies until the early 1990s. In similar fashion, Congress may now wish to revisit its mechanisms for overseeing the Fed.

Shifts in the Fed's Internal Governance

As the Federal Reserve carries out its monetary policy duties, it is directly exercising Congress's powers to regulate money and to borrow directly from the public. Article I of the Constitution states that Congress shall have the power "to coin Money, regulate the Value thereof, and of foreign Coin, and fix the Standard of Weights and Measures."[1] The founders specifically granted these powers to the legislative branch rather than the executive branch. Consequently, the Fed has a unique relationship with the president, whose authority to remove Fed officials is tightly constrained, and with the courts, which have consistently abstained from judicial review. In effect, the Fed exercises its power without any of the usual checks and balances, thereby underscoring the rationale for robust congressional oversight of the Fed's monetary policymaking.

Congress carefully designed the Fed as an independent agency that comprises individually accountable experts whose deliberations would be well insulated from political interference.[2] The seven members of the Federal Reserve Board are presidential appointees confirmed by the Senate to staggered terms of fourteen years and removable only "for cause." In addition, there are twelve regional Federal Reserve Banks that Congress intended to be overseen by, but not subordinated to, the Federal Reserve Board. Each Fed Bank is overseen by its own independent board of directors, who select its president subject to the approval of the Federal Reserve Board.[3] The Fed Bank presidents and the Federal Reserve Board members jointly constitute the FOMC; most of the Fed Bank presidents vote on a rotating basis.[4] Notwithstanding this design, the Fed's monetary policymaking has exhibited a growing degree of uniformity in recent years. As shown in figure 12.1(a), members of the Federal Reserve Board regularly dissented on FOMC decisions from the late 1950s until the early 1990s, but there were no such dissents from 2006 to 2023. That streak was finally broken by Fed Governor Michelle Bowman, who cast a dissenting vote at the September 2024 FOMC meeting.[5]

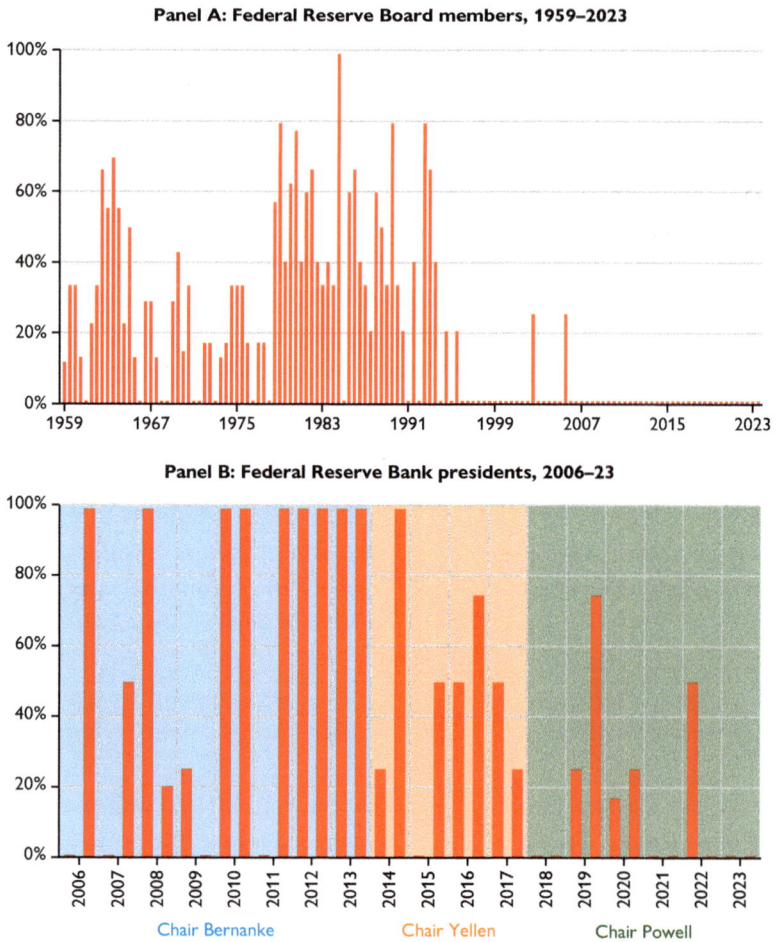

Panel A: Federal Reserve Board members, 1959–2023

Panel B: Federal Reserve Bank presidents, 2006–23

Chair Bernanke   Chair Yellen   Chair Powell

Figure 12.1. Dissenting votes at Federal Open Market Committee meetings.

Note: Panel A shows the percentage of meetings within each semiannual period at which there was at least one dissenting vote by a Federal Reserve Board member, and Panel B provides corresponding information about dissenting votes by Federal Reserve Bank presidents.

Sources: Board of Governors of the Federal Reserve System, Federal Reserve Bank of St. Louis, and authors' calculations. The votes are recorded in FOMC statements posted at: https://www .federalreserve.gov/monetarypolicy/fomccalendars.htm. The history of dissenting votes can be accessed at: https://www.stlouisfed.org/on-the-economy/2014/september/a-history -of-fomc-dissents.

As shown in figure 12.1(b), dissents by Fed Bank presidents were still quite common a decade ago but became increasingly rare thereafter, with no dissents at all from July 2022 through December 2023. Among the incumbent Fed Bank presidents, only one has ever dissented from any FOMC decision: Beth Hammack, president of the Cleveland Fed, dissented in December 2024.

In our law review article, we identify several distinct trends in the Fed's governance that have contributed to the uniformity in its monetary policy-making. In particular, while the Federal Reserve Board is a multimember commission, the Fed chair is not merely "first among equals" but has an out-size role in determining the Fed's monetary policy decisions.

- The Fed chair serves as the Federal Reserve Board's CEO, whereas the other six members of the Federal Reserve Board have nonexecutive roles. Thus, the chair effectively directs the entire staff of the Federal Reserve Board, who produce economic forecasts and other background materials that serve as the focal point for the FOMC's monetary policy deliberations.
- The Fed chair is often the most senior member on the board, further strengthening the centrality of this role. Each vice chair departs after a single four-year term, and other Board members often serve for just a few years before taking a position elsewhere.[6] Instead of serving the staggered fourteen-year terms that Congress intended, new members of the Federal Reserve Board often fill vacant seats, serving partial terms that may last just a few years.
- It has become commonplace for every Federal Reserve Board member to have been appointed by the current incumbent of the White House.[7] These shifts in the Fed Board's composition could undermine public confidence that its policy decisions are being made on a nonpartisan basis.
- The Federal Reserve Board has become increasingly involved in the selection of Fed Bank presidents. For nearly a century, the directors of each Fed Bank carried out this responsibility with little or no involvement of the Federal Reserve Board. Since 2015, however, a Fed Board member has been directly involved in all stages of the selection of each Fed Bank president, and there have been growing concerns that such involvement may effectively dictate the outcome of the process.

Indeed, in its 2019 review of Fed governance, the White House Office of Legal Counsel concluded that Fed Bank presidents are appropriately viewed as "subordinates" of the Federal Reserve Board.[8] However, that conclusion seems directly contrary to the original intent of Congress in designing the Fed's governance.

Shortcomings in the Fed's Accountability to Congress

Monetary Policy Goals and Strategy

Congress has given the FOMC a broad mandate to foster maximum employment and price stability, but the Fed is not required to provide any regular reporting regarding its quantification of these objectives.[9] For example, there are no indications that the Fed engaged in congressional consultations before the 2020 overhaul of its monetary policy framework, when it shifted to an asymmetric tilt toward elevated inflation. Consequently, the operational definition of price stability became more discretionary and opaque, with ambiguity about the horizon over which inflation would be averaged and the duration over which it might remain elevated. Indeed, some former Fed officials have concluded that this framework revision paved the way for the Fed's subsequent inertia in responding to the inflation surge of 2021.[10]

Thus, strengthened reporting requirements could help foster appropriate congressional oversight of such changes. Indeed, some prominent economists have urged the Fed to revise its inflation target upward, to 3% or even higher.[11] Such a change might seem blatantly inconsistent with the Fed's price stability mandate but could be adopted at any time unless Congress imposes more substantial reporting requirements.

Since 2017, the Fed's monetary policy reports to Congress have generally included information about the prescriptions of simple benchmarks such as the Taylor rule, but these reports have provided no explanation for substantial deviations from the policy benchmarks.[12] Moreover, these reports summarize the Fed's baseline economic outlook but do not provide any assessment of material risks or any information about how monetary policy might need to be adjusted if this premise turns out to be incorrect. Ironically, the Fed requires all large and systemically important banking institutions to undergo regular stress tests of their balance sheets, and hence it seems reasonable for Congress to establish a similar regimen according to which the Fed will engage in regular "stress tests for monetary policy."[13]

Balance Sheet Programs

The Constitution vests Congress with the sole authority to "borrow money on the credit of the United States."[14] In recent years, however, that power has effectively been delegated to the Fed, which is now funding its own operating losses by issuing interest-bearing liabilities to the public.

As shown in figure 12.2, the Fed's balance sheet in 2007 was very simple and practically risk-free. Nearly all of the Fed's liabilities consisted of paper currency and bank reserves held at the Fed, which paid no interest, while its holdings of Treasury securities generated a steady stream of interest earnings that were remitted to the US Treasury. Since 2008, however, the Fed's balance sheet has ballooned by a factor of ten and has become far more complex and risky.

Indeed, since fall 2022 the Fed has been incurring unprecedented operating losses that have directly resulted from the securities purchase program that it conducted from March 2020 to March 2022. As shown in figure 12.3, the costs of that program will continue to weigh on the Fed's remittances to the US Treasury for the foreseeable future, and the overall cost to taxpayers is projected to be about $1.6 trillion.[15] Among US public institutions, the Federal Reserve is unique in determining its own accounting rules rather than

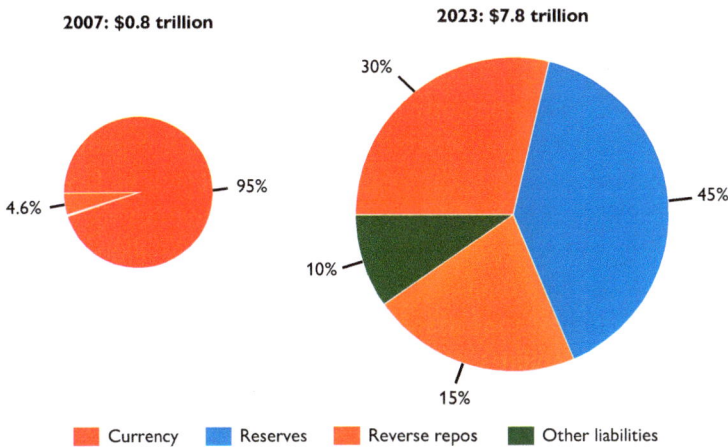

Figure 12.2. The Federal Reserve's liabilities.

Sources: Federal Reserve System Audited Statements (2007) and Unaudited Statements (2023 Q2). All of the Fed's financial statements are posted at: https://www.federalreserve.gov /aboutthefed/fed-financial-statements.htm.

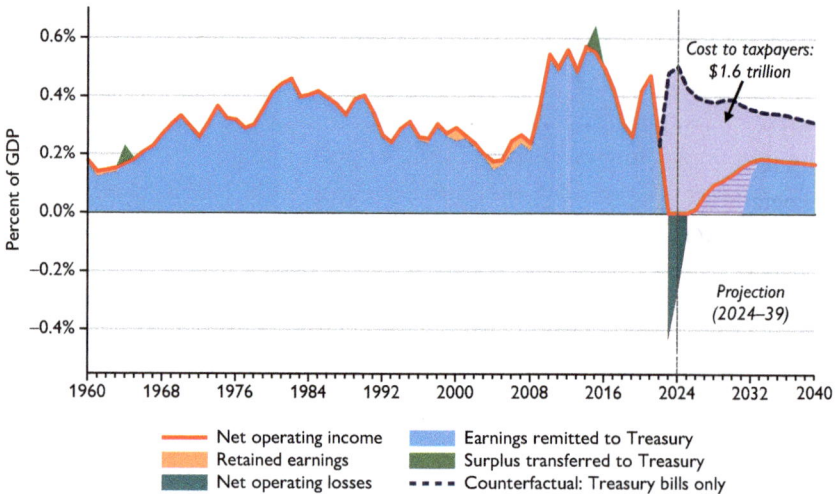

Figure 12.3. Federal Reserve remittances to the US Treasury. The teal, lavender, and hatched lavender regions show the cost to taxpayers of the Fed's recent balance sheet policies; specifically, the hatched lavender region indicates the positive operating income that will be used to repay the Fed's debt obligations accrued during the phase of negative operating income.

Sources: Board of Governors of the Federal Reserve System (remittance data), Bureau of Economic Analysis (nominal GDP data), and the authors' projections. The Fed's remittances are reported in its audited financial statements and unaudited quarterly reports and in its H.4.1 weekly releases; see https://www.federalreserve.gov/releases/h41/.

following GAAP.[16] Consequently, the Fed's operating losses are recorded on its financial statements as a "deferred asset" rather than as negative net worth.

A private institution in such circumstances might well be faced with the prospect of a takeover, bankruptcy, or liquidation. By contrast, the Fed is covering its operating losses by expanding its interest-bearing liabilities: In effect, the Fed is borrowing those funds directly from the public without congressional authorization.[17] Indeed, the Fed's ability to issue practically unlimited amounts of interest-bearing liabilities, outside the constraints of the federal debt ceiling, may be viewed as making the Fed "super-independent" (Bolzani 2022).

Cost-Benefit Analysis

With the sole exception of the Fed, every program of every federal department, office, and agency is audited by the GAO, an independent agency that reports directly to Congress. The GAO not only examines these institutions' financial books but engages in comprehensive performance reviews that foster efficiency and public accountability. By contrast, the Fed is subject only to narrow financial audits conducted by a private accounting firm that has no accountability to Congress or the public.[18] Moreover, the Fed's audits are strictly limited in scope, with the sole purpose of verifying the accuracy of the Fed's financial statements rather than gauging the efficacy or efficiency of programs, as in a performance audit.

The GAO has a strong track record as an effective congressional watchdog. Every specific recommendation that the GAO makes to every federal agency is posted on the GAO's website along with an indication about whether the recommendation was implemented. Thus, the GAO (2022) can document that, over the past decade, about 80% of its recommendations have been followed, and these measures have saved taxpayers nearly $1 trillion.

While the Fed's technical and logistical operations are subject to routine reviews, the GAO is prohibited by statute from auditing the efficiency and effectiveness of the Fed's monetary policy framework or programs.[19] Consequently, the Fed's securities purchases have never been subjected to a comprehensive GAO review. If such a review had been conducted in the wake of previous programs, its findings could have highlighted potential concerns about the efficacy and risks of those purchases.

Though the GAO is an independent agency with an impeccable track record of nonpartisan analysis, a potential concern is whether GAO reviews could exacerbate the risk of political interference in the Fed's monetary policy deliberations. To mitigate this concern, the GAO could be authorized to conduct comprehensive reviews on a fixed annual schedule rather than conducting reviews initiated by requests from congressional committees or individual members of Congress.

Finally, legislators could consider measures to strengthen the independence and broaden the scope of authority of the Fed's IG (inspector general). The Fed's IG could serve as a congressional watchdog for the entire Federal Reserve System, not just the Federal Reserve Board (as is currently the case). In fact, every other major office and agency (i.e., those with operating expenses exceeding $5 billion) has a fully independent IG who is appointed by the president, confirmed by the Senate, and may be removed only by the president for cause.[20] By contrast, the Fed's IG is merely a Fed employee who is appointed by the Fed chair and is removable by a vote of the Federal Reserve Board.[21]

Moreover, current law states that the Fed's IG shall work "under the authority, direction, and control" of the Fed chair while conducting any audit or investigation related to monetary policy. In principle, of course, the Fed chair could direct the IG to conduct a comprehensive evaluation of the FOMC's balance sheet policies and programs. If such an evaluation had been conducted in the late 2010s, following the completion of preceding rounds of securities purchases, an IG report might have alerted Congress that such a program could incur significant costs. However, there is no indication that the Fed's IG has embarked on such an evaluation, even in the wake of the operating losses associated with the latest round of securities purchases.

Strengthening Congressional Access to Internal Fed Information

In carrying out their constitutional duty to oversee the Federal Reserve, members of Congress have raised concerns about a range of issues, including (a) the process of selecting the president of each regional Federal Reserve Bank, especially given the role of those officials as members of the FOMC; (b) the FOMC's management of its balance sheet, especially given recent operating losses; and (c) the FOMC's complacency about elevated inflation in 2021, which set the stage for rapid tightening and major bank failures more recently. However, constraints on legislators' access to internal Fed information have inhibited Congress's ability to carry out inquiries and investigations into such issues.

To facilitate congressional access to sensitive Fed information, it seems helpful to consider how Congress maintains oversight of intelligence activities while ensuring the protection of highly sensitive national security information. In particular, the Intelligence Authorization Act of 1991 instituted the following procedures for congressional oversight of the Central Intelligence Agency (CIA):

- *Routine intelligence activities.* The CIA director and other intelligence officials must ensure that both congressional oversight committees are kept "fully and currently informed" about all noncovert activities, including any significant intelligence failures, and must respond to oversight committee requests by providing all information or material within their custody or control.[22] A parallel set of provisions requires the CIA director and other intelligence officials to keep the oversight committees "fully and currently informed" about all covert activities "to the extent consistent with due regard for the protection from unauthorized disclosure of classified information relating to sensitive intelligence sources and methods or other exceptionally sensitive matters."[23]

- *Extraordinary covert operations.* The president must specifically authorize every covert operation with a written finding that is promptly given to both congressional oversight committees. However, if the president determines that it is essential to limit access to the finding "to meet extraordinary circumstances affecting vital interests of the United States," then "the finding may be reported to the chairmen and ranking minority members of the intelligence committees, the Speaker and minority leader of the House of Representatives, the majority and minority leaders of the Senate, and such other member or members of the congressional leadership as may be included by the President."[24]

Such provisions could serve as a useful template for strengthening congressional oversight of the Fed. In particular, Fed officials could be required to keep both oversight committees—the Senate Banking Committee and the House Financial Services Committee—"fully and currently informed" about the Fed's internal procedures and operations and to provide prompt and complete information in response to all committee requests. Moreover, to protect the most market-sensitive information, the Federal Reserve Board could be authorized to provide such information solely to the chair and ranking minority member of each oversight committee and to the top officials in each chamber of Congress.

More broadly, the US Congress has a constitutional obligation to maintain effective oversight of the Fed. Over the past fifteen years, however, the scope and complexity of monetary policy has outpaced Congress's ability to monitor the Fed's monetary policymaking through existing mechanisms of oversight. In coming years, persistent congressional "undersight" could threaten the delicate balance between the Fed's independence and its public accountability. Potential methods for restoring this balance may well include strengthened reporting requirements, initiation of external reviews by congressional watchdogs, and assurance of congressional access to sensitive information.

Notes

1. U.S. Const. art. I, § 8.

2. Congress identified the key characteristics of an independent agency in 1887 when it created the Interstate Commerce Commission. In particular, an independent agency should have an uneven number of commissioners who are appointed to staggered terms of a fixed period extending beyond the term of the president and who can be removed by the president only "for cause"—i.e., inefficiency, neglect of

duty, or malfeasance in office. In addition, no more than a bare majority of the commissioners should be from any single political party.

3. Each regional Fed Bank's president is selected by six of its directors, of whom three are chosen by commercial banks within that district and three are chosen by the Federal Reserve Board.

4. The Federal Reserve Board members and the Federal Reserve Bank of New York's president cast votes at every FOMC meeting; four of the eleven other Fed Bank presidents vote on an annually rotating basis.

5. See St. Louis Fed (2025).

6. See Levin and Skinner (2024, figure 2A).

7. See Levin and Skinner (2024, figure 2B).

8. This conclusion reflected the Office of Legal Counsel's assessment of a number of factors, including the Federal Reserve Board's influence on the selection of Fed Bank presidents, its scope of control over their budgets and operations, and its practically unconstrained ability to remove them from office. See OLC (2019).

9. The Federal Reserve Reform Act of 1977 and the Humphrey–Hawkins Act of 1978 established specific reporting requirements, but those requirements were practically eliminated by an omnibus bill passed in late December 2000.

10. See Plosser (2021), Eggertsson and Kohn (2023), and Levy and Plosser (2022).

11. See Furman (2023) and Sommer (2023).

12. Such information was omitted from the monetary policy reports that were sent to Congress in June 2020 and February 2021. See Board of Governors (2025).

13. See Levin (2014) and Bordo et al. (2020).

14. U.S. Const. art. I, § 8.

15. Gauging the Fed's remittances in terms of GDP is appropriate because the US economy has grown markedly over the past six decades: Nominal GDP was about $540 billion in 1960 and is now approaching $27 trillion.

16. The Financial Accounting Standards Board determines GAAP for all nongovernmental institutions, including federally chartered enterprises such as Amtrak and Fannie Mae, while the Federal Accounting Standards Advisory Board is responsible for determining GAAP for all federal financial reporting entities, including cabinet departments, offices, and independent agencies such as the Federal Deposit Insurance Corporation and the Securities and Exchange Commission.

17. Since the Fed has authority to issue legal tender, its liabilities are broadly perceived as having the full faith and credit of the US government.

18. The Fed's combined financial statements were audited by Deloitte from 2007 to 2014 and have been audited by KPMG since then. In recent decades, the work of auditing firms has been plagued by recurring performance failures, but analysis of that issue is beyond the scope of this chapter.

19. 31 U.S.C. § 714(b). The Dodd–Frank Act added the provision that the GAO may audit such transactions solely for the purposes of assessing operational integrity,

accounting and financial reporting, internal controls, eligibility criteria, security and collateral policies, and the selection and payment of third-party contractors. 31 U.S.C. § 714(f)(2).

20. The president must notify Congress about the reasons for such a removal.

21. At a congressional hearing in 2009, the GAO's General Counsel Gary L. Kepplinger stated, "We believe that the differences in the appointment and removal processes between presidentially appointed IGs and those appointed by agency heads result in a clear difference in the organizational independence of these IGs" (Kepplinger 2009).

22. 50 U.S.C. § 3092.

23. 50 U.S.C. § 3093(b).

24. 50 U.S.C. § 3093(c).

References

Board of Governors (Board of Governors of the Federal Reserve System). 2025. "Monetary Policy." Board of Governors of the Federal Reserve System. January 8. https://www.federalreserve.gov/monetarypolicy.htm.

Bolzani, Juliana B. 2022. "Independent Central Banks and Independent Agencies: Is the Fed Super Independent?" *UC Davis Business Law Journal* 22 (2): 195–229.

Bordo, Michael D., Andrew T. Levin, and Mickey D. Levy. 2020. "Incorporating Scenario Analysis into the Federal Reserve's Policy Strategy and Communications." Working Paper No. 27369. National Bureau of Economic Research. June.

Eggertsson, Gauti B., and Donald Kohn. 2023. "The Inflation Surge of the 2020s: The Role of Monetary Policy." Working Paper No. 87. Hutchins Center, Brookings Institution. August.

Furman, Jason. 2023. "The Fed Should Carefully Aim for a Higher Inflation Target." *Wall Street Journal*, August 23.

GAO (Government Accountability Office). 2022. Performance and Accountability Report: Fiscal Year 2022. GAO.

Kepplinger, Gary L. 2009. "Inspectors General: Independent Oversight of Financial Regulatory Agencies." Testimony before the Subcommittee on Government Management, Organization and Procurement of the House Committee on Oversight and Government Reform. 111th Cong. March 25.

Levin, Andrew T. 2014. "The Design and Communication of Systematic Monetary Policy Strategies." *Journal of Economic Dynamics and Control* 49 (December): 52–69.

Levin, Andrew T., and Christina Parajon Skinner. 2024. "Central Bank Undersight: Assessing the Federal Reserve's Accountability to Congress." *Vanderbilt Law Review* 77 (6): 1769–1830.

Levy, Mickey D., and Charles I. Plosser. 2022. "The Murky Future of Monetary Policy." *Federal Reserve Bank of St. Louis Review* 104 (3): 178–88.

OLC (Office of Legal Counsel). 2019. "Appointment and Removal of Federal Reserve Bank Members of the Federal Open Market Committee." Opinion for the Assistant Attorney General Office of Legislative Affairs, October 23. https://www.justice.gov/olc/file/1349721/.

Plosser, Charles. 2021. "The Fed's Risky Experiment." Economics Working Paper No. 21116. Hoover Institution. June 18.

Sommer, Jeff. 2023. "The Fed Has Targeted 2% Inflation. Should It Aim Higher?" *New York Times*, March 24.

St. Louis Fed (Federal Reserve Bank of St. Louis). 2025. "A History of FOMC Dissents." *On the Economy* (blog). St. Louis Fed. Last updated February. https://www.stlouisfed.org/on-the-economy/2014/september/a-history-of-fomc-dissents.

13

The Evolution of Postwar Intellectual Leadership on Monetary Policy

James B. Bullard

Postwar Initial Conditions

In his book *The Age of Turbulence,* Alan Greenspan relates an anecdote concerning his days as a graduate student in economics at Columbia University in New York in 1950 and 1951. Greenspan was pursuing an economics PhD, which, he says, was the go-to degree for a person with ambition in economics at that time. His graduate advisor was future Federal Reserve chair Arthur Burns. Burns was a professor and an important figure in macroeconomics, having published a book, coauthored with Wesley Mitchell (1946), on business cycles and their measurement just a few years earlier. Greenspan describes Burns as an "avuncular pipe-smoking professor." He also says Burns liked to challenge the graduate students in class. One day, Burns asked the class, "What causes inflation?" There was no answer. Burns puffed on his pipe. Finally he declared, "Excessive government spending causes inflation" (Greenspan 2008, 37).

Turbulence in Greenspan's personal life caused him to drop out of Columbia. But this pre-monetarism anecdote has stuck in my head as an indicator of the immediate postwar mindset regarding monetary policy— namely, that inflation was entirely a fiscal phenomenon.

A few years later, in 1958, the Federal Reserve Bank of St. Louis hired Homer Jones to be the director of research. This was an attempt, ultimately very successful, by the Bank to enter into the world of academic-style research in order to apply that research to problems in monetary policy. Jones had been a professor of economics at Rutgers University, where Milton Friedman had been one of his students. Friedman (1976, 434) later wrote that Jones "[opened] my eyes to the broader reaches of economics and to the beauties and intricacies of economic theory." The Friedman–Jones alliance meant that the St. Louis Fed entered the intellectual fray with a monetarist research program.[1]

By 1968, this program bore considerable fruit with the publication of "the St. Louis model" of Leonall Andersen and Jerry Jordan (1968). For many years, this was the most widely cited paper in all of macroeconomics. Largely forgotten today, the paper was a technical marvel in its time. Andersen and Jordan had read the Shirley Almon "Distributed Lag" paper that had been published in *Econometrica* in 1965. They used the new technique outlined in that paper to estimate an equation with GDP as the dependent variable with both fiscal and monetary explanatory variables on the right-hand side. The estimation was demanding, and the Bank did not have the computing resources to complete the project. Andersen and Jordan had to ask friends at McDonnell Douglas, a major manufacturer of airplanes and jets, to use their computer. The results indicated that monetary variables were statistically more important than fiscal variables.

Intellectual Leadership Drives Policy

With this and other innovations, including the formation of the Shadow Open Market Committee, intellectual leadership on monetary policy shifted toward monetarist ideas. In 1979, with inflation in the US and around the world running out of control, this intellectual leadership entered the practical policy realm as the Federal Open Market Committee (FOMC) embarked on a "monetarist experiment" under then-chair Paul Volcker. The experiment would put more emphasis on monetary variables and was ultimately successful in vanquishing inflation.[2]

The Volcker disinflation was a searing intellectual experience, the central US macroeconomic event of the postwar era. It leaves a large imprint on today's macroeconomic thinking. The main theoretical lesson was the importance of credibility in achieving satisfactory monetary policy outcomes. That insight came most directly from Finn Kydland and Edward Prescott (1977) in their "Time Inconsistency" paper in the *Journal of Political Economy*. The paper stressed that failure to deliver on promised policy would be understood by an intelligent and forward-looking private sector, ultimately defeating policymaker desires. This insight led to an entire literature on monetary policy games and was cited as part of the Nobel Prize awarded to Kydland and Prescott in 2004.

When we say that the Volcker disinflation was successful, it is in the sense that the chaos of the 1970s was put behind us, and a new era dawned. It was

not just that Volcker ended the high and variable inflation of the 1970s—
the period from the late 1960s to the early 1980s was characterized by significant volatility on the real side of the economy as well. After Volcker, the
1980s expansion was quite long, punctuated by a relatively mild recession in
1990–91, and then another long expansion in the 1990s, followed by another
relatively mild recession in 2001. Later empirical literature would reveal that
the pre-Volcker US economy was more volatile in a statistically significant
sense when compared to the post-Volcker economy for both real and nominal
variables.[3] While there were four recessions in the thirteen years from 1970
to 1982, it would take about forty years for the next four recessions to occur.

The Volcker disinflation was also especially painful. The 1980–82 recession ultimately drove the US unemployment rate to 10.8%, and it created
the impression among a generation of academic economists as well as most
global financial market participants that recessions were necessary if the central bank wished to reduce inflation from a high level. The clear implication
was that one must not let inflation get out of hand, or even begin to get out of
hand. This led to an age of preemptive actual monetary policy. For instance,
European Central Bank president Jean-Claude Trichet often insisted that the
central bank must remain especially "vigilant" concerning inflation developments. As another example, the campaign led by then–Fed chair Janet Yellen
called for increasing the policy rate in 2016 and 2017 even when actual inflation remained below target.

In one of the most important papers of postwar macroeconomics, Thomas
J. Sargent argued in 1982 that expectations alone could be shifted by an agile
policymaker, and that such a shift could be extremely powerful as a policy
tool. This method had the potential to end a high inflation without a recession. Sargent analyzed historical examples from the post–World War I hyper-
inflations in Austria, Czechoslovakia, Germany, and Poland. In each of these
cases, the hyperinflation ended abruptly, *on the day or even on the hour* that a
credible monetary and fiscal regime was put in place in each country. These
disinflations did not have anything to do with Phillips curve effects.[4]

Sargent's (1982) recommendation from the "Ends of Four Big Inflations"
paper was too late to be helpful for Volcker. The Volcker-led FOMC was
not able to end the double-digit US inflation on the day, in the manner that
had been successful in post–World War I Europe. This is because, as Marvin
Goodfriend and Robert King argued in a 2005 *Journal of Monetary Economics*
paper, the Volcker disinflation was "incredible." Volcker had to earn back the
Fed credibility that had been squandered during the 1970s.[5]

Nevertheless, Sargent's insight would prove very useful for the monetary policy response to the postpandemic inflation of 2021–23 in the US, a point in time where the Fed had considerably more credibility.

The Volcker Aftermath

Good things came from the intellectual journey that led to the Volcker disinflation. The searing experience had taught macroeconomists that commitment and credibility were important, perhaps the most important, aspects driving satisfactory monetary policy outcomes. It was also important, as the monetarists had emphasized, to assign responsibility for inflation outcomes to the central bank. It was, after all, Paul Volcker, the Fed chair along with the FOMC, and not the Treasury secretary or the Senate Finance Committee, that ended the inflation.

As these ideas began to be widely understood, some simple extensions began to be considered. If credibility and commitment were important, should the central bank simply state an inflation target and take consistent action to achieve it so that observers of monetary policy could plan accordingly? By the early 1990s, the answer to this question was a clear "yes" and inflation targeting swept global monetary policy. This process was aided and abetted by the European decision in the aftermath of the fall of the Soviet Union, to create, by treaty, a European monetary union (EMU). The implementation and operation of this directive fell to the European Central Bank (ECB), and the meetings during the 1990s concerning how to go about this project contributed importantly to standardizing the lessons from the Volcker disinflation. The ECB would be responsible for inflation in the EMU and would take action to keep inflation low and stable—the original objective was "below 2 percent."

Inflation targeting has generally been viewed as a rousing success.[6] Inflation-targeting countries have tended to have lower inflation and inflation closer to target than they did in the pre-inflation-targeting era. Inflation expectations tended to become more stable around the inflation target, allowing firms to plan more effectively. Countries that bucked the trend, including, at times, Türkiye, Argentina, and Venezuela, ended up with considerable inflation.

New Directions

Imitation is the sincerest form of flattery. Success in St. Louis caused other Reserve Banks and the Board of Governors to get into the academic-style research game beginning in the 1970s. Perhaps most notably, the Federal

Reserve Bank of Minneapolis began to partner with the University of Minnesota and asked some of the professors there to work with the research team at the Bank. This partnership led to a proliferation of new, innovative ideas that are still shaping the contours of macroeconomics today. By the time of the publication of Chris Sims's "Macroeconomics and Reality" paper in *Econometrica* in 1980, and Sargent and Neil Wallace's "Some Unpleasant Monetarist Arithmetic" paper in the Minneapolis Fed's *Quarterly Review* in 1981, intellectual leadership had shifted again. This time the shift was toward deeper and unknown territory.

These papers were methodological in nature. The "Macro and Reality" paper argued that the identification assumptions underlying most macro-empirical work were "incredible." The "Unpleasant Arithmetic" paper made monetarist assumptions but found that because of monetary-fiscal interactions, the policy conclusions could be distinctly non-monetarist. Sargent and Wallace's paper brought up issues about multiple steady states—suggesting, at a practical level, that the macroeconomy could end up converging to different rest points even under market clearing and rational expectations.

The important point was forcefully made, and intellectual leadership was seized: To truly get monetary policy right, we economists were going to have to delve much deeper into the model-building aspect of macroeconomics. The Lucas (1976) critique of econometrics had really hit home: Large shifts in expectations, including expectations about future macroeconomic policy, could cause empirical estimates of policy impacts to be fundamentally misleading.

And indeed, more extensive models were produced, notably when Kydland and Prescott published their paper about the real business cycle (RBC) in *Econometrica* in 1982. Here was a coherent, micro-founded dynamic stochastic general equilibrium (DSGE) model that, the authors argued, fit the macroeconomic data relatively well. And shockingly, there was no effort to include monetary policy in the model at all. Perhaps more shockingly, the equilibrium studied was Pareto optimal, meaning that, despite the business cycles embodied in the model, there was no role for policymakers of any kind to play. When Thomas Cooley and Gary Hansen published their version of an RBC model with money in the *American Economic Review* in 1989, they found that the monetary aspect did not affect the cyclical properties of the model—monetary policy was largely irrelevant. This recalls Ronald Reagan's oft-used lament: "Sometimes I think we should all just go home!"

The lesson was clear. Generally speaking, markets are going to do a very good job of allocating resources in the economy. This is true even when considering dynamic stochastic settings. To study a role for policy, there has to be "something wrong," some aspect of the environment that is preventing the invisible hand from allocating resources efficiently. This "something wrong" came to be known as a "friction." And the most popular friction for monetary economics, for better or worse, came to be the sticky price friction.

Models with Frictions

Michael Woodford described a model economy in his book *Interest and Prices*, published in 2003. He wanted to analyze a fully specified dynamic stochastic economy like Kydland and Prescott, but one that also had an important friction in the form of sticky prices. He stressed in his introduction that he maintained a type of virtual RBC economy underneath his economy with sticky prices. This virtual RBC economy, with its Pareto optimal allocation of resources, would be the observable outcome if either the sticky prices somehow became perfectly flexible, or if the monetary authority followed an optimal policy regime that established the "Wicksellian natural real rate of interest" for the economy—the real rate of interest that would occur if there were no frictions in the economy at all.

The message was that, if one wanted to impute an important role for monetary policy, one had to carefully specify what problem monetary policy is supposed to solve. For Woodford, it is the "sticky price problem." This is what gives Woodford theoretical coherence. But in the realm of practical policymaking, it is far from clear that this is the type of role that is being ascribed to the FOMC. Instead, the FOMC cites the mandates written into US law, which include "stable prices." Woodford's argument was that by pursuing a solution to the sticky price problem, the central bank would end up stabilizing prices.

The New Keynesian model came to dominate discussions of monetary policy, provide intellectual leadership in the field, and provide insight for actual monetary policy discussions. The New Keynesian Phillips curve challenged typical concepts in practical policymaking, because it ascribed a potentially large role (a coefficient near unity) on an expected inflation term, suggesting that the large shifts in expectations described in Sargent's "Ends of Four Big Inflations" paper could indeed impact actual inflation outcomes nearly one-for-one without impacting real variables. The Taylor rule, developed in John Taylor's 1993 Carnegie-Rochester Conference paper, could be incorporated into the New Keynesian framework to give practical recommendations on real-time monetary policy decisions. Monetary aggregates did not play a direct role, but in some circles the model was considered "new monetarist" because of the way it adhered to many monetarist principles, not the least of which is that the monetary authority had the main responsibility for inflation outcomes and had to maintain credibility with respect to those outcomes.

Elimination of Monetary Policy Mistakes?

Many critical views of Federal Reserve policy characterize the FOMC as careening from one policy blunder to another. Little or nothing seems to go right, and each decision by the Committee is a fraught affair that could sink the US economy or lead to unstoppable inflation. These views are summed up in Rudiger Dornbusch's famous quip, "Expansions don't die of old age, they are murdered by the Fed."

Yet we should be careful. In the last twenty years, there have been just two recessions in the US, both of which have clear causes. The Global Financial Crisis stemmed from weaknesses in the US nonbank financial sector, not something under the direct control of the FOMC. And the COVID-19 pandemic was a natural disaster. Did the New Keynesian consensus get enough of the pieces together to inform a reasonably stable monetary policy for the US and other countries? Has the holy grail been attained, to the extent that it can be?

Perhaps. But the most recent candidate for a monetary policy mistake is not the murdering of an expansion, but the fueling of an inflationary outburst in 2021–23 of a type not seen in the US since the Volcker era. How did it happen? I have argued elsewhere that the pandemic should be viewed as a war, and that the combination of wartime deficit finance and low interest rates to support the war effort is known to produce inflation across many different times and places.[7] To end the inflation, fiscal rectitude had to be restored to its prewar level, and in addition, monetary policy had to return to orthodoxy. Both of these conditions occurred as divided government returned after the 2022 midterm elections and the Fed began raising interest rates aggressively during 2022. Inflation began to fall simultaneously with these developments, and without a recession. As Sargent had suggested was possible, the aggressive moves by a credible FOMC during this period shifted expectations back to prepandemic norms to an extent large enough to bring inflation under control.

Challenges Remain

Despite this most recent soft-landing success, all is not well. There are numerous challenges for the future of monetary policy intellectual leadership, and by extension, for the future of monetary policy practice itself. Will these challenges be sufficiently disruptive to overshadow the previously learned wisdom, or will they be seamlessly integrated into some future framework? I cannot say with any certainty.

I will focus on just two such issues, one related to the theory of monetary policy and the other related to the practice. On the theory side, a particularly salient issue is the addition of realistic degrees of heterogeneity into the New Keynesian and related environments, providing enough variability in household income, asset holding, and consumption to approach observed Gini coefficients in the US data. Greg Kaplan, Benjamin Moll, and Giovanni Violante argued in a 2018 *American Economic Review* paper that the addition of realistic degrees of heterogeneity to the New Keynesian world would likely upset many of the key results from that literature. Anmol Bhandari, David Evans, Mikhail Golosov, and Sargent suggested in a 2021 *Econometrica* paper that a Ramsey-type assessment of optimal fiscal and monetary policy in a heterogeneous-agent world would upend many of the existing concepts concerning optimal policy developed in postwar thought. Is it true? Would the addition of realistic heterogeneity change everything?[8]

On the practical policy side, policymakers and advocates of inflation targeting have to contend with the Japanese example. This is an economy with an exceptionally high public-debt-to-GDP ratio, an inflation rate that has been exceptionally low for several decades, and a policy rate that has not been above 0.5% since the 1990s. By conventional analysis, the very low nominal interest rate policy should have generated considerable inflation, but it did not. What is the explanation for this phenomenon?[9] The prepandemic global situation was characterized by EMU economies seemingly poised to converge to the Japanese equilibrium. Would this have been the outcome had the pandemic not intervened? Should we design future monetary policy to avoid such outcomes?

Conclusion

In this commentary, I have argued that the postwar intellectual leadership in monetary economics has shifted over time, and that these intellectual shifts have eventually fed into actual monetary policy decision making. My brief survey suggests that, with regard to theoretical developments, the rise of the "models with frictions" view of the role of monetary policy has had the most widespread influence. The implementation of inflation targeting has had a large and successful practical effect on postwar monetary policy. Whether these pieces of conventional wisdom will survive into the future, however, is in some doubt, because it is relatively easy to identify both theoretical and pragmatic issues that have not been satisfactorily resolved.

Notes

1. For more background on Milton Friedman, see Nelson (2020).
2. See Lindsey et al. (2005).
3. See, for instance, Stock and Watson (2003).
4. See Sargent (1982).
5. This process is described in a recent paper by King and Yang K. Lu (2022).
6. For a recent wide-ranging discussion, see the papers in the Sveriges Riksbank conference, "The Quest for Nominal Stability: Lessons from Three Decades with Inflation Targeting," Stockholm, Sweden, May 23–24, 2024.
7. See Bullard (2024).
8. The paper by Bullard et al. (2024) says "no." Much as with the RBC model, the idea would be that heterogeneity by itself would not prevent markets from allocating resources efficiently—one would need an additional friction to impute an important role for policy.
9. For a discussion of an explanation based on multiple steady states, see Bullard (2010).

References

Almon, Shirley. 1965. "The Distributed Lag Between Capital Appropriations and Expenditures." *Econometrica* 33 (1): 178–96.

Andersen, Leonall C., and Jerry L. Jordan. 1968. "Monetary and Fiscal Actions: A Test of Their Relative Importance in Economic Stabilization." *Federal Reserve Bank of St. Louis Review* 50 (11): 11–24.

Bhandari, Anmol, David Evans, Mikhail Golosov, and Thomas J. Sargent. 2021. "Inequality, Business Cycles, and Monetary-Fiscal Policy." *Econometrica* 89 (6): 2559–99.

Bullard, James. 2010. "Seven Faces of 'The Peril.'" *Federal Reserve Bank of St. Louis Review* 92 (5): 339–52.

Bullard, James. 2024. "The Monetary-Fiscal Policy Mix and Central Bank Strategy." In *Getting Monetary Policy Back on Track*, edited by Michael D. Bordo, John H. Cochrane, and John B. Taylor. Hoover Institution Press.

Bullard, James, Aarti Singh, and Jacek Suda. 2024. "Optimal Macroeconomic Policies in a Heterogeneous World." *IMF Economic Review* 72 (3): 991–1041.

Burns, Arthur C., and Wesley J. Mitchell. 1946. *Measuring Business Cycles*. National Bureau of Economic Research.

Cooley, Thomas F., and Gary D. Hansen. 1989. "The Inflation Tax in a Real Business Cycle Model." *American Economic Review* 79 (4): 733–48.

Friedman, Milton. 1976. "Homer Jones: A Personal Reminiscence." *Journal of Monetary Economics* 2 (4): 433–36.

Goodfriend, Marvin, and Robert G. King. 2005. "The Incredible Volcker Disinflation." *Journal of Monetary Economics* 52 (5): 981–1015.

Greenspan, Alan. 2008. *The Age of Turbulence*. Penguin.

Kaplan, Greg, Benjamin Moll, and Giovanni L. Violante. 2018. "Monetary Policy According to HANK." *American Economic Review* 108 (3): 697–743.

King, Robert G., and Yang K. Lu. 2022. "Evolving Reputation for Commitment: The Rise, Fall, and Stabilization of US Inflation." Working Paper No. 30763. National Bureau of Economic Research. December.

Kydland, Finn E., and Edward C. Prescott. 1977. "Rules Rather than Discretion: The Inconsistency of Optimal Plans." *Journal of Political Economy* 85 (3): 473–92.

Kydland, Finn E., and Edward C. Prescott. 1982. "Time to Build and Aggregate Fluctuations." *Econometrica* 50 (6): 1345–70.

Lindsey, David, Athanasios Orphanides, and Robert H. Rasche. 2005. "The Reform of October 1979: How It Happened and Why." *Federal Reserve Bank of St. Louis Review* 87 (2): 187–235.

Lucas, Robert E., Jr. 1976. "Econometric Policy Evaluation: A Critique." *Carnegie-Rochester Conference Series on Public Policy* 1:19–46.

Nelson, Edward. 2020. *Milton Friedman and the Economic Debate in the United States, 1932–1972, Vol. 1*. University of Chicago Press.

Sargent, Thomas J. 1982. "The Ends of Four Big Inflations." In *Inflation: Causes and Effects*, edited by Robert E. Hall. University of Chicago Press.

Sargent, Thomas J., and Neil Wallace. 1981. "Some Unpleasant Monetarist Arithmetic." *Federal Reserve Bank of Minneapolis Quarterly Review* 5 (3): 1–17.

Sims, Christopher A. 1980. "Macroeconomics and Reality." *Econometrica* 48 (1): 1–48.

Stock, James H., and Mark W. Watson. 2003. "Has the Business Cycle Changed and Why?" In *NBER Macroeconomics Annual 2022, Vol. 17*, edited by Mark Gertler and Kenneth Rogoff. MIT Press.

Taylor, John B. 1993. "Discretion Versus Policy Rules in Practice." *Carnegie-Rochester Conference Series on Public Policy* 39 (December): 195–214.

Woodford, Michael. 2003. *Interest and Prices*. Princeton University Press.

STEVEN J. DAVIS: Those are three engaging talks. While the speakers are coming back to the stage, I will ask the first question, which relates directly to Jim's emphasis on credibility, or its absence in the conduct, successful or unsuccessful conduct of monetary policy. This idea of credibility, the way Jim [Bullard] told the story, it's kind of a nice storytelling after the fact, for when inflation fighting was successful and when it was not, and it sounds persuasive.

If that's really the right way to think about monetary policy, why doesn't the Fed—and central banks around the world—devote enormous energy to assessing in real time the credibility of monetary policy? Central banks do, in fact, look carefully at expectations of inflation, interest rates, and more. But I don't think attention to mean expectations is sufficient to assess credibility.

Expectations derived from financial markets tell you about the beliefs of the marginal participants. Credibility is broader than that. Let me make the point with a concrete example. Recall the situation in the middle of 2020 or late 2020 before the [COVID-19] vaccine was announced. There was tremendous uncertainty as to when the vaccine would become available and how effective it would be. Even in 2021, there was still a lot of uncertainty about how well the vaccine would work.

To assess the credibility of its monetary policy, the Fed needed to know more than what market participants thought of as the expected outcome, because there were a wide range of possible future paths for the pandemic, the economy, inflation, and so on. To understand how market participants expected the Fed to behave under a range of contingencies, to fully assess the credibility of the Fed, we'd need to ask people directly using a survey approach.

If the pandemic lasts so long and requires this much government spending, and here I'm playing off the wartime analogy, will the Fed switch its monetary policy as appropriate when the pandemic's largely in the past? It's very hard to get at that by just looking at financial market data or survey-based point expectations. That leads me to a question.

If credibility is really central, why not try to measure it in a really serious, rigorous, ongoing way—pretty much as a matter of course for central banks?

JAMES B. BULLARD: Well, sure, metrics are great, and I would be all in favor of—if we could get better measures of Fed credibility, then I'd be in favor of getting those.

I do think that if you look at a model and you say, What would the inflation expectation of inflation be five to ten years in the future? It should always be exactly 2%. And you don't see that in the data, you see it diverging from that every so often.

And what we saw, I think, in the first half, second half of 2021 and the first half of 2022, was that those seem to be diverging a little bit and quite a bit over shorter horizons. And I take that as a kind of measure of the credibility of the central bank.

I mean, in the model, that would never happen, because you just have a perfectly credible policy time. But in the real world, traders, financial markets, they start to wonder, "Maybe we're coming into a new era and the Fed won't do its job and somehow rationalize high inflation and just leave it high."

So, I think that was happening in mid-2022, and I've seen some graphs. Actually, Athanasios [Orphanides] has some good charts on this. But once the Fed started raising rates, especially the four 75-basis-point increases in a row, that expectation got quashed right back down to 2%. The Fed was serious, and they were going to achieve the 2% target.

DAVIS: Thanks, let's open it up and see. John Cochrane was first with his hand up, as usual. Then we'll come over here.

JOHN H. COCHRANE: This was great. I'll limit myself to two short questions for Andy.

On dissents, you make an important case, but some institutions are improved by dissents, while some aren't. The Supreme Court uses dissents. I remember many faculty meetings where we fought and fought, but then we all vote the same way, and we agree to forget disagreement for the health of the institution.

The Fed is trying to manage expectations. It's trying to convince people that it's following a predictable rules-based policy. I would think that a constant cacophony of dissents undermines that effort. In foreign policy, the US tries to send a consistent signal, not a cacophony of voices for foreign leaders to hear. You'll remember Larry Summers's interesting talk at the last Monetary Policy Conference arguing against dissent and cacophony on this basis.

A constant cacophony of dissents would lead to more speculation on internal politics. It would lead to more focus on the decision, up and down. It gives the Fed less ability to tie itself to at least the perception of a rule.

You also said that external reviews would be wonderful, and you mentioned the GAO [Government Accountability Office] as a wonderful idea. I like the idea of external reviews too. But as we look across administrative agencies, the ones who get GAO reviews are not all models of apolitical technocratic competence. You mentioned NASA, who can't put up a rocket for under ten times what it costs SpaceX. The FTC [Federal Trade Commission], the SEC [Securities and Exchange Commission], the FCC [Federal Communications Commission], and many other "alphabet soup" agencies are all on various "whole of government" crusades for one thing or another.

The Fed is probably the best-managed government agency I can think of. It's certainly better than all the other financial agencies, that do have reviews. So, I am a little bit worried that this GAO external view hasn't produced wonderful results everywhere else.

ANDREW T. LEVIN: I'm really glad that you asked the first question. Governor Miki Bowman's dissent from the last FOMC [Federal Open Market Committee] decision is very significant.

This is the first time in nearly twenty years that a Federal Reserve Board member has dissented from any FOMC decision, so it demonstrated a remarkable degree of courage. And my personal view is that it was helpful for the Fed. As Governor Waller noted at lunch today, the past few weeks of data have pointed to stronger economic growth, a solid labor market, and the prospect that inflation remains significantly higher than the Fed's target.

Thus, there are now scenarios where the Fed needs to keep interest rates at a plateau instead of an ongoing sequence of rate cuts over the next year. Governor Bowman's dissent helped convey the sense that these FOMC decisions are complex, difficult judgment calls. That's helpful to the Fed, a helpful reminder to the public, and should be helpful to the markets, too.

Indeed, a number of participants at this conference have been dissenters on past FOMC decisions, including Jeff Lacker, Charlie Plosser, Esther George, Tom Hoenig, and Jim Bullard. And in each of those cases, it was a thoughtful, careful dissent, conveying a respectful difference in judgment, which is absolutely appropriate to a public institution whose decisions affect millions of people.

And not only that, but that's what Congress had in mind when the FOMC was established. The design was that a set of independent and individually accountable experts would be making monetary policy decisions. Congress didn't want those decisions to be made behind closed doors and then come out with a pretense of unity like a private board.

Regarding the second question, the Government Accountability Office has saved taxpayers over a trillion dollars. And GAO itself undergoes external reviews by auditors from other countries.

Just like NASA or any of the other agencies you mentioned, GAO will come in and review the Fed. And the Fed may not take all of that advice, but it should still undergo the review.

DAVIS: Okay, in the middle here, and yes, you are still next. And then we'll come over to you.

DAVID PAPELL: This question is for Andy Levin. It strikes me that if you want to have an external review of the Fed, the first step would be to have somebody ask Chair Powell publicly: "Why aren't you doing an external review?" I know you can't ask him that question, and I can't ask him that question, but there are reporters who ask questions at every press conference and could ask him that question. Why don't you contact the reporters who ask tough questions at the press conferences and suggest they ask that question?

DAVIS: So I think that is a suggestion more than a question. Do you want to respond, or Jim, maybe you want to respond?

LEVIN: First of all, I applaud the reporters who are here; I know some of them well. But the unfortunate fact is that the Fed has established ground rules for press conferences, and if a reporter's question is viewed as too uncomfortable for the chair, then that reporter may not be invited back again. And that's very different than press conferences at the White House or other agencies.

And those ground rules are not helpful to the public. Again, this is part of the rationale for Congress to initiate an external review that could encompass the questions about the extent to which the Fed is being challenged in the media.

BULLARD: Yeah, I would just say on this that I certainly got asked about "audit the Fed" many times, and there is a standard answer inside the Fed, which is that there are three groups that are already auditing the Fed.

So you've got an external auditor that does not audit every single year. Then you've also got internal audit, which I found to be actually very effective and very useful inside the Fed. Those are at the various banks; and then you've got the inspector general, and that's been beefed up in recent years, and they're doing even more work than they did before.

So if you actually add up the audit hours, which we did at one point inside the Fed, it's phenomenally high. So it's not this kind of "audit the Fed" idea, which was, "No one's looking at any of this," I think, is not the right view of this. There's a ton of auditing already going on in the Fed, so.

DAVIS: Thank you.

BULLARD: And also, the GAO is the arm of Congress. The reason that they have the inspector general set up is because the Board is an independent agency. So that's just how it's done all around Washington. If you're an independent agency, then you have the inspector general.

The thought has been that you call it an independent agency, then you don't use GAO; use the inspector general. That's the way it's done inside Washington, they could change those.

LEVIN: Christina Skinner and I have specifically addressed this question in our law journal article, which is also available as a Hoover working paper. As a matter of fact, the GAO does comprehensive reviews of every other independent federal agency, including FDIC, SEC, OCC [Office of the Comptroller of the Currency]. The Federal Reserve got an exemption in the 1970s that exempts the Fed's monetary policy function. And that exemption is practically unique. Congress is the Fed's boss, and Congress should reconsider that exemption.

BULLARD: So your paper is probably going to be very useful on this dimension. But actually, now that I think of it, the Fed, there was an audit of the boards of directors, I believe, of the Federal Reserve Banks. My fellow colleagues might remember that. So there was some work on that at one point.

LEVIN: Actually, after the financial crisis, Ben Bernanke gave testimony to Congress in which he said, "We would welcome a GAO review of all of our emergency facilities."

And the GAO did that review, and I think it was helpful. It wasn't perfect, but nothing in this world is absolutely perfect, right?

DAVIS: Let's move on because others want to ask questions. There's clearly been some auditing done and Andy wants more. Okay, so right here, yes.

ROBERT G. KING: So, Robert King, Boston University. I wanted to comment on Andy's presentation, but Steve said something that also required me to make an observation.

For the last four or five years, I've been working conceptually on modeling credibility and reputation in an internally consistent manner, and making explicit comparisons to US inflation data. My conclusion off that is, it's the biggest single thing in terms of understanding the ups and downs of inflation in the United States.

But as part of that process, in ways that are related to what you asked, I did a literature survey, Google survey, etc., and I looked for the phrase "estimated reputation" and "estimated credibility." And I found almost no studies that had that combination of phrases. One, interestingly, happened to be Axel Weber's thesis.

Okay, now, turning, turning to Andy: I think what you say is, is definitely something that the US government should do. But I want to consider the role of the SOMC and its influence on monetary policy—because in a way, it's an auditor, it's a reviewer of practices. And the way in which Federal Reserve information is now provided is that analysts can go back five years later.

And they can look at what were the arguments that were made by the Federal Reserve officials for particular positions and critically appraise them. So if I want to ask, was Jim Bullard a good inflation forecaster or not? And do I like his arguments, yes or no? Everything's there in print.

Now in the way I think about things, I sharply divide the Fed between a monetary authority and a banking/credit authority. And the degree of information we have about the credit dimensions of Fed decision making is so much smaller. Typically an FOMC meeting, or at least some of them, begin in the following way: "Well, let's close the meeting of the Board and open the meeting of the FOMC. That is, let's stop talking by ourselves about huge decisions, and let's go to the open committee."

So we can't really tell anything about the rationales for interventions that, to my mind, in the last several decades, have been far more consequential than the monetary policy decisions.

So even if we can't get Andy's external authority to come in and look at things in detail, if there were standards set for the reporting of the Board in its decision process, I think that would be huge. I think otherwise, we're going to be stuck with a view of the Fed that's well captured by the title of Jeanna Smialek's book, which is *Limitless*.

DAVIS: All right, I need guidance from the organizers here. We're now at sixty minutes. Do you want to go longer, or should we end here? Okay, let me thank the panelists. That was a great discussion. Obviously, there's an appetite for more.

The Conduct of Monetary Policy

Introduction

Robert G. King

I'm Robert King, and I'm filling in for Charles Calomiris, who is regrettably ill and stuck in New York, but is to appear to us virtually later to do a presentation. I'm delighted to introduce the panelists, who are a remarkable combination of individuals whom I've met in many different intellectual contexts.

I well remember reading papers by Loretta Mester on banking, and then later I was delighted that when she became the president of the Federal Reserve Bank of Cleveland, she had the wisdom to appoint one of my former students, Ellis Tallman, as her research director!

Bill Nelson knows more about banking and the Fed than anyone I know: His remarkable knowledge is based on many years of experience inside of the Federal Reserve System. And now at the Bank Policy Institute, he's sharing things more broadly.

Finally, of course, we have Darrell Duffie, who's got a span over financial markets in ways that are preposterous. On the one hand, you have the originator of much of modern financial theory, particularly as applied to derivatives pricing, term structure, and so on. You have the author of *Dark Markets*. And then you have a man who's willing to get his hands dirty with the plumbing of the financial system.

So with that group introduction, I'd like to ask Loretta to talk to us.

14

The Fed's Ample Reserves Monetary Policy Operating Framework

It Isn't as Simple as It Looks

Loretta J. Mester

Over its history, the Shadow Open Market Committee (SOMC) has been very successful at fostering the active exchange of ideas about the economy and monetary policy. Through its efforts, the SOMC has exposed policymakers to new ways of thinking about policy challenges and solutions, thereby offering them some protection against the scourge of groupthink. Aside from the value of the ideas themselves, the SOMC has set a significant example of how to discuss different views in a productive way, with the goal of achieving better policy outcomes. I had the honor to participate in the conference marking the fiftieth anniversary of the SOMC and celebrate its success. This paper is based on those remarks.

In discussing the Fed's current ample-reserves monetary policy operating framework, I will make one simple point: Namely, that the framework is not as simple as the theory suggests.

Monetary Policy Operating Frameworks

A monetary policy operating framework is the method by which a central bank ensures that the policy rate stays within the target range set by the central bank. It concerns how the central bank implements policy, not what the policy is.

In selecting an operating framework, the primary criterion is that the framework allow for effective control of a policy rate that is sufficiently tied to other market rates to allow for reliable transmission of monetary policy throughout the economy. The Fed communicates its policy choice by setting a target range for the federal funds rate, a market-driven rate, determined as the average rate at which banks lend reserves held in their Fed master accounts to one another overnight.

Another desirable attribute of an operating framework is that it be robust to different economic situations (e.g., when policy rates need to move quickly or when the policy rate has been reduced to its effective lower bound). It is also desirable that the operating framework not exacerbate financial-stability problems when they arise, and ideally it should be adaptable to actions that might be taken to address such issues.

Since the time of the Global Financial Crisis (GFC) of 2007–8, the Fed and many other central banks have been implementing monetary policy in a framework that involves a high level of bank reserves, the funds that banks hold in accounts at the central bank. In January 2019, the Federal Open Market Committee (FOMC) announced that it intends to continue to implement monetary policy in an ample-reserves regime, also known as a floor system, in which the Fed achieves its fed funds rate target mainly through setting its administered interest rates, the interest on reserves balances (IORB) rate, and the interest rate on overnight reverse repurchase agreements (ON RRP) (FOMC 2019). The FOMC also affirmed that it would continue to target the federal funds rate as its primary way of adjusting the stance of monetary policy.

This operating framework differs from the one the Fed used before the GFC. Back then the Fed operated in a scarce reserves operating regime, also known as a so-called corridor system, in which the FOMC actively managed the supply of reserves in order to achieve its fed funds rate target.[1]

Both the scarce reserves and ample reserves operating frameworks have proven to be effective during the periods in which they have been used. So, one might ask, why did the Fed change its operating framework after the GFC? This change was necessitated by economic circumstances and the policy choices made in response to those circumstances.

The Evolution of the Fed's Balance Sheet

In January 2007, the Fed was holding less than $900 billion on the asset side of its balance sheet. On the liability side, banks were holding about $20 billion in reserve accounts at the Fed.[2] With reserves this scarce, the FOMC could affect the fed funds rate by making small changes in the supply of reserves via open market operations involving buying or selling short-term Treasuries.

This, coupled with estimates of the demand for reserves, allowed the FOMC to ensure that the fed funds rate was maintained at the FOMC's target. During the GFC and Great Recession, the Fed began lending to banks and other nonbank entities to shore up the economy and financial markets. (See figures 14.1–14.3.) Once the fed funds rate was brought down to essentially zero, the FOMC began purchasing longer-term assets in order to put downward pressure on longer-term interest rates and thereby add further monetary accommodation.[3] As a result of these purchases, the assets on the Fed's balance sheet swelled. Assets rose to over $4.5 trillion in January 2015, their peak during this period, which was a fivefold increase from before the GFC. Reserves, currency, and the US Treasury's account at the Fed (the Treasury General Account, or TGA) were the main liabilities on the Fed's balance sheet. As assets rose, so did reserves. During this period, reserves peaked at $2.8 trillion in November 2014.

At such high levels of reserves, small changes in the supply of reserves have little effect on the fed funds rate, so the Fed could no longer use a corridor system to control its policy rate. In October 2008, Congress gave the Fed the authority to begin paying interest on the reserve balances that banks and other depository institutions hold at the Fed.[4] And this allowed the FOMC to implement monetary policy in a new way. To keep the fed funds rate within its target range, the FOMC used its administered rates, the IORB rate and the ON RRP rate.

In October 2017, the Fed began gradually reducing the size of its balance sheet by allowing assets to begin to run off according to the plan announced in June 2017. In March 2019, reserve levels began to approach the level that the FOMC considered likely to be the level necessary to efficiently and effectively implement monetary policy. Accordingly, the FOMC announced that it would begin reducing the pace at which assets were running off starting in May 2019.

Reserves continued to decline and had fallen to about $1.4 trillion when repo rates and other short-term money-market rates began to spike in mid-September 2019. The market disruption led the Fed to conclude that the level of reserves had fallen below the level consistent with ample reserves, and the Fed began to allow reserve balances to rise again.

When the COVID-19 pandemic hit in March 2020, the Fed again began purchasing Treasury securities and agency mortgage-backed securities (MBS), at first to address market dysfunction in the Treasury market and then to add monetary policy accommodation after the fed funds rate had

Fed balance sheet

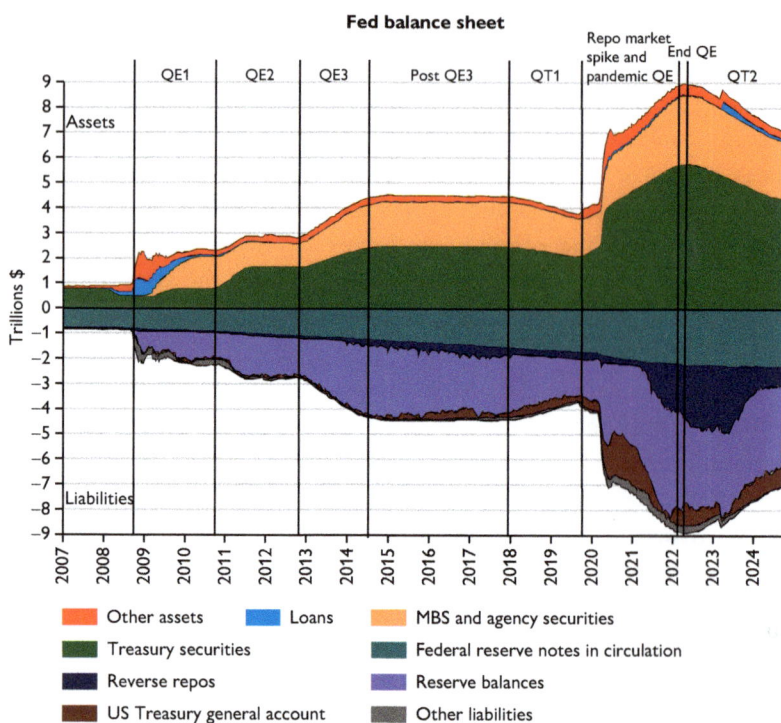

Figure 14.1a. The size and composition of the Fed's balance sheet assets and liabilities have changed significantly since the Global Financial Crisis.

Note: Weekly data; last point plotted is October 2, 2024.

Source: Federal Reserve Board via Haver Analytics.

been brought down to its effective lower bound. By June 2022, the balance sheet grew to nearly $9 trillion in assets, about double its asset size before the pandemic, or about 35% as a share of GDP. There was over $3 trillion in reserves (or about 12% as a share of GDP) and about $2.5 trillion in ON RRPs (or about 10% as a share of GDP).

In June 2022, the Fed began the second normalization of its balance sheet, which is still underway. Since that time, assets have fallen by about $1.8 trillion; ON RRPs are down about $1.7 trillion, but reserves have actually risen a bit (by $22 billion). The Fed's stated intention is to bring reserves down to the minimum level needed to effectively and efficiently implement monetary policy under an ample reserves operating framework where policy rate control is managed primarily by setting the Fed's administered rates.

Assets ($Billions)			Liabilities and Capital ($Billions)		
	Jan 4, 2007	Oct 3, 2024		Jan 4, 2007	Oct 3, 2024
Treasury securities	778.9	4,364.4	Currency	781.3	2,301.7
Agency and agency MBS	0.0	2,284.4	Reserves held by depository institutions	20.0	3,097.2
Loans to depository institutions	1.3	75.5	Reserve repos	29.7	799.3
Other assets	94.4	322.6	US Treasury general account	6.2	823.4
			Other liabilities	6.8	−18.1
			Capital	30.6	43.4
Total	874.6	7,046.9	Total	874.6	7,046.9

Figure 14.1b. The Fed's balance sheet has changed in size and composition.

Source: Federal Reserve Board via Haver Analytics, monthly data.

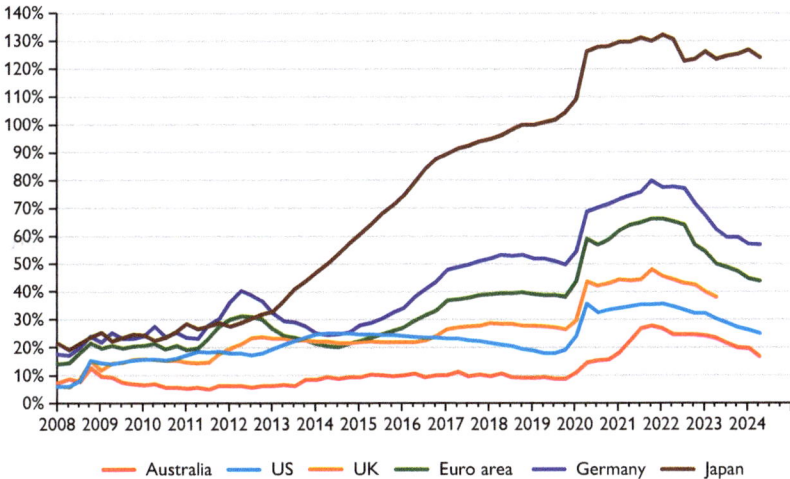

Figure 14.2. Central bank assets as a percent of GDP rose in many advanced economies during the pandemic.

Note: Quarterly data; last observation is 2023 Q2 for UK, 2024 Q2 for the others.

Source: Japan Cabinet Office, Bundesbank, European Central Bank, Bank of England, Federal Reserve Board, and Reserve Bank of Australia, via Haver Analytics.

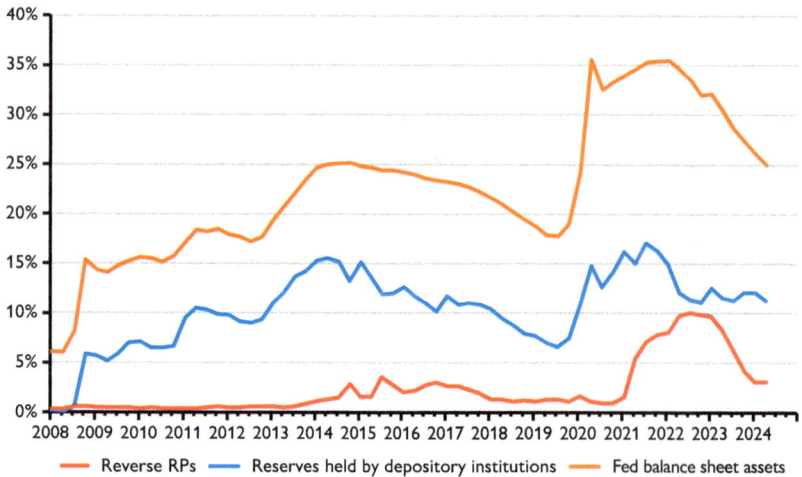

Figure 14.3. Fed balance sheet assets, reserves, and ON RRPs as a percent of GDP rose during the pandemic.

Note: Quarterly data; last observation is 2024 Q2.

Source: Federal Reserve Board via Haver Analytics.

Simplicity of the Ample-Reserves Framework

One of the purported benefits of the ample-reserves framework is that it is simple. And it is—at least on paper. In a world without frictions, banks that need reserves would not want to pay a rate higher than what they could get from borrowing directly from the Fed at its discount window, and banks that have funds to lend would not lend them at a rate lower than the IORB rate, the rate they could get by leaving the funds in their account at the Fed. These arbitrage conditions help nail down the rate at which the demand curve for reserves intersects the supply curve of reserves, the fed funds rate.

When reserves are scarce, banks' demand curve for reserves is relatively steep: Banks are willing to hold more reserves as the opportunity cost of holding reserves—i.e., the fed funds rate falls, and they are willing to hold fewer reserves as the fed funds rate rises. (See the left panel of figure 14.4.) With a steep demand curve, the fed funds rate will change with only small changes in the supply of reserves. In a scarce-reserves system, the Fed estimates the daily demand for reserves and supplies the amount of reserves needed to hit the fed funds rate target.

In contrast, the ample-reserves system does not require the FOMC to actively manage the supply of reserves based on estimates of reserve demand.

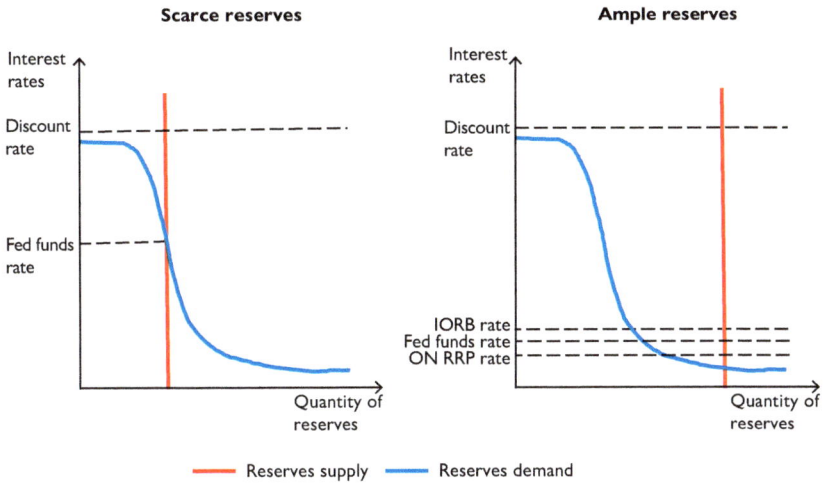

Figure 14.4. The ample reserves operating framework is conceptually simple.
Source: Author's drawing.

(See the right panel of figure 14.4.) When the supply of reserves is ample enough, banks are satiated with reserves. Because they have more reserves than they need for liquidity management and payment services, banks are willing to invest these surplus reserves in other high-quality assets if the market rate is higher than the IORB rate, and they are willing to lend them if they can earn a rate very near the IORB rate. This means the demand curve for reserves flattens out at these high reserve levels. There is no need for the Fed to estimate reserve demand to control interest rates because at these high levels, small changes in the supply of reserves do not affect the fed funds rate. Instead, the Fed controls the fed funds rate by setting the IORB rate, an administered rate, and typical reserve fluctuations do not result in changes in short-term market rates.

In recent years, the US Treasury's cash management practices have led to swings in its account balances at the Fed, which in turn has led to swings in reserve balances. This type of volatility complicates operating a scarce-reserves framework but not an ample-reserves framework. When balances in the TGA increase—say, because the Treasury is issuing Treasury debt, or tax receipts are rising, or the Treasury is building up precautionary cash reserves before a looming government shutdown—the level of reserves in the banking system falls as investors' funds are moved from their bank accounts to the TGA. The simplicity and efficiency of not having to estimate reserve demand on a daily basis in an ample-reserves regime is appealing. I seem to recall that when the Fed was first discussing the longer-run operating framework, there was even talk that such a framework could save on resources because the Fed wouldn't have to employ so many people to estimate reserve demand each day.

Another simplification offered by the ample-reserves system is that it maintains control of short-term interest rates regardless of economic circumstances and in various market conditions. In particular, the ample-reserves system would continue to work when the policy rate has been reduced to its effective lower bound or if the Fed had to provide large volumes of liquidity to alleviate financial system stresses. In these circumstances, the Fed wouldn't have to change its implementation regime to maintain effective control of the policy rate.

But It Isn't as Simple as It Looks

As is often the case, the theory is compelling, but the real world does not always cooperate. The complexity and segmentation of US money markets, as well as differential regulations applied to different financial entities in the money market, imply that the arbitrage assumed in the theory of an ample-reserves system is not seamless. There are frictions. The floor offered by the IORB is made of cork, not marble, so the Fed has had to augment the "simple" ample-reserves framework and still needs to expend resources to monitor reserve demand conditions.

One reason that reality is more complicated than theory is because not every entity transacting in short-term money markets is authorized to earn interest on reserves. Another reason is that banks have shown reluctance to borrow at the discount window when they are in need of funds. The discount window has been stigmatized. This reluctance was most recently shown during the banking stresses in March 2023, when Silicon Valley Bank, First Republic Bank, and Signature Bank failed.[5] This reality led the Fed to augment its ample-reserves framework with two additional facilities, the ON RRP facility and the standing repo facility (SRF).

The Federal Home Loan Banks (FHLBs) do much of the lending in the fed funds market, but they are not eligible to earn interest on their reserve balances at the Fed.[6] (See the left panel of figure 14.5.) So they are willing to lend fed funds at any rate above zero, which puts downward pressure on the fed funds rate. Similarly, money-market mutual funds do not earn interest on reserves, but their lending in the money markets can influence trading in the fed funds market. To ensure that the fed funds rate stays within its target

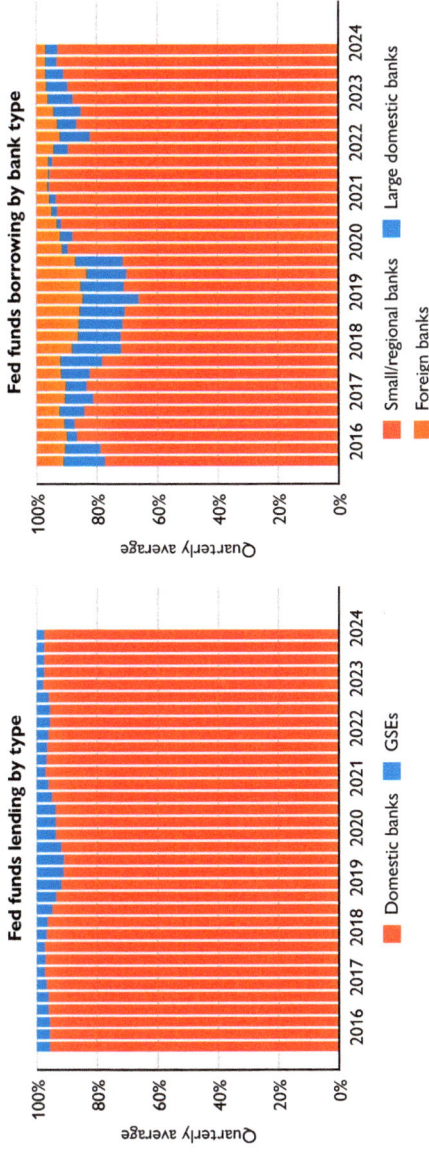

Figure 14.5. GSEs, especially the FHLBs, do the majority of lending and foreign banks do the majority of borrowing in the fed funds market.

Sources: Data from Federal Reserve Board, "Report of Selected Money Market Rates," FR 2420 (left) and FR 2420, NIC Data, Call Report (right); graph reproduced from Anderson and Na (2024).

range, the Fed has adjusted the IORB rate so that it lies slightly below the lower bound of the target range of the fed funds rate. In addition, the Fed set up the ON RRP facility in December 2015 to ensure it would be able to raise interest rates off of the effective lower bound after the Great Recession. This facility allows a broad set of money-market entities, including money-market mutual funds, to lend funds to the Fed overnight against eligible Treasury and agency securities, and agency MBS. By controlling the ON RRP rate in addition to the IORB rate, the Fed can effectively put a firmer floor under overnight interest rates.[7]

In July 2021, the Fed again added to its implementation framework by establishing the SRF.[8] Upward pressure in repo markets, as experienced in September 2019 and March 2020, puts upward pressure on the fed funds rate. The SRF limits this pressure by allowing eligible counterparties, including primary dealers and banks, to obtain funds from the Fed against Treasury and agency securities and agency MBS, at a rate that is set at 25 basis points above the top of the FOMC's fed funds target range. This backstop facility provides an alternative to the stigmatized discount window and helps keep the fed funds rate below the top of the target range. Note that by increasing the substitutability of Treasury securities for reserves in banks' liquidity management, the SRF has the potential to allow the Fed to operate in an ample-reserves framework at a lower level of reserves than it otherwise would.

Practice has shown that another complication with ample reserves is knowing when reserves are ample and not becoming scarce. While not having to estimate reserve demand each day is a benefit of the ample-reserves framework, the Fed does need to understand banks' demand for reserves. It needs to have estimates of the point at which banks' demand for reserves is satiated to ensure that it is maintaining reserve levels sufficiently large to stay in the ample portion of the aggregate reserve demand curve and not allow reserves to fall into scarce territory. This is not necessarily easy, since the demand curve for reserves can shift around.

The spike in repo rates and other short-term money-market rates in September 2019 showed that the aggregate level of reserves is not a sufficient statistic for understanding when reserves are getting scarce; the distribution of reserves across banks also matters. Banks' preferred level of reserve balances can vary by bank size, business model, and liquidity management considerations. In addition, the regulatory burden of maintaining high levels of reserves also varies across institutions (e.g., FDIC assessment fees differ across banks and likely affect their preferred level of reserves). Even if reserve levels are high, if reserves are scarce relative to preferred levels at some banks and ample at others, arbitrage will not necessarily bring the fed funds rate down toward the IORB rate. Moreover, a bank's desired reserve level may change over time (e.g., some banks that are more risk-averse may want to hold higher precautionary reserve levels in stressed market conditions). Roberto Perli, manager of the Federal Reserve System Open Market Account, recently pointed out that frictions in the repo market may also be adversely affecting the redistribution of funding throughout the money markets.[9] In particular, as the repo market has become more concentrated, counterparty risk limits may have become more binding, making it harder for the repo market to work as effectively as it once did to redistribute liquidity. This manifests itself in some ON RRP counterparties utilizing the Fed's facility even when repo rates are higher in the market, since their own counterparties may not be willing to transact with them, having reached their counterparty limit.

As a result of these types of frictions, the Fed has had to monitor conditions in the money markets to ensure that it is maintaining ample-reserve levels as it is allowing assets to run off to reduce the size of its balance sheet. Rather than focusing only on the quantity of reserves, the Fed has been monitoring a set of indicators on reserve conditions that can give some indication if reserves are approaching a scarce level.[10] These indicators include: the stability of the fed funds rate relative to the IORB rate, the sensitivity of the fed funds rate to changes in the supply of reserves, the share of domestic bank borrowing in the fed funds market, the share of payments made late in the day, the average level of daylight overdrafts, and the share of repo trades made at rates above the IORB rate. According to Perli (2024b), aside from the repo market indicator, which has risen noticeably since the spring, all indicators suggest reserves remain abundant.

The Financial Stability Benefit May Be Elusive

Another purported benefit of the ample-reserves system is that it enhances financial stability. In theory, under ample reserves, reserves pay the market rate of interest, so there is no opportunity cost to banks of holding reserves. Therefore, there is little incentive for banks to minimize their reserve holdings in an ample-reserves system. Their willingness to hold higher reserve levels has the potential to reduce liquidity risk in the financial system and foster financial stability.[11]

But as Acharya et al. (2022) and Acharya and Rajan (2023) discuss, an increase in reserves may not increase liquidity because banks with surplus reserves may hoard those reserves in stressed market conditions.[12] This is because banks may have made commitments on their surplus reserves and so are reluctant to give those reserves up.[13] In particular, the authors' research suggests that the expansion of the Fed's balance sheet through asset purchases during the GFC and Great Recession (quantitative easing, or QE) and subsequent shrinkage of the balance sheet (quantitative tightening, or QT) left the banking sector more vulnerable in the face of liquidity shocks and so more dependent on injections of liquidity by the Fed.

They find that when bank reserves expand, banks, in the aggregate and individually, increase demandable deposits and credit lines and decrease time deposits (which are less runnable). But when the central bank begins to shrink its balance sheet via QT, banks do not reverse the increase in demandable claims they took on during QE. (See figure 14.6.) Instead, the ratio of demandable claims to reserves increases for quite a while. This could be because there is inertia within the bank, or it could be because banks have become accustomed to the Fed stepping in and providing liquidity when stresses arise. Whatever the cause, this asymmetric behavior, which the authors call liquidity dependence—in which banks increase demandable claims when reserves increase but do not decrease them when reserves decline—makes the banking system more vulnerable to liquidity stresses and more dependent on central bank interventions. In the authors' view this could have been the deeper cause of the market stresses seen in September 2019 and March 2020, both of which occurred after the Fed had commenced QT.[14]

These results have important policy implications. In particular, if a higher supply of reserves induces greater demand for reserves, it will be more difficult for the central bank to reduce the size of its balance sheet without accepting a greater risk of financial instability. This can be even more problematic if banks have become laxer in their approach to liquidity management because they have become accustomed to relying on reserves that are usually in ample supply. Banks may have less contingency funding in place precisely in the stressed market conditions when they need it. At the very least, policymakers using the ample-reserves regime need to know not only where the satiation point is on a static reserves demand curve, but also that the demand curve for reserves can move around depending on where the central bank is on its balance sheet expansion-contraction cycle. This means that the satiation point for reserves could move abruptly when market conditions change, and what

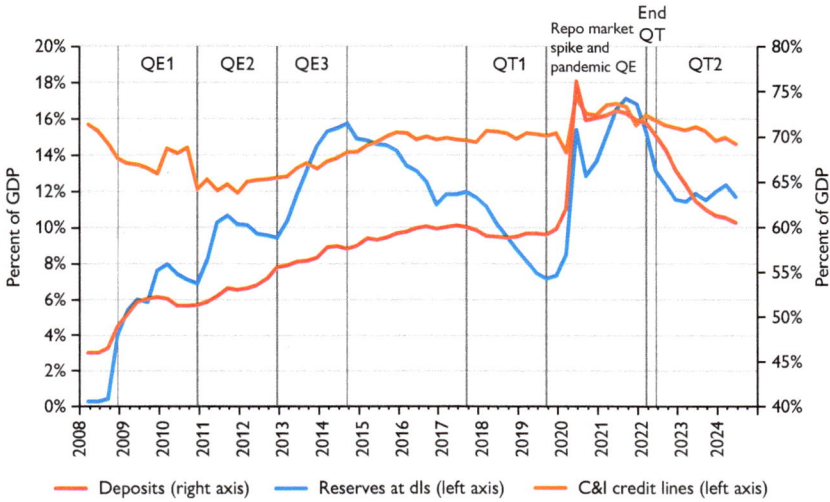

Figure 14.6a. Reserves moved up with QE and down with QT. Bank deposits and credit lines did not move down during QT1 and rose again during the pandemic QE program.

Note: Quarterly data; last observation is 2024 Q2.

Source: Federal Reserve System and FDIC, via Haver Analytics.

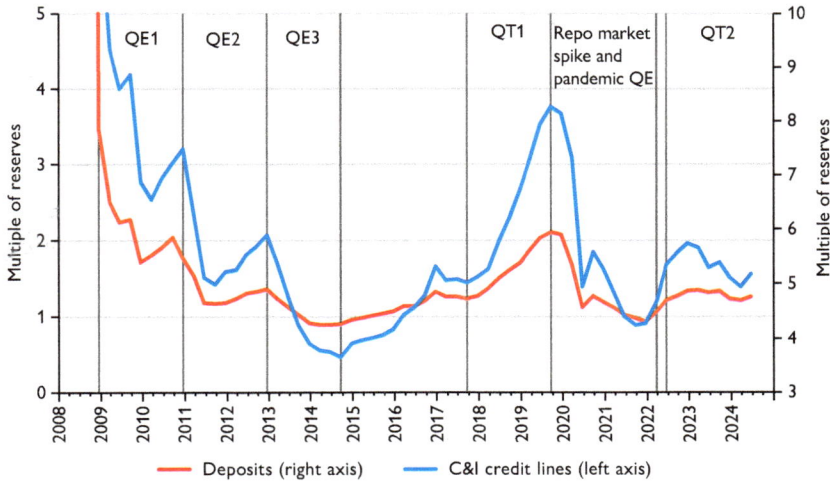

Figure 14.6b. Deposits and credit lines as a multiple of reserves dropped when reserves expanded during QE and rose during QT.

Note: Quarterly data; last observation is 2024 Q2.

Source: Federal Reserve System and FDIC, via Haver Analytics.

looked like more-than-ample reserves may turn out not to be. It also suggests that banks' liquidity claims should be added to the list of indicators the central bank should monitor to ensure that reserves remain ample.[15]

Ample Reserves and the Overnight Bank Funding Market

Borio (2023) also points to some drawbacks of the ample-reserve framework from the viewpoint of financial stability and the overnight bank funding market. The ample-reserve framework entails central banks playing a more significant role in interbank funding markets. Borio argues that the fact that the distribution of reserves, and not just their aggregate volume, matters is a symptom of the fact that banks are much less active in overnight funding markets. The need for reserves to circulate in market stress events, and the possibility they will not necessarily do so, raises the probability that the central bank will be required to inject liquidity more often to calm markets. Norges Bank (the Central Bank of Norway) and the Swiss National Bank, which once used the floor system, have implemented a tiered approach, paying a lower rate as the quantity of a bank's reserves rises, as a way to give the banks some incentive to participate in the overnight bank funding market.[16] The European Central Bank (ECB) also recently reviewed its operational framework and changed from a supply-driven floor system to a demand-driven system, which will limit the ECB's footprint in financial markets and determine the amount of liquidity the central bank provides based on bank demand.[17]

Shrinkage in the overnight bank funding market also has implications for what interest rate the central bank should be targeting. Even though the Fed is using an ample-reserves framework, it continues to communicate its target in terms of the fed funds rate. However, the limited trading in the fed funds market and resulting increase in volatility in that market led the FOMC to discuss alternative potential target rates at their meeting in November 2018.[18] Several Fed policymakers found some merit in considering a shift to the overnight bank funding rate, a more robust unsecured overnight bank funding rate that includes not only fed funds transactions but also certain Eurodollar and certain domestic deposit transactions. In the end, though, the FOMC opted to stay with the fed funds rate as its main way to communicate policy, since it was well understood by the public and market participants.

Political Economy Costs of an Ample-Reserves Framework

In principle, a floor-type operating system does not place a limit on the size of the central bank's balance sheet to implement monetary policy. Plosser

(2018) discusses a number of political economy costs if the central bank's balance sheet can grow to any size, including the potential that Congress or the administration could use the central bank's balance sheet to fund fiscal policy initiatives.[19] Other costs include the potential appearance issue generated from large interest-on-reserve payments going to large banks and to foreign banks; the appearance that the Fed was not able to fully unwind the QE it put into place in the GFC and pandemic, which might lead some to question its use in the future; and the fact the Fed's remittances to the Treasury have been negative since September 2022, which may generate criticism. Such costs are difficult to quantify, but they could create risk to the Fed's reputation and independence.

Fed policymakers have noted such costs. For example, at the December 2018 FOMC meeting's discussion of the long-run operating framework, Chair Jay Powell emphasized the importance of abiding by the agreed-to normalization principle that the balance sheet would be no larger than that which is needed to implement monetary policy effectively and efficiently, given the chosen framework:

I do see this as a high-profile commitment that we need to honor; and doing so, in my view, would do much to support the legitimacy of future large-scale asset purchases—by showing that QE is not just a one-way street to an ever-larger Federal Reserve balance sheet relative to GDP. (FOMC 2018b, 43)

And:

So I do think it's necessary to do what we can to be seen to have worked hard to get to a smaller balance sheet. It's not just that we get down to scarce reserves, it's that we be seen to work hard to do it -- that we take the commitment seriously. (FOMC 2018b, 44)

The switch in calling the regime "ample" reserves from "abundant" reserves was meant to communicate that the Fed will not be allowing reserves to rise without limit, but instead will be seeking the minimum level of reserves that allows the Fed to exercise control over the fed funds rate and other short-term interest rates by setting the Fed's administered rates. This would entail a level of reserves that would include a buffer above the point of scarcity, but not abundantly above that.[20]

Conclusion

My discussion of the Fed's current ample-reserves operating framework is not meant to argue that the scarce-reserves framework is necessarily preferable or that the Fed should go back. For one thing, I think the transition costs of returning to a scarce-reserves system would not be insignificant given the current size of the balance sheet, the current limited transactions in the fed funds market, and the way in which banks have been managing their reserves. Still, I believe it is important to be realistic about the current system. It takes care and feeding. It reflects a choice about the size of the Fed's footprint in financial markets, with the potential that a larger Fed footprint distorts private-sector liquidity risk management practices in a way that is detrimental to financial stability.[21] It has implications for whether the fed funds rate should remain the Fed's reference rate. This suggests that certain features, like tiering, which have been implemented at other central banks that are operating ample-reserves regimes or a hybrid system like the ECB's, should be seriously considered and evaluated in the US context.

The current ample-reserves system is meeting the prime directive—ensuring the Fed has very good interest rate control. But it is good to keep in mind the complexities that the "simple" ample-reserves system entails.

Notes

1. Nelson (2016) and Keister (2012) present excellent discussions of corridor and floor operating regimes.

2. In these figures, reserves includes deposits of depository institutions and term deposits held by depository institutions.

3. Many studies have found that the Fed's various asset purchase programs lowered longer-term yields, although the estimated magnitudes differ across studies and across Fed programs. For a recent study, see Kim et al. (2023).

4. The Federal Reserve Banks were authorized by the Financial Services Regulatory Relief Act of 2006 to pay interest on reserves held by eligible institutions at the Fed, effective October 1, 2011. This date was accelerated to October 1, 2008, by the Emergency Economic Stabilization Act of 2008. See Board of Governors (2025).

5. Since then, many more banks have taken steps to put legal agreements in place and pledged collateral so that they are better prepared to use the discount window. See Barr (2024).

6. According to Afonso et al. (2023), the Federal Home Loan Banks (FHLBs) (which, along with Fannie Mae and Freddie Mac, are the housing-finance-related government-sponsored enterprises, or GSEs) represent about 90% of the total daily lending volume in the fed funds market and US branches and agencies of foreign banks represent between 65% and 95% of the total daily borrowing volume in the fed

funds market. (See the right panel of figure 14.5.) See also Anderson and Na (2024), which is the source of figure 14.5.

7. As of September 18, 2024, the target range for the funds rate is 4.75% to 5.0%, the IORB rate is 4.9%, and the ON RRP rate is 4.8%.

8. See Afonso et al. (2022) for further discussion of the standing repo facility. As of September 18, 2024, the SRF rate is 5.0%.

9. See Perli (2024b).

10. See Perli (2024a, 2024b).

11. See Nelson (2018), Zobel (2022), and Logan (2023) for more extensive discussions of the benefits of the ample reserves operating framework.

12. See also López-Salido and Vissing-Jorgensen (2023).

13. This has been called the "ratchet effect": the supply of liquidity generates its own demand and as supply increases, so does demand. See Borio (2023).

14. As Acharya and Rajan (2023) also point out, banks' shortening the maturity of their liabilities during QE makes it more difficult for banks to finance longer-term assets, thereby undermining the potential beneficial macroeconomic effect of QE.

15. The research also suggests that bank supervisors and regulators may want to consider more state-contingent monitoring, where the "state" is determined by whether the central bank is in a QT or QE phase. For example, during periods of QT, supervisors might want to assume higher levels of deposit-runoff and greater utilization of credit lines in stress tests.

16. Norges Bank (2014, 2) explained that the purpose of switching from the floor system to what they call a quota-based system was to "limit bank demand for central bank reserves and to provide a stronger incentive for banks to redistribute liquidity in the interbank market." The Swiss National Bank also cites support for activity in the Swiss interbank money market, which provides a more robust basis for calculating its policy reference rate, as a benefit of its tiered approach. See Maechler and Moser (2022).

17. See Schnabel (2024).

18. See FOMC (2018a).

19. This is not an ill-founded concern. In light of the two major hurricanes that have hit Florida recently, Nathan Tankus (2024), in a recent opinion column in the *Financial Times*, recommended that the Federal Reserve set up a 13(3) emergency facility to lend directly to municipalities that have been declared in a state of emergency due to natural disasters such as hurricanes. This disaster relief facility would be similar to the Municipal Liquidity Facility, which the Fed established in April 2020 to help state and local governments address the cash flow problems they were facing during the pandemic. Tankus indicates that the new facility would alleviate the potential funding issue caused by the Federal Emergency Management Agency's funding being subject to the federal appropriations process.

20. Afonso et al. (2024) define the level of "ample" reserves as the level that satiates banks' demand for reserves (where the demand curve for reserves is gently negatively sloped) and "abundant" reserves as levels beyond this where the demand

curve is perfectly flat. "Scarce" reserves are levels below the satiation point, where the demand curve is steeply negatively sloped.

21. See Borio (2023).

References

Acharya, Viral V., Rahul S. Chauhan, Raghuram Rajan, and Sascha Steffen. 2022. "Liquidity Dependence: Why Shrinking Central Bank Balance Sheets Is an Uphill Task." Paper prepared for the Federal Reserve Bank of Kansas City's Economic Policy Symposium, "Reassessing Constraints on the Economy and Policy." Jackson Hole, WY. August 25–27.

Acharya, Viral V., and Raghuram Rajan. 2023. "Liquidity, Liquidity Everywhere, Not a Drop to Use—Why Flooding Banks with Central Bank Reserves May Not Expand Liquidity." Working Paper No. 29680. National Bureau of Economic Research. January 2022, revised August.

Afonso, Gara, Gonzalo Cisternas, Brian Gowen, Jason Miu, and Joshua Younger. 2023. "Who's Borrowing and Lending in the Fed Funds Market Today?" *Liberty Street Economics* (blog). Federal Reserve Bank of New York. October 10. https://libertystreeteconomics.newyorkfed.org/2023/10/whos-borrowing -and-lending-in-the-fed-funds-market-today/.

Afonso, Gara, Domenico Giannone, Gabriele La Spada, and John C. Williams. 2024. "Scarce, Abundant, or Ample? A Time-Varying Model of the Reserve Demand Curve." Staff Report No. 1019, Federal Reserve Bank of New York. May 2022, revised April.

Afonso, Gara, Lorie Logan, Antoine Martin, William Riordan, and Patricia Zobel. 2022. "The Fed's Latest Tool: A Standing Repo Facility." *Liberty Street Economics* (blog). Federal Reserve Bank of New York. January 13. https://libertystreeteconomics .newyorkfed.org/2022/01/the-feds-latest-tool-a-standing-repo-facility/.

Anderson, Alyssa, and Dave Na. 2024. "The Recent Evolution of the Federal Funds Market and Its Dynamics during Reductions of the Federal Reserve's Balance Sheet." FEDS Note (article), Board of Governors of the Federal Reserve System. July 11. https://www.federalreserve.gov/econres/notes/feds-notes/the-recent -evolution-of-the-federal-funds-market-and-its-dynamics-during-reductions-of -fr-balance-sheet-20240711.html.

Barr, Michael S. 2024. "Supporting Market Resilience and Financial Stability." Remarks at the 2024 US Treasury Market Conference, Federal Reserve Bank of New York, New York, NY. September 26.

Board of Governors (Board of Governors of the Federal Reserve System). 2025. "Interest on Reserve Balances." Policy Tools, Monetary Policy, Board of Governors of the Federal Reserve System. January 17. https://www.federalreserve.gov /monetarypolicy/reserve-balances.htm#:~:text=The%20Financial%20 Services%20Regulatory%20Relief,%2C%20effective%20October%201%2C %202011.

Borio, Claudio. 2023. "Getting Up from the Floor." Remarks at the Netherlands Bank Workshop, "Beyond Unconventional Policy: Implications for Central Banks' Operational Frameworks," Amsterdam, Netherlands. March 10.

FOMC (Federal Open Market Committee). 2018a. "Transcript of the Federal Open Market Committee Meeting." November 7–8. https://www.federalreserve.gov/monetarypolicy/files/FOMC20181108meeting.pdf.

FOMC. 2018b. "Transcript of the Federal Open Market Committee Meeting." December 18–19. https://www.federalreserve.gov/monetarypolicy/files/FOMC 20181219meeting.pdf.

FOMC. 2019. "Statement Regarding Monetary Policy Implementation and Balance Sheet Normalization." Press release. January 30.

Keister, Todd. 2012. "Corridors and Floors in Monetary Policy." *Liberty Street Economics* (blog). Federal Reserve Bank of New York. April 4. https://libertystreeteconomics.newyorkfed.org/2012/04/corridors-and-floors-in-monetary-policy/.

Kim, Kyungmin, Thomas Laubach, and Min Wei. 2023. "Macroeconomic Effects of Large-Scale Asset Purchases: New Evidence." Finance and Economics Discussion Series No. 2020-047r1. Board of Governors of the Federal Reserve System. Revised August 29.

Logan, Lorie. 2023. "Ample Reserves and the Friedman Rule." Remarks at the European Central Bank Conference on Money Markets 2023, Frankfurt am Main, Germany. November 10.

López-Salido, David, and Annette Vissing-Jorgensen. 2023. "Reserve Demand, Interest Rate Control, and Quantitative Tightening." Working paper. November 1, 2021, revised September 18. https://ssrn.com/abstract=4371999.

Maechler, Andréa M., and Thomas Moser. 2022. "Return to Positive Interest Rates: Why Reserve Tiering?" Speech at the Swiss National Bank Money Market Event, Geneva, Switzerland. November 17.

Nelson, Bill. 2016. "Liquidity and Leverage Regulation, Money Market Structure, and the Federal Reserve's Monetary Policy Framework in the Longer Run." Paper. The Clearing House. September.

Nelson, Bill. 2018. "Understanding the Fed's Implementation Framework Debate." Research note. Bank Policy Institute. November 26. https://bpi.com/wp-content/uploads/2018/11/Understanding_the_Fed%E2%80%99s_implementation_framework_debate_Review05.pdf.

Norges Bank. 2014. "Banks' Assessment of Norges Bank's Liquidity Management System." Norges Bank Papers No. 4. December 12.

Perli, Roberto. 2024a. "Balance Sheet Reduction: Progress to Date and a Look Ahead." Remarks at the 2024 Annual Primary Dealer Meeting, Federal Reserve Bank of New York, New York, NY. May 8.

Perli, Roberto. 2024b. "Balance Sheet Normalization: Monitoring Reserve Conditions and Understanding Repo Market Pressures." Remarks at the 2024 US

Treasury Market Conference, Federal Reserve Bank of New York, New York, NY. September 26.

Plosser, Charles I. 2018. "The Risks of a Fed Balance Sheet Unconstrained by Monetary Policy." In *The Structural Foundations of Monetary Policy*, edited by Michael D. Bordo, John H. Cochrane, and Amit Seru. Hoover Institution Press.

Schnabel, Isabel. 2024. "The Eurosystem's Operational Framework." Speech at the Money Market Contact Group Meeting, Frankfurt am Main, Germany. March 14.

Tankus, Nathan. 2024. "The Fed Should Create a Hurricane Crisis Facility." *Financial Times*, October 9.

Zobel, Patricia. 2022. "The Ample Reserves Framework and Balance Sheet Reduction: Perspective from the Open Market Desk." Remarks at the Cato Institute's 40th Annual Monetary Conference (virtual). September 8. https://www.newyorkfed.org/newsevents/speeches/2022/zob220908.

15

From the Floor Back to the Corridor

Why the Choice of Monetary Policy Implementation Framework Matters

Bill Nelson

The Federal Reserve used to be a much smaller part of the economy and financial markets. Before the Global Financial Crisis (GFC) of 2007–9, the assets of the Federal Reserve equaled 6% of GDP; now they equal 26%. Before the crisis, currency was over 95% of Fed liabilities; now it is 33%, with the Fed now borrowing trillions of dollars from commercial banks, money-market mutual funds, government-sponsored enterprises (GSEs), the Treasury, and foreign official institutions. These extraordinary changes in the size and breadth of the Federal Reserve's interactions with the financial system reflect a change in how the Fed implements monetary policy—that is, how the Fed moves interest rates to where it wants them to be.

The Federal Reserve currently implements monetary policy by creating a vast amount of reserve balances and reverse repurchase agreements, driving the interbank overnight rate down to between the interest rate the Fed pays on deposits of commercial banks and the interest rate it pays money-market mutual funds and GSEs on reverse repurchase agreements. To produce a sufficiently large quantity of Fed liabilities, the Fed needs to invest in a correspondingly large amount of assets.

Because such an implementation regime drives money-market rates down to the "floor" created by the interest rate the Fed pays on overnight borrowing, it is often referred to as a "floor system." The Federal Open Market Committee (FOMC) officially adopted a floor system at its January 2019 meeting, but it had been using a floor system since October 2008. Prior to that point, the Fed had been implementing policy by announcing a new target for the federal funds rate, adjusting the discount rate to one hundred basis points above that target, and continuing to provide just the quantity of reserve balances banks needed to meet their clearing needs and reserve requirements. Because money-market rates ended up in a corridor created by the discount rate and the interest rate the central bank pays on reserve balances (or zero, in the Fed's case at that time), such an implementation regime is referred to as a "corridor system."

Nelson (2024a) discusses how the Fed got so huge and why and how it can shrink. The story of the Fed's growth, and the discussion of how the Fed could shrink without causing market turmoil, are critical components of the overall discussion of the Fed's implementation regime, but readers interested in those issues are referred to the longer paper. This note focuses on *why* the Fed should shrink—why it should implement policy using a corridor system updated to current realities. In particular, the note discusses the extraordinary, often overlooked costs and scant benefits of the current implementation framework.

Costs

Implementing monetary policy using a floor system creates a self-reinforcing cycle that requires the Fed not only to be massive, but to become ever more massive. The dynamic stems from changes in money-market structure, bank behavior, and federal banking agency examiner behavior. It also arises from rising estimates within the Fed about what is normal and by growing ambitions in other parts of the government about potential uses of the Federal Reserve's balance sheet.

To implement policy using a floor system as the Fed originally envisioned, the Fed must supply reserves that exceed the amount the banking system needs by a large enough buffer that reserves supply or demand can rise or fall in line with normal variation without the Fed's taking countervailing fine-tuning action and without the fed funds rate rising or falling. Because the shocks can be large—for instance, on corporate tax day—the buffer needs to be large, about $200 billion.[1]

However, this conceptualization of how a floor system will work was based on an incorrect application of the "Poole model" as shown in figure 15.1. The model, developed by Bill Poole in 1968, describes the relationship between reserve balances and the federal funds rate. Banks maintain reserves to satisfy reserve requirements (currently zero) and to ensure that they do not

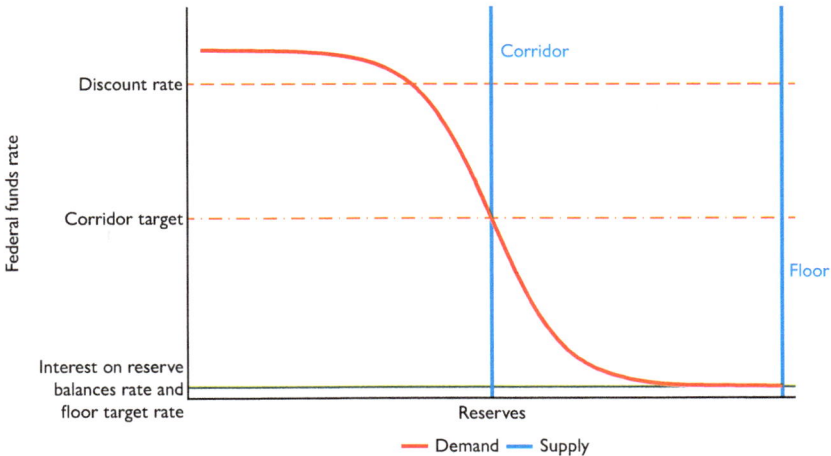

Figure 15.1. Reserve balances and the federal funds rate corridor and floor systems.
Source: Author's calculations.

run an overnight overdraft; following the GFC, banks also hold reserves for liquidity purposes.

When the Fed supplies the quantity of reserves the banking system wishes to hold in aggregate, the fed funds rate clears at the FOMC target rate. When supply falls short, the rate is bid up to a bit above the discount rate, leading some banks to borrow, creating reserves, and clearing the market. If supply ends up too high, the funds rate falls to the interest rate on reserve balances (IORB rate) because all banks have the reserves they need, and no one will lend in the funds market for less than what they can get simply leaving the funds on deposits at the Fed. While the Poole model indicates that the fed funds rate will be pinned to the floor created by the IORB rate when the Fed oversupplies reserves, Poole created the model to describe the behavior of the funds rate *within a day*, not for persistent periods of time. As Poole (1968, 770) noted in the original 1968 paper:

> The model presented here concentrates on these very short-run adjustments. However, it is obvious that the bank must make further adjustments if it experiences persistent reserve drains or accretions.

When the Fed persistently oversupplies reserves, markets and behaviors change in line with the Robert Lucas (1976) critique that policy analysis needs to recognize how the economy will adjust to any new government effort to influence economic outcomes. As seen in figure 15.2, the amount of reserves needed to implement the floor system grows, and because a buffer is needed, the amount keeps growing.

The consequence can be seen in table 15.1, which shows Fed staff's estimate of the quantity of reserves necessary for implementing a floor system.

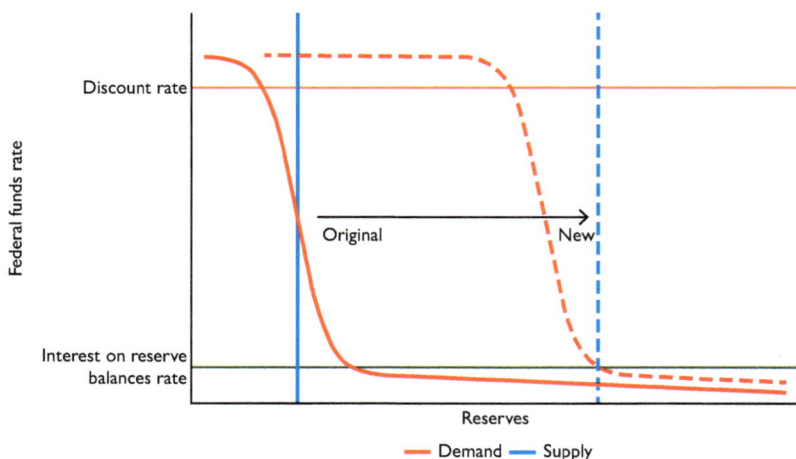

Figure 15.2. Floor system with ratchet.
Source: Author's calculations.

Table 15.1. Fed's estimate of banks' structural demand for reserve balances

Date	Level $ Billions
April 2008	35
March 2016	100
March 2018	600
December 2018	1,000
October 2019	1,500
May 2022	2,300
April 2024	3,000

Source: April 2008 staff memo to the FOMC; March 2016–December 2018 Blue/Tealbooks; October 2019 FOMC directive; May 2022 and April 2024 Federal Reserve Bank of New York projections.

Interbank Markets Deteriorate

One reason why excessive reserves get locked in is because the market mechanism for redistributing reserves between banks deteriorates. Before the GFC, each bank sought to keep reserves to a minimum because the interest rate on reserve balances (zero at the time) was well below the rate banks could earn on other money-market investments or had to pay on money-market borrowings. The Fed adjusted the size of its repo operations with dealers to supply the aggregate necessary amount of reserves. Note that the Fed did not engage in transactions with banks directly (apart from the occasional discount window loan) and dealers do not have reserves. At the end of the day, some banks would have extra reserves, and some would be short of reserves; those banks would trade with each other in the federal funds market until the quantity was redistributed.

Under a floor system, banks do not need to redistribute reserves at the end of the day because most banks have a large quantity of extra reserves. The fed funds market is much smaller and serves a different purpose. The transactions largely consist of loans from Federal Home Loan Banks (FHLBs) to US branches and agencies of foreign banks. The FHLBs have accounts at Federal Reserve Banks but do not earn interest on their deposits; they can, however, lend the Federal Reserve money at the overnight reverse repurchase agreement (ON RRP) facility and earn the ON RRP rate. The branches and agencies can borrow the funds in the fed funds market and invest them in reserve balances on which they earn the IORB rate.[2] The fed funds rate ends up between the IORB rate and the ON RRP rate because the FHLBs and the branches and agencies split the difference between what the branches can earn and the yield on the FHLBs' alternative investment option.

This shift from relying on other banks for liquidity to relying on the central bank for liquidity is why the Norges Bank switched in 2010 from a floor system to a corridor system. When seeking comment on their decision, Norges Bank (2010, 5) noted:

> When Norges Bank keeps reserves relatively high for a period, it appears that banks gradually adjust to this level. . . . With ever increasing reserves in the banking system, there is a risk that Norges Bank assumes functions that should be left to the market. It is not Norges Bank's role to provide funding for banks. . . . If a bank has a deficit of reserves towards the end of the day, banks must be able to deal with this by trading in the interbank market.

Discount Window Stigma Increases

The overabundance of reserves also increases the stigma associated with borrowing from the discount window.[3] Before the GFC, most discount window loans by volume occurred for monetary policy purposes, clearing the market on days when the supply of reserves fell short of demand. After the GFC, the volume of borrowing has fallen sharply, and the borrowing that does occur is mostly for contingency funding purposes. As a consequence, when borrowing does occur, it is more alarming. Banks report that an important reason why they maintain large levels of reserve balances is to reduce to near zero the probability that they would ever have to borrow from the discount window.

Examiners Expect Banks to Have Large Stockpiles of Reserve Balances

As banks' business models adjust to make use of abundant, cheap reserve balances, so do examiners' attitudes toward banks' need for reserve balances. Before the GFC, liquidity was evaluated based on a bank's access to reliable and diversified funding, including access to the discount window. Asset-based liquidity risk-management was considered something that smaller, less sophisticated banks did. After the GFC, liquidity became synonymous with a bank's stockpile of liquid assets, including especially reserve balances.[4] Former vice chair for supervision Randy Quarles has noted that bank examiners' preference for reserves contributed to the abrupt and disorderly end to the previous round of quantitative tightening (QT) in September 2019 (Beckworth 2022).

Examiner expectations also contribute to the one-way ratchet that expands reserves ever further. A chief investment officer of a global systemically important bank (G-SIB) described how his bank increased its holdings of reserve balances rather than reverse repos when the IORB rate was above the repo rate prior to 2018, but he decided against rotating back toward reverse repos when the repo rate rose above the IORB rate simply to avoid having to explain the decision to examiners (Nelson 2020).

The New Normal: A Giant Balance Sheet

The Fed's ever-expanding size is also due to changing views within the Fed on what is a normal use of the balance sheet. In December 2018, when the Committee was debating whether to adopt a floor system permanently, staff told the Committee that about $1 trillion in reserve balances should be necessary. Chair Jerome Powell remarked that if the necessary level of reserve balances turned out to be higher, he would experience "buyer's regret" (FOMC 2018b, 44). The most recent publicly available staff estimates put the necessary amount at $3 trillion, but there have been no expressions of regret.

Similarly, Committee members including then-Governors Powell, Stein, and Tarullo expressed serious misgivings when the ON RRP facility was opened in 2012 about expanding the Fed's set of counterparties to include money-market mutual funds but took comfort from the fact that the facility was supposed to be temporary. Eleven years later, in May 2023, when the ON RRP facility was more than ten times its peak level in 2014, Chair Powell stated that the ON RRP facility was simply doing the job it was designed to do.[5] Indeed, although the ON RRP is still supposedly a temporary facility, the Board's website now describes it as a standard tool of policy implementation.[6]

Fed staff made decisions, evidently without consulting the FOMC, that locked in the floor system—decisions apparently based on the view that there were few costs associated with a massive balance sheet. One such decision was over the size and variability of the US Treasury's account balance. Prior to the GFC, the Treasury kept most of its cash in the banking system, while its deposit at the Fed held roughly steady at about $5 billion. It was held roughly steady because the Treasury and Fed understood that if the balance was highly variable, the Fed would need to engage in large countervailing open-market operations. However, during and after the GFC, Treasury and Fed staff decided to allow the Treasury to expand its balance, which is now about $800 billion, roughly where the Treasury plans to maintain it apart from during debt debacles, when it runs it down.[7] The resulting volatility has been cited by staff several times as a reason why the Committee can't return to a corridor system.[8] The story is similar for the facility the Fed provides to foreign official institutions to place their overnight investments ("the foreign repo pool") (Nelson 2019).

Having an unbounded balance sheet may also have contributed to complacency about the risk associated with large-scale asset purchases ("quantitative easing," or "QE"). Reading and listening to the Fed's explanations for QE4, one gets the impression that it was stumbled into. Begun in March 2020 to address a market meltdown, QE4 gradually morphed into an effort to stimulate the economy (FOMC 2020a), then the Fed locked in the pace of QE with rigid forward guidance (FOMC 2020b).

Because the Fed was investing in longer-term assets funded largely by overnight liabilities, the Fed took on massive amounts of interest rate risk through its QE programs. That was by design. The intent of the programs was to shift interest rate risk from public hands to the Fed's balance sheet, pushing down the term premium on longer-term assets, thereby stimulating the economy. The Fed's balance sheet principles published in 2002 state that interest rate risk is equivalent to credit risk and the Fed would likely only incur substantial interest rate risk after consulting with Treasury and Congress (Board of Governors 2002). However, repeated use begets complacency, and the FOMC now seems to see taking substantial interest rate risk as an unremarkable policy tool.

Sometimes risky investments pay off. In the 2010s, the sluggish recovery resulted in overnight interest rates remaining much lower than had been expected when the Fed purchased longer-term securities in QE1, QE2, and QE3 between 2008 and 2012. As a result, the Fed was highly profitable in the 2010s.

But sometimes risky investments make losses. Starting in 2022, the Fed needed to raise overnight interest rates by more, and to do so more rapidly, than it had done for forty years to combat a sharp rise in inflation. The increase drove the Fed's interest expenses, which are entirely tied to short-term rates, above the interest income it earned on its portfolio of mostly longer-term securities. As a result, the Fed began to make losses in September 2022 and is projected by the New York Fed to continue to make losses until 2025 (New York Fed 2024).[9]

The Fed is making losses even though its monopoly franchises on currency and as banker for the Treasury allow it to fund itself with a substantial amount of interest-free liabilities. The Fed began making operating losses in September 2022 and losses had accumulated to $199.8 billion by September 25, 2024 (Board of Governors 2025, table 6). Over that same period, a portfolio of Treasury bills funded by currency and the TGA would have earned $302.2 billion.[10]

A Dangerous Back Door to the Fed's Balance Sheet

Adopting a floor system has also eliminated a safeguard on the Fed's balance sheet being used by Congress as a source of financing (Plosser 2022; Selgin 2020). If asked to buy this or that security under a corridor system, the Fed could demur by correctly observing that it would lose control of monetary policy if its assets exceeded currency by more than a small amount. At the November 2018 FOMC meetings, Loretta Mester, then-president of the Cleveland Fed, stated, "The lack of an operating constraint on the size of our balance sheet might also generate requests that the Federal Reserve aid specific industries or use the balance sheet to fund government initiatives, as occurred during and since the crisis" (FOMC 2018a, 26). Similarly, at the same meeting, Randal Quarles, then vice chair for supervision, stated:

> Having the FOMC control such a large stock of assets presents what the lawyers in the room will recall from your first-year torts class is called an "attractive nuisance." And for the nonlawyers in the room, an attractive nuisance is an object that a property owner allows to remain on his land when it is obvious both that the object will be dangerous if misused and that misusing it will be irresistibly appealing to passers-by of impulsive and immature judgment, such as children and congressmen. (FOMC 2018a, 34)

Experience has shown that this is not just an abstract concern. The financing plank of the Green New Deal is described as follows:

> As the checks go out, the government's bank—the Federal Reserve—clears the payments by crediting the seller's bank account with digital dollars. In other words, Congress can pass any budget it chooses, and our government already pays for everything by creating new money. (Kelton et al. 2018)

Similarly,

- The Coronavirus Aid, Relief, and Economic Security Act (CARES) of 2020, after encouraging the secretary of the Treasury to implement a program to aid medium-size businesses, states: "Nothing in this subparagraph shall limit the discretion of the Board of Governors of the Federal Reserve System to establish a Main Street Lending Program or other similar program or facility that supports lending to small and mid-sized businesses."[11]
- Saule Omarova, a 2021 nominee to head the Office of the Comptroller of the Currency, proposed that the Fed give everyone accounts. It could then put money into the accounts of businesses if they retained their employees and spent money on "real" goods and services as well as the accounts of underprivileged people, expenditures the Fed would finance by driving its equity negative (Omarova 2021).

- The proposed ECASH Act of 2022 would direct the Treasury to create a digital currency, with costs covered by running an overdraft in a specially created account at the New York Fed.[12]
- And the proposed BITCOIN Act of 2024 utilizes the capital and profits of the Federal Reserve to accumulate a "strategic reserve" of 1 million bitcoins.[13]

Monetizing the Debt

Relatedly, the floor system has also opened the door to the Fed monetizing the debt. It is unclear what "monetizing the debt" actually means. But in 2011, Chair Ben Bernanke was asked by the House Budget Committee if the Fed was monetizing the debt with its large-scale asset purchases. He responded:

> No, sir. Monetization would involve a permanent increase in the money supply to basically pay the government's bills through money creation. What we are doing here is a temporary measure which will be reversed so that at the end of this process, the money supply will be normalized, the amount of the Fed's balance sheet will be normalized, and there will be no permanent increase, either in money outstanding, in the Fed's balance sheet, or in inflation.[14]

At that time, the Fed's normalization principles involved selling the securities acquired during QE to return to a necessary-reserves framework. But the Fed has instead decided to maintain a giant balance sheet, much larger as a percentage of GDP than when Bernanke said there would be no permanent increase. By Bernanke's definition, therefore, the Fed has monetized the debt.

Moreover, although the Fed will never *deliberately* set out to monetize the debt, with the balance sheet unbounded, it is free to respond to developments in a manner that does so. For example, Vice Chair Quarles explained in October 2020 that the Fed may need to continue massive securities purchases because the Treasury was issuing more than financial markets could handle on their own (Derby 2020).

Independence of the Fed at Risk

The independence of the Federal Reserve's conduct of monetary policy relies critically on convention rather than being established by law. Just as the Fed sought to keep Treasury financing rates low at the direction of the Treasury prior to the Treasury-Fed Accord of 1951, future administrations could nominate, and the Senate could approve, Fed Board members with an understanding that the Board would coordinate with the administration in setting interest rates. Because the Fed's balance sheet is now unconstrained, a future administration could also direct balance sheet policy. In fact, the "attractive nuisance" of the unbounded balance sheet could be the catalyst that leads future administrations to forgo the convention of Fed independence.[15]

Relatedly, in recent years there have been many calls (and in the case of the European Central Bank, or ECB, action) to force banks to extend zero-interest loans to central banks to cover central bank losses (Nelson 2024b). The loans would take the form of requiring banks to hold deposits at the central banks on which the central banks would pay no interest. If the central bank funds QE with unremunerated reserves that banks are forced to hold, QE becomes a money maker for the government. The larger the Fed's portfolio, the more the revenue, all without having to raise taxes.

Benefits Are Limited

Both Frameworks Provide Good Interest Rate Control in Normal Times, and Corridor Becomes Floor in Stress Times

An evaluation of the net costs of a floor-implementation regime requires consideration of the benefits as well as costs. Overall, the benefits of the floor system are limited. There is broad agreement that both a corridor and floor system provide good interest rate control in normal times. One purported benefit of a floor system is that it provides better interest rate control in times when the Federal Reserve needs to expand its balance sheet because of emergency lending or asset purchases. While true, a corridor system *becomes* a floor system in such circumstances, as demonstrated by the Fed's experience in 2008 and the ECB's experience in 2009, 2012, and 2015, so it is not necessary for the Fed to implement policy in a floor system *at all times* to reap this benefit.

Monetary Policy Implementation Has Not Become Simpler

Another claimed benefit of a floor system is that it allows for simpler implementation of monetary policy in normal times. Experience has not borne this out. Before the GFC, policy implementation was simple and fed funds rate volatility low. Under the current regime, the Fed and market participants are devoting a huge amount of resources to determining how low reserve balances can shrink without the fed funds rate becoming sensitive to downward swings in reserves. False confidence that the fine-tuning operations were no longer needed led to the severe bout of repo market volatility in September 2019.

The Pre-GFC Implementation Regime Also Satisfied the "Friedman Rule"

Another purported benefit is that the floor system is efficient because it is free for the Fed to create reserves and so it should do so until the fed funds rate equals the interest rate on reserves. As discussed above, it is not true that it is free for the Fed to oversupply reserves—the costs are many and large. Moreover, as explained below, the Federal Reserve was already providing the financial system abundant liquidity using its pre-GFC implementation system.

A deposit at a bank and an undrawn line of credit from a bank are economically nearly identical—both are promises by the bank to provide funds up to some limit on demand. According to what is loosely called the "Friedman rule," it is economically efficient for a central bank to provide the financial system liquidity generously because it can produce the liquidity at low cost. In the pre-GFC regime, the Fed provided liquidity in the form of free lines of collateralized daylight and overnight (discount window) credit. The Fed began offering free lines of overnight credit in 2003 when it converted the discount window into a "no-questions-asked" facility, renamed "primary credit," that financially sound banks could count on to meet contingency funding needs. The lines were and are free. The interest rate on the *draws under the lines* (the primary credit rate) is above market so that banks would choose to use the discount window only as a contingency source of funding. Indeed, if the primary credit rate was too low, and banks used primary credit as an ongoing source of funding, there would be less undrawn line capacity to provide liquidity. Liquidity comes from available funding, not used funding. In addition, beginning in 2008, the Fed began providing financially sound banks free collateralized daylight credit so that banks would use the credit liberally and not withhold payments until late in the day.

The extensions of daylight and overnight credit were and are backed by pre-positioned collateral, primarily business and consumer loans. As a consequence, banks were provided with liquidity (capacity under a line of credit) generously without the Fed's having to maintain a massive portfolio of securities and without banks' having to use up balance sheet space maintaining large deposits at the Fed. Instead, the banks used their balance sheets to make loans to businesses and households that they then pledged to the Fed to back the lines.

Under the floor system, the liquidity is provided by the Fed being the receiver of huge amounts of reserve balances with a corresponding huge portfolio of securities. Many of the costs of the approach are discussed above, but one demonstration of how stuffing bank balance sheets with reserves raises bank balance sheet costs occurred when the Fed stopped its COVID-19-period exclusion of reserve balances from the denominator of the leverage ratio. Even though the Fed paid money funds 10 basis points less on ON RRPs than it paid banks on reserves, the ON RRP facility exploded, as funding the Fed became more profitable for money funds than for banks. And that was just the leverage ratio. Reserve balances also worsen banks' stress-test results and the largest banks' G-SIB surcharges.[16] Those higher bank balance sheet costs translate into lower bank credit supply and reduced economic activity.

Is the Fed Becoming an Outlier?

While expanding the balance sheet through emergency lending and quantitative easing served a legitimate purpose when the federal funds rate was near zero, there is a growing consensus across the major central banks that the costs of a floor system outweigh the benefits. The Bank of Canada, Bank of England, ECB, and Reserve Bank of Australia have all announced plans to reduce reserves until borrowing from the central bank picks up and market rates are a bit above the interest rate the central bank pays on deposits, essentially returning to a corridor system, although they are not using the word "corridor." But as Andrew Bailey (2024) observed recently:

> Generally speaking, as reserves levels grow, the incentives for the banking sector to manage its own liquidity falls. And to the extent that reserve supply crowds out healthy market intermediation in normal market conditions, a large part of the financial system's ability to manage its liquidity will be affected. Mindful of these costs, we do not seek a larger balance sheet than is strictly necessary.

In the same speech, Bailey indicated that there was an active ongoing debate at meetings of central bankers at the Bank for International Settlements (BIS) about the benefits of a floor system. In a podcast in January 2024, Claudio Borio, head of research at the BIS, described the advantage of returning to a corridor system with an active federal funds market and looking to discount-window borrowing capacity as a bank's source of contingent liquidity. In that case, banks first meet their liquidity needs in the interbank market, then prepare for their liquidity needs under stress with collateral at the discount window, as opposed to the current system in which banks meet their liquidity needs with deposits at the Fed:

> Would you like to have a system in which the central bank is a backstop, or would you like to have a system in which the central bank is the mass market maker of first resort, so last resort versus first resort? . . . I think that having a system in which the central bank is a backstop, and a system in which the first line of defense against demands on liquidity is an interbank market, that to me sounds [like], on balance, a better system. (Beckworth 2024)

Looking Forward, Maybe the Fed Is Changing Its Mind Too

There may also have been a quiet, but material, change in how the Fed anticipates conducting monetary policy once it has normalized its balance sheet. Despite the ratchet in the demand for reserves, demand can be reduced, but only by the Fed's 1) reducing supply until money-market rates move a bit above the interest rate the Fed pays on reserve balances, and 2) stopping examiners from requiring banks to hold such high levels of reserves.

The Fed has made changes, and may make more changes, to accomplish no. 2, allowing banks to substitute discount window capacity for reserve balances. Critically, on August 13, 2024, the Fed published a FAQ about how it will enforce the requirement that banks conduct internal liquidity stress tests (ILSTs), the most binding requirement for many banks.[17] Banks not only need to have liquid assets to meet projected needs to pass their ILSTs; they also need to demonstrate that they can *monetize* those assets. The FAQ states that banks can now point to the discount window, standing repo facility, or borrowing from an FHLB as the means by which they would monetize their liquid assets. Consequently, banks can reduce their holdings of reserve balances as the sole means by which they would meet a depositor run. Similar changes, but ones that require a change in regulations, may be in the works (Barr 2024).

Moreover, the Fed may also now be planning on bringing about no. 1, reducing reserve supply until money-market rates are a bit above the IORB rate. Many Fed communications now describe its plan as reducing reserve supply until they are in the zone where the demand curve is sloping up.[18]

Since the flat part of the curve is near the IORB rate, the sloped part of the curve should be mostly above the IORB rate.

In sum, the Fed may also have concluded that the costs of a floor system exceed the benefits and may be taking steps to shrink. If so, the change will become clear over coming quarters as QT continues and reserve balances decline. The rub will come when the Fed has to decide whether it wants to maintain a multi-hundred-billion-dollar buffer of reserve balances over the amount that the banking system needs.

Notes

1. See Board of Governors (2018).

2. Branches and agencies are the predominant borrowers because they do not have insured deposits and therefore do not have deposit insurance premiums. Deposit insurance premiums are based on total bank liabilities, not insured deposits, so they are applied to fed funds purchased.

3. There has been a stigma associated with borrowing from the discount window since the 1920s, and stigma exists for many reasons. See Nelson (2021).

4. See Nelson (2023).

5. When Powell was asked in the press conference following the May 2023 FOMC meeting if the ON RRP facility was making the deposit outflows from banks worse, he responded: "[The facility] is really there to, to help us keep rates where they're supposed to be, and it's, it's serving that purpose very well" (FOMC 2023, 20).

6. Board of Governors of the Federal Reserve System, "The Federal Reserve Explained," https://www.federalreserve.gov/aboutthefed/fedexplained/monetary -policy.htm (accessed February 27, 2025).

7. Maintaining a large cash deposit may give the Treasury more time during debt ceiling debacles if the debt limit had been established based on a level consistent with the higher balance.

8. See, for example, Board of Governors (2018).

9. See also Levin et al. (2022).

10. Cumulative sum of the one-month Treasury bill rate (at a weekly rate) times the sum of the Treasury General Account and Currency Outstanding from the H.4.1.

11. CARES Act, Pub. L. 116-136, 134 Stat. 281 (2020). Section 4003, paragraph (c)(3)(D)(ii), 213.

12. ECASH (Electronic Currency and Secure Hardware) Act, H.R. 7231, 117th Cong. (2022). See also https://ecashact.us/#funding.

13. BITCOIN (Boosting Innovation, Technology, and Competitiveness through Optimized Investment Nationwide) Act, S. 4912, 118th Cong. (2024). Section 9.

14. *Hearing on the State of the US Economy Before the Comm. on the Budget.* 112th Cong. February 9, 2011.

15. See Plosser (2022).
16. See Covas (2021) and Covas et al. (2024).
17. See Nelson and Waxman (2024).
18. See, for example, Afonso et al. (2024).

References

Afonso, Gara, Domenico Giannone, Gabriele La Spada, and John C. Williams. 2024. "When Are Central Bank Reserves Ample?" *Liberty Street Economics* (blog). Federal Reserve Bank of New York. August 13. https://libertystreeteconomics .newyorkfed.org/2024/08/when-are-central-bank-reserves-ample/.
Bailey, Andrew. 2024. "The Importance of Central Bank Reserves." Lecture, London School of Economics, London, United Kingdom. May 21.
Barr, Michael S. 2024. "The Next Steps on Capital." Remarks at the Brookings Institution, Washington, DC. September 10.
Beckworth, David, host. 2022. *Macro Musings.* "Randal Quarles on Inflation, Balance Sheet Reduction, Financial Stability, and the Future of the Fed." Mercatus Center, July 18. Podcast, 47 min., 16 sec. https://www.mercatus.org/macro-musings/randal -quarles-inflation-balance-sheet-reduction-financial-stability-and-future-fed.
Beckworth, David, host. 2024. *Macro Musings.* "Claudio Borio on the Future of Central Bank Operating Systems." Mercatus Center, January 8. Podcast, 50 min., 57 sec. https://www.mercatus.org/macro-musings/claudio-borio-future -central-bank-operating-systems.
Board of Governors (Board of Governors of the Federal Reserve System). 2018. "The Federal Reserve's Long-Run Operating Regime." Memo to the Federal Open Market Committee. October 22. https://www.federalreserve.gov/monetarypolicy /files/FOMC20181022memo02.pdf.
Board of Governors. 2002. "Alternative Instruments for Open Market and Discount Window Operations." Memo, Federal Reserve System Study Group on Alternative Instruments for System Operations. December. Board of Governors of the Federal Reserve System. https://www.federalreserve.gov/monetarypolicy/files /fomc20021201memo01.pdf.
Board of Governors. 2025. "Federal Reserve Balance Sheet: Factors Affecting Reserve Balances—H.4.1." Effective January 16. https://www.federalreserve .gov/releases/h41/.
Covas, Francisco. 2021. "Take-up at the Federal Reserve's ON RRP Facility: Much Larger and More Persistent than Planned, Getting Larger, and the Reasons Why." Bank Policy Institute (blog). June 9. https://bpi.com/wp-content/uploads/2021/06 /Take-up-at-the-Federal-Reserves-ON-RRP-Facility-Much-Larger-and-More -Persistent-than-Planned-Getting-Larger-and-the-Reasons-Why.pdf.
Covas, Francisco, Sarah Flowers, and Brett Waxman. 2024. "Empty Promises: Revisiting the Reasons to Fix the Supplementary Leverage Ratio." Bank Policy Insti-

tute (blog). July 8. https://bpi.com/wp-content/uploads/2024/07/Empty
-Promises-Revisiting-the-Reasons-to-Fix-the-Supplementary-Leverage-Ratio-5.pdf.
Derby, Michael S. 2020. "Fed Official Wonders Whether Treasury Market Can Han-
dle Massive Issuance Alone." *Wall Street Journal*, October 14.
FOMC (Federal Open Market Committee). 2018a. "Meeting of the Federal Open Mar-
ket Committee." Washington, DC. November 7–8. Transcript available at https://
www.federalreserve.gov/monetarypolicy/files/FOMC20181108meeting.pdf.
FOMC. 2018b. "Meeting of the Federal Open Market Committee." Washington,
DC. December 18–19. Transcript available at https://www.federalreserve.gov
/monetarypolicy/files/FOMC20181219meeting.pdf.
FOMC. 2020a. "Chair Powell's Press Conference." Washington, DC. September
16. Transcript available at https://www.federalreserve.gov/mediacenter/files
/FOMCpresconf20200916.pdf.
FOMC. 2020b. "Chair Powell's Press Conference." Washington, DC. December
16. Transcript available at https://www.federalreserve.gov/mediacenter/files
/FOMCpresconf20201216.pdf.
FOMC. 2023. "Chair Powell's Press Conference." Washington, DC. May 3. Transcript
available at https://www.federalreserve.gov/mediacenter/files/FOMCpresconf
20230503.pdf.
Kelton, Stephanie, Andres Bernal, and Greg Carlock. 2018. "We Can Pay for a Green
New Deal." *Huffington Post*, November 30. https://www.huffpost.com/entry
/opinion-green-new-deal-cost_n_5c0042b2e4b027f1097bda5b.
Levin, Andrew T., Brian L. Lu, and William R. Nelson. 2022. "Quantifying the Costs
and Benefits of Quantitative Easing." Working Paper No. 30749. National Bureau
of Economic Research. December.
Lucas, Robert E., Jr. 1976. "Econometric Policy Evaluation: A Critique." *Carnegie-
Rochester Conference Series on Public Policy* 1:19–46.
Nelson, Bill. 2019. "Two Little-Noticed and Self-Inflicted Causes of the Fed's Current Monetary Policy Implementation Predicament." Bank Policy Institute
(blog). October 1. https://bpi.com/wp-content/uploads/2019/10/Two
-Little-Noticed-and-Self-Inflicted-Causes-of-the-Feds-Current-Monetary-Policy
-Implementation-Predicament.pdf.
Nelson, Bill. 2020. "Comment on 'Reserves Were Not So Ample After All.'" Remarks
at the Monetary Policy Conference, Hoover Institution, Stanford, CA (online
conference). October 28. https://www.hoover.org/sites/default/files/hoover
_nelson_remarks_on_cdy_share_1.pdf.
Nelson, Bill. 2021. "Discount Window Stigma: We Have Met the Enemy, and He
Is Us." Bank Policy Institute (blog). August 10. https://bpi.com/wp-content
/uploads/2021/08/Discount-Window-Stigma-We-Have-Met-the-Enemy-and
-He-Is-Us.pdf.
Nelson, Bill. 2023. "Is It Time for a Holistic Review of Liquidity Requirements?"
Report. Bank Policy Institute. February 23.

Nelson, Bill. 2024a. "How the Federal Reserve Got So Huge, and Why and How It Can Shrink." Staff Working Paper No. 2024-1. Bank Policy Institute. February 7.

Nelson, Bill. 2024b. "Should Banks, Thrifts and Credit Unions Be Forced to Make Interest-Free Loans to the US Government?" Bank Policy Institute (blog). July 25. https://bpi.com/wp-content/uploads/2024/07/Should-banks-thrifts-and-credit-unions-be-forced-to-make-interest-free-loans-to-the-U.S.-government.pdf.

Nelson, Bill, and Brett Waxman. 2024. "A Helpful Federal Reserve Board Statement on Bank Liquidity." Bank Policy Institute (blog). August 21. https://bpi.com/wp-content/uploads/2024/08/A-Helpful-Federal-Reserve-Board-Statement-on-Bank-Liquidity_.pdf.

New York Fed (Federal Reserve Bank of New York). 2024. "Open Market Operations during 2023." Report prepared by the New York Fed's Markets Group for the Federal Open Market Committee.

Norges Bank. 2010. "Changes in 'Regulation on the Access of Banks to Borrowing and Deposit Facilities in Norges Bank etc.'" Consultative document. Norges Bank. October 1. Retrieved from https://www.norges-bank.no/contentassets/cfc83348f4574a719dd5a4ce70a48840/consultative_document_06102010.pdf?v=09032017123145.

Omarova, Saule T. 2021. "The People's Ledger: How to Democratize Money and Finance the Economy." *Vanderbilt Law Review* 74 (5): 1231–1300.

Plosser, Charles. 2022. "Federal Reserve Independence: Is It Time for a New Treasury-Fed Accord?" Economics Working Paper No. 22104. Hoover Institution. March 10.

Poole, William. 1968. "Commercial Bank Reserve Management in a Stochastic Model: Implications for Monetary Policy." *Journal of Finance* 23 (5): 769–91.

Selgin, George. 2020. *The Menace of Fiscal QE*. Cato Institute.

16
Rate Corridors Depend on Dealer Balance Sheet Capacity

Darrell Duffie

Thanks very much. As noted by Loretta Mester (2025, in this volume), the target set by the Federal Open Market Committee (FOMC) for interest rates doesn't matter unless the market actually uses interest rates that are close to the target.

I would like to speak about a different problem than the ampleness of reserves. I talked about this at a Hoover monetary policy conference in May. I do not agree with any proposal that the Fed should lower the amount of reserves in the system to the point that banks are forced to deal with less than they feel they need. That's a problematic approach. I was in China in June 2013 when the People's Bank of China (PBOC) swore to its banks that it was going to starve them of reserves because they were too greedy for reserves. When this caused markets to blow up, the PBOC didn't have any other option than to supply the needed reserves. The Fed is always going to supply the needed reserves when it comes to a crunch. So, we can't simply wish down the size of the Fed's balance sheet. I'll come back later with some policy ideas for how to mitigate some of the need for a very large Fed balance sheet.

But I would like to address here a different aspect of monetary policy transmission, not related to William Poole's demand curve, but rather to the capacity of the largest financial institutions to actually lend more reserves, even when they have access to a large quantity of reserves. This is related to their ability to expand their balance sheets given their capital regulations. Just two weeks ago, September 30, 2024, we had the end of a quarter, at which foreign banks must show their regulators they have enough capital. They expand their assets in the middle of each quarter. At the end of each quarter, they shrink their assets so that it looks as though they have enough capital. The most relevant capital requirements for US banks are based on daily averaging. But there is nevertheless a quarter-end impact on US dollar markets, because when those foreign banks pull out of USD money markets at the end of a quarter, there can be significant disruption.

At the September 2024 quarter end, it wasn't a disaster. For example, it wasn't as difficult for money markets as the liquidity crunch of September 2019. But the recent quarter-end behavior of core money markets should have sent shivers through anyone that's monitoring the effectiveness of the implementation of the Fed's policy rates. And it also should give concern to those who are worried about whether financial institutions that actually need money are going to be able to readily get money on future quarter ends.

When large European and other foreign banks reduce their balance sheets at a quarter end, much of the financing that they would have provided must be provided by US banks. There are also some additional demands for borrowing on a typical quarter end, because this is also usually a Treasury issuance day, and US banks do have some quarter-end regulatory requirements.

From figure 16.1, you can see what happens in the repo market, which is the market that really matters for monetary policy transmission, as I'll emphasize later. This figure shows one of the benchmark repo rates, the general collateral financing (GCF) repo rate, which I picked for illustration because it's quite homogeneous, being centrally cleared and based on general collateral.

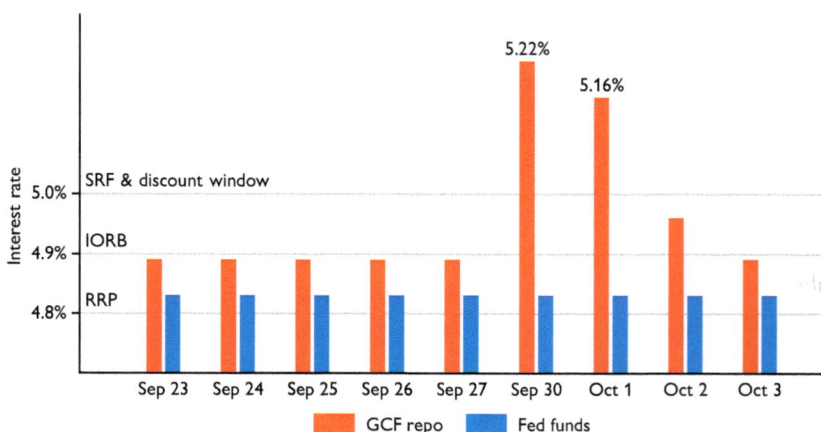

Figure 16.1. The GCF repo rate and the effective federal funds rate (EFFR) on days surrounding September 30, 2024. Also shown are four rates administered by the Federal Reserve: the overnight reverse repurchase facility rate (ON RRP), the interest rate paid by the Fed on reserve balances (IORB), the standing repo facility rate (SRF), and the discount window primary-facility rate.

Source: Federal Reserve Bank of New York (GCF repo), and St. Louis Federal Reserve (FRED) (EFFR).

This benchmark rate illustrates well the shadow price of funding in the repo market. As you can see, the GCF repo rate was very regular until the last day of the quarter, sitting 1 basis point below the interest rate paid by the Fed on reserve balances (IORB).

The stability of repo rates before the end of the quarter represents effective implementation of monetary policy. But then on the quarter end, when capital requirements started to bind on foreign banks, the repo rate shot up to 5.22%, significantly above the IORB. The repo rate was still elevated on October 1, at 5.16%, but then went back down to normal within a couple of days.

This matters. The IORB is designed to be the floor on rates in the Fed's system, as Loretta Mester explains in chapter 14, with a subfloor provided by the reverse repurchase facility rate. There are also supposed to be ceiling rates. The intended ceilings are the discount window rate for banks and the standing repo facility (SRF) rate for repo dealers, the largest of which are subject to bank holding company capital requirements. These large bank dealers can't always step into the market aggressively on quarter ends because their balance sheets are constrained. These dealer banks apparently don't want to go to the standing repo facility to get additional funding. So, for example, the fictitious Bank of Mike Bordo might have said, "Well, I don't really need to pay a high rate like 5.22%. I could go to the Fed and get funding at the SRF rate, which is only 5%." That 22-basis-point difference is a lot in a multitrillion dollar market. But Mike didn't actually arbitrage by getting funding at the SRF. Why wouldn't he take that opportunity? On October 1, $600 billion of repos were conducted at rates above the SRF rate, in fact above 5.14%. But the SRF handled only $100 million that day.

Why wasn't that $600 billion of funding obtained at the Fed, at a much cheaper rate, if the funds had to be obtained? This is also related to stigma— about which Bill Nelson (2025, in this volume) is an expert. It's not a good look for the largest dealer banks to use the discount window and the standing repo facility.

The SRF might have also had some teething problems, because this is the first time that it was actually used. But it is concerning that the facilities that put "safety ceilings" on market interest rates were hardly used. This problem is complementary to any concerns over the ampleness of reserves.

The more basic problem is that the bond market is getting too big relative to bank balance sheets. And that's not the fault of the Fed; it's the fault of the fiscal authority, which is borrowing so much money that the quantity of bonds that need to get financing in the repo market is growing by leaps and

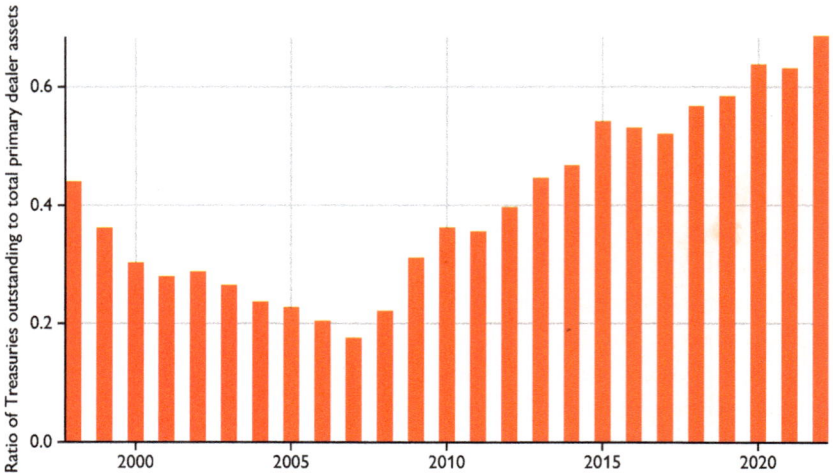

Figure 16.2. The ratio of the total assets of primary dealers in US Treasury securities to the quantity of US Treasuries outstanding.

Source: FRED and public corporate financial disclosures.

bounds relative to the sizes of the banks that intermediate those markets, as shown in figure 16.2.

The vertical axis on this chart is the ratio of total US Treasuries outstanding to the total size of all primary dealer balance sheets. Before the Global Financial Crisis (GFC), the capacity of the market to handle Treasury market intermediation was improving. For example, the quantity of Treasuries outstanding per unit of dealer balance sheet space was going down. That was based on light regulation. The banks would usually have no problem expanding their balance sheets whenever they wanted to, to get a few basis points of arbitrage profit, because they were only lightly regulated for capital. Then, after the GFC, regulators got religion and said: "We need financial stability; we need to regulate these banks for capital." From this point, the balance sheets of most primary dealers grew much more slowly. Meanwhile, the US government was borrowing money hand over fist. We now have roughly four times as much Treasury securities per unit of dealer balance sheet space as on the eve of the GFC. The bond market is just basically too big.

And that's why we saw this blip at the end of last quarter. There's just so much demand for financing relative to the available capital of dealers. What about the fed funds market? Figure 16.1 shows the effective federal funds rate around that time. Wow, the Fed nailed it, 4.83%, day after day, without

Daily transaction volumes ($billions), to scale

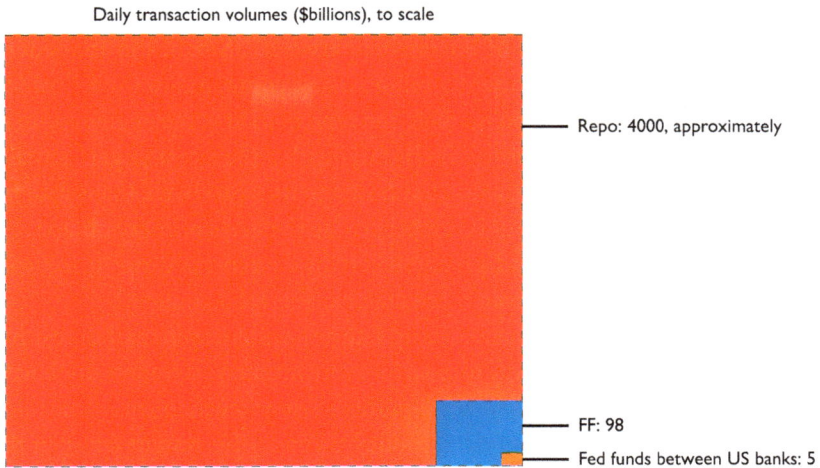

Repo: 4000, approximately

FF: 98

Fed funds between US banks: 5

Figure 16.3. Approximate recent total daily transaction volumes, to scale, in US dollar repo markets, the federal funds market (including transactions between federal agencies and non-US banks), and the component of the federal funds market covering transactions between US banks.

Source: Data from Securities Industry and Financial Markets Association (repo) and FRED (fed funds), via FRED.

budging at the end of the quarter! As Loretta Mester and Bill Nelson discuss in their chapters, the federal funds market is mainly an artifactual market, sitting on the side of major money markets. In my last chart, figure 16.3, I show, to scale, the size of the repo market compared with the federal funds market. The big red rectangle is a recent estimate of daily transactions volume in the repo market. Actually, this is a big underestimate because a lot of repos are now being discovered through new monitoring of the bilateral repo market. Recently, the Fixed Income Clearing Corporation alone cleared $9 trillion of repos in one day—a record.

Let's compare with the size of the federal funds market. That's the small blue rectangle down in the bottom right of the figure, which is about $98 billion when last measured, so, very small relative to the repo market. Most of the federal funds market consists of lending between federal agencies that don't get paid interest on their reserves and European banks that have lighter capital regulations than the largest US banks and do not pay an insurance premium on their liabilities to the Federal Deposit Insurance Corporation. The European banks are basically entering into a negotiation with federal agencies over how to split the interest that the European banks will receive. This is what

I meant by an "artifactual" rate. The tiny orange rectangle at the bottom right of the figure is the amount of borrowing between US banks in the federal funds market. That's only about $5 billion a day, compared to the $4 trillion volume of lending in the repo market. The repo market is the engine room of money markets. That's where the Fed is hoping that the rate it targets actually takes a grip. If the Fed nails the fed funds rate to its target, well, that's nice for communication purposes, but is not otherwise the Fed's primary objective.

So what can the Fed, and policymakers more generally, do to mitigate these concerns without an even more massive Fed balance sheet?

One of the things the Fed can do is update its payment systems. Some other central banks have found a way to get a lot more intraday payments done with a smaller amount of reserves, using liquidity savings mechanisms—meaning incentives and rules that move the money through the system faster in the middle of the day, so that banks don't need to start the day with such large balances of reserves.

Another thing that the Fed could do is to open its standing repo facility to a wider set of counterparties. Loretta alluded to this idea, which was also suggested in a G30 report chaired by Tim Geithner, to which Jeremy Stein, Pat Parkinson, and I contributed. With that, we wouldn't be depending on the capital-constrained banks to intermediate nearly 100% of this market. When funding rates would otherwise blow up, a wider set of market participants could get some funding from the Fed. That's antithetical to concern over the Fed's footprint. Mitigating that concern, the Fed doesn't have to directly face all of its counterparties. The Fed could instead centrally clear its SRF trades, so that it's only facing the central counterparty and doesn't need to vet so many market participants. This would also allow US dealer banks to lower their capital commitments to the repo market by netting their SRF positions with the Fed against countervailing repo positions with other market participants.

Finally, the vast majority of repos don't need to be intermediated on bank balance sheets. We could have an additional segment of the money market in which borrowers and lenders face each other directly, even if they are not banks. This is sometimes called "direct repo," and is an active market in Europe. It's hard for the Fed to mandate this, but it could foster the growth of direct all-to-all trading in the repo market, reducing the bottleneck constraints associated with dealer balance sheet space.

References

Mester, Loretta J. 2025. "The Fed's Ample Reserves Monetary Policy Operating Framework: It Isn't as Simple as It Looks." In *Fifty Years of the Shadow Open Market Committee: A Retrospective on Its Role in Monetary Policy*, edited by Michael D. Bordo, Jeffrey M. Lacker, Mickey D. Levy, and John B. Taylor. Hoover Institution Press.

Nelson, Bill. 2025. "From the Floor Back to the Corridor: Why the Choice of Monetary Policy Implementation Framework Matters." In *Fifty Years of the Shadow Open Market Committee: A Retrospective on Its Role in Monetary Policy*, edited by Michael D. Bordo, Jeffrey M. Lacker, Mickey D. Levy, and John B. Taylor. Hoover Institution Press.

HARALD UHLIG: Maybe this is a question for Loretta Mester or Darrell Duffie or, actually, all three. I am Harald Uhlig, University of Chicago and visiting fellow at Hoover. In the good old times, the federal funds rate was, of course, the key market interest rate. Cash balances and reserves had an interest rate of zero. And the Fed was trying to move that rate up and down. Everybody was staring at that. That was, in Darrell's language, the elephant in the room.

Now, the federal funds rate is no longer central: The interest on reserves is. I am sure the federal funds rate is still important for some players in the market, don't get me wrong. But in the overall scheme of things, it is something that we can pretty much neglect. And I'm even not sure that the repo rates that Darrell showed are all that important.

Once you open the discount window to a larger set of institutions, once you make the discount window equal to the interest on reserves, once you provide more "hand-holding" for the financial market, so that financial market players really use the discount window rather than borrow from private market participants, these issues are gone. Many of these frictions seem small anyways as far as a bigger macroeconomic picture is concerned. Rather, the interest rate on reserves is really the key interest rate, and that's the one that's moving lending conditions up and down. The federal funds rate and the repo rates are a sideshow to that. So why are we still talking about the federal funds rate, is my question, other than for the purpose of examining these rather small frictions?

ROBERT G. KING: So I'm going to trust Jeff Lacker to make his question really short. Then we'll go to John Cochrane, and then we'll have the panel respond quickly and we're going to break.

JEFFREY M. LACKER: I agree that a large Fed balance sheet opens it up as a target for special pleading for people who want to have the Fed participate in credit allocation. This has been a problem under the corridor as well. Ever since the 1951 [Treasury-Fed] Accord, discount window lending has been divorced from monetary policy because the Fed could always sterilize any lending.

And this is why the FDIC and the OCC [Office of the Comptroller of the Currency] came to the Fed for lending for too-big-to-fail banks. And it's why [William] Proxmire pressured the Fed and forced it to start buying agency debt, including the debt of the Washington Metro.

KING: Excellent question. John.

JOHN H. COCHRANE: Thanks, this was wonderful. You have properly focused on the question, "How does the new regime affect interest rates?" The answer I hear is: If you want to nail a price, you need a flat supply curve for all comers. And if you want to fool around with something other than that, you're going to have trouble nailing a price.

But you didn't address the big question of the interest-on-reserves regime. Here, the ghost of monetarism is creaking in that coffin in front of us. Back in the old days, quantities were limited and there was an opportunity cost of liquidity.

Now we live the Friedman rule. We live in a permanent liquidity trap. We're hoping that interest rates transmit to the rest of the economy entirely through prices with no change in quantities, no opportunity cost of liquidity, no rationing the means of transaction, and so forth.

I like that, but I'm a little nervous about it. Does the Fed really have the same control just by raising the interest rate that it had back when it also rationed the money supply? Interpreting history, was 1982 really just about the cost of interest rates on freely provided deposits and loans, or was there something involving the machinery of the financial system? I suspect that the Fed has a lot less control now. What do you think?

KING: Okay, super quick answers.

LORETTA J. MESTER: Right, on the fed funds rate as the target. Harald, yes, you're right, partly if you go back and look at the transcript of that December 2018 meeting, you'll see there was a big discussion about whether we should change the target.

At the end of the day, it was decided not to. One, I think because people were comfortable with the fed funds market, it was all communications. It's how do you communicate? You're exactly right. The control is the administered rates. This is about communicating policy. But the other thing that's an undercurrent there, and Charlie Plosser has talked about this also, is that there are governance issues.

If you were to switch from the fed funds to, say, an administered rate, that's not an FOMC [Federal Open Market Committee] decision, and I think that also played a role in the thinking: Okay, let's keep it, we seem to be able to control it. We can link these short-term money-market rates together and we're controlling them and let's punt on that governance issue.

KING: Yeah. Darrell.

DARRELL DUFFIE: I'll try John's and I'll leave the Proxmire one to Bill.

Well, John, to some extent, it's not really costs and benefits when you're up against the wall. It's not feasible in the current regulatory framework to steer rates by scarcity of reserves because banks are required in the current regulatory regime to prove that they have enough liquidity on their own, without relying on the Fed. So, they have enormous demands for reserves to meet their liquidity needs. We can't really go back to a world in which you could squeeze them down to the point where they just barely have enough reserves to lend to others. The needs that they have for meeting the regulatory requirements and payment needs in the course of a day are orders of magnitude bigger than the adjustments of reserves that the Fed would need to make on a daily basis to target the rate.

So it's just not feasible, as I learned long ago from Don Kohn, in my first encounter with him.

KING: Yeah. I've got to turn to Bill next.

BILL NELSON: Okay, so I'll take a shot at Jeff's question. And I completely agree these pressures existed before, but as I think was Charlie's point—and certainly I agree—back under a corridor system, the Fed could be no bigger than a little bit bigger than the demand for currency, and they couldn't control the demand for currency.

And now under this system, they can be as big as they'd like.

KING: Okay, thank you very much, panel, for an excellent session.

Monetary-Fiscal Issues

Introduction

Michael J. Boskin

We're getting started a bit late and people will start wandering in, but we have a very full panel. We have four excellent speakers who have made important contributions to our subject, which is fiscal and monetary issues, their interaction, et cetera: John Cochrane, Debbie Lucas, Charlie Plosser, and Pat Kehoe.

I'm going to be much more ruthless than previous moderators by limiting everybody to ten minutes, because we're supposed to be done by 5 o'clock and it's five to 4, and we'd like to leave some time for questions and the inevitable one- or two-minute overage when I say time's up. We'll do the best we can, and if we go a little over, I'll apologize.

I'm Michael Boskin, Stanford Economics Department and Hoover Institution. And having listened to some of the panels—I apologize, I missed some of the morning because I was having my eyes dilated. If I call on somebody later, and you're a good friend and I don't recognize you, that's because my eyes aren't fully recovered.

I do want to mention that this occurs against the backdrop of a much richer intellectual history than we were able to discuss so far, including around what the national debt does and deficits do. We'll hear more about that, including ideas of three Nobel Prize winners, one who thought that the major thing about the debt was it had real effects because it decreased the apparent price to taxpayers about what the cost was of funding spending.

We've had Ricardian equivalence reborn. We've had Jim Tobin saying federal debt has different types of characteristics than other financial instruments, especially now that we have TIPS [Treasury Inflation-Protected Securities]. We've had a long history of experiments with different evaluations of them and the like, all the way up to Olivier Blanchard's presidential address to the

AEA [American Economic Association] basically saying: Don't worry about the debt, we can roll it over forever; it's not that big a deal.

I deconstructed that in the *Papers and Proceedings* the next year; if you're interested, I'll send it to you. It doesn't really hold up. Some assumptions are pretty extreme, and we've run the experiment, and interest rates eventually got above the growth rate.

Also, we'll discuss much of what's about to occur, but I think we deserve to mention a few things that have happened. The most important thing is the immense explosion of the national debt in virtually every major economy, and secondly, the tremendous change in what governments are spending on.

When I was an undergraduate, it was still the case that the majority of federal government spending was on purchases of goods and services. And, unfortunately, we need to increase defense spending in a dangerous world. But now the government really is primarily a redistributor of resources. You might say it's a fiscal cross-hauler between people in their peak earning years to those in their retirement, or a little bit to the poor, but mostly big transfers, especially via social insurance and unfunded entitlements, go to the middle class.

And I think it's probably worth just saying, if you'll pardon me from exercising my own opinion about this: Since we're primarily borrowing these days for subsidies, transfer payments, tax credits, and things of that sort, it's worth remembering the original purpose of the federal debt, according to Alexander Hamilton. He argued for the federal assumption of Revolutionary War debt from the states because it was, quote, "the price of liberty." So governments have changed. There are many other things—if I have a chance, I'll mention—that would affect this discussion, but I think it's worth having that in mind as we hear this important discussion of the role of fiscal policy, fiscal policy and inflation, fiscal policy and monetary policy.

So I'm old enough to remember when it was okay to say, and perhaps to get away with saying now, "Ladies first." So, Debbie, I'm going to call on you first.

17

Monetary-Fiscal Interactions

John H. Cochrane

The Recent Inflation

We have just lived through a bout of inflation greater than anything since 1980, after which US inflation was supposedly conquered. Inflation broke out suddenly in February 2021, as illustrated in figure 17.1. Where did inflation come from? The Federal Reserve, remarkably, did nothing for a full year, leaving interest rates at zero. Yet inflation did not spiral upward. Inflation eased just as the Fed lifted interest rates off zero. Why did inflation ease? Standard doctrine says that interest rates must rise above inflation to push inflation down, with a big recession as in 1982. Yet inflation came down on its own despite interest rates below inflation, and with no hint of economic slowdown. As I write, inflation is still persistently above 2%. When will it finally end? Or will inflation resurge, as it did following a similar situation in 1976?

A Fiscal-Theory Interpretation

As a fan of the fiscal theory of the price level (Cochrane 2023), I find it gives simple answers to all of these questions, except of course the last: Inflation will always be hard to forecast.

In the COVID-19 pandemic, the US spent nearly $5 trillion, mostly in the form of checks to people and businesses. The Fed monetized about $3 trillion of that. Not all of that spending was inappropriate. The government did have to face the economic emergency posed by the pandemic and lockdowns. But spend it did.

More significantly, in my view, fiscal policy did not return to normal, or normal levels of dysfunction, after the pandemic waned. The Biden administration passed an additional $2 trillion stimulus in February 2021, quickly followed by the CHIPS and Science Act, the hilariously named Inflation Reduction Act, and more. Unprecedented deficits continued.

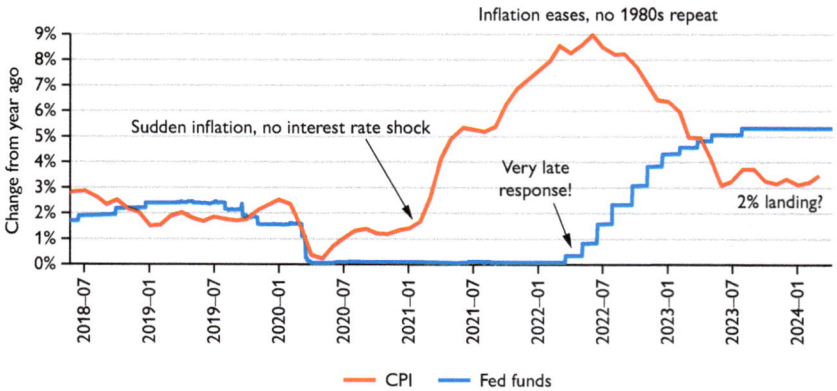

Figure 17.1. Inflation and the federal funds rate.

Source: Board of Governors and Bureau of Labor Services, via St. Louis Federal Reserve (FRED).

The fiscal theory of the price level gives a framework to understand how this fiscal blowout caused inflation. It states that the price level adjusts so that the real value of nominal debt equals the present value of primary surpluses (taxes less spending, not including interest costs on the debt) that pay back the debt. If stockholders see that dividends are unlikely to support the value of their stock, they try to sell and drive down the stock price. If bondholders think that the US will not run surpluses sufficient to repay its debts, the bondholders try to sell too. They try to exchange them for goods and services, driving up the price level. Eventually the real value of debt is inflated back to what people think the government will repay.

Equivalently, inflation comes from too much money chasing too few goods. The government can fight inflation by soaking up money with taxes greater than spending. The government can also fight inflation by soaking up money with bond sales, the classic open market operation. But people are only willing to hold more debt if they think future taxes will exceed spending to repay that debt. So the government can soak up money with current or future taxes. But lacking those, the money causes inflation.

The fiscal theory does *not* say that debt and deficits always cause inflation. It says only that debt and deficits cause inflation when they are greater than expected future repayment. And that repayment can take decades. Figure 17.2 illustrates.

In normal and responsible fiscal policy, the government borrows to finance an emergency (a pandemic, a war, a deep recession) or to invest in productive

No inflation   Inflation!   Inflation!

— Deficit   — Surplus   — Deficit   — Expected future deficit

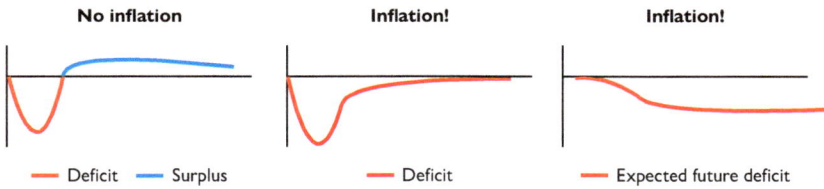

Figure 17.2. Three paths for deficits. X-axis is time, y-axis is dollars, adjusted for inflation.
Source: Author's calculations.

capital (the interstate highway system). Then, the government pays off that debt with small surpluses, over decades. The left-hand panel of figure 17.2 illustrates this pattern. This pattern causes no inflation—the present value of surpluses and deficits does not change.

Well-managed government debt is a good and great thing. It allows governments to meet temporary spending needs without enormous taxes. It allows governments to spread the cost over decades. Governments that can borrow, by effectively promising repayment, can marshal great resources. The left panel of figure 17.2 is what we should expect to see most of the time—debt and deficits in bad times, paid off by surpluses in good times, and little or no inflation.

Trouble brews in the middle panel of figure 17.2. Here the same debt or deficit is not matched by convincing promises of future surpluses. The present value of surpluses declines, and inflation breaks out. This is, roughly, what I think happened in 2021–23.

The right-hand panel of figure 17.2 alerts us to another danger. Even without any current debt or deficit, people can lose faith that the government will repay debt. Inflation springs seemingly out of nowhere. Investors lose faith and a stock can fall for no apparent reason. Inflation, roughly stock in the government, can suffer the same fate.

These observations provide some discipline. It is not enough to point to debt and deficits; we must also ask why people did not expect debt to be repaid, causing inflation. These observations also help us to address the obvious questions, since most debt or deficits do not correspond to inflation: What's different about this time? Why now, but not in 2008?

There is a plausible argument that people this time did not think debt and deficits would be repaid, while they did previously. In 2008, the government promised stimulus now, debt reduction to follow. Some, including myself, chuckled at deficit-reduction promises that always seem to take effect one day after the incumbent leaves office, but at least the government had the decency to make the promise. Nothing like this happened in 2020–23. Congress suspended the PAYGO rules that require cuts in some spending when there are increases in other spending. The zeitgeist was r < g, MMT [Modern Monetary Theory], secular stagnation, don't worry about debt repayment. Treasury Secretary Janet Yellen, arguing for the American Rescue Plan Act in 2021, said the US should go big and not worry about debt, as interest rates were low.

In this interpretation, the deficits of the early Biden administration are particularly significant. The COVID deficits could be seen as classic emergency spending, with an expectation to return to normal fiscal policy when it was over. The huge spending bills of 2021 signaled that nothing of the sort would happen. That inflation eased in summer 2022, when it became clear that additional multitrillion spending bills would not pass, is also significant.

The present-value view also points to discount rates, equivalently interest costs on the debt, as a driver of inflation. A 1-percentage-point-higher interest cost on the debt is, with 100% debt-to-GDP ratio, the same thing as a 1%-of-GDP additional deficit. Following 2008, the US enjoyed nearly a decade of negative real interest costs, with 0% short-term rate and inflation averaging just below 2%. A –2% real interest cost makes a lot of debt sustainable!

The latter mechanism is a serious constraint on monetary policy going forward. Each percentage point of higher real interest rates, undertaken to fight inflation, raises interest costs by 1%, and at 100% debt-to-GDP ratio raises interest costs by 1% of GDP. If Congress does not provide those extra funds, that's an inflationary pressure, offsetting any good that higher interest rates do on inflation.

The bottom line: In 2021–23, people holding $5 trillion of new government debt asked themselves, "Is this a good investment, to save and hold for the future? Or should I get rid of it fast while I can, and try to spend it?" They chose the latter, until inflation brought the value of debt right back to where it was at the beginning.

Fiscal theory is not just storytelling. We write models, quantitative parables of the economy. Models don't prove an idea right, but if you can't write a model, the idea is usually wrong. A model makes sure that the logical ends are tied up, that you respect budget constraints and markets clear.

Figure 17.3 presents a model simulation. I write a simple textbook New Keynesian sticky price model, augmented with fiscal theory. I ask the model what happens if the government runs a 1%-of-GDP deficit, with no plan to repay the debt, and if the central bank leaves interest rates alone.

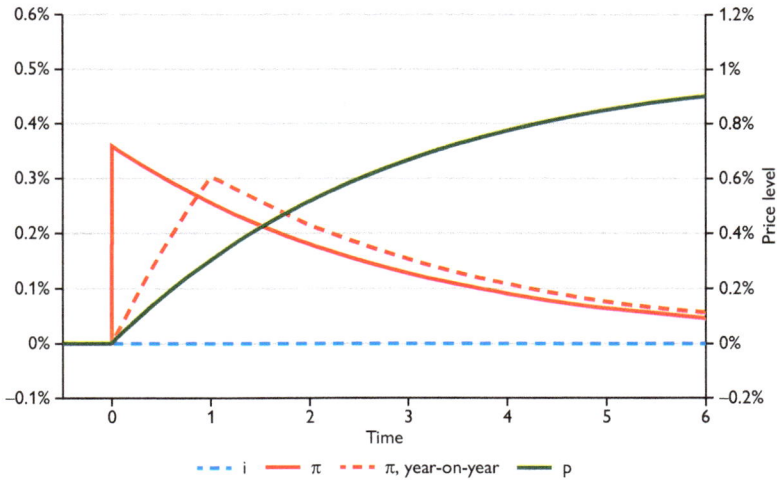

Figure 17.3. Response of a standard New Keynesian model with fiscal theory to a fiscal shock, with no interest-rate response by the central bank.

Source: Author's calculations.

The model is the continuous time version of

$$x_t = E_t x_{t+1} - \sigma\left(i_t - E_t \pi_{t+1}\right)$$

$$\pi_t = \beta E_t \pi_{t+1} + \kappa x_t$$

$$\rho v_{t+1} = v_t + r_{t+1}^n - \pi_{t+1} - \tilde{s}_{t+1}$$

$$E_t r_{t+1}^n = i_t$$

$$r_{t+1}^n = \omega q_{t+1} - q_t$$

where x is the output gap, i is the nominal interest rate, π is inflation, v is the real value of government debt, r^n is the nominal return on the portfolio of government bonds, $\tilde{s}$ is the real primary surplus scaled by the value of debt, q is the price of government bonds, and ω describes the geometric maturity structure of government debt.

Figure 17.3 presents the response to a 1% change in surplus, in the continuous time version of the model.

In response to the fiscal shock, inflation surges. Plotting inflation as change from a year earlier, as we do in the data, inflation grows for a year. Inflation above the interest rate slowly eats away at the value of government debt. In a model without price stickiness, this shock would lead to an instant 1% price level rise, removing that much value from government debt. With sticky prices, the long period of inflation above the interest rate accomplishes the same thing, with the price level rising after a few years. If the government spends, someone has to pay for it. If current taxpayers or future taxpayers do not pay for it, then it must come from the pockets of bondholders, through default, or here via inflation.

So the plot explains the first puzzle of 2021: Inflation surged, even though monetary policy did nothing unusual.

Inflation then eases and fades away, even with no reaction at all by the central bank. In conventional doctrine, the central bank must raise interest rates above inflation, and cause a recession, in order to first keep inflation from spiraling away and then to beat inflation back. In this model, in response to this one-time fiscal shock, once the price level has risen enough to inflate away debt, the force for further inflation is spent. Inflation goes away on its own even if the central bank does nothing. This accords with the puzzle of 2022, that inflation peaked and eased before central banks moved at all, and came back down long before interest rates exceeded inflation, and without any recession.

Central banks are still important in fiscal theory: Figure 17.4 presents the response of the same model to a rise in interest rates with no change in fiscal

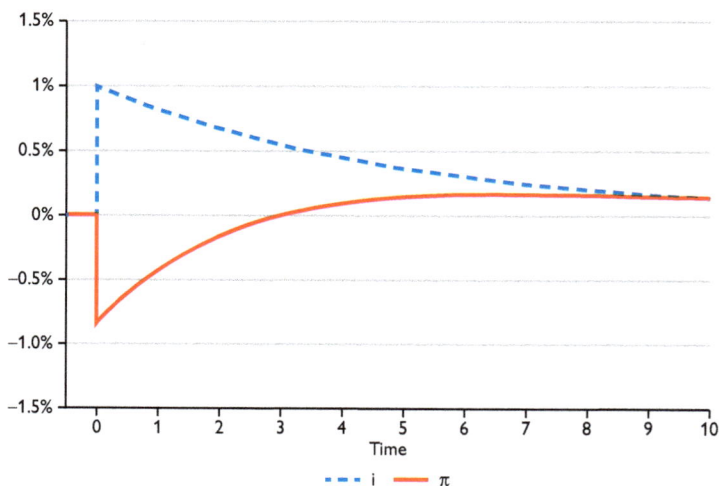

Figure 17.4. Response of a simple New Keynesian model to an interest-rate shock, with no change to primary surpluses. The model includes long-term debt.

Source: Author's calculations.

surpluses. Inflation declines initially, though it rises in the far future. With no change in fiscal policy, monetary policy can only move inflation around through time. The Fed faces what we might call unpleasant interest-rate arithmetic. There must be some inflation to devalue debt, but the central bank can choose when it happens, and whether it falls on long- or short-term bondholders.

Responding to the fiscal shock of figure 17.3 by the monetary response of figure 17.4 is a good thing to do. It leads to a smaller but longer-lasting inflation, which has smaller output effects. Central banks did err, if they did not want inflation, by not raising interest rates sooner. A Taylor-rule-like response remains a very good policy to follow.

Figure 17.4 holds primary surpluses constant. Standard New Keynesian solutions of this model produce greater inflation declines, but they do so by "passively" inducing a fiscal policy contraction (the negative of figure 17.3) along with the interest rate rise. In figure 17.4, I ask what the central bank can do by itself, without inducing tighter fiscal policy.

So, central banks did help to bring rates down faster than they otherwise would have, but at the potential cost of a slightly more stubborn medium-run inflation. That too is roughly consistent with the facts.

Next I examine how other theories of inflation deal with the recent surge and decline.

Money

After forty years in the desert of monetary policy, monetarists are crowing that the money supply rose substantially ahead of the recent inflation. Is money the answer?

The view that the price level is determined by the money supply (MV=PY) suffers a fundamental theoretical flaw: It requires that the government bank control the money supply. If the government does not do so, by following an interest-rate target or otherwise letting money supply be endogenous, MV=PY determines M, not P. But facts are more important than theory.

Fiscal theory and monetarism agree: A helicopter drop of money causes inflation. In fiscal theory, money is just very short-term government debt. But if a helicopter drop came with an announcement that taxes would rise tomorrow, just enough to soak up all the extra money, would there still be inflation? That ought to worry monetarists.

Fiscal theory and monetarism disagree on a different question: What if the government *exchanged* $5 trillion of money for $5 trillion of debt? To a monetarist, money is money: This experiment has exactly the same effect as

giving people $5 trillion of money. To a fiscal theorist, the exchange has no
first-order effect at all. There is no "wealth" effect, just a second-order "portfolio composition" effect.

Indeed, most of the famous examples that money causes inflation result from
money printed to finance deficits. When has too much money caused inflation
for a government whose economy was growing smartly, and whose fiscal affairs
were in good order, but whose central bank bought too many bonds?

Wouldn't it be lovely if the government were to run an experiment for
us? First, exchange $3 trillion of money for debt. Buy $3 trillion of bonds,
and issue $3 trillion new reserves in exchange. (Banks can freely exchange
reserves for cash.) See what inflation this causes. Second, after that has settled
down, print up $3 trillion of new money, and hand it out. Handing money out
counts as transfer payments and adds to the budget deficit. Monetarism says
that these two operations should have exactly the same inflationary effect.
Fiscal theory says that only the second will cause inflation.

Our government just ran just about exactly this experiment. Figure 17.5
illustrates.

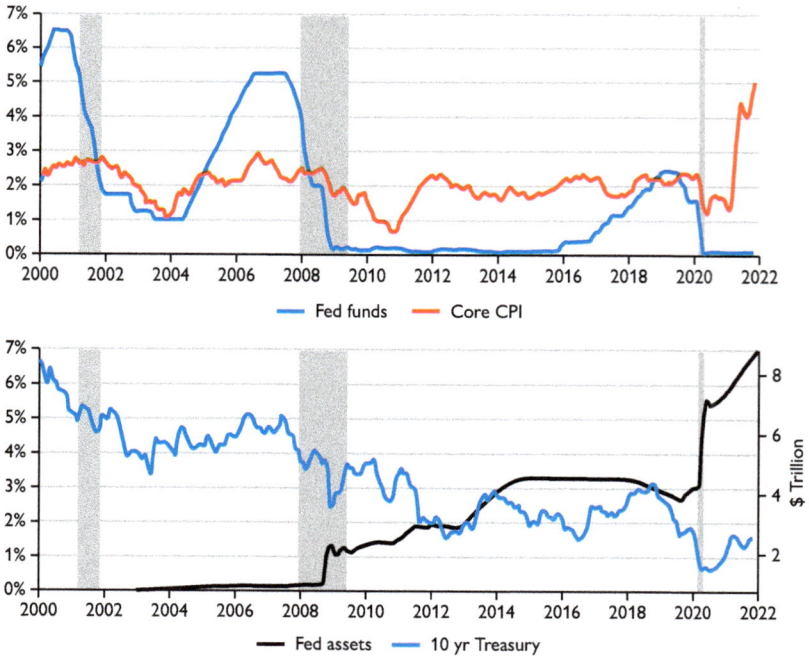

Figure 17.5. Federal funds rate, core CPI (Consumer Price Index), and Fed assets.
Source: FRED.

In the quantitative easing era, the Fed bought more than $4 trillion of bonds in three great waves of quantitative easing. You can see this in the "Fed assets" line. Reserves, a Fed liability, increased the same amount. Before 2008, reserves were below $50 billion. This nearly hundredfold increase in money should have caused hyperinflation. As seen in the "core CPI" line, this massive open market operation had no visible effect at all on inflation.

During and after the COVID-19 pandemic, the Fed bought a similar amount of Treasuries, raising reserves even more, but this time to fund a deficit without any plans for debt repayment. This one caused a wave of inflation, peaking at 8%. It is rare in macroeconomics to be handed such a decisive experiment of such a fundamental prediction that distinguishes theories.

Supply Shocks and Other Stories

Our politicians reacted to inflation with a rousing "round up the usual suspects": monopoly, greed, price gouging, hoarding. More seriously, economists and central bankers have blamed "relative demand" and "supply shocks" (or "supply-chain shocks" if you want to sound fancy) for inflation. In the former, people rotated demand from restaurants to Pelotons in the pandemic, driving up the price of Pelotons. In the latter, production and importation of all sorts of durable goods were hampered by the pandemic.

All of these stories suffer from a common fallacy: They confuse *relative* prices with the price *level*. If you can't get chips to make TVs, or can't make TVs because the factory is locked down, TV prices must go up *relative* to restaurant prices or to wages. We must all get the signal to buy fewer TVs. But why do TV prices go up, rather than wages or restaurant prices go down? Why does the price of *everything* go up? Even more clearly, if demand shifts from restaurants to TVs, why doesn't the price of restaurants go down?

Inflation is a rise in the price level, the common component of all prices that goes up. One does not raise the price level by raising all prices relative to each other!

Inflation always comes from demand. Loosely speaking, we must have the money to pay the higher prices for TVs and the higher prices for restaurants.

Now supply and relative-demand shocks were part of the story. When there is a relative-price shock, some prices must go up relative to others. The government prefers that prices do not go down, on the view that price declines are more economically damaging than price rises. So the government "accommodates" the relative price shock with monetary or fiscal largesse, so that no prices have to actually decline. Hence, in an order-of-events sense, yes, the supply shock led to the inflation. But the supply shock is the carrot that led the horse of monetary and fiscal policy to pull the cart of inflation. The carrot didn't move the cart. In the chain of causality, one might say that it is the pandemic that caused inflation, since it caused the supply shocks that caused the demand response that caused the inflation. Or one might say that a lab leak in China caused the inflation. But people would notice how silly it is to say, "Lab leaks cause inflation." Well, supply shocks are no different.

This point is hidden in standard models. In most New Keynesian models, such as the one I wrote down above, each equation has shocks. In particular, modelers write the Phillips curve as:

$$\pi_t = \beta E_t \pi_{t+1} + \kappa x_t + u_t.$$

They call the disturbance a "supply" shock. Well, you can see how a rise in u_t is likely to produce a rise in inflation π_t. And a formal accounting will find that shocks to this equation do, in fact, account for much of the observed inflation. (Smets and Wouters [2024] is a good example.)

But you still have to ask: How do people get the money to afford the higher prices? Where is the "nominal anchor"? New Keynesian models all do have a nominal anchor, either money-supply or fiscal theory. In some treatments, the central bank issues more money in order to follow the interest-rate target. In others, it issues more government debt. But somebody has to move the nominal anchor! A "supply" shock *without* movement in the nominal anchor doesn't cause inflation.

Monetary-Fiscal Interactions
How do monetary and fiscal policies interact, especially looking forward to the possibility of renewed inflation in the shadow of large ongoing debts and deficits?

Higher interest rates are thought to lower inflation. But higher interest rates make fiscal matters worse, through three channels. First, higher real interest rates mean higher interest costs on the debt. This is a first-order effect: At 100% debt-to-GDP ratio, a 1-percentage-point-higher interest rate means that the deficit rises by 1 percentage point of GDP due to interest costs on the debt. Second, if higher interest rates successfully lower inflation, nominal bondholders receive a windfall, being paid back in more valuable currency. Equivalently, nominal payments do not decline, but nominal tax revenues do decline when inflation declines. Taxes must rise or spending must decline to make up the difference. Third, the whole mechanism by which higher interest rates lower inflation is via a softer economy. But a softer economy—or even a recession—leads to financial bailouts, "automatic stabilizer" payments such as unemployment insurance, lower tax revenue due to lower GDP, and deliberate fiscal stimulus programs.

Thus, higher interest rates pour fiscal gas on the inflation fire, offsetting whatever other inflation-lowering effects they may have.

In all conventional models of monetary economics, a monetary contraction *includes* higher taxes and lower spending, either immediately or in the future to pay off larger debt, in order to pay these additional fiscal costs. It's not accurate to call them "monetary" models of disinflation; they are "monetary-fiscal" models of disinflation, because both monetary and fiscal policy (in present-value terms) tighten to produce disinflation. It's easy enough to see: Look at the plots of real interest rates. If real interest rates rise following the shock, there are higher interest costs on the debt. If inflation goes down, bondholders are paid a windfall. Someone has to pay for these costs, and that someone is taxpayers!

Conversely, what if fiscal authorities do not cooperate, and refuse to raise taxes or lower spending? This is a relevant policy question as well as a theoretical question. A government may not be able or willing to tighten fiscal policy to support monetary policy.

In all current models, *higher interest rates that are not accompanied by a fiscal tightening* (either immediately or in the future—i.e., a rise in the present value of surpluses) *do not lower inflation*. We are left with the frightening possibility that most of what we thought of as the "effect of interest rates" was in fact the effect of induced fiscal tightening, and that central banks may be powerless without that tightening.

Figure 17.6 documents this claim for the standard New Keynesian model. This is the perfectly standard three-equation model, with no fiscal-theory funny business:

$$x_t = E_t x_{t+1} - \sigma \left(i_t - E_t \pi_{t+1} \right)$$
$$\pi_t = \beta E_t \pi_{t+1} + \kappa x_t$$
$$i_t = \phi \pi_t + u_t .$$

In the left-hand panel, I plot the standard exercise, the response of interest rates and inflation to a shock to an AR(1) disturbance, $u_t = 0.7 u_{t-1} + \varepsilon_t$.

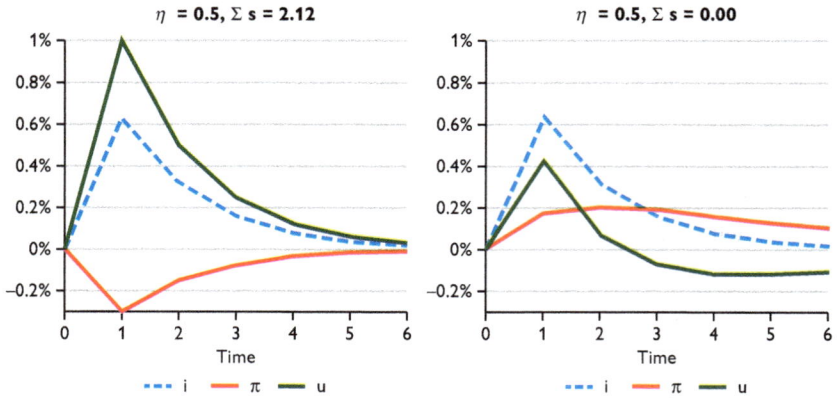

Figure 17.6. Effect of a monetary policy shock in the standard New Keynesian model. Left: AR(1) monetary policy shock. Right: shock reverse engineered to produce the same interest-rate path, but no change in fiscal policy.

Source: Author's calculations.

The interest rate rises, and inflation declines. (Be careful: the *interest rate i* is not the same thing as the monetary policy shock u.) What do you mean, monetary policy alone can't lower inflation?

But look again. The nominal interest rate is above the inflation rate. The real interest rate has risen, and with it, interest costs on the debt. Who paid those higher interest costs? The first-period lower inflation is a windfall to short-term bondholders. Who paid for that? In every New Keynesian model there is a footnote about passive fiscal policy, usually that lump-sum taxes come in to pay any of these costs. It is uncommon to actually calculate what those lump-sum taxes are, or to wonder what happens should they not materialize. Here I calculate those taxes, for a 100% debt-to-GDP ratio. The answer is that primary surpluses must rise by 2.2% of GDP. This is a joint monetary-fiscal disinflation.

What can monetary policy do without fiscal help? The right-hand panel answers this question. In this model there are multiple shock paths $\{u_t\}$ that produce the same interest-rate path $\{i_t\}$. I reverse engineer a different disturbance path $\{u_t\}$ that produces the same AR(1)-shaped interest-rate path $\{i_t\}$ as in the left-hand panel, but requires no change to the "passive" fiscal policy—no lump-sum taxes, please. So, by construction, the path of observed interest rates $\{i_t\}$ is the same in the left- and right-hand panels. (The path of disturbances includes both an interest-rate policy, the observed path of interest rates, and an "equilibrium-selection" policy. Many different inflation paths are consistent with a given interest-rate path, and the interest rate rule includes a component that selects one of those paths. The change in disturbance here changes the equilibrium-selection part without changing the interest-rate path.)

Inflation is different in this simulation. The same observed interest-rate policy, without fiscal support, produces a different inflation. And that inflation *rises*. As promised, higher interest rates without a contemporaneous fiscal tightening do not lower inflation, even in this completely standard New Keynesian model. It is specified and solved in the entirely standard way. I just read and calculated the footnote about lump-sum taxes.

Intuitively, you see that inflation is tied to the interest-rate path. With no change in surpluses, the sum of interest costs on the debt equals the devaluation of outstanding debt by first-period inflation. You can see how an early period of positive interest costs is matched by a later period of lower interest costs. The initial inflation also amounts to a partial default on outstanding debt to pay for the somewhat larger average interest costs.

This example is taken from Cochrane (2024), which investigates many others to make the same point. There is no parameterization of the three-equation model in which higher interest rates lower inflation without fiscal support.

Even in the traditional adaptive-expectations model, higher interest rates cannot lower inflation without fiscal support.

Figure 17.7 displays an example. The model is a traditional adaptive-expectations model. There are no forward-looking terms in the IS curve, and everywhere that there should be a rational-expectations $E_t \pi_{t+1}$, I use past inflation π_{t-1} instead. The model is the continuous-time version of:

$$x_t = -\sigma \left(i_t - \pi_{t-1} \right)$$

$$\pi_t = \pi_{t-1} + \kappa x_t$$

$$i_t = \phi \pi_t + u_t$$

with $\sigma\kappa = 1$; $\phi = 1.5$. I simulate the response to a permanent rise in monetary policy disturbance. Inflation declines. As inflation declines, via the Taylor rule, the interest rate follows along, so we end up at a new lower steady-state inflation. This is an embodiment of the standard story told of the 1980s. What do you mean there is no model of a monetary disinflation?

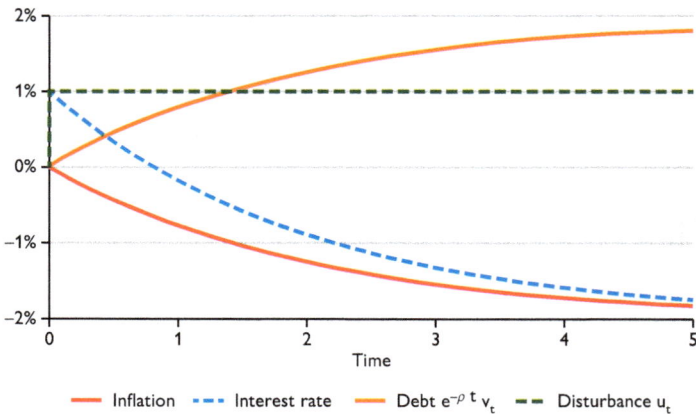

Figure 17.7. Disinflation in an adaptive-expectations model.
Source: Cochrane (2024).

Look again. There is a long period of high real interest rates. Bondholders get paid off in more valuable money. Who pays? If nobody pays, the graph tracks the discounted value of the debt. That value grows forever, meaning that the transversality condition is violated. Without tighter fiscal policy, this is not the answer. Fiscal policy must also tighten to create this answer.

In Cochrane (2024), I work out how inflation responds to interest rates in this model when fiscal policy does not change. The answer is, no path of interest rates can permanently lower inflation without a fiscal tightening. The intuition is straightforward: Higher real interest rates lower inflation, and lower real interest rates raise inflation. But the average real interest rate must be zero if the average change to interest costs of the debt are zero. You can't push inflation down without positive average real interest rates.

Figure 17.4 is the best I can do for monetary policy without a fiscal tightening. Inflation is temporarily reduced but comes back in the end.

What about the 1980s, you ask? Isn't that the paradigmatic case of monetary tightening that vanquished inflation—despite even the notorious "Reagan deficits"? No, that too was a joint monetary, fiscal, and microeconomic reform.

Figure 17.8 presents inflation and the federal funds rate in the Great Inflation and disinflation of the 1970s and 1980s. There were three great surges of inflation. In each event, the Federal Reserve did raise interest rates, and more promptly than it did in 2022. In 1975, inflation eased despite

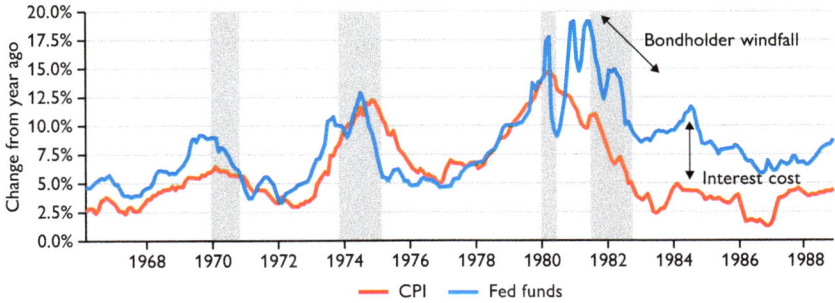

Figure 17.8. Inflation and federal funds rate in the Great Inflation and disinflation.
Source: FRED.

interest rates that fell before inflation fell, another puzzle for standard doctrine. The quiescent period of 1977, with inflation easing but still persistent, may be an ominous reminder of the present moment. Inflation then surged through 1980. The Fed raised interest rates once, and retreated in the face of a sharp recession. The Fed raised rates again, to nearly 20%, and left rates high through a bruising recession. Inflation finally came down by the mid-1980s.

In its conventional interpretation, this is the paradigmatic episode for strong monetary policy, in the form of persistently high interest rates, pushing down inflation. It is usually interpreted through the Old Keynesian dynamics of figure 17.7.

But that isn't the whole story. Notice in figure 17.8 a decade of high real interest rates. These are high interest costs on the debt. Who paid those? Notice that investors who bought bonds at the high yields of 1980 were paid off in dollars worth a great deal more than expected, after inflation fell to 2.5%. Who paid that windfall? Who paid for the deficits induced by the recessions of 1980 and 1982?

Figure 17.9 presents the ratio of primary surplus to outstanding debt. In fiscal theory,

$$\frac{B_{t-1}}{P_t} = E_t \sum_{j=0}^{\infty} \frac{1}{R_{t,t+j}} s_{t+j},$$

surplus relative to debt outstanding is the central measure of the inflationary impact of a surplus, just as total dividends relative to the value of stock outstanding measures the effect of dividends on prices.

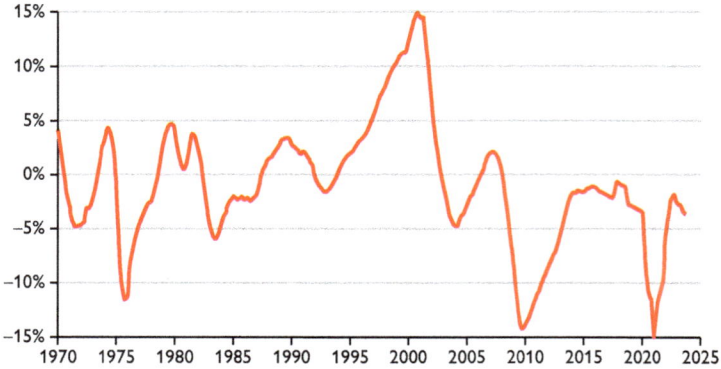

Figure 17.9. Primary surplus divided by federal debt held by the public.
Source: Author's calculations.

The deficits of the early 1970s and mid-1970s were quite large, suggesting a fiscal impulse for inflation. To our focus on disinflation, however, note that the large deficits of the early Reagan years were in fact not quite so large *primary* deficits, especially when one considers the huge recession of the time. Much of the deficit that attracted attention at the time was higher interest costs on the debt. And then surpluses surged. In fiscal theory terms, the present value of surpluses on the right-hand side—the answer to "Who paid?"—is simple: Taxpayers did. By the 2000s, economists were writing papers about what to do when the federal debt was paid off.

The 1980s included a range of fiscal reforms as well as tight monetary policy. The years 1982 and 1986 saw huge tax reforms that lowered the top marginal rate from 70% to 28%, while broadening the base. A Social Security reform put that program on a sound footing for several decades—a particularly noteworthy reform for the present value of surpluses. Fiscal theory is not about current deficits, remember, it is about faith in the government's ability and will to repay debt and run sober fiscal policy over decades. Deregulation, or at least an absence of further regulation, spurred economic growth. For these and other reasons, economic growth accelerated. Tax revenue equals tax rate times income, and higher income generates fiscal surpluses more reliably than any other means.

To emphasize this point, figure 17.10 plots the total surplus relative to the amount of debt, along with the unemployment rate. United States surpluses and deficits are driven almost entirely by the business cycle, not the widely ballyhooed changes in tax or spending policies.

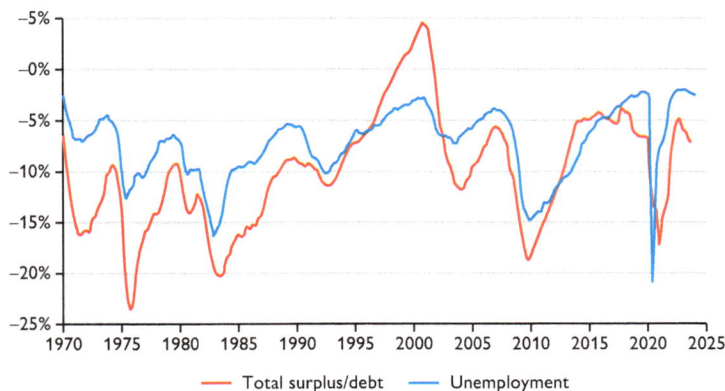

Figure 17.10. Total surplus divided by federal debt held by the public, and the negative of the unemployment rate.

Source: Author's calculations.

The present value of surpluses *did* pay for the disinflation of the 1980s. That's an identity, really, as the right-hand side of the fiscal theory holds generally when discounting by the government bond return. But it's good to see the elements of that identity. Surpluses *did* rise, to pay higher interest costs of the debt, the windfall to bondholders, and the extra debts of the 1980–82 recession. The 1980–84 period represented a joint fiscal, monetary, and microeconomic reform, not monetary policy acting alone. It is a mistake to look at this experience and infer what the Fed can do when acting all by itself.

But 1980 had a 25% debt-to-GDP ratio. We now face 100% debt to GDP. We face expectations of a far larger bailout and stimulus in any recession. A bipartisan Social Security and health expense reform seems a distant political dream. Can the Fed count on this sort of fiscal support if it needs to repeat 1982 to stop the next inflation? The history of Latin America is full of instances in which central banks tried to stop inflation without fiscal cooperation. Inflation fell briefly, then surged again (Kehoe and Nicolini 2021). Will the US Congress, or European governments, sit still for central banks raising their interest costs by multiple percentages of GDP, or will the financial repression of the early post–World War II era return?

The Future

Figure 17.11 reproduces the Congressional Budget Office's (CBO) long-term debt and deficit projections. These are projections, not forecasts or

Next crises?

Federal debt held by the public

Deficits

Primary deficit or surplus   Net interest outlays   Total deficit or surplus

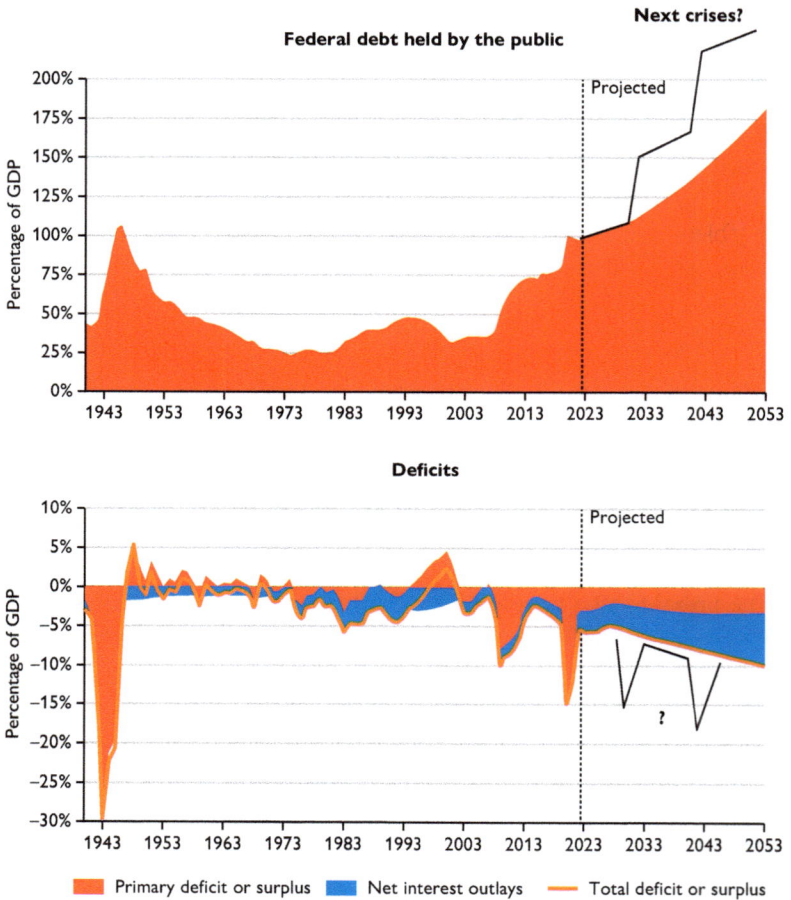

Figure 17.11. Congressional Budget Office (CBO) long-term projections.

Source: CBO and author's calculations. Black lines are author art illustrating what may happen in future crises.

conditional expectations. This will not happen. The CBO says as much, by labeling the debt path "unsustainable." They are projections of what will happen under current law, plus economic assumptions. The only question is how the future will differ from these projections.

The CBO projections are optimistic, in that they assume nothing bad ever happens again. The economic projections do not include the once-in-a-century crises that we seem to have every decade now. Note that the recent run-up in debt happened in two waves: the 2008 financial crisis and the 2020 COVID expansion. The next crisis will surely have a similar effect. So, under current law, something like the black lines is a more likely projection.

The problem is not debt. We can pay off even a 100% debt-to-GDP ratio if we return to small surpluses and strong economic growth. Conversely, if we continue to run 5%-of-GDP primary deficits forever, even defaulting or inflating away the debt will not solve the problem. Indeed, that would make the problem worse: After inflation or default, who will lend us the annual 5% of GDP? The problem is that structural deficit.

The conventional worry is that the indicated smooth path will eventually lead to inflation or debt crisis. I worry about a sharper scenario: What happens in the next crisis? Suppose, say, that China invades Taiwan. Pacific trade stops; a gigantic financial crisis and global recession break out. Our government would want to borrow or print, say, $10 trillion, to bail out, to stimulate, to keep people and businesses afloat, and, this time, to quickly fund military expenses. And all the time, entitlements remain unreformed, and the US throws trillions down various ratholes. Who will give $10 trillion of savings to the US government, believing it will be repaid? Will the experience of 2021–23, in which the same investors took a roughly 10% haircut due to inflation, not weigh on their faith? Will they say no, provoking an even quicker inflation? Will the US even be able to borrow that much? The loss of fiscal space is more worrying than a slow march of full-employment surpluses.

On a smaller scale, the same lack of fiscal capacity is what threatens a coordinated monetary-fiscal reform to contain inflation, should it break out. If there is no fiscal space to pay higher interest costs on the debt, monetary policy is unlikely to be able to lower inflation.

Returning to somewhat normal fiscal policy is not economically difficult. Our economies do not face external threats. Again, pro-growth economic policy is easier than tax hikes or spending cuts. Everything that raises GDP raises tax revenue.

References

Cochrane, John H. 2023. *The Fiscal Theory of the Price Level.* Princeton University Press.

Cochrane, John H. 2024. "Expectations and the Neutrality of Interest Rates." *Review of Economic Dynamics* 53 (July): 194–223.

Kehoe, Timothy, and Juan Pablo Nicolini. 2021. *A Monetary and Fiscal History of Latin America, 1960–2017.* University of Minnesota Press.

Smets, Frank, and Raf Wouters. 2024. "Fiscal Backing, Inflation, and US Business Cycles." CEPR Discussion Paper 19791. CEPR Press.

18

Crumbling Boundaries and the Risks to Central Bank Independence

Charles I. Plosser

The debate over the appropriate relationship between monetary policy and fiscal policy is an old one. However, it has taken on renewed significance since the crisis of 2007–8 as both the Fed and the Treasury have initiated policies that breached accepted norms that had largely been in place since the Treasury-Fed Accord of 1951. My view is that these actions have undermined the institutional arrangements intended to support the independence of our central bank and frayed the boundaries between monetary and fiscal policies.[1]

Sargent (2011a, 2011b) discusses the history and struggles of economists and economic theories to provide guidance as to where to "draw the lines between (1) markets for money and credit, and (2) monetary and fiscal policies." He characterizes these challenges as trying to balance stability versus efficiency. As he says: "Ambiguities and uncertainties about the path forward arise partly because the choices are difficult and involve conflicts of interest that thrust us beyond macroeconomics and into politics." I do not pretend to answer the deep conceptual problems that Thomas Sargent describes. But I do share the view that choices involve conflicts of interest and political economy issues that have important implications for how to "draw the lines."

The economic historian Douglass North was recognized for his work on the role that institutions play in economic growth.[2] He argued that institutions arise as a way for heterogenous actors to constrain interactions among parties, both public and private, to ameliorate frictions and hard to resolve conflicts of interest. These institutional arrangements take the form of laws, contracts, business and corporate arrangements, and even constitutions that establish the institutions of government. The institutions survive because, or as long as, they effectively resolve or manage these conflicts.

The evolution of central banks can be viewed in the same light. Central banks have been around for a long time and the institutional arrangements have evolved. Through much of their history central banks were often private or quasi-private enterprises that operated in a world where the price level was determined by a commodity or metallic standard of one kind or another. In such regimes the central bank, if one existed at all, was often involved with minting metallic coins or executing transactions to maintain the value of the currency in terms of a metallic standard. The gold standard was such a frame-work, serving as a commitment device that tied the hands of central banks, and the fiscal authorities, in ways that helped define the boundaries between monetary and fiscal policies by limiting the scope and potential conflicts for independent monetary policy actions.

Fluctuations in the international price of gold and wartime demands for spending often spurred unwelcome fluctuations in the price level, including disruptive devaluations, often driven by constraints on government budgets and difficulties issuing debt or raising taxes. This fueled a desire by govern-ments to discard the constraints imposed by the gold standard and move to a fiat currency regime that permitted greater flexibility. The freedom to use the printing press (that is, to create fiat money) as a means to finance government spending freed governments from the constraints of the gold standard, yet it also heightened the "stability versus efficiency" tensions and exacerbated the basic conflict between the short-term political demands to finance the gov-ernment's budget and the longer-term demands for a stable currency. While technology and other innovations have changed over time, this fundamental conflict remains at the heart of the institutional design of the central bank and the desire to establish boundaries between fiscal policy and monetary policy.

Thus, the concept of an "independent" central bank has arisen as an insti-tutional response to some of the conflicts of interest and political problems alluded to by Sargent and many others. Whether this is an optimal solution in some economic sense or merely a sufficient solution is not something that we know. The evidence, however, indicates that the more independent central banks have generally yielded better economic outcomes than other arrange-ments that have been tried in the fiat money era. For example, economies that have central-bank functions tightly controlled by the Treasury more often experience episodes of high and unstable inflation and poor economic growth than those economies in which central banks acted with more independence.

In a democracy, an independent central bank does not and cannot mean that it has unlimited or unrestricted powers, nor does it mean that it is unaccountable. The desirable degree of independence is achieved by limiting the goals and the powers of the central bank, and of the fiscal authorities, in ways that seek to address the thorny conflicts of interest. Of course, government maintains the upper hand since it can change the law and thus the institution, but the goal is to make that solution a "costly" one. Put differently, the institutional arrangements seek to tie the hands of both the monetary and the fiscal authorities in ways that make the commitments and the boundaries more credible. Such commitment devices are almost always imperfect and the temptation to resort to discretion, or to violate the boundaries, can be tempting.

The new threats to Fed independence have arisen due to important changes in the use of the Fed's balance sheet initiated by the Fed itself, either alone or in tandem with the fiscal authorities. Some actions were intended to influence the allocation of credit, such as purchases of mortgage-backed securities (MBS) and various lending programs intended to support firms and businesses in the private sector. Such lending is a form of fiscal policy that transfers private risks to public or taxpayer risks.

Other actions by the fiscal authorities explicitly tapped the Fed's balance sheet to fund off-budget spending. The Fed and the Treasury also used emergency provisions in the Federal Reserve Act (section 13[3]) to support private institutions and investors in a manner it had never before exercised.[3] Application of these lending programs, often characterized as "lender-of-last-resort" operations, lacked systematic guidelines governing their use and limitations.

The Fed also adopted an important change in its operating regime. It did so to accommodate the extraordinary increase in its balance sheet due to credit policies and asset purchases in response to near zero interest rates. The new regime pays interest to banks on their holdings of reserves at the risk-free rate while flooding the banks with reserves. The new regime is often referred to as a "floor system," where the relevant interest rate for setting monetary policy is the interest rate paid on reserves (IOR). At that rate, the Fed can, in principle, flood the banking system with reserve without altering its policy rate. The old regime, referred to as a "corridor system," required the Fed to control the quantity of reserves to keep the policy at the target.[4] The changes permit the Fed to use its balance sheet in different and unconstrained ways. In the context of Sargent's (2011b) discussion, it eliminates the wedge between the markets for money and credit.

The highly discretionary actions of its lending activities contribute to moral hazard, incentivizing more risk-taking rather than stability. Along with the new operating regime, these actions contribute to the breaking down of the boundaries between monetary and fiscal policy and place the independence of the Fed at risk, as will be discussed further below.

I want to touch on three interrelated and familiar aspects of the institutional framework that help draw the lines between monetary and fiscal policies, and how the events and policy choices adopted during and subsequent to the 2007–8 recession are affecting the delicate balancing of the conflicts of interest that exist. These issues include (1) governance, (2) mandates or scope of responsibilities, and (3) limitations or constraints on the authorities granted a central bank.

Governance

The political failures of the early attempts to establish a central bank in the US were so distasteful that it took nearly three-quarters of a century after the closing of the Second Bank of the United States before the Congress created the Federal Reserve System in 1913. It was designed as a decentralized institution with a geographical dispersion of semiprivate Reserve Banks and a Board of Governors in Washington. Part of the motivation was to support a more decentralized decision-making process, with a diversity of views and less focus on the financial centers and the short-run politics in Washington.[5]

After the collapse of the gold standard, changes were made in the Fed's governance structure. The Banking Act of 1935 removed the Treasury secretary and the comptroller of the currency from the Fed's governing board; granted governing board members fourteen-year terms; and established a new legal entity, the Federal Open Market Committee (FOMC), to govern the conduct of open market operations (the purchase and sale of government securities). These changes reduced the fiscal authorities' direct participation in the governing board, but granted greater authority to the politically appointed Board of Governors in open market decisions relative to the Reserve Bank presidents. These changes are evidence of the struggle to establish boundaries between monetary and fiscal policy.

The Treasury-Fed Accord of 1951 was an important milestone in support of Fed independence. It was an agreement between the Fed and the Treasury that the central bank would control its own balance sheet rather than tailor its purchases and sales of government securities at the behest of the Treasury.

Governance remains an important element of the institutional design of an independent central bank. In response to some of the criticisms of Fed policies during the Great Financial Crisis (GFC) and the COVID-19 pandemic, you hear suggestions that the Fed needs to be held more accountable.

To some, that translates into "the Fed needs to be more political." For example, it is sometimes argued that Federal Reserve Bank presidents should be political appointees, or that they not be permitted to vote on monetary policy matters. Others have suggested more direct involvement in monetary policy by the executive branch, which would completely vitiate the boundaries and the spirit of the 1951 Treasury-Fed Accord. Such proposals undermine independence by inviting more political interference, exactly the sort of conflict of interest that independence seeks to address. As I argue below, a better way to promote more accountability is to limit or narrow the scope of responsibilities and authorities of the central bank rather than seek greater political interference.[6]

Mandate or Scope of Responsibilities

An important mechanism to support central-bank independence is to limit the breadth and scope of the central bank's mandate. Narrow mandates focus the central bank on limited, well-articulated objectives that make it easier to evaluate the institution's success or failure and thus to hold it accountable. Narrow mandates also serve to discourage or limit the central bank's discretion to use its powers or authorities to justify actions that are not clearly related to the mandate. This also helps provide the central bank with the grounds to resist requests to engage in activities that more appropriately rest with the fiscal authorities. Unfortunately, the trend in the US, and in some other countries, is to expand the scope of central-bank mandates, weakening the institutional framework that supports independence.

When establishing the longer-term goals and objectives for any organization, it is important that the objectives be achievable. Assigning unachievable objectives is a recipe for failure. In the case of a central bank, it could result in the loss of public trust and confidence and thus undermine its effectiveness in achieving its price-stability objective. For example, the active pursuit of the maximum employment dimension of the Fed's so-called dual mandate has been, and continues to be, problematic for the Fed.[7] The FOMC notes in its statement on longer-run goals and objectives adopted in 2012 that "the maximum level of employment is largely determined by nonmonetary factors that affect the structure and dynamics of the labor market." The statement goes on to say that this explains why the Fed does not specify a numerical target for the object. This acknowledges, appropriately in my view, the weakness of the case that maximum employment constitutes an achievable objective for monetary policy or that there is a mechanism for accountability.[8]

The risks and consequences of mission creep or expanding the goals and expectations of monetary policy is not just a recent concern. In his presidential address to the American Economic Association over fifty years ago, Milton Friedman (1968) warned us that "we are in danger of assigning to monetary policy a larger role than it can perform, in danger of asking it to accomplish tasks it cannot achieve, and, as a result, in danger of preventing it from making the contribution that it is capable of making."

Central Bank Authorities and Operating Restrictions

The authorities or powers granted a central bank are frequently aligned with the role and mandates it is assigned. Most countries today operate under a fiat money regime, so central banks are typically given the responsibility to protect and preserve the value or purchasing power of the currency. To achieve this goal, central banks are often given the authority to buy and sell assets to manage the growth of money and credit. The ability to buy and sell assets gives the Fed considerable power to intervene in financial markets not only through the quantity of its assets it chooses to hold but also the composition of those assets.[9]

The Federal Reserve Act broadly constrains the Fed to purchases of US government securities, bought and sold in the open market. The Fed does not have general authority to buy private-sector securities, such as equities or corporate bonds, nor can it buy securities issued by state and local governments. The purpose of these limitations is to prevent the Fed from directly intervening in the allocation of credit, maintaining as neutral a stance as possible with respect to market outcomes. The logic behind this limitation is to protect the Fed from political pressure from private agents or Congress to provide special treatment for particular industries, sectors, or firms. Unfortunately, the willingness of the Fed to use its balance sheet to engage in large-scale purchases of non-Treasury securities opens the door for many parties to seek reasons to call on the Fed for credit support.[10]

Between 1951 and 2007 the Fed followed such a "Treasuries only" policy. About 99% of the growth in the Fed's balance sheet during this fifty-six-year period is accounted for by outright holdings of US Treasury securities. In August 2007, Treasuries accounted for 90% of the Fed's assets. However, by 2015 Treasuries constituted just 55% of Fed assets. By June 2024 Treasuries still only made up 62% of its portfolio. The big difference is accounted for by Fed holdings of MBS.

As mentioned earlier, another operational change adopted by the Fed was to pay interest on reserves. Sargent (2011b) and SOMC colleague Peter

Ireland (2014b) offer insightful discussions of the economic consequences that revolve around stability and indeterminacies of prices when there is no wedge between the markets for money and credit versus the efficiencies gained when that wedge is eliminated. Sargent argues that paying interest on reserves "subverts independence of the central bank and the fiscal authorities." In Plosser (2010b, 2011) and in subsequent papers, I argued that the Fed should seek to shrink its balance sheet and return to a regime similar to it used prior to the GFC. Such a regime could still pay IOR as long as the rate was below market rates so a wedge was maintained between the markets for money and credit.

Many at the Fed and elsewhere emphasize that an advantage of paying interest on reserves at market rates is that it divorces the size of the balance sheet from the Fed's interest-rate policy. This allows the Fed to buy and sell assets to pursue other objectives without altering its interest-rate policy. The "excess reserves" will have to be held by the banking system at the risk-free market rate. This framework is ripe for political abuse and exploitation.[11] What rules would constrain the Fed or the government from flooding the banking system with reserves or allow its unconstrained balance to be used by politicians or the Congress to curry favor with one firm, sector, or industry with government loans? What would prevent the Fed from purchasing large quantities of government debt? The perception or belief that the size and composition of the Fed's balance sheet represented a "new" free parameter to conduct credit allocation or support fiscal policy objectives is dangerous. The Fed would be dragged deep into a fiscal and political quagmire. It is a sure way for the Fed to lose its independence. Is that worth the expected gains in efficiency of a small wedge between the returns on money and the market's risk-free rate?

In Plosser (2022), I describe ways the Fed and Treasury could restore the boundaries. Among the suggestions are to require the Fed to return to a "Treasuries only" portfolio; require the Fed to return to an operating regime that constrains the size of the balance sheet to avoid potential politicization; eliminate or rewrite the emergency lending provision, section 13(3), so that the fiscal authorities have full responsibility and accountability for any lending decisions and residual risk. Independence could also be strengthened if the Fed was more transparent by articulating a set of rules for conducting monetary policy as well as for any credit policies it was authorized to take.

Let me conclude by saying that an independent central bank continues to play an important role in balancing the conflicts of interest among the monetary and fiscal demands of our government. That independence is achieved through constraints placed on the central bank and on the fiscal authorities that draw lines or set boundaries between monetary and fiscal policies. Unfortunately, the boundaries are eroding slowly but surely, and as a result independence will continue to fade.

Notes

1. In 2008 and 2009, Jeffrey Lacker, my colleague at the Fed and now a colleague on the Shadow Open Market Committee, and I began voicing concerns both inside the Fed and more publicly, of the longer-term dangers and risks of the policy approach that was being pursued. See, for example, Lacker (2008, 2009) and Plosser (2008, 2009, 2010a, 2010b, 2012, 2013, 2018). Plosser (2022) presents an overview of the evolution of Fed independence since the 1951 Treasury-Fed Accord and how actions by the Fed and the Treasury undermined the long-standing boundaries between monetary and fiscal policy, and the institutional constraints that help ensure the Fed's independence.

2. See, for example, North (1991). Like 2011 Nobel Prize recipient Sargent, North was awarded a Nobel Prize in Economics in 1993.

3. See Plosser (2022) and Lacker (2025, in this volume) for more detailed discussions of these lending activities and their consequences. It is noteworthy that the Fed did not resort to the discretionary powers of section 13(3) during other episodes of severe financial stress such as the savings and loan crisis, the failures of Enron or WorldCom, the bursting of the so-called tech bubble, or the financial turmoil surrounding the terrorist attack on 9/11.

4. See Goodfriend (2002) and Keister et al. (2008) for a more detailed description.

5. See Lacker (2024) for an interesting discussion of the evolution of the diversity of views at the Fed. He suggests that the decline in dissents by FOMC members reflects a shortage of diverse viewpoints within the Committee.

6. See Plosser (2008, 2013, 2016).

7. The "dual mandate" terminology itself is a peculiar interpretation of the legislative language. In 1978, Congress amended section 2A of the Federal Reserve Act. It instructs the FOMC to "maintain the *long run growth* of the monetary and credit aggregates *commensurate* with the economy's *long run* potential to increase production, so as to promote effectively the goals of maximum employment, stable prices, and moderate long-term interest rates." (Italics mine.) Many discussions about the mandate seem to forget the emphasis placed on the "long run" and instead offer an interpretation that stresses short-run employment and long-term inflation (rather than stable prices).

8. If this is not confusing enough, the Fed revised the 2012 statement on longer-run goals in 2020. It now reads that the "maximum level of employment is a broad based and inclusive goal that is not directly measurable and changes over time owing largely to nonmonetary factors that affect the structure and dynamics of the labor market." Levy and Plosser (2022, 2024), for example, discuss how the change in interpretation adopted by the Fed of this vague mandate influenced a significant

revision in its monetary policy strategy and its consequences. See also Eggertsson and Kohn (2023) and Ireland (2014a).

9. I follow Goodfriend and King (1988) when discussing variations in the central bank's balance sheet. They associate monetary policy with changes in the size of the balance sheet and changes in the composition of assets held as credit policy.

10. Many, if not most, of the lending programs put in place by the Fed could have been done by the fiscal authorities, Treasury or Congress.

11. See Plosser (2018, 2022), Mester (2025, in this volume), and Nelson (2025, in this volume).

References

Eggertsson, Gauti B., and Donald Kohn. 2023. "The Inflation Surge of the 2020s: The Role of Monetary Policy." Working Paper No. 87. Hutchins Center, Brookings Institution. August.

Friedman, Milton. 1968. "The Role of Monetary Policy." *American Economic Review* 58 (1): 1–17.

Goodfriend, Marvin. 2002. "Interest on Reserves and Monetary Policy." *Federal Reserve Bank of New York Economic Policy Review* 8 (1): 68–75.

Goodfriend, Marvin, and Robert G. King. 1988. "Financial Deregulation, Monetary Policy, and Central Banking." *Federal Reserve Bank of Richmond Economic Review* 74 (May/June): 3–22.

Ireland, Peter N. 2014a. "Shifting Perspectives on the Dual Mandate." Position paper, Shadow Open Market Committee, New York, NY. April 14.

Ireland, Peter N. 2014b. "The Macroeconomic Effects of Interest on Reserves." *Macroeconomic Dynamics* 18:1271–1312.

Keister, Todd, Antoine Martin, and James McAndrews. 2008. "Divorcing Money from Monetary Policy." *Federal Reserve Bank of New York Economic Policy Review* 14 (2): 41–56.

Lacker, Jeffrey M. 2008. "Financial Stability and Central Banks." Presented at the Distinguished Speakers Seminar, European Economic and Financial Centre, London, United Kingdom. June 5.

Lacker, Jeffrey M. 2009. "Government Lending and Monetary Policy." *Business Economics* 44 (3): 136–42.

Lacker, Jeffrey M. 2024. "Governance and Diversity at the Federal Reserve." Policy Brief. Mercatus Center at George Mason University. January 8.

Lacker, Jeffrey M. 2025. "Federal Reserve Credit Policy and the Shadow Open Market Committee." In *Fifty Years of the Shadow Open Market Committee: A Retrospective on Its Role in Monetary Policy*, edited by Michael D. Bordo, Jeffrey M. Lacker, Mickey D. Levy, and John B. Taylor. Hoover Institution Press.

Levy, Mickey D., and Charles I. Plosser. 2022. "The Murky Future of Monetary Policy." *Federal Reserve Bank of St. Louis Review* 104 (3): 178–88. First appeared as "The Murky Future of Monetary Policy." Economics Working Paper No. 20119, Hoover Institution, October 1, 2020.

Levy, Mickey D., and Charles I. Plosser. 2024. "The Fed's Strategic Approach to Monetary Policy Needs a Reboot." Economics Working Paper No. 24018. Hoover Institution. May 2–3.

Lucas, Deborah. 2019. "Some Heretical Thoughts on Central Bank Independence." Position paper, Shadow Open Market Committee, New York, NY. September 27.

McCallum, Bennett T. 2010. "The Rationale for Independent Monetary Policy." Position paper, Shadow Open Market Committee, New York, NY. March 26.

Mester, Loretta J. 2025. "The Fed's Ample Reserves Monetary Policy Operating Framework: It Isn't as Simple as It Looks." In *Fifty Years of the Shadow Open Market Committee: A Retrospective on Its Role in Monetary Policy*, edited by Michael D. Bordo, Jeffrey M. Lacker, Mickey D. Levy, and John B. Taylor. Hoover Institution Press.

Nelson, Bill. 2025. "From the Floor Back to the Corridor: Why the Choice of Monetary Policy Implementation Framework Matters." In *Fifty Years of the Shadow Open Market Committee: A Retrospective on Its Role in Monetary Policy*, edited by Michael D. Bordo, Jeffrey M. Lacker, Mickey D. Levy, and John B. Taylor. Hoover Institution Press.

North, Douglass C. 1991. "Institutions." *Journal of Economic Perspectives* 5 (1): 97–112.

Plosser, Charles I. 2008. "The Limits of Central Banking." Speech at the Council on Foreign Relations, New York, NY. October 8.

Plosser, Charles I. 2009. "Ensuring Sound Monetary Policy in the Aftermath of Crisis." Speech at the US Monetary Policy Forum, The Initiative on Global Markets, New York, NY. February 27.

Plosser, Charles I. 2010a. "The Federal Reserve System: Balancing Independence and Accountability." Speech at the World Affairs Council of Philadelphia, Philadelphia, PA. February 17.

Plosser, Charles I. 2010b. "Credible Commitments and Monetary Policy after the Crisis." Speech at the Swiss National Bank Monetary Policy Conference, Zurich, Switzerland. September 24.

Plosser, Charles I. 2011. "EXIT." Speech at the Shadow Open Market Committee, New York, NY. March 25.

Plosser, Charles I. 2012. "Fiscal Policy and Monetary Policy: Restoring the Boundaries." Speech at the US Monetary Policy Forum, The Initiative on Global Markets, New York, NY. February 24.

Plosser, Charles I. 2013. "A Limited Central Bank." Remarks at Cato Institute's 31st Annual Monetary Policy Conference. November. Published in *Cato Journal* 34 (2): 202–11 (2014).

Plosser, Charles I. 2016. "Making the Fed More Accountable—Not More Political." Testimony before the Subcommittee on Monetary Policy and Trade of the Committee on Financial Services. 114th Cong. December 7.

Plosser, Charles I. 2018. "The Risks of a Fed Balance Sheet Unconstrained by Monetary Policy." In *The Structural Foundations of Monetary Policy*, edited by Michael D. Bordo, John H. Cochrane, and Amit Seru. Hoover Institution Press.

Plosser, Charles I. 2022. "Federal Reserve Independence: Is It Time for a New Treasury-Fed Accord?" In *Essays in Honor of Marvin Goodfriend: Economist and Central Banker,* edited by Robert G. King and Alexander L. Wolman. Federal Reserve Bank of Richmond.

Sargent, Thomas J. 2011a. "Drawing the Lines in US Monetary and Fiscal History." Lecture at Wake Forest University, Winston-Salem, NC. February 11.

Sargent, Thomas J. 2011b. "Where to Draw Lines: Stability versus Efficiency." *Economica* 78 (310): 197–214.

19

When Are Central Bank
Policy Actions Fiscal?

Definitions, Examples, and
a Call for Transparency

Deborah Lucas

The Shadow Open Market Committee (SOMC) is often referred to informally as the "Shadow Fed." That more expansive and colloquial moniker may now be the more accurate one. As the Federal Reserve's activities have expanded ever further into the realm of fiscal and regulatory policies, the focus of some SOMC members, mine included, has moved there along with it, and away from more traditional concerns about disciplining interest rate policy.

There are a variety of reasons why the Fed (and other central banks) should avoid crossing the line from monetary to fiscal policy. Those include the ceding of democratic control over government policies to unelected officials, and, in the United States, the lack of constitutional authority for doing so; and the risk to central bank independence should things go awry with those policies. However, there is no general agreement over how, and where, to draw the dividing line.

In my view, questions about which central bank policies cross the line into fiscal policy and what should be done about it are some of the most important and most under-discussed issues in central banking. I've circled back to these issues several times during my tenure on the SOMC, and I want to return to them again briefly here by:

1. Revisiting alternative definitions of when a Federal Reserve action is fiscal, and suggesting a preferred definition and my reasons supporting it;

2. Providing a few examples of Federal Reserve policies that clearly have fiscal elements, and others that by my preferred definition do not;

3. Highlighting the large, indirect, and misleading fiscal effect of how Federal Reserve remittances are accounted for in the federal budget; and

4. Suggesting that, at the very least, the Federal Reserve should be required to become more transparent about the true fiscal and distributional consequences of its policies. Doing so is a prerequisite for applying the mantra of rules rather than discretion in the fiscal sphere of its operations.

Definitions

Stock definitions of monetary and fiscal policy tend to classify a policy according to the identity of the actor taking the action and the type of action. Monetary policy is equated with the actions of central banks. For example, the Federal Reserve states, "Monetary policy in the United States comprises the Federal Reserve's actions and communications to promote maximum employment, stable prices, and moderate long-term interest rates--the economic goals the Congress has instructed the Federal Reserve to pursue" (Board of Governors 2025). In other words, if the Federal Reserve does it, it's monetary. By contrast, fiscal policy is typically equated to a government's tax and spending policies, which in the US are controlled by the legislative and administrative branches. The emphasis is again on the agent taking the action and the types of actions undertaken. Clearly definitions based on the actor or specific types of actions are not helpful for drawing an economically meaningful line between monetary and fiscal policy.

A possible distinction that I was initially sympathetic to is that a central bank policy action is fiscal if its real and distributional effects could be replicated with tax and spending policies. However, that is true of almost all traditional monetary policy actions that have real effects. Perhaps there is an element of truth to that, and monetary policy is simply a carve-out from fiscal policy. Nevertheless, that conclusion is not helpful in identifying the monetary policies that are clearly stepping over a line into the fiscal realm, and hence it is not my preferred definition.

My candidate definition, and the one I focus on here, is this: A central bank policy action is fiscal if it causes a direct transfer of value to or from the federal government. This definition borrows from how the federal budget accounts for revenues and spending. It therefore calls for a parallel between how traditional fiscal actions are accounted for and how the fiscal actions of the Federal Reserve would ideally also be recognized. It avoids the pitfalls of classifying policies based on the actor or on the type of action, or of classifying all monetary policy as fiscal.

Importantly, the phrase "direct transfers" is included in the definition to emphasize that pecuniary externalities arising from Federal Reserve actions would not be considered fiscal under this definition. A pecuniary externality is one arising from price changes. For example, if an open market purchase of Treasury securities lowers interest rates, that has a pecuniary effect that lowers the cost of new Treasury borrowing and thereby transfers value from investors to the government.

Pecuniary externalities are excluded from assessments of the size of fiscal effects of Federal Reserve policies for several reasons: First, pecuniary externalities are the channel by which conventional monetary policy operates, as the example of lowering interest rates via open market operations illustrates. As noted earlier, it would not be helpful to reclassify most Federal Reserve policies as fiscal. Second, the size and duration of pecuniary externalities are extremely difficult to assess, as evidenced by the continuing debate over the effects of quantitative easing. Third, the exclusion creates consistency with the budgetary treatment of traditional fiscal policies because budgetary accounting largely excludes the pecuniary externalities arising from tax and spending policies. Therefore, evaluating the costs of fiscal policy symmetrically across government actors suggests excluding the pecuniary externalities arising from Fed actions.

Examples of Fed Policies with Significant Fiscal Cost

Two concrete examples serve to illustrate policies where I believe that the Federal Reserve has taken a large step over the line, but where there has been surprisingly little recognition of their fiscal nature:

1. Payments of above-market interest on bank reserves; and
2. The uncompensated risk exposure it assumes via the credit facilities it opens and operates during stress periods, notably during the Global Financial Crisis (GFC) and the COVID-19 pandemic.

When the Federal Reserve pays out an above-market interest rate on funds it borrows from a nonfederal entity, subsidies are created that are a form of government spending. In the wake of the GFC and Great Recession, the huge growth of the Federal Reserve's balance sheet was financed by a correspondingly large increase in bank reserves. Those reserves were easily attracted because the Federal Reserve used its newly granted power to administratively set the interest rate on reserves to outcompete other potential borrowers.

How much above market was the rate paid on reserves, and what was the associated fiscal expenditure? Although there is uncertainty about the correct reference rate to use for comparison, the federal funds rate is a relevant point of comparison. That rate would normally be expected to be similar to or a little higher than the IOER (Interest on Excess Reserves) because it entails a small amount of default risk and the IOER does not. As shown in figure 19.1, the IOER was above the effective federal funds rate from 2009 to 2018, sometimes significantly so. That spread allowed banks to take advantage of the artificially high interest rate on reserves by borrowing from other financial institutions without direct access to the Federal Reserve and then lending the funds to the Federal Reserve at the higher IOER rate. Using the federal funds rate as the relevant market rate and applying the premium paid by the Fed over the federal funds rate to outstanding reserves, there was a fiscal transfer to banks of about $21 billion over that period.

The Federal Reserve has increasingly participated in credit policy actions that involve its bearing uncompensated credit risk and thereby providing a

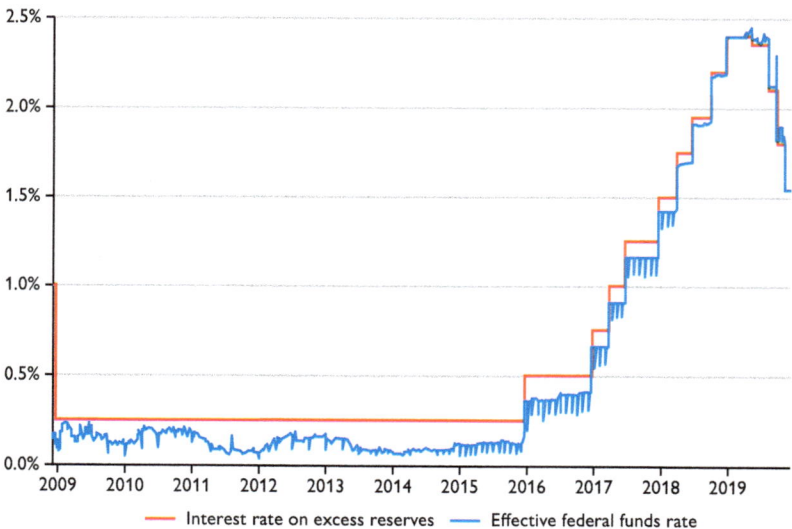

Figure 19.1. Interest on excess reserve versus effective federal funds rate.
Source: Board of Governors, New York Fed, via St. Louis Federal Reserve (FRED).

subsidy to borrowers. That practice started for the first time on a large scale during the GFC and further expanded during the COVID-19 pandemic. The CARES Act, which included a large number of pandemic relief measures, directed the Federal Reserve to create several new facilities that authorized it to directly lend to business and municipalities. Those included the Main Street Lending Program, the Primary Market Corporate Credit Facility, and the Municipal Liquidity Facility. In total, there was authority to buy up to $1.8 trillion of securities in the primary market. Very little of that capacity was used, but had the economic effects of the pandemic been more severe and prolonged, the potential loss exposure would have been enormous. While the Treasury was in a first-loss position on those facilities, my estimates in other work suggest that the residual fiscal cost borne by the Fed was significant.

Examples of Federal Reserve Policies without Significant Fiscal Costs

My suggested definition leaves some Federal Reserve activities squarely on the monetary side of the line that some of my colleagues on the SOMC would argue have significant fiscal elements. In particular, some view central bank purchases of private-sector securities as fiscal. However, under the proposed definition, a policy action only counts as fiscal if it involves a direct cost to the government. When a central bank buys private-sector securities at competitive market prices, such as when the Federal Reserve purchases mortgage-backed securities (MBS) or corporate bonds in the secondary market, those actions are not fiscal. Notably, its purchases of federally guaranteed MBS entail no additional credit risk for the government. Those purchases might increase the price of the securities purchased, benefiting the sellers and ultimately the borrowers at the expense of the government. Nevertheless, because pecuniary externalities are excluded, transactions that occur in competitive markets and that involve an equal exchange of value have no fiscal cost.

Certainly, central bank purchases of private-sector securities could be a bad idea for various reasons, including that they leave the impression that the central bank is overstepping its mandate by engaging in industrial or distributional policy. Relatedly, just because the Federal Reserve is purchasing Treasury securities does not mean the fiscal cost is zero. A fiscal cost would arise if the Federal Reserve were to purchase Treasury securities from the public at an above-market price.

The Federal Reserve first created large-scale emergency liquidity facilities during the GFC. Many of those were reopened during the COVID-19

Table 19.1. Federal Reserve COVID-19 pandemic credit facilities

Primary Dealer Credit Facility (PDCF)

Commercial Paper Funding Facility (CPFF)

Money-Market Mutual Fund Liquidity Facility (MMLF)

Term Asset-Backed Securities Loan Facility (TALF)

Central bank liquidity swaps

Secondary Market Corporate Credit Facility (SMCCF)

Paycheck Protection Program Liquidity Facility (PPPLF)

Temporary Foreign and International Monetary Authorities Repo Facility (FIMA)

Note: Facilities in bold were introduced for the first time during the pandemic. The others were first introduced during the GFC.

pandemic, and new ones were added. Because most liquidity facilities were structured to minimize the uncompensated default losses to the Federal Reserve, they also fall legitimately on the monetary side of the fiscal-monetary line. The facilities listed in table 19.1, which the Federal Reserve operated during the pandemic, all are examples where the Federal Reserve took significant actions affecting credit markets, but where the fiscal costs were minimal. The fiscal costs were minimal because either the transactions occurred at secondary market prices, the loans were highly collateralized, or the Treasury backstopped the losses.

It may be surprising to see the $700 billion Paycheck Protection Program (PPP) on this list. The PPP was administered by the Federal Reserve and was one of the costliest and more controversial fiscal interventions during the pandemic. However, the Federal Reserve's role was limited to administration; the Treasury absorbed the fiscal cost. Certainly, the Federal Reserve's involvement in a program providing large subsidies to businesses made it appear to be involved in fiscal policy, and in my view it was ill-advised to create that perception.

Indirect Fiscal Effect of Flawed Accounting for Federal Reserve Remittances

The final fiscal effect of the Federal Reserve that I want to mention is indirect. It is not the result of the Federal Reserve's policies per se but rather a flaw in the rules governing US federal budgetary accounting. Nevertheless, it creates fiscal distortions, and as far as I know the Federal Reserve has not objected to this practice, at least not publicly.

The issue is that Federal Reserve remittances are booked as revenues in the federal budget and thereby create fiscal space that reduces the budget deficit and accommodates higher spending. The apparent profits grow as the size of the balance sheet grows. That is a problem because that additional fiscal space is illusory. It arises because the Federal Reserve earns a higher rate of return on average on its assets than it pays on its liabilities. However, clearly the action of buying $100 million of Treasury securities with $100 million of reserves in the open market is a neutral exchange that neither creates nor destroys economic value, at least as a first approximation. What is happening is that risk premiums and term premiums are being booked as profit, when in economic terms they are not. It is well understood in budgetary circles that this type of accounting creates a paper money machine for the government to make very real deficits disappear by issuing safe debt and buying risky assets, a dangerous game.

The illusory fiscal space created by Federal Reserve remittances is significant. Over the decade from 2013 to 2023, this reduced reported deficits by $790 billion. Figure 19.2 shows the pattern of those remittances over time.

The large negative effect in 2023 when rising rates increased the cost of reserves over the revenues from portfolio holdings suggests another danger of this practice. Whereas the perception of profits might help protect independence, the risk of large losses that come with a huge balance sheet can also threaten congressional support for that independence.

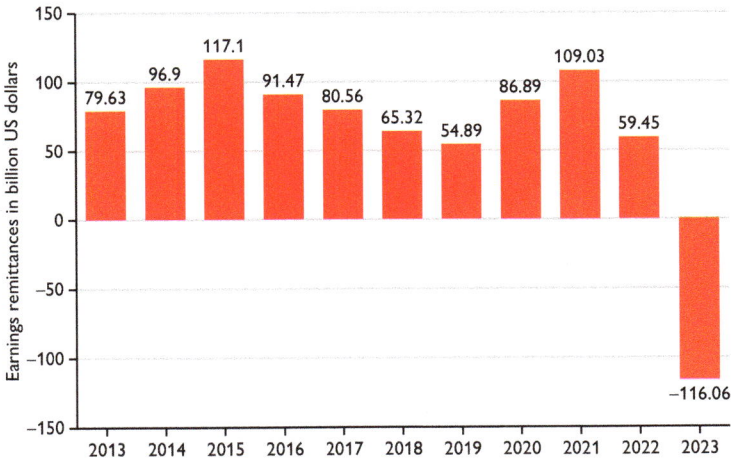

Figure 19.2. Federal Reserve's earnings remittances to the United States Department of the Treasury from 2013 to 2023.

Source: Data from Statista.

What Should Be Done?

Greater transparency and clearer thinking about fiscal and distributional consequences of the Fed's policy is essential for several reasons:

- To hold the Fed accountable to the public and its elected representatives for its fiscal actions;
- to force it to adopt a more explicit cost-benefit mindset in deciding on policy actions;
- to reduce pressures on the Fed to undertake fiscal actions that the rest of the government wants to avoid accountability for; and
- to discourage legislative curtailment of its independence.

A first step would be for the Fed to acknowledge the relevance of these issues and devote significantly more staff resources to addressing them. Harmonizing and improving fiscal and monetary accounting practices is also important to promote transparency and more informed decision making. All of these recommendations are in the spirit of the SOMC's emphasis on transparency and on rules over discretion as a way to discipline the conduct of policy, both monetary and fiscal.

Reference

Board of Governors (Board of Governors of the Federal Reserve System). 2025. "Monetary Policy." Board of Governors of the Federal Reserve System. February 19. https://www.federalreserve.gov/monetarypolicy.htm.

MICHAEL J. BOSKIN: We started fifteen minutes late, so I'm going to reclaim half that. Ask the panelists to come back up really quickly. We'll take a couple of questions. I want to get a couple of quick comments. These are the notes I've taken, questions I'd like to ask: The left side is intellectual history, the right side is what's happened in the economy, and I've only been able to ask a small percentage of them. So, every one of these sessions could have gone twice as long, fruitfully, with a marginal return that was quite substantial. It's not surprising that I have two current colleagues and one former colleague from earlier in my career on the panel.

I agree with almost everything that's been said—almost, not all—but I want to just quickly mention a few and then add a couple of things to start as questions. First, I think Debbie [Lucas] is really onto something important about improving transparency in our budgeting and our information systems about what's fiscal and what's monetary.

We can't really get at what Charlie [Plosser] was arguing for: much greater seriousness about achieving objectives or losing credibility if we aren't able to measure it. By the way, let me put in a plug for more accurate measures of inflation. We're moving in that direction, but now we have a new frontier about what to do about putatively free goods.

Those of you who don't waste your time on the microeconomics of all this, it's quite fascinating, and we'll see where that winds up. One thing that was mentioned by John [Cochrane] at the end, emphasizing cost of growth, is something that I've been involved in. And I think one of the three big changes in postwar evolution in macroeconomics—which are time horizons, expectations, and incentives—is incentives.

And we talked a little bit about incentives in institutions like the Fed, public-choice kinds of things. We didn't talk much about marginal tax rates.

And I still remember advising candidate [Ronald] Reagan and helping him design his tax policies. I'm where 401(k)s and IRAs came from. But in any event, before we had inflation indexing of tax brackets, there was immense pressure to bring inflation down, and there were many reasons to do that.

But in any event, that, I think, was part of the reason why Reagan stuck with [Paul] Volcker. I think that's important to appreciate, that he supported the disinflation plus other things that went on, and John could worry about that. Pat [Kehoe], we have tried fiscal rules. I was involved in one that we had when we lost the nominal anchor of a balanced budget over the cycle.

I developed capital accounts for the federal government. We almost got the president, when I was outside advisor, brought in by Dave Stockman and Marty Feldstein. We almost got President Reagan to order the OMB [Office of Management and Budget] to start producing them. But then Cap Weinberger, then secretary of defense, went ballistic that we'd be giving the Russian secrets by reporting depreciation.

So accounting can get you in trouble in various ways. In any event, we had the Gramm–Rudman [–Hollings Balanced Budget Act], which was basically just projecting you get to a balanced budget. It didn't work, so we extended it. The same thing happened with the Maastricht rules. In 1990, we put in a marginal balanced budget rule called a PAYGO rule, which I think probably made sense.

However, because [George H. W.] Bush agreed to a tax hike in that same deal, it got badly discredited. So I think it's important to focus on that as well. I'd also say that I'm glad John is challenging the central bank canon as a necessary but not necessarily a sufficient condition, that you have to get the funds rate above the inflation rate.

So I think that's something we really do need to grapple with. He has his proposed answer, and we'll see how that penetrates and broadens in the profession over time. Pat, I really like your idea of separating a capital budget from an operating budget; wars are important, and let's hope we don't wind up in a really major one anytime soon.

It's looking risky right now, but we've really underfunded the military for some time. And both in the Obama administration, now in the Biden administration, whatever you think of everything else they did, as a factual matter, they were trying to decrease real military spending.

We certainly need to get a bigger bang for the buck in the military. But when you add the need for increased military spending to the fiscal pressures coming from the impending insufficiency of Medicare and Social Security, there's going to be a serious reckoning that we're going to have to deal with.

I'd add one final thing, which is that there are a lot of statistical—there are many studies by economists. Alberto Alesina, I think, was the main one early on, but many since then, that analyzed successful budget consolidations. And the evidence seems to be that they've been overwhelmingly on the spending side of the budget, not on the tax side, as a broad empirical generalization.

So, I'll end; let's take two or three questions, then we'll have to get on to the next panel. Okay, we've got people in the middle and, I apologize, people on the edges. Maybe we can start in the back row and take those two and see if we have time for one more.

We'll take all the questions at once, and we'll ask the panelists to respond.

MATTHEW KLEIN: I've got a question. I'm wondering why the fiscal response to the financial crisis did not lead to inflation. Was there an implicit assumption that in fact there would be primary surpluses generated then in a way that there was not, with response to COVID?

And then, relatedly, given the implication of interest-rate policy for deficits and primary surpluses, should interest rates in fact have been kept at zero to minimize the inflation post-COVID? Thank you.

DAVID BECKWORTH: This is a question for John. So the FTPL [fiscal theory of the price level] does seem to do a good job explaining the inflation surge and the disinflation.

Now, we're close to 2%, and we still see CBO [Congressional Budget Office] forecasts getting worse and worse. Should we not see inflation going up as a result of that? How do we explain where we are today now that we're seemingly past the inflation surge in disinflation via the FTPL theory?

JACK KRUPANSKY: I'm Jack Krupansky. Back in 2008, the TARP [Troubled Asset Relief Program] plan, the revised TARP plan, where they did forced loans to banks at a high interest rate. Could that have been done by the Fed, or was that inherently fiscal policy?

DAVID ZERVOS: The Japanese debt-to-GDP ratio is 250%. The BoJ's [Bank of Japan's] balance sheet is 140% of GDP.

They've monetized probably 60% to 70% of all JGBs [Japanese Government Bonds]. How does that fit into the fiscal theory of the price level, given that inflation is still low and seemingly running out of steam? Thanks.

BOSKIN: Okay, so, John, several of those were directed at the fiscal theory of the price level. So let's have your concise answer.

JOHN H. COCHRANE: Concise is hard for me! I will advertise that these questions come up often enough that you can find written answers on my website, including an essay about Japan, and a longer essay called "Fiscal Histories" about what's different between 2008 and this time.

The short version is there's lots of reasons why Japan is different from the US. Low interest rates is one of the big ones. We'll see how long that lasts. Japan is fragile. The same debt is sustainable at low rates, but unsustainable at higher rates. And also, Japan—or large debt without inflation anywhere—is not a distinguishing problem for fiscal theory. Every theory says government debt is the present value of surpluses. If it's unsustainable for fiscal theory, it's unsustainable for passive fiscal policy as well. So it doesn't really distinguish theories. Finally, even if something special lets Japan get along at 200% debt to GDP, that doesn't mean Venezuela, Argentina, Greece, Italy, the UK, or even the US can do it.

But there is a good story for Japan. There's also a story for 2008 versus 2021. Fiscal theory emphasizes debt versus expected repayment. You can have a lot of debt as long as there is faith it will be repaid. There were big deficits in 2008, yes. But at least the administration had the decency to say, "Stimulus now, debt reduction later." Nobody even had the decency to say that this time.

We also got lucky from 2008 to 2023 with really low interest rates. Debt service costs matter just like deficits in fiscal theory. The 2008 deficit was much smaller. It was direct government spending, not mailing checks to people. 2008 was a period of very deficient demand. The pandemic was basically a supply shock, like a snowstorm. The economy was not slow because people didn't have money.

With today's deficits, why don't we have Zimbabwean hyperinflation? The CBO numbers are a projection, not a forecast, not a conditional expectation. And they say right there, this is unsustainable. This will not happen. We don't know how it won't happen, but it will not happen that debt to GDP goes up forever.

Why are bond markets still buying the US debt? I think bond markets think this is a great country. Our fiscal mess is a self-inflicted wound. America will surely do the right thing after we've tried everything else, the way we usually do. And when markets lose that faith is when things blow up.

DEBORAH LUCAS: Very quickly, on TARP. It was a completely fiscal action. I think it was about $500 billion of legislative authority. When they decided how they were going to use the money, they decided the only way they could make it really big was to put it at the equity part of the capital structure. So basically, the government was providing very subsidized purchases of things like preferred stock and options from the banks.

And I think there's no way the Fed could have had that large credit-related expenditure without it—well, they wouldn't have even contemplated it, is what I would have said. But there was a lot of fiscal authority that went into that bailout.

BOSKIN: I would just add one quick thing about the fiscal side and the future paying down of the debt.

I had a star undergraduate some years ago who won the university-wide prize for the best undergraduate thesis. He concluded through a variety of consistent vector-autoregression studies that the most stimulative short-run fiscal policy is one that combines a policy to later consolidate the budget with short-run stimulus. Unfortunately, he went off to Goldman Sachs and never published it. Let's hear a big round of applause for all these great speakers.

Federal Reserve Credit Policy

Introduction

Thomas Hoenig

We're going to end this part, before we take a break for our reception, talking about the lender of last resort, too-big-to-fail, and financial systems savior. My favorite topics—and we have some really great people speaking today: Jeff Lacker, who is a former colleague and now current colleague. I've read his material, and he's going to take us down the trail of good intentions and moral-hazard consequences.

We will then turn to Amit [Seru] to discuss too-big-to-fail. We will conclude with Charles Calomiris, who will join us by video to add the final comment on the topic.

20
Federal Reserve Credit Policy and the Shadow Open Market Committee

Jeffrey M. Lacker

While the Shadow Open Market Committee (SOMC) may be best known for its fifty-year record of prescient critiques of the Federal Open Market Committee's (FOMC) conduct of monetary policy, it has also devoted significant attention over the years to the Federal Reserve's credit policy. In fact, the lifespan of the Shadow coincides with a significant growth of the scale and scope of Fed interventions in credit markets. That overlap was not a coincidence—the rising financial instability that provoked Fed participation in rescuing failing banks beginning in the early 1970s is attributable in part to the late-1960s rise of inflation that inspired the birth of the SOMC. The Shadow's critiques of those rescues have been based on a historically faithful understanding of the role of lender of last resort as a critical element of sound monetary policy, concern about the incentive effects of lending precedents, and the principle that financial institution rescues are tangential to the Fed's monetary policy responsibilities and constitute fiscal actions more appropriately assigned elsewhere. Those principles remain all the more relevant in the twenty-first century as the Federal Reserve continues to expand the scope of its credit market interventions.

Both the theory and practice of Federal Reserve lending have changed dramatically over time. At its founding, Fed lending was viewed as the operational mechanism for maintaining monetary stability. The failure to do so in the Great Contraction of 1929–33 is attributable to the flawed Real Bills Doctrine then prevalent within the System. Open market purchases and sales of United States Treasury securities took over as the primary monetary policy instrument after the 1951 Treasury-Fed Accord and lending was relegated to the role of providing occasional accommodation for banks experiencing sudden unanticipated reserve drain late in the day. Discount window lending was routinely sterilized and thus divorced from monetary policy. Beginning in the mid-1960s, the discount window was used to help the FDIC delay the closure of failing banks by providing funds to allow uninsured creditors to exit. The repeated practice of protecting creditors gave rise to expectations that a portion of the financial system was "too big to fail" (TBTF). The scale and scope of the Federal Reserve's credit extension increased dramatically in the twenty-first century. Fed lending peaked at over $400 billion during the Great Financial Crisis (GFC) and extended well beyond the banking sector.[1] The Fed rolled out even broader credit market programs at the onset of the COVID-19 pandemic in 2020 and helped rescue uninsured creditors of failing regional banks in 2023.

This chapter weaves together two narratives. One is the evolution of ideas about how and why the Federal Reserve Banks should play a role in credit markets. Several relatively distinct lending *doctrines*, for want of a better word, can be identified that have shaped and rationalized the Fed's credit market activities. These doctrines vary in the extent to which they are grounded in economic models; some are, some are only loosely, and some have turned out to be wholly fallacious. Most are normative, while some can be interpreted as positive models in a public choice vein.

Federal Reserve lending is at times intertwined with monetary policy, but is fundamentally quite distinct, so clarity about the dividing line between monetary and credit policy is important. I will adopt Goodfriend and King's (1988) crisp distinction. Monetary policy refers to changes in the stock of high-powered money—that is, currency plus bank reserves, the Federal Reserve's monetary liabilities—accomplished by buying or selling Treasury securities in the open market. Credit policy shifts the composition of the Fed's assets by acquiring private obligations, while holding fixed the stock of high-powered money. For example, Fed loans to private institutions or purchases of private securities financed by the sale of Treasury securities ("sterilized") would be pure credit policy. "Credit policy involves the fiscal allocation of public funds in a way that monetary policy does not" (Goodfriend 2011a, 2). Fed lending that is financed by reserve creation ("unsterilized") is a combination of monetary and credit policy.[2] Under the monetary policy operating regime in place prior to 2008 (that is, with no interest on reserves), interest rate targeting required that any reserves added via lending be automatically drained via offsetting open market operations. Note that this definition of monetary policy is narrower than the Fed's definition, which appears to be "any transaction the Fed undertakes to try to influence economic conditions."

Four distinct lending doctrines are discernible in twentieth-century practice and thought. The Fed was founded to provide *Monetary Stability* by expanding the supply of bank reserves and paper currency, via Fed unsterilized lending, in response to shifts in demand, as occurred during banking panics and autumn crop movements in the late nineteenth century. The *Real Bills Doctrine* went further and asserted that credit booms and busts could be prevented if Federal Reserve Banks lent freely but only against short-term, self-liquidating commercial bills arising from real transactions in goods and services. A separate motivation for the founders was *Warburg's Mercantilism*, the desire articulated by the financier Paul Warburg to relocate the financing of US foreign trade—carried out via banker's acceptances—from Europe to New York; central bank lending support was viewed as offsetting foreign central banks' backstop support for their own bills markets. In the mid-1960s a practice emerged of acting as a *Reluctant Samaritan* in one-off cases of financial distress by lending to failing banks, allowing the FDIC to delay closure and let uninsured creditors escape losses. The widening domain of intervention precedents has enlarged the financial safety net over time.

While some continuity with twentieth-century doctrine is evident in the dramatic expansion of the Fed's credit market interventions in the twenty-first century, a case can be made that the expansive new approach to financial stability that emerged in 2007 represented a fundamental doctrinal discontinuity, best thought of as a distinct new lending doctrine. It seems firmly predicated on the idea that laissez-faire banking and financial markets are inherently fragile. As put into practice, however, the doctrine makes virtually no contact with the vast literature on the microfoundations of banking and financial markets in the presence of informational or other frictions. While loosely inspired by a selective reading of that late twentieth-century literature, and by gauzy appeals to Walter Bagehot, the organizing principle underlying current credit doctrine appears to be for the Fed to act as *Sell-Side Savior*, supporting in crises those trying to sell financial instruments, subordinating the interests of market participants with less sanguine expectations about the underlying cash flows, holding funds on the sidelines in anticipation of buying opportunities.

The second narrative thread is the commentary of the Shadow Open Market Committee on Fed credit policy. Consistent with the principles of sound central banking and healthy markets, the SOMC naturally has had much to say. At the Committee's third meeting cofounder Allan Meltzer responded to the bailout earlier that year of Franklin National Bank by calling on the Fed to issue a clear statement of "lender of last resort" policy, which he interpreted narrowly as unsterilized monetary operations because the "unique ability of a lender-of-last-resort is the ability to produce base money on demand" (Meltzer 1974, 36). Anna Schwartz in the 1980s distinguished between "real" and "pseudo" financial crises, the former involving monetary stability and the latter not warranting Fed intervention. She was critical of what she called "misuse" of the discount window to aid failing banks and argued that "the Federal Reserve does not need the discount window to serve as a lender of last resort" (Schwartz 1992, 67). The Committee was certainly on record warning about the growth of financial fragility prior to the GFC; SOMC statements cited the moral-hazard consequences of the Continental Illinois intervention in 1984, and in the early 2000s called out risks emanating from Fannie Mae and Freddie Mac.

Following the GFC, SOMC members expressed concern about threats to the Fed's independence, critiqued regulatory reform proposals, and provided insightful analysis of the emerging central bank financial stability and "macroprudential" programs. Three current and future SOMC members were calling for a Treasury-Fed "Credit Accord" at that time, and a joint statement resembling their proposed accord was actually issued by the Treasury and the Fed in March 2009. Although the Fed has not yet articulated its current credit policy, per se, from the description of its financial stability mandate one can infer a twenty-first-century Fed lending doctrine that sees the Fed as intervening, at its discretion, to remedy financial "distress," "dislocation," and "dysfunction" wherever they might arise. While seemingly inspired by the literature on the microfoundations of banking and financial arrangements, including theories of runs and financial contracting frictions, actual Fed lending practice has made virtually no contact with that literature. No staff analysis compared the possibility propositions detailing the circumstances under which government intervention is warranted in a given theoretical environment with actually observed real-world economic environments. Transcripts and memoirs reveal little or no policymaker interest in the welfare economics of credit market interventions. Indeed, it is not obvious that the Fed's interventions were warranted on economic grounds and most seemed largely distributional. Moreover, in many cases it would be hard to distinguish empirically between market-failure possibility propositions and the fragility induced by decades of Fed interventions. The SOMC's credit policy perspectives may not have left as visible an imprint as those on the monetary policy side, but Fed lending is a heavily contested policy terrain where vested financial interests have more direct distributional stakes.

The paper begins with three lending doctrines that were influential at the founding of the Fed and a brief overview of the evolution of Fed lending practice over the twentieth century, including the rise of "too big to fail." The SOMC's pre-GFC contributions on Fed credit policy are then reviewed. Understanding of the Fed's TBTF lending leads to the fourth doctrine, the Reluctant Samaritan. The associated accumulation of precedents set the stage for the GFC. The influence of the four twentieth-century lending doctrines on the events of the GFC is discussed next, followed by a review of the SOMC's commentary during and after the GFC. After a brief discussion of the Fed's pandemic credit market interventions and the ensuing regional bank failures, the new Fed lending doctrine is explained and discussed.

The Federal Reserve Was Founded to Solve a Monetary Problem

When the Federal Reserve System was founded in 1913, Reserve Bank lending authority was central to an institutional design that was motivated by the shortcomings of existing monetary arrangements (Wicker 2015). Under the National Bank Acts that had structured the US monetary system since 1863, federally chartered banks were entitled to issue their own currency, subject to the requirement that note issues were collateralized by holdings of specified US Treasury bonds. The money stock in use by the public consisted of coins, currency, and deposits at banks. Banks held reserves in the form of coin and currency and deposits at other banks. The public shifted out of deposits and into notes when moving crops to market during harvest season, and when suspicion fell on weak local banks. Because the process of expanding collateralized note issue was costly and time-consuming, currency at times became relatively scarce and hard to obtain. Without a sufficient expansion in note issue, the overall money stock declined.[3]

Tight restrictions on bank branching made for a fragmented banking system—there were over twenty-seven thousand banks in the United States in 1913 (US Bureau of the Census 1975, Part 2, 1019). Clearing and settlement of notes and checks relied heavily on clearinghouses in major cities and the vast web of interbank deposits extending out to small rural banks. When currency was scarce, clearinghouse banks suspended depositor withdrawals (except to deposit at other clearinghouse banks) and sometimes refused country banks' requests to withdraw cash. Clearinghouses would at times issue their own currency substitutes in the form of "clearinghouse certificates," although their legality was in question (Timberlake 1978; Calomiris and Haber 2015).

The design of the Federal Reserve System was influenced by British experience. The Bank of England had an effective monopoly on circulating bank notes and faced a similar fractional reserve problem in crises. The Bank's monetary liabilities—its note issue—was managed through its lending policy and not by purchases of government debt. Bank advances to the government were politically sensitive, given Britain's 1688 constitutional constraints on public finance, and required parliamentary approval. In the US, government bond backing of money had been discredited by the National Bank system and was viewed as inherently inflationary besides. The founders therefore had the Fed's monetary issue backed by loans on or discounts of short-term paper, modelled after the Bank of England (Lacker 2024b).

Henry Thornton ([1802] 1939) and Walter Bagehot (1873) described the crises faced by the early Bank of England as monetary problems, not credit market problems (Lacker 2024b). Taking the constraints on Bank financing of the government as a given, they recommended that the Bank expand its lending when faced with an internal drain. They are very clear that it was expansion of note issue that was the proper objective of the Bank in a crisis. Both Thornton and Bagehot were agnostic about assets acquired to achieve that objective—any asset will do, as long as it's safe. In fact, both noted that expanding note issue by acquiring government securities outright would also be suitable. And both said specifically that the Bank should not lend to failing or distressed entities and that it would be inappropriate for the Bank to attempt to address problems associated with individual institutions in stress or particular segments of the credit market.

Bagehot's strident exhortations were aimed at overcoming the Bank's reluctance to lend into deteriorating credit conditions owing to their for-profit incentive. The Bank's directors were reluctant to concede that they had a public responsibility for monetary stability. Bagehot's cause was as much about governance as it was about policy. In contrast, because the Federal Reserve's profits and losses are ultimately passed through to the US Treasury, the problem with Federal Reserve credit policy today is the opposite—"to limit the Fed's lending reach" (Goodfriend 2012, 48).

A Brief Digression on the Phrase "Lender of Last Resort"

Twenty-first-century central bankers frequently claim that their credit market interventions are in line with a "classic central bank role as lender of last resort," often accompanied by a citation to Bagehot's (1873) *Lombard Street*.[4] For example, in his memoirs, former Fed chair Ben Bernanke recalled that "we saw our responses to the panic as fulfilling the classic central banking role of lender of last resort" (Bernanke 2015, 243). Bagehot never actually used the phrase and neither did Thornton. It seems to have been first used in English by R. G. Hawtrey (1962) in the 1930s (Haubrich 2013).[5] The idea Hawtrey references is the one articulated by Bagehot and more thoroughly by Thornton; when confronted with a banking panic, a central bank should expand, via lending, the supply of the high-powered money (its note issue) over which it has an effective monopoly. Central bank lending in such circumstances must be *unsterilized*, a qualification that was taken as a given by Bagehot but is not typically included in elaborations of his recommendations. Sterilized lending would not have addressed the problems posed by eighteenth- or nineteenth-century panics.

Modern usage of the phrase "lender of last resort" departs from the classical ideas of Thornton and Bagehot in two ways. First, many economists identify the lender-of-last-resort role as supplying additional base money in response to increased demand in a panic, including through open market operations, consistent with Thornton and Bagehot (Humphrey 1975, 1989; Schwartz 1986b; Goodfriend and King 1988; Bordo 1990, 2014b). Second, in the opposite direction, the phrase is often used to refer simply to any central bank emergency lending, whether sterilized or not. For example, by the 1970s, Federal Reserve staff had begun using the phrase "lender of last resort" to refer to emergency lending to "troubled" banks, even in settings in which monetary policy procedures in place resulted in sterilization of discount window advances in order to insulate broader monetary conditions (Board of Governors 1971, 19). Unfortunately, the broader popular usage cloaks central bank credit policy, misleadingly, in the mantle of the time-honored monetary policy prescriptions of Thornton and Bagehot (Lacker 2024b, 38). The historically more accurate phrase "monopoly monetary liability supplier of last resort" would be more faithful to Thornton and Bagehot.

The primary purpose for which the Federal Reserve was founded, therefore, was to act as a "classical lender of last resort" in the historically faithful sense of that phrase. Because of the confusing modern usage, however, I will refer to this as "monetary stability":

Lending Doctrine 1: Monetary Stability (Classical Lender of Last Resort)   When a public shift from bank deposits to notes threatens to reduce the overall money stock and there is some impediment to acquiring government securities via open market operations, the Federal Reserve, as the monopoly issuer of high-powered money in the form of notes and reserve account balances, should lend in order to expand the supply of high-powered money.

The Real Bills Doctrine Led the Fed Astray

The Federal Reserve Act was designed "to furnish an elastic currency" by overcoming the constraints that made it hard to expand the note supply when needed. Beyond that, some of the founders of the Fed had in mind a specific theory of the proper quantitative determination of the volume of Fed lending and note supply. The theory was that note issue "can never be excessive or deficient when issued in the form of loans against short-term, self-liquidating commercial bills arising from real transactions in goods and services" (Humphrey and Timberlake 2019, 1).[6] The aim was to steer bank credit expansion away from "speculative purposes" toward "productive" uses. If money expansion was linked in that way to real activity, the money supply would not exceed demand and would not be inflationary. Banking system credit creation was viewed as tied to money creation, and thus following the doctrine would avoid credit-driven booms and busts. This Real Bills Doctrine, as Lloyd Mints (1945) was later to call it, motivated a set of restrictions in the Federal Reserve Act limiting the types of commercial paper the Reserve Banks could discount from member banks (Hackley 1973).

Lending Doctrine 2: Real Bills   Federal Reserve Banks should lend freely to member banks against short-term, self-liquidating commercial bills arising from real transactions in goods and services.

The fallaciousness of the Real Bills Doctrine was well understood by some early Fed leaders, such as Benjamin Strong, governor of the Federal Reserve Bank of New York from 1914 to 1928. A single "real" transaction could give rise to multiple "real bills" as the merchandise made its way through various intermediaries, each issuing its own paper, on its way to the ultimate purchaser. Moreover, the fungibility of funds meant that collateral requirements might not have any effect on the nature of lending undertaken by the borrowing bank (Chandler 1958, 197–98). Besides, hitching the quantity of a nominal monetary instrument to the nominal quantity of commercial paper offered as collateral had the potential to induce inflationary or deflationary spirals (Humphrey and Timberlake 2019, 9–26; Humphrey 1982; Sargent and Wallace 1975; Hetzel 2022, 35–38).[7] The flaws in the Real Bills Doctrine were also well understood by early British monetary writers, such as Henry Thornton ([1802] 1939, 86, 253–54), who was a member of the 1810 Bullion Committee of the British Parliament, which explained the fallacy.

The fallacy of the Real Bills Doctrine nonetheless continued to influence Federal Reserve actions in subsequent decades, particularly during the disaster of the Great Contraction. The Doctrine led the Fed leadership astray, causing them to misread signals and think that monetary policy was easy when it was actually quite restrictive (Humphrey and Timberlake 2019, 79–85; Friedman and Schwartz 1963, 299–419). In a 1963 letter to Congress, the Board of Governors of the Federal Reserve System finally abandoned the theory and proposed (unsuccessfully) removing the restrictions inspired by the Real Bills Doctrine from the Federal Reserve Act, although Fed officials had voiced skepticism in the late 1940s (Hackley 1973, 191–92; Bopp et al. 1947).

Some Founders Also Wanted the Fed to Backstop the Banker's Acceptance Market

At the time the Fed was founded, international trade by US firms was financed in European financial centers. Short-term obligations would be endorsed by a bank to become "two-name paper," or bills of exchange, which were traded ("discounted") on active markets. In the United States, banks extended credit on promissory notes that were generally not marketable.

Paul Warburg, a financier from a distinguished German banking family who had moved to New York to join Kuhn, Loeb & Co., one of the largest New York investment banks, was one of the driving forces in banking reform prior to the establishment of the Federal Reserve (Broz 1997, 142; Board of Governors, n.d.). His working knowledge of European banking systems made him particularly valuable, including at Senator Nelson Aldrich's famous Jekyll Island gathering that led to the first draft of what became the Federal Reserve Act. Warburg believed it was essential to create a liquid market in bank acceptances—bills issued by firms and endorsed by a bank along the lines of European practice (Broz 1997, 142–59). His case for a broad and liquid market for discounted bills was couched in public-interest terms. He argued that an active discount market would provide banks with a means of adjusting their reserve position by selling or buying bills; promissory notes, in contrast, were unmarketable because of the uncertain creditworthiness of the borrowing firm. An active discount market, Warburg claimed, would also divert reserves invested in stock exchange call loans and thus reduce the extent to which money-market stringency would lead to stock market sell-offs. And it would attract foreign bank investments and tie the dollar more closely to the international financial system, part of a broad Atlanticist agenda to expand America's international diplomatic and economic role (Roberts 2000).

While Warburg couched his argument in terms of the broad public interest, he was very clear that it would have private benefits to the US financial sector as well. After an extensive explanation of the workings of US international trade finance, he decried, in familiar terms, the payments made to European banks:

> It is impossible to estimate how large a sum America pays every year to Europe by way of commissions for accepting such documentary bills, and the other bills with which we shall now deal, but the figures run into many millions. This annual tribute to Europe resulting from our primitive financial system is not merely waste of money, but reflects upon the dignity of a nation of the political and economic importance of the United States. (Warburg 1910, 9)

The pecuniary gains for New York banks were another benefit of bringing trade finance to American shores. A central bank would have a critical role to play in establishing a market for acceptances, according to Warburg. "The central-bank system and the discount system can not be separated," he wrote, "they are absolutely interdependent" (Warburg 1910, 31). A ready market for American paper requires that it can be rediscounted at any moment. "This is insured in nearly every country of the world claiming a modern financial organization by the existence of some kind of a central bank, ready at all times to rediscount the legitimate paper of the general banks. Not only England, France and Germany have adopted such a system, but all the minor European States as well—and even reactionary Russia—have gradually accepted it" (Warburg 1907, 14).

Discount lending by the new Federal Reserve to support the commercial paper market would therefore serve a valuable mercantilist purpose. By subsidizing a New York bills market, Warburg argued, the Fed could counter the support provided by European central banks for their bills markets and help bring valuable financial transactions to American shores.[8]

Lending Doctrine 3: Warburg's Mercantilism   The Federal Reserve should provide backstop price support to the market for banker's acceptances and similar bills of exchange in order to attract and retain the intermediation of short-term financing in the United States.

The founders failed in their quest to create a broad national acceptance market or reduce reliance on stock market loans (Meltzer 2003, 76, 736).

The Fed often operated in the banker's acceptance market in the early years, but that faded in importance after the 1951 Treasury-Fed Accord. By the 1950s, the government securities market, where the Fed was operating quite actively, along with the interbank market for reserve account balances, provided an alternative to stock market call loans for banks to use to adjust their reserve positions. That said, the Fed has been attentive to money-market conditions throughout its history. During the Penn Central crisis in 1970, for example, even though the Fed didn't intervene directly in the commercial paper market, it did explicitly open the discount window to banks while urging them to provide support to their commercial-paper-issuing borrowers that were affected by the market turmoil (Calomiris 1994). And while banker's acceptances and trade finance more broadly did not appear to be instigators in the GFC or the fallout from the pandemic, and were not the targets of direct Fed intervention, the broader commercial paper market was the beneficiary of targeted support from a number of programs implemented in 2008 and 2020.[9]

Fed Lending Practice Evolves over the Twentieth Century

At the founding of the Federal Reserve, discount window lending was envisioned as the primary method of conducting monetary policy, consistent with the Monetary Stability and Real Bills lending doctrines. That changed over the course of the twentieth century. After the 1951 Treasury-Fed Accord gave the Fed greater freedom to operate in the government securities market, open market operations became the main tool of monetary policy. Untethered from monetary policy, Fed lending was free to be deployed for other, nonmonetary purposes.

America's entry into World War I in 1917 drew the Fed in to a supporting role coordinating and managing sales of the Liberty bonds issued by the Treasury (Meltzer 2003, 85–86). The governors (as they were then called) of the Federal Reserve Banks chaired committees organized in each district to promote sales to the general public. In addition, they offered banks short-term loans at preferential discount rates, which enabled member banks to buy short-term Treasury certificates during the periods between bond drives. Discount rates were set below the rates earned on the Treasury certificates, making borrowing immediately profitable. A second type of loan allowed banks to stretch out public payments for bonds. Lending on the security of government bonds was a departure from the Real Bills Doctrine, but Secretary of the Treasury William McAdoo was also chair of the Federal Reserve Board and the Fed had little choice but to pitch in on a patriotic endeavor.

Following the recession of 1920–21, the Fed began making more use of open market operations, in part in order to acquire earning assets to cover Reserve Bank operating costs and in part to move away from passive reliance on the demand for discount window borrowing (Meltzer 2003, 143–44). An awareness emerged, though imperfect, of the relationship between open market operations in bills or government securities and the demand for bank borrowing at the window—sales tended to drive banks to the window to replace lost reserves, purchases tended to induce repayments. System policy discouraged borrowing except "for the purpose of meeting temporary and seasonal needs" (Friedman and Schwartz 1963, 268–69). Open market operations shared center stage in the conduct of monetary policy. At the same time, Reserve Banks began allowing banks to borrow at the window for extended periods, delaying closures that would otherwise have been initiated by owners facing double liability (White 2013).

Real bills thinking was still prevalent, particularly at the Board, at the outset of the Great Contraction of 1929–33.[10] The sustained shift out of deposits into currency drove the money multiplier down. The Fed failed to offset the decline by boosting high-powered money, resulting in a disastrous 35.7% decline in the money stock from April 1929 to April 1933 (Friedman and Schwartz 1963, 333).[11] Fed leaders misread indicators and viewed their monetary policy stance as sufficiently accommodative, despite rapid deflation and elevated inflation-adjusted interest rates (Humphrey and Timberlake 2019).

A debate continues about the waves of bank failures in the Great Contraction. Much of the debate concerns "whether the banking panics were really panics in the sense of illiquidity shocks or whether they reflected endogenous insolvency responses to a recession caused by other forces, such as a collapse of autonomous expenditures or productivity shock" (Bordo and Landon-Lane 2010, 487; see also Calomiris and Mason 2003; Nelson 2020, 2:38–39). A separate set of issues concerns the relative roles of the money stock collapse and the waves of banking failures. Milton Friedman and Anna Schwartz, in A Monetary History of the United States (1963), ascribe a crucial role to the collapse in the money stock and note the contribution of the waves of bank failures to that collapse. Ben Bernanke, in a widely cited 1983 paper, also attributed the Great Contraction to the money stock collapse but found evidence of an additional "credit channel" depressing economic activity, through which bank failures disrupted the information-intensive intermediation process and reduced the economic effectiveness of the banking sector (Bernanke 1983, 257). Friedman and Schwartz disagree:

If the bank failures deserve special attention, it is clearly because they were the mechanism through which the drastic decline in the stock of money was produced, and because the stock of money plays an important role in economic development. The bank failures were important not primarily in their own right, but because of their indirect effect. If they had occurred to precisely the same extent without producing a drastic decline in the stock of money, they would have been notable but not crucial. If they had not occurred, but a correspondingly sharp decline had been produced in the stock of money by some other means, the contraction would have been at least equally severe and probably even more so. (Friedman and Schwartz 1963, 352)

One common misconception about the Great Contraction is that the Fed erred by not lending more freely to banks seeking credit at the discount window. Friedman and Schwartz (1963, 391–99) make clear, however, that the Fed could have conducted open market purchases of Treasury securities, as they did for a time in mid-1932 with salutary effect, or lent to banks by discounting Treasury securities. While acknowledging the disastrous consequences of bank failures, the Great Contraction was a failure of Fed monetary policy, not credit policy.

The Rise of Too Big to Fail

In the 1960s, the Fed began making use of the discount window to help the Federal Deposit Insurance Corporation (FDIC) delay the closure of failing banks. The practice continued, involving larger and larger institutions and ultimately giving rise to the widespread understanding that some banking organizations were "too big to fail." Numerous accounts describe the process. (See Stern and Feldman 2004, and Nurisso and Prescott 2020.) Key features of these interventions are discussed below. The central lesson is that by the time the twentieth century came to a close, there were pervasive expectations that Federal Reserve lending or intervention was likely to insulate short-term creditors from the effects of sizable failing or distressed financial institutions.

Federal Reserve lending to failing banks was often coordinated with or at the request of the FDIC in order to buy more time to arrange for a merger partner, or to delay or avoid the expense to the Deposit Insurance Fund of an outright closure. Fed and FDIC practice when the merger or closure ultimately took place was for the FDIC to repay the Fed loan at par and take back the collateral. As a result, the Fed loan provided the funds for uninsured short-term creditors to exit and avoid losses. If uninsured creditors remained exposed to the bank when it is closed, they would enter into a resolution process alongside the FDIC to recover on the bank's remaining assets. The Fed's loan thus facilitated shifting losses from uninsured creditors to longer-term creditors and/or the FDIC.

Flights from deposits to currency were generally absent in these episodes. Depositors would sometimes flee the failing bank, often serving as the spark for the crisis, but generally to other banks, not to currency. These episodes did not involve declines in the money multiplier or threats to the money stock and thus were not at all crises in the sense envisioned by Henry Thornton or Walter Bagehot. Anna J. Schwartz (1986b) refers to these as "pseudo-financial crises," to distinguish them from true monetary stability crises.

These crisis loans were routinely sterilized—that is, they were financed by the sale of US Treasury securities, not by the creation of high-powered money. If they had not been sterilized, the additional bank reserves would have flowed into the interbank lending market and depressed interbank lending rates, easing monetary policy. The FOMC sometimes did cut interest rates in conjunction with financial crises, but those were deliberate monetary policy actions motivated by fears of a broader deterioration in economic conditions rather than classical monetary distress.

The phrase "lender of last resort" began to be used in conjunction with these one-off crisis loans in the mid-1960s. The Federal Reserve in its 1968 "Reappraisal of the Federal Reserve Discount Mechanism" report used the phrase to describe Fed intervention in individual institution failures. The passage is worth quoting in full:

> Under present conditions, sophisticated open market operations enable the System to head off general liquidity crises, but such operations are less appropriate when the System is confronted with serious financial strains among individual firms or specialized groups of institutions. At times such pressures may be inherent in the nature of monetary restraint, in the sense that monetary policy actions, no matter how impersonally applied, often have, in fact, excessively harsh impacts on particular sectors of the economy. At other times underlying economic conditions may change in unforeseen ways, to the detriment of a particular financial substructure. And, of course, the possibility of local calamities or management failure affecting individual institutions or small groups of institutions is ever-present. It is in connection with

these limited crises that the discount window can play an effective role as "lender of last resort." (Board of Governors 1968, 17)

Note the acknowledgement that open market operations can head off "general liquidity crises"—that is, monetary stability problems of the Thornton-Bagehot variety, necessitating an accommodating expansion in high-powered money. The phrase "lender of last resort" is used instead for Fed credit extension in connection with one-off institutional bailouts—"limited crises"—a usage at variance with the classic lender-of-last-resort idea. Note also the attention to the differential sectoral effects of monetary restraint. The "Reappraisal" was issued just after the famous credit crunch of 1966, in which Fed tightening to attempt to rein in inflation raised interest rates above Regulation Q ceilings and led to sudden financial flows out of banks and into nonbank financial intermediaries. Political criticism of the Fed was sharp, particularly from the housing industry (Haltom and Sharp 2014, 1–2).

The "lender-of-last-resort" phrase was used in the same sense of rescuing individual firms in the communiqué issued by the Bank for International Settlements (BIS) on September 11, 1974 (BIS 1974; *Euromoney* 1974). That tumultuous and pivotal year saw the failure of Franklin National Bank, whose London subsidiary was an active borrower in the Eurodollar market, and of Herstatt Bank, a German bank whose closure in the middle of the trading day left the unsettled legs of foreign exchange trades in limbo.[12] At meetings in Basel of representatives of the G10 central banks, plus Switzerland, questions were raised about which central bank would have the responsibility to be the "lender of last resort" for a bank with cross-border operations (Wallich 1974b, 1974a). The Bank of England wanted clarity that they would not be responsible for supporting Franklin National's London subsidiary and insisted that the central bank of the country of domicile of the parent organization was to be the responsible one. The group reportedly agreed at the July meeting on several points, according to a trade publication report:

- Banks that get into liquidity difficulties within national boundaries will be supported by the central bank concerned.
- Banks that get into difficulties through fraud will not necessarily be bailed out but all deposits will be protected.
- Where the difficulty is at a foreign branch of the bank, the parent bank will be bullied into making good any losses (and if necessary supported by the central bank concerned under 1 or 2 above).

- Where the loss is sustained by an overseas subsidiary, the parent will again be responsible and supported by the central bank if necessary.
- Consortium banks will be supported on a pro rata basis by their parents (again with central bank support if necessary). (*Euromoney* 1974)

In September, the same group released a statement saying it agreed to "intensify the exchange of information between central banks" and that it "had an exchange of views on the problem of lender of last resort in Euromarkets. They recognized that it would not be practical to lay down in advance detailed rules and procedures for the provision of temporary liquidity. But they were satisfied that means are available for that purpose and will be used if and when necessary" (BIS 1974; see also Farnsworth 1974). The statement conveyed a strong backstop commitment but retained maximal discretion.

Principles 1–3 are in line with Warburg's notion of major countries' central banks each providing backstop support for their financial institutions. While Warburg's focus was on support for a market in trade bills and banker's acceptances to match and offset foreign central bank support for their bill markets, the same principle can be seen extended more broadly in 1974. "Too big to fail" for cross-border financial institutions required agreement among central banks on the division of responsibilities.

While Fed credit policy most commonly took the form of direct lending to afflicted institutions, there were times at which the Fed stood back but "encouraged" large member banks to support an ailing market or firm. When the railroad Penn Central defaulted on its commercial paper in 1970, the Fed relaxed long-standing administrative constraints at the discount window to allow banks to lend to their commercial-paper-issuing customers that were not able to roll their paper on previous terms (Calomiris 1994). Similarly, during the stock market contraction of 1987, the Fed "encouraged" banks to lend to equity market dealers facing funding issues (Bernhardt and Eckblad 2013). In 1998, the Federal Reserve Bank of New York organized a private-sector consortium rescue of the hedge fund LTCM (Lowenstein 2011). While these interventions did not involve direct Fed lending to failed institutions, they did utilize the considerable persuasive leverage available to the Fed to protect at least some investors from losses they might otherwise have incurred.

Congressional testimony was an inevitable consequence of the larger and more visible interventions, but the Fed avoided spelling out intended boundaries around possible future interventions. Prior to the early 1980s, member banks had privileged access to the discount window, but the Fed had Depression-era authority to lend outside their ranks and in any event could always lend using a member bank as a conduit. There were no apparent legal bounds on its lending and the Fed would not specify criteria, beyond the vague idea of "distress."[13] The Fed's communication strategy, which came to be known as "constructive ambiguity," conveyed that financial firms should not count on Fed lending support, but the Fed preserved the latitude to intervene at its discretion (Corrigan 1990; Giannini 1999).

The accumulation of cases of Fed-FDIC intervention to insulate various uninsured creditors from losses in failing financial institutions has not gone unnoticed. A voluminous literature notes the obvious moral-hazard effects, which include lower funding costs; excessive size; excessive borrowing, particularly short-term wholesale funding; excessive risk-taking in general; and a competitive advantage for the customers of large financial institutions.[14]

The Shadow Open Market Committee on Twentieth-Century Fed Credit Policy

The high and variable inflation of the late 1960s and early 1970s provided the impetus for the founding of the SOMC. Not coincidentally, however, this corresponded with a rise in volatility in banking and financial markets. Limited deregulation was beginning to increase the scope for competition among banks, and improvements in technology allowed for financial innovation to skirt some regulations (Horvitz 1975). Banks found ways to take on more risk, and the incidence of failures rose. The SOMC, consistent with the principles of sound central banking and healthy markets, naturally had something to say. At the third meeting of the SOMC—held on September 6, 1974, just three days prior to the G10 gathering that released the statement described above—Allan Meltzer (1974) urged the Fed to issue a clear statement of lender-of-last-resort policy. He used that phrase in the classical monetary sense rather than the sense of institutional rescues, and called out the risk of flight from deposits to currency: "The money stock shrinks and interest rates rise. Banks. . . sell assets. . . Bank failures rise, as in the early thirties." Citing Bagehot and the policies of the Bank of England, he cautioned that "prevention of financial panics did not mean then – and does not mean now – that a bank or a large bank should not be permitted to fail. The failure must not spread to solvent, liquid banks or institutions." Meltzer compared the Fed's handling of Franklin National unfavorably to its handling of the

Penn Central crisis in 1970: "In 1970, the Fed did not try to prevent failure; it prevented the failure from spreading through the financial markets. The Fed acted as if it recognized that the lender of last resort has a responsibility to the market and the institutions in the market and not to the particular issuer of securities."[15] Meltzer argued against preventing financial firm failures:

> The appropriate response in the case of temporary illiquidity is for the illiquid bank to borrow in the market. . . . The Federal Reserve has no responsibility to prevent the failure. It should publicly accept responsibility for preventing the panic from spreading through the market. The Federal Reserve should issue a policy statement accepting responsibility as lender of last resort to the financial system and denying responsibility to protect any private financial institutions from the consequences of errors and misjudgments. Such a statement should make clear that the policy will not prevent every failure but will seek to prevent a financial panic. (Meltzer 1974, 1–2)

A half year later, at the next SOMC meeting, Thomas Mayer (1975), then at the University of California, Davis, presented "The Case Against Credit Allocations," a response to several bills before Congress that sought to channel credit away from "inflationary" uses. "It would be foolish," Mayer argued, "to claim that the decisions of the private market are always optimal. But recognition of the weaknesses of market allocations does not suffice to make the case for replacing the free market with government controls." The idea that laissez-faire credit markets are afflicted by imperfections but difficult for government intervention to improve upon would return in the twenty-first-century debates about the "credit channel." If Meltzer and Mayer's guidance had been followed, banking and financial markets might have evolved very different over the next half century.

In May 1984, Continental Illinois nearly failed before being rescued by regulators (Federal Reserve History 2023). A large-scale run by uninsured depositors and other uninsured creditors, "amid rumors that the bank was in danger of failing," led the bank to seek a discount window loan from the Federal Reserve Bank of Chicago. It also received support from a consortium of sixteen large banks, but that was not enough. Two days later, the FDIC, the Office of the Comptroller of the Currency, and the Fed announced a temporary assistance program under which the FDIC guaranteed all depositors and general creditors of the bank and, together with a group of private banks, provided $8 billion in capital. The announcement also stated that "as part of the overall program, and in accordance with customary arrangements, the Federal Reserve is prepared to meet any extraordinary liquidity requirements of the Continental Illinois Bank during this period" (Kilborn 1984). Continental ultimately merged with Bank of America.

At its next meeting after the Continental Illinois failure, the SOMC (1984) policy statement included a section on banking policy in which it decried the rescue and the subsequent statement by the comptroller that the eleven largest banks were deemed "too big to fail," the first official acknowledgement of such. The Committee's statement cited the encouragement to banks to take excessive risks, including international loans, and noted that market discipline would be eroded. "The proper response to Continental's problem was to allow Continental to fail while preventing the effects of the failure from spreading to other banks." That prescription echoes Meltzer's recommendation following Franklin's failure and aligns with the thesis that expanding high-powered money so that the banking system has adequate reserves is the way to diffuse panics while preserving sound incentives. The statement went on to say that "banking history gives many examples to show that large failures do not bring on a financial panic if the authorities lend to the market to prevent a wave of failures. The most recent example in the U.S. followed the failure of Penn Central in the early 1970s" (SOMC 1984, 3).

In the 1980s, the SOMC credit policy thread was taken up by Anna J. Schwartz, SOMC member from the founding. In a contribution to the March 25, 1986, SOMC meeting, Schwartz (1986a) commented on the unfolding LDC (less-developed-country) debt crisis, saying that the "resort to the short-term palliatives that have been relied on to solve the Mexican difficulties do not address the fundamental roadblocks to debt repayment" and that the external debts of Latin American countries "will not be repaid at face value." She urged building up loss reserves, writing down loans to market values, and reforming deposit insurance systems.

In a paper delivered to a Federal Reserve Bank of St. Louis conference titled "Real and Pseudo-Financial Crises," Schwartz brought to bear the understanding gleaned from her lifetime of studying monetary history. "Real" financial crises were "fueled by fears that means of payment will be unobtainable at any price and, in a fractional-reserve banking system, leads to a scramble for high-powered money. It is precipitated by actions of the public that suddenly squeeze the reserves of the banking system. In a futile attempt to restore reserves, the banks may call loans, refuse to roll over existing loans, or resort to selling assets" (Schwartz 1986b, 11–12). In other words, a real financial crisis is the result of monetary instability of the type described by Thornton and Bagehot. The US experience from 1930 through 1933 *was* a real financial crisis, she noted: "A multiple contraction of deposits was enforced by the inability of the banks to acquire adequate amounts of high-powered money" (21). The Fed failed to supply currency or reserves to meet the increased demand, a response that could have been accomplished, as she and Friedman noted in *A Monetary History*, by either lending or open market operations.

Schwartz reviewed historical financial crises in the United States and the United Kingdom and saw no real financial crises in the US since 1933, and none in the UK since 1866 (Schwartz 1986b, 12). Her review of episodes since the mid-1960s labeled "financial crises" led her to conclude that they are not monetary stability problems—she called them "pseudo-financial crises" (25).

> Loss of wealth is not synonymous with a financial crisis. . . . Real financial crises need not occur because there is a well-understood solution to the problem: assure that deposits can be converted at will into currency whatever the difficulties banks encounter. The solution does not preclude failure of mismanaged banks. Recent discussion of moral hazard in relation to real financial crises would be more apt in relation to pseudo-financial crises. They provide the rationale for bail-outs and shoring up inefficiency. Pseudo-financial crises in recent years have generated expectations "that no monetary authority will allow any key financial actor to fail." (Schwartz 1986b, 23, 28)

Schwartz was skeptical about official crisis accounts. "The bugaboo of financial crisis has been created to divert attention from true remedies that the present financial situation demand. . . . It is not financial distress that triggers a crisis. The failure of authorities or institutions to respond in a predictable way to ward off a crisis and the private sector's uncertainty about the response are the triggers of a real financial crisis" (11–12). Allan Meltzer, her discussant at that conference, also emphasized uncertainty about the lender-of-last-resort function and the importance of precommitment (Meltzer 1986). He also emphasized the monetary nature of lender-of-last-resort intervention: "The unique ability of a lender-of-last-resort is the ability to produce base money on demand" (36).

Schwartz was invited to give the 1992 Homer Jones Memorial Lecture at the Federal Reserve Bank of St. Louis and she took the opportunity to discuss "The Misuse of the Fed's Discount Window." (A brief synopsis was presented at the September 1991 SOMC meeting.) Drawing on discount window data obtained by the House Banking Committee, she noted that a very large fraction of discount window borrowers that failed had the lowest possible supervisory rating and that a large number of borrowers had discount window loans outstanding when they failed. Recent practice, she noted, delays closure of failed institutions, increasing losses to the FDIC and ultimately taxpayers. "The time has come," she concludes, "for a truly basic change: eliminate the discount window and restrict the Fed to open market operations" (Schwartz 1992, 59). "The Federal Reserve does not need the window to serve as a lender of last resort" (67).[16]

In the 1990s, Schwartz went on to critique foreign exchange market intervention, the Bretton Woods fiftieth-anniversary commission, the Mexican rescue plan of 1995, and International Monetary Fund (IMF) lending practices more broadly. Allan Meltzer was also an outspoken critic of the IMF (and the World Bank as well), testifying before Congress on the topic and chairing the International Financial Institution Advisory Commission in 1998, which issued a report recommending reforms of the IMF and the World Bank. The incentive effects of the IMF's evolving mission were prominent in his critique:

Since 1971, the IMF has been looking for new things to do. It has now solved its problem by creating moral hazard, allowing international banks to avoid the risks they undertake by imprudent lending. The IMF encourages the behavior that creates the problems. (Meltzer 1998)

Schwartz was similarly critical in a September 1998 SOMC contribution titled "What Future for the IMF?" She also noted the IMF's desire for a "bigger part on the world stage," and cited its role, together with the US Treasury, in fostering a "culture of loans to troubled low-income countries" (Schwartz 1998). Troubled countries can turn to deep international capital markets and borrow at rates reflecting their true credit risk. The IMF rescues, she argued, do not deal with true reform problems. At the March 1999 SOMC meeting, Schwartz (1999) delivered a scathing critique of Stanley Fischer's (1999) address to the American Economic Association advocating for an international lender of last resort, noting that such an entity would be redundant given that national central banks control the creation of high-powered money. Two years later, Schwartz (2001) commented that "three emerging market countries have been in the IMF infirmary: Argentina, Brazil, and Turkey. Despite the critical reviews to which the IMF was subjected in 2000, not much has changed in its response to the pleas for assistance by troubled countries" (1). At the spring meeting the following year, the news release noted that Argentina had failed to address its structural and fiscal problems and urged the IMF to "hold off making further loans until Argentina's internal problems are addressed" (SOMC 2002a).

The policy statement at the Spring 2002 meeting also called out the Fed's warehousing arrangement by which it held foreign currency on behalf of the Treasury when the Exchange Stabilization Fund is exhausted. The arrangement should be terminated, it said, "because it circumvents the intent of Congress with respect to the Exchange Stabilization Fund" (SOMC 2002b). The failure of Enron the previous December, and the resulting focus on corporate governance and transparency, motivated the recommendation, but it also dovetailed with the views of other long-standing critics of the Fed's role in foreign exchange operations, including future SOMC member Marvin Goodfriend (Broaddus and Goodfriend 1996). That context also prompted a memorandum from Lee Hoskins (2002), former president of the Federal Reserve Bank of Cleveland, suggesting a number of other improvements to Fed governance, including decentralizing discount window operations to end micromanagement by the Board of Governors.

In the early 2000s, the SOMC began focusing on the risks emanating from the government-sponsored enterprises (GSEs) Fannie Mae and Freddie Mac. At the Fall 2002 SOMC meeting, the Committee's official statement noted the regulatory advantages and implicit guarantees enjoyed by these GSEs, which encourage excessive risk-taking and distort resource allocation, and recommended privatization. At that meeting Gregory Hess (2002) warned about GSE risk-taking incentives and argued for full privatization and explicit removal of the implicit guarantee. He returned to the subject to argue more forcefully for privatization at the Fall 2003 meeting (Hess 2003). At the May 2004 meeting, he took notice of a December 2003 working paper by Board of Governors economist Wayne Passmore estimating that the housing GSEs receive a 40-basis-points cost of funds benefit from the implicit government guarantee and various other privileges relative to their competitors and yet pass on only 7 basis points in the form of lower mortgage rates (Hess 2004). Hess titled his presentation "Can We Avert the Next Financial Crisis?"—a prescient question in 2004. The policy statement at that meeting, sup-ported by another Hess memo, recommended "to move the supervision and regulation of these GSE's to the Treasury, to explicitly remove the implicit and explicit benefits that they receive and to significantly raise their capital requirements," but ultimately to privatize them (SOMC 2004). In the fall, Hoskins revisited the IMF and the World Bank and urged privatization, again arguing that only national central banks have the capacity to address crises.

Shadow Open Market Committee analysis of issues related to Federal Reserve credit policy generally delivered a sharply critical view of the TBTF rescue lending that began to emerge and grow when the group was founded in 1973, so much so that one member advocated abolishing the Fed's lending authority. The critical perspective was grounded in the historical understand-ing that a central bank, as the monopoly supplier of high-powered money, had a responsibility to deliver monetary stability. That responsibility was origi-nally known as lender of last resort, but central banks had hijacked the phrase and applied it to sterilized lending that was unrelated to monetary stability. Lending in TBTF cases thus falls outside of the Monetary Stability Doctrine. Such lending is also inconsistent with the Real Bills Doctrine, whose propo-nents opposed deposit insurance and Fed lending to failing banks. And it does not fit in with the commercial paper market focus of Warburg's Mercantilism. What sort of implicit doctrine does TBTF lending represent?

Limited Commitment and Fed Lending

As many have observed, in large financial institution failures the Fed faces a time consistency problem (Stern and Feldman 2004, 19–20; Chari and Kehoe 2016). If it chooses a course of action in advance, providing good incentives suggests committing not to rescue the creditors of insolvent institutions. If it cannot commit and can only choose actions ex post, after an institution has gotten into trouble, it may feel compelled to alleviate distress and come to the rescue of uninsured creditors, even in the case of insolvent institutions. James Buchanan (1975) called situations like these "The Samaritan's Dilemma."

In a 1999 paper, Marvin Goodfriend and I took a deeper look at the time consistency problem associated with central bank lending, drawing on insights from the financial contracting literature (Goodfriend and Lacker 1999). Our supposition was that central bank lending is analogous to pri-vate line-of-credit lending, where the presumption would be that contractual arrangements are structured so as to manage the commitment problem effi-ciently from an ex ante standpoint. In contrast, a central bank faces distinctly different incentives and might not be expected to make lending and closure decisions that have the same ex ante efficiency properties. A central bank is a public institution, with profits and losses flowing back to the government, so profit maximization might not be the primary objective. A central bank faces the prospect of being blamed for any financial consequences of failing to lend and will always have difficulty proving the counterfactual that letting a distressed bank fail would not seriously harm markets. The failing institution and its allies—particularly similarly situated firms—may be able to bring pressure on the Fed as well. In addition, delaying or avoiding closure of a financial institution can help deflect attention from supervisory missteps leading up to the problem. The FDIC may be unwilling or unable to accept the up-front cost to the Deposit Insurance Fund from closing a failing bank. Because near-term political fallout and ex post resolution costs are tangible and borrower behavior is sunk, the Fed cooperates in forestalling prominent financial institution closure, even in cases where closure arguably would have been part of an ex ante optimal arrangement.

The limited commitment perspective provides a framework for understanding the rise of TBTF over time. An instance of financial distress leads the Fed and the FDIC to intervene in a way that forestalls financial market turbulence and political costs by allowing uninsured investors to avoid losses. Regulations are tightened to attempt to prevent the occurrence of the risks that were the proximal cause of the crisis. But the newly established precedent increases the probability that market participants perceive of future intervention in similar circumstances. Moreover, the regulatory crackdown encourages financial innovations that bypass the tighter constraints and create potentially fragile financial arrangements on the edge of the domain where future official support might be forthcoming—"shadow banking." The inherent limitations on the effectiveness of risk containment mean that fragility builds up and future crises and intervention become more likely. A self-reinforcing cycle of rescue, regulation, bypass, and crisis leads to an ever-expanding financial safety net (Lacker 2011, 2012b).

Central bankers are not unaware of the moral-hazard effects of the precedents their interventions set and they have a motive to avoid political criticism for bailing out large financial institutions. Their interest in limiting those effects undoubtedly serves to inhibit interventions in some circumstances. Several large nonbank financial institutions have failed without intervention: Drysdale Securities (1982) and Drexel Burnham Lambert (1990) are noteworthy examples. When a large entity is failing, it is almost routine to approach to the Fed for support, as happened when Penn Central failed in 1970 (Brimmer 1989, 5), and in the case of Drexel (Fromson 1990). Stern and Feldman (2004, 80–85) devote a chapter to such cases, arguing that they help illuminate interventions as well.[17]

The Fed's "constructive ambiguity" communication strategy follows naturally from this framework, but it exacerbates problematic incentives. The Fed avoids committing to future interventions in order to discourage the risk-taking that might contribute to future crises. But officials avoid promising *not* to intervene, in order to preserve the flexibility to respond to future crises in a manner that best suits their interests at that time (Corrigan 1990). Board Governor Henry Wallich spelled out the Fed's communication policy in a response to 1974 Senate questions about the provision of emergency assistance:

There are dangers in trying to define and publicize specific rules for emergency assistance to troubled banks, notably the possibility of causing undue reliance on such facilities and possible relaxation of needed caution on the part of all market participants. Therefore, the Federal Reserve has always avoided comprehensive statements of conditions for its assistance to member banks. Emergency assistance is inherently a process of negotiation and judgment, with a range of possible actions varying with circumstances and need. Therefore, a predetermined set of conditions for emergency lending would be inappropriate. (Wallich 1974c, 762)

Preserving optionality leads creditors to attach nonzero probability to being rescued. So when a financial firm faces distress, the Fed's intervention decision shifts the perceived probability of intervening for other similar institutions—upward if it decides to intervene, downward if it does not. Rescues prevent "contagion" by preventing perceived intervention probabilities from falling (Cochrane and Seru 2024, 187).

Limited commitment, then, in the context of late twentieth-century US central banking, yields a distinct lending doctrine:

Lending Doctrine 4: Reluctant Samaritan   Federal Reserve lending decisions are made case-by-case, at its discretion, in order to: mitigate the ex post costs of resolving failing financial firms, especially banks; help the FDIC delay resolution of failing banks; avoid the political fallout of financial market turmoil that might arise if lending is withheld; and minimize the perceived departure from past precedent. Communication strives to minimize expectations of future intervention but preserve maximum discretion.

Marvin Goodfriend and I were struck by the contrast between TBTF lending and the US monetary policy, where the Fed faces the same time consistency problem. Discretionary monetary policy setting without commitment is well known to be suboptimal, but the Volcker Fed was willing to incur short-term costs in order to establish a reputation for fighting inflation (Goodfriend 1997; Goodfriend and King 2005). Goodfriend and I wondered, on the doorstep of the twenty-first century, whether the Fed could pursue a similar strategy by building a reputation for lending restraint (Goodfriend and Lacker 1999, 23–24; Broaddus 2000). I was hopeful, based on Fed leaders' statements that seemed to discourage expectations of future rescues. Federal Reserve Chair Alan Greenspan, in a lengthy speech on "The Financial Safety Net" at the 2001 Federal Reserve Bank of Chicago Conference on Bank Structure, expressed the view that "as a society we ought to explore what we can do at the margin to retain the economic benefits and lower the economic costs of the safety net" (Greenspan 2001b). He spent some time on practical steps to do so, including disclosures to facilitate greater market discipline, but noted that "the additional information will be irrelevant unless counterparties believe that they are, in fact, at risk. . . . The potential for greater market discipline at large institutions is substantial." It seemed to me that reining in the financial safety net might be possible. Goodfriend, on the other hand, was less hopeful. He turned out to be right.

A less hopeful perspective on the possibility of a reputational strategy for limiting lending has led some to look to more formal constraints on Fed credit market intervention. The Federal Deposit Insurance Corporation Improvement Act of 1991 sought to constrain and disincent bank bailouts by requiring certain regulator actions—"prompt corrective action"—for under-capitalized banks, limiting the FDIC to "least-cost" resolution methods for failed banks and limiting Federal Reserve Bank lending to undercapitalized banks.[18] Stern and Feldman (2004) argue that the Act did nothing to fundamentally change regulators' decision making.

The fundamental problem is a consequence of the Federal Reserve Banks' balance sheets. The Fed's ability to manage their liabilities independently is essential to the framework established by the Treasury-Fed Accord for the independent conduct of monetary policy. Yet that independence leaves the Fed's assets under its discretionary control as well. Since lending, once sterilized, does not interfere with monetary policy, the Fed is left exposed to pressure to use the balance sheet for politically favored purposes.

This suggests a broader perspective on the Fed's commitment problem. Compared to the first three lending doctrines, the Reluctant Samaritan is more of a positive theory in the realm of public choice, specifying how an institution like the Federal Reserve will behave given the political environment it faces. It fits naturally into the framework described by Charles Calomiris and Stephen Haber (2015) in their book *Fragile by Design*. They situate central banking within the broader context of the relationship between the state and the banking and financial system, where the central bank is an intermediary, helping the private-sector finance the state and channeling fiscal resources to the private sector in the form of regulatory privileges and various subsidies. Crisis lending on favorable terms to rescue investors in large financial institutions can be seen as an off-budget, rarely visible subsidy that becomes more valuable as the economic environment becomes riskier, as it began to in the 1960s. It also enhances the returns to scale, leading to larger banks, greater implicit subsidies, and broader distortions. From this perspective, the limited nature of central bank lending commitment might be viewed as an endogenous component of the grand political banking bargain Calomiris and Haber describe.

In any event, the expansion of the federal financial safety net in the last third of the twentieth century laid the groundwork for the behavior of financial markets in the twenty-first. Expanding precedents enhanced expectations of lending support and arguably induced greater financial fragility, particularly reliance on short-term wholesale funding, a lending mechanism more likely to elicit rescues. At the end of the century, Federal Reserve Bank of Richmond economists estimated that a total of 44.8% of financial sector liabilities were estimated to be explicitly or implicitly government-guaranteed, based conservatively on previous government actions or policy statements; see table 20.1 (Walter and Weinberg 2002). The potential scale of government intervention was evident, though perhaps not widely appreciated.

The Great Financial Crisis

A decade and a half after the fact, the dramatic financial and banking events of 2007 to 2009 and the Federal Reserve's responses should be quite familiar. Still, it is worth revisiting selected elements of the narrative from the

Table 20.1. Estimated federal financial safety net, 1999, billions of dollars

	Explicitly Guaranteed	Implicitly Guaranteed	Total Guaranteed	Total Liabilities
Commercial Banks	2,203	773	2,976	4,850
Savings Institutions	637	47	684	1,113
Credit Unions	336		336	375
Government-Sponsored Enterprises		2,620	2,620	1,199
Private Employer Pensions	1,805		1,805	2,090
Other Financial Firms				7,723
Total Financial Firms	4,981	3,440	8,241	18,771
Percent of Total Liabilities	26.5%	18.3%	44.8%	100.0%

Source: Walter and Weinberg (2002).

perspective of the lending doctrines identified above and the analysis provided both before and after the crisis by the SOMC.

The Monetary Stability Doctrine and the Great Financial Crisis

The growing recognition of the scale of subprime losses started generating financial market turbulence in early August 2007. It has become commonplace since the GFC to portray the Federal Reserve's responses as "fulfilling the classic central banking role of lender of last resort" (Bernanke 2015, 243). This was certainly an apt characterization in early August 2007, when growing expected losses on subprime mortgages raised counterparty risk in interbank funding markets. Banks' desired holdings of reserve account deposits rose significantly and became more volatile, leading the New York Fed to intervene more frequently during the trading day and in larger amounts. On August 9, an additional $24 billion in reserves were supplied via repo operations—that is, the New York Fed's buying of Treasury securities with reserves and selling them back the next day. Accommodating fluctuations in reserve demand was standard procedure for implementing the FOMC's interest rate target; the difference was the magnitude and volatility of the demand shift that day.[19] These were temporary open market purchases of government securities and would be defined as monetary policy, not credit policy, by Goodfriend and

King (1988).[20] There was no evidence of a public shift out of deposits into currency, so this did not appear to be a broader monetary stability problem.

Later that month, on the evening of August 16, 2007, the Fed lowered the interest rate on discount window loans to 50 basis points above the federal funds rate target from 100 basis points, which had been the norm since the discount window reforms of 2002. The objective was to encourage bank borrowing at the discount window. William Dudley, then-manager of the System Open Market Account, confirmed that any increase in discount window lending that resulted would be sterilized, consistent with the standard interest rate targeting operating regime (FOMC 2007a, 4). Michael Bordo (2009) called attention to the sterilization at the April 2009 SOMC meeting. Thus, increased discount window lending would be completely unrelated to the monetary stability doctrine or any "classic" notion of lender of last resort. All subsequent lending up until October 2008 was sterilized—the Term Auction Facility announced in December 2007, the Primary Dealer Credit Facility announced in March 2008, and the loan to aid the acquisition of Bear Stearns by JPMorgan Chase (JPMC) in March 2008. There were some weaker banks that experienced deposit drains in late 2007 and early 2008, but these just resulted in funds moving from one bank to another and thus would not threaten the money multiplier or the overall money supply. The ratio of deposits to currency was stable and throughout the crisis there was no evidence of the type of fractional-reserve instability cited by Thornton and Bagehot (Lacker 2024b). Thus Schwartz (1986b) would classify this episode a "pseudo-crisis"—that is, not a monetary stability crisis to which the central bank is obliged to respond.

Some accounts of the GFC describe events in the markets for repos and off-balance-sheet asset-backed commercial paper (ABCP) as "runs" and "panics" (Gorton 2008, 2010). Investors pulled away from those markets or demanded shorter tenors and tighter terms. There will be more to say about repo and ABCP runs later on, but here let us address the question of whether the money-like properties of the repo market indicated the need for special central bank response on classic lender-of-last-resort grounds. The answer is clearly "no." Repo market borrowers and ABCP issuers may hold Federal Reserve Bank reserve accounts, either directly or indirectly. And repo market lenders and ABCP holders may have shifted into holding assets backed less partially by Fed monetary liabilities, inducing a movement in a repo version of the money multiplier. But that increase in the demand for Fed liabilities would manifest itself as an increase in the demand for reserve balances.

Indeed, the surge in excess reserve holdings in early August 2007 may have represented such a shift. But again, the New York Fed's standard operating procedure accommodated that demand automatically via open market purchases of Treasury securities, without the need for credit extension to the private sector. This was perfectly consistent with the propositions of Thornton and Bagehot, since both cited operations in government securities as effective means of implementing their recommendations. The Fed was doing all it needed to do, as monopoly supplier of reserve account balances, to respond to any sort of run on repos.

In October 2008, Federal Reserve Banks began paying interest on reserves under authority provided by the Emergency Economic Stabilization Act of 2008. At around the same time, the New York Fed exhausted its ability to sterilize the reserve balances being added by the large and growing credit programs. The Fed's balance sheet and the banking system's reserve balances ballooned, driving the federal funds rate down below the FOMC's target. At the December 2008 meeting, the Committee dropped the target to a range from 0% to 0.25%. While credit extensions were unsterilized after the fall of 2008, as Thornton and Bagehot recommended, they had no direct effect on the quantity of money in the hands of the public. With the banking system's demand for reserve balances satiated, the Fed's balance sheet had become uncoupled from the problematic fractional reserve monetary dynamics that were central to the last-resort lending urged by Thornton and Bagehot (Lacker 2024b).[21] The high-powered money the Fed controlled was no longer scarce.

The Real Bills Doctrine and the Great Financial Crisis

The Fed made no effort during the GFC or the COVID-19 pandemic to limit credit extension to commercial paper arising out of "real" transactions, as the Real Bills Doctrine would require. All of the Fed's special lending programs circumvented the constraints in the Federal Reserve Act motivated by the Real Bills Doctrine. Some programs made use of the authority to make advances to banks (as opposed to discounting paper from banks), while others made use of the authority to make loans to nonbank entities under section 13(3). But the constraints of the Real Bills Doctrine were ignored, consistent with the Fed's formal disavowal of the doctrine in the 1960s (Hackley 1973, 191–92).

While Real Bills prescriptions no longer limit Fed lending, traces of Real Bills thinking are evident in the Fed's approach to financial stability monitoring. That work is focused on "assessing vulnerabilities," including "valuation pressures [that] arise when asset prices are high relative to economic fundamentals or historical norms," "excessive borrowing by businesses and households," and "excessive leverage within the financial sector" (Board of Governors 2024, v–vi). The idea that asset prices can at times rise above "economic fundamentals," perhaps driven by "excessive" borrowing or leverage, echoes the idea that departure from Real Bills principles can lead to "speculative excess," the inevitable collapse of which depressed economic activity (Mints 1945, 207). Michael Bordo at the September 2017 SOMC meeting noted the striking similarity between the Real Bills conception of inflation as driven by asset booms that the central bank should head off and the recent conception of central banks' financial stability responsibilities (Bordo 2017).

More broadly, the essence of Real Bills thinking is that some types of credit are healthier for the economy than others, and banking practice and central bank policies should encourage the productive uses of credit. The Fed's twenty-first-century credit market interventions involved acquiring some sectors' debt obligations instead of holding an equivalent amount of Treasuries. To the extent that such use of the Fed's balance sheet is effective at lowering some sectors' borrowing costs, it is likely to raise borrowing costs in other sectors. Even though the precepts of the Real Bills Doctrine were disavowed by the Fed in the 1960s, the underlying conception of credit markets lives on.

Warburg's Mercantilism and the Great Financial Crisis

The trade bills and banker's acceptances that were the focus of Warburg's mercantilist agenda were not a specific target of the Fed's credit market interventions in the GFC.[22] Some of the Fed's GFC credit market interventions can be seen as at least partially motivated by a desire to preserve and enhance the competitive position of US dollar markets in global banking and finance. Other major countries had long been providing support for their large financial institutions—so-called "national champions." As noted earlier, in 1974, around the time of the birth of Too Big to Fail, the G10 central banks agreed on a demarcation of responsibilities for lending to the overseas affiliates of their major banks. The Fed's provision of dollar funding on favorable terms to foreign banks during the GFC through facilities like the Term Auction Facility (TAF), which was dominated at the outset by branches and offices of foreign banks, appears to be a departure from the 1974 agreement, which held that the home-country parent bank and the home-country central bank would be responsible for the provision of liquidity support of a foreign branch in the United States.

The swap lines the Fed established with foreign central banks also played a role in funding foreign banks' US operations. Under a swap line, the Fed exchanges currencies with a foreign central bank—the purpose being "to enhance the provision of U.S. dollar liquidity."[23] Foreign central banks held large dollar reserves on their own, however, and conceivably could have lent those on favorable terms to their banks. The swap lines instead funneled Fed credit to foreign banks using foreign central banks as conduits, sparing the latter the inconvenience of using their own dollar reserves. Again, this departed from the 1974 agreement and expanded Fed lending across the reciprocal boundaries agreed on in 1974, in alignment with Warburg's broader Atlanticist vision of supporting a robust global role for dollar financial markets.[24] Indeed, one could view the Fed's eagerness to accommodate foreign-bank dollar borrowing demand as aimed in part at preserving the dollar's role as a reserve currency.

The Reluctant Samaritan in the Great Financial Crisis

Key elements of the limited-commitment perspective are evident in how the GFC played out. Federal Reserve decisions were clearly driven by a desire to avoid, ex post, private-sector costs and political fallout, rather than by conformance to a response function policymakers wanted market participants to understand. The moral-hazard implications of interventions were acknowledged but put off, to be dealt with down the road, although those implications did not wait until the next business cycle to emerge and affect unfolding events. At several junctures, the Fed sought to calm markets and "restore confidence," but did so simply by resolving intervention uncertainty in the direction of making future rescues seem more likely. And political considerations, rather than narrow economic analysis, appeared to drive key lending decisions. The narrative centers shifting private estimates of the probability of future interventions, and the Fed's attempt to manage them.

The initial, August 2007, Federal Reserve response to financial market turmoil was *designed* to change expectations about the Fed's stance toward credit markets; it was designed to *increase* the perceived probability of lending, not reduce it as Greenspan had suggested in 2001. The 50-basis-point reduction in the discount rate was intended to reduce the penalty for using the discount window and increase usage. After it was announced the morning of August 17, Vice Chair Don Kohn and New York Fed president Tim Geithner were on a conference call of the Clearing House Association, an organization of the largest banks in the country (formerly known as the New York Clearing

House), to explain the move and try to persuade banks that they should not feel stigmatized going to the window. On the contrary, they argued, it should be viewed as a "show of strength." Only one large bank took up the suggestion over the weekend, but when word of its borrowing leaked out its stock price fell sharply. The next week, the four largest US banks (Citi, JPMorgan Chase, Bank of America, and Wachovia), in a coordinated action, announced simultaneously that they had each borrowed $500 million from the Fed. The Board of Governors also sent letters to three of them granting temporary exemption from section 23A of the Federal Reserve Act which otherwise would have prevented them from sharing the discount window borrowing of their bank subsidiaries with other subsidiaries, such as their broker-dealers.

The Fed's promotional efforts failed to increase discount window lending appreciably. Total borrowing rose from $264 million on August 15 to $2.6 billion the next Wednesday, fell back a bit for two weeks, then spiked at $7.4 billion on September 12.[25] Borrowing remained under $1 billion from late September until mid-December. As noted above, banks were borrowing large amounts from the Federal Home Loan Banks (FHLBs) instead. Borrowing at the FHLBs rose by $237 billion in the second half of 2007, a 36.7% increase, with $150 billion of that increase accounted for by the top ten member institutions (Ashcraft et al. 2010, 553). The Federal Reserve's attempt at intermediation at first could not compete against other government-sponsored enterprises. The Fed had more success with the introduction of the Term Auction Facility, which was open to foreign banks, who were ineligible for FHLB membership.

The Fed's highly visible efforts in 2007 may have failed to appreciably increase discount window borrowing, but they surely tilted private-sector incentives away from taking preventative measures that might have reduced its vulnerability to problems down the road. Capital markets were open for large banks for the next twelve months, and many raised new equity to replace capital written off in recent quarters (Cohan 2009, 398). For example, Lehman Brothers issued $4.0 billion in convertible preferred stock in April 2008, and then in June it raised $6.0 billion in preferred and common stock (FDIC 2011, 31–32). The convertible preferred stock was more than three times oversubscribed, so it could have raised significantly more capital than it did, but it chose not to (Lehman Brothers 2008). The prior month's assistance to the Bear-JPMC merger also would have tilted the willingness of a firm in Lehman Brothers' situation to incur material costs to reduce vulnerabilities. And liquidity management decisions were bound to be affected as well. Large banks using the overnight repo market to fund illiquid assets could have termed out their borrowings or issued additional equity and cut dividends to fund those assets. That might have been costly, but for a solvent firm it should not have been impossible. Convincing market participants that the Fed was more inclined to lend than they might have otherwise thought was bound to have moral-hazard consequences at some point. Policymakers may not have appreciated how soon those consequences would arrive.

Fears of repercussions in the repo market motivated the Fed's decision to lend to Bear Stearns on Friday morning, March 14, 2008, and then on Sunday agree to assist Bear's merger with JPMorgan. Bear had continued to fund illiquid, mortgage-related securities in the overnight repo market, but repo investors began to flee Bear in significant numbers earlier that week. Unwinding the back leg of their overnight repos was up to Bear's clearing bank, JPMorgan; its decision Thursday night to not unwind the next morning forced the Fed to decide whether to lend or not.[26] Following that decision, policymakers feared that if Bear's repos failed to unwind, investors would pull away from other overnight repo borrowers, such as Lehman or Merrill, the two next-largest investment banks. The Fed's intervention succeeded at calming markets by boosting the perceived probability that the Fed would protect repo investors in other investment banks. The intervention itself revealed nothing about the quality of Bear's assets that was not already apparent from the signals given off by Bear's loss of market funding that week. Instead, the intervention simply provided information about the preferences of policymakers. The contagion that policymakers wanted to prevent was the spread of reduced assessments of how likely policymakers were likely to intervene again. The financial safety net now included the top five investment banks.

The moral-hazard implications of the Fed's assistance was noted prominently in a rare public rebuke by former Fed chair Paul Volcker, who said that the Fed's actions "will surely be interpreted as an implied promise of similar action in times of future turmoil" (Volcker 2008, 2). Coming from a former central banker of Volcker's unmatched stature, this was a bracing assessment. And the fact that it highlighted the moral-hazard implications was prescient.[27]

Federal Reserve officials offered virtually no guidance about what to expect in similar future circumstances, consistent with the Reluctant Samaritan's constructive ambiguity communication strategy. Senior executives at Lehman Brothers were said to have been surprised at not receiving the same merger assistance that Bear received. After Lehman was forced, by the government, to file for bankruptcy on September 15, the large assistance package for AIG two days later was another huge, and confusing, surprise. At that point, the need for a clear, publicly announced plan from the Treasury and the Fed for handling subsequent failures was achingly apparent. Up to that point, between Bear, IndyMac, Fannie and Freddie (both taken into conservatorship earlier in September), Lehman, and AIG, six different failures had been handled five different ways. It would have been hard for market participants to predict, based on past actions, how the next financial firm failure would be handled; in particular, where in the capital structure would the cut be made between those rescued and the rest? An announced plan for handling future financial problems would be useful, but it needed to be credible—perceived intervention probabilities were too uncertain. Bernanke and Treasury Secretary Henry Paulson dusted off a plan staff had drafted that summer and went to Congress seeking appropriations for $700 billion. John Taylor (2009) argues persuasively, based on the timing of movements in credit spreads, that the frightening rhetoric used by Paulson and Bernanke to make their case to Congress and the public resulted in a significant deterioration in business and consumer confidence.

While Bernanke and Paulson were appealing to Congress, the decision was made to support all of the debt of Wachovia, including obligations of the holding company and other affiliates, setting a new safety net precedent. The bank subsidiary of Washington Mutual (WAMU) had been taken over by the FDIC and sold on Thursday night, September 25. Holders of the holding company debt would have to seek repayment as part of the holding company's bankruptcy proceedings, along with the FDIC seeking recovery of the costs it incurred inducing a buyer to take over the bank. The following day bondholders began calling Wachovia asking whether the bank would buy back their debt. Such accommodations were often made in normal times in order to maintain investor goodwill, even in cases in which there was no contractual obligation to repurchase the debt. Wachovia's condition had been suspect, due to mounting losses stemming from its acquisition of the California savings bank Golden West, pioneer of the "Pick-A-Pay" mortgage that allowed borrowers the option to skip payments. Wachovia had been slowly bleeding deposits over the summer and the inquiries that Friday posed a dilemma: Cash reserves were dwindling, but refusing a customary accommodation would send an adverse signal that could jeopardize future liquidity. Management turned to the Federal Reserve and Treasury to say that they didn't think they could make it through to the following weekend and thus would have to "be resolved" that weekend. Over the weekend, strategy was discussed by the regulators involved—the Office of the Comptroller of the Currency, the FDIC, and the Fed, including staff from the Board of Governors, and the Federal Reserve Banks of Richmond, New York, and San Francisco (the last two because the prospective bidders were Citigroup and Wells Fargo).[28] Citigroup, it was learned, would be proposing an assisted purchase of the holding company, so a critical policy question on Saturday was whether Wachovia's holding-company debt would get government support, unlike WAMU's. The argument New York advanced for doing so was that without such support "no other large bank would be able to issue debt on Monday morning." That carried the day. Again, intervention steadied markets by raising the perceived probability of future intervention.[29] The financial safety net now included large bank holding companies.

In both the Bear Stearns and Wachovia rescues, policymakers' focus on immediate ("exigent") rather than ex ante considerations was evident. The moral-hazard implications were universally acknowledged, but crisis conditions were viewed as too grim, so dealing with moral-hazard effects was generally left for another day; future legislation or regulatory reforms could prevent the relevant institutions from taking the risks that had afflicted the ones just rescued. Deliberations were never framed in terms of repeated interactions. One did not hear the question posed: "What would we want market participants to believe we would do in similar future circumstances?" An example of this ex post mindset was Chair Bernanke's comment at the very end of the December 2008 meeting: When asked, following a discussion of the Term Asset-Backed Securities Loan Facility program, whether he was "concerned about setting up expectations for the next recession," he said, "Certainly I'm concerned. I'm very concerned. But I'm also concerned about getting through this recession" (FOMC 2008, 237). At the following month's meeting, he spoke in the same vein: "But we are in a situation at this point where past is past and what is sunk is sunk. We have to deal with the situation. And it is very, very important for us to go forward to try to change the legal structure, the regulatory structure, and even Federal Reserve operating procedures in ways that will encourage more-stable systems in the future. But at the moment, the fire is burning, and we have to think about that" (FOMC 2009, 81–82).

The combustion analogy is a perennial motif, with the Fed likened to the firefighter and the homeowners' negligence likened to the sunk effects of past moral hazard (Cochrane and Seru 2024, 171, 186, 190). In fact, *Firefighting* went on to become the title of key decision makers' joint account subtitled

The Financial Crisis and Its Lessons (Bernanke et al. 2019). The weakness in the analogy is the premise that the short-term costs of withholding intervention would be unbearably high—higher than the value of taking the opportunity to start building a reputation for lending restraint. By January 2009, financial markets had seen a year and a half of rescue initiatives, encouraging banks and dealers to make use of the Fed's credit and thus discouraging self-help. At that point, the pessimistic premise might have been pretty reasonable. The question with more lasting significance is whether it was wise for the Fed to push Fed lending so aggressively beginning in August 2007, or whether Greenspan's (2001b) strategy of holding the line on the financial safety net would have been a better course. After all, if Volcker had adopted the firefighter analogy, double-digit inflation might have lasted for quite a while.

The consequential role of shifting intervention expectations was evident in the implementation of the Capital Purchase Program under the Troubled Asset Relief Program (TARP). Announcement of the initial capital purchases at the largest banks in early October meant that private investors contemplating investment in a large bank had to assess the risk of further dilutive purchases by the Treasury. Capital market access was diminished but returned immediately after the release of the Supervisory Capital Assessment Program (SCAP) results on May 7, 2009. The innovative program required the largest banks to submit two-year-ahead projections for their capital positions under baseline and adverse macroeconomic scenarios.[30] For banks projecting a deficiency, further capital had to be raised to close the gap. Treasury pledged to provide the additional capital if needed, but, perhaps more importantly, pledged *not* to purchase more capital in a bank if they could raise the required amount privately. While the "clean bill of health" given by the supervisor-certified loss projections bolstered outlook, the Treasury forswearing further dilution had to have been quite important as well.

The SCAP set an important precedent, in that the included institutions—the nineteen largest banking organizations in the United States—were implicitly deemed too big to fail. Notably, the list included some large regional banks. The smallest traditional bank was Regions at $142 billion at year-end 2009.[31] Viewing that as a candidate TBTF threshold and adjusting for the nearly 40% inflation between 2009 and the first quarter of 2023 yields a value of $198 billion. In other words, based on 2009 precedents, one could presume that a bank with $198 billion in assets in early 2023 is likely to be viewed as too big to fail. Silicon Valley Bank had approximately $212 billion in assets when it failed in March 2023 (Board of Governors 2023a, 2).

Table 20.2. Estimated federal financial safety net, 2009, billions of dollars

	Explicitly Guaranteed	Implicitly Guaranteed	Total Guaranteed	Total Liabilities
Banking and Savings Firms	6,536	7,276	13,812	16,249
Credit Unions	725		725	817
Government-Sponsored Enterprises		6,839	6,839	6,839
Private Employer Pensions	2,799		2,799	3,273
Money-Market Mutual Funds		3,316	3,316	3,316
Other Financial Firms		748	748	12,741
Total Financial Firms	10,060	18,179	28,239	43,235
Percent of Total Liabilities	23.3%	42.0%	65.3%	100.0%

Source: Marshall et al. (2015).

The federal financial safety net expanded along a number of dimensions in the GFC. Prior to the GFC, Fed and FDIC rescues had been limited to chartered banks and thrift institutions. As noted above, GFC interventions established the precedent of backstopping debt at all levels of a bank holding company, not just the bank. In addition, the SCAP implied that safety net support went farther down the size distribution of large banks than previous precedents indicated. And the Treasury and Fed's support for money-market mutual funds and the top investment banks now qualified them for inclusion. As a result of these new precedents, when the Richmond Fed went back after the crisis to estimate the size of the financial safety net, the size had increased to 65.3% of financial firms' liabilities; see table 20.2.

The Dodd–Frank Act of 2010 did little to clarify the scope of the federal financial safety net—the outer boundaries remained ambiguous. The FDIC was given the authority to set up a new mechanism for handling large failing financial institutions, the "Orderly Liquidation Authority" (OLA), but the FDIC's implementation has preserved the discretion to designate qualifying candidate institutions on the fly—that is, in a crisis. Oddly, OLA was not invoked for any of the bank failures of 2023. The newly established Financial Stability Oversight Council (FSOC) was given authority to designate a nonbank entity as a "Systemically Important Financial Institution" and subject them to tighter oversight. That designation carries with it the presumption that they are also too systemically important for the government to let them fail without intervening to protect creditors. The FSOC's relatively discretionary implementation of that authority, together with related litigation, seem to preserve substantial uncertainty about the boundaries of the federal financial safety net, although perceived support probabilities might be quite high for a broad swath of the financial system, given recent rescues. Recent bank failures under the new framework suggest that the Reluctant Samaritan dynamics will continue, and the financial safety net will continue to grow.

Section 165(d) of the Act mandated that large banking organizations submit plans ("living wills") for the "rapid and orderly resolution in the event of material financial distress or failure."[32] Failure to submit a plan deemed "credible" by the Fed and the FDIC (jointly) can result in the imposition of "more stringent capital, leverage, or liquidity requirements, or restrictions on the growth, activities, or operations of the company, or any subsidiary thereof."[33] An industry has sprung up employing an army of lawyers and analysts to help large banks prepare their submissions, which involve lengthy documentation of organizational structure, interaffiliate agreements, and detailed winddown plans. One could think of the living will requirements as prepackaged bankruptcies that can be crafted to avoid relying on governmental resources (Lacker 2012a, 2013). The existence of such plans, approved ahead of time, could conceivably make it easier for regulators to credibly commit to not rescuing investors, thus containing the moral-hazard effect of the Fed's time consistency problem. Instead, implementation of the resolution planning program seems more like preplanning to make FDIC rescues under the OLA as smooth as possible. Industry pressure appears to have led the Fed to allow banks to count discount window access in their resolution plans and their internal liquidity stress tests, which is counterintuitive; regulation is supposed to reduce the moral hazard fostered by reliance on the window, not embed it.

The Shadow Open Market Committee on Fed Credit Policy and the Great Financial Crisis

The events of 2007–9 elicited a flurry of SOMC commentary, with the April 2009 meeting dominated by issues related to the Fed's controversial credit market actions. Michael Bordo compared the GFC to historical financial crises (an object of lifelong research), particularly the Great Contraction of 1929–33 (Bordo 2009). While similar elements are evident—insolvencies and restricted lending, for example—the GFC is not a classic banking panic, Bordo argued, an assessment consistent with Anna Schwartz's (1986b) diagnosis of "pseudo-financial crises." Nonetheless, the Fed greatly expanded the supply of high-powered money, Bordo noted, in accord with Bernanke's interpretation of the Great Contraction. Numerous special credit facilities channeled Federal Reserve credit to particular sectors. "Thus," Bordo argued, "the Fed changed its tactics away from providing general liquidity via open market operations and allowing the market to distribute liquidity to individual firms," shifting policy toward credit allocation in a manner similar to Hoover's Reconstruction Finance Corporation (Bordo 2009, 3). Bordo argued that what was needed was a "bold, decisive and quick resolution of the bank insolvency issue parallel to FDR's banking holiday" (5), something that the capital stress tests then underway offered the prospect of accomplishing.

Also at the April 2009 SOMC meeting, new member Marvin Goodfriend reprised his 1994 argument for an "Accord" for Federal Reserve credit policy (Goodfriend 1994). Such an agreement would be modeled after the 1951 Treasury-Fed Accord that enabled the Fed to conduct an independent monetary policy. "As a long run matter," Goodfriend argued, "a significant, sustained expansion of the Fed credit policy beyond ordinary, temporary last resort lending to banks is incompatible with sustained Fed independence" (Goodfriend 2009). The Fed should therefore stick to a "Treasuries only" policy, he argued, except for limited discount window lending to banks. The Treasury and the Fed should agree on a low long-run inflation objective and should cooperate to shrink the Fed's balance sheet once the crisis was over. The idea of a credit accord had been widely discussed following Goodfriend's original 1994 proposal, but the GFC brought the discussion to the front burner. Within the Fed there was frequent questioning of the proper division of responsibility between the Fed and the Treasury.[34] In early 2009, Charles Plosser was advocating for a credit accord inside the Fed, and both of us were doing so outside the Fed (Plosser 2009; Lacker 2009).

On March 23, 2009, the Treasury and the Federal Reserve issued a joint statement (Board of Governors and US Department of the Treasury 2009) on "The Role of the Federal Reserve in Preserving Financial and Monetary Stability." It looked like the credit accord that Goodfriend, Plosser, and Lacker had been advocating, in that it called for Treasury-Fed cooperation to foster financial stability, and for the Federal Reserve "not to allocate credit to narrowly defined sectors or classes of borrowers." The joint statement also affirmed the need to preserve monetary stability and the need for a comprehensive resolution regime for "systemically critical financial institutions." No mention was made of transferring Fed credit programs to the Treasury, but it included a pledge to jointly seek "legislative action to provide additional tools the Federal Reserve can use to sterilize the effects of its lending or securities purchases on the supply of bank reserves." This refers to authorization for the Fed to issue its own debt, an idea that subsequently fizzled out. I have no direct evidence on whether Goodfriend's proposal or Plosser's and my efforts had any effect—I could not find a mention of the joint statement in either Bernanke or Geithner's memoirs—but I believe both of them were aware of the credit accord proposal and had contacts with Goodfriend in that time frame. Moreover, I believe that they both sincerely shared Goodfriend's concern about threats to the Fed's independence. So my sense is that advocacy by SOMC members before and during the GFC had a strong influence on the Treasury-Fed joint statement. In the end, however, it was not clear how much effect the joint statement had on the actual decisions at the Treasury and the Fed, since the Fed's large-scale acquisition of agency mortgage-backed securities (MBS) was deemed to be consistent with it. Apparently, home-mortgage borrowers were not a "narrowly defined sector or class of borrowers."

At the April 2009 SOMC meeting, Anna Schwartz specifically discussed the March 23, 2009, joint Treasury-Fed statement and applauded its sensitivity to Federal Reserve monetary policy independence. Schwartz (2009) went on to discuss Milton Friedman's view that the Fed should be lodged more firmly within the US Treasury so that the two parties cannot blame each other for failure to achieve macroeconomic objectives. Friedman argued, she said, that "in a democracy it would be wrong to place such concentrated power as the Fed enjoys in a group free from any kind of political control." She disagreed with her late colleague, however, saying that he conceded too much power to the Treasury: "Political control in the hands of uninformed legislators is hardly the summum bonum of a monetary system that provides financial stability and public trust of financial activity."[35]

Regulation and supervision were in the spotlight following the GFC, and the expectation was that Congress, as it had following past crises, would pass remedial legislation. Charles Calomiris (2009c), also added to the SOMC roster in 2009, commented on proposals to reallocate regulatory authority among the Federal banking agencies. He supported the requiring of the Fed to give up its role as microeconomic banking regulator, noting that the US was alone among developed nations in assigning that role to the central bank.

In a second paper for the meeting, Calomiris (2009a) reviewed the origins of the crisis, citing ex ante underestimation of subprime default risk, lax monetary policy, and risk-promoting housing policies during the lead-up to 2007. He urged regulatory changes to discourage too-big-to-fail protection of large, complex banks; provide macroprudential regulatory authority; eliminate subsidies for leveraged housing finance; reform over-the-counter (OTC) clearing and disclosure; improve risk-measurement practices; reform the use of rating agency opinions; and eliminate regulatory limits on concentration in bank ownership. His prognosis for reform in the coming legislative deliberations was mixed—some items on the agenda seem likely to be implemented, while in other areas there is little hope and "great potential for mischief."

By the time of the Fall 2009 SOMC meeting, with the US economy appearing to have bottomed out, the focus turned to how the Fed was going to exit from the extraordinary positions it had amassed via credit programs and asset acquisition. Guest speaker Don Kohn (2009), then vice chair of the Federal Reserve, gave remarks on "Central Bank Exit Policies," providing assurance that the Fed has "the framework to exit" from the unusual policies when it needed to do so. Importantly, he argued, the ability to pay interest on reserves would enable the Fed to raise short-term interest rates even if the Fed's asset holdings were quite high. Lending programs "were designed to wind themselves down as market conditions improve, and are doing so." He also stated that "the Administration has agreed to seek to remove the so-called Maiden Lane facilities from the Federal Reserve's balance sheet," something that did not end up taking place. Athanasios Orphanides (2009), then-governor of the Central Bank of Cyprus and later a member of the SOMC, offered a European perspective on the process of a central bank exiting from a large balance sheet expansion.

Marvin Goodfriend and Bennett McCallum (2009) argued for "Exiting Credit Policy to Preserve Sound Monetary Policy," in the words of their paper's title. They commended Chairman Bernanke for publicly discussing the Fed's exit strategy, and they urged the Fed to go further and declare the intention to return to a "Treasuries only" policy, "with only occasional 'last resort' lending to solvent depository institutions." Moreover, "the Fed should ask the Treasury and the Congress to take the problematic credit assets off its balance sheet in exchange for Treasuries, so that the credit assets can be managed elsewhere in the government, perhaps in a special entity created for that purpose." They also urged modifying regulations to remove the GSEs from the federal funds market or allow GSEs to earn interest on reserve balances—either would eliminate the confusing persistence of fed funds trades below the interest on reserves. Peter Ireland (2013), another twenty-first-century addition to the SOMC, later examined whether the Fed's exit from its extraordinary policy measures was "on track." While noting that "the enormous expansion the bank reserves since 2008 had, for the most part, not translated into rapid growth in the broader monetary aggregates," Ireland urged Federal Reserve officials, and Fed watchers, to pay closer attention to measures of the money supply.

William Poole (2009), then a senior fellow at the Cato Institute and formerly president of the Federal Reserve Bank of St. Louis, highlighted that moral hazard was a much more serious problem following the Fed's interventions. While large financial institutions were cautious for the time being, and the Fed and the Treasury seemed to be aware of the problems they created, "their proposed policies are grossly inadequate to deal with it." In particular, relying on the "bravery of a Treasury secretary or Fed chairman" inevitably means that "any large bank that gets into trouble will be bailed out," echoing the limited-commitment perspective on lending doctrine.

The housing-finance giants Fannie Mae and Freddie Mac, having played a consequential role in the crisis, naturally drew Shadow members' attention. At the September 2009 meeting, Gregory Hess (2009) argued for greater transparency about all aspects of the housing GSEs, and for acknowledgement that "Fannie Mae and Freddie Mac are now part of U.S. Government activities, warts and all." Calomiris, in 2010, described a three-part program for housing-finance reform: (1) Replacing leverage subsidies with means-tested down-payment assistance alongside reduced loan-to-value ratios (and phasing out Fannie Mae, Freddie Mac, and Federal Housing Administration mortgage-guarantee programs); (2) offering means-tested interest rate risk assistance; and finally (3) allowing means-tested, tax-favored savings accounts for would-be homeowners (Calomiris 2010a). The combination would tilt our mechanism for subsidizing homeownership away from subsidizing leveraged homeownership and in the process make for a safer and less fragile system. Means testing would better target subsidies. Hess (2018) would return to the topic at the October 2018 SOMC meeting; he explained the flaws in the conservatorship arrangement and commented favorably on legislative proposals then circulating to resolve the situation.

The circulation of numerous legislative proposals by the fall of 2009 was putting a spotlight on the possibility of changing roles for the Fed. Calomiris pointed out that "the expansive role of the Fed as a financial regulator is out of step with the global trend to separate monetary policy from regulatory policy. Virtually all developed economies have separated their monetary authority from their financial regulatory authority. Such a separation is desirable, as it limits the politicization of monetary and regulatory policy; pressures from special interests in the regulatory arena have led to poor regulatory decision making by the Fed (which fears repercussions from Congress) and those pressures similarly have jeopardized the Fed's independence in managing monetary policy" (Calomiris 2009b, 3). Reforming the resolution of large financial institutions, he argued, should take the form of curing technical problems with the bankruptcy code that discourage its use with financial institutions, and a requirement that shareholders in a failed institution face a complete loss.

Legislative deliberations were well underway in Washington when the SOMC next met in March 2010, and a plethora of proposals were floating around that could affect the regulatory powers and authorities of the Fed. The implications for the Fed's monetary policy independence were a major focus. Marvin Goodfriend (2010) observed that "the Fed's expansive initiatives put the central bank in a cross-fire and created a pressing need to clarify its independent responsibilities." The Fed, he again argued, should return to a "Treasuries only" portfolio. Credit policy, he noted, "exposes the central bank, and ultimately taxpayers, to potentially costly and controversial disputes regarding credit allocation," and "even the acquisition of government agency securities has allocative effects because it steers credit in a particular direction and confers a preferential status enhancing that agency's creditworthiness. . . . Expansive credit initiatives infringe significantly on the fiscal policy prerogatives of the Treasury and Congress and properly draw the scrutiny of the fiscal authorities. Hence, expansive credit initiatives jeopardize central bank independence." In light of proposals for a "pinnacle authority" for financial stability oversight and systemic risk regulation, Goodfriend argued that it should not be the Fed. The decisions such an authority would be called upon to make in times of financial turmoil would be "inevitably political, highly charged, and among the most contentious fiscal policy choices imaginable." Giving such choices to the Fed would put its independence at jeopardy.

At the same SOMC meeting, Bennett McCallum (2010) also spoke on the importance of monetary policy independence and how that relates to the US Constitution. Michael Bordo (2010) argued as well for the importance of monetary policy independence, tracing the history of Fed independence since its founding. Having seen the close cooperation between the chair of the Fed and the secretary of the Treasury in the fall of 2008, his conclusion was that the independence of the Fed had been compromised. To regain its independence, the Fed should wind down its credit facilities, end purchases of mortgage-backed securities and long-term Treasuries, and pursue a successful exit strategy.

Calomiris reviewed the history of the Bank of England and the First and Second Banks of the United States, based on his research with Stephen Haber (Calomiris and Haber 2015) on historical and cross-country banking experiences, noting that the Bank of England was an example of a successful co-evolution of a central bank and its government, while the First and Second Banks never managed to satisfy the political constraints necessary to form a stable consensus about their role and structure (Calomiris 2010c). The Federal Reserve, in contrast, did form a stable bargain that lasted from its founding until it was restructured in the mid-1930s. The lesson he took away, echoing his theme at the previous meeting, was that combining regulatory and monetary policy responsibilities in a single institution poses risks to the Fed's monetary policy independence. He therefore argued against giving too much regulatory authority to the Fed in the wake of the GFC, particularly resolution authority.

When the SOMC met next, in October 2010, the Dodd–Frank Act had been enacted and the Basel Committee had issued its revised capital standards, so it was time to look ahead. Naturally, the path toward implementing regulatory reform drew significant attention. Calomiris (2010b), surveying the field, ventured that "bureaucrats in the future will likely do what they have done in the past: follow the myopic political path of least resistance during a crisis and bail out everything in sight. Knowing that, financial institutions will not take appropriate precautions." The details of the new resolution authority—the FDIC's OLA—would be key. After noting critical failings and omissions in the new regime, particularly any attempt to affix the government subsidization of mortgage risk-taking, Calomiris notes some promising areas for reform: Use interest rates to measure loan default risk; reform the SEC's (Securities and Exchange Commission) credit rating agency regime; require large banks to issue "contingent capital certificates," a type of subordinated debt; and limit the extent of discretionary bailouts of creditors.

At the March 2011 SOMC meeting, Calomiris (2011b) again drew from history; this time from the historical behavior of banks in the 1930s. Declines in loan supply did have significant local effects, but deposit withdrawal appeared to reflect a largely rational and predictable process of deposit market response to deteriorating bank conditions rather than panic per se. Comparing the "run" on asset-backed commercial paper in the summer of 2007, Calomiris noted research by Board staff economists Daniel Covitz, Nellie Liang, and Gustavo Suarez (2013) showing "only about 40% of ABCP issues experienced a run in 2007, implying substantial cross-sectional variation in the perceived risks of different ABCP issuers during the crisis. The same ABCP issuer characteristics predicted variation in the probability of a run on a particular ABCP issue, variation in the widening of the interest spread, and differences in the shrinkage of ABCP maturities" (Calomiris 2011b). The evidence clearly implied that the extent to which an ABCP issuer faced a run or the unwillingness of counterparties to roll over positions was related to their risk profile, consistent with the pattern of depositor withdrawals in the 1930s.

At the October 2011 meeting, reviewing desirable size and structure, transitional dynamics, and macroprudential implications of capital requirements, Calomiris (2011a) concluded that "capital requirements should rise for U.S. and European banks." At the same meeting, amid concerns about a disappointing pace of recovery, Marvin Goodfriend (2011b) warned that "a more intensive use of credit policy by the central bank to stimulate economic activity at present would be politically divisive, potentially costly, and at best subsidize particular sectors at the expense of others without necessarily stimulating aggregate output as a whole."

Regulatory issues continued to garner attention in the years that were to come. At the September 2013 SOMC meeting, Charles Calomiris (2013) commented on the emerging movement to adopt a macroprudential policy regime in which regulatory and supervisory tools are used on a cyclical basis to "cool down or heat up the financial system as needed" to try to combat the financial boom-bust cycles that have become commonplace in recent decades. While sympathetic to the relevance of aspects of financial contracting that can magnify boom-bust cycles, he aligned with those skeptical of the "macropru" program, arguing that the financial system is not inherently fragile and that policymakers should continue to rely on traditional monetary policy tools to stabilize macroeconomic outcomes. In October 2016, presciently in view of the repo market turmoil of September 2019, Calomiris (2016) pointed out the perils surrounding the supplemental leverage ratio.

The delicate political independence of the Federal Reserve, and its relationship to various credit policy and regulatory developments, continued to be a focus of SOMC attention, even after the 2010 passage of the Dodd–Frank

Act. In September 2013, as the world was contemplating the prospect of a new Federal Reserve chair, Marvin Goodfriend provided some advice for the senators that would be conducting confirmation hearings. In light of the dramatic interventions that occurred during the GFC, Goodfriend argued that "the Senate confirmation hearings should ascertain the nominated Fed Chair's inclination toward broad or narrow use of the Fed's operational independence. . . . Failing to constrain the Fed's independent last resort lending reach, in particular, has been and remains counterproductive for financial stability" (Goodfriend 2013, 3). He even wrote some questions for senators to ask the new nominee related to Fed independence, including: "Do you think the Fed should return to the 'Treasuries only' asset acquisition policy it followed prior to the 2007-8 credit turmoil? Explain" (6).

At the following meeting in April 2014, against the backdrop of the Fed's aggressive balance sheet expansion and extension of the maturity of its portfolio, Goodfriend (2014b) highlighted the historical role of the Fed's surplus account as an earnings buffer and noted that "the Fed has long had discretion over its surplus capital and the amounts it transferred to the Treasury." He argued that "the Fed should use that discretion today to suspend transfers and build up surplus capital against the unprecedented interest rate risk on its balance sheet. If the federal debt ceiling were modified to exclude Treasury securities held by the Fed until the Fed can normalize its balance sheet, the accumulation of surplus capital would be costless for taxpayers and the Treasury. However, the build-up of surplus capital against interest rate risk on the Fed balance sheet would better position the Fed to sustain its 2% inflation objective." Attacking the same subject from another angle, Goodfriend (2014a) at the November 2014 SOMC meeting characterized the Fed's quantitative easing program with interest rates at the zero lower bound as a "bond market carry trade." The arithmetic of such trades suggests that the Fed take a forward-looking stance: "Net interest earnings on the front end of the monetary carry trade should be retained—to guard against the central bank having to create reserves (or borrow) to pay interest on reserves or managed liabilities on the back end, and to show that interest expenses are paid for in large part by earnings from the front end." The risks Goodfriend foresaw came to pass in 2022–23, when raising the federal funds rate sharply to combat inflation resulted in negative Fed earnings and large portfolio losses, as documented in detail by SOMC member Andy Levin and coauthors at the April 2022 SOMC meeting (Levin et al. 2022; but see also Lucas 2025, in this volume).

Independence remained a lively subject in May 2017, when Charles
Calomiris reprised for the SOMC his testimony the previous month to the
Subcommittee on Monetary Policy and Trade of the House Committee on
Financial Services (Calomiris 2017).[36] In it he advocated a raft of governance
changes to improve decision making and reduce politicization, including: having at least two governors with significant financial market experience, requiring two staff members to be assigned to each governor, having all Federal
Reserve Bank presidents vote at every FOMC meeting (rather than just five,
per current law), devolving budget authority down to the Reserve Banks, giving the Fed a single mandate for price stability, and mandating a systematic
approach to monetary policy. He would also "prohibit the Fed from holding
securities other than U.S. Treasury securities in its portfolio (except during
emergencies, in the context of assistance approved under its emergency lending powers)," and "remove the Fed from writing and enforcing regulations,"
although "the Fed would still participate in examinations and have full access
to all information necessary to fulfill its role as a lender of last resort."

Calomiris returned to the subject of Fed independence at the September
2019 SOMC meeting, where he presented a paper later published in the
Journal of Applied Corporate Finance. Following the vein mined in his book
with Stephen Haber (Calomiris and Haber 2015), his focus was the interplay between monetary and regulatory policy as seen through the lens of the
grand political bargain around banking and the state. His analysis led him to
the view that "to promote independence along both dimensions of economic
policy, regulatory as well as monetary, two sorts of policy reforms would be
helpful: (1) separation of authority over the two areas into two distinct agencies (to avoid trade-offs that reduce the independence of regulatory policy);
and (2) the establishment of clear mandates and accountability procedures
for each category of policy. In particular, with respect to monetary policy,
the Fed should be required to articulate a systematic framework—such as a
Taylor Rule—that it would adhere to, and which would be subject to (the
Fed's own) revision over time" (Calomiris 2019, 6).

A concern about the Fed's monetary policy independence also was a
theme of the address by Charles Plosser (2019) at the March 2019 SOMC
meeting.[37] His focus was the Federal Reserve's balance sheet and his aim was
to respond to those who were suggesting that because the Fed could pay
interest on reserves, a large balance sheet was relatively costless. Plosser's
concern was that a large balance sheet makes an inviting target for political
actors that want the Fed to use it to circumvent constitutional appropriations

mechanisms for redistributional aims. The resulting political entanglements and controversy would risk damaging the Fed's ability to undertake policy actions that are worthy but in the short term costly. Plosser argued for a balance sheet no larger than necessary to manage a "corridor" operating regime, similar to the pre-GFC arrangements.

The September 2019 meeting also heard some "heretical thoughts" on independence from Deborah Lucas, who joined the SOMC in 2017, in part a response to the book *Unelected Power* by Paul Tucker. Her message, which actually does not seem so heretical, was that "if transparency by independent central banks is a prerequisite for legitimacy in a democratic society, and if central bankers seek to maintain independence, then they should proactively address the fiscal and distributional consequences of their actions to a much greater extent than they do currently. That includes developing standards for measuring and communicating those consequences to the public" (Lucas 2019). With great autonomy comes great responsibility. Lucas knew a thing or two about measuring consequences, having spent time at the Congressional Budget Office (CBO) estimating the fiscal effects of credit programs.

Lucas contributed two presentations of rigorous estimates of the costs of the extraordinary policy interventions of the GFC. Doing so carefully was important because widely reported budget numbers can be misleading. For example, the Fed's remittances to the Treasury surged in the 2010s as its balance sheet ballooned, but that "obscures the financial status of the government by effectively treating as free money the market premiums earned on the Federal Reserve's portfolio that are compensation for the costs of interest rate, prepayment, and liquidity risk that ultimately fall on taxpayers" (Lucas 2017, 1). Drawing on a 2010 study by the CBO, the net present value cost at inception was estimated to be $21 billion.[38] Although that might seem like a relatively modest sum, perhaps surprisingly so, there are a few methodological points to bear in mind. The estimate was on an ex ante fair-value basis. "During that period there was often a considerable difference between market prices and inferred fair value. Had the calculations been done at market prices the reported fiscal costs would have been considerably higher, but still modest relative to the amount of credit extended by the Federal Reserve under the facilities" (8). In addition, by assumption, pecuniary effects—that is, changes in prices or interest rate spreads—were set aside in the construction of that benchmark estimate.

Lucas reported on a more comprehensive approach at the October 2018 SOMC meeting—one that delivers a more sizable sum: "Drawing selectively on existing cost estimates, and augmenting those with additional calcula-tions," she concluded that "the total direct cost on a fair value basis of crisis-related bailouts in the U.S. was about $498 billion" (Lucas 2018, 3). Her work cast light on the distributional effects as well, confirming the insights of the limited-commitment perspective: "As for the incidence of benefits, at the time the bailouts occurred, the largest direct beneficiaries were the unsecured creditors of large financial institutions, most significantly, of Fannie Mae and Freddie Mac. Shareholders benefited less than the popular perception, as most were wiped out" (4). The GFC market interventions were quite large.

Dovetailing with the present paper's focus, at the April 2014 SOMC meet-ing Michael Bordo (2014a) looked back at one hundred years of the Federal Reserve as a lender of last resort, drawing on his contribution to the Federal Reserve centenary research conference held in November 2010 on Jekyll Island, Georgia, marking the famous 1910 meeting there of leading finan-ciers and officials that led to the Federal Reserve Act.[39] Bordo argued that the Fed's effectiveness has evolved significantly, particularly in response to major financial crises, and he highlighted the Fed's initial struggles during the Great Depression, where its actions were often too little, too late. Posing the ques-tion of whether the Fed's GFC lending facilities "worked," he said they did in the sense that the crisis was ultimately allayed, but they "have created prob-lems for the future." The rescues of insolvent financial institutions deemed TBTF "have moved it far away from Bagehot's strictures and opened up a Pandora's box of perils." Among them, he noted, "the Fed's credit policy—a form of fiscal policy—has impinged upon the Fed's independence and weak-ened credibility" (Bordo 2014a, 11). Bordo, in tune with other members of the SOMC since the GFC, emphasized the importance of clear communica-tion and pre-established frameworks for lender-of-last-resort operations.

Also germane to the present paper, in September 2017, Bordo took the opportunity offered by the tenth anniversary of the onset of the GFC to eval-uate the aftermath from an historical perspective. The striking development, he noted, was that "many have argued that the financial stability mandate should be elevated to the same level of importance as price stability and sta-bility of the real macro economy. The definition of financial stability has also changed from the traditional role of the central bank as lender of last resort accompanied by supervision and regulation of the banking system (now referred to as micro prudential policy) to a new role to head off systemic risk to the entire financial system including nonbank financial intermediaries and financial markets" (Bordo 2017, 1). Looking back over the past two centuries, "only two episodes stand out as serious financial crisis related recessions accompanied by credit driven asset price booms: the perfect storms of the Great Contraction 1929–33 and the GFC 2007–2008" (2). His reading of the record suggests to him that financial crises have had many causes, and "central banks should be cautious in a) elevating the financial stability mandate to the same level as price stability and macro stability; b) following [lean against the wind] policies; c) taking on macro prudential responsibilities" (2). "The Financial Stability mandate," he concluded, "could be done by another agency outside the central bank or possibly be a totally separate facility within the central bank as is the case with the Bank of England. This would prevent central banks from engaging in credit policy, maintain their independence from the fiscal authorities and allow them to preserve their main goals which are to provide credibility for low inflation and macro stability" (13).

Looking back, the decade following the GFC saw Shadow members speak out insightfully about the key issues related to Fed lending. The vast increase in credit market interventions raised serious concerns about the Fed's independence and ability to withstand political crosscurrents. The incentive effects of the precedents set during the GFC were highlighted often as well. One SOMC member championed the accurate measurement of the economic magnitude of those interventions. Shadow members also called out the problematic unresolved status of the housing-finance GSEs, still in conservatorship a decade after their failure. Members highlighted deep concerns about possible reassignment of regulatory and supervisory responsibilities, although Dodd–Frank ended up reassigning less than it could have. The central bank movement to take on a "financial stability" mandate was flagged as a clear risk, again citing problematic political exposures that would accompany such a move. Many SOMC members were concerned that the widening of Fed credit market intervention in the GFC along with new financial stability responsibilities would impinge on the Fed's independent conduct of monetary policy in the years ahead. Also noted was the risk to the Fed's future income and net worth from the carry trade built into its large-scale balance sheet. Many of these risks came to pass during the fallout from the next economic shock.

Federal Reserve Credit Policy in the Pandemic

When the magnitude and rapidity of the likely economic dislocations brought by the COVID-19 pandemic became widely apparent in mid-March 2020, the financial market reactions were equally large and rapid. In an extraordinarily uncertain environment, investors sold a wide variety of securities, including

Treasury securities, and moved into cash. The FOMC made a pair of emergency rate cuts, bringing the target range for the federal funds rate down to effectively zero on March 15. The discount rate was reduced to 0.25%, narrowing the spread between it and the top of the target range for the federal funds rate to zero. The Board announced that discount window borrowers could borrow for up to ninety days, prepayable and renewable on a daily basis. On March 12, the Desk announced a $1.5 trillion expansion in repo operations. Following its March 15 meeting, the FOMC announced that "to support the smooth functioning of markets for Treasury securities and agency mortgage-backed securities" the Committee would increase its holdings of Treasury securities by at least $500 billion and its holdings of agency MBS by at least $200 billion. After a March 23 FOMC call, the Committee changed those instructions to the Desk to direct them to purchase Treasury securities and agency MBS "in the amounts needed to support smooth market functioning and effective transmission of monetary policy to broader financial conditions," and to include agency commercial MBS in its purchases as well.[40]

The Fed also dusted off some of the programs it had deployed in the GFC to support the commercial paper market, money-market funds, and primary dealers. The Fed went beyond the scope of GFC interventions, however, "racing across red lines" to launch unprecedented programs to purchase corporate bonds, both from issuers and on the secondary market (Smialek 2023). "They were not overly nice about credit ratings, either, taking on below-investment grade exposure via exchange traded funds" (Lacker 2024c). They launched a program to support municipal securities and eased qualification requirements several times in order to boost participation. Municipal securities were given consideration in 2008–9 but were deemed beyond the pale, given the Fed's long-standing practice of limiting lending to financial institutions. "In fact, just nine months before the pandemic crisis, Powell had pushed back on the suggestion of a progressive member of Congress that the Fed set up a municipal lending program in the next downturn, saying 'I think that's something for Congress to do. I don't think we want to be picking winners and losers'" (Smialek 2023, 208). "And yet, the design of Fed credit programs unavoidably did just that, particularly the municipal bond program, where initial size cut-offs were modified after political blowback" (Lacker 2024c).

The Fed saw a gap between companies big enough to issue bonds, and thus benefit from the Fed's corporate bond-buying program, and the small businesses eligible for the Paycheck Protection Program (PPP), the initiative to make loans through the Small Business Administration and then forgive them. The Fed introduced a program to provide term funding to financial institutions backed by their PPP loans. To fill the gap between bond issuers and small business, the Fed rolled out the Main Street Lending Program, a set of facilities to lend to small and medium-sized businesses and nonprofits.[41] "Not only did the Main Street program involve another nonfinancial credit sector that the Fed had studiously avoided for the previous half-century, but the Fed's announcement was viewed as preempting work underway in Congress to design a similar relief effort. Moreover, when the program was announced, Congress had not yet authorized the Treasury participation that Fed lawyers viewed as essential. Negotiations were going on behind the scenes between the Fed and the Treasury on the design of the program even as Congress was considering program legislation. Indeed, one Senator was promoting his own mid-tier program that was far more expansive than the Fed wanted" (Lacker 2024c).

The Fed's credit policy in 2020 thus broke new ground on two fronts. It intervened in a far broader array of markets, crossing clear precedential boundaries that had previously been viewed as limiting the Fed's lending remit. And the Fed was by many accounts far more deeply entwined in legislative deliberations than before. Prior to the GFC, in accord with long-standing practice, Fed chairs would not comment on fiscal policy proposals other than to repeat that standard endorsement of containing deficits to reasonable levels. This self-imposed restraint was meant to reciprocate, and thereby affirm, deference by the administration and Congress to the Federal Reserve in matters of monetary policy.[42]

It was striking, therefore, to read that Chair Jerome Powell told Speaker of the House Nancy Pelosi to "think big" when it came to the fiscal package being negotiated in mid-March 2020 (Smialek 2023, 181). At that time, the Fed was deeply entangled in the design of credit programs being considered by Congress and the administration, fending off Congress-built programs in favor of their own, and Treasury's, discretionary initiatives. Marvin Goodfriend and other members of the SOMC had warned for years that credit policy ran the risk of entangling the Fed in distributional politics, and it is hard to imagine a more distributional question than who should get federal emergency relief. The advice to "think big" was taken too far in early 2021, as is now painfully clear. In response to the resulting surge in inflation, the Fed maintained an accommodative stance well into the following year. Could the Fed have felt hesitant to pivot from an expansionary policy stance so shortly after enactment of a large fiscal stimulus program that it was, behind the scenes, involved in crafting (Lacker 2024a)? Could this have been an instance of the monetary policy impediment that Goodfriend feared might result from Fed fiscal entanglement? Could this have contributed to the dilatory monetary policy of 2021–22?

The Fed's programs to buy corporate bonds and municipal securities violated long-standing System taboos. Michael Bordo noted at the September 2020 SOMC meeting that the Treasury provided an equity investment equal to 10% of the total program size, using funds appropriated by the CARES Act, in order to absorb a first tranche of losses; this was a welcome departure from what happened during the GFC, he argued, when the Fed undertook credit programs on its own account, without formal Treasury support. Also welcome were the reports that Fed staff resisted some congressional ideas about broader roles in the relief agenda, saying "The Fed can do lending, not spending" (Smialek 2023, 180).

Nonetheless, the break from past precedent of limiting emergency credit market intervention to financial institutions and their obligations rings a bell that cannot be unrung (Heine 2020). The fact that corporate debt issuers did not cause the pandemic does not magically negate moral-hazard effects, as some Fed officials seemed to claim. That would be like saying flood insurance has no incentive effects because homeowners do not cause floods. Over their lifetime, debt instruments can be expected to encounter a variety of circumstances, many—if not most—outside the control of the issuer or the purchaser. Preparation for those circumstances is their own responsibility, or at least it was. After 2020, any unanticipated increase in economic uncertainty that widens bond spreads by enough will raise expectations of Fed intervention to cap and reduce spreads.

The Shadow Open Market Committee on Fed Credit Policy in the Pandemic

The Fed's race across red lines in 2020 raises the critical question: What is the Fed's credit policy? Kathryn Judge, a guest speaker at the September 2020 SOMC meeting, made the case for "Why the Fed Should Issue a Policy Framework for Credit Policy." She argued that, unlike with monetary policy, where the Fed has invested in developing and promulgating a detailed policy statement (though some SOMC members argue nonetheless that clarity can be improved there), "the Fed has no broadly agreed upon framework for credit policy" (Judge 2020, 6). The ambiguity is apparent from a cursory review of the range of pandemic credit market programs. Some were the

Fed's responsibility—corporate bonds and midsize businesses. And some were not—small businesses, for example, where the Fed's role was limited to accepting PPP loans at the discount window. It is hard to see where a bright line might credibly be drawn.

In 2022, even while the inflation surge focused many economists' attention on the Fed's monetary policy responsibilities, members of the SOMC were closely attentive to the credit policy developments of 2020. At the February meeting, Charles Calomiris (2022b) presented a trenchant review of what he called "the institutional devolution of government financial policy." Surveying central bank history back into the late Middle Ages, he portrayed progress up until 2006 as imperfect but evident. Institutional arrangements and political bargains contributed to accountability, established fair rules and procedures, developed implicit or explicit policy frameworks, and balanced internal governance. Calomiris saw the present state as less heartening. The Fed "operates as a state-owned bank" but with unclear authority, its regulatory and supervisory powers "have exploded," and the Fed operates across the Treasury maturity spectrum, muddying what should be the Treasury's responsibility. Fed governance is highly concentrated at the Board, which works closely with one political party. It feels, Calomiris wrote, "like the early 1970s" and "it has to get worse before it can get better."

Michael Bordo, at the November 2022 SOMC meeting, also surveyed the central banking landscape from a historical perspective but came away less despondent. Central banks have learned over time how to achieve monetary stability and a measure of macroeconomic stability through the use of countercyclical monetary policy, he said. "The spread of government guarantees and the development of the 'Too Big to Fail' doctrine in the 1970s converted classic banking panics into fiscally resolved banking crises which involved increasingly larger fiscal costs. Moreover, central banks have recently expanded the lender of last resort function to nonbank financial intermediaries and have used credit policy, a form of fiscal policy, to bail them out" (Bordo 2022, 4). The "present conundrum," as he put it, includes: the expansion of central bank stability mandates to include leaning against credit cycles, which has not historically been successful; falling behind the curve in the inflation surge of 2021—hinting at the historic disaster of the Great Inflation; picking credit policy winners and losers—historically abandoned for threatening independence; and the challenges posed by digitization of finance and money. He draws lessons from history that, if heeded, may brighten the outlook. Central banks need to subdue inflation quickly, beware the threat to independence posed by expanded credit policy, stick to their monetary stability knitting rather than add climate and social issues to their objectives, and explore the promise of digitization.

Bank Failures in 2023

In the wake of the Fed's campaign against inflation, the spring of 2023 saw three regional banks fail as a result of losses on holdings of long-term Treasury securities and later be placed in FDIC receivership: Silicon Valley Bank (SVB), Signature Bank, and First Republic Bank.[43] The first of these went down in spectacularly rapid fashion, with large deposit outflows in a matter of hours. Fed lending then was constrained by the fact that the collateral SVB had pledged to the Federal Home Loan Bank of San Francisco could not operationally be transferred to the Fed in time, so the FDIC was forced to close the bank midday Friday.[44] The Treasury secretary invoked the systemic risk exemption and guaranteed the uninsured deposits. Although the systemic risk clause must be certified bank-by-bank, convincing signals were sent that the secretary would make similar designations going forward, effectively extending implicit deposit guarantees to all similar-size institutions. That weekend, the Fed launched a Bank Term Funding Program (BTFP) offering loans up to one year in maturity against US Treasuries, agency securities, and agency mortgage-backed securities, with no haircuts imposed. Total borrowing soared, both at the discount window and the BTFP, in part as a result of the arbitrage opportunity to borrow at the program rate—the one-year overnight index swap rate plus 10 basis points—and leave the funds on deposit at the interest rate on reserves.

Much has been made of how the failing banks' access to funds was impeded by collateral that was pledged to a Federal Home Loan Bank's being difficult to transfer to the Fed's discount window. A chorus of commentators are calling for an array of efforts to encourage banks to "pre-position" collateral with their Federal Reserve Bank to facilitate emergency lending should they need it, and other efforts to dispel discount window "stigma." The difficulty, however, was that the FHLB would not lend, and it's easy to see why—SVB, like the other banks who failed, was clearly insolvent (Seru 2024). This just highlights the different lending incentives of the private sector and the Fed. Commentators should be asking why the Fed is so eager to lend to insolvent banks that cannot get credit in the marketplace.

Consistent with the Reluctant Samaritan dynamics, the failed banks were on the boundary of the financial safety net. The nineteen largest banks that participated in the SCAP in 2009 were clearly treated as too big to fail. The smallest of those, adjusted for inflation, amounted to a $198 billion bank in early 2023. Silicon Valley Bank had approximately $212 billion in assets when it failed in March 2023 (Board of Governors 2023a, 2), just inside the safety net boundary. Apparently, depositors of Silicon Valley Bank were not sure their uninsured deposits were implicitly protected. Again, fragility is driven by safety net ambiguity.

Where is the new safety net boundary? The smallest of the three failing banks provides an updated upper bound estimate: Signature Bank had about $110 billion in assets at the end of 2022, just before it failed. Reluctant Samaritan dynamics suggest that we should expect: a crackdown on the risky activity that was the proximal cause among similarly situated institutions (although that will be hard as long as held-to-maturity portfolios are full of underwater Treasuries [Jiang et al. 2024]); a solidification of rescue expectations in the territory newly annexed to the safety net; and the emergence of risk and fragility just beyond the new boundaries.

A New Lending Doctrine for the Twenty-First Century?

What principles does the Federal Reserve believe guide its lending in the twenty-first century? What is the Federal Reserve's current lending doctrine? Fortunately, a section of the Board of Governors' website provides some clues (Board of Governors 2025). The Fed now presents itself as operating under a *financial stability mandate*, a broad public responsibility to use its authorities to alleviate financial distress. A financial system provides households and businesses with financing to invest and grow, it says, but

> in an unstable system, an economic shock is likely to have much larger effects, disrupting the flow of credit and leading to larger-than-expected declines in employment and economic activity. . . . In times of crisis, the financial markets that businesses and households rely on may experience severe stress or, in extreme cases, effectively cease to function. . . . Because these markets are vital to the economy, the Federal Reserve—like many central banks—is empowered to take actions that can restore the normal flow of credit needed to support employment and the broader economy.

Under the tab "Responding to Financial System Emergencies" (Board of Governors 2023b), the Board's financial stability web page notes that monetary policy "can support the flow of credit," and then lists dollar funding facilities, emergency lending under section 13(3), and the raft of "special programs" through which the Fed intervened in credit markets (all of which fall under the heading credit policy, not monetary policy, under the definition of Goodfriend and King [1988]). So, an "unstable" financial system underperforms in response to adverse shocks and Fed intervention in credit markets is needed to restore the "normal" flow of credit to improve economic outcomes.

The current articulation of Federal Reserve credit policy principles, together with the record of twenty-first-century credit policy actions, displays some continuity with twentieth-century doctrines.

- Current credit policy shares with the Monetary Stability Doctrine a keen interest in preventing runs that would lead to a collapse of the money stock, as occurred in the Great Contraction of 1929–33, although this interest is implicit and embedded in the apparent goal of alleviating all types of runs. Fortunately, this risk has not arisen since the Great Contraction, deposit insurance and TBTF having significantly dampened the risk of a flight to currency.
- Current credit policy shares with the Real Bills Doctrine the premise that, in the absence of appropriate central bank intervention, credit markets are subject to excessive credit booms and busts that amplify economic fluctuations (Mints 1945, 207).
- Current credit policy shares with Warburg's Mercantilism a preoccupation with short-term wholesale funding markets and a desire to support global dollar hegemony.
- And current credit policy shares with the Reluctant Samaritan Doctrine an aversion to commitment and a focus on mitigating problems ex post.

A case can be made, however, that the expansive new approach to financial stability that emerged in 2007 represented a fundamental doctrinal discontinuity.

- Both stated policy and actual practice now go well beyond what is required for the central bank monetary stability function envisioned by Thornton and Bagehot, even though twenty-first-century policymakers are fond of cloaking their innovations in the mantle of the "classical lender of last resort."

- The Federal Reserve has acquired or lent on financial instruments well beyond the tightly defined set deemed appropriate by the Real Bills Doctrine.
- Similarly, the Fed has intervened far beyond the banker's acceptance market (or even the commercial paper market more broadly) that was Warburg's concern.
- The general reluctance of the Fed in the twentieth century to extend credit too broadly has disappeared. Taboos against lending beyond banking and thrift institutions, or intervening directly in securities markets, are gone. The twenty-first-century Federal Reserve has intervened in markets and institutions considered beyond the pale just a few years earlier.
- Most twentieth-century lending doctrines were grounded in the legal monopoly status of Federal Reserve liabilities. The Monetary Stability and Real Bills doctrines envisioned unsterilized lending aimed at appropriately regulating the supply of monetary instruments that only the Fed could legally supply. In contrast, Fed lending in this century is disconnected from its monetary liabilities. The Federal Reserve Banks were always government-sponsored enterprises as a legal matter; now, as Calomiris (2022b) pointed out at the March 2022 SOMC meeting, the Fed now "operates as a state-owned bank."

Microfoundations?

What accounts for the significant departure from twentieth-century doctrine? One plausible candidate is the influence of ideas. The interventionist perspective of the twenty-first century might reflect in part the influence of several threads of the late twentieth century in economic theory. Building on the achievements of general equilibrium theory in the 1950s, a veritable explosion of literature in the 1970s and 1980s explored models with limited information. Models of financial arrangements in the presence of hidden actions, hidden information about states of the world, or costly information gathering give rise to recognizable financial contracts, such as debt, and recognizable multilateral financial arrangements, such as banks. The models are stark and stripped down and sometimes compared disparagingly to less formal "real world" reasoning, but they make the storytelling visible and disciplined in a way that less formal storytelling is not. Because these models are explicit about the preferences of agents, their endowments, and the technologies they have available to them, including conditions governing the arrival and dissemination of information, one can be more confident in the coherence of the story and can evaluate the efficiency of outcomes and the effects of government interventions on agents' well-being. Motivating a role for government intervention in such models turns out to be surprisingly tricky, however, because for government intervention to improve upon laissez-faire allocations, it must enjoy some sort of comparative advantage, despite being subject to the same informational and technological constraints as private agents. Nonetheless, models of financial arrangements under limited information have demonstrated that in certain models and under certain conditions government intervention is capable of improving on laissez-faire outcomes. Understanding the domains in which these *possibility propositions* hold is important for understanding whether they can be relied upon as a guide to policymaking in any given application. Three types of possibility propositions stand out as influential.

Runs

The celebrated paper by Douglas Diamond and Philip Dybvig (1983) might be the most widely cited explanation for central bank crisis lending. (See Bryant [1980] for an earlier version of the model.) There can be multiple equilibria in their model, one in which depositors do not withdraw funds if they do not need them immediately, which is rational if they expect other patient depositors to exhibit similar patience, and another in which it is rational for depositors to withdraw funds if they expect other depositors also to do so. The first outcome is preferred by all over the second. The authors argue that deposit insurance or central bank lending can rule out the second equilibrium. Diamond and Dybvig's results were the subject of intense scrutiny from the beginning.[45] "As it turns out, the original Diamond-Dybvig framework does not produce clear-cut prescriptions about the value of having in place a discount window facility" (Ennis 2016, 5). Their possibility proposition about the benefits of government intervention has proven to be sensitive to specific details of the model environment.

- One especially critical model feature is that depositors are isolated and cannot communicate with each other at the time they make their decisions about whether or not to run. Neil Wallace (1988) pointed out that this "sequential service constraint" was crucial to the existence of the run equilibrium. If depositors are gathered together at the crucial time, the interaction of patient and impatient depositors leads to efficient outcomes without runs.[46] (See Jacklin 1987.)

- Another crucial feature is the form that deposit contracts can take. Wallace notes, and Diamond and Dybvig acknowledge, that a payment scheme that involves the suspension of convertibility after a certain amount of withdrawal requests, a feature commonly observed in historical bank panics and modern investment arrangements, is sufficient to rule out inefficient bank runs.[47]

- A third feature that is critical to the Diamond–Dybvig result is that the bank and its depositors operate in a closed environment. A government that has access to resources external to the bank and its depositors can provide deposit insurance that defeats runs, but the bank could prevent runs itself if it had the same access, for example, by going to an interbank market.

- A broader challenge for the application of the Diamond–Dybvig model to real-world policy settings is that it is easy to envision other models in which runs occur in response to changes in fundamentals, such as the solvency of the bank (Allen and Gale 1998). Not every sudden surge in deposit withdrawals needs to be the outcome of a Pareto-dominated self-fulfilling prophecy. Some episodes that are typically called "runs" could simply represent efficient depositor responses to updated information about the fundamental condition of their bank.

- Relatedly, there is a vast literature on the historical characteristics of bank runs and failures. The SOMC member Charles Calomiris (2007, 2022a), a leading contributor to that literature, concludes that unwarranted "panic" withdrawals of the type portrayed in Diamond and Dybvig's model have generally played only a small role in bank failures. Rather, withdrawal pressures appear to reflect real concerns about solvency risk at weak banks and do not generally bring about the demise of solvent institutions.

While runs were mentioned quite frequently during the GFC, there was no apparent interest in whether the conditions underlying the Diamond–Dybvig possibility proposition were a good replica of the economic environment we faced—no staff analysis, no briefings, virtually no policymaker inquiries. The idea that a "run" might be occurring or was about to occur was often taken as prima facie evidence that intervention of some sort would provide benefits, even if some costs were involved.

Segmentation
Another literature strand finds a role for central bank lending in the possibility that limited participation across various financial markets may cause market segmentation and "cash-in-the-market" pricing in which financial asset prices are determined by the (limited) funds available to the agents that are actively participating in the market. The essential feature is that a cost of some sort is associated with each "market" an agent participates in, so that in equilibrium agents do not participate in every market. In a version of this type of model with banks, a run may trigger a "fire sale" of bank assets that yields less than the price that would be obtained if participation was not limited (Allen and Gale 1998). A central bank that lends to the bank can prevent the need for the fire sale. Chair Bernanke suggested this type of model as a rationale for the TAF (FOMC 2007b, 147).[48] As a rationale for the TAF, however, several questions immediately come to mind.

- Is the cash-in-the-market feature a realistic representation of the ABCP market in September 2007? There was abundant evidence at the time that substantial funds were "on the sidelines."[49]
- Were banks in dire need of funding in September 2007? There was abundant evidence at the time that they were not.[50]
- Is it possible that rational revisions in risk assessment were responsible for the August shift in financial market conditions? If so, could bank funding positions have been constrained not by the cash in the market but by the views in the market?
- Federal Reserve lending programs such as the TAF were completely sterilized. In models of central bank lending to alleviate cash-in-the-market pricing, it is essential that the additional cash not be offset by reductions in the cash in the market. Did the Fed's sterilizing sales of Treasuries draw cash from outside the fire sale market? If so, what prevents the bank itself from accessing those markets?
- A gap between the fire sale price and the fundamental price gives rise to an incentive for outsiders to participate in that market. How long can that gap persist?
- I know of no quantitative or qualitative assessments by Federal Reserve System staff of the assumptions or predictions of any

cash-in-the-market models. No investigation of barriers to entry, either transitory or persistent, into investing in the ABCP market. No measurement of the amount of idle funds potentially available to invest in the beleaguered sector. No quantitative assessment of "held to maturity" prices of ABCP versus the fire sale prices.

Allen and Gale's possibility propositions seemed to be taken as enough. It was not deemed necessary to compare that perspective to the hypothesis that risks were being rationally reassessed.

Adverse Selection
The perception that discount window stigma is a problem that needs to be addressed was prominent from the beginning of the GFC and was cited as motivation for the strenuous efforts to promote use of the window in August 2007 and the TAF. That perception is still with us today. A cursory attempt to think about modeling the phenomenon provides an alternative perspective. Entities borrow all the time and doing so can reveal information if made known to others. When a large bank receives an equity investment from an overseas entity, market participants are avidly interested in the terms, knowing that due diligence is likely to have provided the investor with material information on the bank's current condition. That revelation may have influenced the bank's willingness to raise equity on those terms. If so, that is a real cost of the transaction and can't be wished away. Put another way, discount window stigma is just equilibrium Bayesian updating in an adverse selection environment.[51]

Careful models of stigma at central bank lending facilities were not available in 2007, but the logic behind them was intuitive and similar models were familiar. Indeed, many FOMC participants at the September 2007 meeting expressed skepticism about whether the proposed TAF would have much of an effect on discount window stigma. When a revised proposal came forward for consideration on a December 6 FOMC conference call, briefing materials contained no meaningful analysis of stigma as an adverse selection problem. Bernanke speculated that the auction format might possibly reduce stigma, but he did not cite that as the primary reason for the facility. The motivation was that getting funding, particularly term funding, had become quite difficult for banks. No staff work addressed the question of any market imperfection that the TAF might address, or whether observations were inconsistent with a well-functioning interbank market reacting rationally to rising counterparty risk. The deciding consideration was simply the desire to reduce bank funding costs.[52]

The Credit View

Ben Bernanke extracted from the outpouring of research on the economics of financial arrangements under limited information a perspective he called the "credit view." His address to a 1993 New York Fed conference provided a comprehensive statement (Bernanke 1993).[53] Two lessons from the new literature stood out to Bernanke: the special nature of banks and other financial intermediaries, and the structure of financial contracts. The first he read as buttressing the premise of his widely cited 1983 article (Bernanke 1983) arguing that Depression-era bank failures extinguished valuable lending expertise and as a result had an independent dampening effect on economic activity, above and beyond the effect of the contraction in the money supply. The second he took as pointing to the critical role of borrowers' balance sheets, particularly when borrowers' net worth constrains economic activity in a downturn. Bernanke (1993, 55) contrasted his credit view with a "money view" that he identified with the conventional IS-LM model, in which monetary policy affects aggregate demand through the effect of the money supply on short-term interest rates. The credit view, he argued, is an alternative channel for the transmission of monetary policy which "allows for more general patterns of asset substitutability" and "can explain the apparent potency of monetary policy actions" (56). He sees a "financial accelerator" in which credit market frictions amplify and propagate nonfinancial shocks and monetary policy impulses (64).

The Federal Reserve's lending policies are directly implicated by the credit view, according to Bernanke. He noted the debate about whether the Fed should "content itself with protecting the money supply"—here he cites Goodfriend and King (1988), but Meltzer (1974) and Schwartz (1986b) were making the same case—or whether it "should act more aggressively to protect lending and other functions of banks (and other financial institutions as well). . . . Clearly," he said, "the issue turns on whether major problems in the banking system or other major institutions would be disruptive to the economy for reasons over and above any effects they had on the money supply" (Bernanke 1993, 61).

The relation between the latter claim and the theoretical literature Bernanke cites is not at all clear. He seems to be saying that if informational frictions make intermediation quantitatively important to economic activity, in the sense that reduction in the scale of intermediation results in reduction in economic output, then government intervention is warranted. The research he cited does not support that assertion. His series of papers with Mark Gertler studied a set of models of financial arrangements under limited information, but outcomes in those environments, as in many such models, are Pareto optimal, as they readily admitted (Bernanke and Gertler 1990, 104–6; 1987; 1989). Informational frictions imply that intermediation is costly, not that government would be any better at it. Bernanke's lecture highlighted a model (Akerlof 1970) in which a market "could break down completely" (Bernanke 1993, 52), and yet agents in the model are doing as well as they possibly can, given the circumstances and constraints they face. Bernanke and Gertler (1990, 106) argued that their model supports a case for subsidized central bank lending in financial panics, because it increases (bank) borrower net worth and thereby reduces the agency costs associated with informational frictions. Reducing those agency costs can increase per capita output even if it comes at the expense of transfers from other agents. Such transfers resemble "bailouts" of debtors, they argued.

I know of no staff research before, during, or after the crisis that aimed at quantifying the social-welfare trade-offs involved in this credit channel rationale for intervention, nor was the magnitude of transfers acknowledged in program proposals.[54] As with other strands of the microfoundation literature, there was no direct contact in policy deliberations to models in the credit view literature, aside from Bernanke's reference to the book by Allen and Gale (2007) in September 2007. The specific circumstances under which intervention was useful in particular theoretical models were of no apparent interest. Nor was the question of whether the assumptions of particular models about the physical, informational, and legal environment contributed to a persuasive replica of observed banking and financial markets. Instead, broadly inspired by the microfoundations literature, the *potential* for remediable inefficiencies in some models seemed to rationalize a sweeping impulse to intervene whenever perceived "distress" exceeded a subjective qualitative threshold for particular financial institutions or markets. When pressed, a gesture toward possibility propositions was deemed analytically sufficient.

Even if Fed staff took seriously the application of well-specified models of financial arrangements to the data and looked for market imperfections that might warrant official intervention, they would have to contend with the powerful competing hypothesis that observed financial fragility was the result of expectations of official intervention, built up over decades of accumulated precedents. Heavy reliance on short-term demandable wholesale funding, "over" leverage, credit "booms," would seem like predictable effects of the decades of rescue precedents. Whether these fragilities were inherent features of modern financial markets or induced by the financial safety net was not on the agenda.

Without meaningful contact with explicit underlying models, the financial stability program is left untethered, dependent on subjective words like "distress," "dysfunction," and "strained." These descriptive terms connote some sort of theoretically modeled market failure, but they have no clear economic meaning outside of a given model, and central bank financial stability practitioners have not provided us with their model. We are left without any principles to guide assessments of things like "how distressed" is sufficient to require intervention, or when is a market "not functioning"? If prices and quantities both fall, could that be a market functioning the way it should when the facts change, when uncertainty rises, when expected future cash flows fall? Staff provides no quantitative estimates of discrepancies between fire sale prices and fundamental values. During the GFC, virtually all of the staff's efforts were devoted to program design and implementation. They seemed well aware that sharing quantitative estimates of fundamental values would have raised a host of uncomfortable questions, such as "How long do you expect that discrepancy to last?" and "Why should your estimate be accorded more confidence than the collective wisdom embodied in market prices?"

Politics

A second candidate explanation for the twenty-first-century shift in Fed credit doctrine is politics. The distributional nature of Fed credit policy choice places the Federal Reserve at the very center of the fraught and fluid relationship between banks and the state, the history of which Calomiris and Haber (2015) so vividly describe. In their cross-country, historical review, Calomiris, Marc Flandreau, and Luc Laeven (2016, 48) describe the evolution of central banks' lender-of-last-resort role as "the outcome of a political bargain" and argue that the political environment in a given country is a "key driver" (49) of the timing of its emergence. Early twentieth-century credit policy owed as much to politics, such as that expressed in Warburg's Mercantilism, as it did to theoretical ideas, such as the age-old Real Bills Doctrine. The evolution of Fed credit policy in the second half of the twentieth century was also a product of its political environment and governance.

Having an independent balance sheet with which it could intervene, after the Accord, without monetary policy consequences, left the Fed exposed, in possession of a vestigial tool of keen interest to the banking industry but subject to a serious time consistency problem. The Reluctant Samaritan fed and was fed by the growth of large banks, but might have struggled, by itself, to meet the challenge of subprime losses in 2007, given the induced fragility of the system.

The influence of politics and the inherent fragility perspective seem to have been complementary. The credit view emerged alongside of and rationalized the growing interventionism of central banks. It extrapolated from fashionable new economic theories that interpreted Fed-induced financial fragility as an inherent property of a laissez-faire system, to be remedied ex post by discretionary technocratic credit market interventions and ex ante by macroprudential regulators and financial stability monitors. In 2007, the credit view's commitment to interventionism dovetailed with the self-interest of Wall Street and exacerbated moral hazard. The resulting turbulence provoked a fierce populist backlash, but for now the inherent fragility view seems to have prevailed and become the establishment view.

The Pursuit of Financial Stability in Practice

The credit market interventions during the GFC and the pandemic were redistributional, a fact often lost sight of during the crises. While interventions are frequently criticized for being capricious, a broad pattern is discernible, and it is striking. Sellers of ABCP benefited, not the opportunistic investors looking for bottom-feeding opportunities to buy the paper for less. Borrowing banks (that is, banks selling interbank obligations) were aided by the TAF; other banks were disadvantaged—those that could have earned a spread by lending to other banks rather than holding the Treasuries that the Fed sold to finance the program. Similarly, borrowing dealers benefited from the Primary Dealer Credit Facility at the expense of potential lenders who wanted compensation for risk-taking. The assistance for the Bear Stearns merger was a transfer to help prop up the price of toxic securities, and to aid the sale of Bear's shares to JPMC shareholders. The AIG rescue supported a seller of default insurance. Similarly, other credit programs aided borrowers or security sellers and took away profit opportunities from investors that had money on the sidelines, waiting for prices to fall to levels they saw as warranted. These interventions all had in common that they transferred resources to the sellers of claims of various types, who were unable to obtain funding or sell securities at prices they viewed as satisfactory, in circumstances in which the fundamental value of those claims was unusually uncertain. This suggests an apt characterization of the Federal Reserve's new twenty-first-century lending doctrine:

> **Lending Doctrine 5: Sell-Side Savior**   The Federal Reserve intervenes in any credit market at its discretion to restore the *normal* flow of credit to borrowers when financial markets experience *stress*. Interventions are designed to be seen as fair.

The wording is adapted from the Board of Governors website titled "Responding to Financial System Emergencies," including the undefined italicized terms.[55] The term *normal* is taken to mean noncrisis, non-recessionary times with low unemployment and low uncertainty. As with the Reluctant Samaritan lending doctrine, the Fed's credit policy actions are chosen ex post, without precommitment. In contrast to the Reluctant Samaritan Doctrine, however, the domain is broad and any credit flow is in scope. Circumstances are ostensibly limited to occasions when financial markets are experiencing "stress," but the Fed reserves the discretion to define that as it sees fit. Note that minimizing political blowback from nonintervention, a key objective for the Reluctant Samaritan, is omitted here, reflecting how supportive the Fed's political environment now is toward intervention. Instead, the political imperative is to intervene in ways that are perceived to distribute benefits *fairly* across business and household sectors. Popular attitudes toward potential beneficiaries, particularly in the financial sector, are likely to be important in assessing fairness; hedge funds, for example, became societas non grata in the 2000s and it would likely generate political criticism if they benefited from targeted rescues. Small businesses, on the other hand, perennially evoke political sympathy, even if credit programs targeting them tend to generate adverse ex post publicity around cases of fraud or abuse.

The Shadow Open Market Committee

The SOMC has witnessed and illuminated the remarkable evolution of the Fed's lending over the last fifty years. Members highlighted the importance of Monetary Stability and pointed out how Fed lending had strayed from and was no longer needed for that purpose. They counseled humility and transparency in credit policy, advocating for clearly articulated principles and limits. Members predicted the housing-finance crisis and ambiguity-induced turmoil of the GFC. Members warned that a swollen Fed balance sheet risked large losses if inflation emerged. Members cautioned that credit market intervention put monetary independence at risk and might inhibit the Fed in an inflation fight; the record suggests that may have happened. Members called for an explicit statement by the Treasury and the Fed about respective credit policy responsibilities, a call that was heeded, though with somewhat disappointing results. Above all, SOMC members have collectively deepened our understanding of Federal Reserve credit market activities.

Prospects for a Volckeresque recovery of the Fed's reputation for more limiting lending, as many SOMC members have advocated for over the years, appear dim. Sell-Side Savior Doctrine moves decidedly in the opposite direction. A legislative solution, as suggested by Anna Schwartz, seems hopelessly lacking in political support. Marvin Goodfriend and I (1999) conjectured that successively more costly financial crises could prompt political demand for pullback and reform, just as the late-1970s inflation, combined with the recognition, championed by the SOMC, that the Fed was responsible for the bad outcomes, built political support for Volcker's disinflationary campaign. Instead, in the next crisis the Fed blamed the fragility on markets, the way Arthur Burns shifted responsibility for inflation to a raft of special factors. The success of the SOMC campaign against inflation provides an example, however, of how a patient, relentless pursuit of the truth can bear fruit. The ability of ideas and understanding to exert, from time to time, a constructive influence on the evolution of Federal Reserve doctrine and practice provides perhaps the best basis for a hopeful outlook.

Notes

1. Source: Board of Governors of the Federal Reserve System (US), Assets: Liquidity and Credit Facilities: Loans: Primary Credit: Week Average, retrieved from FRED, Federal Reserve Bank of St. Louis; https://fred.stlouisfed.org/series/WPC, February 24, 2023, and author's calculations. The peak was reached in October 2008.

2. A stricter definition would classify anything beyond holding short-term Treasury securities (T-bills) as credit policy. Members of the SOMC have noted the fiscal/distributional consequences of the Fed's operations in longer-dated Treasury securities, and some have advocated a "bills only" monetary policy (Lacker 2022).

3. If M is the total stock of money in the hands of the public, consisting of coins, notes, and deposits; H is high-powered money (coin and bank notes); r is the ratio of bank reserves to deposits; and d is the deposit-currency ratio; then $M = H(1+d)/(1+rd)$. A shift from deposits to currency (a decline in d) requires an offsetting increase in H to avoid a contraction in the money stock (Friedman and Schwartz 1963, 790–92).

4. This passage closely follows Lacker (2024b).

5. Sir Francis Baring published a pamphlet in 1793 using the French phrase "*dernier resort*" to describe the Bank of England's position in the crises of 1793 and 1797. See Lacker (2024b, 5).

6. The definitive accounts of the Real Bills Doctrine are Mints (1945) and Humphrey and Timberlake (2019). See also Humphrey (1982), Hetzel (2014), and Lacker (2019).

7. Sargent and Wallace (1982) interpret the Real Bills Doctrine as central bank lending policy (or open market operations) that accommodates fluctuations in the demand for credit and present a model in which that policy dominates a "quantity theory" policy that stabilizes the central bank money supply. There is no distinction in their model between different private credit instruments, however, and thus there are no bills that are not "real." Moreover, credit markets and the process of production and distribution are not rich enough to assess Strong's critique.

8. Warburg's views were shared by other New York financiers such as Frank Vanderlip, president of National City, the largest bank in New York; and Benjamin Strong, president of Bankers Trust and later the first governor of the Federal Bank of New York; along with allies such as Senator Aldrich (Broz 1997, 148, 151; Meltzer 2003, 76).

9. Trade finance became a delicate political issue with the outbreak of World War I. Warburg, then a member of the Federal Reserve Board, clashed with Strong, governor of the Federal Reserve Bank of New York, over the interpretation of Federal Reserve Act provisions regarding acceptances. "Until late 1916 each professed disinterest in the probable effect of particular policies on the Allies, maintaining that the only relevant concern was how best to promote American economic interests. Predictably, though, Strong's suggestions were likely to assist, and Warburg's to impede, the Allied war effort" (Roberts 1998, 594). Federal Reserve credit policy became entangled in politics at the very beginning.

10. For accounts of Fed policy in the Great Contraction, see Friedman and Schwartz (1963, 299–419); Hetzel (2022, 142–92); Humphrey and Timberlake (2019, 79–100); and Bordo et al. (1995, 2002).

11. Friedman and Schwartz calculate that the change in the deposit-currency ratio alone would have produced a decline in the money stock of 37%, the change in the deposit-reserve ratio would have produced a decline of 20%, and the interaction of the two would have produced a rise of 10%. The stock of high-powered money did increase, but only enough to produce a rise of 17.5% in the stock of money.

12. For accounts of the Franklin National failure, see Spero (1980) and Sinkey (1977). "In many ways Franklin was a turning point, indicating a new way for how banks would be resolved and the lengths to which banking agencies would go in avoiding the least hint of financial instability, with minimal evidence presented of actual disruptions that would occur absent a bailout" (McKinley 2011, 68).

13. See commentary by Charles Calomiris (2012) at the April 2012 SOMC meeting, and Calomiris and Meltzer (2016).

14. For an overview of the literature, see Stern and Feldman (2004), Benston (1995), and Kaufman (1990, 2014). For a recent review of the voluminous empirical literature, see Strahan (2013).

15. See note 12.

16. Her coauthor Milton Friedman (1960, 30–35) took the same position in *A Program for Monetary Stability*.

17. In November 2008, LandAmerica, a mortgage title insurance company based in Richmond, Virginia, approached the Federal Reserve Bank of Richmond about lending assistance. The request was denied, and it filed for bankruptcy on November 26.

18. Federal Deposit Insurance Corporation Improvement Act of 1991, Pub. L. 102-242, 105 Stat. 2236, §142.

19. Excess reserves jumped from an average of $1.7 billion from December 12, 2002, to August 1, 2007, to an average of $9.2 billion over the two-week period ending August 15, 2007. Federal Reserve Bank of St. Louis, Excess Reserves of Depository Institutions, retrieved from FRED, Federal Reserve Bank of St. Louis; https://fred.stlouisfed.org/series/EXCSRESNW, February 24, 2023, and author's calculations.

20. Bernanke later described the New York Fed's intervention on August 9, 2007, as consistent with the "lender-of-last-resort concept" (Bernanke 2015, 144).

21. See Ennis (2018) for a model in which monetary conditions are unchanged over a broad range of reserves supply in the presence of interest on reserves. See also Ennis and Sablik (2019).

22. The Fed did roll out programs to bolster the broader commercial paper market.

23. For example, the New York Fed credits the Bank of England with a dollar account balance, while the Bank of England simultaneously credits the New York Fed with an equal value sterling account balance.

24. The support provided to AIG beginning on September 16, 2008, may have been influenced by international considerations, as well, along the lines of the 1974 agreement in Basel; some foreign banking organizations had substantial exposures to AIG just before they failed (McDonald and Paulson 2015).

25. Board of Governors of the Federal Reserve System (US), Assets: Liquidity and Credit Facilities: Loans: Wednesday Level [WLCFLL], retrieved from FRED, Federal Reserve Bank of St. Louis; https://fred.stlouisfed.org/series/WLCFLL, September 5, 2024.

26. Tri-party repo clearing banks (JPMorgan Chase and Bank of New York) extend intraday credit to dealers; so if a dealer is not expected to fully fund their overnight position at the end of the day, the clearing bank has an incentive to refuse to unwind in the morning. See Ennis (2011) for a model of strategic interaction between a tri-party repo clearing bank and a central bank over a failing dealer, the importance of the clearing bank's provision in intraday credit, and the related issue of the Fed's provision of intraday credit to the clearing banks.

27. I gave a speech in London in early June 2008 questioning whether financial fragility was inherent or induced by the moral-hazard effects of central bank

intervention, which was taken by the financial press as a critique of the Bear Stearns assistance (Lacker 2008).

28. See Bair (2012, 95–105) for an account of regulatory agency discussions that weekend.

29. Citigroup's bid for Wachovia proposed federal support in the form of a "ring fence" in which a designated set of assets would be guaranteed by the FDIC, the Treasury, and the Fed. Specifically, losses on the designated asset pool beyond a minimum threshold would be divided between the FDIC and the Treasury up to a second threshold, beyond which they would be borne by the Federal Reserve Bank of New York. Prior to consummating the acquisition by Citi, Wells Fargo submitted a revised bid that required no government support, which the FDIC accepted Thursday night, October 2. The same ring-fence arrangement was used to assist Citigroup itself later that fall and was proposed for Bank of America in January 2009. The latter was not consummated after the May release of the results of the Supervisory Capital Assessment Program dramatically improved market conditions for the large banks. In both ring-fence agreements, if losses were large enough to require the Federal Reserve to absorb some, the mechanism for doing so was to be a nonrecourse section 13(13) loan from the Reserve Bank in an amount that exceeded the posted Treasury securities collateral by the amount of the loss to be absorbed.

30. Since loan loss provisions looked ahead twelve months, this meant three-year-ahead projections were effectively required.

31. State Street was smaller but the outsize role it plays in clearing and settlement drove its TBTF status.

32. The requirement applies to bank holding companies larger than $50 billion in assets, as well as certain nonbank financial companies.

33. Dodd–Frank Wall Street Reform and Consumer Protection Act, Pub. L. 111-203, 124 Stat. 1376 (2010).

34. Lawrence Ball (2018) provides an account of decision making regarding Lehman Brothers that raises pointed questions about the relationship between the Fed and the Treasury.

35. "Summum bonum" is Latin for "the highest good."

36. His testimony drew upon "prior work, including a coauthored 2015 Shadow Open Market Committee (SOMC) presentation to Congressional staff written by Charles Calomiris, Greg Hess, and Athanasios Orphanides."

37. See also Plosser (2017).

38. She was a coauthor of the study while working at the CBO.

39. Bordo, along with William Roberds, co-organized the conference and co-edited the conference volume (Bordo and Roberds 2013). In that volume, see especially Bordo and Wheelock (2011). On lender of last resort, see also Bordo (2014b).

40. See Cochrane and Seru (2024) for a critical analysis of the Fed's approach to Treasury market functioning.

41. The name harked back to critics who said the Fed was rescuing "Wall Street" in 2008; then-Fed chair Ben Bernanke claimed it did it to rescue "Main Street."

42. For example, the January 2001 testimony of Alan Greenspan (2001a) to Congress in support of the tax proposals of incoming President George W. Bush was seen as such a noteworthy departure from practice that Greenspan prefaced his remarks with the statement that "I speak for myself and not necessarily for the Federal Reserve," a standard disclaimer for other Fed officials but highly unusual for the chair.

43. On the failure of Silicon Valley Bank, the most prominent case, see Seru (2024), Quarles (2024), and Duffie (2024).

44. The Fed did extend substantial credit to the bridge bank set up by the FDIC as receiver for SVB.

45. For a thorough survey of much of the subsequent literature, see the First Quarter 2010, Special Issue of the *Federal Reserve Bank of Richmond Economic Quarterly*, particularly the review essay by Huberto Ennis and Todd Keister (2010). See also the survey of models of discount window lending by Ennis (2016).

46. Note that the sequential service constraint is violated in the famous bank run scene in Frank Capra's 1946 movie *It's a Wonderful Life*.

47. This insight was later deepened by Ed Green and Ping Lin (2000, 2003), who derived the optimal partial suspension bank deposit contracts in a version of the Diamond–Dybvig model. Eighteenth-century Scottish banks issued "option notes" giving the bank the right to delay redemption of their notes for up to six months, with interest; see Goodspeed (2016) and Pressnell (1956). These were later prohibited by legislation. Suspension of convertibility of deposits into currency were frequent during late nineteenth-century US banking panics (Calomiris and Gorton 1991; Wicker 2008). Many modern investment arrangements feature "gating" or other restrictions on immediate withdrawals.

48. Bernanke also tutored US senators about fire sales while testifying in favor of the TARP legislation in the fall of 2008. He asked the members to think of complex mortgage-related securities as having two different prices: one, a "fire-sale" price that it would fetch today if sold quickly into an illiquid market, the second, the "hold-to-maturity price"—"what the security would be worth eventually when the income from the security was received over time" (Bernanke 2015, 314).

49. For example: "Hedge funds and private-equity firms, the most visible scratch-and-dent buyers this year, have moved to the sidelines because of the deep uncertainty in the mortgage market" (Berry and Terris 2007).

50. For example: "'All the big banks have plenty of capital and plenty of deposits, so they do not need to go to the window,' said James Reichbach, a managing partner at Deloitte & Touche in New York. Bert Ely, an independent analyst in Alexandria, Va., said, 'Banks are saying we don't need 5.75% money. We can borrow cheaper in the fed funds market'" (Rehm 2007).

51. For models of discount window stigma, see Ennis and Weinberg (2013) and Ennis (2019) and the citations there. For a nontechnical exposition, see Ennis and Price (2020). Models of adverse selection are notoriously sensitive to assumptions about what allocations qualify as equilibria; different assumptions can result in different conclusions about whether government intervention can improve outcomes in adverse selection models of lending markets (Lacker 1994).

52. I wrote a letter to my colleagues prior to the meeting pointing out the weaknesses in what I thought was the best theoretical rationale for the TAF (Lacker 2007).

53. The conference was called "Colloquium on the Credit Slowdown in the Recent Recession" and was held at the Federal Reserve Bank of New York on February 12, 1993. The proceedings were published in the *Federal Reserve Bank of New York Quarterly Review* volume 18, issue 1 (1993).

54. See Lucas (2018) for rigorous estimates of Fed credit program costs.

55. "In times of crisis, the financial markets that businesses and households rely on may experience severe stress or, in extreme cases, effectively cease to function. Employers often rely on these markets to raise the cash they need to meet payroll and cover near-term operating costs. These markets also serve households as investment options for their savings or to facilitate loans to buy cars and homes or to attend college. Because these markets are vital to the economy, the Federal Reserve—like many central banks—is empowered to take actions that can restore the normal flow of credit needed to support employment and the broader economy" (Board of Governors 2023b, first paragraph).

References

Akerlof, George A. 1970. "The Market for 'Lemons': Quality Uncertainty and the Market Mechanism." *Quarterly Journal of Economics* 84 (3): 488–500.

Allen, Franklin, and Douglas Gale. 1998. "Optimal Financial Crises." *Journal of Finance* 53 (4): 1245–84.

Allen, Franklin, and Douglas Gale. 2007. *Understanding Financial Crises. Clarendon Lectures in Finance Series.* Oxford University Press.

Ashcraft, Adam, Morten L. Bech, and W. Scott Frame. 2010. "The Federal Home Loan Bank System: The Lender." *Journal of Money, Credit and Banking* 42 (2): 551–83.

Bagehot, Walter. 1873. *Lombard Street: A Description of the Money Market.* Scribner, Armstrong & Co.

Bair, Sheila. 2012. *Bull by the Horns: Fighting to Save Main Street from Wall Street and Wall Street from Itself.* Free Press.

Ball, Laurence M. 2018. *The Fed and Lehman Brothers: Setting the Record Straight on a Financial Disaster.* Cambridge University Press.

Benston, George J. 1995. "Safety Nets and Moral Hazard in Banking." In *Financial Stability in a Changing Environment,* edited by Kuniho Sawamoto, Zenta Nakajima, and Hiroo Taguchi, 329–85. Palgrave Macmillan.

Bernanke, Ben S. 1983. "Nonmonetary Effects of the Financial Crisis in the Propagation of the Great Depression." *American Economic Review* 73 (3): 257–76.

Bernanke, Ben S. 1993. "Credit in the Macroeconomy." *Federal Reserve Bank of New York Quarterly Review* 18 (1): 50–70.

Bernanke, Ben S. 2015. *The Courage to Act: A Memoir of a Crisis and Its Aftermath.* W. W. Norton.

Bernanke, Ben S., Timothy F. Geithner, and Henry M. Paulson. 2019. *Firefighting: The Financial Crisis and Its Lessons.* Penguin Books.

Bernanke, Ben S., and Mark Gertler. 1987. "Banking and Macroeconomic Equilibrium." In *New Approaches to Monetary Economics: Proceedings of the Second International Symposium in Economic Theory and Econometrics*, edited by William A. Barnett and Kenneth J. Singleton. Cambridge University Press.

Bernanke, Ben S., and Mark Gertler. 1989. "Agency Costs, Net Worth, and Business Fluctuations." *American Economic Review* 79 (1): 14–31.

Bernanke, Ben S., and Mark Gertler. 1990. "Financial Fragility and Economic Performance." *Quarterly Journal of Economics* 105 (1): 87–114.

Bernhardt, Daniel, and Marshall Eckblad. 2013. "Stock Market Crash of 1987." Federal Reserve History. Effective November 22. https://www.federalreservehistory.org/essays/stock_market_crash_of_1987.

Berry, Kate, and Harry Terris. 2007. "Scratch-and-Dent Supply to Grow as Prices Shrink." *American Banker*, August 6.

BIS (Bank for International Settlements). 1974. "Statement of Central Bankers." *New York Times*, September 11.

Board of Governors (Board of Governors of the Federal Reserve System). 1968. "Reappraisal of the Federal Reserve Discount Mechanism: Report of a System Committee." Board of Governors of the Federal Reserve System.

Board of Governors. 1971. "Reappraisal of the Federal Reserve Discount Mechanism, Volume 1." Board of Governors of the Federal Reserve System. https://fraser.stlouisfed.org/files/docs/historical/federal%20reserve%20history/discountmech/bog_reappraisal_discount_197108_vol1.pdf.

Board of Governors. 2023a. "Review of the Federal Reserve's Supervision and Regulation of Silicon Valley Bank." Board of Governors of the Federal Reserve System.

Board of Governors. 2023b. "Responding to Financial System Emergencies." Board of Governors of the Federal Reserve System. Last modified April 23. https://www.federalreserve.gov/financial-stability/responding-to-financial-system-emergencies.htm.

Board of Governors. 2024. "Financial Stability Report." Board of Governors of the Federal Reserve System.

Board of Governors. 2025. "Financial Stability." Board of Governors of the Federal Reserve System. Last modified January 22. https://www.federalreserve.gov/financial-stability.htm.

Board of Governors. n.d. "Paul M. Warburg." People, Federal Reserve History. Accessed August 5, 2024. https://www.federalreservehistory.org/people/paul-m-warburg.

Board of Governors and US Department of the Treasury. 2009. "The Role of the Federal Reserve in Preserving Financial and Monetary Stability Joint Statement by the Department of the Treasury and the Federal Reserve." Press release. March 23. https://www.federalreserve.gov/newsevents/pressreleases/monetary20090323b.htm.

Bopp, Karl R., Robert V. Rosa, Carl E. Parry, Woodlief Thomas, and Ralph A. Young. 1947. *Federal Reserve Policy*. Postwar Economic Studies No. 8. Board of Governors of the Federal Reserve System.

Bordo, Michael D. 1990. "The Lender of Last Resort: Alternative Views and Historical Experience." *Federal Reserve Bank of Richmond Economic Review* 76 (1): 18–29.

Bordo, Michael D. 2009. "The Great Contraction and the Current Crisis: Historical Parallels and Policy Lessons." Position paper, Shadow Open Market Committee, Washington, DC. April 24.

Bordo, Michael D. 2010. "The Federal Reserve: Independence Gained, Independence Lost. . . ." Position paper, Shadow Open Market Committee, Washington, DC. March 26.

Bordo, Michael D. 2014a. "Has the Federal Reserve Learned to Be an Effective Lender of Last Resort in Its First One Hundred Years?" Position paper, Shadow Open Market Committee, New York, NY. April 14.

Bordo, Michael D. 2014b. "Rules for a Lender of Last Resort: An Historical Perspective." *Journal of Economic Dynamics and Control* 49 (December): 126–34.

Bordo, Michael D. 2017. "An Historical Perspective on Financial Stability and Monetary Policy Regimes: A Case for Caution in Central Banks Current Obsession with Financial Stability." Position paper, Shadow Open Market Committee, New York, NY. September 15.

Bordo, Michael D. 2022. "The Evolution of Central Banks." Position paper, Shadow Open Market Committee. November 11.

Bordo, Michael D., Ehsan U. Choudhri, and Anna J. Schwartz. 1995. "Could Stable Money Have Averted the Great Contraction?" *Economic Inquiry* 33 (3): 484–505.

Bordo, Michael D., Ehsan U. Choudhri, and Anna J. Schwartz. 2002. "Was Expansionary Monetary Policy Feasible during the Great Contraction? An Examination of the Gold Standard Constraint." *Explorations in Economic History* 39 (1): 1–28.

Bordo, Michael D., and John Landon-Lane. 2010. "The Banking Panics in the United States in the 1930s: Some Lessons for Today." *Oxford Review of Economic Policy* 26 (3): 486–509.

Bordo, Michael D., and William Roberds, eds. 2013. *The Origins, History, and Future of the Federal Reserve: A Return to Jekyll Island.* Cambridge University Press.

Bordo, Michael D., and David C. Wheelock. 2011. "The Promise and Performance of the Federal Reserve as Lender of Last Resort 1914–1933." Working Paper No. 16763. National Bureau of Economic Research. February.

Brimmer, Andrew F. 1989. "Distinguished Lecture on Economics in Government: Central Banking and Systemic Risks in Capital Markets." *Journal of Economic Perspectives* 3 (2): 3–16.

Broaddus, J. Alfred. 2000. "Market Discipline and Fed Lending." Remarks before the Bank Structure Conference, sponsored by the Federal Reserve Bank of Chicago, Chicago, IL. May 5.

Broaddus, J. Alfred, and Marvin Goodfriend. 1996. "Foreign Exchange Operations and the Federal Reserve." *Federal Reserve Bank of Richmond Economic Quarterly* 82 (1): 1–19.

Broz, J. Lawrence. 1997. *The International Origins of the Federal Reserve System.* Cornell University Press.

Bryant, John. 1980. "A Model of Reserves, Bank Runs, and Deposit Insurance." *Journal of Banking and Finance* 4 (4): 335–44.

Buchanan, James M. 1975. "The Samaritan's Dilemma." In *Altruism, Morality, and Economic Theory*, edited by Edmund S. Phelps. Russell Sage Foundation.

Calomiris, Charles W. 1994. "Is the Discount Window Necessary? A Penn-Central Perspective." *Federal Reserve Bank of St. Louis Review* 76 (3): 31–55.

Calomiris, Charles W. 2007. "Bank Failures in Theory and History: The Great Depression and Other 'Contagious' Events." Working Paper No. 13597. National Bureau of Economic Research. November.

Calomiris, Charles W. 2009a. "Prudential Bank Regulation: What's Broke and How to Fix It." Position paper, Shadow Open Market Committee, Washington, DC. April 24.

Calomiris, Charles W. 2009b. "Reassessing the Role of the Fed: Grappling with the Dual Mandate and More?" Position paper, Shadow Open Market Committee, Washington, DC. September 30.

Calomiris, Charles W. 2009c. "The Allocation of Regulatory Authority." Position paper, Shadow Open Market Committee, Washington, DC. April 24.

Calomiris, Charles W. 2010a. "A Three-Part Program for Housing Finance Reform." Position paper, Shadow Open Market Committee, New York, NY. October 12.

Calomiris, Charles W. 2010b. "Beyond Basel and the Dodd–Frank Bill." Position paper, Shadow Open Market Committee, New York, NY. October 12.

Calomiris, Charles W. 2010c. "Restoring Monetary Policy Independence: The Risks of Regulatory Reform." Position paper, Shadow Open Market Committee, New York, NY. March 26.

Calomiris, Charles W. 2011a. "Bank Capital Requirement Reform: Long-Term Size and Structure, the Transition, and Cycles." Position paper, Shadow Open Market Committee, New York, NY. October 21.

Calomiris, Charles W. 2011b. "Monetary Policy and the Behavior of Banks: Lessons from the 1930s for the 2010s." Position paper, Shadow Open Market Committee, New York, NY. March 25.

Calomiris, Charles W. 2012. "A Fed Scorecard for the Last Decade, and Its Implications for the Future." Position paper, Shadow Open Market Committee, New York, NY. April 20.

Calomiris, Charles W. 2013. "Reducing the Risks of the New Macro-Prudential Policy Regime." Position paper, Shadow Open Market Committee, New York, NY. September 30.

Calomiris, Charles W. 2016. "The Microeconomic Perils of Monetary Policy Experiments." Position paper, Shadow Open Market Committee, New York, NY. October 7.

Calomiris, Charles W. 2017. "Reforming the Rules That Govern the Fed." Research paper No. 17-41. Columbia Business School, Columbia University. https://doi.org/10.2139/ssrn.2946931.

Calomiris, Charles W. 2019. "How to Promote Fed Independence: Perspectives from Political Economy and History." Position paper, Shadow Open Market Committee, New York, NY. September 27.

Calomiris, Charles W. 2022a. "Bank Failures, The Great Depression and Other 'Contagious' Events." In *The Oxford Handbook of Banking*, 3rd Ed., edited by Allen N. Berger, Philip Molyneaux, and John O. S. Wilson. Oxford University Press.

Calomiris, Charles W. 2022b. "The Institutional Devolution of Government Financial Policy." Position paper, Shadow Open Market Committee. February 11.

Calomiris, Charles W., Marc Flandreau, and Luc Laeven. 2016. "Political Foundations of the Lender of Last Resort: A Global Historical Narrative." *Journal of Financial Intermediation* 28 (October): 48–65.

Calomiris, Charles W., and Gary Gorton. 1991. "The Origins of Banking Panics: Models, Facts, and Bank Regulation." In *Financial Markets and Financial Crises*, edited by R. Glenn Hubbard. University of Chicago Press.

Calomiris, Charles W., and Stephen H. Haber. 2015. *Fragile by Design: The Political Origins of Banking Crises and Scarce Credit*. Princeton University Press.

Calomiris, Charles W., and Joseph R. Mason. 2003. "Consequences of Bank Distress during the Great Depression." *American Economic Review* 93 (3): 937–47.

Calomiris, Charles W., and Allan Meltzer. 2016. "Rules for the Lender of Last Resort: Introduction." *Journal of Financial Intermediation* 28 (October): 1–3.

Capra, Frank, dir. 1946. *It's a Wonderful Life*.

Chandler, Lester V. 1958. *Benjamin Strong: Central Banker*. Brookings Institution.

Chari, V. V., and Patrick J. Kehoe. 2016. "Bailouts, Time Inconsistency, and Optimal Regulation: A Macroeconomic View." *American Economic Review* 106 (9): 2458–93.

Cochrane, John H., and Amit Seru. 2024. "Ending Bailouts at Last." *Journal of Law, Economics & Policy* 19 (2): 169–93.

Cohan, William D. 2009. *House of Cards: A Tale of Hubris and Wretched Excess on Wall Street*. 1st Ed. Doubleday.

Corrigan, E. Gerald. 1990. "Testimony before the United States Senate Committee on Banking, Housing and Urban Affairs." 101st Cong. May 3.

Covitz, Daniel, Nellie Liang, and Gustavo A. Suarez. 2013. "The Evolution of a Financial Crisis: Collapse of the Asset-Backed Commercial Paper Market." *Journal of Finance* 68 (3): 815–48.

Diamond, Douglas W., and Philip H. Dybvig. 1983. "Bank Runs, Deposit Insurance, and Liquidity." *Journal of Political Economy* 91 (3): 401–19.

Duffie, Darrell. 2024. "Silicon Valley Bank and Beyond: Regulating for Liquidity." In *Getting Monetary Policy Back on Track*, edited by Michael D. Bordo, John H. Cochrane, and John B. Taylor. Hoover Institution Press.

Ennis, Huberto M. 2011. "Strategic Behavior in the Tri-Party Repo Market." *Federal Reserve Bank of Richmond Economic Quarterly* 97 (4): 389–413.

Ennis, Huberto M. 2016. "Models of Discount Window Lending: A Review." *Federal Reserve Bank of Richmond Economic Quarterly* 102 (1): 1–50.

Ennis, Huberto M. 2018. "A Simple General Equilibrium Model of Large Excess Reserves." *Journal of Monetary Economics* 98 (October): 50–65.

Ennis, Huberto M. 2019. "Interventions in Markets with Adverse Selection: Implications for Discount Window Stigma." *Journal of Money, Credit and Banking* 51 (7): 1737–64.

Ennis, Huberto M., and Todd Keister. 2010. "On the Fundamental Reasons for Bank Fragility." *Federal Reserve Bank of Richmond Economic Quarterly* 96 (1): 33–58.

Ennis, Huberto M., and David A. Price. 2020. "Understanding Discount Window Stigma." Economic Brief No. 20-04. Federal Reserve Bank of Richmond. April.

Ennis, Huberto M., and Tim Sablik. 2019. "Large Excess Reserves and the Relationship between Money and Prices." Economic Brief No. 19-02. Federal Reserve Bank of Richmond. February.

Ennis, Huberto M., and John A. Weinberg. 2013. "Over-the-Counter Loans, Adverse Selection, and Stigma in the Interbank Market." *Review of Economic Dynamics* 16 (4): 601–16.

Euromoney. 1974. "What Was Agreed in Basle." October.

Farnsworth, Clyde H. 1974. "10 Nations Plan Bank Aid to Shore Up Confidence." *New York Times*, September 11.

FDIC (Federal Deposit Insurance Corporation). 2011. "The Orderly Liquidation of Lehman Brothers Holdings Inc. under the Dodd–Frank Act." *FDIC Quarterly* 5 (2): 31–49.

Federal Reserve History. 2023. "Continental Illinois: A Bank That Was Too Big to Fail." Time Period: The Great Moderation, Federal Reserve History. Last updated May 15. https://www.federalreservehistory.org/essays/continental-illinois.

Fischer, Stanley. 1999. "On the Need for an International Lender of Last Resort." *Journal of Economic Perspectives* 13 (4): 85–104.

FOMC (Federal Open Market Committee). 2007a. "Transcript of the Conference Call of the Federal Open Market Committee." August 16. https://www.federalreserve.gov/monetarypolicy/files/FOMC20070816confcall.pdf.

FOMC. 2007b. "Transcript of the Meeting of the Federal Open Market Committee." September 18. https://www.federalreserve.gov/monetarypolicy/files/fomc20070918meeting.pdf.

FOMC. 2008. "Transcript of the Meeting of the Federal Open Market Committee." December 15–16. https://www.federalreserve.gov/monetarypolicy/files/FOMC20081216meeting.pdf.

FOMC. 2009. "Transcript of the Meeting of the Federal Open Market Committee." January 27–28. https://www.federalreserve.gov/monetarypolicy/files/FOMC20090128meeting.pdf.

Friedman, Milton. 1960. *A Program for Monetary Stability*. Fordham University Press.

Friedman, Milton, and Anna J. Schwartz. 1963. *A Monetary History of the United States, 1867–1960*. Princeton University Press.

Fromson, Brett Duval. 1990. "Did Drexel Get What It Deserved?" *Fortune*, March 12.

Giannini, Curzio. 1999. "'Enemy of None but a Common Friend of All'? An International Perspective on the Lender-of-Last-Resort Function." Essays in International Finance No. 214. Department of Economics, Princeton University.

Goodfriend, Marvin. 1994. "Why We Need an 'Accord' for Federal Reserve Credit Policy: A Note." *Journal of Money, Credit and Banking* 26 (3): 572–80.

Goodfriend, Marvin. 1997. "Monetary Policy Comes of Age: A 20th Century Odyssey." *Federal Reserve Bank of Richmond Economic Quarterly* 83 (1): 1–22.

Goodfriend, Marvin. 2009. "We Need an 'Accord' for Federal Reserve Credit Policy." Position paper, Shadow Open Market Committee, Washington, DC. April 24.

Goodfriend, Marvin. 2010. "Clarifying Central Bank Responsibilities for Monetary Policy, Credit Policy, and Financial Stability." Position paper, Shadow Open Market Committee, New York, NY. March 26.

Goodfriend, Marvin. 2011a. "Central Banking in the Credit Turmoil: An Assessment of Federal Reserve Practice." *Journal of Monetary Economics* 58 (1): 1–12.

Goodfriend, Marvin. 2011b. "Fiscal Dimensions of Inflationist Monetary Policy." Position paper, Shadow Open Market Committee, New York, NY. October 21.

Goodfriend, Marvin. 2012. "The Elusive Promise of Independent Central Banking." *Monetary and Economic Studies* 30 (November): 39–54.

Goodfriend, Marvin. 2013. "The Chair's Succession and the Fed's Future." Position paper, Shadow Open Market Committee, New York, NY. September 30.

Goodfriend, Marvin. 2014a. "Monetary Policy as a Carry Trade." Position paper, Shadow Open Market Committee, New York, NY. November 3.

Goodfriend, Marvin. 2014b. "The Relevance of Federal Reserve Surplus Capital for Current Policy." Position paper, Shadow Open Market Committee, New York, NY. March 14.

Goodfriend, Marvin, and Robert G. King. 1988. "Financial Deregulation, Monetary Policy, and Central Banking." *Federal Reserve Bank of Richmond Economic Review* 74 (3): 3–22.

Goodfriend, Marvin, and Robert G. King. 2005. "The Incredible Volcker Disinflation." *Journal of Monetary Economics* 52 (5): 981–1015.

Goodfriend, Marvin, and Jeffrey M. Lacker. 1999. "Limited Commitment and Central Bank Lending." *Federal Reserve Bank of Richmond Economic Quarterly* 85 (4): 1–27.

Goodfriend, Marvin, and Bennett T. McCallum. 2009. "Exiting Credit Policy to Preserve Sound Monetary Policy." Position paper, Shadow Open Market Committee, Washington, DC. September 30.

Goodspeed, Tyler Beck. 2016. *Legislating Instability: Adam Smith, Free Banking, and the Financial Crisis of 1772.* Harvard University Press.

Gorton, Gary. 2008. "The Panic of 2007." Working Paper No. 14358. National Bureau of Economic Research. September.

Gorton, Gary. 2010. *Slapped by the Invisible Hand: The Panic of 2007.* Oxford University Press.

Green, Edward J., and Ping Lin. 2000. "Diamond and Dybvig's Classic Theory of Financial Intermediation: What's Missing?" *Federal Reserve Bank of Minneapolis Quarterly Review* 24 (1): 3–13.

Green, Edward J., and Ping Lin. 2003. "Implementing Efficient Allocations in a Model of Financial Intermediation." *Journal of Economic Theory* 109 (1): 1–23.

Greenspan, Alan. 2001a. "Testimony of Alan Greenspan: Outlook for the Federal Budget and Implications for Fiscal Policy." Presented at the US Senate Committee on the Budget. 107th Cong. January 25. https://www.federalreserve.gov /boarddocs/testimony/2001/20010125/default.htm.

Greenspan, Alan. 2001b. "The Financial Safety Net." Remarks at the 37th Annual Conference on Bank Structure and Competition of the Federal Reserve Bank of Chicago, Chicago, IL. May 10.

Hackley, Howard H. 1973. *Lending Functions of the Federal Reserve Banks: A History.* Publications Services, Division of Administrative Services, Board of Governors of the Federal Reserve System.

Haltom, Renee, and Robert Sharp. 2014. "The First Time the Fed Bought GSE Debt." Economic Brief No. 14-04. Federal Reserve Bank of Richmond. April.

Haubrich, Joseph. 2013. "Comment on 'The Fed's First (and Lasting) Job: Lender of Last Resort.'" *Forefront,* June.

Hawtrey, R. G. 1962. *The Art of Central Banking.* Frank Cass.

Heine, Garrett. 2020. "Has 'Moral Hazard' Been Fueling the Corporate Bond Market?" Morningstar, Inc. October 30. https://www.morningstar.com/funds /has-moral-hazard-been-fueling-corporate-bond-market.

Hess, Gregory D. 2002. "Is It Time for Fannie Mae and Freddie Mac to Cut the Cord?" Position paper, Shadow Open Market Committee, Washington, DC. November 18.

Hess, Gregory D. 2003. "It's Time to Privatize Fannie Mae and Freddie Mac." Position paper, Shadow Open Market Committee, Washington, DC. November 10.

Hess, Gregory D. 2004. "Can We Avert the Next Financial Crisis?" Position paper, Shadow Open Market Committee, Washington, DC. May 3.

Hess, Gregory D. 2009. "Fannie Mae and Freddie Mac: The Houseguests That Stayed Too Long." Position paper, Shadow Open Market Committee, Washington, DC. September 30.

Hess, Gregory D. 2018. "Fannie Mae and Freddie Mac—Re-Loaded." Position paper, Shadow Open Market Committee, New York, NY. October 19.

Hetzel, Robert L. 2014. "The Real Bills Views of the Founders of the Fed." *Federal Reserve Bank of Richmond Economic Quarterly* 100 (2): 159–81.

Hetzel, Robert L. 2022. *The Federal Reserve: A New History.* University of Chicago Press.

Horvitz, Paul M. 1975. "Failures of Large Banks: Implications for Banking Supervision and Deposit Insurance." *Journal of Financial and Quantitative Analysis* 10 (4): 589–601.

Hoskins, Lee. 2002. "Fed Governance." Position paper, Shadow Open Market Committee, Washington, DC. April 15.

Humphrey, Thomas M. 1975. "The Classical Concept of the Lender of Last Resort." *Federal Reserve Bank of Richmond Economic Review* 61 (January/February): 2–9.

Humphrey, Thomas M. 1982. "The Real Bills Doctrine." *Federal Reserve Bank of Richmond Economic Review* 68 (September/October): 3–13.

Humphrey, Thomas M. 1989. "Lender of Last Resort: The Concept in History." *Federal Reserve Bank of Richmond Economic Review* 75 (March/April): 8–16.

Humphrey, Thomas M., and Richard H. Timberlake. 2019. *Gold, the Real Bills Doctrine, and the Fed: Sources of Monetary Disorder, 1922–1938.* Cato Institute.

Ireland, Peter N. 2013. "Is the Fed's Exit on Track? Assessing the Indicators." Position paper, Shadow Open Market Committee, New York, NY. September 20.

Jacklin, Charles J. 1987. "Demand Deposits, Trading Restrictions, and Risk Sharing." In *Contractual Arrangements for Intertemporal Trade,* edited by Edward C. Prescott and Neil Wallace. University of Minnesota Press.

Jiang, Erica Xuewei, Gregor Matvos, Tomasz Piskorski, and Amit Seru. 2024. "Monetary Tightening and US Bank Fragility in 2023: Mark-to-Market Losses and Uninsured Depositor Runs?" *Journal of Financial Economics* 159 (September): article 103899.

Judge, Kathryn. 2020. "Why the Fed Should Issue a Policy Framework for Credit Policy." Position paper, Shadow Open Market Committee, New York, NY. September 30.

Kaufman, George G. 1990. "Are Some Banks Too Large to Fail? Myth and Reality." *Contemporary Economic Policy* 8 (4): 1–14.

Kaufman, George G. 2014. "Too Big to Fail in Banking: What Does It Mean?" *Journal of Financial Stability* 13 (August): 214–23.

Kilborn, Peter. 1984. "Saving a Bank: How the US Pitched In." *New York Times,* May 18.

Kohn, Donald L. 2009. "Central Bank Exit Policies." Remarks at the Shadow Open Market Committee, Washington, DC. September 30.

Lacker, Jeffrey M. 1994. "Does Adverse Selection Justify Government Intervention in Loan Markets?" *Federal Reserve Bank of Richmond Economic Quarterly* 80 (1): 61–95.

Lacker, Jeffrey M. 2007. "Letter to Ben S. Bernanke, Donald L. Kohn, Members, Board of Governors, and Members, Conference of Presidents." December 5. https://fraser.stlouisfed.org/files/docs/historical/frbrich/presidents/lacker/20130118_talf_dissent.pdf?utm_source=direct_download.

Lacker, Jeffrey M. 2008. "Financial Stability and Central Banks." Presented at the Distinguished Speakers Seminar, European Economics and Financial Centre, London, United Kingdom. June 5.

Lacker, Jeffrey M. 2009. "Government Lending and Monetary Policy." *Business Economics* 44 (3): 136–42.

Lacker, Jeffrey M. 2011. "Committing to Financial Stability." Presented at the George Washington University Center for Law, Economics and Finance, Washington, DC. November 5.

Lacker, Jeffrey M. 2012a. "A Program for Financial Stability." Presented at the Inaugural George and Susan Beischer Address, The Banking Institute, UNC School of Law, Charlotte, NC. March 29.

Lacker, Jeffrey M. 2012b. "Understanding the Interventionist Impulse of the Modern Central Bank." *Cato Journal* 32 (2): 247–53.

Lacker, Jeffrey M. 2013. "Ending 'Too Big to Fail' Is Going to Be Hard Work." Presented at the Council on Foreign Relations, New York, NY. May 9.

Lacker, Jeffrey M. 2019. "From Real Bills to Too Big to Fail: H. Parker Willis and the Fed's First Century." *Cato Journal* 39 (1): 15–31.

Lacker, Jeffrey M. 2022. "The Fiscal Costs of Quantitative Easing: A Case for Bills Only." Presented at the Shadow Open Market Committee Conference, Chapman University, Orange, CA. June 24.

Lacker, Jeffrey M. 2024a. "Governance and Diversity at the Federal Reserve." Policy Brief. Mercatus Center at George Mason University. January 8.

Lacker, Jeffrey M. 2024b. "Last Resort Lending: Classical Thought vs. Modern Practice." Research paper. Mercatus Center at George Mason University. October 29.

Lacker, Jeffrey M. 2024c. "Racing through Red Lines." *Business Economics* 49 (1): 64–66.

Lehman Brothers. 2008. *Q2 2008 Update.* June 4. https://web.stanford.edu/~jbulow /Lehmandocs/docs/DEBTORS/LBHI_SEC07940_514735-514759.pdf.

Levin, Andrew T., Brian L. Lu, and William R. Nelson. 2022. "Quantifying the Costs and Benefits of Quantitative Easing." Working Paper No. 30749. National Bureau of Economic Research. December.

Lowenstein, Roger. 2011. *When Genius Failed: The Rise and Fall of Long-Term Capital Management.* Paperback. Random House.

Lucas, Deborah. 2017. "Fiscal Consequences of the Federal Reserve's Balance Sheet." Position paper, Shadow Open Market Committee, New York, NY. September 15.

Lucas, Deborah. 2018. "The Financial Crisis Bailouts: What They Cost Taxpayers and Who Reaped the Direct Benefits." Position paper, Shadow Open Market Committee, New York, NY. October 19.

Lucas, Deborah. 2019. "Some Heretical Thoughts on Central Bank Independence." Position paper, Shadow Open Market Committee, New York, NY. September 27.

Lucas, Deborah. 2025. "When Are Central Bank Policy Actions Fiscal? Definitions, Examples, and a Call for Transparency." In *Fifty Years of the Shadow Open Market Committee: A Retrospective on Its Role in Monetary Policy,* edited by Michael D. Bordo, Jeffrey M. Lacker, Mickey D. Levy, and John B. Taylor. Hoover Institution Press.

Marshall, Liz, Sabrina Pellerin, and John Walter. 2015. "Bailout Barometer 2009 Revised Estimate." Federal Reserve Bank of Richmond. Last updated October.

https://www.richmondfed.org/-/media/RichmondFedOrg/research/national_economy/bailout_barometer/pdf/bailout_barometer_2009_revised_estimate.pdf.

Mayer, Thomas. 1975. "The Case Against Credit Allocations." Position paper, Shadow Open Market Committee, Washington, DC. March 7.

McCallum, Bennett T. 2010. "The Rationale for Independent Monetary Policy." Position paper, Shadow Open Market Committee, New York, NY. March 26.

McDonald, Robert, and Anna Paulson. 2015. "AIG in Hindsight." *Journal of Economic Perspectives* 29 (2): 81–106.

McKinley, Vern. 2011. *Financing Failure: A Century of Bailouts.* Independent Institute.

Meltzer, Allan H. 1974. "Failures of Banks and Other Financial Institutions." Position paper, Shadow Open Market Committee, Washington, DC. September 6.

Meltzer, Allan H. 1986. "Real and Pseudo-Crises: Comment." In *Financial Crises and the World Banking System,* edited by Forrest Capie and Geoffrey E. Wood. Macmillan.

Meltzer, Allan H. 1998. "Asian Problems and the IMF." Position paper, Shadow Open Market Committee, Washington, DC. March 16. Reprinted in *Cato Journal* 17 (3): 267–74.

Meltzer, Allan H. 2003. *A History of the Federal Reserve. Vol. 1: 1913–1951.* University of Chicago Press.

Mints, Lloyd W. 1945. *A History of Banking Theory in Great Britain and the United States.* University of Chicago Press.

Nelson, Edward. 2020. *Milton Friedman and Economic Debate in the United States, 1932–1972, Vol. 2.* University of Chicago Press.

Nurisso, George C., and Edward Simpson Prescott. 2020. "Origins of the Too-Big-to-Fail Policy in the United States." *Financial History Review* 27 (1): 1–15.

Orphanides, Athanasios. 2009. "Central Bank Exit Policies." Remarks at the Shadow Open Market Committee, Washington, DC. September 30.

Plosser, Charles I. 2009. "Ensuring Sound Monetary Policy in the Aftermath of Crisis." Presented at the US Monetary Policy Forum, University of Chicago Booth School of Business, New York, NY. February 27.

Plosser, Charles I. 2017. "The Risks of a Fed Balance Sheet Unconstrained by Monetary Policy." Economics Working Paper No. 17102. Hoover Institution. May 4.

Plosser, Charles I. 2019. "Balance Sheet: Exposures, Risks, and Financial Difficulties." Position paper, Shadow Open Market Committee, New York, NY. March 29.

Poole, William. 2009. "Exit Policies from the Financial Crisis—to What?" Position paper, Shadow Open Market Committee, Washington, DC. September 30.

Pressnell, Leslie Sedden. 1956. *Country Banking in the Industrial Revolution.* Clarendon Press.

Quarles, Randal. 2024. "Silicon Valley Bank: What Happened? What Should We Do About It?" In *Getting Monetary Policy Back on Track,* edited by Michael D. Bordo, John H. Cochrane, and John B. Taylor. Hoover Institution Press.

Rehm, Barbara A. 2007. "A Window of Opportunity? Some Wonder." *American Banker,* August 22.

Roberts, Priscilla. 1998. "'Quis Custodiet Ipsos Custodes?' The Federal Reserve System's Founding Fathers and Allied Finances in the First World War." *Business History Review* 72 (4): 585–620.

Roberts, Priscilla. 2000. "Benjamin Strong, the Federal Reserve, and the Limits to Interwar American Nationalism Part I: Intellectual Profile of a Central Banker." *Federal Reserve Bank of Richmond Economic Quarterly* 86 (2): 61–76.

Sargent, Thomas J., and Neil Wallace. 1975. "'Rational' Expectations, the Optimal Monetary Instrument, and the Optimal Money Supply Rule." *Journal of Political Economy* 83 (2): 241–54.

Sargent, Thomas J., and Neil Wallace. 1982. "The Real-Bills Doctrine Versus the Quantity Theory: A Reconsideration." *Journal of Political Economy* 90 (6): 1212–36.

Schwartz, Anna J. 1986a. "External Debt and the Banking System." Position paper, Shadow Open Market Committee, Washington, DC. March 25.

Schwartz, Anna J. 1986b. "Real and Pseudo-Financial Crises." In *Financial Crises and the World Banking System,* edited by Forrest Capie and Geoffrey E. Wood. Macmillan.

Schwartz, Anna J. 1992. "The Misuse of the Fed's Discount Window." *Federal Reserve Bank of St. Louis Review* 74 (5): 58–69.

Schwartz, Anna J. 1998. "What Future for the IMF?" Position paper, Shadow Open Market Committee, Washington, DC. September 14.

Schwartz, Anna J. 1999. "Is There a Need for an International Lender of Last Resort?" Position paper, Shadow Open Market Committee, Washington, DC. March 8.

Schwartz, Anna J. 2001. "The IMF Infirmary." Position paper, Shadow Open Market Committee, Washington, DC. October 15.

Schwartz, Anna J. 2009. "Boundaries Between the Fed and the Treasury." Position paper, Shadow Open Market Committee, Washington, DC. April 24.

Seru, Amit. 2024. "What Can We Learn about Financial Regulation from Silicon Valley Bank's Collapse and Beyond." In *Getting Monetary Policy Back on Track,* edited by Michael D. Bordo, John H. Cochrane, and John B. Taylor. Hoover Institution Press.

Sinkey, Joseph F., Jr. 1977. "Identifying Large Problem/Failed Banks: The Case of Franklin National Bank of New York." *Journal of Financial and Quantitative Analysis* 12 (5): 779–800.

Smialek, Jeanna. 2023. *Limitless: The Federal Reserve Takes on a New Age of Crisis.* 1st Ed. Alfred A. Knopf.

SOMC (Shadow Open Market Committee). 1984. "Policy Statement." October 10.

SOMC. 2002a. "Shadow Open Market Committee News Release." April 15.

SOMC. 2002b. "Policy Statement." April 15.

SOMC. 2004. "Policy Statement." May 3.

Spero, Joan Edelman. 1980. *The Failure of the Franklin National Bank: Challenge to the International Banking System.* Columbia University Press.

Stern, Gary H., and Ron J. Feldman. 2004. *Too Big to Fail: The Hazards of Bank Bailouts.* Brookings Institution Press.

Strahan, Philip E. 2013. "Too Big to Fail: Causes, Consequences, and Policy Responses." *Annual Review of Financial Economics* 5 (1): 43–61.

Taylor, John B. 2009. "The Financial Crisis and the Policy Responses: An Empirical Analysis of What Went Wrong." Working Paper No. 14631. National Bureau of Economic Research. January.

Thornton, Henry. (1802) 1939. *An Enquiry into the Nature and Effects of the Paper Credit of Great Britain (1802) Together with His Evidence given before the Committees of Secrecy of the Two Houses of Parliament in the Bank of England, March and April, 1797, Some Manuscript Notes, and His Speeches on the Bullion Report, May 1811.* Reprint edited by Friedrich A. von Hayek, George Allen, and Unwin.

Timberlake, Richard H. 1978. *The Origins of Central Banking in the United States.* Harvard University Press.

US Bureau of the Census. 1975. *Historical Statistics of the United States: Colonial Times to 1970.* US Government Printing Office.

Volcker, Paul. 2008. "The Economic Club of New York." Remarks at the Economic Club of New York 101st Year, 395th Meeting, New York, NY. April 8. Transcript at https://www.econclubny.org/documents/10184/109144/2008VolckerTranscript.pdf.

Wallace, Neil. 1988. "Another Attempt to Explain an Illiquid Banking System: The Diamond and Dybvig Model with Sequential Service Taken Seriously." *Federal Reserve Bank of Minneapolis Quarterly Review* 12 (4): 3–16.

Wallich, Henry C. 1974a. "Notes on BIS Governors' Meeting of July 8, 1974, Attachment B, Memorandum of Discussion." Report, Board of Governors of the Federal Reserve System. https://www.federalreserve.gov/monetarypolicy/files/fomcmod19740716.pdf.

Wallich, Henry C. 1974b. "Notes on BIS Governors' Meeting of March 11–12, 1974, Attachment B, Memorandum of Discussion." Report, Board of Governors of the Federal Reserve System. https://www.federalreserve.gov/monetarypolicy/files/fomcmod19740319.pdf.

Wallich, Henry C. 1974c. "Statement before the Permanent Subcommittee on Investigations, Committee on Government Operations, US Senate, October 16, 1974." *Federal Reserve Bulletin* 60 (11): 757–63.

Walter, John R., and John A. Weinberg. 2002. "How Large Is the Federal Financial Safety Net?" *Cato Journal* 21 (3): 369–93.

Warburg, Paul M. 1907. "Defects and Needs of Our Banking System." *New York Times Annual Financial Review,* January 6.

Warburg, Paul M. 1910. *The Discount System in Europe.* National Monetary Commission. Government Printing Office. https://www.jstor.org/stable/1171787.

White, Eugene N. 2013. "'To Establish a More Effective Supervision of Banking': How the Birth of the Modern Fed Altered Bank Supervision." In *The Origins, History, and Future of the Federal Reserve: A Return to Jekyll Island*, edited by Michael D. Bordo and William Roberds. Cambridge University Press.

Wicker, Elmus. 2008. *Banking Panics of the Gilded Age*. Cambridge University Press.

Wicker, Elmus. 2015. *The Great Debate on Banking Reform: Nelson Aldrich and the Origins of the Fed*. Ohio State University Press.

Amit Seru

It is truly an honor to discuss this paper; it is exceptionally rich and insightful. I gained a great deal from it and hope to contribute to the discussion by focusing on one key aspect that resonates with several of the paper's central themes: governance.

The Federal Reserve's role in shaping monetary and credit policy has evolved significantly, influenced by shifts in economic thinking, market dynamics, and governance challenges. The governance of an institution like the Federal Reserve is critical because it embodies the delicate—and at times precarious—balance between public interest and private economic interests in regulation. This balance is aptly captured by George Stigler's famous observation: "As a rule, regulation is acquired by the industry and is designed and operated primarily for its benefit." It serves as a cautionary reminder of the challenges in maintaining impartiality and effectiveness in regulating industries, particularly in the banking sector. I will argue that several recent actions by the Fed have introduced vulnerabilities, particularly in its governance and the credibility of its independence. In my analysis, I will emphasize the persistent tension between rule-based and discretionary decision making.

The chapter masterfully traces the Federal Reserve's evolution from its foundational role as the "Lender of Last Resort" to its current position as a "Financial System Savior," highlighting the transformation of its credit policies. It compellingly argues that while the Fed's early mandate was rooted in doctrines such as the Real Bills Doctrine and Warburg's Mercantilism, its role has expanded significantly over time. In particular, the emergence of the Too Big to Fail paradigm has reshaped its approach to financial stability, presenting both opportunities and challenges. This evolution reflects the intricate interplay between economic theory and practical governance. For instance, the Federal Reserve's response to the 2008 financial crisis marked a pivotal shift, employing unconventional monetary tools to stabilize the economy.

These developments underscore the growing complexity of the Fed's role and its increasing reliance on discretionary measures.

Governance and Independence Issues

Maintaining the credibility of independence is a cornerstone of effective governance. The Federal Reserve's unique governance structure, featuring three classes of directors, seeks to balance public accountability with private-sector expertise. This design provides distinct advantages, such as enhanced information gathering about the economy. However, it also introduces vulnerabilities, particularly the risk of regulatory capture.

These vulnerabilities have been widely noted, including in the 2011 Government Accountability Office report, which highlights significant connections between Federal Reserve directors and the financial sector (GAO 2011). This revolving door dynamic is further compounded by the frequent movement of personnel between the Fed and the private sector, raising concerns about the institution's ability to maintain impartiality. Figure A illustrates an analysis I conducted, examining the flow of employees from the Fed to various private-sector roles—financial, nonfinancial, and others. As shown, there is a substantial transition of personnel from the Fed to the private sector. While such movement can have benefits, such as enabling the Fed to attract a vibrant and skilled talent pool, it also amplifies concerns about the Fed's independence.

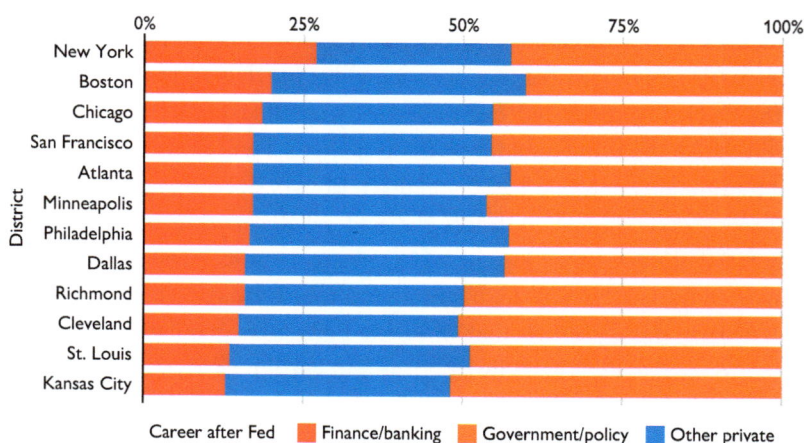

Figure A. Movement of personnel between the Federal Reserve and private sector, following the methodology in Agarwal et al. (2014).

Source: Author's own data.

To safeguard its credibility, the Federal Reserve must uphold foundational principles of good governance: (1) *commitment*, emphasizing a preference for rules over discretion, as highlighted by John Taylor's decades of research; (2) *reputation*, built on consistent and principled decision making, especially during challenging times; and (3) *transparency*, to ensure accountability and public trust.

Unfortunately, I would argue that the Fed's credibility and independence have been undermined. A lack of commitment, reflected in an overreliance on discretion, has frequently eroded its reputation for making tough, impartial decisions. These challenges are further compounded by insufficient transparency in many of its actions. Let me elaborate on these points with examples from research I've conducted in collaboration with others.

The practical implications of discretion in governance are starkly evident in the Federal Reserve's supervisory practices, particularly in the use of CAMELS ratings, a critical tool for assessing bank stability. These ratings evaluate banks across six dimensions: capital adequacy, asset quality, management quality, earnings quality, liquidity, and sensitivity to risk. Each dimension is scored on a scale of 1 to 5, with 1 being the best and 5 the worst, culminating in a composite score that blends the individual ratings. These scores play a pivotal role in policy decisions, such as determining deposit insurance premiums and approving bank expansions.

Every financial turmoil or crisis has historically led to increased regulation around bank supervision. Many of these regulations prescribe what banks can or cannot do, leading one to assume that such a rule-laden framework would leave little room for discretion in supervision—especially following the surge in regulatory complexity introduced by the Dodd–Frank Act. However, this assumption would be incorrect. Rather than simplifying oversight, the proliferation of rules has created a more complex regulatory environment, often allowing for discretionary interpretation.

In our research, we examine how much of the variation in CAMELS composite ratings is driven by the individual components. One might argue that certain components, such as management quality, are inherently more subjective, while others are less so. Our findings reveal that management quality accounts for a striking 49% of the weight in composite CAMELS ratings (see figure B). This indicates a significant degree of discretion in these supervisory evaluations.

This reliance on discretion introduces substantial variability, as evidenced by differences in ratings assigned by state and federal regulators. When the same bank is evaluated by both, discrepancies often emerge, reflecting

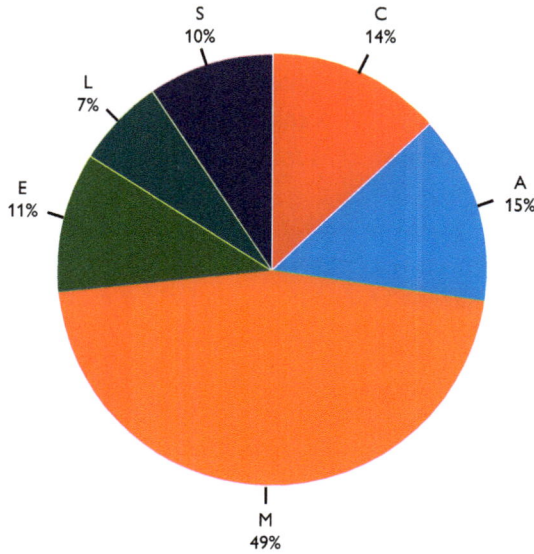

Figure B. Discretion in CAMELS ratings: weight on each subcomponent in the composite CAMELS rating.

Source: Agarwal et al. (2024).

divergent interpretations and priorities. In other words, the fragmented responsibilities within our current regulatory framework, characterized by overlapping jurisdictions, allow for the same rules to be interpreted in markedly different ways. This pervasive use of discretion across the regulatory landscape not only amplifies variability but also creates significant uncertainty for banks navigating the system.

This reliance on discretion has further eroded the credibility of the Federal Reserve by enabling it to avoid addressing fundamental issues through decisive, rule-based action. One of the most critical and persistent concerns in banking is *high leverage*, where even small asset losses can jeopardize a bank's viability. The 2023 turmoil underscored this systemic risk once again. High interest rates depressed the value of assets—particularly marketable and liquid securities—and threatened the solvency of numerous banks. Yet these risks were neither surprising nor insurmountable; they could have been mitigated by enforcing rules that required banks to maintain higher equity buffers.

Instead, the Fed has leaned on discretionary measures, often interpreting solvency crises as liquidity issues. And it did it yet again in the recent turmoil. This approach has resulted in the proliferation of subsidies within the banking sector, leaving it increasingly fragile. Such reliance on discretion has also led to the expansion of Lender of Last Resort facilities, which have shifted from being exceptional tools to standard responses. Over the past two decades, this mission creep has normalized liquidity interventions, regardless of whether they were truly warranted, further entrenching vulnerabilities in the financial system.

These practices have understandably raised significant questions about the Fed's governance. Consider the failures of Silicon Valley Bank and First Republic in the 2023 turmoil. The Federal Reserve's report on the causes of these failures focused overwhelmingly on liquidity issues, referencing the term over three hundred times, while giving scant attention to the solvency concerns that were at the core of these banks' collapse. Unsurprisingly, this liquidity-focused narrative has been eagerly adopted by industry participants to argue against higher equity capital requirements, as proposed in the Fed's Basel III Endgame reforms. By framing solvency as a nonissue in its own report, the Fed inadvertently undermined its case for stricter capital regulations, enabling the industry to push back more effectively.

Innovation in the financial sector provides another example. Fintech, payments, and private credit are transforming the landscape, yet the Fed has been notably slow to adapt. Industry rhetoric often highlights the potential risks of innovation to profitability, which appears to have influenced the Fed's cautious stance. The ongoing debate over Central Bank Digital Currencies, for example, underscores the broader tension between fostering competition and protecting incumbent institutions.

Lastly, the Fed's balance sheet remains a critical issue. Despite its commitments to unwind unconventional monetary policies, decisive action has been obstructed by industry lobbying. This hesitation not only delays essential reforms but also undermines the Fed's credibility, reinforcing perceptions that it opts for a softer, industry-favored approach rather than making tough, necessary decisions.

Conclusion

In conclusion, this paper is an essential read for anyone interested in these critical issues. My remarks have centered on governance, a dimension deeply intertwined with the paper's themes. The Fed's unique structure demands an exceptionally high standard of credibility, which has been undermined by excessive reliance on discretion and a hesitation to make difficult decisions. To safeguard the institution's long-term effectiveness, addressing these challenges through meaningful governance reforms—including a potential reset or reorganization—is imperative.

References

Agarwal, Sumit, David Lucca, Amit Seru, and Francesco Trebbi. 2014. "Inconsistent Regulators: Evidence from Banking." *Quarterly Journal of Economics* 129 (2): 889–938.

Agarwal, Sumit, Bernardo C. Morais, Amit Seru, and Kelly Shue. 2024. "Noisy Experts? Discretion in Regulation." Working Paper No. 32344. National Bureau of Economic Research. April.

GAO (Government Accountability Office). 2011. *Federal Reserve System: Opportunities Exist to Strengthen Policies and Processes for Managing Emergency Assistance (GAO-11-696).* July 21.

Charles W. Calomiris

The first thing to say about Jeffrey Lacker's excellent paper is a simple thank you. On behalf of the entire Shadow Open Market Committee (SOMC), I am grateful to Jeff for the breadth of his treatment of the SOMC's five decades of discussions of lender of last resort (LOLR) policies. I am also grateful to my SOMC colleagues for giving me the chance to comment on his thorough and thoughtful review and explain the evolution of my own thinking and research on this topic.

The SOMC's contributions to the debates over the proper structure and use of LOLR powers are, as Lacker's paper shows, quite diverse. In fact, if one were looking for an example of the openness of our committee to different perspectives on an important set of policy questions, our discussions of the structure and use of the LOLR would be a prime example. As such, this diversity of opinion is a sign of the healthy intellectual breadth of the SOMC over its five decades and the mutual respect its members have shown for each other throughout our history.

It is useful to divide SOMC perspectives on the LOLR into two opposing viewpoints: One sees the proper objectives of the LOLR as narrowly limited to ensuring the stability of the aggregate money supply, and consequently, the tools needed to achieve its objectives are limited to open market operations. The other (broader) view sees the LOLR's proper objectives extending beyond the stabilization of the money supply, with particular emphasis on credit markets, including assistance targeted to individual banks or borrower classes. To achieve those interventions the LOLR would have to use the discount window, and potentially other tools.

As Lacker's discussion notes, the narrow view of the purpose and toolkit of the LOLR goes back at least as far as Friedman and Schwartz's classic 1963 *Monetary History*, in which they explicitly argue that during the Depression, the key Federal Reserve failure was allowing the sharp contraction of the aggregate money supply. In their view, the collapse of bank credit and the failure of banks would not have been important if that credit collapse and those failures had been countered by a sufficient expansion of high-powered money that would have kept the total money supply from falling. That view was reprised in Anna Schwartz's (1992) classic article, reflecting the refinements of the argument by Marvin Goodfriend and Robert King (1988).

The broader view of the LOLR, at least in my mind, goes back at least as far as the seminal work by Raymond Goldsmith and Ronald McKinnon in the 1960s and 1970s, and by Brunner and Meltzer's general equilibrium conception of the many dimensions linking the real economy and the financial system (see, for example, Brunner and Meltzer 1990).[1] The development of information economics in the 1970s and 1980s also played a fundamental role in providing microeconomic foundations for that broader view, which is particularly visible in Ben Bernanke's (1983) Nobel Prize–winning discussion of the cost of credit intermediation as a major magnifying factor during the Great Depression. All of those influences had major effects on my thinking about the LOLR when I began to think about this topic in the early 1980s.

In my mind, the central points of departure for the broader view of the LOLR are the recognition that (1) bank credit serves a vital role in the economy, separate from the aggregate money supply; and (2) the credit supply of individual banks (which possess different information, are engaged in distinct client relationships, and do not always overlap geographically), generally are not perfect substitutes for one another. According to the broader view, preventing aggregate bank credit from declining, and preventing localized shocks from producing contractions in credit supply by important groups of credit suppliers, are important objectives of an LOLR that seeks to preserve the stability of the credit system and its contribution to the productive allocation of capital in the economy.

Empirically, the literature on bank credit supply during the Depression showed that state-level contractions of credit supply mattered greatly for reducing relative income in states suffering especially great bank distress (Calomiris and Mason 2003), which demonstrates the general proposition that the aggregate supply of money is not a sufficient statistic for understanding how the banking system matters for output.

The Great Depression also was a testing ground for a new kind of LOLR intervention, purchases of bank preferred stock by the Reconstruction

Finance Corporation (RFC)—analyzed by several recent studies, including Calomiris et al. (2013). All the studies of the RFC find that it proved successful in stabilizing local bank credit supply, and because assistance was offered selectively and combined with bank governance constraints, the RFC did not entail major fiscal costs.

During the Depression, collateralized lending by the Fed was understood to have limited consequences for stabilizing banks that had lost significant equity capital, because such lending subordinated depositors' claims on bank assets that were used as collateral. Some observers claimed that this effective subordination not only failed to encourage credit supply expansion but may even have spurred depositor runs on banks.

More generally, the broad view of the LOLR (e.g., Calomiris et al. 2016) envisions the need for a wide range of tools—collateralized lending, credit guarantees, "lifeboats," preferred stock purchases, and common stock purchases—which are able to address different shocks of different severity. Compelling evidence that efficient interventions by the LOLR include a broad toolkit comes from many historical examples, including two in Canadian banking history before it had established the Bank of Canada as its central bank. In 1906 and 1908, the incipient banking crises in Canada led the Bank of Montreal to organize a coalition of banks to take over weak banks because of concerns about spillover effects from allowing them to fail. One way to understand those two private, voluntary interventions to bail out failed banks is that they were attempts to avoid the possible spillovers survivors can suffer from failures. What's especially interesting about those two interventions is that they were selective. Generally, weak Canadian banks were allowed to fail, but in some cases, externalities were perceived by banks themselves as sufficiently large to warrant spending their own resources to intervene. That history of selective Canadian bank action cannot be understood from the perspective of money-supply stabilization.

The theoretical and empirical literature on bank credit supply since Bernanke (1983) also recognizes how recessions, in general, produce loan losses that erode bank equity, which can substantially magnify recessions because bank equity is expensive to raise. This implies that monetary expansion, per se, may not be an effective tool for expanding the supply of credit when bank risk management is the binding constraint on the supply of credit. Banks with expanding deposits but limited equity choose to hold cash rather than expand credit, and this was a common experience during the Depression, and in recent years (Calomiris and Wilson 2004; Jiménez et al.

2012; Aiyar, Calomiris, and Wieladek 2014a, 2014b, 2015; Aiyar, Hooley, et al. 2014; Baron et al. 2021).

Assistance from the LOLR via the discount window has also been used to support an expansion of the supply of bank credit to put out fires occurring outside the banking system. Targeted discount window assistance passed through banks was used in 1970 to stabilize the newly emerging commercial paper market in the wake of the failure of a commercial paper issuer, Penn Central. The Federal Reserve Bank of New York let money center banks know that they could access the window freely, without fear of a nonpecuniary penalty, to pass on credit to commercial paper issuers experiencing refusals to roll over their paper in the wake of Penn Central's failure. That crisis was soon resolved as it became clear that other commercial paper issuers were financially sound. Interestingly, after the Penn Central crisis, bank-provided backup lines of credit (with implicit backing from the Fed's discount window) became a permanent feature of the commercial paper market (Calomiris 1994). Open market operations would have been an inferior tool for dealing with the Penn Central shock for two reasons: First, expanding the money supply would have been a blunt instrument that would have worked through all interest rates rather than through the spread in a particular segment of the market (bank loans to commercial paper issuers). Second, it would have been difficult for the Fed to know when to end that hypothetical monetary stimulus to address the temporary positive shock to bank credit demand; in contrast, by using the discount window the Fed could target credit to a group experiencing a shock (commercial paper issuers) without disrupting the overall stance of monetary policy, and remove that special access to the discount window once it saw commercial paper issuers returning to the commercial paper market.

Despite our disagreements over the role and form of LOLR assistance, SOMC members always agreed on a fundamental point that puts them squarely at odds with the Fed: LOLR assistance should be provided through a systematic and transparent approach to policy. To maximize its impact and to avoid abuse of assistance through unwarranted credit subsidies, the Fed should formulate, announce, and follow an LOLR policy framework. To whom will credit be provided, under what circumstances, and how?

For the narrow view of the LOLR, that is an easy question to answer: The Fed should stick to stabilizing the money supply as part of a systematic approach to monetary policy. For the broad view of the LOLR, the Fed could articulate (but never has articulated) a set of principles to guide the use of the discount window, or to explain circumstances where the discount window is an inadequate tool (which implies a need for Treasury, not Fed, intervention). I emphasize that a broad approach to the LOLR does not mean that there should be no limits on Fed discretion, nor does it mean that the Fed should be able to get away with saying nothing in advance to constrain its lending policies to banks. An LOLR policy description should specify how the terms for Fed assistance will be determined and provide at least a rough description of the circumstances where traditional discount window lending to banks is appropriate. It should also define the circumstances in which it may need to provide credit to nonbanks, or non-collateralized credit to banks and nonbanks, and how it would approach those actions. If it were willing to do so, there would be much better grounds for restoring the broad authority over lending that was taken away from the Fed after the 2008 crisis (Calomiris et al. 2017).

As part of defining the proper role of its assistance to banks, the Fed also should note the limitations of lending to banks to resolve their problems. As we learned during the Great Depression and the 2008–9 banking crisis, banks that are in severe distress need more than collateralized loans to address their problems, and wrongly providing such loans can even be counterproductive to banking system stability. The Fed should point to the circumstances where only the government can act to provide assistance, as it did through the RFC or the Troubled Asset Relief Program (TARP). As part of such a policy statement, the Fed, in concert with the Treasury, would make explicit the proper role and structure of non-Fed assistance, and the lessons that should have been learned from the RFC and TARP experiences about how assistance should and shouldn't be provided (Calomiris and Khan 2015).

Whenever Allan Meltzer testified before Congress about the LOLR, he took the opportunity to point out that the Fed has never provided even rough guidance about the policy framework it uses to implement LOLR policies, which he always regarded as a serious deficiency. As Mark Carlson's (2025) book on the Fed's early experience as the LOLR shows, the Fed experimented with its LOLR powers during the 1920s, and its LOLR policies varied greatly across Reserve Banks. Indeed, some Reserve Banks did not strictly adhere to limits on their statutory powers. But the Fed did not perform a systematic analysis of its LOLR policies to learn from abuses of discretion, or to develop a set of policy rules informed by its successes and failures. That failure contributed to the Fed's failure to act properly as a LOLR during the Depression. I would say that the Fed has never performed such an analysis or indicated what it has learned as an LOLR from its own successes or failures, which means that the market cannot benefit from being able to expect warranted support, and incentives in the market are adversely affected by the moral hazard invited by anticipated LOLR excesses based on observing prior Fed overreach. The social costs stemming from the Fed's failure to formulate a consistent, empirically informed framework for the LOLR has been a consistent theme of criticisms provided by all members of the SOMC, irrespective of whether they advocate a narrow or broad LOLR role. In that regard, the SOMC's discussions of LOLR mirror one of its primary criticisms of Fed monetary policy: its failure to specify a systematic framework to guide constructive actions and constrain abuses of discretion.

Note

1. One can go back much further to find roots of this broad view. Henry Thornton, Walter Bagehot, and other nineteenth-century authors saw the LOLR as stabilizing credit, not just money in the narrow sense. Although they used the phrase "money market" to describe the shocks to which the LOLR needed to respond, that phrase had, and still has, a broader meaning than the market for the medium of exchange. Indeed, in a financial system dominated, as Britain's was in the nineteenth century, by the banker's acceptance—a financial instrument that served both as a loan and a medium of exchange—it was not even possible to conceive of, or distinguish empirically between, separate disturbances to money and credit.

References

Aiyar, Shekhar, Charles W. Calomiris, John Hooley, Yevgeniya Korniyenko, and Tomasz Wieladek. 2014. "The International Transmission of Bank Capital Requirements: Evidence from the UK." *Journal of Financial Economics* 113 (3): 368–82.

Aiyar, Shekhar, Charles W. Calomiris, and Tomasz Wieladek. 2014a. "Does Macro-Prudential Regulation Leak? Evidence from a UK Policy Experiment." *Journal of Money, Credit and Banking* 46 (s1): 181–214.

Aiyar, Shekhar, Charles W. Calomiris, and Tomasz Wieladek. 2014b. "Identifying Channels of Credit Substitution When Bank Capital Requirements Are Varied." *Economic Policy* 29 (77): 45–77.

Aiyar, Shekhar, Charles W. Calomiris, and Tomasz Wieladek. 2015. "Bank Capital Regulation: Theory, Empirics, and Policy." *IMF Economic Review* 63 (4): 955–83.

Baron, Matthew, Emil Verner, and Wei Xiong. 2021. "Banking Crises without Panics." *Quarterly Journal of Economics* 136 (1): 51–113.

Bernanke, Ben S. 1983. "Nonmonetary Effects of the Financial Crisis in the Propagation of the Great Depression." *American Economic Review* 73 (3): 257–76.

Brunner, Karl, and Allan Meltzer. 1990. "Money Supply." In *Handbook of Monetary Economics, Vol. 1*, edited by Benjamin M. Friedman and Frank H. Hahn. North-Holland.

Calomiris, Charles W. 1994. "Is the Discount Window Necessary? A Penn-Central Perspective." *Federal Reserve Bank of St. Louis Review* 76 (3): 31–55.

Calomiris, Charles W., Marc Flandreau, and Luc Laeven. 2016. "Political Foundations of the Lender of Last Resort: A Global Historical Narrative." *Journal of Financial Intermediation* 28 (October): 48–65.

Calomiris, Charles W., Douglas Holtz-Eakin, R. Glenn Hubbard, Allan H. Meltzer, and Hal S. Scott. 2017. "Establishing Credible Rules for Fed Emergency Lending." *Journal of Financial Economic Policy* 9 (3): 260–67.

Calomiris, Charles W., and Urooj Khan. 2015. "An Assessment of TARP Assistance to Financial Institutions." *Journal of Economic Perspectives* 29 (2): 53–80.

Calomiris, Charles W., and Joseph R. Mason. 2003. "Consequences of Bank Distress during the Great Depression." *American Economic Review* 93 (3): 937–47.

Calomiris, Charles W., Joseph R. Mason, Marc Weidenmier, and Katherine Bobroff. 2013. "The Effects of Reconstruction Finance Corporation Assistance on Michigan's Banks' Survival in the 1930s." *Explorations in Economic History* 50 (4): 526–47.

Calomiris, Charles, and Berry Wilson. 2004. "Bank Capital and Portfolio Management: The 1930s 'Capital Crunch' and the Scramble to Shed Risk." *Journal of Business* 77 (3): 421–56.

Carlson, Mark. 2025. *The Young Fed: The Banking Crises of the 1920s and the Making of a Lender of Last Resort*. University of Chicago Press.

Friedman, Milton, and Anna J. Schwartz. 1963. *A Monetary History of the United States, 1867–1960*. Princeton University Press.

Goodfriend, Marvin, and Robert G. King. 1988. "Financial Deregulation, Monetary Policy, and Central Banking." *Federal Reserve Bank of Richmond Economic Review* 74 (3): 3–22.

Jiménez, Gabriel, Steven Ongena, José-Luis Peydró, and Jesus Saurina Salas. 2012. "Macroprudential Policy, Countercyclical Bank Capital Buffers and Credit Supply: Evidence from the Spanish Dynamic Provisioning Experiments." Discussion Paper No. 2012-011. European Banking Center. May 1.

Schwartz, Anna J. 1992. "The Misuse of the Fed's Discount Window." *Federal Reserve Bank of St. Louis Review* 74 (5): 58–69.

THOMAS HOENIG: We have a couple minutes. Well, we'll make a couple of minutes, put it that way, for, say, three questions, and then we'll let everyone respond.

LORENZO GIORGIANNI: Thank you. Amazing presentations. I don't want to derail the conversation away from the main topic.

But I think that, looking forward, one risk is that the next big crisis might be a debt crisis, a type of run on Treasuries. If investors smell that risk and we start having wobbles in the Treasury markets, I guess the Fed will come in and intervene under the guise of some market-functioning issue.

So how do you think about that part of the financial stability mandate of the Fed? What are the rules of the road? Seems to be a very fuzzy area where repeated interventions there might actually induce significant moral hazard.

JACK KRUPANSKY: Hi, I'm Jack Krupansky. Real simple question on Silicon Valley Bank. Before that happened, I thought bank runs were just a thing of the past, the 1930s or something. How frequent do you think actual bank runs will be in the future? And isn't there some way—Silicon Valley had assets, so couldn't the Fed have taken the assets but kept the depositors whole so that we don't have this banking integrity concern?

I don't want to protect the bank, but I want to protect banking integrity so people don't have to feel like they have to run in a panic.

HOENIG: Okay, we'll let Jeff reply and then Amit.

JEFFREY M. LACKER: Thank you to Charlie Calomiris and Amit Seru. I really appreciated your comments, Charlie. We have a lot to talk about offline sometime, but I appreciate your generous spirit. The Fed does intervene at times in the Treasury market, saying they have concerns about market functioning. At a certain level I know what they're talking about. At a certain level, I don't. At the level of a model with preferences, endowments, and technologies spelled out, I'm not quite sure I get it. And again, it goes back to this question of how should markets behave when the real economy is really uncertain?

About runs, there's a good paper by Jonathan Rose, 2015, a working paper at the Board of Governors, that documents the runs in the Great Financial Crisis. He shows they were all runs from one bank to another. The runs like we had in the Great Depression, where people took their money out and took currency home with them—those are things of the past. Runs are a real thing and they're less about people showing up in line than they are about large depositors that have access to a bunch of different banks that just move their money to another bank.

But thank you for those questions.

AMIT SERU: I want to emphasize one key point: While much attention has been focused on Silicon Valley Bank, it's important to recognize that many other banks share similar vulnerabilities. These institutions face the same risks of runs or the threat of runs due to their large holdings of uninsured deposits and heavily depressed assets. This isn't fundamentally a liquidity issue; when assets remain depressed for a year or more, it becomes a solvency issue. We can label it as a liquidity problem, but that's precisely the crux of my argument—it's not.

HOENIG: Agree.

CHARLES W. CALOMIRIS: I wanted to just answer the question directly about what the FDIC could have done.

They have the capability to pay out a large percentage of uninsured deposits, even though the bank has failed. So in the case of Silicon Valley Bank, for example, the FDIC knew that it could have paid out 90% of uninsured deposits with the bank failing. And so the notion that somehow it was needed, as Secretary [Janet] Yellen said to bail out the bank so that they could pay out 100 cents on the dollar was just completely unnecessary, and it really showed how political this bailout was. So the answer to your question is yes, it could have been solved a different way.

HOENIG: Thank you all very much. Thanks to the panel, for all their work. Thank you.

Influences of the SOMC and
Others Outside the Fed

Introduction

We've come to the last panel of the day, on the influences of the SOMC and others outside of the Fed. I just wanted to start by saying that often what you hear at SOMC meetings is that monetary policy would be better informed, and a lot of missteps may be avoided, if the Fed more seriously incorporated a more diverse range of viewpoints and frameworks into its deliberations and decision-making processes.

So I applaud the organizers for assembling this extraordinary group: Donald Kohn, Roger Ferguson, Bob Heller, and Esther George. They collectively bring many decades of practical experience and wisdom to be able to shed light on how and when outsiders have had a meaningful influence on the Fed. So the question really is: Does the Fed really listen?

And let me start to get some answers to that question by handing it over to Don Kohn.

21

From the SOMC to the FOMC

How Ideas Filter into the Fed, with
Special Reference to the Taylor Rule

Donald Kohn

Multiple channels have long existed for ideas to filter into the Federal Reserve from the Shadow Open Market Committee (SOMC) and others outside the Fed, but how they have been received and processed has changed over time. That has reflected both changes in receptivity inside the Fed and shifting relevance of the outside academic ideas for real-world policymaking. Work by SOMC and other researchers on policy rules gradually gained more prominence in policy discussions over the 1990s and early 2000s, but for a variety of reasons, policymakers have resisted close adherence to any of the suggested policy rules.

Channels of Influence

When I started at the Federal Reserve in the early 1970s, alternative perspectives on policy were making their way into the institution, though not getting the open-minded consideration they deserved. Given their backgrounds and interests, policymakers and staff will naturally pay attention to the views of others about policy strategy and to the academic research on topics relevant to policy. Moreover, when I joined the Board staff in 1975, the Board met regularly with a group of outside academic experts, including such luminaries as Paul Samuelson and Milton Friedman, who opined on current policy as well as economic developments of interest to policymakers.

Many policymakers come from academia or financial markets, bringing what they learned there. The SOMC, for example, has contributed a number of former members to the Federal Open Market Committee (FOMC)—Bill Poole, Charlie Plosser, Jerry Jordan—who have not hesitated to argue their perspective in FOMC meetings.[1] All of these were Reserve Bank presidents, highlighting the role of the Reserve Banks in broadening the considerations going into monetary policy, leaning against tendencies for groupthink at the Board of Governors to dominate policy; in this respect, Reserve Bank presidents play a role similar to that of external members of the Monetary Policy Committee at the Bank of England. For example, the Federal Reserve Bank of St. Louis led the charge on introducing elements of monetarism into the policy debate in the 1970s. And historically, though not in recent decades, the Federal Reserve Bank of New York was often at odds with the Board perspective on monetary policy.

Research staffs at the Reserve Banks and the Board have largely been recruited from academia and come with the perspective of their advisors and mentors. Milton Friedman students in influential staff positions at the Board in the late 1970s and early 1980s included Steve Axilrod, Dave Lindsey, and Tom Simpson, all of whom contributed to the monetarist experiment of 1979–82. And later Monetary Affairs, the division I ran that is charged with providing monetary policy advice to the FOMC, was partly populated with John Taylor students.

Receptivity to Outside Influences

For outside research and ideas to affect policymaking, they need to find an open-minded audience inside, and the ideas need to be useful in the policy process, growing out of an understanding of that process and the needs of policymakers. In my view, progress has been made on both of those fronts over recent decades, and the result has been increasingly productive interactions of the Federal Reserve and outside observers—even if the advice is not followed as tightly as those commentators and researchers would like.

When I joined the Board's staff in 1975, Arthur Burns was chair, and he had a very limited tolerance for discussion and publication of ideas that might raise questions about the way monetary policy was being run under his leadership. Governors and Reserve Bank presidents were strongly discouraged from discussing monetary policy in public, especially if their views deviated a bit from the current internal received wisdom. Articles in Reserve Bank publications by Bank staff needed to be cleared with Board staff, and Board staff themselves were not permitted to publish academic work that might raise questions about the conduct of policy. These practices continued under William Miller and Paul Volcker and were very gradually relaxed under Alan Greenspan.[2]

Today, policymakers often give speeches and interviews that suggest their views might not be completely aligned with the leadership of the Committee—despite the small number of formal dissents. And staff publications and working papers appear to be largely unconstrained in suggesting new angles for analyzing policy-relevant issues. As noted, the restraints gradually eroded under Greenspan and this loosening gathered momentum under Ben Bernanke and Janet Yellen, perhaps reflecting an openness to and appreciation for research carried over from their academic backgrounds.

The paucity of dissents at FOMC meetings in recent years is perhaps a concerning indicator that alternative perspectives don't get full airing at FOMC meetings. That may be a product of differences being smoothed out in the consensus building that precedes the meeting, but that would make them less subject to a full-table discussion. On the other hand, the speeches and publications suggest an institution with an intellectual environment that welcomes serious consideration of alternative perspectives—much more so than it did thirty or forty years ago.

Sometimes the lack of consideration of academic ideas is caused by the ideas themselves. Real business cycle analysis that dominated macroeconomic academic writing in the 1980s, with its emphasis on productivity shocks causing business cycles, did not align with the lived experience of the FOMC, especially after the very tight monetary policy of 1980–82 so clearly caused the deep recessions of 1980–82, which in turn reduced inflation.

And the Shadow Open Market Committee's focus in the 1980s and early 1990s on policy rules operating through the monetary base was never going to resonate with the FOMC, given the dominance of foreign holdings of US currency in the level and variations of the base, and the well-established strategy of implementing policy by changing interest rates. In a presentation to the SOMC in 2015, Ben McCallum (2015) noted that by placing interest rates at the center of monetary policy, the Taylor rule opened up dialogue between the Federal Reserve and academics.

Increased Federal Reserve transparency has played an important role in fostering better dialogue between Fed insiders and researchers and observers outside the Fed. Roger Ferguson's (2025) contribution in this volume reviews a number of the steps the Fed has taken to become more transparent about its decisions and their rationale. The better outsiders understand the Fed, the more useful and informed will be their analysis.

Case Study: How Policy Rules Worked Their Way into Policy Discussions

Getting the FOMC to pay more attention to interest-rate-focused monetary policy rules has been a major goal of the SOMC. Those rules are also an interesting illustration of how outside ideas can work their way onto the policy process.[3]

Although John Taylor's late 1992 piece putting forward the Taylor rule is a seminal landmark in the rules literature and sparked a virtual industry of rule suggestions, work at the Fed on rules and rule-like behavior predated this contribution. In the late 1970s, researchers at the Board were fitting "reaction functions," finding regularities in how the FOMC responded to new information.[4] Indicative of the ongoing work, in June 1992 the Federal Reserve held a conference on "operating procedures and the conduct of monetary policy" that contained a lot of policy rule material, including an examination of McCallum's rule. McCallum (1993) and John Taylor (1993) wrote the summaries of the conference.

In the 1990s, the Division of Monetary Affairs (MA) worked increasingly on policy rules, especially after 1993, when I spent a semester at Stanford, enjoying John's hospitality and being subject to his relentless proselytizing. Janet Yellen and Larry Meyer were important supporters of this work and MA regularly sent a Rules Memo to the Board, but not to the FOMC. By late in the decade, policy rules played an increasingly important role in the Bluebook, the staff document discussing policy alternatives, which went to all FOMC participants. For example, the Taylor rule was used to model policy responses to various shocks presented in alternative simulations. And the Taylor rule informed the monetary policy assumptions that underlay the staff forecast of the economy in the Greenbook. In 2004, my successor began to include in the Bluebook a table and charts on rule results on a regular basis.

As vice chair and then chair, Janet Yellen continued to reference policy rules, giving several speeches on them, albeit with important caveats that I will discuss below. For example, in one speech at Stanford she presented three rules—Taylor, balanced approach that puts added weight on variations in output or employment gaps, and a changes rule that ties changes in the policy rate to changes in output and inflation gaps without needing to take a stand on the long-term level of the policy rate (Yellen 2017). And under her leadership in 2017, the Federal Reserve began to include a box in its semiannual monetary policy report comparing the path of the funds rate to the output of a variety of rules.

Policymakers recognize the advantages of regular and predictable policy geared to achieving their long-run goals of price stability and maximum employment. But the direct role of rules in policymaking has been limited;

they have been characterized as at most "guideposts" by Alan Greenspan or "broad guidelines" by Janet Yellen. They have given a variety of reasons for their resistance to stricter adherence.[5]

1. "They [rules] assume the future will be like the past" (Greenspan 1997), but shocks hit the economy that weren't encompassed in the period in which the rules were tested. Greenspan, in 1997, gave as examples the stock market crash of 1987, the credit crunch of 1990–92, and the productivity acceleration in the second half of the 1990s. Yellen (2017) cited surprises in fiscal policy and foreign growth.
2. Relatedly, new policy circumstances arise that can influence the appropriate setting: time at the zero lower bound constraint; changes in the Fed's balance sheet; risk management considerations.
3. Many policy rules use current or past values of output or inflation on the right-hand side—best practice monetary policy targets a forecast.
4. Many rules are highly sensitive to assumptions about the equilibrium values for interest rates (r^*), unemployment (u^*), or the level of potential output (y^*). Yellen highlighted the effects of different assumptions about r^*, which was estimated to have declined substantially over time, and changing estimates of u^*.

Greenspan's resistance is especially interesting inasmuch as he, and Paul Volcker before him, ran the monetary policy John Taylor found to be rule-based and successful.

In other work, I have identified the key aspects of monetary policy from 1982 at the end of the monetarist experiment to 1997 that restored price stability over time while damping cyclical fluctuations (Kohn 2024). First, Chairs Volcker and Greenspan were tightly focused on restoring price stability as the principal job of monetary policy. Second, to do so after 1982 they didn't try to put the economy in recession to reduce inflation rapidly, but they were forward-looking, generally acting on forecasts for the next few quarters, seeing it as essential to preempt any potential uptick in inflation after the experience of the 1970s. Third, they paid very close attention to inflation expectations as a gauge of how they were doing in restoring price stability. And fourth, they responded to unexpected developments flexibly.

Adhering to broad principles like these may be as systematic and rule-based as successful policy realistically can get.

Notes

1. The current makeup of the SOMC is further evidence that SOMC-compatible ideas had channels into the policy process. Of the eleven current members of the SOMC, three were FOMC policymakers (James Bullard, Jeffrey M. Lacker, and Plosser), and three were Board staff members (Gregory Hess, Andrew Levin, and Athanasios Orphanides).

2. See Robert Heller's contribution in this volume (chapter 23) for an example of Paul Volcker's limited tolerance for public discussion of policy by other policymakers. There were, however, many more dissents from FOMC decisions in the Burns, Miller, Volcker, and early Greenspan eras than there have been in recent years. Those dissents are evidence that alternative views were being expressed in the FOMC, and the dissents also were a way to communicate those views to the public, as their rationale was explained in the minutes of the meeting (St. Louis Fed 2014).

3. This section has benefited greatly from input from Athanasios Orphanides.

4. In my memory, they were not allowed to publish the results because they reflected badly on how policy had been run in the 1970s.

5. What follows has been drawn from Yellen (2017) and from Greenspan (2017). I've added a few thoughts of my own into the mix.

References

Ferguson, Roger W., Jr. 2025. "Influences of the SOMC and Others Outside the Fed." In *Fifty Years of the Shadow Open Market Committee: A Retrospective on Its Role in Monetary Policy*, edited by Michael D. Bordo, Jeffrey M. Lacker, Mickey D. Levy, and John B. Taylor. Hoover Institution Press.

Greenspan, Alan. 1997. "Rules Versus Discretionary Monetary Policy." Remarks at the Fifteenth Anniversary Conference of the Center for Economic Policy Research at Stanford University, Stanford, CA. September 5.

Kohn, Donald. 2024. "Comments on 'Lessons from History for Successful Disinflation,' by Christina D. Romer and David H. Romer." Paper prepared for the "Inflation in the COVID Era and Beyond" conference, National Bureau of Economic Research, Cambridge, MA. May.

McCallum, Bennett T. 1993. "Concluding Observations." In *Operating Procedures and the Conduct of Monetary Policy: Conference Proceedings*, edited by Marvin Goodfriend and David H. Small. Finance and Economics Discussion Series, Board of Governors of the Federal Reserve System.

McCallum, Bennett T. 2015. "Remarks on John Taylor's Contributions." Shadow Open Market Committee, New York, NY. March 20.

St. Louis Fed (Federal Reserve Bank of St. Louis). 2014. "A History of FOMC Dissents." *On the Economy* (blog). St. Louis Fed. September 16. https://www.stlouisfed.org/on-the-economy/2014/september/a-history-of-fomc-dissents.

Taylor, John T. 1993. "New Directions in Monetary Policy Research: Comments on the Federal Reserve System's Special Meeting on Operating Procedures." In *Operating Procedures and the Conduct of Monetary Policy: Conference Proceedings*, edited by Marvin Goodfriend and David H. Small. Finance and Economics Discussion Series, Board of Governors of the Federal Reserve System.

Yellen, Janet L. 2017. "The Economic Outlook and the Conduct of Monetary Policy." Speech at the Stanford Institute for Economic Policy Research, Stanford, CA. January 19.

22
Influences of the SOMC and Others Outside the Fed

Roger W. Ferguson Jr.

The topic—"Influences of the SOMC and Others Outside the Fed"—is in many ways an ironic one. If we have learned anything from the past fifty years, it is the importance of "independent central banks." A simple definition of "independence" might be "the freedom from outside influence." In fact, the Shadow Open Market Committee (SOMC) was founded at a time when the Fed had been freed from one form of outside influence—the need to support Treasury borrowing during World War II, which ended with the 1951 Treasury-Fed Accord—but confronted other outside influences. The early 1970s were a time when the Fed faced immense political pressure—an outside influence applied successfully by the Nixon administration on Arthur Burns, ultimately to the regret of the nation as inflation took hold. One of the goals of the Shadow Open Market Committee was to provide a framework that would guide monetary policy and, presumably, reduce the influence of external parties such as Congress and the executive branch.

Adding to the irony, modern-day central bankers are notoriously proud of their ability to avoid outside influences. Montagu Norman, the iconic governor of the Bank of England from 1920 to 1944, was fond of the phrase, "Never explain, never excuse." I recall a situation during my tenure as vice chair of the Board of Governors in which there was pressure on the relatively new European Central Bank (ECB) to reduce rates. Wim Duisenberg came to the Bank for International Settlements and repeated a phrase that rings in my ears: "We hear, but we do not listen."

In some ways, Paul Volcker, one of the most revered Fed chairs, embodied the high point of this disregard of outside influences. In the pursuit of price stability, the Fed was famously faced with the strongest protest in its history. Indebted farmers demonstrated with their tractors, circling the Fed's Constitution Avenue headquarters in Washington, DC, and home builders mailed two-by-fours with strong, in some cases scatological, messages addressed to Chair Volcker. More substantively, and perhaps a victory for the SOMC, the Volcker Fed adopted a "monetarist-inspired" policy of targeting money supply resulting in the rates John Taylor (2025, in this volume) highlighted and two deep recessions, all clearly leading to public outrage.

However, because the Fed was targeting the money supply and not interest rates directly, it could argue that the rates that were the source of discomfort were simply the results of supply and demand forces beyond its control. The Volcker Fed was also famously comfortable with opacity and seemed to strongly believe that policy worked best when it surprised markets, and presumably other outsiders. Interestingly, the public, particularly journalists, also seemed to accept, however reluctantly, the notion that monetary policy should be literally and figuratively shrouded in a cloud of opaque cigar smoke emanating from a "temple" not open to mere mortals.

So, I start by noting how much the thinking of sophisticated and soberminded policymakers has evolved over the past fifty years. Why has the concept of outside influence, and more broadly outside interaction, become an accepted concept at "bastions of orthodoxy" such as the Hoover Institution? To understand the answer to this apparent contradiction, I find it useful to segment "others outside the Fed" into three groupings: academics, other central bankers, and financial markets.

Academic Influence and the Practice of Central Banking

Let me start with the influence of academics. The Shadow Open Market Committee might be considered ground zero for academics. However, there are other academic or quasi-academic groupings that focus on topics of importance to the Fed, such as the Group of Thirty, the Bretton Woods Committee, and the Global Interdependence Center's (GIC) College of Central Bankers. These groupings and many individual academics have played a useful role in trying both to influence Fed thinking and to enhance Fed impact. The influencing part is embedded in the history of the SOMC itself. The intellectual rigor that the SOMC and the broader community of monetary scholars brought to the debate at the founding of the SOMC forced the Fed to recognize that nonmonetary forces such as the power of labor unions and oil price shocks were not the proximate cause of the inflation being experienced in the 1970s.

Perhaps most fundamental to the functioning of central banking is the concept of "price stability" itself. This simple concept has evolved significantly due to the influence of academics and related groupings. Paul Volcker famously thought that the Fed's price stability mandate required zero inflation. However, thanks to seminal academic work, we have come to understand that price stability now means inflation somewhat above "zero." Academics, supported by experience, found that price stability defined by a small, positive level of inflation allows for more fluid wage setting (with the possibility of decreasing real wages without cutting nominal wages), avoids measurement errors, and avoids the zero lower bound (hopefully). In the euro area, where inflation is measured as a weighted average of the inflation of all member countries, the 2% target enables the implications of any differences between countries to be addressed. Having a target of 0% would mean some member countries might risk having negative inflation (i.e., deflation). In the United States, a nonzero inflation target has allowed for goods disinflation or deflation even as we seem to have a bias toward persistently positive services inflation. I will return to the topic of price stability's being defined as slightly positive inflation shortly.

Related to the concept of price stability at low, but positive, inflation is the concept of rules-based policy, as is so powerfully expressed by John Taylor and the Taylor rule. Variations of the Taylor rule have been adopted as a framework both for driving policy discussion and for critiquing the actions of policymakers. The debate around the FOMC table has been strongly enriched by bringing a rules-based argumentation, even if policy itself is not guided exclusively by the rule.

One must hasten to add explicit "inflation targeting" to these notable examples of academics driving Fed and other policy thinking. We think of inflation targeting as having emerged only in the 1990s, but there were versions of "inflation targeting" from the early twentieth century. Irving Fisher proposed a "compensated dollar" system in which the gold content in paper money would vary with the price of goods in terms of gold, so that the price level in terms of paper money would stay fixed. In his *Tract on Monetary Reform* (1923), John Maynard Keynes advocated what we might now call an inflation-targeting scheme. Keynes recommended a policy of exchange rate flexibility, appreciating the currency in response to inflation and depreciating it in response to deflation, allowing internal prices to remain more or less stable. In this, Keynes also anticipated the foreign exchange transmission channel for monetary policy in an open economy. However, these early and rudimentary concepts of inflation targeting fell into disrepair during the Bretton Woods period, in large part because of the fixed-exchange-rate regime that prevailed. However, with the end of the Bretton Woods era, the need for a publicly recognized anchor became more pressing. Academics contributed importantly to this debate by demonstrating a link between an explicit inflation target and well-anchored inflation expectations. This has led to a much deeper understanding of the "expectations channel" as an independent and important channel of the transmission of monetary policy.

Of course, in addition to adding to our understanding of the theoretical underpinnings of monetary policy, academic economists have been central to recent debates on the correct stance of monetary policy. The debate that raged about the inflation that followed the COVID-19 pandemic between those who saw the inflation as "transitory" and those who saw it as "permanent" is just the most recent example of how the Fed and academic economists are engaged with each other.

Before leaving the important role of academics in influencing the Fed, let me hasten to add that the groupings of academics that I mentioned earlier—the Group of Thirty, Bretton Woods Committee, and GIC's College of Central Bankers—have been willing supporters and amplifiers of the Fed and its policy efforts. Through reports with titles such as *Central Banking and Monetary Policy: Principles and the Way Forward; Banking Conduct and Culture;* and *Enhancing Financial Stability and Resilience: Macroprudential Policy Tools and Systems for the Future,* these groupings attempt to support and amplify the positive work of the Fed, other central banks, and regulators globally.

Central Bank Influences and Inflation Targeting

While academics have provided much of the raw material that has fed progress in Federal Reserve policymaking, other central banks have played an important role. Many are well aware of the role of the Reserve Bank of New Zealand, followed by the Bank of Canada and the Bank of England, in developing and advancing the practice of setting an explicit, numerical inflation target. I will not relive that very important history. For more than a decade after many other central banks adopted an explicit inflation target, the Fed had not formally adopted such a target, even though for much of this time, the Fed seemed to settle implicitly on a 2% target. The Fed's official adoption of a 2% target only occurred in 2012. As a policymaker I was skeptical of adopting a point estimate inflation target. I believed that the FOMC could raise rates sufficiently to reduce inflation to the desired target, but that central bank tools, by themselves, could prove insufficient to raise inflation if it fell below that desired 2% level.

Financial Markets and the Need for Transparency

Financial markets are the third, and possibly most powerful, outside influence with which the Fed and other central banks must contend. The Federal Reserve was not founded to take responsibility for monetary policy. However, the Federal Reserve Act did allow the Reserve Banks to buy and sell government securities in the open market. By the early 1920s Fed officials recognized that these purchases and sales influenced market interest rates and credit conditions. In 1923, the Fed's leaders formed the Open Market Investment Committee to determine open market operations for the entire System, and the Fed began to conduct monetary policy. The influence of the Fed on markets and vice versa has been well established for one hundred years. What has changed is the attitude of central banks, particularly the Fed, in how they wish to "work" with financial markets. This is another way to discuss "transparency." I will dedicate the remainder of my remarks to this important topic.

As I said in the opening, across the fifty-year lifespan of the SOMC, the Fed and other central bankers gradually came to recognize that more transparency in policymaking was inevitable, and perhaps even a welcome development. If market participants understood the Fed's desired policy stance and likely moves, policy would be more effective. That effectiveness, emanating from influencing market expectations, gradually came to be seen as another tool of policy.

I have already mentioned Paul Volcker's preference for leaving markets in suspense, even after policy decisions were made. Far from exhibiting nefarious behavior, Volcker and his colleagues probably believed that their internal discussions were more robust without the prospect of disclosure. They also worried about unintentionally strong impacts from disclosure. In a 1970s lawsuit, the Fed argued that immediate disclosure of its actions "would significantly harm the Government's monetary functions" (Federal Reserve History 2024). The potential risks included unfair profits, outsize price changes, and more costly open market operations. Instead of issuing a statement describing its policy actions, the FOMC expected markets to infer its intent by observing open market policy actions. During the early 1960s, the FOMC disclosed its monetary policy only once per year, in the Board's Annual Report. This disclosure was required by the Federal Reserve Act. The 1966 Freedom of Information Act required the FOMC to disclose its actions with a ninety-day lag. In 1975, the Committee decided to shorten the lag to forty-five days, and it shortened the lag again, to thirty days, in 1976.

Volcker's successor, Alan Greenspan, was also thought to be squea-mish about the emerging trend toward central bank transparency. During Greenspan's tenure, journalists and market participants were rumored to ana-lyze the size of his briefcase on FOMC meeting days for some sort of signal as to whether he would push for an interest rate cut. Greenspan facetiously claimed that he could "mumble with great incoherence." He observed in 1993 that "the Federal Reserve has a reputation, along with other central banks of being secretive" (Federal Reserve History 2024).

I would assert that, contrary to this caricature of Greenspan's nearly two decades as chair as a period of opacity, it was actually a period of experimen-tation and progress on the path to transparency. Greenspan certainly resisted the adoption of a formal 2% target, while supporting (or at least acquiescing in) an implicit 2% target. However, and importantly, Greenspan supported several innovations that allowed markets to better understand Fed policy-making. During Greenspan's tenure the Fed went from saying nothing on the outcomes of policy decisions to saying quite a bit on policy.

Before Greenspan, as discussed, changes in communication were gradual and often forced by legislative requirements. During Greenspan's tenure, the FOMC formed two working groups on transparency. The FOMC decided to issue increasingly detailed statements and issued them in a policy-relevant time frame—i.e., on the day of the FOMC meeting. Those statements started by simply stating the fed funds target—a major shift in policy framework from the money-supply control that was the tool favored by the Volcker Fed, which had the advantage of allowing the Fed to disclaim any responsibility for the level of interest rates that caused so much pain. The practice of the FOMC disclosing its actions the same day of its meetings started in February 1994. The now-familiar practice of issuing a statement after every meeting, regardless of whether a change in policy had been agreed on, began with the February 2000 meeting. Additionally, the FOMC statements evolved during Greenspan's tenure to include disclosure of the FOMC votes and brief state-ments of the rationale for dissents, if any. Critically, the FOMC also experi-mented with differing phrasings of what future policy moves seemed most likely, while trying to avoid making commitments. These were initial, but critical, efforts toward official "forward guidance."

Of course, the FOMC has progressed on the journey toward transpar-ency since 2006 by building on the base that the Greenspan Fed laid. Chair Bernanke viewed the Fed as being behind other central banks in the move toward transparency. As mentioned, under Bernanke, the Fed adopted an explicit inflation target in 2012. Bernanke held the first post-FOMC press conference in 2011. While the FOMC had long used language that revealed the Committee's expectations of future policy, using phrases such as the "tilt" in the 1990s, the FOMC formally began using "forward guidance" after the 2007–9 financial crisis. The persistent use of such "forward guidance" as a formal tool of policy had the desired effect of influencing longer-term rates in a direction that supported easing financial conditions.

If the Greenspan Fed has been misunderstood in terms of the degree of openness to transparency during normal policymaking, Greenspan himself has certainly been credited with understanding the importance of transparency and working to control market expectations during periods of crisis. During the stock market crash of October 1987, Greenspan said, "The Federal Reserve, consistent with its responsibilities as the Nation's central bank, affirmed today its readiness to serve as a source of liquidity to support the economic and financial system" (Federal Reserve History 2013). The value of these types of declarative statements during moments of crisis and dislocation has been well established by subsequent crises. Shortly after the terrorist attacks of September 11, 2001, the Fed issued a simple statement that is credited with calming markets: "The Federal Reserve is open and operating. The discount window is available to meet liquidity needs." In the summer of 2012, financial markets were concerned about the possibility of an imminent breakup of the euro. Mario Draghi (2012), the president of the ECB, on the morning of July 12, 2012, uttered a few words that immediately defused the market concern. He said: "Within our mandate, the ECB is ready to do whatever it takes to preserve the euro. And believe me, it will be enough." In the aftermath of this statement, the spreads on government bond yields of Spain, Italy, and Greece—the so-called peripheral countries—dropped back toward normal levels after a three-year upward trend.

Conclusion

Central bank independence has become the norm for most modern economies. However, "independence" does not mean being free of all external influences. Academics, other central banks, and financial markets have been implicated in both theory and practice of central banking. Whether it is understanding the nature of inflation itself, debating the current conjuncture, or pushing for greater transparency, outside forces have acted upon the Fed. The Shadow Open Market Committee is one of several institutions that have played a role in driving the Federal Reserve in both the understanding of the causes of inflation and in the practice of central banking.

References

Board of Governors (Board of Governors of the Federal Reserve System). 2001. Press release. September 11.

Draghi, Mario. 2012. Speech at the Global Investment Conference, London, United Kingdom. July 26. https://www.ecb.europa.eu/press/key/date/2012/html /sp120726.en.html.

Federal Reserve History. 2013. "Stock Market Crash of 1987." Time Period: The Great Moderation, Federal Reserve History. November 22. https://www .federalreservehistory.org/essays/stock-market-crash-of-1987.

Federal Reserve History. 2024. "Transparency." Topic: About the Fed, Fed Governance, Federal Reserve History. August 5. https://www.federalreservehistory .org/essays/transparency.

Keynes, John Maynard. 1923. *A Tract on Monetary Reform*. Macmillan and Co. Ltd.

Taylor, John T. 2025. "Rules Versus Discretion over the Last Fifty Years." In *Fifty Years of the Shadow Open Market Committee: A Retrospective on Its Role in Monetary Policy*, edited by Michael D. Bordo, Jeffrey M. Lacker, Mickey D. Levy, and John B. Taylor. Hoover Institution Press.

23
The Shadow Open Market Committee and Its Role in Monetary Policy

Some Personal Observations*

Robert Heller

Karl Brunner and the Origins of the SOMC

Karl Brunner, who along with his student Allan Meltzer was the founder of the Shadow Open Market Committee (SOMC), was a distinguished professor of economics at the University of California, Los Angeles when I joined that faculty in 1965—almost six decades ago. I was lucky enough to have an office near Karl's office in Bunche Hall on the UCLA campus. Just about every day, after we returned from lunch at the Faculty Club, it was very quiet on the eighth floor of Bunche Hall as many of the older professors took a little nap. But more often than not, their siestas were interrupted when Karl Brunner opened his office door and blew a small bugle—Karl called it a Swiss *Waldhorn*—that he kept in his office. Typically, the bugle call was followed by Karl's booming voice yelling down the corridor: "Jerry—where are the regressions?"

Dutifully, Jerry Jordan, who was his research assistant and whose office was at the other end of the long corridor, would come racing down the hallway with a stack of IBM printouts of the latest research results showing the influence of the money supply on prices or some related topic. As you all know, Jerry Jordan became the director of research of the Federal Reserve Bank of St. Louis and president of the Federal Reserve Bank of Cleveland, as well as a member of the SOMC.

*I am grateful to Frank McCormick for comments on an earlier draft and to Dan Van Dyke of the Rosen Consulting Group for assistance with the graph.

Having obtained my PhD at University of California, Berkeley, that was my real introduction to monetary economics and the significance of the money supply in monetary policymaking.

The influence of Karl Brunner on my thinking was further enhanced by Milton Friedman, who was a frequent visitor to UCLA—especially during the winter months, when it snowed in Chicago. Thanks to these discussions with Karl Brunner and Milton Friedman, I became a firm believer in the importance of controlling the money supply to achieve a stable price level (Heller 2015, ch. 13, ch. 15).

Money Matters

Milton Friedman popularized the dictum that "inflation is always and every-where a monetary phenomenon." I find it therefore inexplicable that the word "money" is not even mentioned once in the Fed's most recent Monetary Policy Report to Congress. Even more astonishing, you will look in vain for the word "money" in any of the statements published by the Federal Open Market Committee (FOMC) during the last four years. It is nowhere to be found!

This is abundant evidence that today's Fed pays no attention to the money supply and its role in the economy. If Milton Friedman were alive today, he would be aghast!

It was not always this way. Almost half a century ago, the Humphrey–Hawkins Act of 1978 actually *required* the Federal Reserve to set targets for the growth of the monetary aggregates and to report these benchmarks to Congress twice each year.[1] When Chair Paul Volcker tackled the inflation-ary surge of the late 1970s and early '80s, he did so by focusing firmly on the control of the money supply.

At the same time, the high interest rates of up to 20% engendered by the inflationary surge—together with the regulatory restrictions on interest paid on demand deposits by banks and savings and loan associations—led to a record-high number of bank failures and the almost complete elimination of the savings and loan industry. I remember these catastrophic events very well because I had a front-row seat as chair of the Fed's Committee on Bank Supervision and Regulation. Every year during my tenure we experienced approximately eight hundred bank failures—or about 2,500 in total.

Into the breach stepped numerous newly created nonbank financial ser-vice institutions whose liabilities were not counted in the traditional defini-tion of the money supply. Consequently, the heretofore tight relationship between the money supply as defined by the Federal Reserve and inflation broke down, and money supply targeting lost its attractiveness. But as Karl Brunner (1983, 40, 51) has pointed out, there is an important distinction between the official definition of the money supply and what people actually use as a medium of exchange. It is that latter concept that is important for actual economic behavior and should be used in the analysis of the relationship between money and prices. As the Fed was unable to produce such a dynamic time series of the money supply, it began to focus on interest rates as a control variable to reach its congressionally mandated goals of price stability and maximum employment.

But I would argue that even if the money supply is no longer used as a control variable, it is still most useful as an indicator of financial conditions in the economy. Paying attention to the money supply would have almost certainly helped the Fed avoid the recent surge in inflation.

Figure 23.1 shows the money supply, M2 (the red line), for the last few years as well as the inflation rate as represented by the Core PCE index (the blue line). Even an economic greenhorn will recognize the tight correlation between the two time series. Karl Brunner and Milton Friedman, as well as numerous SOMC researchers, devoted much of their work to prove in detail the causal linkage between money and prices.[2]

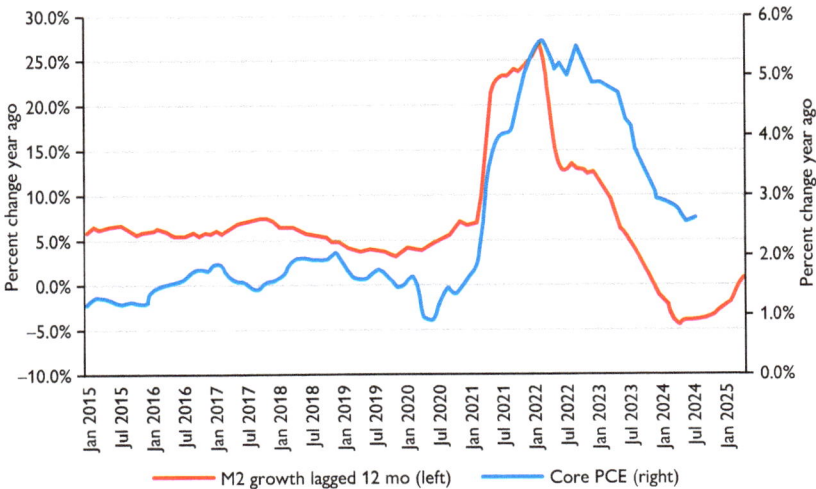

Figure 23.1. Core PCE inflation vs. M2 growth lagged.

Source: Federal Reserve Bank of St. Louis (FRED). I am grateful to Dan Van Dyke for help with this graph.

For the Fed to ignore these findings amounts to a virtual dereliction of duty. Indeed, if the Fed had at least paid rudimentary attention to the money supply during the last few years, the recent bout in inflation would not have gotten out of hand and might have been much better controlled—if not entirely avoided.

The Goal of Price Stability

The Federal Reserve Act directs the Federal Reserve to "maintain long-run growth of the monetary and credit aggregates commensurate with the economy's long-run potential to increase production, so as to promote effectively the goals of maximum employment, stable prices and moderate long-term interest rates." The Fed refers to these three goals traditionally as the "dual mandate."

For many years now, the Fed has interpreted the congressional mandate for "stable prices" as being consistent with 2% inflation. However, with a 2% inflation rate, the price level will actually double every thirty-six years. Over a normal lifespan of some seventy-two years, the price level will therefore quadruple. I would argue that very few people would characterize this state of affairs as "price stability."[3]

Also, it is virtually impossible for any policymaker to hit a point target like a 2% inflation rate precisely. So the Fed will almost always be accused of erring on either the high or the low side of the inflation target. It might therefore be much more advisable to specify a target range of 0%-to-2% inflation as the goal of monetary policy (Heller 2017, 250–51).

Policy Signaling

When I joined the Federal Reserve Board in 1986, Paul Volcker was the chair—and he ruled the Fed with an iron hand. Not only was he determined to bring inflation back under control, but he also had a tight rein on what could be said by the other Board members about policy. Preston Martin was the vice chair of the Board, and when he gave a speech about possible solutions to the international debt crisis, Volcker publicly rebuked him and told the press that he found Martin's remarks "incomprehensible" (Rosenblatt 1985). Totally chagrined, Pres Martin resigned from the Federal Reserve Board soon thereafter.

Preston Martin's resignation created a vacancy on the Board, and soon President Ronald Reagan appointed me to fill that vacancy. In those days, Federal Reserve decisions on monetary policy were tightly guarded secrets—even *after* they had been made. There was an entire coterie of "Fed watchers" on Wall Street that made its living by "reading the tea leaves" and attempting to discern whether the Fed had actually changed policy or not.

I vividly recall one episode where the FOMC had not changed policy at the regular FOMC meeting. As usual, the formal directive gave the chair and the Open Market Trading Desk some latitude to tighten or loosen policy ever so slightly in the inter-meeting period. We were all surprised when on April 29, 1987, Chair Volcker arranged a special conference call of the FOMC and told the committee that "we were playing things rather cautiously but not really changing the borrowing target in any overt or non-overt way . . . but there was erring on the side of restraint" (FOMC 1987, 1). He continued with: "And I think that I should confirm that we have had a small snugging or tightening, or whatever word seems appropriate at the time" (2).

I had never heard the term "snugging" before and so, after consulting with my Webster's Dictionary, I learned that he had tightened policy without telling the FOMC about it ahead of time. As Volcker himself stated, he and the trading desk did so in an "overt or non-overt way"—but without asking for a formal FOMC approval of this change in policy.

Not long thereafter, I talked with a reporter about current monetary policy. The next day, Volcker called me into his office, and he told me in no uncertain terms: "If you don't keep quiet about monetary policy, I'll ruin your professional reputation!" Because I did not want to follow in Pres Martin's footsteps, I kept forthwith quiet about monetary policy.

As time passed after this episode, Paul Volcker and I became good friends, as we both believed in the importance of stable prices and zero inflation for the health of the American economy. That was the ultimate goal that we both tried to achieve.

The "closed-mouth policy" of Chair Volcker's era stands in stark contrast to today's FOMC, where all the members frequently give speeches "signaling" what future monetary policy actions undertaken by the Fed might look like. As a result, all the professional Fed watchers are nowadays trying to discern how policy is likely to change in the near future—as opposed to whether it had actually changed. The only difference is that these days markets may change a few days before a Fed action is actually taken, while during the Volcker days the markets would react soon after the policy change was actually made. The difference amounts to a few days. But one may also say that markets nowadays react more to rumors and expectations rather than actual facts. In my mind, it is very doubtful that this is a better state of affairs.

The Fed Gets a Flag

When I joined the Board, I was lucky enough to be assigned the best office in the entire building: the corner office on Constitution Avenue and 20th Street. It had a head-on view of the Washington Monument. The director of supply services, Robert Frazier, helped me move in and made sure that I had everything that I needed. When he kept insisting that there must be something else that he might be able to do for me, I finally asked him: "All right, why don't you get me some of those flags like Chairman Volcker has behind his desk?" He quickly begged off and said: "I cannot do that—those are the chairman's *personal* flags from his service at the US Treasury."

I responded to him: "Fine, then just get me an American flag and a Federal Reserve flag!" His answer was: "Governor, I cannot do that either—because the Federal Reserve does not have a flag." I was surprised at that answer but was content to get my American flag.

Shortly thereafter, Chair Volcker appointed me as the administrative governor. In those days, that task was usually assigned to the most junior member of the Board. It occurred to me that I was now in a position to get the Federal Reserve an official flag—similar to those used by the many government agencies nearby.

So I called Bob Frazier back in and told him about my plan. When he asked what kind of design I had in mind, I replied: "Well, something like all the other government agencies have, like the State Department or the Treasury Department." Bob came back a few days later and told me: "Well, the State Department does not have a flag either!" I asked him what the banner on top of their building was, and he replied: "They told me that they display their seal on cloth."

That gave me an idea. I had him make a few photocopies of the official seal of the Federal Reserve Board and took these papers home with me. Then I gave them to my son Christopher and my daughter Kimberly, along with a set of crayons, and asked them to design a flag for the Fed.

Nine-year-old Chris, who was very much enamored with pirates in those days, came back with a rather bold design that really looked like a pirate flag (figure 23.2). But my daughter Kimberly Allison, who is now a professor of medicine right here at Stanford, came up with an elegant design that showed the official seal on a stylish blue background surrounded by a golden rim (figure 23.3).

Figure 23.2. My son Chris's proposed design for the Federal Reserve Board flag.

Source: Robert Heller, personal archive.

Figure 23.3. My daughter Kimberly's design, which was developed into the final Federal Reserve flag.

Source: Robert Heller, personal archive.

Figure 23.4. The Heller family with the Federal Reserve flag.
Source: Robert Heller, personal archive.

I took Kimberly's design back to the Fed, and the graphics department produced the final design for the Federal Reserve flag. The Board of Governors adopted the flag officially on June 22, 1987; figure 23.4 shows the proud family holding up the new flag of the Federal Reserve System. It is probably the only lasting contribution that I have made to the Federal Reserve System.

But considering that the current FOMC members continue to disregard the important contributions by Milton Friedman, Karl Brunner, Mickey Levy, Michael Bordo, and the many other members of the Shadow Open Market Committee on the importance of the money supply for economic policymaking, I should probably have suggested to the Board to adopt a slightly different flag—a flag that would have always reminded the Federal Reserve's policymakers of keeping a close watch of the money supply.

This flag might have looked like figure 23.5.

Such a flag would constantly remind the Federal Reserve Board that *money matters* in making monetary policy. The current FOMC committee does not seem to have taken that lesson to heart, as the money supply is never discussed or even mentioned in any of the post-meeting FOMC statements of the last four years.

Figure 23.5. Imagined rendering of the Federal Reserve flag with a reminder to keep an eye on the money supply.

Source: Robert Heller, personal archive.

The inflationary episode of the early 2000s could have easily been avoided if the Fed had paid even rudimentary attention to the money supply increases engendered by its own policies. Milton Friedman was probably turning in his grave! Thank you very much.

Notes

1. Full Employment and Balanced Growth Act of 1978, Pub. L. 95-523, 92 Stat. 887. Also see Dorn (2019).

2. See, for instance, Bordo (2023) and Ireland (2023), as well as Warsh (2024).

3. For a history of the 2% inflation target, see Heller (2017, 248–50).

References

Bordo, Michael D. 2023. "Monetary Aggregates Still Matter." Position paper, Shadow Open Market Committee. October 20.

Brunner, Karl. 1983. "Has Monetarism Failed?" *Cato Journal* 3 (1): 23–62.

Dorn, James A. 2019. "Myopic Monetary Policy and Presidential Power: Why Rules Matter." *Cato Journal* 39 (3): 577–95.

FOMC (Federal Open Market Committee). 1987. "Conference call." April 29. Transcript available at https://www.federalreserve.gov/monetarypolicy/files/FOMC19870429confcall.pdf.

Heller, Robert. 2015. *The Unlikely Governor*. Maybridge Press.

Heller, Robert. 2017. "Monetary Mischief and the Debt Trap." *Cato Journal* 37 (2): 247–61.

Ireland, Peter N. 2023. "US Monetary Policy, 2020–23: Putting the Quantity Theory to the Test." Position paper, Shadow Open Market Committee. October 20.

Rosenblatt, Robert A. 1985. "Martin's Comments on International Debt Called Incomprehensible: Volcker Rebukes Fed Vice Chairman." *Los Angeles Times*, June 21.

Warsh, Kevin. 2024. "Interest Rates Are a Sideshow in the Fed Drama." *Wall Street Journal*, July 29.

24

Consensus and Dissent

Influences on Monetary Policy Deliberations

Esther L. George

For many years, I have appreciated the engagement and exchange of diverse ideas and the desire of the Shadow Open Market Committee (SOMC) to achieve better policy outcomes for the nation. A number of its members (John Taylor, Allan Meltzer, Ben McCallum, Michael Bordo, Marvin Goodfriend, Debbie Lucas, Athanasios Orphanides, Mickey Levy, and many others) have been influential voices at the Federal Reserve Bank of Kansas City's Jackson Hole Symposium over the years.

On the eve of the Federal Open Market Committee's (FOMC) policy framework review, the SOMC (and others) will have yet another opportunity to weigh in on how the FOMC should think about its monetary policy strategy, tools, and communication practices. Over the past five years, since the last framework review, significant changes have occurred in the economy because of a global pandemic and the monetary and fiscal response that followed. Incorporating lessons learned from the experience of that episode range from supply shocks, inflation dynamics, balance sheet policies, and the use of forward guidance, to name a few.

This quintennial review also offers an opportunity to consider the central bank's communications and decision-making process itself. One aspect that the SOMC (among others) has noted is a growing decline in dissents from the FOMC's decisions. A working paper by Gauti Eggertsson and Don Kohn (2023) also mentions the lack of dissent among policy voters between September 2020 and June 2022, raising questions of whether the FOMC's very consensus-driven process suppressed an effective challenge to the majority view during this period. Indeed, Chair Jerome Powell (2024) himself recently acknowledged that "the good ship 'Transitory' was a crowded one with most mainstream analysts and advanced-economy central bankers on board."

Congress designed the Federal Reserve System to address concerns about its accountability and authority. The compromise was to decentralize its structure with a geographic dispersion that establishes a distribution of governance responsibilities and encourages independent and diverse perspectives in decision making. That structure has proven durable and remains intact today. So, largely, has the central bank's mission for monetary policy, supervision and regulation, and payment services to banks.

The FOMC is by design a large committee of nineteen individuals who bring their own views and backgrounds to the policy table. Each of these policymakers can and do express these views publicly through speeches and interviews. As a result, there have been times when FOMC participants have been criticized for creating a cacophony of voices. In a 2016 speech, Powell addressed this critique, noting "the public expression of our diverse views helps sustain public support for the Federal Reserve as a public institution. Those members of the public who disagree with our policy should know that their concerns are given voice in our deliberations. But there is a tradeoff here that needs to be managed: On the one hand, the effectiveness of policy is thought to depend on the public's understanding of the Committee's consensus. On the other hand, the expression of diverse views may sometimes make it difficult for the public to see that consensus" (Powell 2016).

Enhancing transparency and communication has been a focus of the FOMC for some time. Since 2007, the FOMC has sought to enhance the public's understanding of the individual participants' views. Four times a year, each of the nineteen participants submits an anonymous individual forecast in the Summary of Economic Projections (or dot plot), which offers the public a sense of the range of opinions about inflation, employment, growth, and the appropriate policy settings for the federal funds rate. But the ultimate expression of this range of views comes from the FOMC's decisions at each meeting when twelve of the nineteen participants cast a vote on the stance of monetary policy by registering a "yes" or "no" vote for the policy option being considered. A unanimous vote signals little daylight among the voting members—a strong consensus in support of the policy action. When a dissent is registered, the FOMC's statement notes who disagreed with the decision and why.

Synthesizing the diversity of views across such a large committee is a task that falls to the FOMC chair. Indeed, the current chair has generally gotten high marks for his ability to build consensus. No previous chair has led with fewer dissents (Lacker 2024). This record of consensus building is especially remarkable given the uncertainty associated with the global COVID-19

pandemic shock and the extraordinary surge in inflation. It has not gone unnoticed by market participants, academics, previous policymakers, and the press.

It was my experience that FOMC deliberations did allow for robust debate
and consideration of various viewpoints before reaching a decision. Policy
choices and strategy reflected this input. It was also true in my experience that
presenting a unified front was viewed as enhancing the credibility of monetary policy decisions and providing stability to financial markets. Consistent
messaging also is valued by market participants, particularly during times of
heightened uncertainty and economic stress.

Having a diversity of views present at the policy table can challenge conventional thinking and shape good policy choices. Coming from someone
who pulled the dissent lever from time to time as a voting member of the
FOMC, it may come as no surprise that I also feel strongly that public trust
and central-bank credibility depends on the transparency of these diverse
views, and intellectual honesty in expressing them not just internally but also
publicly. It is in the public's interest to have the FOMC's policy decisions and
its disagreements visible to the public.

A dissenting vote gives the public important insight to the nature of the debate
that led to the policy decision. In fact, at the September 2024 FOMC meeting,
a voting member dissented. While the nature of the policy disagreement was
explained, the dissent drew particular attention because it was the first time in
nearly two decades that a Federal Reserve Board governor voted against the
majority. When dissents are unusual, the public might fairly question whether
the FOMC's otherwise unified front is the result of groupthink and a desire for
conformity rather than the result of a thorough consideration of alternative economic and policy perspectives. It is a question that the Federal Reserve should
take seriously, I think, as it has done in other instances where perceptions and
appearances have the potential to undermine public trust in the institution.

Some have suggested that the Committee's use of forward guidance could
have influenced FOMC voting patterns. Used extensively since the Great
Financial Crisis, forward guidance is intended to influence financial and economic conditions in the short run by describing future monetary policy. It
creates a binding commitment for the central bank if it is to be credible.

Others have argued that the collegial and consensus-driven culture among
Fed policymakers reflects the basic nature of a committee and its membership. As described in 2008 by Carnegie Mellon professor Allan Meltzer
(a founder of the SOMC): "It's a club, and the members of the club tend to
be supportive of a club, and particularly of the chairman. It's not popular to

dissent" (Grynbaum 2008). During times of political divisiveness or attacks on the central bank, some have speculated that members may feel it is particularly important to close ranks in support of the institution and its leadership.

There are other dynamics beyond the FOMC itself, however, that I believe serve to reinforce a very strong consensus-oriented culture among its members. In particular, the Reserve Banks' operating model has evolved in a manner that emphasizes the need for a strong culture of collaboration and consensus in governance and staffing of their operations.

This shift began in the 1990s when the Reserve Bank presidents took steps to lower their operating costs by consolidating technology investments. As the banking landscape changed, additional moves toward consolidation were made in some of the core aspects of Reserve Bank operations, such as payments system services to financial institutions. Offering a standardized national approach in these areas also led to the development of a different governance model—one that would substitute the established independent decision making within a single Reserve Bank for oversight by a committee of presidents from multiple Reserve Banks. From an operational perspective, these initiatives helped to achieve the goal of creating a system-wide business model for nationwide services across market segments and geographies. The changes understandably prioritized efficiency and financial stewardship.

With this change, however, the Reserve Banks undertook an important, and necessary, cultural shift. Rather than optimizing decision making and outcomes at the individual Reserve Bank level, as had been the mode of operation historically, the culture transitioned to one designed to optimize "one System." As might be expected, this business model also emphasized new aspects of governance and leadership required of Fed leaders, as evidenced in the job description for a Reserve Bank president:[1]

> While each Reserve Bank operates as a distinct legal entity, the success of the System depends upon effective collaboration among the Reserve Banks.... The intellectual and operational partnership among Reserve Banks has several dimensions relevant to the President's role. Among them:
>
> - *Individual System Contributions*: Contributing to the debate and decision-making process at the Conference of Presidents on issues that transcend the purview and authority of individual Reserve Banks, recognizing the duty to ensure that decisions on

such matters reflect the broad interests and strategies of the System. Leading or contributing to System-wide committees, projects, or other efforts to ensure that the best ideas and thinking
from across the System are identified. Building consensus, reaching decisions, implementing decisions, and assessing results in all
leadership assignments.

- *Support for Coordinated System Direction*: Ensuring high-quality
execution of System initiatives assigned to the Philadelphia Fed.
- *Staff Contributions*: Identifying and elevating the profile of Philadelphia Fed staff with the experience, interest, and ability or
potential for leadership roles on System-level mandates, initiatives, subcommittees, task forces, and other project work.

Each of these explanations offers possible rationale for the waning votes of
dissent. Forward guidance as a policy instrument, the very nature of committees and their leadership, and the evolution of the Reserve Bank operating
model and governance mechanisms point to the premium placed on consensus. It is a reality that fosters the effective functioning of the central bank.

A strong culture of consensus by itself should not be misread as undue
deference or loyalty. On the other hand, some view dissent as a "high bar"
and, for that reason, believe disagreements and debates on policy options are
best carried out internally rather than cast as a public dissent. That approach
strikes me as running the risk of making FOMC participants merely advisors
and undermining their public duty of voting independent views. Certainly,
an overly consensus-driven culture could make the FOMC less effective in
responding to future economic challenges or crises.

How the FOMC strikes a balance between unified decision making and
dissents is critical to good policy decisions and public trust. For that reason,
the trade-off is worth examining as the FOMC revisits its monetary policy
strategy, tools, and communications practices.

It's also an issue the SOMC is well positioned to weigh in on, as it has for
half a century. I look forward to that tradition being carried forward in the
spirit of achieving sound policy outcomes for the US.

Note

1. Position and Candidate Specification. President and Chief Executive Officer. Federal Reserve Bank of Philadelphia. October 24, 2024, https://www.philadelphiafed
.org/-/media/FRBP/Assets/Institutional/presidential-search/FRB-Philadelphia
-President.pdf, 7.

References

Eggertsson, Gauti B., and Donald Kohn. 2023. "The Inflation Surge of the 2020s: The Role of Monetary Policy." Working Paper No. 87. Hutchins Center, Brookings Institution. August.

Grynbaum, Michael M. 2008. "Fed Loses Its Unified Voice." *New York Times*, April 9.

Lacker, Jeffrey M. 2024. "Changing Governance Practices Seem to Have Reduced the Diversity of Views at the Federal Reserve." Presentation, Shadow Open Market Committee, New York, NY. April 5. Available at https://www.jeffreylacker.org/recent-writings.

Powell, Jerome H. 2016. "A View from the Fed." Remarks at "Understanding Fedspeak," Brookings Institution, Washington, DC. November 30.

Powell, Jerome H. 2024. "Review and Outlook." Remarks at the Federal Reserve Bank of Kansas City's Economic Policy Symposium, "Reassessing the Effectiveness and Transmission of Monetary Policy." Jackson Hole, WY. August 23.

DEBORAH LUCAS: Great, thank you very much.

Good, we're going for a while longer, this is a hardy group, okay. And I can't help but ask this, maybe I'm channeling a little John Cochrane, but it's also my own interest. I think a theme that came out of what many people said today in many different ways is that we believe that fiscal policy is one of the main determinants of prices.

And just imagine that there is kind of an outside consensus on that; Do you see that as something that can somehow find its way more fundamentally into what the Fed does? Because I think a lot of us have said it is important for a long time, and somehow when I listen to the Fed, I don't hear it reflected back at all, so I'm curious if anyone is willing to comment on that.

I don't think it requires taking a position for or against fiscal policy, but rather: Is there a way of incorporating it into the communication framework in a way that's meaningful and not threatening to the Fed?

ROGER W. FERGUSON JR.: Go on, Don.

DONALD KOHN: So I think fiscal policy is hugely important for aggregate demand and sometimes for supply, depending on tax levels and things like that.

But I don't think, just reflecting on John's discussion, you're going to find someone from the Fed saying, we don't control the price level, it's those guys in Congress and the president. So I think part of the culture of the Fed, and I hope this continues, is that we are responsible for price stability, that is our responsibility, that's what the Federal Reserve Act says, and we are going to exercise that.

Now I do think that it was surprising in 2020 and 2021 that there wasn't more discussion; I mean, I don't know what happened at the FOMC [Federal Open Market Committee] meetings. We haven't seen the transcripts yet, but there was practically no discussion in the minutes of the—particularly in 2021—the huge fiscal stimulus along with the opening of the economy as [COVID-19] vaccines came in.

So there was a surge, a very V-shaped thing, and I think the Committee—interesting to hear Chris's comments on this. And Loretta's [Mester], the committee was counting on its forward guidance to tell it when to raise rates and it didn't need to comment on fiscal policy. And the forward guidance was, in my view, misguided in a number of directions, so they were relying on a poor thing.

But I also think there was a break from the [Paul] Volcker/[Alan] Greenspan era and to some extent the [Ben] Bernanke era; all three of them talked about the implications of fiscal policy for interest rates. So you can do what you want with your budget, but I'm telling you what's going to happen to interest rates you raised.

Greenspan famously said: You raise taxes, interest rates will be lower than they would otherwise be. Volcker worried about the dual deficits and all that, twin deficits and all that kind of stuff. So I think the Fed to some extent has pulled back too far from commenting on the implications for the macroeconomy of the fiscal policy.

And then my last point is, we had a discussion—John included—about how important interest payments on the debt are going to become, and that it's really going to put extra pressure on the Federal Reserve. So both the Democratic senators won't be able to get their spending increases and the Republican senators won't be able to get their tax cuts, so this is going to intensify the political pressure on the Federal Reserve.

And I think it's so important that we maintain the independence of the Federal Reserve from short-term political pressures, and I really worry about people's ideas about how that might be eroded.

FERGUSON: I sort of push a little bit back on your question—which, Don, elaborate on this—but the entire setting of monetary policy has got to take into consideration the fiscal impulse.

And the models are completely built around this, so this notion that somehow or another it's not relevant, it's central to my experience, the way monetary policy is made. I agree with Don completely in that it is, I think, legitimate in a neutral way for the Fed to have a point of view that if the fiscal

authority does one thing, this might have implications in ways that will influence what the Fed is going to do or how the economy is likely to unfold. I
think that's a very legitimate comment to have, or for them to have. I think the
challenge, and we saw certainly with Greenspan—I don't know others—that
you'd go to Congress, join Humphrey–Hawkins, or semiannual testimony.

And you get these debates back and forth, trying to get the chairman to say
something that seemed to lean one way or the other around a fiscal debate, I
think that's a very dangerous place for us to be. The other thing I point out is
something that came up today that I think we do have to think through very
clearly, which is this tendency now that people recognize.

That the Fed can use its balance sheet and have been asked to drive certain kinds of policies—to put a real limitation on how far that goes, because
that will open a massive door. And I was very pleased to hear many people
today talk about that, because I think it's really important for the academic
community and others to be quite clear about how one should think of the
limitations there. Because in the world in which fiscal school limitations are
going to become paramount, the thought that the central bank is going to be
this massive sovereign wealth fund, I think, is going to just continue to rise in
pressure. So that's the thing. I worry less about fiscal policy per se, and much
more about something that might be described as fiscal dominance, or the
misuse of the Fed's balance sheet for this broader range of tools.

Both parties are going to be looking for that. And that, I think, is what
strikes me as the real worry that one should have going forward here.

LUCAS: Right. Well, yeah, let me open it up a little bit, take a few questions.
Go ahead.

BILL NELSON: So I think my career at the Fed spanned the period before there
were any announcements at all after the FOMC meeting, through a period
where quite elaborate statements were being made.

And my perception at least was, the more elaborate the statement was, the
further in advance of the committee meeting the decision effectively had to
be made, because the statements needed to be prepared, the ground needed
to be laid for them. And so my question is: Is there an inherent trade-off
between transparency and the openness to dissent and debate?

FERGUSON: Not sure there's a trade-off there. I mean, people have to come and
have a point of view. For sure, though, I think you do point to one of these
problems. And when I was there with Don, I chaired two of these committees

on transparency, and trying to figure out how he did all of this thing, and made it also real time.

And so you well know, and Don certainly participated in quite a bit in that; I'm not sure how it runs now, but it used to be that there'd be a little break and then we would go and sort of try to rework the statement as much as possible. I'm not sure I'd describe the statements as being elaborate.

I think, if anything, they've gotten a little shorter. And I've observed under Chairman [Jerome] Powell that there's a relatively small number of changes that are made. So in some sense, I think they've become—it's not a critical comment, it's become a little bit more formulaic than they were when we first started doing them when I was there.

And so I will see how they evolve. But I think you put your finger on a really difficult point, which is, you want them to be a good record, a one-page record of the meeting, picking up as much of the nuance as you can. But at the same time, there's this process of having to get them done.

The only other thing I'd add on this transparency thing is then having to also be prepared for the press conference, which comes half an hour after the meetings are over. And that creates a huge dynamic in terms of getting all the statements lined up and some clarity around what the Q and A is going to be.

I've been very impressed with how well, frankly, the Fed has been able to do that, because that puts even more pressure on the chairman and the committee to get itself organized around what the message is going to be.

LUCAS: Governor Waller, go ahead.

FERGUSON: We need to hear from Chris.

CHRISTOPHER J. WALLER: So I'm always very hesitant to make comments.

FERGUSON: We need to hear from you.

WALLER: What I'm going to say, I've said publicly already, so it's not new, but I'll just reiterate. So I'm just going to comment on fiscal policy stuff. So both Chair Powell and myself have made public comments about the fiscal deficit's not being sustainable.

I mean, we can sit there and look at when deficits—and this came up today in the session Pat Kehoe or some others had said—when you're running deficits of 6% to 7% of GDP and primary deficits of 2.5% to 3%, this is not sustainable when, when you're doing it in peacetime.

Now, I'm not going to tell Congress how to fix that problem. And that's what we avoid. Maybe some of our European colleagues are much more blunt, but they're a super national organization and they can't get away with this. But it is just arithmetic.

You can't do this. And we've made it very clear. My remarks today were about when the supply of Treasuries starts outgrowing the demand for Treasuries, this is going to push up long-term rates. It's just math. It's not anything, and I'm going to have to deal with it.

The second point is there's a lot of talk about central bank independence. And I've always taken the view that the best way to maintain my independence is not to criticize my masters. You deal with fiscal policy, I'll deal with monetary policy. When I start telling you what to do with fiscal policy, you have every right to start telling me what to do with monetary policy.

The third point is, and this was my very first speech as a Fed governor, there was a narrative going around in the spring of '21, when we were at the zero lower bound, that the Fed would never get off of it because the debt had grown so big that the interest expense would be so large, the Fed would never raise rates.

And I said at that time, guess what? When we have to raise rates, we'll do it. And we did. So I'm not too worried about that concern. I'm done preaching.

LUCAS: Great. Okay, I've been told that it's time for people to enjoy their dinner and the conversation at their table.

Let's give everyone a big hand. Thank you. Mickey wants to say something. I want to thank the organizers for an amazing conference today.

MICKEY D. LEVY: On behalf of the Shadow Open Market Committee, I want to thank John Taylor, Marie-Christine Slakey, and the Hoover events team, and everything about Hoover's generosity in hosting this fiftieth anniversary of the Shadow.

We also want to thank all of the participants, including all of the current and past Fed members, and all the participants who contributed so much of their time and effort into making this a very rewarding conference. And I'll just conclude: Marilyn Meltzer, you were with this at the beginning, and my strong hunch is Allan [Meltzer]'s doing high fives now.

My hunch is he's very happy, and he's looking forward to the future of the Shadow Open Market Committee. Thank you very much.

About the Contributors

Michael D. Bordo is a Board of Governors Professor of Economics and the director of the Center for Monetary and Financial History at Rutgers University. He is the Ilene and Morton Harris Distinguished Visiting Fellow at the Hoover Institution. He has held previous academic posts at the University of South Carolina and Carleton University in Ottawa, Canada, and was a visiting professor at Cambridge, Princeton, Harvard, and other universities. Bordo was also a visiting scholar at the International Monetary Fund; the Federal Reserve Banks of St. Louis, Cleveland, and Dallas; the Federal Reserve Board of Governors; the Bank of Canada; the Bank of England; and the Bank for International Settlements. He is a research associate of the National Bureau of Economic Research and a member of the Shadow Open Market Committee. He has published eighteen books on monetary economics and monetary history, most recently *The Historical Performance of the Federal Reserve: The Importance of Rules* (Hoover Institution Press, 2019). He is the editor of a series of books for Cambridge University Press, *Studies in Macroeconomic History*. He has a BA from McGill University, an MSc in economics from the London School of Economics, and a PhD from the University of Chicago.

Michael J. Boskin is the Rose and Milton Friedman Senior Fellow on Public Policy at the Hoover Institution, the Tully M. Friedman Professor of Economics at Stanford University, and a research associate at the National Bureau of Economic Research. He is the author or editor of more than 150 articles and eighteen books, most recently *Defense Budgeting for a Safer World* (Hoover Institution Press, 2023) and *American Federalism Today* (Hoover Institution Press, 2024). As chair of the White House Council of Economic Advisers (1989–93), he helped resolve the Third World debt and the savings and loan crises, expand global trade, introduce emissions trading in environmental regulation, and implement rules to control government spending while protecting the defense budget. On candidate Ronald Reagan's tax policy task force, he helped develop policies toward lower marginal tax rates, tax bracket inflation indexing, accelerated depreciation, and IRAs and 401(k)s. He later chaired the CPI Commission, whose report transformed the way government statistical agencies around the world measure inflation, productivity, and real GDP. His research continues to focus on a broad array of important policy issues.

James B. Bullard, former president and chief executive officer of the Federal Reserve Bank of St. Louis, was chosen in 2023 as the inaugural dean of the reimagined Mitch Daniels School of Business at Purdue University. Bullard is charged with inspiring, further developing, and implementing Purdue's redefined approach to undergraduate, graduate, executive, and research programs—preparing tomorrow's business leaders and entrepreneurs at a top-ranked business school grounded in the principles of free enterprise and a free-market economy that generates opportunities and prosperity, and in the hallmarks of a well-rounded Purdue education, with an emphasis on tech-driven, analytics-based business success. At the St. Louis Fed, Bullard earned significant praise and accolades for his long-standing leadership and innovative thinking as part of the Federal Open Market Committee in guiding the direction of US monetary policy. One of the nation's foremost economists and respected scholar-leaders, Bullard was the longest-serving Federal Reserve Bank president in the country and was ranked as the seventh-most influential economist in the world in 2014.

Charles W. Calomiris is codirector of the Institute for Research in Economics at the Heritage Foundation, Henry Kaufman Professor Emeritus at Columbia Business School, professor emeritus of international and public affairs at Columbia's School of International and Public Affairs, and chief economist of Mina Analytics. He recently served as chief economist and senior deputy comptroller at the Office of the Comptroller of the Currency. Calomiris is a research associate of the National Bureau of Economic Research. He was a distinguished fellow at the Hoover Institution, where he codirected the Initiative on Regulation and the Rule of Law for many years. He was a member of the Advisory Scientific Committee of the European Systemic Risk Board and has been a visiting scholar or consultant to many central banks and regulatory agencies. Calomiris received a BA in economics from Yale University and a PhD in economics from Stanford University.

John H. Cochrane is the Rose-Marie and Jack Anderson Senior Fellow at the Hoover Institution. He is also a research associate of the National Bureau of Economic Research and an adjunct scholar of the Cato Institute. Before joining Hoover, Cochrane was a professor of finance at the University of Chicago's Booth School of Business and previously taught in its Economics Department. He served as president of the American Finance Association and is a fellow of the Econometric Society. He writes on asset pricing, financial regulation, business cycles, and monetary policy. He has also written articles on macroeconomics, health insurance, time-series econometrics, financial regulation, and other topics. His books include *The Fiscal Theory of the Price Level* (Princeton University Press, 2023) and *Asset Pricing* (Princeton University Press, 2001, rev. 2005). Cochrane frequently contributes essays to the *Wall Street Journal*, *National Review*, *Project Syndicate*, and other publications. He maintains the *Grumpy Economist* blog. Cochrane earned a BA in physics at the Massachusetts Institute of Technology and his PhD in economics at the University of California–Berkeley.

Steven J. Davis is the Thomas W. and Susan B. Ford Senior Fellow and Director of Research at the Hoover Institution, and senior fellow at the Stanford Institute for Economic Policy Research. He is an economic advisor to the US Congressional Budget Office, elected fellow of the Society of Labor Economists, and consultant to the Federal Reserve Bank of Atlanta. He cofounded the Economic Policy Uncertainty project, the US Survey of Working Arrangements and Attitudes, the Global Survey of Working Arrangements, the Survey of Business Uncertainty, and the Stock Market Jumps project. He co-organizes the Asian Monetary Policy Forum, held annually in Singapore. Before joining Hoover, Davis was on the faculty at the University of Chicago Booth School of Business, serving as both distinguished service professor and deputy dean of the faculty.

Darrell Duffie is the Adams Distinguished Professor of Management and professor of finance at Stanford University's Graduate School of Business. He is a research fellow of the National Bureau of Economic Research and a fellow of both the Econometric Society and the American Academy of Arts and Sciences. Duffie is a past president of the American Finance Association and chaired the Financial Stability Board's Market Participants Group on reference rate reform. He is an independent director of Dimensional Fund Advisors and a member of the leadership teams of the G30 working groups on

Treasury Market Liquidity, chaired by Timothy Geithner, and Bank Failures and Contagion: Lender of Last Resort, Liquidity, and Risk Management, chaired by William Dudley. Duffie's most recent book is *Fragmenting Markets: Post-Crisis Bank Regulations and Financial Market Liquidity* (De Gruyter, 2022). In 2024, Duffie began teaching a new course at Stanford, "The Future of Money and Payments."

Roger W. Ferguson Jr. is the Steven A. Tananbaum Distinguished Fellow for International Economics at the Council on Foreign Relations. He is the immediate past president and chief executive officer of TIAA. Prior to joining TIAA, Ferguson was head of financial services for Swiss Re and chairman of the Swiss Re America Holding Corporation. Ferguson is the former vice chair of the Board of Governors of the Federal Reserve System. He is currently the chief investment officer at incubation firm Red Cell Partners, where he is also a director and chair of the Investment Committee. Ferguson began his career as an attorney at the New York City office of Davis Polk & Wardwell and was an associate and partner at McKinsey & Company. He is a member of the Smithsonian Institution's Board of Regents and a fellow of the American Academy of Arts and Sciences. He serves on the boards of Alphabet, Corning, and International Flavors and Fragrances. Ferguson is also active as an advisor and board member with various private fintech companies. He serves on the boards of the Institute for Advanced Study, the Memorial Sloan Kettering Cancer Center, and other nonprofits. Ferguson holds a BA, JD, and a PhD in economics, all from Harvard University.

Esther L. George was president and chief executive officer of the Federal Reserve Bank of Kansas City and a member of the Federal Open Market Committee from 2011 to 2023. Her Federal Reserve System service spans more than forty years, including considerable experience as a bank supervisor. In 2009, she served as the Federal Reserve's acting director of banking supervision and regulation in Washington, DC. George was actively involved in the Federal Reserve's work to ensure the smooth and efficient functioning of the nation's payment system, including leading the effort to establish instant retail payments known as the FedNow Service. She has hosted the Kansas City Fed's annual Jackson Hole international Economic Policy Symposium. George currently serves on the boards of the Hallmark Corporation, the Ewing Marion Kauffman Foundation, the Peterson Institute for International

Economics, the National Bureau of Economic Research, the Committee for a Responsible Federal Budget, and the Kansas City 2026 FIFA World Cup.

Charles Goodhart has had long a career alternating between academia and work in the public financial sector. He has served academic positions at Cambridge University and the London School of Economics. He has been a specialist monetary economist, focusing on policy issues and financial regulation at the Bank of England, including at its Department of Economic Affairs and Monetary Policy Committee.

Robert Heller began his career as a professor of economics at UCLA. Subsequently, he became chief of the Financial Studies Division of the International Monetary Fund and served as senior vice president and director of international economics at Bank of America. President Ronald Reagan appointed him as a member of the Board of Governors of the Federal Reserve System in Washington, DC, where he served together with chairs Paul Volcker and Alan Greenspan. He then became an executive vice president of VISA International and president and chief executive officer of Visa USA. He has served as chair of Marin General Hospital and on the boards of several public and private corporations. He is also a staff commodore of the San Francisco Yacht Club. He is the author of seven books on international economics and finance. His autobiography is *The Unlikely Governor* (Maybridge Press, 2015).

Gregory D. Hess serves as president and chief executive officer of IES Global, a leading not-for-profit study-and-intern-abroad organization. With a consortium of 270 US-based colleges and more than 240 global partner universities, IES Global supports more than eleven thousand students annually at more than thirty centers across twenty countries. Hess holds a BA with high honors from the University of California–Davis, and a master's and PhD in economics from Johns Hopkins University. Prior to joining IES Global, he served as the sixteenth president of Wabash College (2013–20) and dean of faculty at Claremont McKenna College (2007–13). Beginning his career as an economist at the Federal Reserve Board, Hess has since taught at leading institutions, including Carnegie Mellon University, the University of Kansas, Cambridge University (St John's College), Oberlin College, and Claremont McKenna College.

Robert L. Hetzel is a retired economist from the Federal Reserve Bank of Richmond, which he joined in 1975. As senior economist and research advisor, he counseled the bank's president on matters concerning participation in Federal Open Market Committee meetings. He has written three books on the history of the Federal Reserve System: *The Monetary Policy of the Federal Reserve: A History* (Cambridge University Press, 2008); *The Great Recession: Market Failure or Policy Failure?* (Cambridge University Press, 2012); and *The Federal Reserve: A New History* (University of Chicago Press, 2022). He is a senior affiliated scholar at the Mercatus Center of George Mason University and a fellow in the Institute for Applied Economics at Johns Hopkins University. He received an AB and a PhD from the University of Chicago, where he was in the Money and Banking workshop and did his thesis work under Milton Friedman.

Thomas Hoenig is a distinguished senior fellow at the Mercatus Center at George Mason University. Hoenig previously served as vice chair of the Federal Deposit Insurance Corporation from 2012 to 2018; and as president and chief executive officer of the Federal Reserve Bank of Kansas City and a member of the Federal Reserve System's Federal Open Market Committee from 1991 to 2011.

Peter N. Ireland is the Murray and Monti Professor of Economics at Boston College, where he teaches courses on macroeconomics and financial economics for undergraduates and doctoral students, and a member of the Shadow Open Market Committee. His writing and research focus on monetary policy and its effects on the economy. Before joining the faculty at Boston College in 1998, Ireland held a teaching position at Rutgers University and worked as a research economist at the Federal Reserve Bank of Richmond. He received undergraduate and graduate degrees in economics from the University of Chicago.

Otmar Issing was the chief economist and a member of the Executive Board of the European Central Bank from 1998 to 2006. From 1990 to 1998, he held the same positions at the Deutsche Bundesbank. Before joining the two central banks, he was a professor at German universities. From 2006 to 2018, he was the president of the Center for Financial Studies at Goethe University, Frankfurt. He acted as chair of the Expert Group on the new Financial Order appointed by Chancellor Angela Merkel; he served on the High Level Group of the European Commission chaired by Jacques de Larosière and on the G20 Eminent Persons Group on Global Financial Governance. Among many awards, he received the High Cross of the Order of Merit of the German Republic.

Robert G. King is a professor of economics at Boston University, having previously held professorial positions at the University of Rochester (1978–1993) and the University of Virginia (1993–2000). He is a consultant to the Federal Reserve Bank of Richmond, a research associate of the National Bureau of Economic Research, and editor of the *Journal of Monetary Economics*. He spent his childhood in Manchester, Connecticut; Jupiter, Florida; and Bethesda, Maryland. At Brown University, he studied economics, mathematics, and history while earning BA, MA, and PhD degrees. Over the course of his career, he has taught macroeconomics, financial economics, and monetary economics to BA, MBA, and PhD students.

Donald Kohn holds the Robert V. Roosa Chair in International Economics and is a senior fellow in the Economic Studies program at the Brookings Institution. Kohn is a forty-year veteran of the Federal Reserve System, serving as a member and then vice chair of the Board of Governors from 2002 to 2010. He also served as an external member of the Financial Policy Committee at the Bank of England from 2011 to 2021.

Jeffrey M. Lacker served as president and chief executive officer of the Federal Reserve Bank of Richmond from 2004 to 2017. He is currently a member of the Shadow Open Market Committee and a senior affiliated scholar at the Mercatus Center at George Mason University. From 2018 to 2022, Lacker was a distinguished professor in the Department of Economics at the Virginia Commonwealth University School of Business. In 2022, Lacker was inducted into the Global Interdependence Center College of Central Bankers. He was an assistant professor of economics at the Krannert School of Management at Purdue University from 1984 to 1989 before joining the Richmond Fed in 1989 as an economist. Lacker received a BA in economics from Franklin & Marshall College and a PhD in economics from the University of Wisconsin.

Andrew T. Levin is a professor of economics at Dartmouth College. His research has been highly influential, with a total citation count that ranks among the top dozen monetary economists worldwide. He has been a regular visiting scholar at the International Monetary Fund; an external consultant to the European Central Bank; an external advisor to the Bank of Korea; a scientific advisor to the central banks of Norway and Sweden; a consultant to the government of Australia's review of the Reserve Bank of Australia; and a visiting scholar at the central banks of Canada, Japan, Netherlands, and New Zealand. He has also provided technical assistance to the central banks of Albania, Argentina, Ghana, Macedonia, and Ukraine. He worked at the Federal Reserve Board for two decades, including two years as a special advisor to the chair and vice chair on monetary policy strategy and communications, and he was an advisor at the International Monetary Fund prior to joining the Dartmouth faculty. Levin holds a PhD in economics from Stanford University. Levin has been a member of the Shadow Open Market Committee since 2019 and was a visiting scholar at the Hoover Institution during the summers of 2022, 2023, and 2024.

Mickey D. Levy is a visiting fellow at the Hoover Institution and a long-standing member of the Shadow Open Market Committee. He is also a member of the Council on Foreign Relations. Levy is a past member of the Financial Research Advisory Committee of the Office of Financial Research. From 1998 to 2013 he was chief economist at Bank of America, where he was on the executive asset, liability, and finance committees. Currently he runs a consulting firm (MDL Insights) and a website (mickeydlevy.com). He conducts research on monetary and fiscal policies and on how they influence economic and financial market performance. He has authored numerous articles on the Federal Reserve, the effectiveness of monetary and fiscal policies, and those policies' interactions with and influences on the business cycle, credit conditions, and inflation. His articles appear frequently in the *Wall Street Journal* and in various policy journals. He testifies often before the US Congress on various aspects of monetary policy and banking regulation, credit conditions and debt, and fiscal and budget policies.

Deborah Lucas is the Sloan Distinguished Professor of Finance at the Massachusetts Institute of Technology Sloan School of Management and Director of the MIT Golub Center for Finance and Policy. Her current research focuses on developing and applying frameworks to assess the costs and risks of credit guarantees and other types of government financial support. She is a research associate at the National Bureau of Economic Research, a senior fellow at the Asian Bureau of Finance and Economic Research, and a member of the Shadow Open Market Committee. She is an elected member of the National Academy of Social Insurance, the National Academy of Public Administration, and an elected fellow of the Econometric Society. She is on the board of the Chicago Mercantile Exchange and P/E Investments. Previous appointments include chief economist, assistant director, and associate director at the Congressional Budget Office. She received her BA, MA, and a PhD in economics from the University of Chicago.

Loretta J. Mester was president and chief executive officer of the Federal Reserve Bank of Cleveland from June 1, 2014, through June 30, 2024. In that role, she participated in the formulation of US monetary policy and oversaw more than one thousand employees based at the Bank's Cleveland office and branch offices in Cincinnati and Pittsburgh. Mester is an adjunct professor of finance at the Wharton School of the University of Pennsylvania. She has taught in the undergraduate finance and MBA programs at Wharton and in the PhD program in finance at New York University. Mester is a trustee of the Cleveland Clinic, a trustee of the Musical Arts Association (Cleveland Orchestra), a director of the Council for Economic Education, and a director of the Haverford Trust Company. Mester graduated summa cum laude with a Bachelor of Arts degree in mathematics and economics from Barnard College of Columbia University. She earned MA and PhD degrees in economics from Princeton University, where she was a National Science Foundation Fellow.

Bill Nelson is an executive vice president and chief economist at the Bank Policy Institute, where he oversees research and analysis in support of the advocacy of the institute's member banks. Previously he served as executive managing director, chief economist, and head of research at the Clearing House Association and chief economist of the Clearing House Payments Company. Prior to joining the Clearing House in 2016, Nelson was a deputy director of the Division of Monetary Affairs at the Federal Reserve Board, where his responsibilities included monetary policy analysis, discount window policy analysis, and financial institution supervision. He has published research on a wide range of topics, including monetary policy rules; monetary policy communications; and the intersection of monetary policy, lender-of-last-resort policy, financial stability, and bank supervision and regulation. Nelson earned a PhD, an MS, and an MA in economics from Yale University and a BA from the University of Virginia.

Athanasios Orphanides is a professor of the practice of global economics and management at the Sloan School of Management at the Massachusetts Institute of Technology and cochair of the board of governors of the Asia School of Business. He is also an honorary advisor to the Bank of Japan's Institute for Monetary and Economic Studies, a member of the Shadow Open Market Committee, a research fellow at the Centre for Economic Policy Research, a senior fellow at the Center for Financial Studies, and a research fellow at the Institute for Monetary and Financial Stability. Before joining MIT Sloan in 2012, he served a five-year term as governor of the Central Bank of Cyprus and was a member of the governing council of the European Central Bank. Earlier, he served as senior advisor at the Board of Governors of the Federal Reserve System, where he began his professional career as an economist.

Charles I. Plosser, a visiting fellow at the Hoover Institution, served as president and chief executive officer of the Federal Reserve Bank of Philadelphia from 2006 until his retirement in 2015. He has been a longtime advocate of the Federal Reserve's adopting an explicit inflation target, which the Federal Open Market Committee did in January 2012. Before joining the Philadelphia Fed in 2006, Plosser served as dean of the University of Rochester's Simon Business School from 1993 to 2003. He has been a research associate of the National Bureau of Economic Research as well as a visiting scholar at the Bank of England. Plosser served as coeditor of the *Journal of Monetary Economics* for two decades and cochaired the Shadow Open Market Committee with Anna Schwartz. His research and teaching interests include monetary and fiscal policy, long-term economic growth, and banking and financial markets. Plosser earned PhD and MBA degrees from the University of Chicago.

Condoleezza Rice is the Tad and Dianne Taube Director and the Thomas and Barbara Stephenson Senior Fellow on Public Policy at the Hoover Institution. She is also the Denning Professor in Global Business and the Economy at Stanford's Graduate School of Business and a founding partner of international strategic consulting firm Rice, Hadley, Gates & Manuel LLC. Rice served as the sixty-sixth US secretary of state (2005–9) and national security advisor (2001–5) in the George W. Bush administration. She previously served on President George H. W. Bush's National Security Council staff and as Stanford University's provost. She has been on the Stanford faculty since 1981 and has won two of the university's highest teaching honors. Rice is a fellow of the American Academy of Arts and Sciences and has been awarded over fifteen honorary doctorates. Born in Birmingham, Alabama, Rice earned her bachelor's degree, cum laude and Phi Beta Kappa, from the University of Denver; her master's degree from the University of Notre Dame; and her PhD from the Graduate School of International Studies at the University of Denver, all in political science.

Georg Rich taught economics for a decade and served as chair of the economics department (1972–74) at Carleton University in Ottawa, Canada. He next joined the Swiss National Bank and was promoted to director and chief economist. Rich later became an honorary professor at the University of Bern, Switzerland. He also taught a course at the Graduate Institute of International and Development Studies in Geneva. He has published widely on monetary matters, including studies on Canadian monetary history and Swiss monetary policy. Born in Schaffhausen, Switzerland, Rich pursued his undergraduate studies at the University of Zurich and obtained a PhD in economics from Brown University.

Amit Seru is a senior fellow at the Hoover Institution, the Steven and Roberta Denning Professor of Finance at Stanford's Graduate School of Business, a senior fellow at the Stanford Institute for Economic Policy Research, and a research associate at the National Bureau of Economic Research. He was formerly a tenured faculty member at the University of Chicago's Booth School of Business. Seru's primary research interest relates to financial intermediation and regulation. He has served on several editorial boards and was most recently a coeditor of the *Journal of Finance*. He has received various National Science Foundation grants and the Alexandre Lamfalussy Senior Research Fellowship from the Bank for International Settlements, and was named as one of the "Top 25 Economists under 45" by the International Monetary Fund in 2014. He has presented his research to US and international regulatory agencies. His research has been featured in leading economic journals and major media outlets. Seru earned his PhD in finance from the University of Michigan.

Christina Parajon Skinner is an associate professor at the Wharton School, University of Pennsylvania, where she is also codirector of the Wharton Initiative on Financial Policy and Regulation. She is presently an affiliate fellow at the Stigler Center at the University of Chicago's Booth School of Business and a research member of the European Corporate Governance

Institute. Before joining the faculty at Wharton, she served as legal counsel at the Bank of England, in the Financial Stability Division of the Bank's Legal Directorate. She is an expert on financial policy and regulation, with a focus on central banks and fiscal authorities. Her research pursues questions surrounding central bank mandates, monetary and fiscal policy, capitalism and financial markets, and the constitutional separation of powers. Skinner's work is international and comparative in scope, drawing on her experience as an academic and central bank lawyer in the United Kingdom. Her research has been published in the *Columbia Law Review, Duke Law Journal, Vanderbilt Law Review, Harvard Business Law Review*, and *Georgetown Law Journal*, among other leading academic journals. Skinner earned her JD at Yale Law School and her bachelor's degree, cum laude, from Princeton University's School of Public and International Affairs.

George S. Tavlas is the alternate to the governor of the Bank of Greece at the Governing Council of the European Central Bank and a distinguished visiting fellow at the Hoover Institution at Stanford University. He was director general and chief economist at the Bank of Greece from 2010 to 2013, and a member of the bank's General Council and the Monetary Policy Council from 2013 to 2020. Previously, Tavlas was a division chief at the International Monetary Fund. He also worked as a senior economist at the US Department of State, and as an advisor for the World Bank and the Organisation for Economic Co-operation and Development. He was a visiting professor at Leicester University, and a visiting scholar at the Brookings Institution, the South African Reserve Bank, the LeBow College of Business at Drexel University, the Becker Friedman Institute at the University of Chicago, and Duke University's Center for the History of Political Economy. His book, *The Monetarists: The Making of the Chicago Monetary Tradition, 1927–1960*, was published by the University of Chicago Press in 2023.

John B. Taylor is the George P. Shultz Senior Fellow in Economics at the Hoover Institution, where he chairs the Economic Policy Working Group, and the Mary and Robert Raymond Professor of Economics at Stanford University. He also directs Stanford's Introductory Economics Center and cochairs the Faculty Council of the Stanford Emerging Technology Review. He served as senior economist on the president's Council of Economic Advisers; as under secretary of the Treasury for international affairs; as president of the Mont Pelerin Society; and on the G20 Eminent

Persons Group on Global Financial Governance. His most recent books are *Principles of Economics*, tenth edition (with Akila Weerapana; FlatWorld, 2023); *Choose Economic Freedom: Enduring Policy Lessons from the 1970s and 1980s* (with George P. Shultz; Hoover Institution Press, 2020); and *Reform of the International Monetary System* (MIT Press, 2019). Among his many awards are the US Treasury's Alexander Hamilton Award and Distinguished Service Award, the Medal of the Oriental Republic of Uruguay, the Truman Medal for Economic Policy, the Bradley Prize, and the Hayek Prize for his book *First Principles* (W. W. Norton, 2012). Taylor received a BA in economics, summa cum laude, from Princeton and a PhD in economics from Stanford.

Christopher J. Waller took office as a member of the Board of Governors of the Federal Reserve System on December 18, 2020, to fill an unexpired term ending January 31, 2030. Prior to his appointment at the Board, Waller had served as executive vice president and director of research at the Federal Reserve Bank of St. Louis since 2009. In addition to his experience in the Federal Reserve System, Waller served as a professor and the Gilbert F. Schaefer Chair of Economics at the University of Notre Dame. He was also a research fellow with Notre Dame's Kellogg Institute for International Studies. From 1998 to 2003, Waller was a professor and the Carol Martin Gatton Chair of Macroeconomics and Monetary Economics at the University of Kentucky. During that time, he was also a research fellow at the Center for European Integration Studies at the University of Bonn. From 1992 to 1994, he served as the director of graduate studies at Indiana University's Department of Economics, where he also served as associate professor and an assistant professor. Waller received a BS in economics from Bemidji State University and an MA and PhD from Washington State University.

Kevin Warsh is the Shepard Family Distinguished Visiting Fellow in Economics at the Hoover Institution and a lecturer at the Stanford Graduate School of Business. He is a partner of Stanley Druckenmiller at Duquesne Family Office LLC and serves on the board of directors of UPS and Coupang, the leading Korean e-commerce company. Warsh is a member of the Group of Thirty and the Panel of Economic Advisers of the Congressional Budget Office. Warsh conducts extensive research in economics and finance. He issued an independent report to the Bank of England proposing reforms in the conduct of monetary policy in the United Kingdom, recommendations that

Parliament adopted. Warsh served as a member of the Board of Governors of the Federal Reserve System from 2006 until 2011. He was the Federal Reserve's representative to the Group of Twenty and the Board's emissary to the emerging and advanced economies in Asia. In addition, he was administrative governor, managing and overseeing the Board's operations, personnel, and financial performance. Prior to his appointment to the Board of Governors, Warsh served as special assistant to the president for economic policy and executive secretary of the White House National Economic Council (2002–6). Previously, Warsh was a member of the Mergers and Acquisitions department at Morgan Stanley in New York, where he served as vice president and executive director. Warsh received his AB from Stanford University and his JD from Harvard Law School.

Axel A. Weber is president of the Center for Financial Studies, Goethe University, Frankfurt, Germany. He is the chair of the Visa Economic Empowerment Institute, chair of the advisory board of Raisin GmbH, chair of the Trilateral Commission Europe, and a member of the Group of Thirty. He also is a member of the Temasek International Advisory Council and senior advisor for CVC Advisers Limited and Boston Consulting Group. He was chairman of UBS Group AG (2012–22), president of Deutsche Bundesbank (2004–11), and a member of the Governing Council of the European Central Bank.

David C. Wheelock is a senior vice president and policy advisor at the Federal Reserve Bank of St. Louis, where he has been employed since 1993. He previously served as the bank's deputy director of research. Wheelock was previously a faculty member at the University of Texas at Austin and a visiting scholar at the St. Louis Fed. He has written articles on banking and monetary policy topics for professional journals and Federal Reserve publications, and is an authority on the history of the Federal Reserve and the Great Depression. He is the author of *The Strategy and Consistency of Federal Reserve Monetary Policy, 1924–1933* (Cambridge University Press, 1991). Wheelock received his BS degree in economics from Iowa State University and his MS and PhD degrees from the University of Illinois Urbana-Champaign.

About the Hoover Institution's Economic Policy Working Group

The Economic Policy Working Group brings together experts on economic and financial policy from the Hoover Institution and elsewhere to study key developments in the US and global economies, examine their interactions, and develop specific policy proposals.

For twenty-five years starting in the early 1980s, the US economy experienced an unprecedented economic boom. Economic expansions were stronger and longer than in the past. Recessions were shorter, shallower, and less frequent. GDP doubled, and household net worth increased by 250% in real terms. Forty-seven million jobs were created.

This quarter-century boom strengthened as its length increased. Productivity growth surged by one full percentage point per year in the United States, creating an additional $9 trillion of goods and services that would never have existed. And the long boom went global, with emerging-market countries from Asia to Latin America and Africa experiencing the enormous improvements in both economic growth and economic stability. Economic policies that place greater reliance on the principles of free markets, price stability, and flexibility have been the key to these successes.

Recently, however, several powerful new economic forces have begun to change the economic landscape, and these principles are being challenged, with far-reaching implications for US economic policy, both domestic and international. A financial crisis flared up in 2007 and turned into a severe panic in 2008, leading to the Great Recession. The economic expansion that followed that Great Recession lasted for more than a decade but ended severely as the forces of the coronavirus pandemic hit the US and world economy in 2020, leading to another recession. This episode and the slow economic growth during the ongoing recovery raise fundamental questions about the role of economic policy. How we interpret and react to these forces—and in particular whether proven policy principles prevail going forward—will determine whether strong economic growth and stability return and again continue to spread and improve more people's lives or whether the economy stalls and stagnates.

The Economic Policy Working Group organizes seminars and conferences, prepares policy papers and other publications, and serves as a resource for policymakers and interested members of the public.

About the Shadow Open Market Committee

The Shadow Open Market Committee (SOMC) was established in 1973 by Karl Brunner, Allan Meltzer, and Anna Schwartz (Milton Friedman's coauthor of *A Monetary History of the United States*). The committee was dedicated to alerting the public and the Federal Reserve to the deleterious effects of the Great Inflation of the 1970s and to advocating a return to sound rules-based monetary policy as the way to restore price stability. In subsequent years, the SOMC became a very influential force in guiding the Fed in its return to price stability. Since that time, the SOMC, composed of leading academic economists, has continued its critical analysis of Fed policy and promotion of reforms to improve monetary policymaking. This conference celebrated the half century of accomplishments of the SOMC by bringing together its current members, prominent Hoover senior fellows, present and past Federal Reserve officials, and key foreign central bank leaders.

Index